# *Gooney Birds & Ferry Tales*

# *Gooney Birds & Ferry Tales*

## The 27th Air Transport Group in World War II

Jon A. Maguire

and the Men of the 27th ATG

**Schiffer Military History**
Atglen, PA

**Dust jacket and color profile artwork by Steve Ferguson, Colorado Springs, CO.**

The painting on the dust jacket depicts events of April 12, 1945, when a 321st Transport Squadron C-47 flown by Lts. Joe Maguire and Barker was hit by flak after delivering a load of 55 gallon gasoline drums to Gutersloh. On the return trip the crippled ship was bounced from behind by an Me 109 somewhere over the northern edge of Amsterdam near the Zuider Zee. Maguire and Barker were able to make it back to England and made an emergency landing at Woodbridge Air Field. The complete story appears on pages 114-115.

*Dedication*

*This work is dedicated to former 27th ATG Historian Marvin Diehl, with appreciation for all the work he did to preserve the memories and secure forgotten decorations for his World War II comrades, to General George J. Eade, USAF (Ret), with appreciation for his efforts in obtaining the long overdue decorations, and to my dad.*

Book Design by Robert Biondi.


Library of Congress Catalog Number: 98-85737.



Printed in China
ISBN: 0-7643-0592-1

We are interested in hearing from authors with book ideas on military topics.

Published by Schiffer Publishing Ltd.
4880 Lower Valley Road
Atglen, PA 19310
Phone: (610) 593-1777
FAX: (610) 593-2002
E-mail: Schifferbk@aol.com.
Please write for a free catalog.
This book may be purchased from the publisher.
Please include $3.95 postage.
Try your bookstore first.

# Contents

# Introduction & Acknowledgements

This project has probably been in the works for about forty years. At least from the time I was old enough to say, "Tell me a story about when you flew airplanes in the war, Daddy!" I grew up asking my father, Joe Maguire, about the 27th ATG, as well as his cousin, Ralph Jenks, when I would see him at holiday family gatherings. Dad and Ralph were both pilots in the same group, during the same time period, yet their duties were very different and they were not stationed at the same bases most of the time. The more questions I asked the more complicated the answers became. Were you in the 8th Air Force? Were you in the 9th Air Force? Were you in USSTAF? Did you fly C-47s? Did you fly fighters? Bombers? Were you in England, France, Italy, Africa, Russia? The answer to all of those questions for a member of the 27th ATG could be yes!

I suppose every kid of my generation, whose dad was a vet, asked the question, "What did you do in the war, Daddy?" I probably asked it more than most. Dad would tell me stories and show me pictures. As I grew older I wanted to know the men who were in the pictures. Finally, one of those men called my dad and said he was in Oklahoma City (our hometown) for the 27th ATG reunion. It was Joe Stevens, Dad's best buddy from those days. It had been almost 50 years since they had last seen each other. Needless to say, it was a great reunion, and we have not missed one together since.

As I slowly became known to the members of the group they welcomed me with open arms, and shared their stories with me. There is nothing quite as captivating as seeing the heart and soul of a 21-year-old flyer shine through the eyes of a 75 or 80-year-old man, as he recounts those exciting days as if they were yesterday – not 50 years ago. Some of those men I now consider among my best friends.

The original historian of the group was Marvin Diehl. Marvin's deteriorating health forced him to relinquish the job after many years of outstanding service to the group. Much of his work is reflected in this book. When Marv resigned I was honored to be asked to carry the torch forward and serve as the new 27th ATG historian. As I listened to the stories and anecdotes year after year, I realized that it would be unfortunate not to record them for posterity. This was ultimately the inspiration for this book.

Writing the history of the 27th Air Transport Group was almost an impossible task. During the war this group was in an ongoing state of change, adapting to meet the needs of a constantly changing battle front. Members of one squadron were continually on detached service to other squadrons. Different parts of the group were stationed at many bases in the ETO during the same time period. Some squadrons were assigned to the 31st TG for periods of time, so the history is quite intermingled with that group. At least when writing a history of a bomb group, or fighter group, they were at the same place, at the same time, for the most part, performing the same task. Not so with the 27th ATG, as this work will document.

The 302nd Transport Wing, United States Strategic Air Forces (USSTAF), is a unique organization. The 27th ATG and the 31st TG made up the wing. The 27th originated in 8th Air Force Service Command, while the 31st originated in the 9th Air Force. They came together under USSTAF to serve the ferry and transport needs of the Army Air Forces in the European Theater of Operations (ETO). To my knowledge, this was the only transport unit which was not part of Air Transport Command (ATC).

The focus of this work is not to tell the technical history of names, dates, and places, although this is included with the reprint of the original 302nd Wing unit history found at the front of this volume – this is an exact facsimile reprint of the book published in the ETO, at the end of the war. This will provide the reader the "official" version of the story. The real focus, however, is on the personal anecdotes and stories of the individuals in the group. The 27th ATG was made up of people, and these are stories about people. The stories are happy, sad, frightening, serious, and, for the most part, true ... at least as true as fifty years of memories will allow! I have done minimal editing to these recollections as I wanted them to be in the words of the men and women who lived them. These were men and women who worked very hard at a job which was greatly unnoticed at the time and has certainly been left out of mainstream history books. The 302nd Transport Wing had over 100 airplanes at the Battle of the Bulge, many of which were from the squadrons of the 27th ATG. To my knowledge, this is the first time this has been recorded in "the history books." They deserve to be remembered.

A large majority of the photographs in this work are seen here for the first time. The color aircraft profiles record for the first time the unusual, and colorful markings of some of the aircraft of this organization.

I hope this work will be of interest and of value to historians and modellers, but most of all, I hope it honors and preserves the memories of the 27th Air Transport Group, and those who served.

This work would never have been possible without the efforts of many contributors. I would first like to thank my dad and mom, Joe and Jeanan Maguire, for inspiring me to start this project many years ago. Thanks to my wife, Rhonda, son, Sean, and daughter, Megan, for putting up with me being away from the family so much during this project. Special thanks must also go to former 27th ATG Group historian Marvin Diehl. His years of research and hard work made this job much easier than it would have been. Marvin gave me full access to all the materials he assembled over the years. My good friends, Greg and Carrie Skaggs, were a tremendous help in transcribing some of the stories for me and in contributing the fine drawings which appear at the beginning of each chapter (Greg can be contacted through the author, via Schiffer Publishing, for inquiries about his art work). Steve Ferguson did the color profiles and cover art, and can also be contacted through Schiffer.

My good friend and fellow aviation historian, Mick Prodger, with Fernado Cortez of the "Hangar 9" Museum at Brooks AFB, San Antonio, TX, provided great assistance with material on flight nurse Reba Whittle. Thanks to Bob Biondi and the staff at Schiffer for help with scanning, editing, and design. Also thanks to Schiffer, for having the faith to do this project.

Most of all, thanks to those members of the 27th Air Transport Group who have contributed material and photographs. Without you, this would not have happened. Names appear in alphabetical order: Vincent Alexander, Bert Astrove, Harold Bonser, Victor Boynton, Fay Brandis, Rose (Mrs. Walter) Butkus, John "J.J." Canning, Clarence "Kit" Carson, Joe Cioffi, Donald Clark, Joe Clemow, Richard Cook, John Dargin, Jr., Marvin Diehl, Donald Diehm, Raymond Dlouhy, George J. "Jim" Eade, Jake Eckert, John "Joe" Ellis, Gordon "Gordy" Fisher, Fred Garcia, Howard Gilberg, Jacques Gordon, Charles Harbaugh, Jr., Houston Hubble, Dillard "Red" Hyden, G. Ralph Jenks, Walter Jones, Art Kane, Ingwer "Ket" Ketelsen, Hal Kinkade, Werner Koethe, Robert Lawrence, Richard Lill, Ted Lucas, Thomas Lynch, Joe Maguire, John McDowell, Larry McGuire, Robert Merritt, Richard Mollwitz, Solomon Padia, Harry Protzeller, Ben Ramsey, John Schneider, Jr., Richard "Dick" Seebers, Joe Stevens, Howard Stillwell, Harold Susen, Burl Taylor, Franklyn "Frank" Terry, Leslie Veit, Robert Patrick "Paddy" Walker, William White, Dudley Willis, and V.M. (Mrs. Raymond) Zych.

Also thanks to Carroll V. Glines for allowing me to use portions of *The Amazing Gooney Bird: The Saga of the Legendary DC-3/C-47*, Magnus Jansson, of *Aftonbladet*, Von Gilbert, Westinghouse Public Relations, Jerry Rep, *Friends Journal*, USAF Museum Association, Captain Kjell Agren, Swedish Air Force, for permission to use portions of *Flygoperation Balchen*, by Jan Waernberg, Valerie A. Whittle, Joe Cioffi, Editor, *Ferry Tales*, Jette Olsen, Peter Lindroos, J. Michael Goodwin, Jeff Ethell, William D. Edwards, Mike Davidson, John Campbell, and Mike Conner.

# The Official History of the 302nd Air Transport Wing, United States Strategic Air Forces

*(Reprint of original WWII era Unit History)*

# DEDICATED TO THOSE WHO REMAIN BEHIND

## Killed

2d Lt Charles Agbashian
Sgt Mario J. Agnese
2d Lt Vernon F. Albrecht
T Sgt Cecil A. Allen
1st Lt John M. Allen
Sgt Anthony F. Bellini
2d Lt John H. Boss
Cpl Chester D. Bright
Pvt Leslie A. Butler
1st Lt Donald K. Cameron
2d Lt Herman C. Carey
2d Lt Warren M. Chapman
M Sgt Loyd F. Cheek
1st Lt James P. Christy
Cpl Alphonse V. Cogozza
1st Lt Charles B. Congdon
S Sgt Raymond Copell
S Sgt Victor C. Corson
1st Lt Burl J. Creech
S Sgt John L. Demmer
1st Lt Clyde A. Depuy
1st Lt William J. Dien
1st Lt Ronald B. Dorrington
Cpl Henry H. Eagan
Sgt Cecil A. Edmonds
S Sgt Addison W. Fain Jr
1st Lt Robert C. Fife
2d Lt Max I. Fogg
Capt Charles Francis
1st Lt Frank S. Frazer
Sgt Ottie L. French
2d Lt R. L. Garkie
1st Lt Theodore E. Garland
1st Lt Richard O. Gasperoni
2d Lt Hillyer C. Godfrey
Cpl Henry A. Gorecki
2d Lt William G. Gough
Cpl Harold W. Grubb
Sgt Robert L. Hadley
2d Lt Algie M. Hill

1st Lt Eugene H. Howard
2d Lt David R. Hughes Jr
1st Lt Donald L. Hunter
Cpl Howard Hutchinson
2d Lt Kenneth W. Johnson
F/O Edward Johnston
Sgt Sam. F. Joseph
2d Lt Summen A. Killgore
Cpl Claude King Jr
2d Lt Robert Knowles Jr
2d Lt Daniel C. Lardin
2d Lt Alva W. Leeper Jr
2d Lt Douglas C. Legear
1st Lt Walter L. Lenox
F/O Willard Leutenegger
Cpl Hyman Levitsky
T Sgt William P. Lulf
1st Lt William B. Lustig
Capt Howard B. Lynch
2d Lt Jimmie Mah
1st Lt Winfield H. Malone
F/O Kenneth A. Maloney
1st Lt James C. Martin
Cpl Henry A. Mazzie
2d Lt Clyde K. McDow
1st Lt Bernard J. McGuire
S Sgt Kirk H. McLoren
Pvt Rex J. Measom
Capt Loren L. Miles
Sgt Charles Miller
Capt Everett L. Miller
F/O John V. Monasmith
2d Lt Craig C. Moore
Sgt Walter A. Morin
Pvt Wilbur L. Murray
2d Lt Ralph M. Nathan
Sgt Robert S. Norris
1st Lt Roy H. Parker Jr.

1st Lt Howard R. Pedersen
Capt John P. Perrin
1st Lt Richard L. Pogue
1st Lt Rex L. Pond
1st Lt William H. Powers
2d Lt Joe F. Quintana
2d Lt Dennis E. Robinson
2d Lt Ralph H. Robinson
2d Lt Robert G. Robinson
2d Lt Richard R. Rolfe
2d Lt Richard C. Rowe
F/O Samuel P. Rubinowitz
F/O John R. Runnells
F/O Eugene S. Rybaczek
S Sgt Harry Segal
2d Lt William J. Shaffer
1st Lt Sampson Sharff
S Sgt George F. Sherman
2d Lt Roy J. Shilling
2d Lt Redene W. Simenson
2d Lt Robert Smillie
2d Lt Floyd Smith
Cpl Jerome T. Smith
Cpl Julius J. Sope
2d Lt William L. Starch
Pfc Merl E. Stutesman
Cpl James F. Syron Jr
1st Lt Benjamin A. Taylor
Cpl James D. Todd
F/O Oliver E. Tudor
F/O William H. Vallee
Sgt Edward V. Vermillion
T Sgt John J. Vojcik
1st Lt Edwin E. Walker
1st Lt Claude H. Weid
S Sgt P. W. Weltner
Pfc Edward M. White
T Sgt Stanley L. Wisneskie
2d Lt George A. Wood
Pvt Nick Yaksich

## Missing

1st Lt Herman Adolfae
1st Lt William G. Bavin
S Sgt Wilfred S. Belk
S Sgt Clarence R. Benge
1st Lt Robert B. Blackler
2d Lt Elmer F. Born Jr
1st Lt Malcolm S. Brown
S Sgt Robert L. Campbell
S Sgt James R. Carroll Jr
T Sgt Eugene J. Conroy
2d Lt Raymond E. Davis
T Sgt Joseph A. Filkins

Sgt Joseph C. Fiset
2d Lt David L. Forbes
2d Lt Ted M. Freeman
1st Lt Reeves K. Gauthier
1st Lt Glenn E. Goodwin
2d Lt Kenneth V. Halverson
Sgt LeRoy W. Holliday Jr
T Sgt John T. Huddy
2d Lt Raymond E. Jones
2d Lt Gordon J. Kinsella
T Sgt William E. Kirwan
1st Lt John D. Lampman Jr

1st Lt Paul E. Mellers
Capt Everett L. Miller
2d Lt Kelly R. Moutray
Sgt Floyd R. Myers
T Sgt John A. Neilson
1st Lt Ermene Pallatine
1st Lt Ralph T. Parker Jr
S Sgt Charles D. Pavlak
2d Lt Donald S. Phillips
1st Lt Robert T. Reed
2d Lt Wallace M. Smyth
Pvt William H. Westeimier

# FOREWORD

A good organization is one which is able to carry out efficiently an assigned task regardless of the difficulties involved. Since I was new to this command on that late afternoon of Christmas Eve 1944, it was with uncertainity that I obligated the wing to have 100 airplanes at Istres by day break of the following day. The results of that mission are well known and from that day forth I never accepted an unusual or difficult commitment with other than the utmost confidence that it fulfilled beyond the highest expectations.

The 302d Transport Wing proved on enumerable occasions that it was a good organization. Its record of airlift and ferrying during the months of March and April proved that it was the top transport organization anywhere. These are records which everyone of you - clerks, cooks, drivers, as well as ground and air crew members - should be very proud. They would not have been attained had not each of you been competent, energetic, resourceful and at all times willing to contribute more than your share to get the job done.

I am aware of the difficulties under which you have operated for the past seven months-the cold, the ice and snow, and above all the hazardous flying conditions. In spite of these and many other hardships, you kept our striped tail transports flying so well that we were commended by practically every major command in this theater.

This wing is now nearing the completion of its task. Organizations and personnel have been reassigned-some to other theaters, some to home and others to the occupational forces. No matter where you go, I know that you will perform your duties with the same spirit and determination that you have in the past. This booklet is intended to be a reminder to you of your tour in the "E.T.C."; of your buddies and friends who shared your hardships as well as your pleasures. In later years when as a free citizen in a free country, you glance through its pages I sincerely hope that it will serve to remind you that then as now each of us must do our share, and more, in order that we may live in a free country - a peaceful country.

Martin A. Bateman

MARTIN A. BATEMAN,
Colonel, Air Corps,
Commanding.

## TABLE OF CONTENTS

The appreciation of the entire command is expressed to you who have helped to compile this material -

Unit Historians
Statistical Sections
Public Relations
Photographers
901st Engineer AF Hq Co

A 27th Group aircraft calls at Grove, Home of the 31st Group and the ETO's largest air terminal, for a load of freight.

## THE 302D TRANSPORT WING, WHEN COMPOSED OF THE 27TH AND 31ST GROUPS, BECAME AN ORGANIZATION EQUALLED BY NONE OTHER

The 302d Transport Wing made its first official appearance in the European Theater of Operations on 5 December 1943. Few people, if any, will recall this date in connection with the wing for this was a paper appearance only. It wasn't until 6 July 1944, thirty days after the invasion of the European Continent, that Col Charles W. Steinmetz assumed command of the wing and commenced organization of his headquarters.

The original plan was to have assigned to the wing some ten transport units equipped with Douglas C-47 type transport aircraft. There were many times later in the history of the wing that pilots, air crews and ground crews, as well as many high officials wished there had been ten such organizations to carry out the mission of resupply by air of army and air force units on the continent and the evacuation of casualties and escaped prisoners to hospitals in the United Kingdom, for the work performed by the command exceeded by far the expectations of the original planners.

Although many units of the 302d Transport Wing, as it was known Victory in Europe Day, had been in operation within the United Kingdom since August 1942 as carriers of mail, passengers and cargo, and other units had commenced their direct continental support on D plus five day, the wing itself was still in its infancy. For an infant however, it had performed a man-sized job, for in nine months aircraft of the wing carried over 95,000 tons of materials.

In this period of time, three commanders led the organization in its important mission. On 1 September 1944, the 302d Transport Wing was reassigned to the Air Service Command of the United States Strategic Air Forces in Europe and Colonel Leslie P. Arnold formerly of Eastern Air Lines, and one of the pilots to make the first round the world flight, was appointed commanding officer by Major General Hugh Knerr. Three months later Colonel Martin A. Bateman, a young command pilot who had formerly been executive officer of the Base Air Depot Area of the Air Service Command, was appointed commanding officer, and Colonel Arnold was reassigned to the Zone of Interior, to return to the commercial airline.

The transport wing's aircraft have hauled an endless variety of cargo in support of the forces that for so long slugged it out with the "Jerries". They have carried winter overcoats, ammunition, overshoes, bayonets and helmets. They have lugged flares, rockets, bombs, tires, belly-tanks, tanks, propellers, airplane engines and instruments for fighter-bomber squadrons; wire laying equipment, cables, communications apparatus and even telephone poles for the Signal Corps; radio equipment, gasoline and tank tracks for the armored divisions of the Third Army; land mines for the Corps of Engineers; ordnance for the Twelfth Army Group; tons of maps for the Infantry; penicillin, sulfa drugs, whole blood and blood plasma for the Medical Corps; propaganda leaflets for the Psychological Warfare Division. In addition to this, ferry organizations of the command have moved every type of aircraft used in the theater from ports of entry or assembly depots to combat units of the Eighth, Ninth and even the Fifteen Air Forces.

Normandy

"D Day" found the 302d Transport Wing still on paper. The 31st Transport Group was located at Grove, Berkshire and the 27th Air Transport Group was spread all over the United Kingdom but had its headquarters and two squadrons near London at RAF Station Heston.

It was "D plus 5" when the 31st Transport Group first stuck its nose into the continental affairs as Colonel Carl Feldman, then Commanding Officer, touched down with a loaded C-47 on the dust swirled runway on the Normandy beachhead. After the delivery of supplies on board, the aircraft was loaded with allied casualties to return to waiting ambulances in England. From that date to Victory in Europe Day, the transport aircraft of the Wing have never ceased in their endless flights, carrying supplies to the continent and returning wounded to England.

A special picked cadre from this group was sent to the airstrip on Omaha Beach under the leadership of Major Milton E. Evans, Operations Officer, to organize the receiving of air freight and the assemblying of evacuees. This airstrip was nothing more than a "wide open spot" right next to the beach, dusty and within range of enemy small arm fire, but its business surpassed that known to any other airdrome in the theater to that date. It passed the London airdromes of Hendon and

Heston and the Air Transport Command airdromes of Prestwick and St. Mawgan. It was later referred to by correspondents and generals, "G.I.s and Gobs", as well as by those who operated it as "the busiest airdrome in the world".

The Wing headquarters was organized just prior to the closing date of this campaign. Colonel Logan T. McMenemy was named Traffic Control Officer and Lt Col Robert O'Hara, Operations and Training Officer. Later Colonel McMenemy was named Executive Officer; Lt Col O'Hara, Chief of Administration; and Lt Col Orie W. Coyle, who was transferred from the 27th Air Transport Group, where he had been supervising operation of intra-island air travel for the organization, Chief of Operations. Plans were immediately drawn up for the operation of existing terminals and the installation of standard terminals in liberated countries. The primary function still remained the transport of passengers and cargo as designated by the Ninth Air Force. The 31st Transport Group increased its operations by adding to its call list the air strip at Colleville.

During the first fifty-one days of operations, which extends just slightly over the last days of the Normandy campaign, over 7,000,000 pounds of cargo was flown from England to France, over 4,000 passengers were transported both ways, and 11,574 casualties were evacuated to the United Kingdom hospitals.

## Northern France

It was during the campaign of Northern France that the Wing was reassigned from the Ninth Air Force to the United States Strategic Air Forces in Europe. It was also during this campaign that the Wing was assigned the 27th Air Transport Group, and moved most of all its units to the continent, or, as it was known then, to the "far shore".

The considerable increase in cargo and passenger traffic and evacuation of wounded during the month of July as compared with June, continued during August. The total tonnage amounted to over 8,000,000 pounds, which exceeded the two previous months combined. The largest increase requiring better air travel service was the rise in the number of casualties to be evacuated. The figure grew correspondingly with the enlargement of allied battle operations on the continent. In August over 13,500 men were moved back to

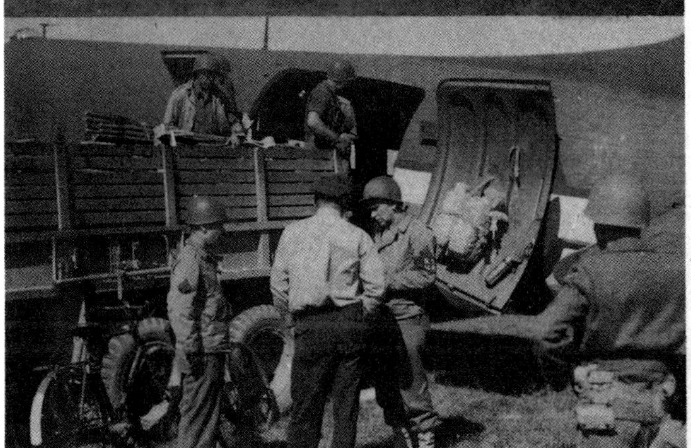

**Above: Destination - Germany.**
**Below: Return of litters to continent for Medical Corps.**

the United Kingdom by aircraft of the Wing.

The time required for loading, unloading, stacking and manifesting cargos was greatly reduced with the improvement in method and with the growing experience of officer and enlisted personnel.

The landing strip at Colleville was enlarged and therefore capable of taking a larger number of aircraft. The airstrip at Quercueville, near Cherbourgh was opened on the 8th of August. During this month, operations commenced at Biniville; Bolleville; Beille, east of Le Mans; Montdesir, north of Orleans; and, just shortly after the liberating of Paris, the capitol and queen city of France, aircraft of the Wing were unloading their freight at Le Bourget, the famous airdrome on which Charles Lindbergh landed on his trans-atlantic flight.

The chief difficulty encountered by the Wing during this campaign was the lack of communication between the United Kingdom and the "far shore", and on the "far shore" itself. Radio communications were not only overloaded by many different commands and organizations, but further, were frequently jammed by the enemy. "Far shore" strips were acquired and abandoned in such quick succession that proper teletype communications could not be had. For these reasons, not only was coordination between the United Kingdom and the "far shore" terminals made difficult, but transmission of strength reports, statistical reports and other important data was considerably delayed and frequently cause confusion. The scheduling of aircraft and relaying of information pertaining to traffic could not, therefore, be done with the

**Above: Loading freight at Greve, 1945.**
**Below: Down Town Ticket Office, Cherbourgh**

desired coordination between terminals.

In addition to transport between England and the continent, a courier service was maintained in the United Kingdom. A similar service was instituted on the continent, making stops twice daily at sixteen Ninth Air Force stations. Many special flights were carried out on the continent, in the United Kingdom and between the two.

With the reassignment of the Wing to the United States Strategic Air Forces in Europe and the joining forces of the two groups the 31st Transport Group, which had primarily been fully occupied in "cross channel" operations, and the 27th Air Transport Group, which had been hauling passengers, mail and cargo from the date of provisional activation of its units in the theater in August of 1942, an organization equalled by none other was formulated, abundantly equipped with trained forces, and eager to apply itself to the colossal tasks of operating rapidly expanding aerial supply lines.

The command consisted then of two transport groups, and the 1001st Service Group, which was a provisional organization commanded by Major Chauncey P. Pond, and later by Lt Col Harry W. Sichard.

Colonel Arnold who assumed command just two weeks prior to the close of the campaign, named Colonel Laurence B. Hickam as Chief of Operations for the Wing, and Lt Col James Douglas as commanding officer of the 27th Air Transport Group, filling the position he had vacated.

The 31st Transport Group was moved from Grove to the Normandy peninsula, with its headquarters at Querqueville. The 27th Air Transport Group commenced cessation of its United Kingdom business and set its sights at the new field, that of operation on the continent. Squadrons were moved from their various "homes" all over the United Kingdom to Grove and then proceeded to move one at a time to Le Bourget airdrome near Paris.

Perhaps one of the most remarkable skylines ever to be established in the history of aviation was the "petrol to Patton" system. When the ruins of the bridges of choked French highways blocked ground transportation, when no railroads ran into the interior of France, when General Patton and his Third Army awaited precious gasoline with anxiety, the machinery of air transportation was set into motion. Fleets of C-47s, augmented by converted Flying Fortresses and Liberators were quickly organized and the shuttle from gasoline depots in the United Kingdom and from the pipe line from ship to shore at Querqueville to the Third Army was under way. From the loading of the gasoline to the unloading on shell torn fields, taken only a few hours before the transport's arrival, the operation was precise and marked with the enthusiastic cooperation of pilots, both our own and these on temporary duty with the command, radiomen, engineers, ground crews and RAF crews of RAF Station Lyneham. A

Above: 302d Transport Wing Passenger Terminal at Querqueville, August 44.

Below: Air evacuation from Germany by C-46, Curtis Commandos.

great deal of credit for the successful completion of this operation goes to that group of some four hundred "casuals" who were then on DS, that dreaded state of being, with units of the Wing, and who later were assigned to bring the Wing to its peak in personnel force for operations.

While new flying schedules were instituted and personnel of the combined groups were being reshuffled for greater efficiency, several detachments were transferred to continental bases. Arrangements were made by higher headquarters whereby aircraft and crews would be placed on duty with the Wing from Air Transport Command.

Units moved from old to new stations quickly, and speedily adapted themselves to new and more difficult working conditions and environment. From all of this it might appear that the 302d Transport Wing, during this time was primarily faced with a paper war and a checker game affair of moving units about in the United Kingdom and in France, but during the month of September over 21,000,000 pounds of cargo was carried in addition to over 50,000 passengers and 9,000 casualties evacuated.

The close of the Northern France Campaign found squadrons and detachments of the three groups of the Wing operating from Northern Ireland to Southern Cornwall of England, from London to Southern France, Belgium and Holland, and moving into the airdromes that surround Paris.

## Rhineland

The campaign Rhineland, the longest of the besieged campaigns

Above: Wing Headquarters, Paris, France. Below: Return of liberated Frenchmen to their homeland after five years in German concentration camps by wing aircraft

of the European war, lasting from 17 September 1944 to 21 March 1945, covered nearly half of the Wing's history in the sense of time alone. It was during this campaign that the Wing carved its deepest impressions in the military journals, for the loads carried by the "gooneybirds" were not of high figures in the term of pounds but they were constant in their arrival on the "far shore". It was during this campaign that the Wing "dug in" for future operations, and that the strength of the organization reached its peak to meet operational requirements.

The Paris airdrome of Le Bourget was opened by a detachment

of the Wing headquarters which had been formed at Querqueville. Upon their arrival at the famed airdrome, the 320th Transport Squadron of the 27th Air Transport Group was found busily engaged in evacuating wounded from the combat areas, utilizing approximately twenty UC-64, Norsman for the mission. Lt Col Leon R. Brownfield was the first Commanding Officer of the field, ably assisted by Lt Col Eugene H. Callahan as Executive Officer, and Capt Jack L. Jones as Adjutant.

The 10th Airdrome Squadron, commanded by Major Arthur Kline, moved its force with the detachment then headed by Lt Col Callahan in rebuilding the field to receive the remaining units of the 27th Air Transport Group. The 1001st Service Group was moved from Warton, Lancashire and quickly established itself at the Paris Air Terminal only to be soon thereafter disbanded.

The 311th Ferrying Squadron of the 27th Air Transport Group was attached to the First Tactical Air Force and stationed at Istres, near Marseilles, in Southern France. This squadron was placed under the operational control of "First TAF", as it was then known, and busied itself with hauling supplies for the air force units and organizations of the Seventh Army and the evacuation of wounded to station and general hospitals in the Riviera area. The 325th Ferrying Squadron of the 27th Air Transport Group remained in the United Kingdom and continued the operation of intra-UK airlines and a passenger terminal at RAF Station North Holt. The 87th Transport Squadron was transferred to the Base Air Depot Area to supply that organization with air transportation needed for depot use. These two squadrons, the 325th Ferrying and the 87th Transport, are the only two organizations of the Wing that were never stationed on continental soil. Later the 87th Transport Squadron was reassigned to the Wing and placed in the 31st Transport Group.

One hundred crews and aircraft of the Air Transport Command were placed on duty with the Wing for a ninety day period to increase the operating capacity of the organization. This was a strain on the operating capacity of the organization. This was a strain on the administrative sections throughout the squadrons, groups and the Wing headquarters but it provided for more air lift to move the needed supplies to the

Above: General Jones during command inspection at Greve, 1945.
Below: Air freight terminal at Greve

fighting units. Many of these crews requested reassignment to the various squadrons of the wing at the completion of their temporary duty. Many of the friends made during this campaign included officers and men of that command. A number of them are included on the killed and missing roll of the Wing. These crews erased the nickname "ATC-allergic to combat", as far as their buddies were concerned.

On the 10th of November the headquarters of the 31st Transport Group moved from Querqueville to Chartres, France, where it was joined by the 313th Transport Squadron, which moved up from Bolleville, and the 314th Transport Squadron, which moved north from Maupertus. The following day the 312th Station Complement and the 310th Ferrying Squadron were reassigned from the 27th Air Transport Group to the 31st Transport Group and moved from Grove, England to Chartres. This strengthened the operating capacity of the first continental operating group and more evenly distributed the number of aircraft employed by the Wing.

Shortly after the move of the 31st Transport Group, Colonel Feldman was reassigned as commanding officer of the 27th Air Transport Group, carrying with him Lt Col Wendell I. Covalt, Major Ted Bennett and Captain John Moore as executive, operations officer and adjutant, respectively. Lt Col James H. Douglas, who had formerly commanded the group returned to the Zone of the Interior. Lt Col Henry C. Allen was made the new commanding officer of the 31st Transport Group with Lt Col Carey C. Harmon later appointed deputy for administration and Major Mitt Evans, deputy for operations.

**Above: "Petrol to Patton" - converted B-24s and B-17s loading for flight.**

**Below: Air evacuation of French casualties from Germany.**

With all of the moving about by units of the two groups in the month of November, aircraft of the Wing still carried over 13,000,000 pounds of cargo, 17,000 passengers and 6,500 evacuees. For twenty-five days of the month, Wing aircraft were used to carry package gasoline to the Twelfth Army Group, which was made up of the Third, First and Ninth Armies. Thirty-five aircraft were dispatched for the first day's operation with Lt Col Kenneth A. Reecher making an initial run to see that operations and off-loading procedures were functioning smoothly. Lt Col Reecher was then assistant to Colonel Hickam in Wing Operations. During the period of this operation, 2,377,668 pounds of gasoline were hauled to the army group. Air evacuation increased over the previous month due to the installation of evacuation procedures at Le Bourget to provide aircraft returning to the United Kingdom from the Paris area with loads of allied casualties destined for the hospitals near Membury and Ramsbury in England. A total of 287 flights were made in air evacuation this month.

In the earl days of December, Colonel Martin A. Bateman was appointed commanding officer of the Wing and immediately set upon a plan to make all operations and administration top in efficiency or non-existant. His new staff soon read: Colonel Patrick N. Beville, Deputy for Administration; Lt Col Kenneth A. Reecher, Deputy for Operations; Major Hubert O. Johnson, Jr, Chief of Personnel; Major Harold F. Priddy, Chief of Supply and Maintenance; and Major Noah H. Holbrook, Adjutant General. Colonel Laurence B. Hickam, and Lt Cols Theodore V. Moore, George Cussens, Allen G. Russell, Arthur O. Pittenger and Joseph E. Derham returned to the Zone of the Interior for reassignment.

During the month of December the 31st Transport Group returned to its original home - Grove, Berkshire in England. Priority air cargo was building up at that station and soon reached the highest known in the theater. The Grove air freight terminal soon became the second largest terminal in the world, second only to that where air freight is collected for flights over the "hump" in the China-Burma-India Theater.

With the move of the 31st Transport Group back to Grove, the 1001st Service Group was disbanded and the 519th Service Squadron was assigned to that organization, and also returned to England.

December was the first of three bad weather months, but the non-operational time was well utilized in the betterment of the over-all command in operations and administrations alike. Whereas the number of passengers transported and the amount of freight carried decreased, the number of evacuees flown from France and the amount of soldier's mail carried increased over November. A special operation performed by the Wing is described in the Campaign Ardennes.

Captain Ernest Wagner of the Wing Operations staff proposed a plan of installing air intransient

Above: Major Edward J. Heng, Wing Inspector General, 1 September '44 to 25 February '45

Below: Colonel Laurence B. Hickam, Deputy Commander for Operations, 1 September '44 to 13 December '45.

HEADQUARTERS
UNITED STATES STRATEGIC AIR FORCES IN EUROPE
Office of the Commanding General

28 December 1944.

SUBJECT: Commendation

TO : Commanding General, Air Service Command

1. With great satisfaction I desire to commend the Air Service Command and the 302nd Transport Wing in particular for the effective manner in which they met an emergency on December 24th. in transporting troops from Marseille to Strip 82 and Nancy-Essey.

2. The late hour when this project was received, the collection and dispatching of the aircraft and the accomplishment of the mission in minimum time reveals a high degree of organization and management. The manner in which this mission was performed reveals credit not only on the Air Service Command but the Air Forces in Europe at large.

CARL SPAATZ
Lieutenant General, USA
Commanding

1st Ind.

20122
HQS, ASC-U.S. Strategic Air Forces in Europe, APO 633, U. S. Army
28 December 1944.

To: 302nd. Transport Wing (Thru: Commanding General, Continental Air Depot Area, APO 744, U.S. Army)

1. The above commendation is forwarded to the 302nd Transport Wing

C. P. KANE
Brig. Gen., USA
Commanding

DEC 29 1944

DEC 30 RECD

depots at the two main airdromes of operation of the Wing. These later materialized in the light of the 102d and the 103rd Intransient Depot Squadrons (Provisional) The units were covered by authorized bulk allotments of personnel. Captain John Dengel, an "old timer" in the handling of air freight, after representing the 27th Air Transport Group at Burtonwood for over a year, was placed in charge of the continental squadron.

The first of the year found many enlisted men who had seen long service in the theater returning to the United States under the Very Heavy Bombardment program. This was a program whereby personnel from overseas commands could be utilized to replace others who were assigned to very heavy bombardment groups or to actually fill these groups after a short leave at home. The Riviera Rest Homes were opened; first for officer personnel and later for enlisted personnel. Those who were lucky enough to have seven days of sunshine and relaxation in the Southern playground of France found that it could be a restful week or it could be the build up for a week's rest "back at the base".

The 27th Air Transport Group moved from Le Bourget to Villacoublay, a distance of approximately five miles by air travel, and returned their famed field to the French Air Forces.

Ferrying of replacement aircraft in the theater for the Eighth Air Force had formerly been a duty of the 27th Air Transport Group and for the Ninth Air Force a duty of the 31st Transport Group. Upon the formation of the Wing, composed of the two groups, the duty was given to the Base Air Depot Area to insure the delivery of these aircraft but the Wing was still required to furnish the pilots who flew in these operations. In February the Wing was once again charged with the full duty of ferrying. The 1302d Ferrying Squadron was formed as a provisional organization later to be replaced by the 310th Ferrying Squadron, which was reassigned to direct wing control from the 31st Transport Group. During the remainder of the Rhineland Campaign this squadron ferried over 4,000 aircraft from storage depots in the United Kingdom and ports of entry to combat units of the Eighth, Ninth and First Tactical Air Forces and assisted combat units in the movement of some 1500 others. These aircraft consisted of every type used in the

Above: Loading personnel at Heston for shipment to "far shore".

Below: Destination - Omaha Beach!

European Theater. Heavy losses in the ground forces, exceeding reinforcements sent from 'the Zone of the Interior, caused a necessary drawing from the available and physically fit men of the service and air forces in the theater. During the Rhineland Campaign over 250 men were drawn from the service squadrons, the truck company, headquarters squadron, and the flying squadrons as well, to supplement the number furnished by other commands. Along with these went many of the original members of both groups as the reassignment was limited to personnel of the last four grades and many worthy men had been held in these grades due to lack of position vacancies in their squadrons.

After a great deal of discussion and a bit of debating, a policy was initiated by the Commanding General, United States Strategic Air Forces in Europe, which allowed for the return of flying crews of this command to the Zone of the Interior after completion of over 1500 flying hours and two years service in the theater, and who were recommended for rest and rehabilitation by their flight surgeon. So it was, that in February and March, crews departed from each group for the United States for a period of rest and then reassignment to transport duties. Major Gregory Thomas, and Lts Bertrom Myers and Douglas Saunders of the 27th Air Transport Group and Captain Donald Schearhorn and Lt William Albrecht of the 31st Transport Group, were among the first to be returned under this plan.

In March preparations were made to assist the Troop Carrier command in the evacuation of its share of casualties during the time that command was on oper-

Above: The 310th Ferrying Squadron wins Wing Track Meet, Paris, 1945.

Below: Brig Gen C.P. Kane presents Wing Flying Safety Trophy to Col Feldman, 27th Air Transport Group, and Captain Lancaster, 86th Transport Squadron.

ational missions. Over seventy-five per cent of the aircraft of the Wing were used in this function. The close of the Rhineland Campaign and the opening of the Central Europe Campaign was little noticed, for there was probably less distinction in these two campaigns than any others, for the allies were on the move and the Elbe River was the goal.

### Ardennes

In December of 1944 when the German high command risked the might of all of their forces in one strong attack against the allied armies which had succeeded in liberating France, Luxemburg and Belgium and were preparing for their drive into the land of the Boch, General Eisenhower's troops were forced to withdraw and prepare for the counter offensive.

Though the Wing played only a small part in the successful completion of this counter offensive, here is the story that will long be remembered by those who took part. The story begins at 1630 hours on the afternoon of December 24th, when the Wing was alerted. Squadron radios crackled with instructions. Planes already in the air with various military cargoes were recalled to their home bases and told to unload and stand by.

An hour later word was flashed that 100 planes were to proceed from bases at Grove and Le Bourgett to Istres, near Marseilles in Southern France. There they were to pick up hundreds of tank mechanics and technicians and fly them to advance airfields in the battle area where General Patton's Third Army was fighting.

Freight men tugged and sweated to unload the big Douglas transports of their cargoes. Airplane engine specialists, radio mechanics and other ground crew men swarmed over the C-47s, giving them a last-minute check before take-off. It was a race against time and the weather, for a fog was fast threatening to close at least one base.

The first of the transports took off at 2030 hours on Christmas Eve. By 2200 hours the whole aerial armade was on its way. And several hundred air corps men spent their Christmas eve in the air. Meanwhile at the destination airfield, where the highly-trained troops were to be loaded, the 311 Ferrying Squadron sprang into action. Forty thousand gallons of gasoline had to be trucked from nearby supply dumps, and clerks, cooks and carpenters all pitched in to do the job. Flying control corralled extra jeeps and put them on tap to direct aircraft to dispersal areas.

The moon was riding high in the sky that night when the airliners began to arrive. Smoothly and precisely they landed and pulled into parking areas to which they were directed by radio, signal lights, and jeeps.

Ground crews went to work on the planes almost as soon as the props stopped spinning. Gas trucks drew alongside and replenished spent fuel supplies.

By 0800-that was Christmas morning-the servicing was completed, just as the tank men began to arrive. Twenty minutes later the first plane, with its cargo of men, raced down the runway, nosed into the air, and headed for the battlefront. From then until 1430

PERFORMANCE RECORD

| Data | March | April |
|---|---|---|
| Assigned and Attached | 5,442 | 5,450 |
| A.W.O.L. | 2 | 2 |
| Courts Martials | 39 | 29 |
| Transferred to Ground Forces | 30 | 183 |
| | | |
| Flying Hours | 18,310 | 23,257 |
| Accidents per 1000 Hours | .22 | .08 |
| Transport Aircraft Assigned | 166 | 163 |
| Comm Flight Aircraft Attached | 54 | 87 |
| | | |
| Aircraft Ferried | 2,357 | 2,238 |
| Tons cargo hauled | 9,168 | 14,048 |
| Casualties evacuated | 40,067 | 36,008 |
| Passengers carried | 16,090 | 21,067 |
| | | |
| Total tonnage carried, including passengers, evacuees, mail and cargo | 15,655 | 20,278 |

Figures as compiled by statistical control sections of each group, separate squadron and wing headquarters.

hours Douglas Transports took off in a steady stream on the troop carrying assignment. Some of the planes even managed to get in a second trip to the front that day.

Before noon the vitally needed tank mechanics and specialists were pouring out of the C-47s into an airfield within earshot of an artillery duel along the western front.

The whole troop transport operation was completed in less than 24 hours. Not a man nor a plane was lost.

Throughout the campaign, the Paris to Luxemburg daily flight continued carrying on board priority mail, passengers and cargo, essential to the fighting units in that area. From airfields surrounding this great battle ground Wing aircraft assisted in the evacuation of casualties after the delivery of a ship load of gasoline, ammunition or medical supplies.

Above: Loading organizational equipment for move to "far shore".
Below: Shipment of whole blood to front.

CENTRAL EUROPE

March found the entirety of the armed forces of the allies as well as those of the Soviet Union racing into Germany. The 302d Transport Wing was in this lineup and played its part in the race by carrying over a million pounds each day during this month to the front line units.

With every possible blow being thrown at the retreating Germans, the aircraft of Troop Carrier Command were withdrawn for operational missions during most of this campaign. This increased the load of casualties for the wing to evacuate to rear hospitals. During March over 40,000 were carried out of the combat area, and during April and the first week of May a similar number were evacuated. During one period of this campaign, over seventy-five per cent aircraft assigned to the Wing were used in this phase of operation.

Three C-46 Commandos were assigned to the 31st Transport Group to increase the moving capacity from Grove and other shipping points in the United Kingdom. These aircraft were capable of carrying over 9,000 pounds on each trip and often chalked up loads of 27,000 pounds to the "far shore" in a single day, with a similar tonnage of casualties returned to the United Kingdom. On these days pilots and crews of the coveted aircraft would rise before many cooks and K.P.s were catching their "forty winks" and take off for the front before 0300 hours in order to complete three round trips for the day.

Over 4,000,000 pounds of ammunition were carried to fighter units which had expended their supply and were carrying only bombs on their sorties over enemy lines. Often the fighter aircraft were refueled and rearmed with the transport's cargo before the wing aircraft cleared the field.

In April the service organizations which had seen long and hard duties from Scotland and Cornwall to Warton, Normandy and the Seine were disbanded in favor of the activation and organization of two service groups. The 370th Air Service Group, commanded by Lt Col W. L. Covalt, was detailed to support the 27th Air Transport Group. The 371st Air Service Group, commanded by Lt Col C. C. Harman, was assigned to the 31st Transport Group for its support.

During this campaign the wing was charged with maintaining a communications flight for SHAEF Air Staff at Reims. A detachment of the 311th Ferrying Squadron, which had been reassigned from the 27th Air Transport Group to Wing control for the operation of the U.S. Strategic Air Force Communications Flight at Toussus Le Noble, was formed under the direction of Capt Michael Adams. The 311th Ferrying Squadron, then commanded by Major James Lyons, was maintaining communications flight for three of the major headquarters of the theater.

The wing reached its highest mark during the sixty day period of March and April and were carrying on this record on V-E Day. Aircraft of the organization carried 35,000 tons of passengers, mail, cargo, evacuees, and liberated prisoners and displaced persons. This included over 75,000 evacuees; 40,000 passengers; 45,000,000 pounds of freight and one and a half million pounds of soldiers' mail. During this period over 4,500 aircraft were ferried by the 310th Ferrying Squadron, communications flights maintained and assisted in flying over 85 various types of aircraft, over 200 men were reassigned to the ground forces as reinforcements, the total flying hours for the command exceeded 40,000 hours, thirteen aircraft were away in Sweden and Russia on secret missions, and the strength of the command reached the lowest point witnessed since the previous October. Brigadier General I.W. Ott, Commanding General of the Central Air Depot Area, the command to which the wing was assigned during this period recommended the entire organization for the award of the meritorious service plaque. An interpretation of the regulation by the Judge Advocate of Air Technical Service Command declared that the wing was too large an organization to be awarded this citation. Groups and separate squadrons were eligible for such recognition but not the wing as a whole.

The wing, in less than nine months, had carried 95,000 tons of passengers, evacuees, mail and cargo and ferried over 9,000 aircraft. It was commended by each of the higher air force headquarters of the theater and by many of the ground and service force and headquarters. The hornet tail - black and yellow striped C-47s - had covered the United Kingdom, and the European and West Asiatic Continent.

HEADQUARTERS UNITED KINGDOM BASE
COMMUNICATIONS ZONE
EUROPEAN THEATER OF OPERATIONS
UNITED STATES ARMY

APO 413
28 April 1945

SUBJECT: Commendation

TO : Colonel M. A. Bateman, Commanding Officer, 302nd Transport Wing, APO 744, US Army

1. Please allow me to express the appreciation of the Visitors' Bureau of this Headquarters, as well as my personal thanks, for the splendid services rendered by Detachment "A" 97th Airdrome Squadron, 31st Transport Group, towards assisting the many hundreds of combat officers on leave here from the Continent during the past several months. The Visitors' Bureau would have been unable to properly service these officers had it not been for the efficiency and helpfulness of this Detachment.

2. It is our desire
Boyd A. Thomas and Lt. Richard
Department, and Lt. Eldridge H.
Johnson of the Traffic Departme
eration have so successfully aid
Bureau. I would be grateful if
officers the appreciation of bo
the Visitors' Bureau.

HEADQUARTERS 12TH ARMY GROUP
APO 655

330.13 (AG-O)

8 June 1945

SUBJECT: Commendation.

THRU : Commanding General, Air Technical Service Command Europe, APO 744.

TO : Commanding Officer, 302nd Transport Wing, APO 744.

1. The Army Group Commander wishes to express to all personnel of the 302nd Transport Wing his deep appreciation of their tireless effort and outstanding achievement in transporting cargo, passengers and mail to and for elements of this command. The contribution of pilots, of ground crews and of administrative personnel were of inestimable value in hastening the defeat of the enemy.

2. It is realized that many of the missions flown by the 302nd Transport Wing have been hazardous in the extreme. In spite of all obstacles, the record of this organization in meeting prescribed schedules has been in accord with the highest military tradition, and reflects great credit upon all concerned.

C. R. LANDON
Colonel, AGD
Adjutant General

RECEIVED JUN 1945 HQ. A.T.S.C.

AAF-379, APO 633, US ARMY, 15 JUNE 1945.

Forces in Europe, AAF-379, APO 633, US Army.

his appreciation for the outstanding ser-
period it was under his command.

RECEIVED 15 JUN 1945

Major, AGD,
Adjutant General.

JUN 15 1945

\- 1 -

Supreme Headquarters
ALLIED EXPEDITIONARY FORCE
Office of the Supreme Commander

18th June, 1945.

Dear Colonel Bateman,

I wish to commend you and the air and ground crews of your Command for the fine job of flying repatriated allied personnel which you have done.

The record of your Wing in helping in the liberation of allied repatriates and without a single casualty or serious accident, deserves the highest praise.

Please convey to your staff and to your crews, my sincere thanks and heartfelt commendation for a job well done.

Sincerely

Colonel Martin A. Bateman,
The Commanding Officer,
302nd Transport Wing.

HEAD
134TH REINFORCE
APO

373.

SUBJECT: Employment of aviation.

TO : Commanding Officer, 302nd Trans

1. It has been a mutual pleasure f
speed our efforts to defeat the German Ar

2. During the months of March, Apr
received personnel totaling almost nine t
ration of your command. The facilities w
in successfully completing our vital miss
forcements to units of the United States

3. It is understood that your service to our organization, because of redeployment, will be decreased, and we know that you will try in every way to meet every request and commitment, and that insofar as facilities are available you will succeed.

4. On behalf of my staff, I wish to thank you and your organization for the never failing efforts and cooperation which you have extended to us. It has been a genuine pleasure to work with you.

RECEIVED AG 302nd TRANSPORT WING 9274

Lloyd C. Dean
LLOYD C. DEAN
Lt Colonel, Air Corps
Commanding

\- 1 -

ARTERS
ER OF OPERATIONS
TATES ARMY
Chief Surgeon
887

16 June 1945

From the beginning of the European Campaign in Normandy, all the way across Western Europe, the service rendered the Medical Department by your Transport Wing has been of invaluable aid. The rapid delivery of whole blood, biologicals, drugs and other critical items, and the swift evacuation of casualties to our hospitals in rear areas, has made it possible to save countless lives that otherwise would have been lost.

I want to take this opportunity to thank you and each member of your command for your wholehearted cooperation,. For flying long hours, landing on inferior fields, often directly behind the front lines and in extremely bad weather, I would like to thank personally each pilot and crew member of the 302nd Wing; and for making aircraft available in all cases of emergency, the operations staff of Wing, Group, and Squadrons:

My sincerest appreciation to the 302nd Wing for your contribution to the Medical Service in this Campaign.

PRHawley
PAUL R. HAWLEY
Major General, USA

27

Group CO, Lt Col Reecher and Maj. Moore go over a weighty problem.

## THE WORKHORSE OF THE WING -- 27TH AIR TRANSPORT GROUP.

The 27th Air Transport Group, the first such organization in the European Theater of Operations, was officially formed in April of 1943 as part of the VIII Air Force Service Command. Upon activation it consisted of the Headquarters Squadron, 86th and 87th Transport Squadrons, and the 519th and 520th Service Squadrons.

Some nine months earlier however, this organization began to form. So it was, that the organization was actually in operation when it was given official recognition.

Just how the idea materialized in the Eighth Air Force Headquarters was never definitely settled, but there were at one time three transport aircraft on detached service from a Troop Carrier organization to a flight section of the service headquarters - three aircraft that started the group and never returned to their original organization. Captain James Briggs was one of the pilots of these aircraft and on pass when he met his former bomber commander in a London Hotel. Two days later Captain Briggs and crew were working for a Major Arthur J. Pierce of the VIII Air Force Service Command.

The field of opportunity was wide open and the small organization soon grew from a three aircraft one, to a widespread unit receiving replacement aircraft and combat crews from the United States at Prestwick under Major Matt G. Carpenter, to ferrying aircraft from Burtonwood and Warton under the direction of Major Remlin and Captain J.E. McDonald. A communications flight was formed for the headquarters personnel at Heathrow under the direction of Lieutenant Jack Kille and operations of passanger and freight transport service at Hendon Airdrome, London, was under the supervision of Major Frank Crowley.

The invasion of North Africa caused the development of still another activity, this time in Cornwall. There Lt Col Carpenter, who was moved down from Prestwick, took over the operation of three detachments employed in dispatching and receiving replacement aircraft and supervising the shipment of freight by air to that theater.

In April when the group was activated, the title, 86th Transport Squadron, was given to that unit at Hendon. The ferry organization at Warton was activated as the 87th Transport Squadron. The unit in Cornwall was named the 519th Service Squadron, and that at Prestwick the 520th Service Squadron. No sooner were they officially named, than each went far over its authorized strength.

In the winter of 1943, additional units were added to the group. These included the 320th and 321st Transport Squadrons and the 311th, 312th and 325th Ferrying Squadrons. These added to the units already in operation went to compose a strong service organization capable of performing almost any mission in the field of transport or aircraft ferrying.

Major Pierce who had advanced to Colonel turned over his group to Colonel Leslie P.Arnold, an expert in commercial aviation, and returned to the United States for assignment toa Tactical Bomb Group.

Under Colonel Arnold, Lt Col Carpenter was named Deputy Commander. He was succeeded as Commanding Officer of the 519th Service Squadron by Major Allen R. Russell. Major Joe Stenglein was placed in command of the 310th Ferrying Squadron at Warton and took over from the 87th Transport Squadron the ferrying duties.

The 87th Transport Squadron suplimented the service of A.T.C. in hauling priority freight to the theater by flying converted B-24s to and from Wright Field at Dayton, Ohio. This was a trip fought for by every pilot and crew of the group.

The 86th Transport Squadron continued its steady grind of hauling passengers and mail in and out of London, calling at Prestwick, Langford Lodge near Belfast, North Ireland, Warton, Burtonwood, and later St Mawgan in Cornwall.

The group using the 10th Airdrome Squadron, the 86th Transport and the 325th Ferrying Squadron operated Heston airdrome until after the first six months of the Continental invasion. In August 1944, the pilots of the 86th Transport Squadron averaged over 100 flying hours each; the 310th Ferrying Squadron made over 3,000 deliveries; Lt Harry Oberholtzer drew a secret assignment carrying him to Teherran, Bari, Cario, Casa Blanca and Russia; and the 325th Ferrying Squadron was still operating traffic detachments all over the United Kingdom.

### Group Staff to Wing

When the 302d Transport Wing was reassigned from the IX Air Force Service Command to the Air Service Command of the U S Strategic Air Forces in Europe and Col Arnold was named commanding officer to succeed Col Steinmetz, he carried with him from the 27th

Air Transport Group the majority of his staff officers.

Lt Col James Douglas who had been Group Engineering Officer was named commanding officer to succeed Colonel Arnold. The group headquarters moved from Meadowbank, near London, to Grove, the station then recently evacuated by the 31st Transport Group. Squadrons that had formerly been operating on their own as independent units were moved to the station in order to provide opportunity for group organization and prepare for the final move to France. The 320th Transport Squadron, commanded by Major Lyons, preceded the other units to the bombed airfields of France, moving into Le Bourget shortly after the liberating of the Paris area. The unit was employed in aerial evacuation from tactical units. The 86th Transport Squadron were ordered to "rough it" by moving into tents in "buzz bomb alley". The 311th Ferrying Squadron, employed as a transport organization, was kept busy hauling gasoline from Lyneham and Chipping Ongar. The 310th Ferrying Squadron again in September moved over 3,000 replacement aircraft. The 321st Transport Squadron under Major James Briggs moved to Grove from North Ireland and went into training, studying the use of the army .45 caliber automatic and basic Franch. The 325th Ferrying Squadron, charged with intra-United Kingdom activities, carried over 500 tons.

The following month, October, crews from Air Transport Command were attached to all of the flying squadrons. The 321st Transport moved over 1,000 tons and Captain William Boyd, Squadron Engineering Officer, was sent to France to prepare for the arrival of the unit at Le Bourget. The 310th Ferrying Squadron became a transporting unit after placing ferry crews sufficient to continue that operation on detached service with the Base Air Depot Area. The 311th and 312th Ferrying Squadrons were soon known as radio training schools, training over half of the operators, ground and aerial, for the whole group. The 86th Transport Squadron, with Lt Daniel Early Jr moved its ground echelon to France.

In November, the 87th Transport Squadron, which had moved from Warton to Chipping Ongar to cope with the gasoline being hauled to General Patton's tank units, moved to Grove and was then reassigned to the Base Air Depot Area. The 311th Ferrying Squadron moved to Istres and was at-

Above: Col Leslie P. Arnold, Commanding Officer, September - November, 1944.

Below: Ferry pilots receive assignments.

tached to the First Tactical Air Force - provisional. The group moved its headquarters to Le Bourget and was in the process of preparing for continental operations when Colonel Carl Feldman was assigned as commanding officer, replacing Lt Col Douglas, who returned to the Zone of the Interior. Colonel Feldman had formerly commanded the 31st Transport Group.

Colonel Feldman appointed Lt Col W. L. Covalt, Deputy Commander; Major Theodore Bennett, Operations Officer; and Captain John Moore, Adjutant. All of these officers were reassigned from the 31st Transport Group. Lt Colonel Morton Freed continued in the capactiy of Materiel Officer for the organization.

Colonel Feldman brought with him a policy of "Results Not Excuses" and this soon began to pay dividends.

The group was well quartered in large apartments near the field, in buildings formerly occupied by the German troops. The 86th Transport Squadron pitched a tent near the flight line to offer protection against the winter winds and mud for its crew chiefs. This squadron carried over 745 tons, plus 1168 evacuees and 3000 passengers during November. Warrant Officer W. D. Mc Cormick, the squadron's favored adjutant, was awarded the Bronze Star Medal for meritorious services in that capacity. Major Carroll's 312th Ferrying Squadron transported over 1,600,000 pounds during the month, and the 325th Ferrying Squadron in moving from North Holt to Grove cancelled no regular runs nor delayed the regular passenger schedule. The 310th Ferrying Squadron was reassigned to the 31st Transport Group at Chartres.

The 311th Ferrying Squadron in Southern France learned its main

Above: Col A J Pierce, first group commander, and Col Leslie P Arnold, his successor.

lesson "to fly high and fast" as one aircraft was lost in moving the squadron to its new location. Even before it got well settled, rumors, and they were plentiful in that squadron, began to tell of a future move of the unit to India.

## Le Bourget Home for Winter

The group soon settled for the winter at Le Bourget and operational figures commenced to rise. Two problems faced the maintenance crews throughout the long cold months - mud and blower clutch failures.

The 325th Ferrying Squadron was reassigned to the 31st Transport Group, evening the number of units of each type in each organization. Then, only the 311th Ferrying Squadron was absent from the group's station.

In the 86th Transport Squadron, old timers holding well deserved ratings were at the same time, as in other squadrons, holding back the advancement of other deserving men. Pfc Fred A. Schimpfle was one of these, having served as a superior crew chief for twelve months with the squadron. It was this squadron that furnished the bulk of the personnel for Project "A" in Sweden. This personnel was later transferred to units under Wing control due to their extended and unforseen absence. During December the 321st Transport Squadron boasted 97.8 per cent of its aircraft operational. The 312th Ferrying Squadron carried over 1,500,000 pounds of cargo 3800 evacuees and 1700 passengers.

The group played its part in the Ardennes campaign by furnishing half of the aircraft for the Wing's mission of carrying tank experts from Istres to Northern France by receiving and refueling all the aircraft engaged - utilizing the maintenance section of the 311th Ferrying Squadron stationed at Istres; and, by continuing the Paris to Luxembourgh daily scheduled flight, carrying priority passengers, mail and cargo.

Also during the winter Captain Hartwell Lancaster replaced Major Phillip Parkinson as commanding officer of the 86th Transport Squadron, who transferred to A.T.C. Captain Lancaster and and Lieutenants Gerald Denman and Sarkis Samarian made a special flight to Iceland. Lieutenant Harold Linville was named Operations Officer replacing Captain Lancaster.

The Very Heavy Bombardment Program offered opportunity for some men of the group to return to the United States. Among these were Staff Sergeant Roger Ansink and Staff Sergeant Alec Hayes. Hayes had been overseas two and one-half years and had been a member of the 321st Transport Squadron since the day of its activation.

Villacoublay

Just as Le Bourget airfield was beginning to regain its color and the mud was not quite so plentiful, action was brought to a head to return the field to the French Air Force, Villacoublay, another field just on the outskirts of Paris was selected as the new home. Units started moving in February and continued throughout March. The 321st Transport Squadron, profiting from past experiences, having its equipment listed in order of priority for movement, and for the past year having studied moves and the ease with which they could be accomplished, found little difficulty in completing its change of station. All units were blessed

Above: Prime Minister Winston Churchill and Lt Gen John Lee, Heston, 1944
Below: "Buzz Bomb Alley".

with mud on their arrival however, for it was plentiful.

The 311th Ferrying Squadron placed its flying crews on detached service with other squadrons of the groups, pending its move to rejoining the group. Captain John Howard was sent to Villacoublay in charge of the advanced party to receive the squadron, and shortly thereafter Major Thomas moved his unit to its new station.

The 320th Transport Squadron, for its work in evacuation, using C-64 type aircraft, was commended for its performance by the Theater Surgeon General. This squadron was in the meantime reequipped with C-47 transports.

No sooner had the group began to breathe a bit at its new station, when the "all out" period began and the air freight figures piled higher and higher. The 86th Transport Squadron, the last unit to move from Le Bourget, won the Wing's Squadron Flying Safety Trophy. The 27th Air Transport Group won the Wing's Group Trophy. These were for the three month period of January, February and March.

Master Sergeant John Boone was elected President of the Enlisted Men's Council for the Headquarters Squadron. Ted Malone broadcast to the people of the United States on the work of a number of the men of the organization.

The 86th Transport Squadron sent two special flights to Italy. Master Sergeant John G. Dea, Captain Frank Kontour's, noncommissioned officer in charge of maintenance, was highly praised by the squadron when it won the Wing Trophy.

The 311th Ferrying Squadron was assigned a new commanding officer in Major James Lyons. He was succeeded as commanding officer of the 320th Transport Squadron by Captain Lloyd Shields. The 311th in its operations flew to to advanced units so far ahead of intelligence reports that often pilots used maps from the "Stars and Stripes" to find enemy locations.

Lt Col Matt G Carpenter and Maj Allen C Russell, first and second commanders of 519th Service Sq and "service" staff officers.

The 320th Transport Squadron doubled its February operations, flying a total of 1686 flights during the month.

The 321st Transport Squadron commenced training for night flights. These were planned for use between London and Paris. The last week of March was spent by this squadron shuttling ammunition to front line units from Grove, flying ten long hours each day. Captain Boyd developed a system of maintenance check that paid dividends by keeping his record above 95 per cent.

During these increased operations, the ground forces were compelled to draw on non-tactical units of ground and air forces. Being service in classification and duty, though daily coming close to combat operations, personnel were drawn from each of the organizations.

In April, the last heavy month, the 311th Ferrying Squadron was reassigned from the group to Wing Control to operate various communications flights. Many of the aircraft and crews of this squadron however were reassigned to other squadrons of the group.

Master Sergeant Forrest Blood was among the officers and men used in forming the new service group, organized to support the transport organizations. Lt Col Covalt, the transport organization's executive, was made commanding officer of this new organization.

The 86th Transport Squadron lost one of its most experienced crews when Lieutenants Mellers and Lampman, Technical Sergeants Ruddy and Filkins while carrying 5,000 pounds of 100 octane gasoline to frontline units disappeared.

The 312th Ferrying Squadron developed its maintenance section to such a degree of proficiency that an engine change was made in eighteen hours, the aircraft never being carried as "U/S". Three aircraft of the squadron were fired on by flak battries of the German Luftwaffe, causing minor damages. Flying seventeen aircraft, the squadron totaled over 2,500 hours for the month, averaging 150 hours on each transport.

All squadrons were introduced to new faces as personnel formerly of Troop Carrier Units or Medium Bomb Units were transferred in to replace crews of Air Transport Command who returned to their parent organizations.

New Commanding Officer

Lieutenant Colonel Kenneth A. Reecher, who had completed a tour of B-17 bomber missions, a tour in Russia with USSTAF's Eastern Command, and who was formerly Deputy for Operations of the Wing, succeeded Colonel Feldman as Commanding Officer of the Group when the latter returned to the United States in hope of an assignment to a very heavy bombardment combat unit.

During the closing days of the European War one of the main missions of the group was the return of released allied prisoners of war and the repatriated

Above: LeBourget Passenger Terminal, 1944.

Below: Maj Ted Bennet, Oprs Officer and Col Carl Feldman, Comdg Officer.

citizens of many of the United Nations, including thousands of French and British in particular.

In the very first day of operations, more than 700 worn and tired but smiling sons of France were brought from a collecting point in Germany into Villacoublay where they were greeted by an eager and enthusiastic French reception committee.

For most of these repatriates, it was the first time they had set foot on French soil in five or six years. Their frail bodies and deeply lined faces gave ample testimony to the treatment they had been forced to undergo as forced laborers under the Nazi warlords. Their gratitude needed no vocal expression - it was clearly evident in the sparkling eyes and tired smiles.

Released allied prisoners of war, too, were brought to Villacoublay on the first leg of their journey homeward, and many were carried still further to the port of embarkation at Le Havre. Like the repatriates, their faces told a story of hardship and privation.

In 26 months, the 27th Air Transport Group carved its name deep into the journals of Uncle Sam's air arms in the European Theater of Operations. Long before D-Day, it had helped to set the stage for the invasion, hustling supplies throughout the United Kingdom - England, Scotland, Northern Ireland and Wales. Its big C-47s had roamed far from home to undertake emergency missions in almost every corner of Europe.... to Swedan, to Italy, to Iceland and even into Africa and Russia. They winged their way across the Atlantic to bring back urgently needed material. When the Allied forces began to forge their way across the continent, the 27th carried gasoline, blood plasma, whole blood, ammunition, and other high priority cargo wherever it was needed on the battlefields in France and Germany.

Lt Col James Douglas

Even V-E Day failed to hault the activities of the 27th Air Transport Group and while operational air force units paused for a well deserved rest, the 27th continued to fly into Germany to bring back liberated prisoners of war and repatriates.

The record of the 27th Air Transport Group will long remain a tribute to the men who worked so untiringly that Victory in Europe might not be delayed by so much as a single day. It is a tribute not alone to pilots and air crews, but to every man who did his job... the ground men, mechanics, cooks, clerks, carpenters and all those who made up this great team called the 27th Air Transport Group.

Maintenance on the smallest to largest of A/C has been performed by the 370th.

## MADE UP OF UNITS BORN IN THE UNITED KINGDOM AND ONE FROM THE U.S. THE 370TH AIR SERVICE GROUP SUPPORTED THE 27TH AIR TRANSPORT GROUP

The 370th Air Service Group wasn't even a month old when the Russian and allied armies met at the Elbe River but it wouldn't be fair to tell of the performances of this group of men who were the other half of the Continental forces of the 302d Transport Wing for only this short period. Formed on 12 April 1945, this service organization was attached to the 27th Air Transport Group to support it in maintenance of aircraft and automotive vehicles and supply it with everything from soup to nuts. It took over the housekeeping duties of Villacoublay and operated the traffic and freight section which handled close to a million pounds of freight and 15,000 passengers each month.

Just when the organizations which formed the 370th Air Service Group were first melded together to form one team in support of the flying organization would be hard to say. The 520th Service Squadron had behind it a great record of receiving replacement and combat aircraft from the United States while at Prestwick, Scotland from August 1942 to the Spring of 1944, when it went to Warton to play its part in the Service Section and later the provisional 1001st Service Group. The 10th Airdrome Squadron, though changed little upon the activation of the group had operated Heston airdrome near

London and shared in the manning of Querqueville and Le Bourget. The 1988th Quartermaster Truck Company, since it departed from Jefferson Barracks September of 1942, had seen service at Burton on Trent, throughout Cornwall, Warton and Heston and Le Bourget. The 312th Station Compliment was one of the original units of the Wing. The 1385th Military Police Company came to the command at half strength in March. The 2127th Engineer Fire Fighting Platoon had stood guard over airdromes at Querqueville and Istres. The 20th Mobile Repair and Reclamation Squadron had in seven short months, made a place for itself on the rolls by supporting the "petrol to Patton" line of B-17s and B-24s at Lyneham and Chipping Ongar and by dispatching its mobile teams throughout the United Kingdom and France. It was hard to get used to the lack of individuality and to the required team play that the organization of the service group brought, but soon the esprit de corps was the same as that found formerly in any of these service units.

520th Service Squadron

This squadron found itself at Warton in the Service Section when the 302d Transport Wing took command of the 27th Air Transport Group. The technical supply section was busy assemblying spare parts in expectance of 65 new C-47s. A number of C-53 type aircraft were converted to "VIP" aircraft for use by the transport groups on special flights. In September the squadron began to grow in strength, gathering personnel from Russia, France, Lyneham, Langford Lodge, and just about every other place where men could be found in Air Service Command. The 1st Service Group was formed as a provisional unit to serve both transport groups with Major C. P. Pond, Jr, named as the commanding officer. Captain Roger Hicks replaced Major James Lyons as commanding officer of the squadron, and Captain William Buhler was named Engineering Officer for the "Willow Run of England". Lt S. C. Schaller and Sgt D. E. Krahl departed for France with a ten day level of supplies as the advanced supply section of the group. The next month the squadron commenced to leave in force for the Continent, leaving behind a unit just strong enough to function until operations commenced at Le Bourget. In December the provisional group which had been redesignated as the 1001st disbanded and the service units split to give direct support to the two transport organizations. The 520th was assigned to the 27th Air Transport Group and charged with third and fourth echelon maintenance of this group's aircraft. Before the disbandment of the squadron Captain David Hollyfield replaced Major Hicks, when the latter was named personnel officer for the transport group.

10th Airdrome Squadron

The 10th Airdrome Squadron remained a separate squadron under the new group. Between the covers of its morning reports nearly half the names of personnel in service units throughout the 302d Transport Wing will be found for it had furnished personnel for the operation of Heston under Major Arthur B. Kline, Querqueville under Majors Ralph Pickering and L. F. Smithers, Istres under Major Harold White, and Le Bourget and Villacoublay under Captain Jay A. Shroyer. The squadron sent a detachment to Brussels headed by Lt M. G. Smith, Jr, to expedite the handling of freight and passengers transported there by the command. Before the formation of the group it was the squadron's duty to operate the base quartermaster and ordnance, however the main task became the operation of special aircraft and the traffic terminal which was the largest air passenger terminal in the theater. This was operated under the guidance of Captains J. L. Dingel and Carl Neisweinder. Strong in operation on V-E Day, the squadron had seen many changes and locations since the day 1st Sgt Richard Walsh reported at Heston to reorganize the unit.

1988th QM Truck Company

One of the oldest service units in the theater air force, the company had hauled ammunition, bombs, personnel, clothing and food supplies, and air corps spare parts throughout England, Ireland, Scotland and Wales, and shuttled pierce steel planking from Normandy to Le Bourget, and the "Stars and Stripes" and "Yank" magazines to the front when transportation was scarce. It had operated base transportation sections at Predannack, Portreath, St Eval and Trebelzue, Warton, Heston, Le Bourget, Grove and Villacoublay. It had seen every type of trucking service possible in nearly ever place possible. At Warton in one month Cpl Paul Honath and Pvt Joseph Best repaired over 400 tires for the company. At Heston Lt L. J. Halbrook and Staff Sergeant James Gantt operated a motor pool serving the United Kingdom airline out of London. It too had a detachment at Istres. It was one of the few units that retained its original commanding officer from the time it hit the theater until the time it was disbanded. Captain Walter M. Trauger arrived a "shave tail" in command of the unit and stood faithfully with the organization through its trials and tribulations.

312th Station Compliment

Originally scheduled to mann air terminals of the command, this organization found itself first in one group, then in another, and finally included in the melding of the 370th Air Service Group. The squadron furnished base personnel at Grove until the 31st Transport and the 27th Air Transport Groups both had moved to the Continent. After a brief stay at Le Bourget, it was reassigned to the 31st Transport Group to mann Chartes. When this Group returned to England, the Squadron returned to the 27th Air

Above: 10th Airdrome Fire Section B-26 crash, Heston.
Below: Gen. Lee's aircraft 873

Transport Group and later moved to Villacoublay with that organization. Captain William H. Lausman assumed command when the squadron reached France and later Captain Russell G. Oien was placed in command. The squadron superiorly manned and operated its installations. It was ably guided by 1st Sgt Louis E. Dennis who served as cook and mess sergeant before being made 1st Sgt.

20th Mobile R & R Sq

Assigned to the Wing to support the gasoline shipment to the Third Army, the first station and temporary home for this squadron was RAF Station Lyneham, in September 1944. From there the squadron was moved to Chipping Ongar to carry on similar duties, and then to Grove. The squadron was under the leadership of Major Fred Griffith. From Grove the unit was moved to France with other units of the 27th Air Transport Group, and under the guidance of Major Fred Olander and Captain Frank Kelley dispatched mobile teams to any part of the theater where wing aircraft were in distress. A mobile team was dispatched to Istres; two were returned to the "U.K." The squadron won the Wing Basketball Tournament, defeating the 31st All Stars, 44 to 26.

Other Units

Little can be said of Lt Carroll Peabod's 1385th Military Police Company as a unit for it had just one month previously joined the Villacoublay group. The men were quick to learn the ways of the Continent and with support of what few experienced police were on hand and the aid of war dog teams Captain J. L. Hinkel, Lt Peabody, and Lt Kenneth Hawkins organized a strong police unit to insure base security. The 2127th Engineer Fire Fighting Platoon commanded by Captain Jack Williams, like all fire departments - little though of except

Above: Service Squadron hangar at Le Bourget, 1944.
Below: Engine Repair Shop, Warton, 1944.

when needed to fight fire - stood by faithfully, keeping guard over the field.

New Group

The formation of the 370th Air Service Group was nothing more than regrouping of functions formerly performed by various units. Lt Col W. L. Covalt was named commanding officer and Captain Trauger commander of the headquarters and base services squadron. Captain Holyfield was designated commanding officer of the 631st Air Materiel Squadron and Captain Kent L. West, formerly assistant engineering officer for the transport organization, commander of the 807th Air Engineering Squadron. Captain Shroyer continued as commanding officer of the 10th Airdrome Squadron.

Gen Koenig Govenor General of Paris and his pilot Capt Ira Sullivan, one of many special projects performed by the wing.

FERRYING REPLACEMENT AIRCRAFT AND FLYING COMMUNICATION FLIGHTS ALONG WITH SPECIAL PROJECTS CARRIED THE WING OVER EUROPE, AFRICA AND ASIA

To the 302d Transport Wing was delegated any and all jobs that resembled air transportation and ferrying by Air Service Command. Among the various projects were the detaching of flying personnel to the Base Air Depot Area test flight sections to ferry aircraft throughout the United Kingdom, the detaching of ten crews and transport aircraft to an undisclosed destination on a top secret project, later called Project "A", the detaching of seperate crews to fly high officials, and the operation of communications flights for various headquarters of the air forces and the air staff of the Supreme Headquarters of the Allied Expeditionary Forces.

## Communications Flights

The duty of operating communications flights was one that had followed the 27th Air Transport Group since the days of the provisional activation of that organization. One of its first units operated a flight from Heathrow Airdrome, near London, for the Eighth Air Force Headquarters and the Eighth Air Force Service Command. This airdrome is now the largest serving commercial traffic in London, equipped with long lagoons to receive amphibious aircraft. From Heathrow the flight was moved to Hendon and operated by the 86th Transport Squadron; and from there to Heston where the

325th Ferrying Squadron assumed the operation of the activity. By this time however, the Eighth Air Force had moved and the United States Strategic Air Forces in Europe with its Air Service Command headquarters utilized the operations. When the allied forces invaded the continent and advanced parties of the top air force headquarters moved to the Paris area, a new organization was established to operate the flight section.

Personnel assigned to the wing headquarters squadron and placed on detached service at Tous Le Noble (A-46) in Detachment "B", and later the 1302d Airdrome Squadron, a provisional unit, under the leadership of Captain Michael Adams, made up the new organization. Initially maintaining just over thirty various aircraft in December of 1944, by April of the following year this organization was trying in every way to keep over eighty aircraft of fourteen varieties in the air for staff officers of USSTAF and Air Service Command.

Starting in September of 1944, Capt Adams, assisted by Captain D. G. Martin; as executive officer; Captain Ed Granger, as operations officer; and Chief Warrant Officer L. R. Crotty, as adjutant and personnel officer, soon put the badly bombed field into shape to receive and dispatch the highest rank of the theater. In February of the following year over fifty U.S. generals arrived or departed from this station. Over one each day kept the little field alive with readiness and ever striving for better appearance.

In April 1945, the 311th Ferrying Squadron was reassigned from the 27th Air Transport Group and assigned to this station to assume the operation of the communications flight. For the first time in over two years an authorized organization had been detailed to operate this function. That same month the Wing was detailed to establish a communications flight for the Air Staff of SHAEF Headquarters at Reims, where the armistice was signed. Major James Lyons, who then commanded the 311th Ferrying Squadron, assigned Capt Adams to this detachment. Ably assisted once more by Captain Martin, this detachment moved forward and operated at Reims until that headquarters moved to Frankfurt. Lt Wickey will long be remembered by all who called requesting air craft from the headquarters served, for as operations officer, he filled a key-stone job around which the entire station operated.

Other members who played important rolls at this busy airstrip were S/Sgt Thompson, M/Sgt Knerr, M/Sgt Bernstein, and M/Sgt Drybough.

## Ferrying

Originally occupying half of the activities of the 27th Air Transport Group, ferrying of replacement aircraft in this theater has always been a major and important function. Major Remlin was the first director of ferrying for the 27th Air Transport Group back in 1942. At one time all ferrying squadrons assigned to that organization were used in ferrying rather than transport work as was later necessary. The 326th Ferrying Squadron of the 31st Transport Group performed the movement of newly arrived or modified aircraft for the Ninth Air Force.

In the fall of 1944, the Base Air Depot Area was charged with this responsibility for Air Service

Command but the Wing was required to furnish the pilots and crews who actually moved the aircraft. Originally assigned to the 310th Ferrying Squadron, these crews were reassigned throughout the entire command to even the load carried by each squadron and group then heavily engaged in transport work.

In February 1945, the Wing was once again charged with the operations. Major Gayle Schooling was placed in charge with Capt Fay Brandis as assistant at Warton and Captain Howard Nichols assistant at Burtonwood. This new organization was a provisional one known as the 302d Ferrying Squadron. Shortly thereafter, the 310th Ferrying Squadron was withdrawn from the 31st Transport Group and again put to ferrying. The personnel then engaged by Major Schooling were assigned to the unit and the 310th, the original organization

employed in ferrying in the theater was once more on its well known job.

Lt Stephen Hupka was named adjutant; Chief Warrant Officer Crotty, personnel officer; Lts Kenneth A. Jones, Robert Hartzell, and Wilton Hodges, flight leaders at Burtonwood; and, Lts Thomas Smith, Joseph Sabinske and Cecil E. Price, flight leaders at Warton. Captain Brandis was named squadron executive officer and remained in charge at Warton. Captain Nichols was named squadron operations officer.

At the same time crews were delivering aircraft to depots and combat units, they were often leading newly arrived combat crews to home stations, crews who were unfamiliar with the weather pecularities and terrain of England and France. The big story for the fighter pilots was the moving of some 66 "Thunderbolts" and "Mustangs" from Casablanca, Morocco to Warton.

The following is a three month record of the Squadron:

| Month | Ferried | Combat Aircraft Led to Bases |
|---|---|---|
| Feb | 2,194 | 949 |
| March | 2,357 | 741 |
| April | 2,238 | 420 |

Project "A"

In November 1944 the Wing was instructed by USSTAF Operations to select the ten best aircraft, manned by ten well experienced crews, and prepare these for a secret mission. Mystery surrounded these crews and all who

Above: Ferry pilots showing capacity of B-17 taxi aircraft.
Below: Ferry pilots in Ireland at morning briefing.

handled any part of the task. Originally assigned to the 27th Air Transport Group, the crews were later reassigned while absent to the 310th and 311th Ferrying Squadrons.

Definitely known was that the crews, later supplimented by ground crews, were on a job called Project "A" and that it was far north. The latter was known from the type of equipment and clothing carried on each aircraft.

Shortly after V-E Day the first crews, including Captain Meritt and Master Sergeant Levy returned to the command and told the story. These ten aircraft, under the command of Captain Holliman, were stationed in far north Sweden near the Norwegian border. Their primary mission was to support Norwegian 'police' units. Among the loads carried by the flight other than 'police' troops, was a hospital unit, hay for the horses used by the resistance forces, paratroopers, and food and clothing.

Each of the members of this task force learned to ski. A few witnessed fighter attacks by Finnish and German aircraft. All spent the winter near the thermometer which read from thirty to forty degree below zero - Centragrade, which is approximately fourteen degrees below zero as we read the scale.

Other Operations

Other wing operations included the Wing Headquarters and Headquarters Squadron, commanded by Major Leo Domijan in England and in France by Captain Edward Heinsimer.

The advanced detachment of the Wing Headquarters set its office on the Champs Elysees in September of '44, while street fighting still occurred in some sections of Paris.

Above: Ferry pilots checking latest briefing "poop" and weather.

Below: Ferry pilots file clearances prior to take off at squadron.

During the time of the rapid expansion of service units in the winter of 1944, Captain Walter Hopper, and Lieutenants Robert Brett and Maxwell Sturtz operated a command replacement or reinforcement pool at Meadowbank.

The following stations or airstrips operated as detachments of the Wing Headquarters at one time or another: Istres, Querqueville, Le Bourget, Toussus Le Noble and the ferry section at Burtonwood and Warton.

Grove, England. This freight terminal is second only to the terminal flying supplies to China over the "Hump".

THE 31ST GROUP HAS LEFT AN ENVIABLE RECORD IN ITS PATH THROUGH ENGLAND, FRANCE AND GERMANY.

The three months of October, November and December of 1943 were the labor months for the 31st Transport Group at Grove, Berkshire in England, for it was then the headquarters and five squadrons were activated, manned and organized. Among these units were the 313th, 314th, 315th and 316th Transport Squadrons and the 326th Ferrying Squadron.

Col Carl Feldmann was appointed commanding officer by the Commanding General of the Ninth Air Force Service Command, the command to which the group was then assigned. The first commanding officer was an officer of the Regular Army; a command pilot with some thirteen years of service. He was a member of the first task force to land in the United Kingdom and a veteran of the famous Polesti oil refinery raid.

The group was activated with one lone aircraft - the famous "Baby Dumpling", a veteran of battles against African heat and burning sands. The "Babe" was symbolic as a beginning, for on V-E Day she was still carrying her share of the supply and evacuation burden. It was the "Babe" that carried the 10,000th patient from Normandy.

From that winter the group grew and expanded, groaned from new loads and constantly prepared for the invasion so long awaited. Each cargo flight in the United Kingdom was but a prelude to bigger things ahead. Pilots were trained to fly under similated combat conditions -- to hug the ground and to recognize emergencies. Other units of the group were sent out to live under field conditions.

Fighters and bombers were ferried by the 326th Ferrying Squadron, under the command of Lt Col Henry C. Allen, from assembly areas to attack strips. The 315th and 316th Transport Squadrons, commanded by Major Albert Hansen and Captain Robert E. Ahlin, were inactivated, but the 315th carried on as a provisional organization, flying the cargo and mail and transporting passengers throughout the United Kingdom for the Ninth Air Force.

Each step forward was a drive toward invasion. Suddenly the tempo increased. New aircraft were added, mechanics worked the clock around painting black and white invasion stripes on the transports, and a special assembly crew was called in to work a twenty-four hour shift installing litters, magically converting the "sky trains" to "flying ambulances" capable of carrying 24 litter patients or 27 ambulatory patients. They were the "mercy planes" of World War II.

By "D Day" the group was a potent force. June 11th brought the first test, and this by the commanding officer, as Col Feldman landed the first transport on the beach at Omaha. From then on the airstrip was a 31st show. The queens of the sky swept in dumped their loads and took aboard wounded allied soldiers for the hospitals in England. The field operations were placed under Major Milton Evans, and T-1 became "the busiest airdrome in the world".

Lt Col Allen was relieved as commanding officer of the 326th Ferrying Squadron and named air executive of the Group. He was succeeded by Captain Francis W. Foreman. The squadron later transferred to the IX Air Force Service Command after the group had been assigned to the 302d Transport Wing and the Air Service Command, of the United States Strategic Air Forces in Europe.

There was little effect on the group when the 302d Transport Wing was placed over the organization as a command headquarters for there still remained active only the 31st Transport Group in the Wing. After three months of operating to the airstrips in France, the group had recorded over 13,000 tons of cargo, 27,000 evacuees, and 41,000 passengers transported.

## Group Moves to France

Led by the 313th Transport Squadron, the group made its way to airstrips in Normandy. The headquarters was located at Querqueville, a former Luftwaffe fighter base just south of Cherbourgh.

Shortly after the completion of the move, the group was reassigned with the wing to the Air Service Command, operating for the United States Strategic Air Forces in Europe instead of the Ninth Air Force alone. New faces were seen - newly assigned personnel to assist in maintenance and ATC crews attached for operational duty.

Evacuation aircraft of the group were inspected by General Eisenhower and Admiral King. Transports of the group assisted in the hauling of thousands of gallons of gasoline to the Third Army during the battle for France and to the thunderbolt units pounding at the Germans during the siege of the Falaise gap.

With the front ever nearer to Germany, group aircraft delivered hundreds of pints of life giving blood plasma and whole blood to field hospitals. To the fighting men went bayonets, rifles, grenades, combat rations and rubber shoes to war against trench foot. Belly tanks, cramming planes so tightly that pilots and crews entered their planes through escape hatches, were flown to tactical units, increasing the striking range of thunderbolts, mustangs, and lightnings, escorting bombers and coordinating strafing attacks with the ground forces. Army medics demanded toilet seats, and toilet seats were carried by the 31st aircraft. Engineers ordered fence posts and received them, and the Quartermaster called for chicken wire, receiving same on priority shipment for road matting. "Red Ball" trucks brought hot freight to the 31st airstrips, who in turn flew it to the tactical units. France was busy in an American way and the Americans with the 31st Transport Group were on their way to Germany.

New C. O.

November of 1944 found all the units of this group again on the move. This time Chartres (A-40) was to be the new home, but only for a few short weeks. The 313th Transport Squadron moved north from an airstrip near Bolleville and LaHaye du Puit, the 314th left Manupertus and the headquarters left their former Russian barracks at Querqueville to make themselves at home in the Travelers' Insurance Building. The 310th Ferrying Squadron equipped with nineteen C-47s, four B-17s and three B-24s was reassigned from the 27th Air Transport Group and also moved to Chartres from Grove. The headquarters squadron had formed Detachment "A", consisting of the personnel formerly assigned to the 326th Ferrying Squadron, and this too moved forward. At the new base there was mud, mud and more mud. There was mud in the supply, mud in engineering, mud in the mess and mud to spare.

The move from Normandy was interesting for those who came by road, and a bit difficult for the ground echelon of the 314th Transport who were troubled with breakdowns of their decontamination units and their five ton tractor flat bed trailer.

After a few days spent in preparing the field for a "home" Col Feldmann was reassigned as Commanding Officer, 27th Air Transport Group. With him he carried a few of the "old timers" to compose his new staff. Lt Col Wendell L.Covalt, Major Theodore E. Bennett and Captain John Moore were among these.

Lt Col Allen, who had commanded the 326th Ferrying Squadron at

Above: Loading .50 caliber ammunition destined for fighter strips of Ninth AF.

Below: Loading belly tanks for delivery to fighter strips.

activation and later been named air executive assumed command of the group. He named Major Milton Evans Deputy Commander and Major Walter Shea Operations Officer. Lt Harold Trott was named Assistant Adjutant to Major Robert E. Cochran to replace Captain Moore.

Still new in the drivers seat when Colonel Martin A. Bateman was made Commanding Officer of the Wing, Lt Col Allen was instructed to return the 31st Transport Group as quickly as possible to Grove where the air freight terminal was rapidly becoming the world's second largest.

The return of the group to its birthplace offered opportunities for consolidation of many of its activities. Consolidated messes were opened. A production line maintenance was initiated, primarily manned by the 519th Service Squadron but supplemented by engineering personnel from each flying squadron.

The 314th Transport Squadron in moving was required to pack its canvas while still wet and found it necessary to dry the same at Grove in large niesen huts, using stoves and blower fans. The 313th sent aircraft and crews to Italy on special projects and the 310th sent the same to Russia. The 325th Ferrying Squadron disbanded its traffic detachments throughout the United Kingdom and appointed Captain Ian W. Miller executive officer when Captain Cameron was assigned to Biggin Hill as Commanding Officer of the unit there.

On Christmas Eve when the Wing issued the call for a hundred transports to standby for a high priority assignment, aircraft bearing the white triangle were enroute to depots and airstrips all over the United Kingdom and France. Radios at Grove commenced

Above: Evacuation of ambluatory patients.

Below: Evacuation of litter patients.

to buzz. Aircraft half way accross the English Channel turned and "high tailed" for home. With final instructions issued, aircraft took off for Southern France to rush the needed tank experts to the fighting front just south of Luxembourgh. This was one of the greatest hauls ever made by the units of the group. Just how much it meant in turning the rolling tide of the German counteroffensive cannot be measured.

The 313th Transport Squadron dispatched five aircraft on a special trip into the Mediterranean Theater, traveling to Harrington, Brindisi, Torretto, and Rome, covering 14,675 air miles.

The 87th Transport Squadron which had formerly belonged to the 27th Air Transport Group but reassigned to the Base Air Depot Area for a months service was returned to the Wing and assigned this time to the 31st Group.

The winter at Grove threw a lot of mud at the organization. A mud control project was instigated and soon with great care, Grove was not only one of the largest U.S.bases in the United Kingdom as well as the largest air freight terminal but also one of the best groomed.

In January 63 men left the group for the United States under the Very Heavy Bombardment Program carrying off some of the original cadre personnel. The 87th Transport Squadron carried over 500 tons during this bad weather month. Captain Paul Morris was named executive officer of the 310th Ferrying Squadron, relieving Captain C.A.Rawls. The 314th Transport Squadron, dividing its aircraft and crews into two flights, set as a goal for the flight carrying the largest figures a party at the expense of the loosers. Captain Clifford Byrne, operations officer of the 325th Ferrying Squadron, returned to the Zone of the Interior having served with that unit for some six months after completing a tour of operations. T Sgt Charles Ruby of the same squadron returned under the VHB plan.

The following month, February, saw another group of faces disappear from the station as the group was called on for reinforcements for the ground forces. Each squadron furnished its share and soon under the stress found its technically trained personnel on squadron details. Major Robert Ahlin was relieved of commanding officer of the 313th Transport and made head man of the 325th Ferrying Squadron, replacing Major Allen Lind who became Assistant Group Operations Officer. Captain Laverne Huston succeeded Major Ahlin as commanding officer of the 313th and detailed two special flights to Rome. The 310th Ferrying Squadron which had been furnishing all personnel used by the Base Air Depot Area of the Air Service Command for ferrying replacement aircraft to tactical units and storage depots reassigned the majority of this personnel to other ferrying squadrons of the Wing. This equally balanced the number of ferry crews furnished by each group and each of the four ferrying squadrons. Along with the unfavorable weather, seven one-hundred hour inspections, two two-hundred hour inspections, one aircraft in the depot for a 1200 hour inspection, major repairs on still another aircraft,

Above: One of the World's largest freight air terminals, Grove.
Below: Interior of one of the air terminal hangars, Grove.

and engine changes on two aircraft required because of blower clutch failures, the 313th Transport Squadron still marked up 1,064 hours for its aircraft flying time for the month.

Central Europe Drive

March saw the opening of the Central Europe Campaign and the "all out" drive of all allied armies and air forces crushing the German might.

In this month alone the group carried a third of the total tonnage it had moved in the entire year of 1944. It carried two thirds more evacuees and spent one-fifth more time in the air. From this, it can be seen that all available space on board each aircraft was utilized to maximum efforts. An empty aircraft meant a drop in morale of the crew. Poor loading and unloading crews meant the same for this prolonged the stay on the ground.

Major Lind led a flight to Russia on another special mission. Captain J.C. Pimentel was named Group Operations Officer when Major Shea was placed in charge of operations at Biggin Hill. Captain Cameron assumed command of the 314th Transport Squadron; Major Harold Paulin, the former commanding officer, having been transferred to the 310th Ferrying Squadron when Major Brooke was detailed to General Spaatz's flight section at Reims, near SHAEF Headquarters.

Captain Hoerner was promoted to Major and the 87th Transport Squadron began to take a number of first places. They claimed to be the first to land a transport in Germany. Air Inspectors of the Central Air Depot Area rated the squadron as one of the best of that command. Lieutenant Nathan Corman flew 161 hours that month and Lt Francis Nowak, 156. Corporal Nicholas Marotta,

Above: C-46 at loading ramp, Grove.

Below: Loading patients for evacuation to hospitals in United Kingdom.

a radio operator, flew 163 hours. This squadron was one of the first to have a C-46 "Commando" assigned. "Dumbo", as it was named, and on his initial trip carried over 10,000 pounds each way.

The 313th Transport Squadron also was assigned a "Commando" and started in to give crews transition training in expectance of additional numbers.

The 314th Transport Squadron won the station basketball championship. It had twenty-one pilots to top 100 hours flying during the month, and carried over 877 tons of passengers, evacuees, mail and cargo. A typical trip made by transports of this organization was from Grove to Nancy, carrying ammunition; from there to Pompey, near Nancy, for a load of gasoline destined for

Mainz, near Weisbaden; and from there to an advanced airstrip for a load of evacuees to return to England; finishing the day by carrying a load of freight to the air terminal or mail for the next morning's flight, to Grove. Late chow was a custom and not an unusual event.

In the 325th Ferrying Squadron, Staff Sergeant Roland Dittl and Sergeant Robert Strock started in on the information, education and orientation program by leading the unit in a number of weekly discussion groups.

The 310th Ferrying Squadron, still flying the largest number of aircraft in the group, carried over 4400 evacuees and over 1000 tons of cargo.

To replace the pilots leaving the organization after an extended period of detached service from ATC, new officers were reassigned from the reserve previously held by Troop Carrier Command and from a number made available when medium bomber groups, flying B-26s, were converted to bomber-attack groups equipped with A-26s. These new organizations required only half the number of pilots as the old.

In April, group aircraft flew over 12,000 hours, carried over 10,000 tons, and moved over 6,000 passengers and 20,000 evacuees. This was the last big month. It was in this month that the allied forces beat down their last final blow.

The 310th Ferrying Squadron was relieved from assignment to the group in which it had gloriously served for five months and once again returned to its initial job of ferrying. Few of the personnel of this organization employed in transport activities went to Burtonwood with the change, and Major Paulin who had commanded the unit was named Group Operations Officer. Captain Pimentel returned to the United States.

Staff Sergeant Earnest Gonzales led the 87th Transport Squadron for flying time records that month, putting in 171 hours at the radio. The 313th Transport Squadron hauled high ranking German prisoners from the Ninth Air Force Prisoner of War Interogation Section at Wiesbaden to London where they were interogated by allied authorities. The 314th Transport Squadron with fourteen transports flew 2432 hours, averaging 173 hours for each aircraft for the month.

## Close of War

The close of the European War

Above: Barracks at Querqueville.

Below: Col Feldman and Lt Col Covalt, CO and Ex, 1944.

found the 31st Transport Group still doing business at the same station where it had been formed a year and a half before. But the story that was written in those intervening months will make a scintillating chapter in the history of logistics in World War II.

What began at Grove as a few hangers and a trickle of supplies developed into the largest air freight terminal in the European Theater of Operations... largest in the world except for a similar installation in Burma serving planes flying "The Hump"

Almost every conceivable type of equipment cleared through this giant depot and into the ample fuselages of the C-47s. And most of the material went to fill "rush orders" for fighting units on the Continent. There was everything from .45 caliber pistols to rockets, machineguns and trench morters. There was winter clothing for the doughs at the front, there were overshoes, eggs, oranges and combat rations. There was de-icer fluid and portable hangers for operational air force units.

In those long, work-filled months, the 31st Transport Group posted a number of "firsts" that will long serve as a measuring stick with which to gauge the activities of the group. It was first to establish an air freight and evacuation strip on the Normandy beachhead. It was first to evacuate wounded from Germany. It was first to evacuate wounded from the other side of the Rhine. It was first to ferry the A-26 attack bomber in the European Theater of Operations.

Air transport of supplies could never have hoped to take the place of the Liberty Ships that

Above: Cargo dumped, aircraft stand by for casualties for return flight.
Below: Air evacuation from Ninth Armoured Division.

plied the channel. But it did get a tremendous amount of critical cargo where it was needed ...and did it more quickly than any other known means of Military transportation.

The men at the front have paid silent homage to the C-47s of the 31st Transport Group as they landed with urgently needed supplies. And many a man owes his life today to the speed with which he, as a wounded combat soldier, was returned from the from the front to a base hospital in the rear.

The story of the 31st Transport Group is the story of a good job well done.

Cold hands, cold tools, and freezing weather makes an outdoor engines change at Grove a "cussing bussiness".

## EXPERIENCES OF CORNWALL AND WARTON WELL QUALIFIED THE 371ST AIR SERVICE GROUP TO SUPPORT THE 31ST TRANSPORT GROUP

The 371st Air Service Group, like the 370th, was less than a month old when V-E Day was announced. In support of the 31st Transport Group at Grove and furnishing the housekeeping installations of the theater's largest air freight terminal, the group had since December of 1944 been in operation under various titles. The main neculeus of the new group was the 519th Service Squadron, which was one of the oldest organizations of the Wing. Personnel were also drawn from the 97th Airdrome Squadron and a limited number from the 1988th Quartermaster Truck Company and the 20th Mobile Repair and Reclamation Squadron, both of which were attached to the 27th Air Transport Group. The 2005th Engineer Aviation Fire Fighting Platoon and the provisional military police company was incorporated into the group to complete the organization of a smooth operating maintenance and supply depot and a station compliment which operated a station for larger than a normal service group would be expected to maintain.

Prior to the move to Grove in the winter of 1944, the units had performed service in as many varied places as other units of the Wing. Until that time the 31st Transport Group had operated on its own, without service support, from Grove to Normandy, and from there to Chartres.

### 519th Service Squadron

The 519th Service Squadron was activated in Cornwall near Land's End at RAF Station Portreath in April 1943. It was one of two service squadrons organized and assigned to support transport activities which ranged from handling freight and passengers at air terminals and repair combat aircraft in the field by use of mobile units, to the dispatching of replacement aircraft and tactical units to North Africa during that campaign.

The commanding officers of this unit read like a who's who list in the 27th Air Transport Group. The first was Lt Col Matt G. Carpenter, who later became Deputy Commander of the group. He was followed in turn by Major Allen G.Russell, who was the first officer of the command to receive the distinguished service cross. Captain Dale C.L. Honeycutt followed the Major, and was in turn followed by Captain Timothy A.De Eulis, who remained in command until the disbandment of the squadron.

In Cornwall the squadron was split for a time into three elements. One unit, containing the headquarters section, was located at Portreach, dispatching fighter aircraft to Africa in connection with the "Torch" movement and assisting tactical units of the Eighth Fighter Command in refueling and maintaining thunderbolts used on sorties in support of bombers pounding the U-Boat pens at Brest and St Lezaire. S second unit was located at St Eval, north of Newquay, receiving heavy replacement aircraft, B-17s and B-24s from the US over the South Atlantic route. The third unit was a small number of air corps personnel with a detachment of the 1988th QM Truck Co at Predannack, dispatching fighter aircraft to North Africa. Among those performing duty at first one station and then another, as required, were then Captain James Briggs, Lieutenants Posie Clinton, Merton Crockett, William Buhler, Richard Flemming, H.O. Johnson, Jr, M Sgt Clifton Mellott, 1st Sgt George Mettey, Sgt John De Luca, Cpl Robert Gorey.

From Cornwall, the squadron moved into the service section at Warton and later became a part of the 1st and the 1001st Service Groups (Provisional). The squadron furnished the headquarters personnel for this group. It was then Pfc Elmer Hanners and Pvt John Darling beyond the call of normal duties, assisted in the evacuating of children from a British school destroyed when a B-24 crashed blindly into the building. From Warton the squadron moved to Le Bourget, crossing the channel on LSTs and landing at Utah Beach after a rough trip that turned nearly every member's stomach and made them soon forget about the next meal but worry a bit over the last. When the move back to England was made, the squadron transferred all of its equipment to the 520th Service Squadron and started in again at Grove to reassemble tools, machines, vehicles, etc. The order from then on was "PLM", or "production line maintenance". An organization was set up under Major William Neff, the 31st Transport Group Engineering Officer, to handle all third echelon maintenance, plus a bit more, and all engine changes for the four squadrons of the group. Captain Fleming organized the air corps supply section, ably assisted by Captain James Freeman. So it was that this squadron ended only 200 miles from where it was born, but had traveled and operated over a 1000 miles route.

### 1031st MP Company

Organized when the units returned

to Grove, this provisional company maintained base security under the guidance of Lt Leonard Lippman. The company was originally made up of men available from any source but later, through reassignment and replacement, personnel were found more capable of properly performing the duties of a military police company, securing the base at entrances, patroling nearby villages, and standing guard over special aircraft.

97th Airdrome Squadron

The 97th Airdrome Squadron, which furnished a number of personnel for the organization of the group and later was one of the squadrons of this same group, operated under the command of Captain Laverne Huston. The primary mission of this unit was to furnish transient alert crew service on the flying line under the guidance of M Sgts Kenneth Doncho and Howard Thompson; operate airdrome control, where T Sgt Ray Johnston and thirteen others were employed; base quartermaster under Captain Joe Marshall and, base transportation under Captain Hichman Baker. This squadron also supplimented to personnel assigned to the maintenance depot operated by the 519th Service Squadron.

T Sgt Edward Nydon, who was an ex-combat flight engineer and who had flown over 35 missions without an abortion, was placed in charge of maintaining readiness for flight on all fighter aircraft ferried to the station to await favorable weather for continued flight to France. S Sgt Earl O'Neal and his refueling crew in February, refuelled an average of 63 aircraft each day, and the following month the entire servicing section handled an average of 95 aircraft each day.

Other Units

When the service group was formed, personnel and equipment of the 2005th Engineer Aviation Fire Fighting Platoon were reassigned to the Headquarters and Base Services Squadron, and the unit, in name only, was transferred to another command. This platoon had moved from England to Normandy and from there to Chartres and back to England.

The 1988th QM Truck Co sent a detachment of men and vehicles to Grove in February of 1945 to assist in the traffic problem then prevailing. This group was under the charge of S Sgt James Lilly, and were included in the new transportation section of the service group. Likewise, the 20th Mobile Repair and Reclamation Squadron had two mobile teams in the United

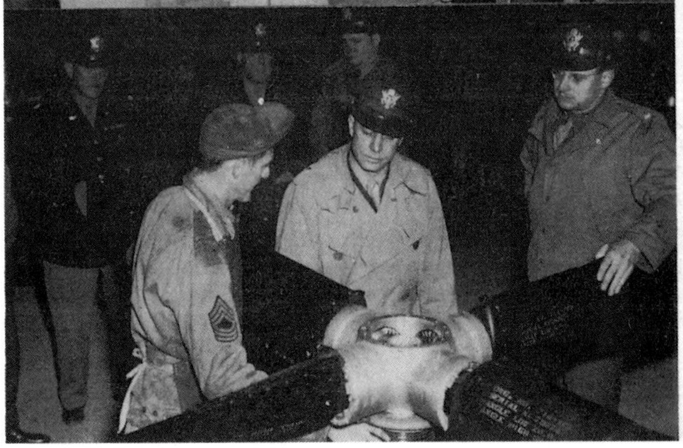

Above: Lt Fleming and Air Corps Supply personnel of 519th Service sq.
Below: Gen Jones, inspecting maintenance shops at Grove.

Kingdom under the charge of Warrant Officer Herchell Wheat, servicing wing aircraft downed away from home. This personnel was reassigned to the new organization.

Too much cannot be said of that small group of men that operated the London Traffic Office and the traffic and freight sections at North Holt and later Biggin Hill. They operated under every name in the book but it was under the name of Detachment "A", 97th Airdrome Squadron, commanded by Captain John Cameron in January 1945, that the organization began to function smoothly and pass through record numbers of personnel. Lieutenants B.O. Johnson, E.H. Silsley, Boyd Thomas, Richard Ivory, and Warrant Officer Robert Bower were a few of the "laborers" at this stop on the theater airline. In March Captain Cameron was reassigned to command a transport squadron and Major Walter Shea was placed in command.

Above: 1031st MP Co of the 371st Air Service Group at Grove, Berkshire.

Below: T Sgt Nard and Lt. Crockett.

### Group Staff

When the group was formed, officers were drawn from many units at Grove to staff the headquarters and command the new units. Lt Col Carey C.Harman was named commanding officer. He was well acquainted with the duties involved for as ground executive officer for the 31st Transport Group he was charged with the base housekeeping and the supply and maintenance. Major Robert Cochran, formerly the transport group's Air Inspector, was named group executive and commanding officer of the Headquarters and Base Service Squadron. Captain John Compton, formerly the personnel officer of the 31st Transport Group, was named group adjutant. Captain Richard Fleming who had supplied wing units from the beginning of operations was named commanding officer of the 632d Air Material Squadron, but soon afterwards went on thirty days leave to the United States where he was found on V-E Day. Captain James Freeman assumed command in his absence. Captain Timothy De Eulis was placed in command of the 808th Air Engineering Squadron. Captain Edward Lundak, who had replaced Captain Huston as commanding officer of the 97th Airdrome Squadron when the latter was placed in charge of a transport squadron, retained command of his unit until it moved to Biggin Hill minus personnel later in the month. After this move he was appointed S-3 officer of the service group. The group in order to simplify administration, was initially assigned directly to the 31st Transport Group.

CAPT. FRANK NORTON

ABOVE: COL. TIM McCOY, LT. COL. HARMAN, MAJOR EVANS

LEFT: LT. D. SMITH

ABOVE: GROVE COMMUNICATIONS SECTION

LEFT: AWARD OF AIR MEDALS IN 27TH

OFFICERS AT HENDON

CPL.S KEITH & BERK· LT. HARDIN

ABOVE: FERRY CREWS ABOARD TAXI A/C
LEFT: WING COMMUNICATIONS ·· MEADOWBANK

GENERAL MARSHALL

HESTON CARPENTERS

LT. ALBRECHT & CREW

86TH SQUADRON INSIGNIA

ABOVE: CAPT. SHAHAN, MAJ. PITTINGER & MAJOR JOHNSON
RIGHT: M/SGT. ADAMS

M.P. COMPANY – GROVE – '45
PHILADELPHIA GROUP – WARTON – '44

CAPT. DANIELS

LT. SAUNDERS & PFC WEBSTER

ABOVE: SGT. COLLINGWOOD AND LT. TERREL

LEFT: MAJOR STANGLEIN

'DOC' MARTIN "FILL IT OR PULL IT?"

31ST CONTROL ROOM

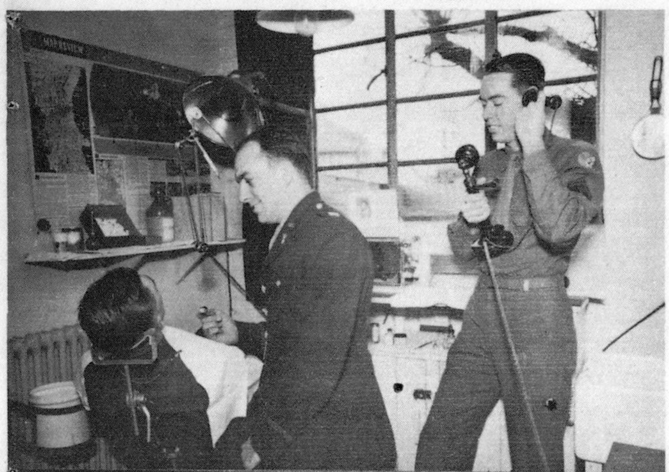

CAPT. JAMES D. BRIGGS

CONTROL TOWER LE BOURGET

ABOVE: HESTON BASEBALL CLUB

LEFT: LT. NOWAK

ABOVE: DEDICATION OF CHAPEL AT LE BOURGET
LEFT: PVT. JENNERS & LT. McGUIRE

IOTH AIRDROME PARTY

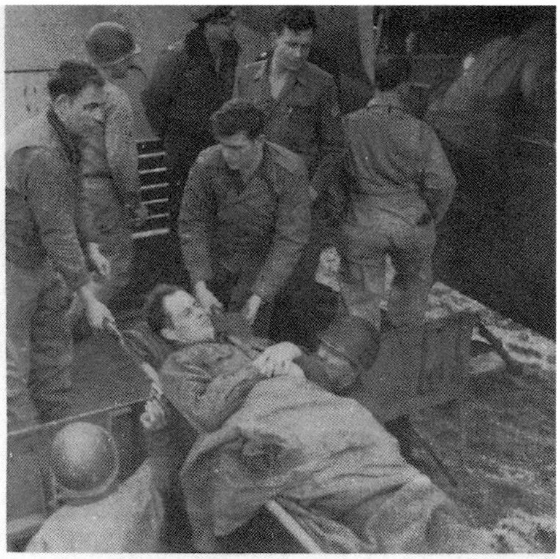

AIR EVACUATION

RIGHT: CAPT. BAKER

ABOVE: 86TH TRANSPORT SQUADRON ENGINEERING SECTION

CAPT. MILCH

HAVE A COKE?

27TH UNIT C.O.'S MEET AT HESTON '44

ABOVE: SGT.'S LUFT AND ALCORN AT CHECKERS ··· GRASSI AND WHITFIED KIBITZ ···

ABOVE: GEN. MILLER, MAJ. ALDEN AND CAPT. PARKINSON

RIGHT: 31ST GP. SPECIAL SERVICE GREENBERG

BELOW: NURSES AT GROVE

BELOW: TRANSPORTATION SECTION HESTON

CAPT. HAIGH

SALUTE THE SOLDIER PARADE

MAJOR MOORE

SGT. FITZPATRICK & LT. SAUERS

OFFICERS AT WARTON '44
VIVIEN LEIGH AT GROVE '45

GEN. WOOD PRESENTS SOLDIERS MEDAL TO CAPT. CURTIS

COFFEE FROM A.R.C. - GROVE

ABOVE: FIRE FIGHTING .. LE BOURGET
LEFT: CAPT. & SGT. CLINTON

ABOVE: WING HQ. BASKETBALL TEAM
LEFT: UNLOADING GASOLINE .. GUTERSLOH

COL. FELDMAN
& CPL. WOOD

E.M. & NURSES AT GROVE

ABOVE: FAREWELL PARTY AT OSTERLY
LEFT: RHUMBA BOYS

COL. BATEMAN &
COL. PAT BEVILLE (O.B.)

MAJ. PRIDDY & WING COLORS

DELIVERING GASOLINE TO ORLY
SEPTEMBER '44

CAPT. KENNEDY & GLADYS JONES

ABOVE: GENERAL MILLER PRESENTS
MAJ. RUSSELL WITH D.F.C.

RIGHT: SGT. BARRON

LANGFORD LODGE TRAFFIC SECTION
MEADOWBANK BARBERS

COLONEL ARNOLD & GEN. OTT

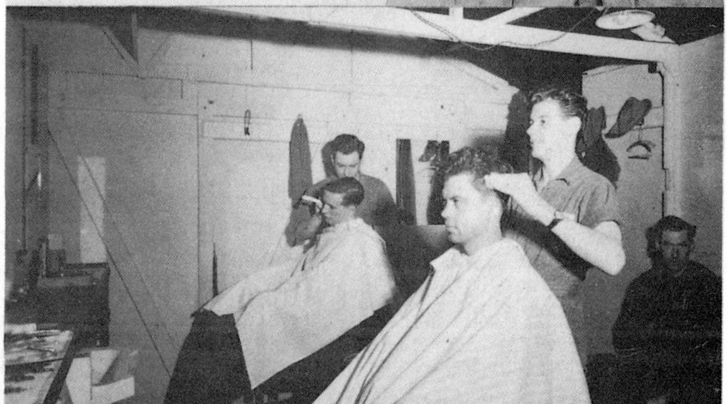

CPL.'S GRANSHAW & MAWHINNEY & LT. ROZNNES

MRS. SPELLER

CPL. CARNES & VIVIEN LEIGH

GEN. JONES INSPECTS AT GROVE

MEETING OF TRAFFIC OFFICERS '44

CAPT. BRANDIS

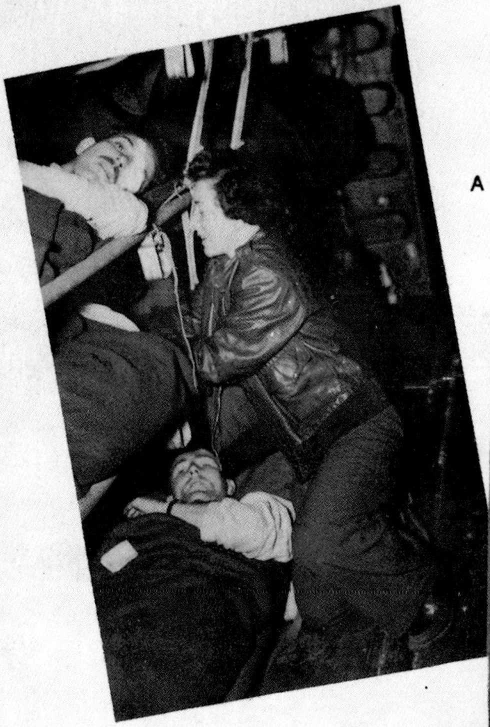

AIR EVACUATION

ABOVE: 520TH SERV. SQ. BASKETBALL TEAM

LEFT: BING CROSBY AT HESTON

ABOVE: 816TH AIR EVACUATION SQ.
LEFT: DIGGIN' GREASE PIT QUERQUEVILLE '44

CPL. BENGE
LT. TRENHOLM &
S/SGT. LEITL

CAPT. JOHNSON & T/SGT. RIVENBARK

ABOVE: UNLOADING AT QUERQUEVILLE
LEFT: WING HQ. MEADOWBANK

SGT. GILBERT &
LT. RINEHART

SGT.S BARGH & MEIROSE & WAC

LINK TRAINER CREW
VILLACOUBLAY '45

LT. SICO & LT. WILLIAMSON

ABOVE: AIR EVACUATION
RIGHT: MAJ. 'DOC' HASEWINKLE

811TH AIR EVACUATION SQ.
PARTY AT WAC BILLETS - PARIS - '44

CPL. PYLE & CAPT. TRAUTMAN
A-46 - '44

PRESENTATION OF SOLDIER'S MEDAL TO PFC HAROLD KOONTZ

CAPT. ZIPPER

CREW ON GUTERSLOH FLIGHT

CHRISTMAS IN 'HUT 5'
HAPPY BIRTHDAY PETE GURA

CHAPLAIN NELSON

LEFT: CAPT. IAN MILLER & SGT. L. CAMPBELL

ABOVE: 10TH AIRDROME RISKS A FEW RED CROSS DO-NUTS

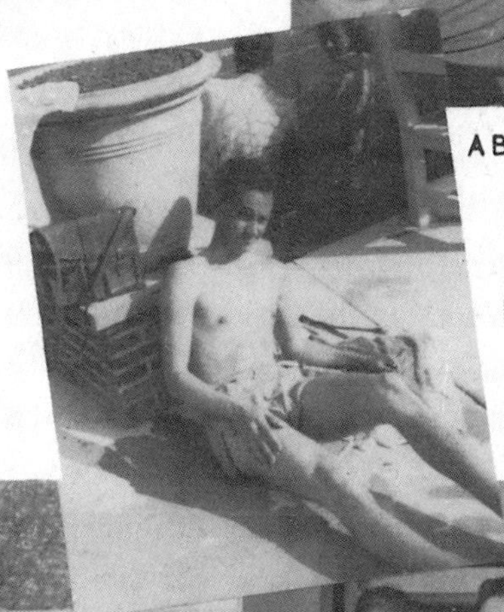

LEFT: JACK JONES AFTER 33 MONTHS IN THE ETO

BELOW: MAJ. BUHLER AND MAJ. RYDSTROM

ABOVE: 31ST ALL STAR BASKETBALL TEAM

T/SGT.'s BRENTLINER & GORDON & LT. KITOS

BRIEFING AT HESTON '44

FRED ASTAIRE AT HESTON

31ST MOTOR POOL GROUP

JACK DEMPSEY AT HESTON

LT.'S O'BRIEN, BURA, SPIDEL & PFC THOMPSON

GEN. SPAATZ & GEN. DOOLITTLE HESTON '44

PRESENTATION OF SOLDIERS MEDAL TO PFC CLARENCE OWINGE

CAPT. RAMSEY

M/SGT. MARSHALL, T/SGT & MRS. HAZLEWOOD

LT. KEENEY

DEDICATION OF 87TH'S DAY ROOM THE 86TH AND THE KELLEY SISTERS

31ST SPECIAL SERVICE

CAPT. OIEN

COL. BATEMAN RECEIVES CROIX DE GUERRE

PILOTS OF 326TH FERRYING SQ.

TURKEY DAY AT MEADOWBANK

PFC MARDEN & CAPT. GORDON

LT. COL. CALLAHAN

ABOVE: 10TH AIRDROME AERO CLUB

LEFT: CAPT. DE EULIS

ABOVE: 27TH P.X. STAFF

LEFT: HAVE A BIG ONE!

QUERQUEVILLE TRAFFIC SECTION

WOJG McCORMICK

RIGHT: COL. BATEMAN & LT. COL. ALLEN

ABOVE: RADIO MEN OF FERRYING CREWS

"FILTHY FIVE"

CROSBY, KEPLER & ALLARD

BROOKWOOD CEMETERY

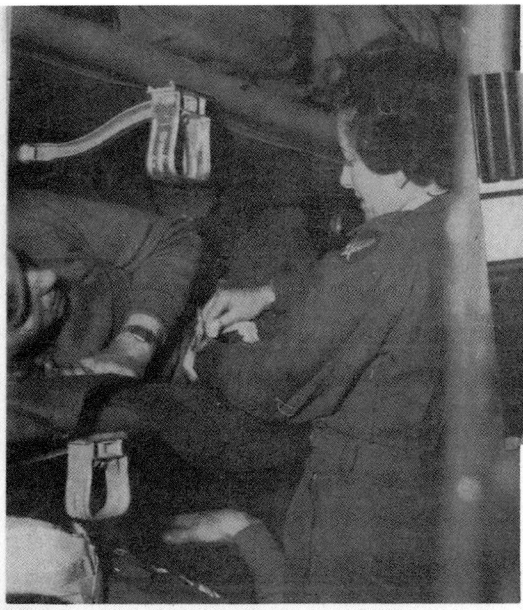

LT. DYER

F/LT. VILES, CAPT. GENUNG AND SGT. ELDRED

AIR EVACUATION

27 TH BASE UTILITIES
25 STRIPES AT LE BOURGET

MAJOR REMLIN

PASSENGERS & CREW AT GUTERSLOH

WOJG LEONARD

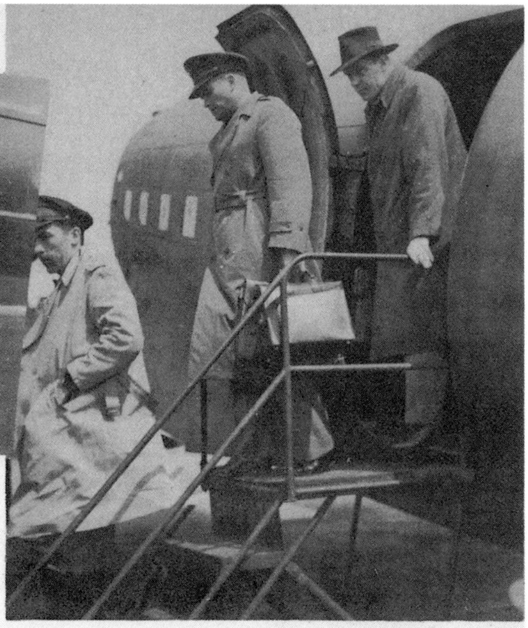

GENERAL OTT

UNLOADING AT QUERQUEVILLE - '44
CHRISTMAS PARTY FOR ENGLISH CHILDREN

CAPT. SHIELDS

# 302D TRANSPORT WING

COL. M. A. BATEMAN

HQ. 302D T. WG.

WAC DET. HQ. SQ. 302D T. WG.

HQ. SQ. 302D T. WG.

DET. 'A' 310TH FERRYING SQ.

310TH FERRYING SQ.

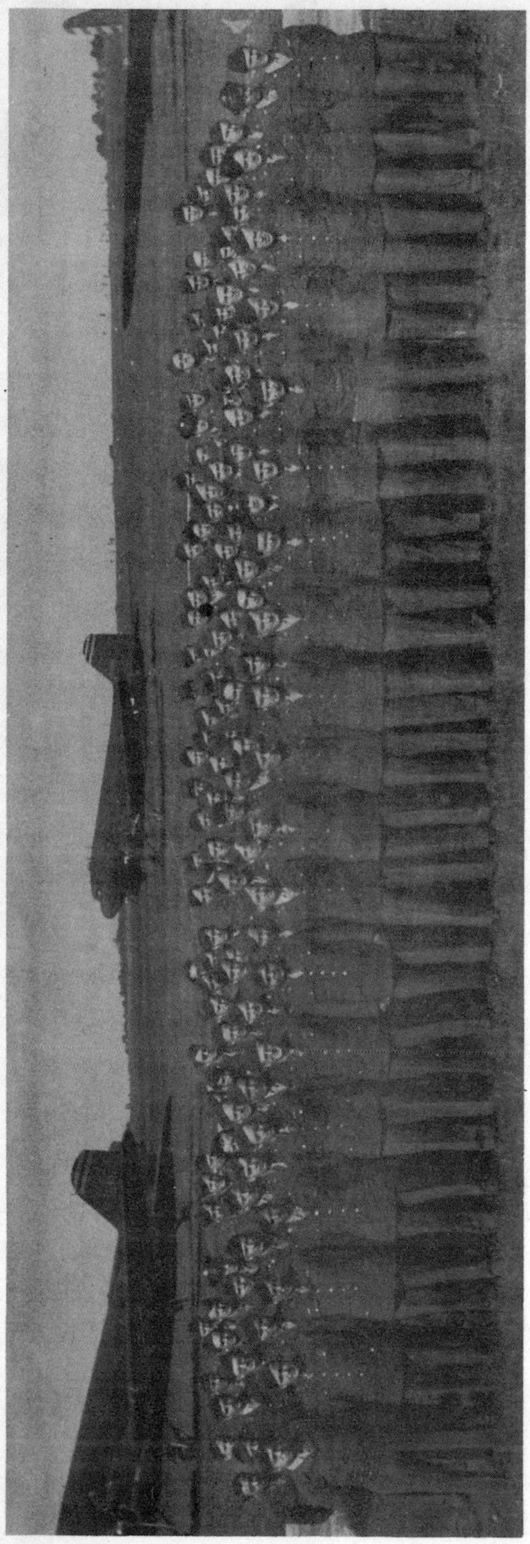

311TH FERRYING SQ.

# 27TH AIR TRANSPORT GROUP

LT. COL. KENNETH A. REECHER

HQ. & HQ. SQ. 27TH AIR TRANSPORT GP.

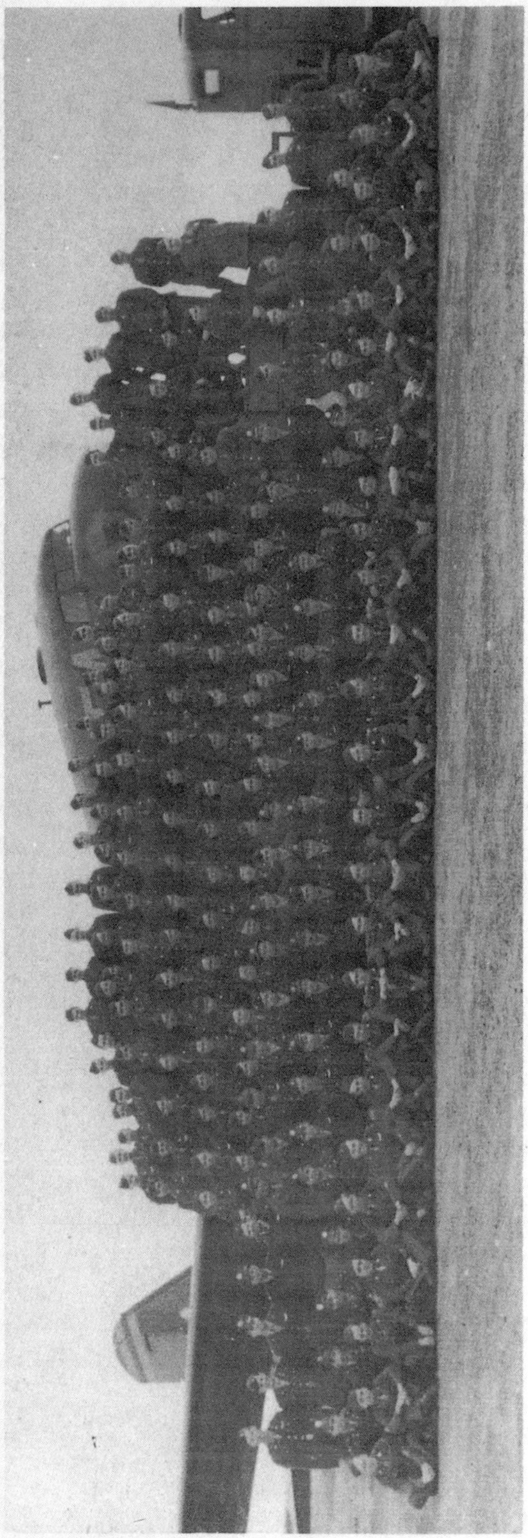

86TH TRANSPORT SQ.

320TH TRANSPORT SQ.

321ST TRANSPORT SQ.

312TH FERRYING SQ.

# 370TH AIR SERVICE GROUP

LT. COL. W. L. COVALT

HQ. & BASE SV. SQ 370TH AIR SV. GP.

ABOVE: 807TH AIR ENGINEERING SQUADRON BELOW: 631ST AIR MATERIEL SQUADRON

10TH AIRDROME SQ.

# 31ST TRANSPORT GROUP

COL. HENRY C. ALLEN

HQ. & HQ. SQ. 31ST TRANSPORT GP.

87TH TRANSPORT SQ.

313TH TRANSPORT SQ.

314TH TRANSPORT SQ.

325TH FERRYING SQ.

# 371 S.T AIR SERVICE GROUP

LT. COL. C.C. HARMAN

HQ. & BASE SV. SQ. 371 ST AIR SV. GP.

632D AIR MATERIEL SQ

808TH AIR ENGINEERING SQ.

*Chapter 1*

# One Man's View of the 302nd TW: From Start to Finish

I first heard Richard M. Cook's name in 1994. My dad called and said that he had received a letter from a guy living in England who was a radio operator in the 321st. He had written my father because my dad was one of the officers who had censored Richard's mail during the war. We met in 1995 at the 27th ATG reunion in Cocoa Beach, Florida.

In May of 1996 Richard wrote to then Group historian Marvin Diehl with his story for the "Member's History Files." After I became historian in late 1996, I was going through the files and found this great account of the early days and development of the 27th ATG. Richard served in the unit from its inception and was in the Ferry and Transport Section, 8th AF Service Command, the 86th Transport Squadron, the 320th Transport Squadron, the 321st Transport Squadron, and the 325th Ferrying Squadron. The following account of Richard's broad range of experiences will provide the reader with a solid overall perspective of the 27th ATG and its development throughout the war.

**27th Air Transport Group**
**Air Section**
**Ferry and Transport Section**
**Eighth Air Force Service Command**
**APO - 635**

World War II began in September of 1939 when Germany attacked Poland. On the 7th of December, 1941, the Japanese bombed Pearl Harbor and U.S. bases in the Philippine Islands. On the 8th of December at 4:30 PM President Roosevelt declared war on Japan.

At that time, I had previously enlisted in the United States Army Air Corps. After completing my recruit training I was assigned to the 90th Bomb Squadron (L), 3rd Bomb Group, Hunter Field, Savannah, Georgia. The squadron was assigned B-18A Bombers, which were later replaced with the Douglas A-20 Light Attack Bombers. After completing the Radio Operator and Maintenance Course at Scott Field, Illinois, I was classified as a "qualified" Radio Operator/Maintenance Technician. In May 1942 I was transferred from the 90th to the "Air Section" of the 8th Air Force Service Command, Savannah, Georgia.

The Eighth Army Air Force was created as a part of the United States Army Air Force in Savannah, Georgia, on the 28th of January, 1942. The History of the 27th Air Transport Group dates from early April 1942 when the Air Section of the Eighth Air Force Service Command (AFSC) was established at Savannah. The first units of the Air Force Service Command left the United States on May 22, 1942. We crossed the Atlantic in three "sub-groups" to ensure that the "whole" group would not be lost to submarine action.

The group to which I was assigned arrived in England in the early part of June 1942 via Drew Field at Tampa, Florida. My group departed New York "in convoy" on the 30th of May, 1942, aboard the SS *Manargo*, the slowest ship in the convoy. The other two groups departed after us, and they arrived at Grennock Bay, Scotland, before us. We arrived on the 9th of June. That night we traveled by train to High Wycombe, Bucks., about 25 miles west of the city of London. We had a two mile "hike" up Daws Hill (with all of our gear) to the base at Daws Hill Lodge, once the seat of English nobility, which later became part of the evacuated Wycombe Abbey Girl's School. We had a bowl of mutton stew as our reward. A few days later we were transferred to the Eighth Air Force Headquarters at Bushey Park, which was located across the Thames River from the town of Kingston, London. From here I was transferred to Hendon Aerodrome at Colindale, in London.

*A group of men of the 27th ATG. Richard M. Cook is on the back row, fourth from left, under the propeller hub. The officer standing second from left, is Phil Parkinson. Third from left, is Vinnie Carboni. The others are not identified.*

On my arrival at Hendon Aerodrome I was amazed at the number of barrage balloons around Hendon Aerodrome and within the Colindale area. They resembled a small bloated airship, without any engines or control surfaces. Each balloon was tethered to a ground anchor with a wench to allow the balloon to be reeled down to the ground for inspections, maintenance, and other requirements. The purpose of the balloons was to prevent the German aircraft from attacking specified military and civilian targets.

The barrage balloons made the approach and landing at Hendon somewhat more complicated than normal. One of our pilots did make a mistake once, catching the balloon anchor cable about four feet from the end of the right wing tip. He managed to correct the aircraft's flight path, recovered control, and landed safely.

The Air Section of the 8th Air Force Service Command (AFSC) was charged with all the transport and ferrying activities within the Command. Lt.Col. Glyne M. Jones was named as Chief of the Air Section. One of his first acts was to contact the Air Technical Section of ETOUSA (European Theater of Operations, USA) and immediately request that the Eighth Air Force Service Command assume all flying activities operated by them. These operations consisted of theater priorities for all trans-Atlantic travel under the supervision of the Adjutant General, ETOUSA, plus the reception and the dispatch of all trans-Atlantic passengers. This included ATC, Pan American Airways, American Export Airlines, BOAC and RAF movements, and, if possible, the shuttle of trans-Atlantic passengers to and from reception and distant aerodromes. It was also suggested that arrangements be made to assume internal ferrying operations of all aircraft flown to the United Kingdom, as well as those assembled within Langford Lodge, formerly a large Country Estate located in Northern Ireland and operated by Lockheed Aircraft Corporation and the Burtonwood Depot, located outside of Warrington, in the northwestern part of England.

The AFSC established its own flying units to meet its own particular needs. An Air Transport and Ferry Organization was created in July 1942, specifically to provide services between various 8th AFSC bases and other Eighth Air Force bases. This Ferry and Transport Service, 8th Air Force Service Command, was delegated the total responsibility of transporting by air, "all passengers, mail, and cargo, plus the ferrying of aircraft within the European Theater of Operations." On the 15th of April, 1943, this service became the 27th Air Transport Group.

*27th ATG C-47 loading at Honnington.*

*Ready for takeoff.*

*Radio announcer, Ted Malone, in his program, "Top of the Evening," recounted some of the early history of the 27th ATG.*

**WESTINGHOUSE PRESENTS**
**"TOP OF THE EVENING"**
**TED MALONE SPEAKING FROM OVERSEAS**
**FEBRUARY 21, 1945**

Hello, there. This is Ted Malone overseas.

Somebody told me once that an enemy force could never capture Washington, D.C., because, in the first place, they would get lost. The maze of streets would get them so tangled up, they would never get in.

The more I learn about the armies of the World, the more I am convinced they enjoy similar virtues. The groups and divisions, regiments and brigades are so complicated, even the postmen get confused. Part of this may be planned to baffle the enemy – but some of it, I found, just happens.

Somewhere, for some reason, a new kind of force or organization is needed, and promptly it is born, named, numbered, and goes to work, and that is how the Army grows.

One of the most colorful examples of this is an air force made up of adventurous young pilots under a colonel who is a legend in himself. The name of the organization, released only this month, is the 27th Air Transport Group, and the colonel, a fabulous character right out of a book who has ridden everything from submarines in the Pacific to combat planes, while chasing the Desert Fox over Africa – the Colonel, admired, respected, and loved by all his boys – is a steel-muscled young Midwesterner from Sabetha, Kansas, Colonel Carl R. Feldman.

By the way, I have a small wager with the Colonel just now, a hundred francs – two bucks I think that would be in Sabetha – on the question of Gooney Birds. Colonel Carl (Halliburton) Feldman swears, "I saw Gooney Birds from a periscope off Wake Island in the Pacific."

"Gooney" sounded like a gag, so I denied it on principle and accepted the wager. And if some of the Colonel's friends in Sabetha, or other ornithological experts on Goonies don't come to his rescue, two American eagles will wing my way.

The 27th Air Transport Group came into existence about as casually as the wager between the Colonel and myself. Two Air Corps officers, a captain and a major, who used to fly together back in the States, happened to meet in a London hotel one night, and they had an idea. There was a definite need for some sort of organization to carry priority passengers and supplies overseas – a transport group – and they proposed to start one.

James D. Briggs of Long Beach, California – then a captain, now a major – thus became one of the two charter members of what has grown to be one of the most versatile and valuable flying organizations on the Continent: the 27th Air Transport Group. Today, with more than five-hundred officers and at least twice as many enlisted men, the 27th ATG flies out wounded, transports supplies, and ferries planes to and from all corners of the European battlefield.

I just spent one of my most interesting weeks overseas, eating, sleeping, and flying with this great gang of kids, and I can assure you that anything that has to be done in the air, they can do, and most of the time, they're doing it. Every man in the outfit is a story in himself. The Colonel; his tall, clean-cut, executive officer with a B.S. from Purdue, Lieutenant Colonel Wendell L. Covalt, from Kokomo, Indiana; his Operations Officer, a sleek, black-haired young Major from Milwaukee, Ted Bennet (but don't let his good looks or his youth fool you: Bennet has been around; he is a veteran of eight major combat engagements).

He was with Colonel Feldman, the CO, in a B-24 Bomber Group, headed for China when they were put to work in Africa helping drive Rommel out of the desert and into the Mediterranean. Major Bennet was also a member of the battle squadron that bombed the Ploesti oil fields, on that first memorable flight. His plane was hit and forced down in the desert, half-way back to his base, but the Major and the crew were luckily rescued, and they go on making more history – Bennet, with the 27th ATG.

Yes, every man in that outfit is a story – even the Adjutant, Captain John J. Moore. Adjutants, with their mountainous burdens of paper work, are notoriously lacking in any sense of humor, but not the Irish Captain of the 27th. Even the Sergeants like him, and that is the acid test. True, when burly, black-haired Master Sergeant Jenkins from Dallas, Texas, heaved a snowball at his Adjutant, relations were strained at the moment – but rough weather is an old story to the boys at the base, and like the planes, they always get through.

When they asked for plates for the mess hall, the truck arrived with a load of captured German soup bowls. It wasn't what they ordered, but it would do until they got to Berlin, the boys decided, and used them.

Major Briggs, a charter member of the 27th, though young in years, is one of the oldest men in service. At twenty-four, the Squadron CO has been in the Army eight years, next May. He was the pilot of the first American plane to be flown over when the Eighth Air Force came to England in June 1942. Jimmy enjoys telling the story of his arrival that stormy June day. Apparently word had spread that the American Eighth Air Force was coming over, and rumor fed on rumor, until it was expected that the sky would be black with planes. Actually, only a few were sent in on that first experimental flight. They got separated on the way over and landed on different fields. The base where Briggs landed was decorated, and crowded with RAF fliers, ready to welcome the American armada, when the Major, then a Captain, circled and brought in his one lone bomber for landing.

It had been a grueling flight, and Briggs insisted he was a little groggy when the RAF officials climbed aboard, and with considerable ceremony, one much-decorated gentleman introduced himself as Lieutenant Commander Briggs. The captain, startled, replied, "Well, I'll be doggone! Why, I'm Captain Briggs." All formality immediately dropped at the base, and the Yankee legend began.

The day I arrived at the base, Major Briggs had just returned from one of the typical assignments the 27th takes on. He and another Squadron CO, Major Joel Carroll of Kansas City, Missouri, had just taken a flight of war-weary bombers to southern Italy. And "war-weary" was a good way to describe them, both Briggs and Carroll assured me. Because the heaters didn't work, they nearly froze, and because the superchargers on one and the engines on another didn't function as they should, part of the flight almost ended in tragedy. But they found a place to sit down and they did some repair work, and eventually the airplane was delivered.

The pilots of the 27th have ferried planes to Africa, Russia, Sweden, and I almost said China. If they haven't done the latter, I am told on good authority they have a dozen pilots practicing the chop sticks and learning to mess up their K-rations until they turn into chop suey.

But ferrying planes is only one of their jobs. The 27th ATG is one of the most impressive passenger airlines in Europe. They have hauled in thousands of tons of cargo and hauled out thousands of wounded. And yet their story is less a list of figures than a legend of pilots – boys and men who fly anything, anywhere the Army needs it.

*(More of Malone's commentary appears in Chapters 5 and 7.)*
*Richard Cook's account continues:*

**86th Transport Squadron**
**27th Air Transport Group**
**Hendon Aerodrome, Colinade, NW9**
**London, England**

The initial personnel of the 86th Transport Squadron, 27th Air Transport Group were stationed at RAF Hendon Aerodrome, Colindale, NW 9, London, England. I was assigned from Bushy Park to Hendon in the early part of July 1942. We started with eight pilots, several radio operators, aircraft mechanics, and other support personnel.

The maintenance and enlisted flying crew sections were located on one side of one of the two large hangars. Navy personnel occupied the other side. A Polish fighter squadron occupied the other hangar. These two large hangars are now the major part of the RAF Air Museum, located on the old Hendon Aerodrome at Colindale.

Various aircraft were loaned from the Royal Air Force – chiefly Oxfords, but including an Avro Anson, an "Argus," and a "Dommie" (de Havilland Dominie). In the late summer of 1942 a Lockheed Hudson was made available. Also, about this time three C-47s with pilots were temporarily assigned, i.e. "on loan."

After arrival, I, along with other Radio Operators, was given training by RAF instructors in the airborne radio operational procedures used in the British Isles. We received our initial flight training in a British Anson, using a long trailing wire antenna. I logged my first flight as a qualified "Airborne Radio Operator" in a C-47 on August 18, 1942. Our operations began to expand. From July 22 1942 until the end of 1943 over 4,296 tons of cargo and nearly 20,000 passengers were carried. This initial organization later became the 86th Transport Squadron, 302nd Transport Wing.

The military situation of the Allies in early summer of 1942 could be summarized by the optimistic as bad. U-Boats were cutting heavily into shipping, and everywhere the Allied armies were in retreat. As a consequence, the Eighth Air Force's objective in the European Theater was the establishment of a massive air force to strike at the very heart of the German industrial sectors. Despite the high shipping losses, vast amounts of war material were being landed and all types of military aircraft were being ferried across the North Atlantic in ever increasing numbers. All the rail, truck, and other transportation facilities within the United Kingdom were greatly over worked. A vital need arose for an Air Transport Service to fly (1) high priority traffic within the United Kingdom, (2) passengers,

*Gooney Birds of the 86th Squadron.*

*86th TS, C-47.*

mail, and cargo to and from important geographical locations within the United Kingdom, and (3) for a ferry service to deliver military aircraft from the depots and ferry terminals to operational fields within the United Kingdom.

The Eighth Air Force Service Command was allotted the task of creating the service to fill these needs. Major General Frank, commanding the 8th Air Force Service Command, directed Major Aurther J. Pearce to form a provisional group to be known as the "Ferry and Transport Service." In August 1942 Major Pearce assigned Major Frank C. Crowley to Hendon to assume command of our small detachment of selected officers and enlisted men with the assigned task of creating an airline to operate from that Aerodrome. Major Crowley, an able executive and an expert pilot backed by 27 years of flying experience, was a wise choice. With three Douglas transports and associated equipment, and with our personnel consisting of only 13 officers and 30 enlisted men, an "airline" came into existence.

Scheduled flights were soon in operation between Hendon Aerodrome (the London Terminal) and important military locations throughout Northern Ireland, Scotland, and England. Despite the shortage of flying equipment and trained personnel the "airline" attained early success. From August 1942 until it became the 86th Transport Squadron, 27th Air Transport Group, AFSC on the 15th of April, 1943, this airline carried over 12,000 passengers, 144,000 lbs. of priority mail, and over 3.6 million pounds of air freight. These record traffic movements were completed without any casualties and a record of no forced landings due to mechanical or engine failure. However, on one flight our pilot did overshoot the end of the runway, at a base somewhere in southern England. When we came to rest, the perimeter road was behind us. I do not know why, but someone started laughing, then we all started laughing for several minutes before any effort was made to get out of the aircraft. When we stopped laughing we found that we had to go out of the top hatch.

Among passengers of note were Secretary of the Treasury Morganthau, Admiral Starke, and Ambassador Winant, as well as hundreds of other prominent people. On the 9th of November 1942 we flew Mrs. Eleanor Roosevelt, the President's wife, to Northern Ireland from Hendon and returned on the 13th. I was lucky enough to have been the radio operator on this trip. I have her signature on a pound note along with that of Bob Hope and others.

Sometime around the beginning of September the local British Telephone Exchange at Colindale invited the members of the RAF Sgt.'s Mess at Hendon to their annual Red Cross Exchange Dance. This was being held at the Red Lion Pub at nearby Edgware. This is when and where I first met my future wife, Doris Eleanor (Atkins) Cook. On the 6th of November we became engaged.

When the "Air Section" was activated at Hendon Aerodrome the three C-47s we received came with their crews "on temporary loan" from the Troop Carrier Command. One of the conditions of the loan was that "if they needed the aircraft they would be returned." On the 8th of November 1942 the Allies landed in North Africa. During the invasion more aircraft were lost than anticipated. Troop Carrier Command quickly called for their aircraft. As the crews originally came with the aircraft, the question arose as to whether they wanted the crews, also. Consequently, our commanding officer decided to take a gamble and send different crews. I was among the "chosen few."

On the 17th of November 1943 the three aircraft took off from Hendon and landed at Hurn Airport near Bournemouth, on the south coast of England. The next day the aircraft were loaded with "combat-ready troops," along with their equipment and supplies. The flight crews were briefed for the flight to North Africa. We then flew overnight to an airport located along the coast of Algeria, North Africa. It was a beautiful flight, with a full moon and rolling white clouds. We skimmed the clouds, staying low in case we were attacked. We landed to refuel and then continued on to Oran. We spent two nights there. The first night we slept on the hangar floor. The next night we decided to sleep on the ground, beneath the airplane, as we felt that the ground would be softer. On the second day our worries were over, as we were ferried back to Gibraltar. Shortly thereafter we were put on a boat back to England. My pilot on this trip was Lt. Lancaster. I arrived back two days before my 21st birthday.

On the 8th of February, 1943, Doris and I were married. Thirty days later, on the 10th of March, I was sent on TDY to the southwest part of England. While there my throat began to ache. I thought I might have Mumps, but kept quiet, as I did not want to be stuck in the hospital there. After I returned home, three days later they went down on me and I was put in a British hospital at Mill Hill, near the base. Later I was taken from the Mill Hill Hospital to the Air Force Hospital at Kingston. I was put on a liquid diet for several days and was not allowed out of bed. Several days later I was finally discharged from the hospital.

**320th Transport Squadron (C&M)**
**27th Air Transport Group**

The 320th Transport Squadron (C & M) was activated 1 November 1943, per General Order No.52, Headquarters, VIII AFSC. The primary

*A Gooney Bird of the 320th TS stuck in the mud.*

mission of the squadron, as indicated by its name, was the hauling of cargo and mail, with the emphasis on cargo. On the date of activation there were no personnel assigned, but on 7 November, 1943, forty-seven enlisted men arrived. Of these 47 men, Sgt. Robert J. McGinnis had the honor of being the first enlisted man assigned, by virtue of his orders, dated 5 November 1943, one day ahead of the other forty-six. The first officer assigned was Lt. Harold B. Slusher, who reported for duty on 10 November 1943 and assumed command. On 12 November 1943, 1st Lt. DeJay J. Shriner reported for duty, and on the 23rd of November, Capt. James D. Briggs reported, along with other assigned personnel, and assumed command upon arrival. I reported along with Capt. Briggs. By the end of November the strength of the organization was 14 officers and 96 enlisted men.

Under the command of Capt. Briggs the 320th Transport Squadron built up an enviable record hauling cargo. Hauling was done by trucks when the weather was bad, or when aircraft were not available. This procedure led to the formation of a "Traffic Section," which worked in conjunction with the Transportation Section. This played an important part in the operation of the organization. Although the Traffic Section was an unauthorized section according to the TO, the shortage of aircraft left no other alternative.

Under the direction of 2nd Lt. Robert H. Mellinger, his nine able assistants, and Sgt. Herbert S. Hall, the Traffic Section managed to contract for and deliver some sixty to seventy thousand pounds of freight per month. The loading and unloading of the aircraft and trucks was being done by the remaining fifteen enlisted men who made up the section, under the supervision and the push of the diminutive S/Sgt. Walter "Shorty" L. Stroth.

On the 5th of December, 1943, the 302nd Transport Wing made its first appearance on paper only, without a Commanding Officer. This was to replace the "Air Section" of the 8th Air Force Service Command. On the 21st of December, I went home to Doris on an 8 day leave over Christmas. On 29 December 1943, Capt. Briggs was transferred from the 320th and was assigned as Commander of the 321st Transport Squadron, which was located in Northern Ireland. I returned to the Base on the 30th of December and Captain Briggs informed me that I was in the group of personnel

*Lt. C. Johnson, Lt. J. Couch, Cpl. Elliott, Lt. T. Lynch, Lt. R. Ramer, Lt. E.W. Hille, and Lt. G.R. Batedorf, 320th TS, Le Bourget, 10/44.*

*Batdorf, Couch, Chelchowski, Rogge, and Ramer, of the 320th TS.*

that was being transferred to the 321st Transport Squadron (C & M) with him. We moved shortly after the 1st of January, 1944.

**The 321st Transport Squadron**
**27th Air Transport Group**

The 321st Transport Squadron was activated at AAF Station 239 under the authority contained in Paragraph 1, Section 2, General Order No. #52, Headquarters, 8th Air Force Service Command, 1 November 1943, as amended by section 2, General Order #54, 8th Air Force Command. The primary duty assigned to the organization was the "Taxi" service to return the ferry pilots back to the depots, with secondary duties of hauling freight and/or passengers. The squadron also performed the special duties of providing transportation on numerous occasions to VIPs, such as Major General Hezlett, Brigadier General Collins, Brigadier General Hill, and, in addition, operated the Air Traffic Office of the 27th ATG at AAF Station 239.

In early January 1944 the squadron was transferred to Langford Lodge Air Depot at Aldergrove, Northern Ireland. This was a large depot managed by the Lockheed Aircraft Corporation. At the time of its activation the organization was under the command of Major Leo H. Johnson, with Captain C. Palma as Administration Officer, Capt. Joel A. Carrol as Operations Officer, 1st Lt. Arthur J. Harris as Technical Supply Officer, First Lieutenant Harry A. Coblar as Engineering Officer, and Sergeant Fred C. Sehaid, Jr., as First Sergeant. 2nd Lt William H. Strickland replaced Lt. Coblar as Engineering Officer on the 28th of November.

After Major Briggs assumed command the key personnel of the 321st were as follows:

| | |
|---|---|
| Major James D. Briggs, | Commanding Officer |
| Capt. R.C. Henderson, | Operations Officer |
| 1st Lt. DeJay J. Shriner, | Administration Officer |
| 1st Lt. Arthur J. Harris, | Technical Supply Officer |
| 1st Lt. William C. Boyd, | Engineering Officer |
| 1st Lt. Harold B. Beilmer, | Communications Officer |
| M/Sgt. Charles H. Fore, | First Sergeant |
| M/Sgt. John C. Booth, | Chief Aircraft Inspector |
| M/Sgt. Marvin L. Torry, | Line Chief |
| T/Sgt. Richard M. Cook, | Communications Chief |

My flight logbook shows that I made my first flight on a CB-24 aircraft on January 9, 1944. These aircraft were modified to carry cargo and

*Captain Schleich, standing in front of a 321st TS C-47.*

supplies. This assignment – flying in B-24s and C-47s – continued throughout 1944. According to my records, on the 6th of June, 1944 (D-Day), powdered eggs were replaced by "REAL EGGS" for breakfast. We were living in Nissen Huts, 14 men per hut, and we had to walk about a half mile each way to the mess hall to eat and to take a shave and shower. The major accomplishment of the squadron at that time was the delivery of aircraft and the operation of a "Taxi Service" for the 27th ATG.

This squadron had numerous obstacles and problems to overcome. Originally, the biggest problem was the vague and indefinite assignment of aircraft, not only by number, but also by type. This was solved with the initiation by 27th Group Headquarters of "Aircraft Assignment Orders." The problems relating to this situation, of unsuitable personnel and the wrong types of tech supply parts, were overcome with time. Over a period of months the B-24 specialists and mechanics were gradually trained to maintain the aircraft being used. Shifting personnel was a constant diffi-

*Pilots of the 321st TS at the close of the war.*

*321st Operations Officer Jim Rinehardt takes a quick break after a tough day.*

culty, however, disrupting the organization of the unit and necessitating the training of replacements. The men available for such replacement training became scarce, and of increasingly inferior ability and aptitude, until surplus personnel were non-existent. A man could not be obtained for training to replace another man in a certain section of the squadron (who may have become ill or transferred) without removing him from some other section which might have been in dire need of his services, also. The last of the major problems was that of technical supply items for our own aircraft. Part of the reason for the lack of supplies is really explained by the low priority rating of the unit. However, every effort was made to obtain sufficient parts to keep the aircraft in the air a maximum number of hours each day. In spite of all the obstacles, the 321st's performance in carrying out its assignments steadily improved. This was shown by the constant increase in passengers and freight as indicated in the chart below.

The following is a monthly comparative analysis of the various activities in the Air Traffic Section:

| Month | Personnel | Passengers | Cargo |
|---|---|---|---|
| Feb | 234 | 146* | 57,653* |
| Mar | 1601 | 168* | 71,436 |
| Apr | 2034 | 501 | 682,094 |

*These figures for February and March were incomplete due to the fact that some pilots failed to turn in all of their manifests during these months, therefore, these figures are actually larger than shown.

In general, morale in this unit was good, improving with increased operations. The men had access to an Aero Club, several post libraries, athletic equipment, and two or more motion pictures and other types of theatrical entertainment each week.

Doris and I began discussions about her coming to Northern Ireland to visit toward the end of January. I found out that we could stay in a village called Lisburn, about 17 miles from Belfast. The room would cost one pound sterling ($4.00) per week. At the end of the visit Major Briggs gave me permission to accompany Doris back to London due to her pregnancy and the fact that travel was very difficult.

On a trip to London, on the 6th of June, 1944, I was given a day's leave to visit Doris at the maternity home (Wilcote House) near Oxford. On the way to the maternity home the taxi driver told me that the invasion of Europe had begun.

The ground war in Europe intensified, and on July 18, 1944, St. Lô, France, fell. The action was so fierce that not one house was left standing. General Patton had made his break through. By the sixth of August he had raced south and completely cut off the Brittany Peninsula. During this time his 3rd Army was moving so fast his gas supply lines could not keep up with him and gas had to be flown in to 3rd Army. On each trip we carried in ten 55 gallon drums of gasoline. We then flew to a hospital site to pick up the wounded personnel and return them to the hospitals in England. This was done every day.

After D-Day (June 6th, 1944) the Germans began using a more terrifying weapon against England. This weapon was called the "Buzz Bomb," and the German's name for it was the "V-1," short for "Vengeance Weapon 1." After a preset distance a clock/timer mechanism locked the elevators in the down position, and the bomb would dive to the ground and explode.

The V-1's initial launch date was fixed for midnight on June 12, 1944, at an initial rate of two missiles from each of about 40-50 launch sites. Only ten missiles were fired in the first salvo, after a four hour delay. Half crashed, and of the other five, one landed in the Channel, while the other

*321st TS C-47 piloted by Joe Maguire, somewhere over France.*

*Some of the Pilots of the 321st TS, at Le Bourget.*

four reached England just after four o'clock in the morning on June 13th. It is estimated that a total of over 8,000 V-1 rockets were fired. Of these, over 2,000 misfired or crashed soon after launching. Roughly 4,000 of the remainder were brought down by various defenses. With this weapon the Germans could not discriminate between the military and civilian population.

On the 8th of September, 1944, the Germans began using another weapon, called the V-2. It was a rocket type weapon with a peak speed of 3,500 miles per hour, a range of approximately 200 miles, and reached a height of approximately 60 miles during the trajectory. You never heard or had any warning that this one was coming. Neither the V-1 or the V-2 was a military weapon designed for a specific target. It was a very inhuman attempt to demoralize the English civilian population.

In the first part of July we made a trip to Heston. As Doris was still in the maternity home, I brought the crew chief home with me. I told him that he would be safe from the buzz bombs. That night a buzz bomb landed very near the house. The only plaster that fell in the whole house fell on him in his bedroom.

On the 27th of June, 1944, Cherbourg, France, was captured; of more immediate interest to me, however, was the birth of our son, Stephen. Doris had been evacuated from London for the birth. She returned on July 11 from the nursing home. The maternity home implored her to stay, but she wanted to return home to her family. Her parents had a Morrison Shelter erected in the dining room. Needless to say, she slept in the shelter with the baby every night, and they used it many times during the day when they heard the buzz bombs coming.

Around the middle of July I was sent to Heston for three days, seeing our son Stephen for the first time. The buzz bombs were very bad, and I was very worried about Doris and the baby.

After some time the buzz bombs were superseded by the V-2s. The first V-2 rocket fell in London on the 8th of September, around 7 PM. They arrived at about 3 times the speed of sound. Consequently, there was no public warning. Later on, with practice, the coastal radars were able to give 3-4 minute's notice before the rocket's impact.

On 6 July, 1944, the 302nd Transport Wing was assigned a commander. It was assigned to the 8th Air Force Service Command (AFSC) and commenced operations on the 1st of September, 1944. The 27th ATG became a part of the 302nd Wing. During September 1944 we were seeing a lot of Belgium. On the 23rd of August, Paris was taken. Around the 21st of September I spent my first night in Paris. By the end of September I had accumulated over 700 flying hours in the ETO (European Theater of Operations). I have no record of the amount of flying time after that. Around this time I was transferred to the 325th Ferry Squadron.

*A C-47 returns from a days work.*

*Waiting for another load.*

**325th Ferrying Squadron**
**27th Air Transport Group**

The Battle of the Bulge began on December 16, 1944. The German High Command risked the might of all their forces in one strong attack against the Allied Armies, which had succeeded in liberating France, Luxembourg, and Belgium. General Eisenhower's troops were forced to withdraw and prepare for the counter offensive.

Under cover of darkness the German 38th Division struck along a fifty mile front on December 16th, 1944. Mechanized units overran several of the U.S. First Army's positions and drove the Allies almost to the Meuse River in the southern Ardennes. When asked to surrender at Bastogne, the surrounded General McAuliffe said those famous words, "Nuts." It was called the "Battle of The Bulge" because of the bulging shape of the German breakthrough on the map.

The first night mission in the history of the squadron was performed during the month of December 1944 in support of the Battle of the Bulge. The story begins on Christmas Eve at 16:30. Festivities had just gotten under way when Squadron Operations was ordered by Group Operations to get every available aircraft ready to takeoff as soon as possible for a secret mission to Marseille, France. The mission was to fly emergency reinforcement troops up to the front lines. In a matter of seconds the ping-pong and poker games broke up and the bar was closed. The pilots and crews were set up as the aircraft were being checked out by the ground crews. By 1830 hours crews for fourteen aircraft had been selected, fed, and reported for squadron briefing. Group briefing followed, and by 1930 hours all crews were in their respective aircraft, awaiting take-off signals.

The mission proceeded successfully, except for one aircraft which turned back. The moon was riding high in the sky that night when the aircraft began to arrive at their destinations. Ground crews went to work on the planes as the props stopped spinning. As soon as the servicing was completed the planes were loaded with personnel and cargo. Soon they were airborne and on their way to the battle front. By Christmas morning all thirteen aircraft of the 325th had completed their mission and returned safely to the base, just in time for Christmas dinner and a belated celebration. This trip was an excellent morale booster to the men of the squadron who, by it, felt that they were a little closer to actual conflict with the enemy. The experience of flying wounded or airborne troops close to the front line helped make the men directly involved feel closer to the men who were actually trading high explosives and bullets with the Germans. The whole operation was completed in less than 24 hours. Not a man or plane was lost. (There were over 100 aircraft from the 302nd Transport Wing involved in this operation. See Chapter 5 for the complete story.)

I missed the night mission on Christmas Eve, because our aircraft stopped at Heston on a return trip from the continent and we stayed over night. I went home to see Doris and the Family. A heavy, freezing fog came in over London during the night. We were unable to takeoff the next morning and were stranded there for two days over Christmas and Boxing Day. The only clothing I had was the flying suit that I was wearing.

By the 27th of December the Allies had halted the German Offensive.

Toward the latter part of 1944 the Military came out with a rotation program that allowed personnel who had been in the European Theater of Operations more than 30 months to rotate back to the States. I elected to return. I was transferred from the 27th Air Transport Group in England to Enid, AAF, Enid, OK. I was given a "delay-in-route," i.e. leave. Doris followed two months later. After Doris arrived we had a Rest & Recreation leave at the Coral Reef Hotel in Miami Beach, Florida. Sometime in March 1945 I arrived in Enid, Oklahoma. Doris followed some time later. I was discharged from the United States Army Air Forces in August, 1945.

# Chapter 2

# The Transport Squadrons: 86th, 87th, 320th, and 321st

The transport squadrons of the 27th ATG were the 86th, 87th, 320th, and the 321st Transport Squadrons. Their job descriptions were essentially the same: do what needs to be done, when it needs to be done. Another veteran described it as "Anything, Anywhere, Anytime." The 86th and 87th were the first two transport squadrons in the 27th, activated in 1942. They were later joined by the 320th and 321st in late 1943. These are some of their stories.

**Theodore M. "Ted" Lucas, Radio Operator, 86th Transport Squadron:**

Before departing the States, I was assigned to Hunter Field, Savannah, GA, and crewed a B-18. We would fly up to Bolling Field in Washington, D.C., on Mondays, spend the week there, and fly back to Savannah on Fridays. We did this for several months. At the time, I did not know this was the preliminary stage of the 8th Air Force.

I was part of the original cadre of the AAC group that was first to arrive in England. We embarked from Boston on the HMS *Andres* and stopped at Halifax to pick up some RCAF types. We had to remove all insignia that reflected Air Corp. I guess they did not want us to be identified as USAAC if something happened to us. We crossed the Atlantic in convoy, dropping part of the convoy at Iceland. We docked at Liverpool and went to High Wycombe to a former girl's school which had become 8th Bomber Command.

In spite of not wearing Air Corp insignia, we were surprised to hear "Lord Haw Haw" welcome us to England, on the radio, a few days after we arrived.

Finally, we were sent to RAF Hendon when some C-47s were delivered to us. My flight records indicate we started flying in October of 1942.

We received a plush C-53 (military DC-3) for flying VIPs. We flew many generals, etc. Once we flew Foreign Secretary Anthony Eden. We also once flew Eleanor Roosevelt to visit one of her sons who was stationed at a base in the Midlands. (Editor's note: This was probably Elliott Roosevelt, who was CO of the 25th Bomb Group at Watton.) Flight Engineer Norman Benoit and I crewed a C-47 assigned to fly General Carl Spaatz when he was first assigned to the 8th Air Force. We flew all over England as he inspected airfields, etc. Shortly before D-Day, we flew "Ike" to the south Coast of England, to check on invasion preparations, I suppose.

I was part of two 86th crews that delivered two C-47s to Russia from France. We flew across North Africa to Tehran, then on into Russia. We delivered one plane to Piryatin and one to Poltava in the Ukraine. Then we hitch-hiked back to France.

Early on, the Allies were building air bases so fast that they were not even on the maps. Crews arriving in B-17s and B-24s would get lost and end up wandering all over the Midlands. To help with the situation, a navigator and I, who were familiar with the countryside, were sent to Land's End at St. Mawgan and St. Eval. Many of the bombers were arriving there. We would fly in the lead ship to the base, drop them off, and fly back to Land's End in a Cessna.

While at St. Eval, a B-26 with a flight of P-38s arrived bound for North Africa at the invasion. The B-26 radio operator apparently became ill, and I was sent in his place. We arrived safely at Oran, and I hitched back to St. Mawgan/St. Eval on a B-17 being ferried to England by way of Gibraltar.

Shortly after D-Day, we landed at Airfield A-21, St. Laurent sur Mer, France, which at that time was designated as E-1, the first U.S. airfield on

*This photograph was taken at the pyramids at Giza near Cairo. Left to right: Sgt. Martin, flight engineer, Ted Lucas, radio operator, Sgt. Carboni, radio operator, an unnamed flight engineer, and one of the navigators that accompanied us.*

the continent, located atop Omaha Beach. We spent the night sharing our plane with some reporters who were covering the invasion. I sent a poppy that I picked up next to E-1, home to my mother. I could not tell her where I was, but I mentioned Joyce Kilmer (poet and journalist killed on a French battlefield in WWI) in my letter, and apparently she got the message. How the censors let that get through amazed me. She had that poppy framed, and I still have it. It is a little faded, but still in good shape.

We also landed at Orly, Paris, right after the liberation. A Cessna landed first to see if we could land on the grass. The runways were covered with bomb craters. We spent a great week in Paris. At the bar in the Hotel Scribe, my pilot introduced me to Ernie Pyle, who was there covering the liberation.

Operations clerks did not keep complete records on enlisted crew members, but my flight records indicate we were flying out of RAF Hendon, assigned to Headquarters Squadron, 8th Air Force. My records of March 1943 show us assigned to Headquarters Squadron, 8th Air Force, attached to Headquarters Squadron, 8th Air Force Service Command. The first reference to the 86th Transport Squadron, 8th Air Force Service Command, is on my flight record for June of 1943.

My last flight in the ETO is recorded as June 21, 1945, with total flight time of 1,022:10. All my flights were not recorded, such as the B-26 flight to Oran, the B-17 flights to the Midlands, the Russia flights, etc.

I stayed in the Air Force for 20 1/2 years and retired as Chief Master Sergeant and Communications Chief at Andrews AFB. Total Flight time at retirement was about 10,000 hours.

*Richard Lill, 28 November 1944, outside apartments in Paris. The Original notation on the back reads, "B.T.O. (Big Time Operator) in the ETO. Please notice the leather jacket. I spent a lot of time, in a lot of supply rooms, before I got that. Anytime I want to keep my feet warm, but don't want to move, I put those boots on. One look will tell you why."*

**Richard A. Lill served as a radio operator in the 86th and 320th Transport Squadrons:**

I served with two Squadrons of the 27th for 3.5 months in 1944/45. I was not, however, assigned directly to the group. I and many other radio operators were with the group on "detached service" from the Air Transport Command. We were all sent to the European Theater in what seemed to be a rush movement of 100 new C-47s, with perhaps 150 mostly inexperienced crews, from Nashville, in early to mid October 1944. By the time we got to Prestwick, the urgency of the movement appeared to have vanished, and we were sent to Grove, England, and later assigned to the 27th ATG and moved to Le Bourget Airdrome outside Paris.

I flew with the 27th from November 1, 1944, to February 24, 1945, at which time I went back to the ATC at Metfield, England. I have my radio log sheets from Jan 1 to February 24, 1945, but I have no record of the flights in November and December. For about 2 weeks in December I was on a "ground station" at Le Bourget, but that apparently was discontinued, as we did very little.

I routinely was on flights to England with a variety of cargo, and to front line airfields with medical supplies, and many times returned with wounded. My logs detail this up until February 13, 1945, when we were ordered to start sending our messages in code. From that point on, I know where I flew, but know nothing of the cargo.

Separately, the 27th in Paris participated in the Christmas Day delivery of tank technicians to Patton's 3rd Army. I did not make that flight, but I remember it.

*Loading a wounded soldier on an 86th TS C-47.*

*A "Gooney Bird" of the 321st TS, going to work from a grass airfield in France.*

*Loading wounded.*

**Much of April, 1945, was spent flying gasoline and supplies of all descriptions to advanced bases, and air-evacuating American wounded. This article from *Stars and Stripes* describes some of the activities of the group in that period:**

**C-47s Take Gas and Supplies to 9th at Elbe**
by Arthur W. White, *Stars and Stripes* Staff Writer

ADVANCED SUPPLY FIELD, Germany, April 15, 1945 - The workhorses of the Air Force cargo carrying C-47s lumbered over the Rhine again yesterday with life-giving gas for the 9th Army thrusting across the Elbe River.

Unarmed and unescorted, and stinking with gasoline fumes that a single bullet could have touched off, they flew in around the Ruhr pocket to the most forward supply field in northwest Germany. Before the props had stopped turning the first jerry cans were hustled into neat stacks on the field to await the tanker trucks that would haul them forward, and within 12 minutes the planes had taken off again and were heading back to Belgium for another load.

The C-47s which drew the gas assignment were from Col. Carl R. Feldmann's 27th Air Transport Group. From March 15th to yesterday they hauled a daily average of 54,000 gallons of high-octane gas for planes and tanks to front-line airstrips.

**40,000 Wounded Flown Out**

In addition, 4,000,000 rounds of 50 caliber ammunition were delivered to tactical air and ground armored units, and 1,400 tons of plasma blood and medical supplies to field hospitals. Forty thousand wounded were flown out on the return trips.

The first gas load brought into Germany by 2/Lt. Dick Ambrose, of Norton, KS, and his co-pilot, 2/Lt. Vincent Furan, of St. Louis, MO, took American fighter-bombers straight back into combat.

As they waited for their ship to be unloaded, four P-47s short of gas came in for an emergency landing on the battered field. They had just returned from a strafing attack on a fortified village, northeast of Hanover, which was holding up the advance of a 9th Army column.

The gas from Ambrose's transport went straight into the P-47s, and 20 minutes later they were back in the sky. While skirting the Ruhr pocket, Eddie Segar of Carlton, SC, and Ken McKenzie of Eufaula, AL, Ambrose's engineer and radio operator, took turns craning their necks in search of black specks high up.

The day before, while hauling gas south of the pocket, Ambrose and the rest of the bunch hedge-hopped for hours as German fighters circled high in the area. Small arms fire from the ground hit several planes in the squadron, but the gas wasn't touched and all got back safely. When they landed at their home base near Paris, Ambrose found the branch of a tree wrapped around the plane's tail.

**Another pilot remembered those gas flights to Patton:**

As the Americans moved across France and into Germany, we were flying C-47s and stripped down B-17s. Patton was on the move and outrunning his supply lines. We hauled gas in five gallon jerry cans. By 10:00 every evening, Patton's H.Q. called telling us what landing strip he would have control of and what time in the morning he would control it. We would schedule our crews to be landing at these strips within 30 minutes of Patton's set time. All these gas hauls were flown at tree top levels via a well defined corridor. We flew low to escape detection from the air, however, this exposed us to occasional sniper fire from the ground. One bullet into a fuselage full of gas cans would blow the plane sky high. I preferred the B-17s because they were faster. The few (fortunately) planes that crashed were caused by weather; the crews became lost passing over the front lines or were hit by sniper fire. Bullet holes in the wings were not uncommon. We would land straight in, unload our gas, often into tanks still firing from the edge of the field. Our takeoffs, regardless of the wind direction, would be away from the front lines, because at times there may not be enough distance to make a turn. Then, back to load up for another trip. Patton

*2nd Lt. Dick Ambrose, 321st TS.*

always kept his word to have the landing strip in time, and we kept ours to get him gas in time. It was meaningful to be that involved in a successful campaign, all the way to the Elbe River.

**Joe D. Maguire, C-47 pilot of the 321st Transport Squadron, recalls events of April 12, 1945, on one of the gas resupply missions:**

As this story unfolds, you will understand why I have never had a problem remembering the date, April 12, 1945!

Our orders that day were to fly a load of 55 gallon drums of aviation gasoline to Y-99, a recently captured Luftwaffe airfield, at Gutersloh, Germany, which was now one of our front line fighter bases. During the war, C-47 crews flew a great number of gasoline supply missions to General George C. Patton's tanks and to advanced fighter bases. At the time, we young "supermen" felt these missions to be routine, and they were flown with little anxiety. In reality they were quite dangerous, as one well placed round could ignite the whole plane!

*A stripped down B-17 gas tanker, or taxi. Note the yellow and black stripes, at the top of the vertical stabilizer indicating the aircraft is part of the 302nd Wing. Also note that all guns have been removed to conserve weight. This aircraft was involved in an accident which occurred when the gear switch was thrown by mistake.*

We took off, loaded from our field at Villacoublay, Paris, flying to Liege, Belgium, and turning to Gutersloh. We could see several cable tethered balloons off to our right, and soon, sixteen P-47 fighters, in flights of four aircraft each, passed below and in front of us. The air was filled with smoke and the smell of cordite. Thank goodness we did not see any German fighters and vice versa! The Luftwaffe was getting pretty scarce this late in the war.

We located and landed at our destination. Our drums of gasoline were soon unloaded, and we were back in the air. The gear was up and we were gaining altitude, then WHAM! BANG! It was a solid flak hit in the left wing which severed the control cables. There was a temporary lapse in conscious thinking while survival instincts took over. I lost our exact location, but was well aware of our general vicinity.

I was first pilot with the load coming in, and Lt. Barker, who was newly transferred to our squadron from another unit, was co-pilot. One of my crew was Sgt. Bouchier, and regretfully, I cannot recall who the other man was that day. We changed crews about every flight, which makes it difficult to remember a specific one. On the trip out, Barker was pilot and I was the co-pilot, when we were hit. Initially orders were given to put on parachutes, but I returned to the left seat and determined that I could control and fly the airplane. We did not want to go back through the area where we had been, so I started gaining altitude and heading for England. While gradually gaining altitude and heading for England, we passed over the north side of Arnhem and were over the Zuider Zee on the north edge of Amsterdam. Anxiety swelled within us again because of the flak barges below us. It was about this time, when out of nowhere, at ten to eleven o'clock high, a fighter hit us with a 20mm cannon shell just behind the bulkhead where the radio operator sat. The explosion left the cargo area looking like a salt shaker! The crew identified the fighter as a Me-109. The German made two more passes from behind our airplane. As we would see his tracers, I would cross controls and slide away from the path of fire. The left wing got riddled, but the self-sealing tanks worked well. (That was the first I knew we had self-sealing tanks!) By now, we were heading out to sea and the fighter broke off the attack. Talk about "luck'o the Irish," no blood was drawn. Fortunately, this late in the war, the Germans did not have many experienced pilots left. If that fighter jockey had been half decent, we would have been history.

As we approached England, we got on the World Guard (emergency radio system) and hollered "Mayday Mayday!" I had a conversation with the English operator, in the course of which he asked, "How many Angels are you?" In my exited and frustrated state, I told him there are none on the plane! I, of course, soon figured out that he wanted my altitude. After giving him my best estimate of latitude and longitude, we were soon met by RAF Bristol Beaufighters and a RAF PT type rescue boat. The Beaufighters led us to Woodbridge emergency air field on the coast of England. I remember at that point, my greatest concern was whether or not my tires were shot out. I buzzed the tower, and they told me the tires looked OK, but decided I better land "hot," just in case. As it settled down, we found out the tires were fine.

We went into the base and met an English interrogator. He said something to the effect of, "Well, I guess you lads have had it today. I hate to be the one to tell you this, but President Roosevelt died today." On top of that,

*Flak damage to left wing of C-47 flown by Lt. Joe Maguire and Lt. Barker on 4/12/45. Right: Maguire and Barker, glad to be back on the ground at Woodbridge Airfield in England, 4/12/45.*

I later found out that my home city back in the States, Oklahoma City, had been hit by a tornado that day!

Fifty years later, at a 27th ATG reunion, I learned that the Gooney Bird we were in that day was later used for spare parts!

**That was a tough day in the air, but when asked about his most difficult flight, Joe relayed the following:**

"One of the toughest days of my life was a day we flew a load of wounded men from a makeshift grass field along the edge of the Danube river. We had to fly those guys back to a hospital at Prestwick, Scotland. Due to the type of injuries of the patients we were flying, we could not fly very high.

When we got to Prestwick, there were already twelve planes stacked up and the fog was thick. The pressure on the ground controller was tremendous.

Most of us 321st Squadron pilots, at that time (and many other pilots of the 27th ATG and the 302nd Wing), had a special ILS (instrument landing system) card or license, which we called the "Rainbow Card" because it had several different colors on it. It was for the SCS-51 system, which was being installed in the ETO late in the war. That system allowed us to fly during "socked in" conditions.

As quickly as possible, I got into the stack and got myself set up with the ground control approach guy, and he didn't mess around very long. All I did was tune in, and I told the radio operator to come up front. We did exactly what the guy on the ground said. I remember I kept the plane at a constant rate of descent, and I made the turns when he told me to make them, and pretty soon he told me to let the gear down. I let the gear down, and pretty soon he said put the flaps down and that I had better start rounding out and looking up. It all was falling into place, and when I finally did look up, there was the runway. You could have taken my shirt off and wrung sweat out of it when I got on the ground!"

**Maguire remembered his move to Grove Airfield, because it brought with it a special reunion:**

My first assignment with the 321st was at Heston Aerodrome in London. We soon moved to Grove, near Wantage, England. We landed just before lunch. We parked the aircraft and made for the mess hall. As I entered, my eyes made immediate contact with those of Ralph Jenks, who was a Pilot in the 310th Ferrying Squadron. Ralph's throat was wrapped due to a Strep throat, but in a most surprised and hoarse voice, he said, "Well, Son!" (Son was a sort of nick name he called me at the time).

This was my cousin, who I grew up with. His mom and dad, my aunt and uncle, as well as he and his older sister, Irene, gave me lots of attention growing up and had a positive influence on me.

Ralph and I left Oklahoma City on the same train for military service, along with our high school pal, Dolph Farrand. Ralph and I were together through Preflight, but were separated, going to different Primary, Basic, and Advanced Flight Training schools. Then, out of the blue, there we were together in the 27th ATG in England. (Our buddy Dolph ended up flying B-25s with the famous "Burma Bridge Busters" in the CBI theater.)

What a happy event that was for Ralph and me, and what a small world. That was 1944, and over 50 years later, we are still in the 27th ATG (veterans organization). Ralph is, at this time, President of the group. We have a great time, although sometimes there is sadness, as we learn of the loss of another old buddy. The memories are powerful, happy, and sad, like those of a large family.

**Joe Maguire also remembered a captured German motorcycle used by the pilots of the 321st:**

*Loading more wounded on a 27th ATG C-47.*

*Lt. Joe D. Maguire at Le Bourget, Paris.*

*Ralph Jenks, Joe Maguire, and Dolph Farrond at Sheppard AAF, Texas, for basic training.*

*Ralph Jenks and Joe Maguire together as Cadets at College Station, Texas.*

*Joe Stevens and Joe Maguire while in training with 1st Troop Carrier Command at Sedalia, MO.*

As we had the Germans on the run, late in the war, a lot of the things they left behind were pretty neat trophies. We had acquired a captured SS motorcycle. It was all black and chrome, as I remember. One day I took it out for a ride, and when I got it up to speed, found out the hard way that it had been in a wreck! The front forks were apparently sprung, because it began to vibrate and shake badly. It was all I could do to get it shut down and get off of it without killing myself!

That was the end of that story, until fifty years later, I was having dinner at my son's house with my good friend, Joe Stevens, who was one of my fellow pilots in the 321st. We started reminiscing about our war years, and somehow that motorcycle came up. It was then that I found out, for the first time, that my buddy Joe had run the bike into a pole and sprung the forks on it! We had a great laugh about that one.

**Joe Stevens' version of the story goes like this:**

The Germans were retreating, and some of our crews were returning with the "spoils of war," such as motorcycles and cars. We had one motorcycle at our billet. One afternoon, when I wasn't flying and no one was around to observe, I thought I would try to ride the motorcycle.

Though I had never ridden a motorcycle, I knew I could ride a bike – and heck, I could fly an airplane – so, what would be the problem?

After getting the bike started, I managed to get it in gear and headed off down the road. I hadn't gone more than a couple of hundred yards when a pole jumped out in front of me, bringing me and the motorcycle to a sudden halt. Picking myself and the bike up, I started it up and headed back up to the billets. I noticed that the motorcycle didn't want to track straight, and after I dismounted, I could see that the front forks were badly out of line.

I never mentioned it to anyone until a few years back when I was visiting with my friend, Joe Maguire. He was telling me about the motorcycle with the sprung forks, which nearly did him in when he got up to speed ... It was then that I came clean.

**Joe Stevens served as a pilot with the 321st Transport Squadron from August of 1944, until the end of the war. He shared the following recollections:**

After graduating from pilot training, January 7, 1944, I was assigned to a Troop Carrier wing at Bergstrom Field in Austin, TX, for C-47 Transition training. Nearly a month was spent there to determine if we could qualify for first pilot or be assigned as co-pilot. I was fortunate, and was assigned to Sedalia, MO, for further training. The training at Sedalia consisted of several phases, including single and double glider tows, dropping paratroopers, resupply drops over ground targets, and pick up of a downed glider. Training Command wanted power pilots to have a better understanding of the glider pilot's situation, so we were given some dual time in gliders. I made a total of five flights, including the ground snatch. It was thrilling to say the least, and I came away with a better understanding and respect for the glider pilot.

After nearly five months at Sedalia, my crew consisted of Joe Maguire, co-pilot, John McCann, flight engineer, and John Powers, radio operator. We reported to Baer Field, Fort Wayne, Indiana, where we were assigned a new C-47B (No 43-16389) for our flight to England. We departed Baer Field, August 25, 1944, and flew 6 1/2 hours to Dow Field, Bangor, Maine, where we overnighted. We left Bangor August 26th, and flew 4 1/2 hours to Goose Bay, Labrador. At Goose Bay, the fuselage auxiliary tanks were

*Left: This is one of three portraits Joe Maguire sent home to his wife Jeanan during Christmas 1944, at the time of the "Battle of the Bulge." Maguire traded a Paris photographer fresh fruit from his rations to pay for the portraits. Right: Lt. Joe Stevens at Le Bourget, Paris.*

topped off, and we departed for Iceland on August 28th. The Weather Officer said we might encounter a little ice, maybe enough to make a cocktail. Well, he was wrong. About halfway through the 8 hour 15 minute flight, we used up all of the prop deicing fluid, and for the rest of the flight we had to cycle the props to remove the ice from them. Our navigator was unable to get any fixes because of the weather. Out of 8 hours and 15 minutes flight time, 6 hours was on instruments. We RONed (Remained Over Night) at Reykjavik, Iceland, and departed for a 6 hour and 25 minute flight to Nutts Corner, Ireland, which was an alternate due to weather at Prestwick, Scotland. After landing at Nutts Corner, our new C-47B was taken from us and we were flown to England.

After arriving in England, some of the crews were assigned to 9th Troop Carrier Command and others to USSTAF, Air Service Command, 27th Air Transport Group, at Heston. I have always felt fortunate that it worked out the way it did and I was not assigned to Troop Carrier Command, as I knew of some crews that were lost shortly thereafter.

*Joe Stevens relaxing at a pub and enjoying an English brew.*

**Joe will always remember the night he was Corporal:**

My good friend Jerry Nesbitt, from my hometown, was stationed at Burtonwood as an aircraft mechanic. The one flight that I made there was an "overnighter," and I looked Jerry up.

Jerry wanted to show me the town and visit his favorite pub. There was only one obstacle. I didn't have a uniform, only my flight coveralls. We were able to get a uniform that fit me, from one of his barracks mates. The problem was, he was a Corporal. So I went to town dressed as a Corporal. I wonder what would have happened to an officer for impersonating an enlisted man if he were stopped by the M.P.s?

**Fresh eggs were a precious commodity to GIs as the powdered version left a little to be desired. Joe Stevens, being the resourceful guy he is, shared the following story:**

After several months of powdered eggs, I had a hunger for fresh eggs. I knew that Operations had a L-4 on the field at Villacoublay, and I had flown J-2 "Cubs" and Luscombe aircraft before joining the Air Force. After filling my duffel bag with chocolate, soap, and cigarettes, I went to Operations and talked them out of the L-4.

Taking off from Villacoublay, I flew east toward Reims, looking for any farm that might have chickens. After about an hour and a half of flying and making several landings, I hit the "mother load" of fresh eggs. After negotiating with the farmer and his family, I had enough eggs so that everyone who was at our billet had two fresh eggs each.

The little L-4 had a 65 horsepower motor, carried only 12 gallons of fuel, and had a top speed of 75 m.p.h., burning 4 gallons of fuel per hour. On the way back to Villacoublay, I had such a strong headwind that the G.I. trucks on the roads were passing me. I had flown some 2 1/2 hours and didn't want to chance running out of fuel over the middle of Paris, so I landed at Le Bourget to refuel. Early on in my flying career, I was told by my instructor that the only time you can have too much fuel on board is when your plane is on fire. I have heeded his advice ever since.

**One of Steven's "close calls" came on a flight to Luxembourg with Bob Bailey as co-pilot. The dates are very hazy and conflicting, but the event is real and remembered!:**

It started out as a somewhat routine flight, except for the weather, which was overcast skies with ceiling 300 to 400 feet en route, and the destination Luxembourg called for ceiling of 1,500 feet. The crew consisted of myself as pilot, Bob Bailey, co-pilot, John McCann, crew chief, and Alphonse Cogozza, radio operator. We had a French Lieutenant as a passenger who was in the U.S. Intelligence Service.

The flight was made on top of the overcast with a planned time and distance letdown after passing a radio fix, some miles south and west of Luxembourg. A letdown was initiated after passing the fix. Descending through 1,500 feet we were in the clear. Upon looking down, we could see what looked like the German Siegfried Line of pill boxes, so a climb was started and a return to the radio fix. A new approach was started with a more rapid rate of decent and a shorter time. I was confident that this would put us right over our destination.

Upon descending into the clear, right over an airfield, I was surprised to see flak filling the sky! A climb up through the overcast was immediately made, and when we broke out on top, it seemed like we were surrounded by bursts of flak! We were hit, and the left engine was damaged, rendering the throttle and prop control useless. One burst in the left wing was just outboard of the wing tank. There were several bursts in the fuselage, one hitting the radio compartment and wounding the radio operator in the leg, although not seriously.

Realizing the precarious situation we were in, the French Lieutenant began tearing up the documents in his briefcase.

After assessing the damage as best we could, we decided to head for a fighter strip near Verdun. When we arrived over the airfield at Verdun, we were advised that the field was below minimums. After I explained our

*Joe Stevens, in the cockpit of a 321st TS, C-47. The "lemon drop" on the cowling was the 321st squadron insignia.*

situation, we were given permission to land. The ceiling was about 500 feet with 1 mile visibility. A letdown was made, and we came out right over the airfield. A close in pattern was made to keep the runway in sight. The landing was uneventful, as the landing gear and brakes operated normally, although we had no way of knowing this before hand.

I can remember wishing that I had a manhole cover for a seat cushion to protect the future family. Maybe that wasn't too bad a wish. I still have a large piece of flak that was lodged in my seat cushion as a souvenir of the flight.

As a side note - The radio operator, Alphonse Cogozza, was killed about a week later on January 18, 1945, in a C-47 crash near A-54. He was the radio operator on a crew with Lt. Roy Shilling, as pilot, which crashed with a load of flight crews who were rotating back to the States. All on board were killed except for four passengers.

*Radio operator Alphonse Cogozza, and co-pilot F/O Robert Bailey, stand beneath the flak hole, in the left engine nacelle of the C-47, piloted by Joe Stevens. The damage rendered the throttle and prop control useless.*

**Walter "Alley Oop" Jones served as a flight engineer with the 87th TS and the 310th and 311th Ferrying Squadrons. He remembered flying gas for General Patton in B-17s:**

I flew a lot of gas over to France for General Patton, but 'till I read about a request for information on "Operation Blondie" I never knew it had a name! It's been over forty-three years since all this took place, and my mind, like the rest of me, doesn't work as well as it used to, but maybe I can still give some fairly accurate information.

I was a flight engineer with the 87th Transport Squadron at the time, as I recall, when flight crews from the 87th Transport and the 310th Ferrying Squadron were sent to two bases for this operation. (Other squadrons from the 27th ATG were also involved). One of them was an RAF station, called Lyneham, and the other, which I went to, was Chipping Onger. It was near Chelmsford, as I remember. When we arrived, there were a lot of war-weary B-17s sitting on the hardstands, with some service group installing bomb bay fuel cells in them. The planes were mostly just the way they had come back from their last missions. The secret ops equipment had been removed, but they still had guns installed, half full ammo cans, and spent shell casings on the floors. Quite a few had flak damage and bullet holes in them. There were also some maintenance people present. These men apparently were from bomb groups, and I'm sure we never would have rolled a wheel without those guys. We all went to work getting the planes operational, and a day or so later some were ready. My crew took off the second day, headed for France, with a load of gas for Patton's troops.

*Joe Stevens looking back from the pilot's seat of a C-47.*

I can't recall the name of the strip where we landed. You very rarely landed at the same place twice in those days. Some of the strips were regular runways, but a lot of them were just large fields that had been bulldozed flat and PSP put down. Some strips just had large wire mesh that came in big rolls. This sure played hell with tires and wheels. The control towers were either mobile types or just a jeep with a radio in it. Once we had arrived in France things were like always. We got in line and waited for a fuel tanker to unload us. We had to keep an eye on those guys, lest they take our reserve fuel. They'd take all they could get! If you let those guys have too much you could wind up swimming the last twenty miles back to England!

Sometimes French farmers would come around with a jerry can, wanting some fuel for their tractors. Sometimes we gave them some. I'll bet those old Fordson tractors made a few fast laps around the fields on that aviation gas before the valves burned out!

After the Red Ball Express got going we just phased out hauling gas. When I left Chipping Onger, I had been there about five or six weeks. The planes were still there. I don't know what happened to them.

The flight crews mostly stayed together. I went to Grove, then to Chartres, France, back to Grove, and then to Villacoublay Airdrome near Paris. I stayed there till it was time to go home. I landed in the States on Christmas morning 1945 for the best Christmas present I ever had.

**The following story, also from Walter Jones, was published in *The Amazing Gooney Bird: The Saga of the Legendary DC-3/C-47* by C.V. Glines. (It appears hear, courtesy of C.V. Glines):**

In September, after the breakout at Saint Lô, we flew gasoline to General Patton before the Red Ball Express was set up. We also flew rockets, blood plasma, and other critical items to France, and took wounded men and German prisoners to England on the return trips.

The day I want to tell you about started like any other day. I was the flight engineer assigned to this C-47, and we were to take a load of high-ranking officers of some armored division to Metz, France. The trip over was uneventful, until we landed at a strip that was made to accommodate a squadron of P-47 "Jugs." The strip was a common one for France at that time, with steel matting runways, narrow taxi strips, and lots of tents. We landed just behind a flight of fighter planes, and my pilot, being unfamiliar with the layout of the field, started to follow them around the taxi strip. We didn't get very far. The strip passed all right for the Jugs, but was too nar-

German POWs loading wounded into C-47s.

row for the C-47. We hit both wing tips on some good-sized trees growing along the strip. The tail came up in the air and bounced back a couple of times as we came to a jolting halt. I ran back to open the door and got the ladder down and was almost trampled in the stampede of passengers trying to get out of the plane.

After we had all piled out and looked the plane over, I was all for putting it on a red cross (making an X on the maintenance form with a red pencil to indicate the plane was unsafe for flight until repairs were performed), pulling it over to one side, and leaving it there until some service squadron could come and fix it or cannibalize it for spare parts. It was beyond my capability to fix it, so all I wanted to do was get out of there on the next plane going back to our base.

The left wing was turned up at about a 60-degree angle for about a foot and a half. The right one was torn and mangled from the nut plates on the wing all the way up to the tip, and back to the last spar that holds the aileron on. It was a mess, to say the least, and I would have bet anything I had then against a discharge that that C-47 wouldn't fly again until both wing tips and maybe both wings had been replaced.

But the captain looked it over and told me to get the crash ax from the ship. Then he got up on the right wing and started chopping the torn metal away from our right wing tip. He chopped off all that he could get at, and then we got some mallets and hammers and beat the jagged ends back inside what was left of the tip. It was an awful looking thing, with jagged metal sticking out all over. Then he used his pocket knife to cut off one piece of rubber deicer boot that was hanging down.

Going over to the left wing tip, we beat and beat on that one trying to straighten it out, but we didn't do much good. The thing was cocked up in the air about 60 degrees. We were tired of pounding on it. It was then that the captain told me we were going to fly it back to Heston. Well, you can imagine what I felt like telling him; but I was young and foolish, so we piled in and taxied to the Operations tent. He told them he was going to takeoff in spite of the accident we just had, and filed his flight clearance.

As I was pulling the ladder up, a commander from the Royal Navy came running up, puffing like an old ferry boat. He wanted a lift back to England and had just heard we were leaving. What a sailor was doing that far away from the ocean, only the King knew.

I told him about our damage and pointed to the wing, which looked like it was going to flap. He hesitated a minute, uttered a few "Bless my souls," then decided that if we were crazy enough to fly the ship that way, he was crazy enough to go with us.

He was a rather portly man, to say the least, and we certainly had a time getting him strapped in a parachute. We finally made it, but he looked like a sack of potatoes, he was bulging so much from the chute straps.

By the time we were at the end of the runway to takeoff it looked as though every man at the base was there to see us kill ourselves trying to get that clobbered bird into the air.

Well, sir, that old airplane took off and climbed like it was new. We climbed to about 7,000 feet and cruised at 130 miles per hour. I really expected to see that right aileron and the rest of the wing tip go at any second. I could see it fluttering and starting to bend. I told the pilot about it, and he slowed down a little bit. The ship flew remarkably well, considering its condition. It required only about three degrees of aileron trim, which we attributed to the left wing tip being bent up.

When we landed at Heston and taxied up to Operations, I think all of the brass in the United Kingdom was out there. They could hardly believe we had flown that C-47 in that condition from Metz, France, to London in one piece.

In our excitement over the trip, we had completely forgotten about the commander. I found him stretched out under a couple of blankets fast asleep. It's wonderful what ignorance will do sometimes. Our predicament didn't worry him a bit. He got up, stretched, thanked me, and plumped down the steps just like he was getting off a streetcar after a day at the office.

When we got the C-47 back in the shops and started to change wing tips, we could see how lucky we were. That last spar and one aileron mounting bracket had been cracked. Another inch and we would have had to change the whole wing because it would have ripped all the nut plates out that fasten the wingtip to the wing.

I often think back on that day, and I wouldn't do it again even if I could. But the C-47 will always have a soft spot in my heart as the best airplane ever built, and I will always remember my association with it. No one will ever be able to tell me that another plane can be as forgiving. I know!

**J.C. (Jake) Eckert was a pilot in the 87th TS and the 310th FS. Jake was also involved in flying gas to Patton:**

An old copy of my flight record shows C-47A flights almost every day from 5 September, into the first week of October, 1944. Notes scribbled on the old records say "Gas and Supplies to 3rd Army, southern England to northern France."

Not all were "Gas Runs." Occasionally, we were assigned a nurse. (They couldn't go along on the gasoline deliveries.) When we had a nurse on board, we would hold up a makeshift cardboard sign with NURSE painted on it in the windshield of the airplane. Then we would be directed to the Field Hospital area, to have our supplies unloaded and to take aboard wounded GIs for transportation back to England. Some of those flights were pretty grim.

The gas runs were a bit different, though. Finding the pasture or the field where the trucks were parked awaiting our arrival wasn't always easy. Then, too, there was always the danger of flying too far east. Fortunately, I never did. I remember, though, that a Lt. Parker was not so fortunate. He and his crew landed too far east. I have to assume they were taken prisoner.

Landing on rough cow pastures was a bit hilarious at times. There we were with a plane load of five gallon jerry cans filled with gasoline, bouncing all over the place, while we were wrestling the old "Gooney Bird" to a stop. Couldn't miss a few broad smiles from those rugged looking tank guys when we arrived at their trucks to be unloaded. Unload they did, and off they'd go, heading east. Some way to fight a war! I don't believe we lost any crews on those runs, except for Lt. Parker, as mentioned before.

Our crew was comprised of Lt. Arthur Ford, myself (pilots), and I believe Sgt. Alvin Fisher, crew chief. No navigator or radio man.

*Gilberg in the cockpit of a Gooney Bird.*

*Right: Howard Gilberg at Maghaberry April, 1944.*

*Below: The painting on the back of Howard Gilbergs A-2 jacket. The motto over the "angel" says, "Anything with Wings."*

Let me add a note of gratitude to those guys in the Depot and in Flight Test. Seldom did we ever have to turn back an aircraft for any reason. Those of us in the 87th Transport Squadron (Later the 310th Ferrying Squadron) rarely had any trouble in accomplishing the mission we were assigned to do in the many types of aircraft we were flying. Weather and other things were problems, but the aircraft rarely gave us any trouble.

**Howard Gilberg was a Pilot in the 320th Transport Squadron. He well remembers D-Day:**

One of the interesting stories that I can relate occurred June 6, 1944, D-Day. I had a load of star shells and bomb fuses that I was supposed to deliver some place down where the invasion forces were leaving from. I presume these were to go over on the boats. A crew chief and I were in a C-64, and unfortunately, as I found out later, my carb heater wasn't working. On takeoff, at about 2 or 300 ft, the engine cut out. Directly in front of us was a town, so I turned to the left, because I saw a space between two

*C-64, #43-5392 of the 320th TS, after Howard Gilberg made a successful emergency landing on D-Day, 6 June 1944.*

hangars. When I got through the hangars, right in front was a large field running parallel to the airport. I was able to land the plane without damage, and we stopped at the end of the field in front of a haystack. When we got out, my crew chief kissed the ground and promised never to fly again. To my knowledge, he transferred to a ground assignment and never did. The plane was not damaged, so after they unloaded the cargo and found out what had gone wrong, they took off and flew it back to the field. (I can't remember the crew chief's name, but I can visualize him to this day.)

**Marvin A. Diehl served as a flight engineer with the Group in WWII. After the war Marvin was the Group Historian and provided countless hours of service to the 27 ATG Veteran's Group and its members. This work is largely the result of his efforts. This is Marvin's story:**

I entered the service on March 12, 1943, from Lehighton, PA. I was sent to Indian Town Gap, and after a few days I got my GI issues from the government.

I was ordered, with a few other fellows, to proceed to Miami Beach, Florida. Gordon Merluzzi and a fellow from Jim Thorpe were the only ones I knew. The rest of the fellows that left Lehighton ended up in New Jersey for their 6 weeks of basic training. I got stuck in Florida, but we had good weather most of the time, so I really couldn't complain. After 6 weeks of basic training, I was sent to Embry Riddle School of Aviation at Coral Gables, Florida.

I tried to take the test for flight school. Our drill Sergeant, who was from Georgia and getting quite old, said they only wanted small men for fighters. He said I was too tall and weighed 200 lbs. However, I only weighed 180 lbs., so he had lied to me. I didn't find that out until later. I still remember Miami, and our rifle range at 19th Street. After 3 months at A&E Mechanic School, I made corporal. So a few of us went back to the beach and found out we now outranked our old instructor, who was still a P.F.C. After A&E school they sent four of us to Lynn, Mass., for a month of turbo super charger school. We couldn't go to town often, since we weren't paid much. We were getting $50.00 a month.

After that school, they sent us down to Kelly Field, San Antonio, Texas. I spent about 2 weeks there waiting to be shipped overseas. We thought we were going to the Far East, since we were fitted with khaki clothes. By now I was beginning to realize how our government operated. Instead, we were shipped on a troop train, through the middle west, and finally arrived in Chicago. We left the good old U.S.A. and went into Canada.

We came across at Niagara Falls, and then, back to the U.S.A. again. We came down through New York, into Pennsylvania, and what do you know? We stopped in Lehighton (my hometown) to change engines. They wouldn't let us talk to anyone. I got the porter to call my mother and father to come to the station, hoping that maybe I could see them one more time before going overseas. I never did have a furlough while I was in the service. Unfortunately, when the whistle blew I saw my dad's old 1928 LaSalle heading for the station, and we never did get to talk.

We headed for Camp Kilmore to be shipped overseas. I spent 14 days in a convoy, going over to Liverpool, England. Now it was starting to feel like a war, with sub alerts, storms, drills on ships, and landing at Liverpool,

England. There was never a light showing. It was dark that night when we unloaded. It was raining, and noisy from all the feet moving, the whispering, and a hup two-three-four to the trucks. Finally, we boarded a train, to a place called Honington, A.A.F. #375. We had just received it from the British. The 1st S.A.D. (Strategic Air Depot) and the 320th Transport Squadron were the first American units to operate from Honington. We had good food at Honington – a good field all around for us. I must say the Army Air Force spared me from K.P. duty. I had K.P. twice in basic and three times overseas. My rank of Sergeant, then Staff Sgt., helped a lot.

Honington was a well maintained, former British fighter base and repair base. It had four large hangars, and we were billeted in brick buildings. The 364th Fighter Group arrived after us, and they were to live in tents until the end of the war.

The 364th had P-38s, and later converted to P-51s. I was in a casual pool in the later part of October 1943. I was placed in the 320th Transport Squadron on November 1, 1943, when it was activated. Everybody was a stranger to me. Some of my first pilots were: F/O Jack Couch, F/O Harold Rogge, 1st Lt. Grant Schleich, Richard Ramer, and F/O John R.S. Morgan.

Morgan was the pilot for Glenn Miller when they disappeared on a flight from Twinwood Farm to Le Bourget, Paris. John R.S. Morgan was in the 35th Air Depot Squadron, at Alconbury, at that time. When I flew with him a few times, he was in the 325th Ferrying Squadron, attached to the 320 TS Morgan was not the best pilot, especially when the weather got bad. He could get lost very easily.

I attended the funeral at Brookwood Cemetery, near Cambridge, England, of Lt. Malone, M/Sgt. L. Cheek, and Cpl. Henry Mazzie. All three men were killed when their UC-64 hit the tower at King Alfred's Church. F/O Couch was the investigating officer of the crash.

While I was with the 320 TS, stationed at Honington, I saw many a B-17 crash land. It was mostly a grass field and a depot. They would salvage or repair the B-17. Sometimes a P-38 or P-47 would also crash land after a mission. The 320th's main job was to fly and deliver needed material to different bases in the East Anglia section of England. There were over 100 air bases in a 100 mile area. Sometimes you would takeoff, and before you reached 400 ft. you were getting too close to the next air base.

*Marvin Diehl with a UC-64 Noorduyn Norseman of the 320th TS. The yellow and black checkerboard cowling, was the squadron marking of the 320th.*

My first scare in an airplane was in an Avro Anson. We flew right behind a group of B-17s trying to get altitude. I thought the Anson was going to fall apart from the prop wash!

The next scare occurred when I was in one of three UC-64s, flying together, low on gas, with everything socked in. We were getting ready to head the planes for the ocean and bail out, when one of the UC-64s saw a hole open up. Lt. Chachowski with Sgt. Palermo saw the hole first, and they dove for it. The other planes followed. We were last through the hole, but we may have been first to land. As we were landing on a runway, that the other two aircraft also had landed on, they passed us, going in the opposite direction! They had some words with each other, but nothing ever excited my pilot, Harold Rogge. He was always calm, with that pipe he always sucked on. He was a good pilot.

I almost forgot to tell you about Fish & Chips. This was a piece of fish and French fries, wrapped up in a newspaper, like an ice cream cone. We were not supposed to buy any, at first, as there wasn't much food in England. I never did like England too much. The beer and ale was always

*Left: Flight engineer Marvin Diehl of the 320th TS August, 1944, England. Center: 320th pilot, F/O Jack Couch. Couch served with the RCAF prior to transferring to the USAAF, in 1943. Right: Rogge, Evans and Stroh, 320th TS, March, 1945.*

warm, and most of the food was cold. It just wasn't to my taste, from down on the farm.

I remember in September '44 when we left Eccles, (AAF #548) to go to Le Bourget, Paris. There were twenty UC-64s, and we landed, one right after another. The field had all kinds of ribbons to land and taxi on, as it had been mined by the Germans. The airplane, in front of Harold Rogge and me, slowed down after landing. Harold got on the radio and said to keep the UC-64 moving, or, "I'll eat your tail off." I mean there was not much room left, and we could have done just that. I still remember crossing the channel from Eccles. I was glad when that trip was over, but later on, flying back and forth from France to England, it didn't bother me much anymore. I can still see those White Cliffs of Dover. They were white, and straight up and down, 50, maybe 100 ft. at places.

I still remember going down to St. Mawgan one time. On the return trip, we flew along the west side of England, but not for too long, as we saw all the ships preparing for the Invasion of France. Well, we got challenged, as we were not supposed to be there. We didn't know the colors of the day right away, and it wasn't long before we saw black puffs (flak) all around us. We shot the colors of the day out of our very pistol, and were on our way out of there! We were in a Lockheed Hudson V. We had six of them at one time, and we got rid of all of them.

*F/O John R.S. Morgan. Morgan was the pilot of the UC-64 which was lost with Major Glenn Miller on board. Morgan had been an RCAF pilot before transferring to the USAAF in 1943.*

After we arrived in Paris, we had trouble the first couple of days. The Germans had poured concrete down the waste lines, and the plumbing would not work. It was altogether different living in France, compared to England. In France there were still some Germans around in civilian clothes, and you could not trust the French too much, as they would steal you blind. However, there were still some good French people. I remember one Frenchman telling us they had just shot a sniper, who had hidden up in the roof of the hangars the day before we arrived, in the first part of Sept. '44. Paris had been liberated on Aug. 25, 1944.

My close encounter with death was with Lt. Hugh MacKenzie. We made a trip up to Liege, Belgium, for wounded, but could not get any on our return trip, because the weather was bad. We took off in a C-64 with three high ranking French officers. We stayed under the overcast, as to go up through it would mean we would have to come back down through it again. Lt. MacKenzie said, "You watch the trees below us, and if they get any closer, tell me." I kept watching, and soon, I said, "They are getting closer !" At that time, I looked through the wind shield, and there it was, a tree in front of us! Lt. MacKenzie pulled the stick back, and we mushed though the trees. I saw my whole life pass in front of me! He kept the C-64 flying, and I had my hand on the ignition switch. If we would have crashed, I would have tried to shut off the electricity to the engine to prevent a fire. He did a good job at saving our lives. We got on top of the clouds, and we checked our damage, which included the wing, tail wires, gas gauge, and torn fabric on parts of the airplane. When we got back to Paris, we wanted to fire a red flare to let the tower know we were in trouble, but they said no, since we had no wounded on board. They let us come straight in. The plane was used for parts later on. This happened on December 3, 1944.

I always hated to go to Liege, Belgium, as the coal piles were 200 to 500 feet high. I had some nosy pilots, as we had to fly low over St. Lô, buzzing the French in the fields. Sometimes they would throw pitch forks or anything they had at us as we buzzed them. I made many a trip to Cannes, and Nice, France, and we would Red-X the airplanes and stay overnight.

Another close encounter was missing the first approach to Cologne, Germany Airfield. On second approach, the pilot kept his eye on the field so he wouldn't lose it in the bad weather. We were awfully low. The C-47

*Left: Marvin Diehl in the cockpit of a UC-64A. Below: 320th Norsemen, on the flight line at Le Bourget.*

started to shake, and we knew it was ready to stall. The pilot, co-pilot, and I all reached to advance the throttles. I could look down, and we were no more than 300 feet away from some burned and bombed out buildings.

I'll always remember the Remagen Bridge still standing. I don't know what we were doing up so far, but I remember Stuka dive bombers trying to destroy it. We got out of there in a hurry!

One of the trips was to Pilsen, Czechoslovakia. General Eisenhower was parked beside us, but we had to stay at our airplane. The General left, as he was there to see his son. We had time to spare, so the four enlisted men from the two C-47s started to walk into Pilsen. At that time, about 10 Russian soldiers came up the road and motioned for us to get off the sidewalks. We had to step in the gutter to let them pass, and we didn't see anymore of them as we returned to our C-47s. A lot of experiences all over Europe.

Another dangerous place to fly was over the Jersey Islands, in the Channel. The Germans never did surrender them until after the war. We lost a couple of planes from our outfit there, and a few men were killed.

I was also on that trip from Marseille or Istres Airfield on Christmas Eve, 1944, when the moon was full. We had 106 C-47s, from our group, go there that evening and pick up young G.I.s (tank mechanics). They had just arrived from the States and thought they were going to a refresher course. Little did they know, they were going close to the front lines to repair tanks and help in the Battle of the Bulge.

I got to go in one Concentration Camp and turned around and left after half way through it. I also remember going to Hamburg, Germany, to go through submarines. I was again half way through one when I had to get out on the deck again. It was no place for me. I saw much of Europe when it was leveled. Today I wouldn't know it.

On our trip home we went to Le Havre, but there were no boats for us. Our CO said, "We are going home for Christmas." He got a train with 40x8 box cars, put us in it, and we started for Marseille, France, on the Mediterranean. We left Marseille December 3, and arrived in New York on December 23, 1945. We had a storm for 3 days and made no mileage. We were at the same place for 3 days. It was so bad one day, we were eating and the ship listed so far that everything that was on the table wasn't there anymore, as it all slid on the floor. That was it. They closed the kitchen, and we had K or C rations. I don't remember which one.

There are many more stories, but they will fade away, never to be told again.

**Tom Lynch served as a squadron navigator with the 320th for a period of time. Here is his story:**

I flew 34 combat missions with the 389th Bomb Group between March 6, 1943, and June 24, 1943. I was a navigator on a B-24 "Liberator." My crew returned to the U.S., and I was assigned to the 27th Group for a non-operational tour. This meant I could be held for 90 days, but no combat. I reported to the group at Heston. I was told that my non-combat role would be to navigate "war weary" bombers back to the U.S., take a 10 day leave, and repeat the process until my 90 days had expired. Needless to say, I was less than thrilled over this. I was sent to the ATC base at Valley, Wales, for a refresher course in celestial navigation. I returned to Heston and awaited orders. Days went by, and nothing happened. I complained, and was promptly assigned to the 320th Transport Squadron at Honington, where they shared the base with a P-51 group.

The 320th was equipped with UC-64 (Noorduyn Norseman) aircraft and served as the "UPS" in England. Daily missions included flights with high priority cargo to air bases all over the UK. Each mission would include from five to ten landings. In August of 1944, the outfit moved to Le Bourget in Paris. You can imagine what 24 of these planes in formation

*A UC-64 in flight as seen from another UC-64.*

*Loading wounded at Nancy, France, 1944.*

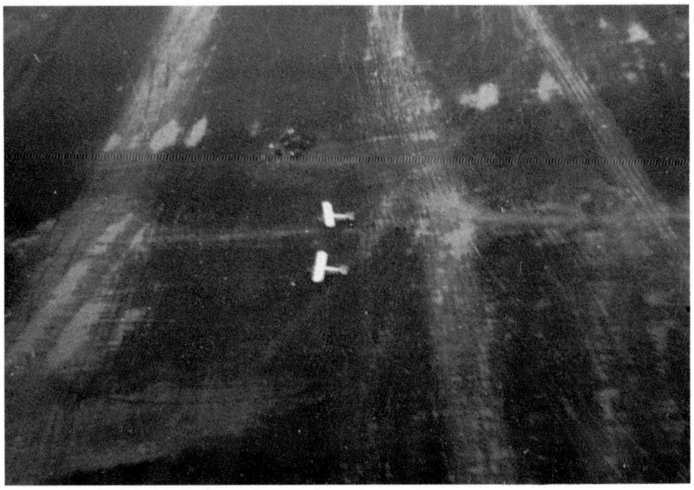

*Two Norsemen on a makeshift landing strip in a French farmer's field.*

looked like. It must have alerted the Luftwaffe! Our ground echelon was delayed on the move, and we were forced to scrounge up an old French tanker for our fuel and had only one jeep for ground transport. We were housed in an apartment building recently vacated by the Germans and had no running water.

Our missions were a little more chancy in France. We flew to forward grass strips and did not know exactly where the front lines were on any given day. We delivered blood to the front and evacuated wounded where larger planes could not land.

I left the 320th in November of 1944 and returned to the U.S. I left the Army in 1945 after the end of the war. After three years as a civilian, I reentered the Army and made it my career. I retired after thirty years of service as a lieutenant colonel. My career took me back to Europe, where I was able to revisit our targets of 1944. I also served in Iceland, Brazil, Okinawa, and Vietnam.

As for the 320th, I can only salute the skill of the pilots under very trying circumstances. In today's world no one could imagine what it was like to fly in all kinds of weather with only a compass and basic instruments. There were no navigation aids and no weather information. All navigation was by pilotage and map reading. They normally flew alone, so they had to handle everything. These pilots did not get DFCs or Air Medals as combat crews did, but, in my opinion, they earned them.

**Leslie E. Veit served as a flight engineer with the 86th Transport Squadron. At the urging of his wartime C.O., Major Philip Parkinson, who became a close friend after the war, he wrote and self published a booklet called "The Forgotten Men of the Eighth Air Force." His story is, in many ways, typical of a lot of young airmen of the 27th ATG in World War II, and excerpts from it are reproduced here with his permission:**

THE DAY OUR WORLD ENDED

May 1943. Greetings from Uncle Sam. I WANT YOU! Report for induction on May 20th. My world, as I had known it, just came to an end as I was sworn in. I was now in the Army of the United States! June 3rd, Report to the National Guard Armory at 33rd & Lancaster, for transport to induction center. That day Jane's tears flowed like the fountain at Logan Circle. I must admit my own were very close to the surface.

New Cumberland, PA, was just across the river from Harrisburg, but I must confess, I felt more like I "was up the river" for a long sentence. There, we were poked, prodded, analyzed, and given an IQ test and our fates determined. We were put on a train and headed south. Our first sign of civilization was at Louisville, Kentucky. We GIs were not allowed off the train. The next thing we knew we were in Mobile, Alabama, and taken to Keesler Field near Biloxi, Mississippi.

We were examined again, bent over and spread, then given shots enough to make many men sick. Some of the tough guys even fainted. Then we were placed in training squadrons, under drill sergeants who spoke an entirely different language. The one I had was a lanky Texan who spoke Army with a Texas accent. I never could understand him. I just followed the crowd. You bump into some nice people that way, but you can also catch a lot of hell from the drill sergeant!

Close order drill in loose sand is murder on the legs, but they toughen up real quick. Along with all the PT we had under the hot Mississippi sun, we got lean and mean. One day it was so hot on the drill field that men were dropping right and left from the heat. The base CO never stopped the drilling until all the beds in the hospital were full. The aid crews were so busy, they just dragged the dead ones to the edge of the field and covered them with blankets. Drilling was not called off, until heat cases were being

*Enlisted men of the 320th. The original caption on the back of this picture reads, "Kenny, Joe, Kupinsky, and me (Diehl)."*

put in the medics barracks. Imagine the uproar that would cause in today's Army. Congress would spend days and days investigating, but as it was war time, nothing was made of it.

After the completion of basic training, we were shipped a whole 12 miles to Gulfport, Mississippi, for aircraft mechanic training. That was right down my alley, as I was naturally inclined to anything mechanical. I made good scores on all my subjects, except one. In engine run-up phase I heard that Jane was in labor, and I was so worried I walked out of the test. The sergeant was a good guy, so instead of flunking me out, he asked other instructors how I had done. They all replied, "top of the class," so he gave me a passing 70 for the test. That knocked my average for the school down some, but I at least made it through. I had a good average all through school. Even found an error in a text book drawing. We showed it to the school commander, and he said, "keep quiet about it, 5,000 men have taken this course and none found it. It will take another 5,000 to find it again."

After the completion of training at Gulfport we were shipped to Long Beach, California. There we were billeted on the grounds of the Douglas factory, at the Long Beach Airport. Each day we were to study a specific

*320th Squadron navigator Tom Lynch, October, 1944.*

section of the C-47. We were even given guided tours so we could see how certain specific assemblies were put together. All told it was a very interesting month. Since we were in advanced studies we had no KP! A civilian contractor ran the mess hall, and it was the best food we had had since being inducted.

### MY FIRST AIRPLANE RIDE.

Part of our training at Long Beach consisted of going along for a ride in a fresh C-47. This was a new, off the line plane that had not yet been flown. Boy were we nervous. The Army acceptance pilot took us over the San Bernardino mountains. There he put the plane through its paces. First, kill one engine and feather the propeller, then restart that one and repeat the process with the other engine. Needless to say, without knowing what was going to happen we were understandably shaken up.

After a few stalls to see if the wings stayed on and other maneuvers, we returned to the airport, the pilot signed for the plane, and it became the property of Uncle Sam. Just imagine all the money spent in training before finding out if I would become airsick or not. You can't do your job properly if you are sick.

After two months at Long Beach we got orders to report to Sedalia Army Air Field in Missouri. The shipping orders were called a delay-in-route. It gave us time to go home for a few days before reporting in. I got to see my new son for the first time! Gads he was tiny, but you should see him now. Knowing this flight crew training was our last stop in the States, before going overseas, I arranged for my wife, Jane, and Les, Jr., to come to Sedalia for the three months I would be there. Now, Sedalia was a mixed up place. It was called Sedalia AAF because that was the largest town nearby. However, it was actually in Knobnoster, but the train didn't stop there. So, we got our mail through Warrensburg.

### THE SEDALIA DAYS

I was lucky enough to draw as crew Lou Ruffio, pilot, who had been a truck driver for Pepsi-Cola on Long Island, Paul Hagerup, co-pilot, fresh out of school, and George Mortenson, radio operator. I say lucky to draw them, because we were training in troop carrier work, and Lou and Paul were of the opinion that a plane should not be lost just because the pilot or co-pilot was out of commission. So, whenever the conditions permitted, I flew as co-pilot, and in some cases as first pilot. Naturally, when we were flying tight formations and/or towing gliders, the professional pilots took over. I did, however, have the pleasure of getting in a lot of stick time.

Some of our formation flying was, to say the least, very tight, especially as we all got accustomed to working and flying together. I have seen formations so tight that the wing tips of our plane were even with the horizontal stabilizer of the lead plane, and our wings overlapped by the length of the ailerons. That is some very tight flying! Of course, when we towed gliders we loosened up considerably, as the tow rope would oscillate and have the tail of the plane really swinging back and forth. We were taught that when we were preparing for glider towing to slack off the control cables to the rudder and elevators. They told us at the factory that a C-47 could stretch as much as 3 or 4 inches under the stress of pulling two gliders.

### THE SNATCH AND GRAB GAME

One phase of training called for us to do a pickup of a downed glider. Since tow ropes were one inch nylon and very expensive, we reused them until they broke. The usual procedure was this. Two poles were set up before the downed glider, a loop of nylon rope was hung over them, and then a section was attached to the glider.

Our pick up plane was equipped with a boom, similar to that, which later, was used for refueling. In the front of the cabin was a very large reel of cable. The reel was equipped with a drag brake, similar to what they use on fishing reels, but big. The cable passed through the floor and passed over a steel plate. Above the plate was a sharp cold chisel with an explosive charge behind it. The cable then passed down the pole, and a clip on the pole held it in place, with the large hook turned down.

As the engineer, I was to lay on the floor and lower the boom as we approached the downed glider. I would then arm the explosive charge. As the rope was hooked, the boom was raised again, and then I watched the cable drum as it unwound. If it got to the last layer without coming to a stop I was to hit the panic button and sever the cable. I would watch to see how we were doing. When the drum slowed to a stop as it should, we knew we had a glider in tow. I would then disarm the panic button, and after we dropped off the glider at home base, I would rewind the cable and secure the hook.

We spent our last days at Sedalia on a bivouac at our alternate field. We had to sign our furlough papers before going on the trip. I then discovered that we were spending 3 days of our furlough on the bivouac. I gathered all of the enlisted men around, and we all agreed that we would take the 10 days we signed for and come back late. As we were preparing to end the exercise, we were told we would be dropping parapacks at Sedalia. I discovered a fuel leak that had gas in the belly of the C-47. Lou and I discussed the problem. We decided that I would release the packs manually so as not to use the electrical relays in the bottom of the plane. He used the jump master signal lights to let me know when to drop the packs. We did not blow up! We landed safely, and I reported the leak to the crew chief and took off to get Jane and Jr. and go home.

### STARTING OVER

After the three months at Sedalia it was time to take Jane and Les, Jr., home to Philadelphia. After a week at home came a very tearful farewell. D-Day was a month behind us, and we could not be sure that we would ever see each other again. On returning to Sedalia, I was reduced to yard bird for reporting late from furlough. I tried to demand a court martial to expose the injustice of spending 3 days of the furlough on a bivouac. No luck. They put us on a train for Ft. Wayne, Indiana. There we were fitted with our parachutes and assigned a new C-47. Knowing the difficulty of changing the filters on the R-1830 Pratt & Whitneys, I went to the local Sears store and bought a flex socket to fit the retaining nuts. It made the job so much easier that I had to carry the socket in my pocket at all times to keep it from being stolen.

During our preflight briefing we were instructed on all the hazards of the trip to England. We were thoroughly instructed on the use of the six fuel tanks in the cabin. If the fuel valves were not turned in the proper sequence, an airlock could develop, and you can't call AAA if an engine quits over the ocean.

Our first stop was Presque Isle, Maine. There we spent the night, had breakfast, then did a preflight and daily on the bird, and took off for Goose Bay, Labrador. We got up the next day to the word that, although the weather was beautiful in Goose Bay, the weather was very bad over the ocean and Iceland. So, while everyone else had a ball in the rec room, I checked the flight log and found 20 hours were on the plane. I proceeded to pull a 25 hour inspection, much to the amusement of the others goofing off. I wanted to know my bird.

While at Goose Bay I saw my first Mosquito Bomber. The plane buzzed the runway, then pulled up in a vertical climb and at about 1,500 feet, the thing just disintegrated. We heard later that it had a vibration problem and that an RAF pilot and a DeHavilland mechanic were trying to find it. The largest pieces to come down were the engines. It rained Spruce and Balsa pieces like falling leaves for the next ten minutes. One parachute did open, and the man came down head first, as he was tangled in the shroud lines.

The man came down head first right for the runway. I started running as fast as I could to try and break his fall, as he was unconscious. Just before he hit, a stray gust of wind came out of nowhere and blew him off into some soft sand. I did not quite make it in time to break his fall. I was short by about ten yards. As the ambulance was on the way by then, I did not touch him, as my knowledge of first aid was minimal to say the least.

The next day we got the word Reykjavik, Iceland, was clearing. Go for it! So 52 planes took off at two minute intervals and headed out to sea. We had a navigator that was borrowed from the ATC to light the way. He taught me the use of the drift meter and other things, and let me help navigate over. On arrival at Reykjavik we went into the operations office to check in. Then I damn near had an attack of the same kind. The sign read, "All Aircraft will have a 25 hour inspection performed before leaving this base!" I was really shook up, as the weather was lousy, misty rain, and some fog to make it real miserable. On complaining to the officer in charge, he said, "If you did one in Goose Bay you don't have to." Man, I rushed in with my forms to show it had been done. That is when I got the last laugh. Everyone else was out in the rain, while I stayed in the warm. I did take one walk around the field for exercise, and I saw a man with a shovel digging a shovel full, kicking something in, then covering it up. I asked him what he was doing, and he said that a B-24 had the tail break off on takeoff, and that it flipped and came down upside down and blew up. He was burying the pieces. He said the bigger pieces were put in a box and buried properly. He was just getting the pieces they missed earlier. He was so practiced at this he could tell where the pieces came from. He showed me a piece about a quarter inch thick and said it was a piece of a skull, that came from the forehead as it was thicker. My first real look at the hazards of flying! The next leg was to Prestwick, Scotland. The rain and fog lifted, so we took off the next day bound for Scotland, but the fates decreed otherwise.

## CROSSING THE NORTH ATLANTIC

As we were about halfway there, we received word that the field at Prestwick was fogged in. We were routed to an alternate at Nutts Corner, Ireland. On the way, Lou did a no-no. He flew over a convoy. Within seconds a Navy Wildcat (Grumman F-4-F) was coming at us. Fortunately, the radio man, who was in charge of signal codes, had the right color flares in the very pistol. I grabbed it, put it in the port, and fired. The Navy wagged his wings and passed right over us. Landing at Nutts Corner was uneventful, as the weather was clear there. Then the Army did something that I never could understand. Instead of allowing us to fly the planes on to the depot, they loaded us into a hodgepodge of airplanes and took us to England. Then they had to fly ferry crews over to Ireland to get the planes to England. A friend told me after the war it was to keep us from going over the border into the Irish Free State and being interned for the duration.

At the replacement depot half of us were sent to the Air Service Command, while the rest stayed in Troop Carrier Command, which we had trained for. We had never heard of the Air Service Command, but it turned out to be the luckiest thing to happen to us. The group that stayed in Troop Carrier Command had heavy casualties in the Holland Invasion, in part thanks to Gen. Montgomery being so bull headed. His Intelligence told him the Germans were ready for them, so he sent a reconnaissance plane to overfly the proposed landing zone. The Germans were smart enough not to shoot it down, so "Monty" gave the orders to go ahead. The Germans had a real turkey shoot, and our boys were the turkeys.

*The squadron insignia of the 86th TS on a C-47 nose.*

## LIFE IN THE 86th TS, HESTON AIRDROME

We arrived by train to the London suburbs and were then trucked to the airfield. We had wanted to keep all of our luggage with us on the train, but were told to put it in the baggage car. The British are very efficient! Well, our things never showed up at Heston. After six weeks in the same clothes, we were getting ripe, to say the least. So, one of our pilots started from our starting point and headed to London, checking every baggage car he saw on a siding. He found our things sitting on a siding in the middle of nowhere. Boy were we glad to get our things. A shower never felt so good.

We were billeted in tents at the edge of the field and used the sanitary facilities in a building nearby. We were told it was an orphanage before the war, but the children were evacuated to a safer area. I guess we were expendable, as the base was right on the edge of Buzz Bomb Alley. We then settled down to a routine of delivering gas and ammunition to Patton and hauling back his wounded.

What later turned out to be a sore spot for us was this. The flight nurses who cared for the wounded were from Troop Carrier Command and were classified as combat personnel. This qualified them for the Air Medal for every 25 channel crossings. That, later on, counted as points for discharge. When the weather was too bad to risk the lives of the wounded, we flew the supplies over and came back empty. In fact, we flew when the fighters and bombers stayed on the ground with the sea gulls. Yes, even the sea gulls were walking some days. Some days we took off by compass from a marker on the edge of the field. The fog was so thick that only one plane at a time was allowed to taxi on the field.

The 86th Transport Squadron was one of the few cargo outfits in the ETO with a squadron insignia. Our CO, Maj. Parkinson, had been an aid to Maj. Gen. Miller and knew Gen. Eisenhower, so when he went into London and asked the creator of the "Sad Sack" cartoon character to draw him one with a big box on his back, it was not hard to get Gen. Eisenhower's OK to use it as a squadron insignia. We are justifiably proud of our insignia. The original picture is still in the possession of Major Parkinson.

## THE LUCKY BREAK

One day I was in Operations when a captain walked in and said, "I need a plane for about 3 or 4 days." Operations said who are you? He replied that he was an aide to Eisenhower. "Yes sir, and how long do you want it?" Since mine was the last plane on the field in service, I got the job.

I had a real interesting three days moving Eisenhower's staff, including his chef, valet, all the WACS, and his private flock of chickens. When it came time to load his file cabinets, two MPs with Thompsons watched every move of mine. You would have thought I was wearing a NAZI uniform. We got everything moved OK and delivered to a field near Versailles where his new headquarters were. Then, off to the north of England to pick up spare parts for his personal B-25. It was a rare model to the ETO, so any parts not the same as were used on B-25s in the ETO were stocked for his personal plane. On our final night there (for the life of me I can't remember the name of the town), I went out with Ike's flight engineer. As he said goodbye to the townspeople he had befriended, it called for opening a fresh bottle. Man, did we get loaded! The next morning as I wandered out to the landing strip where the Gooney Bird was tied down, I heard a plane circling above the ground fog.

I had my radio man raise the plane and talked to the pilot. They were very low on gas and they thought there should be a field below them. Since they did not have enough gas to get to a field that was clear, I got an idea. I told the pilot the field elevation, the barometer reading at that minute, and that we had about a 100 foot ceiling after he would break through the fog. I gave him the runway heading and told him I would fire very flares from the left side of the end of the runway, and told him to signal when he saw them. On the third shot he said they saw them. Firing as fast as I could reload, I guided him in. He came right over my head for a perfect landing.

EMBARRASSING MOMENTS

One night several of us were in a pub near Heston when a really good looking RAF girl came in. We never noticed her patch showing branch of service. When our guys started to rap on the table, talking in code, they got a surprise. The British were in the war long before we were and they could use code far better than we could. When she picked up a spoon and started rapping out a message in code, they were astounded! My buddies got red in the face, got up, and walked out of the pub. Later in our tent, I asked why they left. They replied, "She called us every dirty name we ever heard, then threw in some that were new to us! But boy could she send!"

THE GREAT TRAIN WRECK

On one trip that had taken us to the North of England, we were heading back to Heston just cruising along enjoying the ride, when I saw a train jump the tracks. I tapped the pilot on the shoulder and pointed it out to him. He looked at the map for the location, called our base on the radio, and gave the map coordinates. They called an Army base nearby, and we had ambulances and aid personnel there before the British knew they had a problem. The train was traveling slow, so no cars overturned. They just were jumbled across the tracks. One of the popular jokes of the day was about a little old lady on a train. She complained to the conductor that she could walk faster than the train was going. He replied, "Get off and walk." She said "No use. My family won't be down to the station to meet me until they hear the train pull in."

One day while riding the Underground into London, I did notice double deck army bunks on all the platforms. Upon inquiring, I was told that they were home to people who had been bombed out of their homes. The GI duffel bags on the end of the bunk held all their worldly possessions, yet I had never heard of a single person being robbed. Our British cousins suffered much and complained less than many at home where they were safe from bombs. So much for the British Bull Dog spirit. They were hardy people.

WHO'S ON FIRST?

One day I was called into Operations and told to make sure I had loading ramps aboard. Because of their size, we usually left them out unless we knew for sure we would be hauling a jeep or big gun. The pilot was also given some orders. We took off and went to another field where we picked up a jeep. It had the entire back taken up with a huge radio set. We also picked up the ground control personnel to operate the radio.

We took off and the pilot showed me the instructions. We were to fly a prescribed course, to avoid German guns, then land at Brussels. We were told to land straight in and to be sure to land between the tapes the engineers had laid out. That was the only area swept of mines. We followed the instructions and landed straight in without turning over the city. After we landed and shut off the engines, we could hear the guns in town. The whump of the mortars, the deep cough of our .50s, and the rattle of other small arms fire. Now we knew why they said land straight in and not to go over the city.

After unloading the jeep and personnel we had a little time to kill. As I walked (carefully) around the area, I saw a junkyard of wrecked planes, mostly ours. There was an old Belgian man. With his broken English plus hand signs, we communicated. I saw one B-17, badly shot up, that had parallel grooves in the belly. He explained that the plane carried wounded and that the others would not bail out and leave them. The fog was very heavy as they let down. By some miracle, they came down in the only spot in Belgium where such a thing could happen. A railroad was on a high embankment with no poles or trees in the way. The plane came down through the fog and landed right on the tracks and slid along for a couple of kilometers.

Later the newspaper *Stars and Stripes* had a headline that read, "TROOP CARRIER FIRST AGAIN," then went on to say that Troop Carrier planes were making regular flights into Brussels, less than 48 hours after the Germans left. Here I was there a full 24 hours before them and set down the people who guided the Troop Carrier people in. There ain't no justice! The 86th TS was there FIRST, I know.

THE BIG BANG - SEPT. 8th. 1944

The first V-2 to hit England landed a few miles from Heston. I was in the hangar rebuilding a carburetor when the ground shook so bad the workbench walked out from the wall about four inches! What a creepy feeling. One minute you are working at the bench, the next minute you are waltzing Matilda! After finishing the rebuild, and getting my plane back in service, I was told that a new kind of rocket had struck. Later we flew over the spot, and the crater was big enough to hold a small cottage.

TOUGH DUTY

We ran a VIP airline between Scotland and Paris via Heston. Crews would start at Heston, go to Paris, and RON at the Hotel Metropole. Then, return to Heston, drop off and pick up passengers, and proceed to Scotland, where they would stay overnight. They would again return to Heston and change airplanes and crews. Everyone wanted that duty, as it meant an overnight stay in Paris. Oui La-La! The Moulin Rouge was in full swing, as was the Rue-De-Pigalle

We also had the mail run into Cherbourg. That had to be the worst place to land in all of France! Because of the hill paralleling the coast, we always landed with a cross wind. The old hands at it would crab into the wind to the right of the runway, then when over the end, would straighten out, and the wind would drift you to the runway. A pilot making the trip for his first time literally sweat blood. It was real hairy! To make it worse, it was a steel mat runway, which was nearly always wet with ocean spray. However, the mail from home was the best morale builder we had, so the trip was worthwhile.

BUZZ BOMB ALLEY

A month or so before I had arrived at Heston, a buzz bomb hit the field. It came just as the CO, Maj. Parkinson, was landing. Needless to say, it must have been an exciting landing for him. It also killed two of our men and blew the roof off of a hangar.

At Heston, we lived in tents with concrete slabs, like patio blocks, for a floor. We had the legs of our bunks folded under and the bunks on four bricks, to keep low in case of a bomb blast. There were sand bag walls around the tents, and a slit trench right outside the doorway. Once a bomb came so close, I bounded out of bed and jumped into the trench, right on top of a tent mate. His language lit up the area. Another night one hit so close that the vibration made my bunk slide off the bricks on one side, so I spent the rest of the night sleeping on a tilt. I was too lazy to get up and fix it.

Another time, I was doing a 25 hour inspection on my plane when the sirens sounded. As usual, we kept on working, but keeping a sharp ear for the sound of the buzz bomb. As it approached the field the ram-jet cut off. Now buzz bombs were unpredictable. When the engine cut off they could do one of four things, drop like a rock, glide straight ahead, or peel off right or left. When it cut off I laid flat on the concrete apron to be below the blast. Then I realized the landing gear could buckle, so I ran from under the plane and flattened out again. It is amazing the silly things you will do in times of stress. I raised my head off the concrete apron and blew away the dust, then flattened out again. Silly, wasn't it?

The bomb peeled left into a row of houses across the street from the hangar, so we all climbed up on the roof framework and watched the fire brigade do their thing. Life at Heston was, to say the least, exciting. But it had its compensations, as there were several really good pubs nearby. We would have a couple of pints of 'arf-n-'arf, and then we could sleep through most of the night. Except when one landed real close.

*Enlisted men's tents at Heston. Note, sandbags to protect the men from "buzz bombs."*

*Le Bourget before the war.*

## THE Le BOURGET TIMES

Whether it was because so many tires were going flat in the Paris area, or the brass just wanted a touch of the Paris night life, I am not sure, but we moved to Le Bourget in the fall of 1944. When we first arrived the apron in front of the hangars was littered with ammunition. The first order from the CO was, DON'T TOUCH! Naturally, there is always a wise guy in the crowd that knows better. One night he was trying to dismantle the fuse of a 20mm round and it went off. We found his thumb a week later when moving bunks to GI the floors. We then were billeted in what had been the French Air Cadets barracks.

The hangars were a mess. What our bombers did not do, the Germans tried to do. They were of all reinforced concrete construction. The Germans placed demolition charges on every other support column. The concrete blew away, the rebars bent, and the hangar stood up. Later the French workers just placed new forms in place and poured fresh concrete, making the hangars as strong as ever.

We were moved into an apartment complex just across from the main entrance of the field. Upon being assigned our rooms, four men to an apartment, we discovered the toilets full of concrete. Having been in construction, I started sounding the concrete to estimate its thickness. Imagine my surprise, there was only about one inch over a lot of newspaper. Getting a hammer and cold chisel from my tool box, I soon had the toilet cleared out. Passing the word to my next door neighbors, hammers and chisels were busy all over the place. The next thing was to trace down the water pipes and get them working. By nightfall we had running water and flushing toilets. Man, we had it made.

Many times I cooked K-ration meals in the cabin heat ducts, as we missed many meals otherwise. After some complaints from the crews, the CO ordered at least one serving line in the mess hall must stay open until

*Right: Le Bourget tower when the 27th ATG occupied it, after the Germans had left.*

all crews were accounted for. Some would RON at another field, but the line stayed open until they called in and all others were home. Man, we were really living then, hot meals for a change!

TAKING CHANCES

Shortly after we moved into Le Bourget we heard some rumors about a L-5 liaison plane flying under the Eiffel Tower. Some weeks later when I had a pass to go into town, I heard a roar in the sky – it was a P-47 Thunderbolt in a shallow dive. It went right through the arch at the base of the Tower. Since I was less than a block away I had a fairly good view. That shook up a few people to say the least.

The field at Le Bourget was pockmarked with filled in bomb craters. The only trouble was they were never properly compacted, so when it rained, they got very soft. Rather than zig-zag around to miss them, I had a simple solution. When I saw a soft spot ahead, I just gave the engines full throttle, dumped full flaps, and literally flew across them.

One of the pilots from the 87th tried to adopt my method, only he was going too slow to start with and sunk in. His left prop hit the ground, and the nose section of the engine broke off. The prop came cartwheeling through the cockpit far enough to cut into the left leg of the co-pilot. You can imagine what the pilot looked like. That did instill in me a sense of caution, as far as soft spots were concerned.

One day while my plane was getting a 100 hour inspection, I decided to see the countryside. I "borrowed" a 6X6 from the motor pool, drove through a bomb crater that had taken out part of the wall, and explored the area around the field. I had just gotten back to the motor pool and parked the truck when a sergeant who was looking for me saw me climbing out of the truck. He angrily asked where I had been. I said I was just napping on the seat. A little white lie beats a court martial any day.

A LITTLE SCARE

When we moved to Le Bourget there was a Junkers tri-motor (Ju 52) parked on the ramp, along with the aforementioned ammunition. It was the German equivalent to our C-47; the workhorse of the Army. I had never seen a German plane in the skies until one day, a He 111 gave us all a real scare. All the C-47s were lined up wingtip to wingtip, a perfect setup for a strafing run. All our .50s were in storage so they did not need to be kept clean all the time.

The German circled the field a couple of times, scaring the hell out of most of us, until he left and went to Paris. I did not personally see the damage, but was told he hit the railway station, a hospital, and the Red Cross building.

*Bombed out hangars are visible, at Le Bourget, in 1944.*

*86th TS CO Major Philip Parkinson with flight crew, Le Bourget, 1945.*

A REAL SCARE

One rainy day Captain Lancaster, our Operations Officer, came out to my plane with a radio man. He said I have some local stops to make, nothing much, you can be my co-pilot for the trip. After several stops at different fields, we landed on one grass strip that was really soggy. On running up the engines prior to takeoff he said, "Your parking brakes don't hold." I looked out the window and saw they were holding, we were just sliding in

*Ben Swank in front of damaged hangars at Le Bourget.*

*Enlisted quarters at Le Bourget. The room indicated was radio operator Bill White's.*

*86th TS C-47 undergoing 100 hour inspection at Le Bourget, 1945.*

*Joe Maguire, in front of a German Ju 52, at Le Bourget.*

the wet grass. I mentioned this, but evidently the pilot never heard me. He gunned the engines and took off with the wheels locked. We used up all the runway in the process. We landed at Orley field, on a concrete runway, with the wheels locked. Thank God for the downpour. The inch of water on the concrete was all that kept us from being a statistic on the KIA list. The Gooney Bird slid along with the tail in the air so high we could look out the windshield at the runway. The tail came down with a resounding kerwhump, and we looked at each other with that "what happened" look. Then we realized what had happened. Lanc had not heard me say the brakes hold OK and took off without releasing the parking brake lever. I take responsibility for this myself, for it is the flight engineer's job to keep the pilot from screwing up. That's what they put us there for.

OBSERVATIONS ON PARIS

I was in town on leave when they re-lit the eternal flame under the Arc-De-Triumph. I never saw so many people before in my life. The Champs Elysees was wall to wall for blocks on either side of the Arch. It was almost impossible to move, the crowd was so thick.

They called Paris the city of lights, and I found out why. Even so soon after the Germans leaving, it was lit up so bright the cars did not need their headlights. In fact, it was against the law to use headlights in the bright areas. Only parking lights were permitted. I saw one Gendarme step out in front of a car with headlights on and take his night-stick and knock out the headlights. I guess that was less trouble than writing a ticket.

The thing I liked most was the outside urinals. All the main streets had kiosks, just a roof and a circular wall open at the bottom so you could look under to see if it was occupied. There were about six urinals around a central post. I never did find out where the ladies went. I do remember that most smaller bistros had unisex rest rooms. You better remember to button up before you exited the stall. It sure was a shock the first time I met a lady as I was leaving. You get used to it, though.

The smaller side streets had none. Just signs that read "Defense-De-Uriner." That means don't do it on the wall. Curb your "Dog." That took a little more getting used to – going in the gutter with people walking by. As I said to one Frenchman, "If it's good enough for you, it's good enough for me." After all, you can only hold just so much "din Rouge." It seems that the French had a very blasé attitude about such normal body functions.

At the end of the Paris occupation, many of the German soldiers shed their uniforms and donned civilian clothes, in an attempt to slip out of town unnoticed. One of my buddies found a pair of new German Army boots that were just his size. Thinking to be a little different, he took to wearing them into Paris as his dress shoes. You must try to understand the feelings of the people of Paris. They had been under German oppression for several years. When members of the Maquis spotted him, they thought he was a German who had a stolen GI uniform. They were ready to shoot him right on the spot. It took a lot of fast talking through an English speaking Frenchman for us to convince them that he was indeed "American." P.S. He never wore them into the city again!

The Maquis, or French Forces of the Interior (FFI), had the FFI logo painted on the doors of their cars. Whenever a shot was heard they seemed to come right up out of the sewers. They were right on the spot! Many of the French who had been collaborators would kill a GI if they had the chance. Paris had an average of a killing a night for a while after the liberation.

The French had a unique way of dealing with the "girls of the night" who had taken German boyfriends. They shaved their heads! I saw many a girl, who was recognized by someone in the crowd, get her wig pulled off. Then there would be a mad chase through the streets, as the crowd ran after her. They sure could be nasty when they got riled up.

When we first arrived at Le Bourget, we got some dirty looks from the people in the area, because when USAAF planes bombed the airfield and the German barracks at the edge of the field, many bombs missed their targets and homes were destroyed in the proximity of the field. It was not until we explained that we only hauled supplies, not bombs, that we were more welcomed.

*C-47 at Le Bourget.*

The Maquis even took over guard duty on the perimeter of the field. Our MPs only looked after the main gate. It was nice for us, because they did KP in exchange for their meals. It was a good deal both ways.

FOG BOUND or ANSWERED PRAYERS

Many times we would tank up on gas in the morning and then keep a close check on consumption, as flying with half full tanks would allow us to haul almost a half ton more cargo to the front. On one flight to supply what was later known as the Battle of the Bulge, we were heading back to Le Bourget when we got word the field was fog bound. The nearest open field was two hours time away. The pilot asked me, "How is our gas?" I checked the fuel gauges and replied, "We have about a half hour left." On talking to the field control tower we learned that they had clear vision on the ground. The fog was about a hundred feet above the ground. My pilot advised the tower of our situation and started to circle the field. Then we noticed, sticking up through the fog, a gold cross. That gave us a good landmark, as we knew the location of the church in relation to the field. As we circled the field, we were questioned about the wisdom of our actions. The pilot replied, "If we are going to crash from lack of gas, we are going to do it where you will find us."

I sat down at the navigator's table, bowed my head, and made the most fervent prayer of my life. "Dear God, get me down out of this mess, and I won't come up into your territory any more." Well, you can believe it or not, but moments later a hole opened up in the fog, and we could see the field below us. The pilot made like a dive bomber, and we went down through the hole. He hedge hopped around under the ceiling and landed safely.

Being of a curious nature, after we were parked and the engines shut down, I climbed up on the wing and looked into the gas tanks. All I saw was wet tank bottoms. What little gas we had left was at the back end. I doubt that we could have stayed up more than a few minutes more. They say there are no atheists in foxholes. I can guarantee, there aren't very many in the air, either.

Being of a forgetful nature, as most of us are, I flew the next two days. Then, shipping orders came in transferring me to a unit in the UK. I never flew again as a crew member. Now that raises a question. Was it divine intervention or an Army SNAFU that grounded me?

Finally our transportation was arranged and we bid goodbye to Le Bourget and Paris. I ended up at Burtonwood Base Air Depot in the North of England. It was a good location, in that it was out of range of the German bombers. It was a real lousy location weather-wise. They averaged 100 flying days a year. When the weather did clear, the flying activity was very intense. I saw one P-51 takeoff with vapor trails coming from the wingtips. The pilot must have noticed them, too, for as soon as he had the landing gear up, he did a slow roll as he climbed away from the field. It left a giant corkscrew in the air. What a sight to see.

After asking for a plane to crew and being refused, I settled down to weeks of boredom, interspersed with occasional KP duty. I shoveled a lot of coal at the mess hall. What a mess hall we had there! The Army messed up and put a man who had been a restaurateur in civilian life in charge of the mess hall. What he did with the rations that the Army gave him, you would not believe. In fact, it became so well known, that crews would find excuses to stay long enough for a meal. Someone placed a sign over the door reading "The Gourmet's Shangrila."

Les Veit was transferred to Grove Air Depot in England with the 808th Air Engineering Squadron.

*808th Engineering Squadron at Grove. Les Veit is the tallest man in the back row.*

WHAT MAKES A HERO ?

As someone once said, "It is ordinary men, doing the most extraordinary things, in times of stress." That may very well be true. Please allow me to show another side of it.

On a trip to an advance fighter base to deliver much needed ammunition and other supplies, an interesting thing happened. As we waited for a truck to come and unload our plane, my pilot walked over to the P-51 at the end of the runway, poised for takeoff. He talked to the pilot in the P-51, and they compared notes as to their jobs and their respective planes.

After our plane was unloaded, I signaled my pilot that it was time to go. As he turned to leave, he wished the P-51 pilot good luck, then added that it sure took guts to fly one of the fighters. The answer may surprise you as it did me. The fighter pilot said, "Hey man, you are the ones with the guts! I have one of the fastest, most maneuverable planes in the sky. I have six .50s to shoot with, self sealing gas tanks, armor plating at my back, and if all else fails, a parachute to get out with. You guys fly one of the slowest planes in the air, with gas tanks you could shoot through with a .22. You have no armor plating and no guns. You guys are the ones with the guts."

Could it be that courage, like beauty, is in the eye of the beholder? How do you define the intangible?

*(More of Les's story can be found in chapters 5 and 8.)*

**Charles H. Harbaugh, Jr., served as a Pilot in the 311th FS and the 87th TS. He offered the following recollections of his service:**

In the mid-1930s, throughout military prep school and military college, I was keeping a keen eye on the news of the gathering war clouds in Europe. My father, a surgeon, studied there and taught us to speak French by requiring French to be spoken at the table.

In military school, my French teacher was a gentleman from France, a graduate of the Ecole Militair, and he moved with his new wife to a country home one mile from ours. He also moved a 1928 or '29 Arrow Sport biplane with a LeBond engine onto his property, and there I spent many afternoons flying with him off of his private strip, which also included a hangar for the plane. He also had an interest in cars, and somewhere had acquired an old 1930 or '31 very large Buick Roadster, ie. – two doors, side curtains, a rumble seat, side mounts, and a trunk rack on the back. It was big and long and a beauty worth a fortune today.

Approaching draft age, I had no desire to be in the Infantry or the Coast Artillery, as I was in ROTC. So I started out for the Army Air Corps.

My father wouldn't hear of that, and when I told him my plans and that I didn't need to register for the draft, he escorted me to the registrar's office to be registered by one of my mother's students. On the side, I made my application to the Air Corps, and after diligent practice, signed my father's name to the consent forms, complete with the MD behind it.

I got off to Richmond for the physical and mental test. I remember the Sergeant giving the mental test and telling us if we were up on current events, we had nothing to fear. Breezed through that. The physical was something else. There was a problem that I was not intelligent enough to know something was wrong with me. Back home, I was looking up the problem in my father's medical books, and he wanted to know what that was all about. The jig was up; I had a great father (and mother), and he immediately arranged for the operation and, while surprised about his signature on the application, he thought it was a good facsimile.

After recuperation, it was back to Richmond with the application, this time signed by my father with a wish for God's speed. A couple of months later, I was called to active duty and off to Miami.

Here was my first run-in with the Army way. I (and others, too) was supposed to go directly to Cadets. Not so. We went to regular old Army basic and to a College Training Detachment (CTD). I merely went, made no protest, and wound up in Springfield, Ohio, my father's hometown, and Whittenburg College, his Alma Mater. Here among family the three months were enjoyable. My father's health deteriorated, and I slipped home one weekend to see him the last time. I still see him proudly standing on the railroad platform at MRB as I headed back for Springfield.

Off to San Antonio – what a place.

Because of my father's health, I asked to be transferred to the Eastern Command, but only got as far east as East St. Louis, Missouri, at Parks Air College. I wasn't very happy about that, as Parks had a reputation throughout the training command, for being tough – if not the toughest – flying school. I had a prince of an instructor, Jack Starkweather. He had six students. Three in the morning and three in the afternoon. He washed two out in the morning and two out in the afternoon. He had a new and beautiful wife, but I think he was so jealous of her that he wouldn't even let the cadets meet her. So maybe there was a method to his madness, get home sooner. One funny event happened there. A corn field was right beside the airfield and no fence between the two. Some cadet undershot and came down in the corn. The corn must have been right high, as all you could see was the tail advancing toward the field and the prop slinging ears of corn. When he came out of the corn, he was still flying about a foot off of the ground. He landed successfully, but had several holes in the leading edge of the PT-26.

My father died while I was at Parks and was buried in Springfield. I was out for two weeks, but came back and passed on to Independence, Kansas, another tough flying school, flying BT-14s. Few people know that plane. It was an advanced version of the old BT-9 and the same basic plane as the AT-6, with fixed and narrower gear and a 450 HP engine. It was a ground looping fool, as they say, and you flew it until you chocked it and cut the engine.

My instructor and the two cadets that slept on both sides of me were killed the first night of night flying. Nobody assigned me to another instructor, and near the end of the time there, I was turned down on check ride. The Squadron Commander called me in and asked who my instructor was. When I told him Lt. Fitzgerald, he said, "Yes, but who was my instructor after he was killed?" I told him I didn't have one. So he said he would fly with me on a check ride. Evidently I flew it well. On the ground he said to me, "Anyone who can fly like that without an instructor has passed this phase. You are the first one sure of to advance."

*87th TS pilot Charles Harbaugh, Jr. at Grove Airfield near Wantage, England.*

Advanced at Waco, Texas, was no trouble. I especially liked formation flying, but not the instrument training and the Beech AT-10.

Flying school was over. Two close buddies were with me all the way through, Harold Harlow and Kenny Halverson. Harold's sister, Jean Harlow, pinned on my bars and my mother, my wings.

Here again came another of the Army's dirty tricks. Nothing was said, when I signed up, about Flight Officers, but a number didn't get commissions, for no reason other than a number. I remember, at the swearing in as an officer, we were discharged as an Aviation Cadet, and for a short time were out of the Army. The swearing in officer mentioned it and advised against not taking the oath. I really believe if I had been in that situation, I would have refused the oath. Fortunately, I was not.

I knew any officer – and I was now an officer – could check out supplies at Tech. Supply, so I went off to Tech. Supply and signed out a chute and a B-4 bag. This was an old pre-war bag and I still have it.

I don't remember where I got to, but I picked up a ride on a B-24 to Pope Field, NC. A P-51 landed right behind us and parked beside us. I climbed up on the wing to look inside. A WASP (female pilot) was inside, and I was quickly told I was not allowed to look. "This is a restricted plane!" I didn't lose any time telling her to go fly a kite.

Home on leave with orders to report to Sedelia AAF, Knobnoster, Missouri. That I did, taking my old Chrysler with me. On the road near Indianapolis, on a CAVU day, an American Airlines DC-3 flew by, not over 500 ft. I could easily read the name and numbers on it. Well, it won't be long till I'll be flying one, too. Although I put in for B-17s, I've never regretted flying this great old bird and the outfit in the ETO. Sedalia lasted three months, and I was assigned to be a co-pilot with Ray Ryan. While Ray was running around at night with Mary, I would go down to engineering and get a repaired ship and fly and fly. I had so much time, I was offered a crew, but elected to stay put. Kenny and I were still together. While at Sedalia, I got word that my old instructor, Jack Starkweather, was at Berry Field, Tennessee. I decided to hop a ride over there for a weekend. I found Jack OK, and I got to meet his wife. I also found a number of former instructors there from Parks Air College. They had been taken into the Army Air Force, as flight officers with service pilot's wings. They were apprehensive about meeting their former pupils, as each of them was now outranked by their former cadet students. I didn't give them any advice.

*Left: Operations at Grove, including the 87th TS, taken from the tower. In Charles Harbaugh's words, "Notice the mud on the roads. When we first went there, there was so much mud that the brakes would not control the planes on the taxi ways and the roads were as bad. An order was put out that anyone driving off the hard top would be put to work with a shovel and broom, cleaning the roads. Some were put to work, including officers, doing just that. An I.G. came along, saw the officers and put an end to that. The officers out there said they would sit off any punishment. I didn't have any transportation at the time, so I didn't get in on any of the broom details." Right: Entrance to the officer's mess, station side, at Grove in 1958.*

Jack was a prince of an Instructor, and I had no problems with him. After the war, flying around, I would see Jack's name signed "StarkWX," on airport sign-in sheets. He was killed in a Twin Beech crash, flying out of Cape Girardo, MO. His passenger, the daughter of the company's president, survived.

After sweating out east or west, we finally got off to the ETO. Baer Field, Presque Isle, picked up a navigator, and off to Goose Bay. On the downwind at Goose Bay, exactly opposite at the center of the field, an explosion rocked the ship. A British Mosquito blew up in the air. We flew the pattern, taxied to the far end of the runway, and half way back, to where we parked. No hurry to get out, but standing in the door, little pieces of plywood were floating down. People were running, and I looked up and a chute was about 100 ft. up. Wirtz said the man in the chute was hanging upside down. My recollection was that he was all red, covered with blood. The meat wagon picked him up immediately, but the plywood kept on floating down. The time from the explosion until the survivor was on the ground seemed like an awfully long time. Wirtz tells me he was looking right at the Mosquito when it exploded. We flew to Meeks, Iceland, direct. We didn't have any desire to land at BW1 on the trip. WX was decent, but the mud at Meeks was not. Meeks to Nutts Corner, North Ireland, where we left a new C-47B we brought to the ETO. I can't remember how we got to Scotland, but, shortly, we were on the train to London, and ended up at Heston Airfield. I had to get to downtown London, mainly to see how accurately the news had portrayed the bomb damage. Compared to what we did to German cities, the damage was minor.

We were not at Heston very long, until we moved to Grove and the 311th Ferrying Squadron. My Form Five shows two weeks as a co-pilot, and then I was checked out to the left seat. Then came the famous "P-51 deal." After the check ride with Major Thomas (311th CO) he told me to go over to the depot and get a plane and fly one of them, probably slow time after overhaul. The only plane there, besides a L-5 and a L-4, was a P-51. I checked with their operations, and, gathering a chute, a couple of hours studying the manual, the line chief and I fired up, and I took off on the short runway. With minimum power, I immediately climbed out to do airwork. After two hours, I was back to land. Being over cautious and knowing P-51s had a habit of dropping a wing landing, I wasn't satisfied with the first attempt and added power for a go around. I gave it too much power, too abruptly, and flipped it up on one wing. I merely corrected and went back upstairs for more airwork. The second approach still didn't satisfy me, so I went back around and landed normally on the third try, greasing it in. My first inkling of anything wrong was John Howard's question, "Do you consider yourself checked out in a P-51?" My answer to his remark, "I flew it." Then Gregory Thomas called me in and royally chewed me out. That didn't impress me much, as I had been through my rat year at VPI, but his last remark, "I'm going to ground you and transfer you out of the squadron," did impress me. To this day, after reading Stillwell's article, and the 311th methods of check out or rather bouncing around in B-17s, without an instructor, learning to fly that bird, I have never understood Thomas' chewing. He never threatened a court martial. He was decent enough to acknowledge that he had ordered me to the depot and mentioned that I was never told what to fly. I was only told to go get a plane and fly it. Then came the trip to Meeks, and I heard Thomas made a speech at Prestwick, "This will separate the men from the boys." He was the only one who turned around and didn't make it.

*The tower at Grove as it appeared in 1958.*

After the war, I picked up an accident report of a DC-6 going into the marshes, with four dead engines, at what was then called Idlewild. I read the report several times before I realized the captain was Gregory Thomas. No fault of his – someone had put the wrong fuel in the takeoff injection

*Grove operations area from the tower. The 87th Sqdn. was on the extreme left in this picture.*

*Nissen hut living quarters at Grove.*

system. All survived. I later learned he was lost on a flight off of Taiwan in a cyclone.

Before the trip to Iceland, I was sitting around with nothing to do and the 311th was starting to move to Istres. Halverson was flying one of the planes, and I asked him if I could go along. He said, "Sure, but I'm leaving at five in the morning." I fully intended to go, but simply didn't wake up, so I missed the flight. Halverson hit the mountains in Spain and all were lost. Herkey and Betty were married when we were in East St. Louis. I had a number of letters from her, but never had any news to tell her when I wrote back. He had a son born just a few weeks before. It took me 50 years to find Ray Ryan, and I have also been looking for Betty and their son all this time, to no avail.

While Thomas was away on the trip to Iceland, I went to group headquarters and told them I was to be transferred. They knew it, so they put me in the 87th. The quarters were much better, on the depot side of the field, and they had a much better mess and officer's club. It was too far to walk to operations, so we were taxied in a plain old GI truck.

I had acquired a motor scooter. I found a bunch more at Langford Lodge and spent time restoring it. In the 87th only Major Hoerner and I had private transportation. I had the others stored in the wooden barracks next to ours and fixed it up nice. I even found a pint can of shiny O.D. paint at Burtonwood. The base Adj. told me one night they were investigating where I was getting gas for it. I put his mind at ease, "I go down to the motor pool once a month and get one gallon, about all it holds, and the motorpool Sgt. puts it on the next truck he gases up." That was the last I heard of that. For some reason, I once put 100 octane in it, because the air compressors in the Maintenance hangar, where they were stored, used 100 octane only. I was going around the perimeter one night, right in front of the tower, and it just beautifully coasted to a stop. I pushed it to the hangar, got the tools out of the compartment, and took the head off. There was no top to the piston, and no parts of it to be found. It had disintegrated. I had one awful time, the next few days, talking the Sgt. that had the air compressors out of a piston he had in the window, in full view.

Martin Chaves was the 87th's Engineering Officer, and he came around and asked me for one of the other six motor scooters I had to fix up. He said it would help me if anybody got after me for it. I told him he was certainly welcome to one or more. I had had to sign for them at Langford Lodge, and that piece of paper got me a title for it here in Virginia. Yes, I brought it home.

I had it in the plane once in France and was riding down the ramp, way behind a French ceremony, with flags flying. A large number of those guys broke ranks to come see me ride by. I went on, but didn't hear anymore about that.

In the 87th, we had barracks made of wood, which were certainly much nicer than a Nissen Hut. Phil Eisenwinter, Jim Walsh, and I lived in the last one on the row. We divided it with a living room and a bedroom. The bedroom had an extra bed. We used it once in awhile for someone RON. In this wing there were two other pilots from Winchester who used it. We had two pot-belly stoves, and each night we laid a small fire in the bedroom. We took turns in the morning firing it off, and in ten minutes we had a nice warm room to dress in. The barracks were right on the road to the town of Wantage.

Phil "Ike" Eisenwinter and I would get on the train and go into London. He had a pair of custom made shoes made. They were big, but he said comfortable, and the last time I talked to him, he still has them.

On our flights to Y-35 (Compiégne/Margny), I always tried to get there first. For some stupid reason, the wheels couldn't figure out how I did it, without using unauthorized power (I religiously flew it by the book). Even the flight leaders flew with me and wouldn't take the left seat. I simply climbed to 12,000 feet, picked up a good tail wind, half way across the channel, started down carrying 30" all the way, and sometimes up to 250 MPH or more, and I was there first, usually. Getting out of Y-35 early made the rest of the day easy.

One CAVU day in particular, half way in from the coast, I started picking up scud, so I got down on the ground. It got thicker and thicker,

*Reindeer Officer's Red Cross, in London.*

*Left: Jenkins, walking toward camera, Nick Flocus to his right with head turned, and two other pilots of the 87th. Someone had backed an ambulance into their airplane and damaged the aileron. "This was a casualty flight out of Aachen and was one of my first trips to Germany. One of the flight nurses can be seen in the background. Only two men were killed on all of these flights. That was when our 87th TS C-46 caught on fire in flight and crashed, killing all on board." – Harbaugh. Right: "Lt. Jenkins leaning against the wing of a C-47. I believe this was taken on one of our first trips to Germany, around Aachen. "Jenk" was my co-pilot most of the time in the 87th. He was an excellent pilot." – Harbaugh*

until it was solid at 100 feet, then visibility was unlimited. I goofed and didn't get slowed down enough to land and had to go around. Of course, I had to go around that hill. Next approach, I made it without any trouble and landed. Phil came over on top and asked the tower for the WX. Back came, 600 feet and unlimited visibility. Back came Phil, "Damn, I'm on top at 600 feet." I told him go back out and get under it and there was no problem. Everybody else heard that and poor old "Ike" was way down the line when he got parked. I was sitting in the cockpit and looked out, and Ike was going across the runway with those big shoes on, to have a word with the tower operator.

Burtonwood Air Depot – we made frequent trips, empty, from Grove to pick up loads for the far shore. My mother had written that Johnny Smoke was stationed there and suggested that I look him up. My sister and I grew up with Johnny and his sister, and we had double dated some. I went to the warehouse where he was supposed to work and his buddies knew where he was goofing off. Not knowing me or what I was after, they started yelling "Smoke, there is a Lt. looking for you." We found him, however, before he could get out of the big box he was sleeping in.

Burtonwood had some zero-zero fogs and someone had taught me their landing system there. On the top of the tower there was a radio beacon. With the ADF (Automatic Direction Finder) you crossed the runway and the tower at 1,000 ft., 90 degrees to the runway. (At 1,000 ft., you easily cleared the slag piles.) You then flew on 15 seconds and turned 90 degrees left. Another 15 seconds, and a left 90 degrees put you on base leg. You then let down to 500 feet, and in 10 seconds turned for the runway, all the time with the ADF pointing to the tower. I guess the caravan could hear us coming and fired flares like mad. As you can see, we made it successfully. Sometimes, we did have to rack it around at 200 ft. to get lined up, but never had to go around. On one trip, when I went to the tower to clear, they were not going to let us takeoff as we were way below minimums. After some pushing the clearing officer said, "Aw, what the hell, if you can land in this you can sure takeoff," and off we went.

On a flight somewhere close to Berlin, we landed at an all grass field with all of the buildings pretty well hidden in pine trees. I understood it to be Germany's equivalent of our Wright Field. We were met by a Brigadier General, who informed us he was commandeering our ship, and we would have to RON. This was the first time I had encountered this, and I told him we had explicit orders not to comply. He said he had cleared it with the Wing, so I had the R/O confirm it. We stayed overnight. Next morning the ship was loaded for Burtonwood and the General came by with a set of German periscope binoculars, on a tripod, to be delivered to the CO at Burtonwood, who I'm sure was a friend. He made me sign for them, with name, rank, and serial number. He also ordered me to deliver them, in person, and have the CO at Burtonwood sign the same receipt I had signed. He was determined that they get to the right person! On the ramp at Burtonwood, we set them up and looked at the slag piles. They appeared close enough to reach out and touch. (The piles were not dust, as they appeared from a distance. They were actually huge boulders, about the size of a small car.) I delivered the binoculars in person, as ordered, and had him sign for them. I got a good look at the colonel's office, which I had heard about. He had shelves all around the office. As each new plane arrived, he had the clock removed and placed in his office for safe keeping, until the plane left. He had quite a supply of clocks there.

Another trip from Burtonwood, we climbed out and leveled off at about 4,000 feet between layers, with unlimited visibility 1,500 ft. above and below us – so off to Beachy Head direct. Somewhere along the flight a group of B-17s came up through the undercast en mass. We were surely in their way and B-17s were being racked around like fighters, with the navigators throwing red lights at us. I decided it would be better if both of us were not moving all over that patch of sky. When Hoerner asked me what I did, I told him, "I took it off of auto pilot and flew straight and level." He agreed that was right, and after all I was there first. It was scary, B-17s were everywhere.

On another flight, on the same track right over London, on a clear day, the right engine went "Briiiit." I worked the mixture to no avail, and the crew chief was there instantly when it made the same noise again. I told him I thought we should feather, and I remember his words, "I do, too." We lost no time getting George off and had it secured in less than 45 seconds. (I have only lost one other engine in my lifetime, which was on a DC-4.) We were at my usual 10,000 ft., so it was downhill to Grove 60 miles east. I called Foible (radio call sign for Grove) on VHF and told them our troubles. I suppose everyone in the UK and Germany heard that transmission. Chaves later thanked me for saving the engine, as he had an unusually good maintenance record – so good, Wright Field had authorized him to go above recommended TBO. I don't remember what the trouble was, probably a broken valve.

*Left: "A captured German half-track, probably at Y-64 in east France. Y-64 is where Fogg and DuPuy were shot down by ground fire, on final approach to land. We were told to land from the west, regardless of wind, as the enemy lines were at the edge of the field. They either didn't listen or didn't hear and were killed." – Harbaugh. Right: A C-47, off the hard top, at Grove. "We had to borrow balloon jacks from the British to get it back up, and dig a hole under the wing tip to prevent damage." – Harbaugh*

My mother wrote that Pete Hilmelright, who I sat next to in school, had been shot down and was MIA, and the War Department didn't give his mother very much information. She asked me if I would try to find out something. He was flying P-61s, so I stopped at the only field in Belgium that I thought had them. I was taxiing in at a crawl, as the ramp was very narrow. The ramp was alive with people, and they signaled that I wasn't going to clear a B-26 nose. I stopped, got out, and was met by the CO. He was so happy I hadn't torn the nose off of one of his planes he congratulated me and told me all he knew about Pete. He had rolled the plane over to bail out and the radar operator got out OK. They thought Pete had hit the horizontal stabilizer and never opened his chute. His body was found and years later was buried in the National Cemetery in Winchester.

We picked up a load of wounded in Germany to bring back to Chipping Onger, England. The weather forecast was good, but as soon as we got off of the Continent, we ran into a fast moving, "textbook" front. It was forcing us down, and we went by Reading at about 200 feet. We had to pull up into it and called Foible (Grove). They diverted us to a RAF field on the south coast, and we landed in clear skies. The RAF treated us royally. Their doctor, a four striper (Group Captain) and his staff met the plane, examined each wounded man and moved them all to the base hospital awaiting the ambulances coming after them. The crew went to the Ops. Office and the ship was taken care of and refueled. I didn't see the nurse and her technician until the next morning, and I assumed she went to the hospital with the wounded. She complained that I didn't pay enough attention to her, and after that I was assigned a regular nurse. I believe she was their CO, but anyway, no more nurse complaints. This one was great.

One night, approaching Grove in decent weather, we passed Harwell in full view, and when we called Foible to land it was zero-zero. We got clearance to land at Harwell and again we were treated royally. Since they didn't have a late mess, as we did, they drove us in a car over to Grove. The plane was loaded there during the night and refueled, and we left from there the next morning.

Someone in the outfit found the Daunou Hotel, 6 Rue Daunou, in Paris, a half a block from the opera. I don't know where I had been or why I was by myself, but I was coming up the Rue de L'Opera walking one night right after the liberation of Paris. It was dark, very little street light, and I was scared, as there were still Germans in Paris. I had my .45 cocked in my pocket, but made it back to the hotel. That was 1944. My mother and sister were there later, my daughter stayed there, and this fall my wife and I were back with our grandson. When I wrote them for a reservation they called me in the States to confirm the reservation. Certainly not the Ritz, but an ideal place to stay in the very heart of Paris.

*(More of Charles Harbaugh's recollections are found in Chapters 5 and 8)*

*Chapter 3*

# The Ferrying Squadrons: 310th, 311th, 312th, 325th and the 2920th (Provisional)

The ferrying squadrons were tasked with delivering aircraft all over the ETO, and sometimes beyond. Bomber and fighter aircraft were flown from Gander, Newfoundland, or other bases via the "Great Northern Route," to bases, including Nutts Corner and Langford Lodge Air Depot (LLAD), in northern Ireland. These brand new ships were refitted and modified at these bases, and then ferry crews, usually three or four men, would deliver them to front line combat units as combat loss replacements. The ferrying squadrons always knew the loss rates after a raid, as they flew the replacement ships.

They also doubled as transport squadrons at times. The pilots assigned to these squadrons had to be very versatile. One day they might fly a B-17, and the next day a P-51 or P-38. Many times, they were handed a manual and told to deliver the airplane. If they were lucky they might get some ground instruction. This made for some very hairy situations!

**Robert P. "Paddy" Walker transferred from the RCAF to the USAAF and was attached to the 310th Ferrying Squadron in mid 1943. He flew out of Warton, before transferring to the 25th Bomb Group (Recon Special) at Watton, where he became a highly decorated OSS pilot. Paddy was (and still is) an avid letter writer. He was kind enough to go through the scrap book his mother had kept and pull out some excerpts from his letters, which give us great insight as to what life was like in the 310th at Warton.**

*EXCERPTS – Letters Home*

*September 30, 1943*: "Today was pay day, but I missed it and dinner, too – out on a trip. Incidentally, my co-pilot knows Jenny Simms and quite a few other celebrities. He used to work with them in California. It's funny, you know, he's a 1st Lt. outranking me, but I'm still captain of the old Forts – they're wonderful planes."

*October 9, 1943*: "Things over here are still the same. I'm 1st pilot on Fortresses, delivering them here and yon. This co-pilot of mine is quite a card. He used to be with NBC and worked with Jack Benny for seven years – Bob Hope – and all that crowd. They used to go out on parties in Hollywood – at least Virgil was among the invited guests. He was engaged to Janet Blair, the gal that played the role of Eileen in the show, "My Sister Eileen," for a year or so. They broke off the engagement, and just before coming overseas he married a French actress – pure French, according to him. Virgil knows a whole crew of movie stars and has written to a couple of friends of his to get me some autographed photographs. Speaking of movie stars, I saw Clark Gable at his base the other day as he buzzed by on his motor bike. Welch and Walcott are at his base and say that he is just one of the boys."

*October 28, 1943*: "Dear Mom and Family, You should see me now – sitting with my back propped against the head of the bed, shoes and tie off, leather coat thrown over my feet – this stationery is on a clip board, and I'm writing away! One of your letters has just arrived, the first in some time, and I'm anxious to get an answer off to it. Having just eaten, the top button of my pants had to be unbuttoned – bloody uncomfortable! The wall on my right is covered with pinup girls from *Esquire* – *Yank* – newspapers, etc. That little picture of Madeline on Riley Boy is also pinned up there. The walls are so doggone bare that a little color had to be added – (It also keeps the hut a bit warmer!). Just below all those pictures stands a

*F/O (later Lt.Col. ) Robert P. Walker shortly after his transfer to the USAAF from the RCAF, in 1943.*

table covered with junk – kinda like my desk at home used to look like. From here can be seen a box of tobacco, pipe holder, tin can (ash tray), a RCAF writing pad, a dirty handkerchief – (I wiped some ink up with it), an officer's hat (the operational, beat-up type), a cigar box, a book on meteorology, a knife, a leather strap, my red flannels (Yep!), etc. In other words, it's a mess, this table of mine: guess that's why I'm writing here – can't find space on the table. Incidentally, the chair isn't much better – there's a khaki shirt, bathrobe, tie, and blouse over the back of it.

It's just 1800 hours, or 6 p.m. The BBC has just come on, (BBC newscast); the news is pretty good over here these days with the Russians driving westward toward Germany. I hope they stop when they reach the Channel. There was a traveling PX here yesterday, so I went down and bought myself a couple of shirts, three sets of underwear, a pair of gloves, and a long camel-hair colored overcoat. The coat fits well, and is really smart looking. They didn't have any shoes my size, or I would have gotten another pair. One pair of mine is having half soles and heels put on them. It takes ten days to three weeks to get them back – I'm off again – rambling on – talking (should say writing) about nothing in particular and everything in general – hope you won't mind.

This barracks block isn't divided into rooms – we're all in together – fourteen of us – (not counting the mice). Speaking of mice – well these take the cake – The doggone things find our rations, then get in single file to wait their turn to get at them. We have quite a system worked out to combat them, though, (thought up by "The Character," a RCAF transfer who has finished his tour and has the British DFC), – [l/Lt. Kingdon Knapp] – When we hear a mouse by "The Character's" bed, a signal is given to a fellow across the way, who promptly shines a flashlight on the spot where the noise is coming from. "The Character" immediately throws a shoe, brick, or something at the creature (We haven't gotten any yet!). One of the fellows even took a couple of shots at one with a .45 automatic one night – but he missed, too! – Speaking of the devil – one just walked by! The rat!

I'm pretty tired tonight – had a pretty rough trip today with the weather and all, flying over water to boot. My eyes feel like they have a couple of lead weights hung on them – other than that though I'm in fine shape – may be putting on a little weight – who knows? Boy, these Fortresses are honeys, wonderful to fly, and handle beautifully to be as big as they are. Incidentally, I have the honor of being the youngest first pilot in the squadron – not that it means anything – but it's something to write about anyway.

Well, a bull session on airplanes has developed. Everyone talking about the kind of plane they are going to buy after the war. Get a bunch of pilots together and you'll always have bull sessions. One of the fellows who is married was telling about a letter he got from his wife. This guy has been flying for years, and in the letter his wife said that she wanted to see the day when he would wake up in the morning and not look out the window to see what the weather was like. It's funny, but that's about the first thing we do in the mornings – raise the black-out curtain and take a look out the window. It never fails! Well, the bull session is increasing. There are two guys sitting here on my bed now, and three more perched about elsewhere. It's really getting deep now! The flight commander of fighter flight just came in with a bottle of whiskey in his hand and a cigar in his mouth. He put the bottle away and left to go to the post theater.

Gosh, it doesn't seem like Xmas is almost here again, but when you look at the calendar, there it is, big as life. I sure would like to see a Xmas tree all lit up like we used to have at home. We'll probably have a party or something here, or maybe I'll go to someone's home this time.

If this letter doesn't make sense, don't blame me. The discussion is getting so that you can't hear yourself think – really loud."

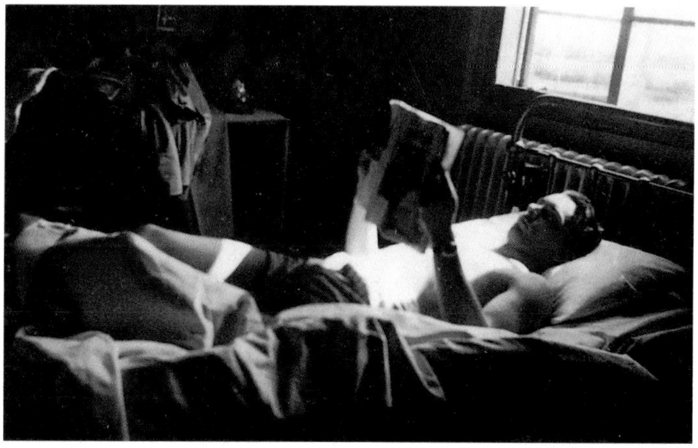

*Walker on his bunk at Warton.*

*Left: F/O Jack Couch and F/O Walker wearing their new English tailor made, American uniforms. Both men transferred from the RCAF in 1943. Right: "Pat" Walker and "The Character" Kingdon Knapp. Note the British DFC ribbon on Knapp's chest. King was killed in combat flying an A-26 "Invader" in Korea.*

*October 29, 1943*: "The other night I walked into the mess and sitting at the table was Bruce McMurchy – [Canadian, in RCAF in Canada with me] – you wouldn't know him, but he was in Manning Pool, I.T.S., and Chatham with Charles and me. – [Charles D. Jordan, who hitch hiked to Canada with me]. We went out – had a few beers – went to a dance – and talked over old times – who was alive out of our old gang and what not. There are surprisingly few left. One of the fellows "got it" returning from a sweep about a month ago. He had seven victories to his credit. Two of them are in Alaska – flight lieutenants. [equivalent to captain in USAAF].

A letter arrived from Bud Moessmer today – he was telling me about Joe Seguin, who used to be with us in Canada. "Little Joe" is over here somewhere. Olie Jarvis, Bud's friend from St. Louis, who washed out and was at Trenton when I was, is now a Captain in the Air Force. He took a discharge, and got his wings in the States. Another one of the old fellows, Al Lochland, who washed out and went as an Air Gunner now has five "Jerries" to his credit and the British DFC and the Victoria Cross, Britain's highest medal. The old boys are doing all right for themselves.

*Left: Knapp and Walker, in front of a B-17 "taxi." Center: Walker and F/O "Pee Wee" Morgan. Morgan was the pilot of the UC-64 that disappeared with Glenn Miller. Right: F/O Robert Morgan.*

My situation here is the same – dull. To be perfectly frank, I don't like it here and would give anything to get on combat, but all my beefing doesn't phase them one bit. I'm only attached to this squadron, and as long as I'm only attached to this squadron, I can't get any promotions. It's a hell of a set up, and if there's any way of getting out of it, I'm going to do it. Today I went back to the Replacement Center from which I was posted, to see the CO, but he wasn't there. The Adjutant listened patiently to my complaints, and advised me what to do – it's worth a try anyway.

You should see this barracks. You never saw so much junk for so few fellows – footlockers, barracks bags, bed rolls, Val-packs, helmets, bicycles hanging from the ceiling, etc. – and the guys – what a bunch of madmen! It's impossible to think in here, let alone write a letter. There's so much noise in here now that you can't hear yourself think."

*October 31, 1943* (2920 Ferry Squadron): " One of the boys in our midst, who also transferred from the RCAF, is known as "The Character," and he certainly lives up to his name. He has the British DFC, as he was on operations with the RAF, and did some splendid work. You have to do something pretty doggone good before the British will turn loose one of them. "The Character" transferred before he finished his tour, therefore his last missions were done in the American uniform. The other day he received the Air Medal and Oak Leaf Cluster. It was funny the way the medal was presented to him. Instead of making some sort of presentation, the CO just called him in and gave it to him. It sure made me mad – shucks – any fellow that deserves a medal certainly deserves some sort of presentation, even if it's just calling attention to the fact that he has received it. This certainly wasn't the case.

My laundry and cleaning came back today – in my laundry was a note – to wit: "Dear Pat, We three girls have fallen for your red sweater, have you got any more like it? I can assure you that we would be very grateful. If and when you have finished with it would you like to pass it over? Please send along c/o the three packers, 30, 31, and 6."

The funny part of it is that the red sweater they are speaking of is the top part of my red-handles! Guess I'll have to get in touch with the girls to see what the score is."

*November 16, 1943*: (310th Ferry Squadron) "Tonight I'm duty pilot. – The other day I was over at the station where "Pee Wee" is now stationed. [F/O Robert Morgan]. I just happened to drop in there and remembered afterward that he was there. Well, I wandered over to his office, yes, he has an office, as a matter of fact, he is in charge of air transport at this particular station. Anyway, when he saw me, he nearly had a fit, it was the first time I had seen him in several months. Immediately, he began taking me around introducing me to practically every officer on the station. You would never guess who his buddy is, a major from Austin, Major Rice, and a heck of a good guy. Well these guys take me to a little place for supper where we have eggs ... with shells! When I wasn't looking, the major would put his eggs on my plate – when it all ended up I had eaten five eggs. Guess it sounds funny to be talking about such things, but over here they are a rarity. To top this all off, there were a couple pieces of apple pie which were very good – very.

My co-pilot these days is King Knapp, DFC (British), Air Medal and Oak Leaf Cluster. King finished up his tour with the RAF. We get along good together, I guess, because we think along the same lines about a lot of things. I don't know how long he will be flying with me, but I'm afraid not for very long. He is new here, and has to rest up six months before they will send him back on combat duty, and in the meantime, he will be checked out on these jobs we fly here. He is known in our barracks as "The Character" because of some of his sayings and what not. He's always getting the hot-foot, a frog in his bed, or something of the sort."

"The Character" and I managed to get into town this afternoon, and while there a funny thing happened. We had just had some tea and were walking down the street very innocently when all of a sudden King stopped and asked me if I thought he was drunk. He was far from that as he hadn't touched a thing, and I told him that if he were drunk it was the cheapest one I had ever seen – for free. On asking him what brought forth such a question, he pointed down the street a way. It was then that I thought that I was intoxicated as well, for there not more than a hundred yards down the street – so help me – there walking single file down the street, were five ELEPHANTS. It was such a surprise to us that we ended up going to the aquarium and zoo – believe it or not."

*December 24, 1943*: "Guess who I saw today over in Ireland? [It was] Jimmy Doolittle – brass band and all. He had arrived from (somewhere) and was going (somewhere) and was played in, with an Army band. General D. was all smiles and seemed to be in the best of spirits. The band played him a couple of numbers, and then he got into his car and drove away – escorted – "natcherly." After Jimmy left we all piled into our trucks to go out to our planes, and the band played the Air Force song – you know the one – "Off you go, into the wild blue yonder" – or something like that. It kinda made you feel good to know that the band was playing a piece for our bunch. Oh well, you can't carry a brass band around to keep your spirits up, can you?

Everyone is out tonight, except Lausen, who is asleep, and Pedro. By the way Pedro is a fuzzy little brown, black, and white kitten that has no more sense than a monkey. It's the most playful thing you ever saw. The minute you step in the door, he's after you. He will hide behind a flying boot or something and spring out at you as you walk by. (Incidentally, he's a she!) Pedro belongs to Knapp – where he got the name is beyond me, but the kitten certainly knows it. You can't call, "kitty, kitty, kitty" and get her attention, or get her to come to you if you want it. You've got to yell, "Hey Pedro – come here!" and "she'll come scooting. Right now she is asleep on my winter flying jacket which is on my bed."

*January 2, 1944*: "Tomorrow and the next day are my days off – guess Ket [Ingwer Ketelsen] and myself will go to a little town up north where he has some friends, and where Americans are scarce. This little town where we are going is pretty quiet – a dance at the dance hall every night. Ket's friend sings in the orchestra. She has a cute little blond girl friend whose name is, O'Shaughnessy – a real Irish gal."

"An order came out a while back saying that we were to fly in weather which would be, in some instances, "washed out" for combat squadrons, so I reckon our work is pretty important. It's too bad that our outfit doesn't get some kind of recognition for its work – without a doubt it deserves some merit, or at least a "thank you" from someone."

*Lt. Ingwer "Ket" Ketelsen.*

"I just got in a while ago – was caught away from base last night. "Ket" was posted to another station. Now I have another co-pilot – a chap named, Douglas, 1st Lt. of the old Eagle Squadron.

After transferring from the RAF, he flew with Col. Peterson's squadron on "ops." He's that 23 year old full colonel, also formerly of the RAF"

"We had a two and a half hour trip – all through bad weather – Another chap was flying on my wing, but when it got to where he couldn't see me and I him – well, he turned back. We stooged on through the stuff on instruments most of the time and got the ship delivered. We stayed overnight, and finally managed to get back tonight."

*May 15, 1944*: "Pete, King, and I are still waiting for our orders transferring us to this Mosquito squadron to come through. It shouldn't be long now. This morning there was an article in the paper over here telling of a RAF "type," who flew from Canada to England, coast to coast, in five hours and thirty-nine minutes – a distance of some twenty-two hundred miles. That's an average of four hundred miles an hour ground speed. You've got to admit that he wasn't wasting any time passing over the "puddle." Well, that's what I'll be flying (soon, I hope), and will be depending on that factor for the type of work I'll be doing – speed. One thing about it, Mom, I'll probably get home a lot sooner by finishing up a tour on this

*Ketelsen and Walker, in front of a B-17 taxi ship probably "Slap Happy."*

*King Knapp and Ket Ketelsen.*

work than if I remained here. Believe me, Mom, I'm really eager for this deal – as mentioned before, it's one of those things that a pilot dreams about. King saw the colonel today and he said that the next he'd see of us was when we reported to his squadron for duty. In other words, our transfer is going according to plan. I might add that we are the envy of about every pilot here. They are wishing that they were RAF trained now."

"It's almost midnight – the crap game is over – blackout shades have been drawn for some time, and the rest of the fellows are in bed – so – that means I'll have to close for now."

*June 25, 1944*: "At last I'm on a combat squadron – at long last – and feel as though a great weight has been lifted from my shoulders. You know that I wasn't pleased with the work that I had been doing, although the experience, as far as I'm concerned, has been very beneficial to me. You know the type of aircraft that I am now flying, and you can no doubt imagine I am really pleased to be flying it. It's a "honey' of a kite, and I do mean, "honey." They say that you have to treat all aircraft like a woman, that is, except this one – which has to be treated like a lady – and a very respectable one."

"This morning I flew up to my old base [Warton] in one of these kites to pick up my laundry – as well as to build up my time – and you should have seen their eyes pop when Walker landed and taxied up to the line. Boy, were some of them jealous!"

**Pat Walker also related the following story which is sadly remembered by many of the men:**

One of the villages near the base at Warton was Freckleton. When I was first assigned to Warton in June 1943, it was a new outfit made up of guys just over from the States and a bunch of us who had transferred over from the RAF and RCAF. It was designated as the 87th ATG (Provisional), later becoming the 27th ATG. I left Warton in May 1944 for combat assignment to Watton. In August 1944 a B-24 crashed into an elementary school in Freckleton, killing thirty-eight little children. Some of the G.I.s from Warton helped rescue the surviving children from the schoolyard. One of the little girls who survived the crash has been visiting me with her husband on their trips to the States for about the last ten years. On one of their trips they were in this part of the country, and looked me up. My name was in the BAD-2 (Base Air Depot-2) Roster. She had been made an associate member of the BAD-2 Association at their first meeting in Blackpool. She is Valerie (Preston) Whittle.

My friend, Wiley Noble, is the Secretary and one of the founders of the 3rd Strategic Depot Association. That depot, which repaired battle damaged B-24s, was on the opposite side of Watton, where I flew the "Mossies." A close friend of Wiley's was a pallbearer of one of the little coffins at the communal burial of the children at the Freckleton cemetery. He saw the name, "Sonya," on the coffin that he carried, and vowed to name a future daughter he might have in her name. This happened, and she also is a close friend of Wiley's. He happened to call me while they were visiting me, and wanted to talk with Valerie, to tell her this story. He also asked whether she would write up a little synopsis of how she remembered that day for an article in the 3-SAD newsletter. Enclosed is a copy of what she wrote.

PLANE CRASH INTO SCHOOL AT FRECKLETON, ENGLAND, AUGUST 23, 1944 – by: VALERIE A. (PRESTON) WHITTLE

Background lead-in to her story by: Lt.Col. Robert P. Walker, USAF (Ret)

On August 23, 1944, two B-24 aircraft which had undergone maintenance at the USAAF Base Air Depot Number 2, Warton, England, were ordered up for test flights. Soon after these aircraft had taken off and were in the process of testing, a local storm rapidly developed. It evolved into a very serious storm with gale winds, heavy blowing rain, low clouds, and minimum visibility. The pilots were ordered by the control tower to land immediately. One B-24 managed to land safely at the Warton Air Base. The second B-24, while attempting to make a low approach to land in the blinding rain and poor visibility, crashed into the Freckleton school house. Valerie (Preston) Whittle was a seven year old student attending class in the school when the crash occurred. This is her story of that event:

It was August 23, 1944. I was seven years old, and my brother, George, was five. It was the first week back at school following the summer break, and George had just started school for the first time.

At about 10 a.m. that morning the sky darkened and we had a severe thunderstorm. It was raining very heavily, and the storm was directly overhead. I remember brilliant flashes of lightening and a terrific loud crash. Then flames appeared outside the windows. We didn't know what had happened, but the school teacher led us into the cloakroom adjacent to our classroom and from there we escaped through a window into the school yard. From here we ran into a playing field at the back of the school, which was surrounded by a six foot high wall. We stayed there until some G.I.s arrived and climbed over to us and handed us over the wall. I couldn't find my brother. The classroom he was in was at the front of the school and had been destroyed by the crashed Liberator. Two children from that class survived, thirty-eight perished.

Valerie A. Whittle
March 6, 1996

**On the lighter side, Walker recalled some of his flights with the 310th:**

One morning at Warton, I was going to make an early morning takeoff to deliver a B-17 to a base in East Anglia. My other two crew members – co-pilot and flight engineer, were late. After a long wait, and they didn't show up, I decided to deliver the B-17 solo. I started engines #3 & #4 from the co-pilot's seat, then moved over to the left seat and started #1 & #2. I flew it solo to the base, and the jeep driver who came out to pick up the delivery crew to take us to the control tower didn't believe me. He had to go look inside the plane to verify I had flown it alone. He shook his head all the way to the tower. (This is a true story – I swear!)

Another time King Knapp – ex-RAF with British DFC, was flying as my co-pilot on a B-17 pick-up from Langford Lodge in Ireland. He needed four engine time since he had done an RAF tour on Wellingtons (2 engine). On the way across the Irish Sea toward the Isle of Man, he mentioned that his girlfriend (later wife) lived on a golf course in Scotland, which her father managed or owned. We decided to divert to Scotland and say hello. We found the course and clubhouse where they lived. King, flying from the right seat, buzzed the house several times until they all came outside and waved. They figured it was King. On the last buzz job, he knocked off part of the chimney with the right wing tip. Then it was time to leave! Our story was that some "yahoo" taxied into us and hit our wing tip!

One other time, I flew a B-24 to Lands End, and was then to pick up another one to deliver to Marrakech, Morocco. That plane wasn't there, and I needed to get back to Warton. There was a Lockheed Hudson the RAF had in their charge that they wanted moved back to some American base. I volunteered (even though I had never been inside a Hudson except on guard duty as a basic RCAF Cadet at St. Hubert, Quebec).

They pulled it out of the hangar, a sgt. showed me the cockpit, and I flew it back to Warton. My first and last flight in an A-29 Hudson. It was a cinch to fly, but I had some explaining to do to Major Joe Stenglein, my CO at the 310th, at Warton – he forgave me!

**"Paddy" Walker also recalled some fancy taxiing of B-17s – in reverse!:**

My story about backing B-17s into hardstands may sound like fabrication, but I assure you it is true. I either heard some of the pilots discussing it at Warton, or someone demonstrated it to me. Some of the "parking places" didn't have room to taxi in and turn around without the tail possibly hitting something. In these cases, the ground crew would hook up a tug to the tail wheel and tow it in. The tail wheel on the B-17 will rotate 100 degrees when unlocked, which allowed for it to be backed up. By holding the brake on one side only, and using the outboard engine on that side you could swing it around about 45 degrees. Then you would do the same on the other brake and outboard engine. This way you could sort of fish-tail it back into the hardstand. After getting in, you would taxi forward just enough to get the tail wheel straightened out, and lock it. Really! I did this on occasions just to show off to the ground crew who didn't believe that it could be done. War stories! They will never end.

*Left: Lt. Ingwer C. "Ket" Ketelsen. Right: Ketelsen, preparing to deliver a P-47D.*

**Ingwer "Ket" Ketelsen was also a pilot in the 310th FS. He shared the following memories and photographs:**

I came overseas with the 49th Service Group. This was a mobile aircraft repair unit, consisting of two repair squadrons, and a headquarters squadron. The repair squadrons were equipped to go into the field, with mobile tools and equipment, and repair downed aircraft. Each squadron came complete, even to having a "test pilot" to fly the repaired craft. I was one of those pilots, as well as Adjutant of one of the squadrons. Well, when we arrived in the UK, the repair squadrons and their valued equipment were sent to non-mobile, base situation, and the headquarters squadron, was absorbed into the whole resultant mishmash. Fortunately, it was a concept that could make the change and worked out very well, so far as the war effort was concerned. Leadership positions were somewhat mixed up for a while. Our Group Commander, a full colonel, was assigned to Base Supply. It didn't last, however, for he was given a B-26 group. I later transferred to the 310th.

When I first arrived at the 310th, I flew with F/O Robert P. "Pat" Walker, an ex-RCAF Pilot, out of Warton.

*Members of the 310th Ferrying Squadron who made the trip to Casablanca.*

I remember one trip, when a group of pilots of the 310th was flown to Casablanca, in one of our B-17 taxi ships to bring up a bunch of P-47 and P-51 fighters that had been brought over to the ETO on a carrier. At least that was the "scuttlebutt" that drifted our way, at the time, so far as I can recall. At any rate, we all picked up our planes and flew our first leg to Algiers, together. From there, a few of the "better swimmers" opted to fly directly over the Mediterranean to Marseille, while others of us took the Sardinia-Corsica route. All made it safely back to Burtonwood.

*Back row: Lt. Peres, Lt. Ketelsen, Lt. Herman Estrada. Second row: Lt. Lionel Palmer, Lt. Earnest G. Garrett, Lt. Vincent Alexander. Seated on ground: Lt. Clarence W. Fightmaster. Photo taken in Algiers.*

During the months of January and February, 1945, a number of pilots of the 310th were involved in ferrying "war weary" B-24s to the southeast coast of Italy. I was involved in taking three of the B-24s to Italy. The first one was a real "boneyard special!" We picked it up at Langford Lodge, Ireland, and returned it, forty-five minutes out, for oil pressure problems. Among other things, we had runaway props on takeoff from Marseille, erratic engine instrument readings, and we lost an engine before arrival at Manduria. After delivery we carried orders to use any air transportation available to get us back to the UK, sort of an official authorization to "hitch-hike" our way home. It could take a week or more to do this. The last trip, at least the last trip that I know of, a taxi ship was sent to pick us up. Nearing Rome on the return, all the crews aboard, to the last man, detected noises coming from those "Gooney Bird" engines that cried out for us to RON and have them checked out. The engines sounded much better after a night in Rome!

Lt. James E. Lemon was a good friend of mine from my hometown. We grew up together and always dreamed about flying someday. He was the best man at my wedding. I knew he was in Italy flying B-24 combat missions, so I looked him up and dropped by to see him. We spent the night

*"The Crew" in Algiers: Lawrence, Jenks, Krutsch, and Jacobs.*

*Tunis, Libya: Gaw, Bugg, Belot, Jacobs, Krutsch, Trees, and Jenks.*

*Ket Ketelsen and Earnest Garritt saw the Casbah together in Algiers.*

*Ketelsen with his crew for the first two trips to Italy, in B-24s.*

*J.J. Canning with a local policeman in Casablanca, April, 1945.*

*310th Squadron members waiting to board the taxi after a night in Rome.*

*Ketelsen with B-24 "Bashful Marion."*

at his base and our two crews got acquainted. Public Relations at his base got wind of our visit and our home town paper got pictures and a news article to commemorate our meeting. I was to see him once more on my third B-24 delivery a couple of weeks later. About a month later, I learned that he was killed when he lost two engines on the same side shortly after takeoff with a full load of bombs. He managed to hold control until his crew could get out, but perished when he tried to make it out, so his co-pilot related.

**The author of these "ferry tales," who served in several different squadrons of the 27th ATG, both ferrying and transport, preferred to remain anonymous. The names of individuals in the stories have been edited out at his request, but all of the stories are true. This man was actually trained as a fighter pilot, but was assigned to ferrying aircraft upon arrival in the ETO:**

A small group of fighter pilots came to England via Queen Elizabeth and Glasgow, in late 1942. Fighter Command needed planes more than pilots, so we were assigned to Burtonwood to deliver P-39s, etc., to Duxwold and other bases in Southern England.

Lousy winter weather made for few flights, so we eager beavers volunteered for anything. I lucked out with a L-4 to go near London. Hell – I wasn't proud, just hungry. Typical winter weather kept me low and slow. Lower ceilings and poor viz had me low along roads and railroads. RR tracks disappearing into tunnels kept the flight exciting. It became more exiting as I became lost and low on fuel. Finally, a RAF air base appeared, so I landed for fuel and to find out where the hell I was. I located a fuel truck – by taxiing into it! I put my right wing tip into the truck's windshield. This upset the RAF field commander, and later my CO, and gave me a reputation that was slow to be forgotten.

Low ceilings and lousy viz were a constant hazard. We were often forced to fly low along the coast, eyes searching for barrage balloons. Lost again, as was often the case, I once stumbled over London in a P-47. The balloons were above, lost in the clouds. Dropping wheels and flaps, slowing to almost stall speed, I dodged a couple of balloon cables and exited to the countryside. I landed at another RAF base, reoriented myself, and flew on.

Poor weather took its toll. We lost two P-38s in the moors north of Warton. Some sheep farmer had heard engine sounds in the nearby hills and we spent two days hiking and searching in the mist and drizzle. We eventually found them – or pieces of them. They had hit hard and blew into many parts. It is unnerving to pick up a flight boot with the foot still in it.

*Left: Ket Ketelsen with lifelong friend, Lt. James E. Lemon at Lemon's B-24 base in Italy. Lemon was killed about six weeks after this picture was taken. Right: Ket Ketelsen fighting the ever-present mud at Burtonwood, in the Spring.*

Two days later, a couple of good friends of mine (I had stood up for one of them as he was getting married in Florida, just before leaving) were flying P-47s to southern England. Bad weather forced them to climb into the clouds, hoping to get on top. They collided, and both chutes got tangled in falling wreckage. It is tough duty packing belongings and writing notes to family.

Constant low ceilings and bad visibility forced us to navigate by rivers and railroads. Burtonwood and Speke (Liverpool) were both big air depots with a large river and many railroads leading in. After getting to know the approaches, it was not unusual for some of us to have landed and be taxiing to the parking area before the control tower could see us on the ground. On one trip into Warton in a P-39 with a belly tank, which made for sloppy handling, I made three passes at an upwind landing, finally saw a piece of the runway too late to land, so I hauled it around tight, came in fast downwind on the wet runway, and skidded to a stop about 20 feet from a stone hedge.

Not too far from us, at Woodvale, was a RAF base with a Polish squadron flying Typhoons, a British fighter plane. They were fearless pilots and loved to dogfight with us. We would bomb their control tower with paper bags of human waste, then wait for them to come up and dogfight. I blew an oil line in one of these dogfights and had to land my P-47 at their base. The windshield was black with oil, so my landing with side vision only was not very smooth. There was much good-natured ribbing by the Poles as they had "shot me down."

Whenever two or more of us delivered planes to the same destination, it was only natural to fly close formation. We took off in pairs with the lead plane navigating and the rest "tucking-in" close; especially nearing our delivery point. Occasionally, one of us would tap our wingman's wing tip with ours just to say "hi." In preparation to landing, we would line up echeloned to the right, buzz low over the runway, peel up and land, one right behind the other. On such a maneuver, only left turns would be made, as a right turn would force the fourth guy out down pretty low. On one such low pass, our leader was bringing us in at 250 m.p.h., I was the fourth guy out, "tail-end Charlie," and was looking through the other two canopies, practically reading the leader's instruments. He did not feel properly aligned with the runway and made a slight correction to the right. This forced me lower, and I felt a slight jar of the plane. Glancing ahead, I was on the ground. I leveled my wings, slid under the other three planes, came up on the left and speeded up and landed. My right wing tip light was smashed. I had demolished a boundary fence post and the controllers thought I was in the ground. My leader apologized, but was grounded for two weeks.

Another P-47 experience occurred during takeoff, flying on one of my buddy's wings. This guy is still the best pilot I have ever known. He has that smooth touch with any airplane he flies. We were to deliver two P-47s near London and could take a couple of days to sightsee. Luggage space in a fighter plane is nil, so we carried our overnight bags on our lap. On takeoff, in formation, naturally, his bag slipped to the floor. In retrieving it, he moved the control column to the right, turning into me. I hauled back and up, then settled back on his wing. He was grinning at me, saying "oops."

P-39s gave us the most trouble. One lousy day I picked up a P-39 in Ireland destined for our base, now at Warton, near Blackpool, England. Low ceilings and poor visibility were usual across the Irish Sea, plus my rough running, bucking engine made me nervous. Finally, I reached land, the north coast of Wales, and hunted for any field to land and work on the engine. The first field would be it. It was a small grass training field for Tiger Moths, the British, open cockpit, bi-wing trainer. I checked the "T" (traffic indicator), dropped the gear, and sloshed to a skidding stop at the field's edge. The English did not think I would be able to get in and knew I would not be able to get out, but worked on the engine anyway. I did some readjusting, tightening, plug changing, and it sounded good enough for me, for the time being. I asked them to hold the traffic. They had the "meat wagon" and fire truck ready, and I headed diagonally across the muddy field, taking the longest run I could get, regardless of "T" or wind direction. I brushed the bushes, but was on my way North. The gremlins struck again as the malfunctioning Allison engine, coughing and sputtering, kept me below 500 feet. If I could have reached 1,000 feet, I would have headed the P-39 towards the sea and bailed out. I finally reached Warton, landed straight in, downwind, with the brakes locked. I burned out both tires, climbed out, and told operations where they could shove this particular airplane.

The British anti-aircraft guns in Liverpool liked to practice tracking targets. One Sunday, we were called to send some planes over Liverpool

*Bell P-39 "Airacobra" fighter.*

*310th members Stenglein, Eade, Anders, Gildersleeve, Brandis, Bromly, and Stewart.*

*Lts. Langhorn Gee and Jimmie Andrews with a P-47 "Thunderbolt", commonly called the "Jug."*

P-47s at an operational fighter base.

for tracking. We rounded up a B-24 and a couple of fighters and headed out. I was flying a P-38 with drop tanks under each wing. I made a couple of medium altitude runs over town and swung over the harbor. Suddenly, there was a flak burst ahead of me, then another behind me – I was being boxed in. A boat in the harbor had not been notified we were "friendlies" and that this was a practice. This ticked me off, so I rolled the P-38 over, dove straight down, and dropped a wing tank on each side of the boat. I think I scared them more than they scared me. That was the last tracking practice allowed.

P-38s were fun to fly and fun to taxi. With the super chargers on top of the engine nacelles, close to the cockpit, they sounded just like a big Buick as you gunned them on the ground. We modified an older P-38, putting in a jump seat behind the pilot. Someone or some part often had to be delivered to Fighter Control Headquarters quickly. It was usually an exciting ride for the passenger, as we hugged the ground all the way, hopping over trees, fences, and buildings – just having fun.

Landing gear problems ... About five feet off the ground, in a P-39, my gear warning horn sounded. I gave it the gun, used the emergency gear system, and landed. We would get surprises like that often. Landing at a bomber base in a B-17, I called for gear down. My co-pilot flicked the toggle switch and called "gear down" on his side. I took a quick peek and verified my side. However, on final approach, we were met by flares and red lights. I went around, rechecking gauges and indicators. All looked okay, but checking for a wheel on my side, I noticed no gear. I had missed really seeing for "wheels down" the first time. The co-pilot went to the bomb bay and began to crank the gear down manually. Half way through the procedure, I flipped the switch again, the gear motor took hold, and almost broke my co-pilot's arm with the twirling crank. I apologized later.

B-26s were another thrill of an airplane to fly. The early, short wing, Martin Marauder "Flying Coffin" claimed more than its share of young pilots. On takeoff, full power, slow speed, and losing an engine, you had seven seconds to crank in full rudder trim or you were on your back. I lost a good friend when an engine failed him in a B-26 on takeoff. Fay Brandis flew a B-26 "Demon Deacon" as our taxi ship and would pick us up at fighter and bomber bases to bring us back to Warton. We often had 20 to 30 guys aboard. I was glad Fay was a good pilot. Many B-26s were picked up at Newcastle, Ireland. I had been assigned a new co-pilot, a service pilot, fresh from the States, who had flown nothing larger than small training planes. He was in his late 30s or early 40s on his first trip in Europe. We were to pick up a B-26 in Newcastle and take it to southern England. I checked the plane out, fired up the engines, and taxied to the end of the runway for takeoff. This particular runway ended at the edge of the Irish Sea. The B-26 does not fly off the runway, you have to ease it off. Unannounced to my co-pilot, and to have some fun, I had planned to fly low that day, as I often did, just for the joy of it. Thus, roaring down the runway, I made no attempt to lift the plane into the air. At 140 m.p.h., nearing the end with nothing but water ahead, I glanced at my new co-pilot. He had a firm grip on the arm rests, eyes wide and pushing as far back in his seat as far as he could get. Just at the end of the runway, I reached over and raised the gear, while we kept right on going, at the same height, out over the Irish Sea. We never got higher all the way to the coast of Wales. The propeller tips kicked up spray, leaving a wake as we swerved around boats rather than over them. Over land, I hung on the tree tops, whizzing by church steeples and tall smoke stacks, and finally greased it on the runway at our B-26 base. The co-pilot had not said a word, just watched, and sweated clean through his uniform. A rough welcome to the war. I later apologized. He meanwhile got thoroughly drunk, but flew with me again.

Another B-26 flight, which happened later in the war, comes to my mind. I took a mechanic and a co-pilot to Marseilles, southern France, to pick up a B-26 that had landed with engine trouble. We checked it out on the ground and got tower clearance to leave. In a B-26, right behind the

Ferrying new B-26 "Marauders."

*Lts. Brandis, Rawls, Brumley, and Smith at Warton, 1943.*

*Brandis, Fisher, Jones, and Rawls at Warton.*

pilot in the ceiling, is a bracket for holding a very pistol (flare gun) for signaling through the top of the cabin. On my takeoff, at about 60-70 m.p.h. down a very bumpy runway, the flare gun fell from the bracket and exploded in the cockpit, filling it with burning flares and smoke. I hit the brakes, cut the engines, and opened the side windows poking my head out to see where to stop. Smoke billowing from the windows alerted the fire trucks, and they roared out to extinguish the flares. When all cleared up, we returned to the end of the runway and took off for England. It was an exciting couple of minutes.

I learned a lesson, the hard way, in a P-38. This fighter had the advantage of being able to use the lower engine in tight turns to out maneuver an opponent, but it was heavy on aileron control. As a result, Lockheed came out with a hydraulic aileron booster for dog fighting, giving the pilot a delicate touch on the stick. A friend and I took up the first modified P-38s with a caution note not to try the boosters below 1,500 feet altitude. I was flying his wing when he engaged his boosters at about 1,000 feet. Next thing I knew, he had flipped over and dove straight into the ground. I climbed to about 5,000 feet before flipping my booster switch. I slowly made gentle turns to get the feel of it, finding control much more sensitive and delicate, good for prolonged maneuvers.

Not all of our flying was hairy. We did have fun – usually at someone else's expense. Much of our flying was delivering a variety of aircraft from the Lockheed Modification Center at Langford Lodge, Ireland, to bases in England. The British used the Irish Sea as a training area for their naval pilots. They had converted a small freighter into a flat-top, and with their little Tiger Moths, practiced carrier landings. Returning from Ireland in a B-17 one nice summer day, my co-pilot spotted one of those little flat tops with its planes in the pattern practicing. I dropped the big bomber down to about 600 feet and approached the pattern, dropping my wheels and half flaps. Pandemonium broke out as I joined the pattern. Tiger Moths split out every which way as red lights and flares shot up from the converted carrier. I turned off base leg onto the final, lowering full flaps as if in preparation to land. My bomber seemed as big as their ship. Sailors on the deck of the flat top scurried, moving planes and raising flags! About 50 feet from the fantail, I applied full power, raised the gear and flaps, and we laughed all the way back to England. I guess they were too busy to catch my number, or my CO would have had me on the carpet!

In Northern Ireland, Langford Lodge, Lockheed ran a repair and modification center. We were in and out of there often with P-38s. Lockheed's number one test pilot, Tony LeVier, would occasionally put on a show for us. That P-38 became a part of him during his precision aerobatics. His

*R/O, Bill White, turning the prop on a Martin B-26.*

*Major Norman Eisenberg, Site 13 Commander, Ray Dlouhy, flight engineer on the "Demon Deacon", Fay Brandis, pilot of the "Demon Deacon", and Captain Foreland, civil engineer, Warton, 1944.*

landing would be coming in low over the runway threshold, pull straight up and over, drop wheels and flaps, landing out of the loop. I never tried it.

Through a stroke of luck, I had an opportunity to fly the British Mosquito. I can not remember how or why I was picked. I had never seen or been in one, but a Mosquito showed up at Burtonwood and was needed at a RAF base in East Anglia. This plane is a sleek, twin engine fighter bomber, used as a night fighter or a long range low level bomber. It had conventional tail wheel landing gear, inline liquid cooled Rolls Royce engines, and was damn fast. It had typical British awkward air brakes, and the plane was made of laminated wood. After a brief cockpit checkout by a British pilot, I fired up and taxied out. I zig-zagged along the taxiway as forward visibility is poor in a taildragger. Weaving down the runway, building up speed to get the tail up and have rudder control, I finally become airborne. I played around cautiously, at altitude, until I got the feel of the plane, then went down on the deck all the way to the RAF base. The Mosquito was fast and maneuverable, and I thoroughly enjoyed it. Hated to get out after delivery. Too bad more American pilots did not have a chance to fly this airplane.

More than once, modification centers would screw up an airplane. I remember idling on the end of a runway at Warton, checking the magnetos in a B-24 prior to takeoff. The side windows were open, and it was a nice day. I heard a strange crackling, fluttering noise and looking out and up, I watched a P-51 fall into the ground just across the river from the base. The depot had tried to add another gun mounting in the wing and weakened the wing spar, which failed, and we lost another pilot.

While I am still reminiscing of small planes, another favorite day for me comes to mind. I had in Ireland my "personal" P-39. This was a light African camouflage reject from which I had removed the guns, armor plate, and most radio equipment to lighten the ship, making it more maneuverable and responsive. The British were preparing air support for the Anzio beach head and needed practice for the Spitfire defenders. A target was set up on a point of land in a large lake in Northern Ireland. We were asked to stage a mock attack in a variety of aircraft. I rustled up a P-38, B-24, A-20, assorted other airplanes, and I flew my P-39, on which I had painted "Slugger," the nickname of my wife. While other planes flew higher, and the Spits intercepted them, I never flew higher than the tallest trees. I went down highways, through villages, around woods, and being familiar with the area, could pop in on the target time and time again, hearing the British on the radio telling their Spits, "Just been hit by the 39 again." Later that evening at the RAF base, they gave me good natured hell, but that light, well camouflaged P-39 they just could not spot, even when they were only 400 feet above. A memorable day.

Lockheed Hudsons were American twin engine transport planes modified by the British. We got them back, still with the RAF air brake system, using them out of Ireland hauling freight and personnel to southwest England. This called for flying over the Irish Sea, along the mountainous coast of Wales and into the estuaries of the southwestern tip of England. All was pilotage or dead reckoning, as radio navigation aids were not yet available to our type of flying. The 100 foot and 200 foot ceilings and poor visibility did not give us much time to react when suddenly face to face with a rocky mountain. We did not always get through. We lost a few on

*Lockheed P-38 "Lightning" on operations with a fighter squadron.*

*DeHavilland's "Wooden Wonder", the Mosquito. This example is one of the few American flown "Mossies" of the 25th Bomb Group (Recon Special) out of Watton.*

*Left: Langford Lodge. Right: Control tower in Ireland.*

the Welsh mountains. That was to be expected, but some of us "old dogs" had learned "new tricks" to save our hides.

I flew into almost all of the B-17 and B-24 bases in England at one time or another. Often I would be at one of those bases when our bombers would be returning from raids deep into Germany. I would watch as ambulances clustered around the shot up planes, wounded and dead were removed, then fire hoses would wash out debris and parts of human bodies. These crewmen spent hours, day after day, going through hell, returning with parts of their closest buddies. The trauma they suffered for three years had to be at least equal to the pressures of Vietnam, but we have never heard them complain or make demands. Of course then, they did not have (and probably would not have wanted) the TV and media to cash in on their sorrows. The hard sell for ratings was not as prevalent in those days, and we could heal ourselves quietly.

I am about to brag, but only once, about my best landing – and this one was special. The B-24 had serious problems when forced to ditch in the North Sea. There was no escape hatch in the aft section behind the bomb bay area. Being a high wing, four engine bomber, when ditched and settling in the water, the complete fuselage submerged. The B-17, with its low wing configuration, would float very briefly with the fuselage above the waves, and the crew could exit – if they were fast. A modified escape hatch for a B-24 was designed at the Lockheed Center in Ireland, and they wanted it rushed to Hethel, a B-24 base in East Anglia. The weather was terrible for flying. There were low clouds and no visibility over all of England. No planes were flying anywhere, but I was asked to give it a try. I got a co-pilot and engineer, plus a general, who insisted on going along. I took the B-24 off with enough fuel to return if necessary. We reached the middle of England flying above the clouds and were being guided lower to sneak under the clouds and on to Hethel. The air controllers screwed up on their DF (direction finder) headings. The first things we saw were trees and woods almost catching our wings. They had let us down into a hilly wooded area. I pulled up and out of there quickly. The General, riding in the radio operator's seat, peering out the little window next to the number 3 engine, was in a cold sweat. I explained the controller's error, and we would dead reckon to Hethel and try a let down there. It was flatter country. Hethel tower heard us fly over, low in the clouds and with about a 300 feet ceiling and low visibility. I let down, saw ground, and found the airport. I made a tight fighter approach pattern and landed. The General, watching the landing gear and wheel on his side, told me later "As we skimmed over the runway threshold, the wheel barely touched the surface, slowly started to rotate, and picked up speed, as the B-24 eased lower on the extended gear struts." He never "felt" us touch down, and finally realized we were firmly on the ground when I was braking for the turn off to taxi. It was perfect timing for the best landing I ever made. I am glad the General was not along for the many really raunchy landings I have since slopped in on.

*A group of the 310th waiting to be picked up by the taxi ship, after delivering planes, somewhere in East Anglia. It appears they are ready to critique the landing of the "taxi driver" pilot – a common practice, the evaluation of which, was generously shared with that taxi pilot!*

The B-24 was not only a nice airplane to land, it was a great plane to taxi. Having wide gear with a nose wheel, we could whip that baby around the taxiways just using the two inboard engines, screeching our tires on the corners. Late one afternoon, I was called to deliver a high priority part to a RAF base near London. It was a lousy day, and I knew I would have to scurry to make it back by dark to get into our field. Needless to say, I was impatient. The little "follow me" jeep, which met me at the end of the runway after I landed at the RAF base, became the object of my impatience. I tailgated him in the big B-24. The faster he went, the faster I taxied behind him. He finally peeled off the taxiway, close by the tower after reaching a speed I am sure was over 60 m.p.h. and me right on his butt. I stopped the airplane, kept the engines idling, and hopped out with my package. There was the jeep driver, a RAF Wing Commander, who proceeded to chew me out, up one side and down the other – and I had it coming. If he had blown a tire or hit the brakes, I would have squashed him with the B-24. He followed up with a letter to my CO – another chewing out and lousy flight assignments followed.

*Delivering new B-24s.*

The B-17 is a forgiving airplane and I enjoyed flying it. At Langford Lodge, Ireland, they had a three story building which was all glassed in at the top. It was the flight control or tower. The building was near the intersection of the two long runways. Three guys directed airport traffic from the tower. With a co-pilot and an engineer, I had taken a B-17 aloft to check out some reported malfunctions. All checked well, so the engineer went aft to the tail gunners seat to enjoy the ride. We were about 6,000 feet up, when curiosity got the better of me and I began to feather (shut down) the engines, one after the other. The bomber light on fuel and armament continued to fly well even with only one engine operating. So, I feathered it, too. There was sudden silence in the big B-17. I could talk with the engineer, 60 feet back in the airplane, although he did not have much to say, except four letter words. The plane continued to glide, losing about 1,000 feet per minute at 150 m.p.h.. I could not resist a temptation, so nosing over into a dive up to 250 m.p.h., I snuck up on the control tower from behind and swished over their heads about 20 feet above. Climbing up, I began restarting the engines. Fortunately, they all came on line and we landed without incident. Another chewing out by the base commander, but the co-pilot and engineer will remember that ride ... and, so did I.

Some flying excitement occurred even when I was not flying. This time it took place while I was in the control tower described in the preceding paragraph. We were assigned some complete tour (25 mission) B-24 pilots to help deliver P-47s. I had given one of these pilots, a tall slow speaking Southern boy, a cockpit check, briefed him on the fighter plane, and went up in the tower with a couple of guys to watch his first takeoff and landing. He fired up and taxied from the dispersal area to the end of the inactive runway. A B-24 was idling its engines at the intersection of the active runway, waiting for traffic to clear. We gave him the flashing green light signal clearance to taxi down the inactive runway. The P-47, with its conventional tail wheel, is blind taxiing straight ahead. We soon realized he was not zig-zagging for visibility and he was picking up speed – he was taking off – with this B-24 parked on the runway ahead of him. When he finally raised his tail and saw the big bomber dead ahead, he had no choice but to attempt a takeoff, ready or not. The P-47 staggered off the runway, its wheels bounced off the horizontal stabilizer of the B-24, its propeller cut gashes in the top of the fuselage, the wheels then hit the top of the B-24 wings, and it lifted into the air, mushing toward the control tower. We jumped from the tower railing to the next level and onto the ground running. The P-47 roared above, eventually gaining speed and altitude. The pilot circled twice and came in smooth, with only a broken brake hose to show for damage. He was cool as a cucumber, no doubt the result of his Ploesti Oil Field raid experiences. The B-24 was totaled out, and the crew still shaking two days later. So was I.

To check out in a new type of fighter or bomber aircraft usually meant a briefing, a cockpit check, a familiarization ride, and practicing some takeoffs and landings. We did not always have that opportunity. A case in point. The first A-26 landed in Langford Lodge, Ireland, in 1944. This was a medium twin engine bomber between the A-20 and the B-26. Heavier, faster, and greater bomb load than the A-20, but lighter, more maneuverable, and versatile than the B-26, and a lot safer. Fay Brandis was sent over from Warton, England, to pick up the A-26 and deliver it south. However, his CO said he had to be checked out first. I was in Ireland at the time and he asked me to check him out. Neither of us had ever flown or even seen an A-26. Our check out consisted of climbing in the airplane with the flight manual, and page by page we started the engines, taxied to the runway, and took off ... I was reading and Fay was flying, all the way to England. He dropped me at Warton, I found another plane, and flew back to Ireland. Fay delivered the A-26 to southern England. We were now both checked out in the A-26.

I had an opportunity to bring a war weary B-17 back to the States in 1944. These were beat up, old bombers being sent back to Tinker Air Depot, Oklahoma, for complete rebuilding. The route back was England to Marrakech, Morocco, to Dakar, Africa, to Natal, South America, to Belem, on the Amazon River, to Georgetown, Guyana, to Arecibo, Puerto Rico, to Homestead, Florida, to Tinker Field. My co-pilot was a tall, easy going Texas boy. We also brought a navigator, engineer, and radio operator. We took off from England at night over the ocean, by-passing France to avoid German night fighters, and landed at Marrakech at dawn. We rested briefly, and continued south over the African desert to Dakar. Our navigator pointed out the airstrip, and I landed avoiding cows and natives along and on the runway. No Americans around, no gas trucks, no airplanes, no trucks, just natives. We had landed on an abandoned airstrip. We took off and found the correct airport nearby. The crew hailed a truck, and we all went for a swim in the ocean, with the natives. A big skinny dip. The next day was east over the Atlantic towards Natal. Right in the middle of the ocean, the oil pressure on our Number 3 engine began dropping, so we shut it down. No big deal, except we knew if we landed at Natal with an engine feathered, they would hold us on the ground until it was repaired, and that could take days. We were only given ten days to deliver the B-17, visit our homes, and get back to England on a C-54 transport. Time was precious. As we approached Natal, we started Number 3 engine, just letting it idle while we landed and taxied to parking. The engineer loaded it with oil, and the following morning, we fired up heading north to the States. Number 3 still idled for takeoff, but once clear of the airport, we shut it down, saving it for landing in Belem. This bothered the ten U.S. sailors I had picked up in Natal for a lift home. It bothered them more when we headed low over the Amazon jungles of Brazil straight towards Belem. We were supposed to be following the coast in case of trouble, but that took too long. Thus, we leap frogged all the way home, landing at Tinker Field with Number 3 feathered, reporting we had just lost it on the last leg of the trip. Three hours later, my crew was refreshed and heading in different directions for a brief, but wonderful, break in the war.

Any extended flight away from the daily routine was relished. One such flight was a B-24 to be delivered to southern Italy. All this with four or five days off in Rome on the return. I had a little Italian guy from the Bronx, New York City, as my co-pilot (later to be killed in a B-24 crash). Our second stop was Naples, and after securing our B-24, we roamed the streets searching for a good Italian meal. The co-pilot spoke the language, but with the war recently going through town, and late in the evening, we were unable to find any eating places open. Finally, he, chatting with a young Italian, said the boy's mother would cook us a meal if we would

*A B-24 of the 459th BG, 15th Air Force, in Italy.*

pay. A deal was made, and up an alley we went, a couple flights of stairs, and were in a sparsely furnished room, drinking Vermouth, awaiting our spaghetti. It came and was delicious. Our only mistake was departing via the kitchen, where we almost lost the whole meal. A hole in the floor served as garbage disposal, sink, toilet, whatever. Dirty laundry covered the kitchen counter, and the odor overwhelmed us. The Vermouth must have saved us from the germs. Later, however, on our R & R (rest and relaxation) in Rome, we had many good meals with wine and salads (something we had not had in years), and breads and desserts. I spent two hours in a barber's chair getting the works – shampoo, facial, haircut, shave, manicure. We hated to leave for England, but the war continued.

Not all flights were of a military nature. I flew a couple of midnight requisition flights. One was a C-47 from Paris to Scotland. Some of our older guys had become involved with the black market and talked me into this particular pick-up in Glasgow, Scotland, late one evening. Only later, after I had been guided to a remote parking area and saw my cargo being loaded, did I realize we were carrying almost three tons of Harris Tweed. Landing in Paris, well after midnight, we were met by trucks at the far end of the runway, unloaded, and I taxied to the ramp. I was given a bolt of this prize woolen cloth as "thanks" for my help. I gave it to a French couple who worked in our mess hall. She was especially appreciative, and soon modeled a suit and coat she had tailored from the tweed. Some other guys were dealing in gold bullion. I never got involved.

A slightly illegal, but "just cause," flight was a furniture requisition from our old English base at Grove. Upon moving to Paris, we opened an enlisted men's club, but needed furnishings. We remembered the nice stuff at the RAF base where we had been temporarily quartered. A raid was planned, coordinated with some air force trucks in England, and another unlighted, midnight flight was made. I again parked my C-47 in a remote area, and we were soon stripping the RAF club of 5,000 pounds of chairs, tables, sofas, lamps, radios, and several cases of British ale. Much of this had to be quietly snuck below the lighted windows of the M.P.s. Our NCO club was pleased with the furnishings, and I do not believe the English ever did find out how their club disappeared.

As the Germans were driven back, we had some leisure time and would occasionally deviate from our assigned flights. Once, with loading ramps aboard my empty C-47, I flew south landing at a little airstrip near the Swiss border. A unit of U.S. Engineers were stationed on the field. I offered to take them up for rides if they could find some goodies to take back to my boys in Paris. It took several flights to give them all a ride, and they got a great kick out of it. My co-pilot and I were invited for supper while the engineers put some things in the airplane. After a good meal, we returned to our C-47 to find loaded aboard a BMW convertible roadster, four motorcycles, heaps of German uniforms, guns, binoculars, and swords. What a haul! I could not thank them enough. The guys at home went crazy when I unloaded. I saved a couple pistols and a sword for myself.

Take the combination of bad weather, a heaterless airplane, and a cold winter day, and you have got troubles. Such was a flight from Burtonwood to Paris in a B-24 with only an engineer as my co-pilot. A 300 foot ceiling on takeoff with 12,000 foot tops was a warning of things to come. Higher meant colder, and breaking out on top, we realized the cabin heaters were not working and we were becoming cold. Not being dressed for subfreezing temps, our hands and feet soon became numb. I gave my engineer/co-pilot some quick lessons in flying, and he soon was able to at least maintain straight and level at altitude. We took turns flying and warming our hands under our arms or fanny. En route, our radio compass failed, so it was dead reckoning to Paris. Weather there was 400 feet ceiling and a couple of miles visibility, however, I could not let down with the Eiffel Tower, radio towers, and tall buildings nearby. We continued south hunting for breaks in the cloud layers. We dropped a couple thousand feet both to seek ground and get warmer. Never did get warm, but did find a break and snuck under the clouds heading for Paris. The B-24 had picked up a load of ice, so we were a bit sluggish. Finally, still frozen, we worked our way to Paris, where the runway was also frozen, solid ice. Coming in as slow as possible, I put the big bomber on the numbers and began braking. No response, so using only the inboard engines, I skidded the B-24 around until we were sliding down the runway backwards, then applying power we came to a stop before sliding off the end or sides. This was a long time before reversible propellers, so I reversed the airplane. I never wanted to try that again.

*Me 108, with an Me 110 in the background.*

A light airplane flight was in a Messerschmitt 108. We had found the little airplane in a French hangar. It was a 4 place, low wing, German executive plane. All the instruments and controls were labeled in German, but we found one of our mechanics to get it running. Once running, we climbed in and pushing/pulling levers and controls, we managed the little plane into the air. By pulling a lever or flipping a switch, then seeing what happened, we could label everything in English. This was a neat and fun little airplane, and we were figuring how to dismantle, crate, and ship it home when a colonel took it from us.

**Bill White served as a radio operator with several different squadrons in the 27th ATG. Bill related a few of his memories:**

While serving in the 27th ATG, I was assigned to the following squadrons: 310, HQ, 86 and 314.

As a flight radio operator, I participated in over 800 flights with many fine pilots. My first pilot was Flight Officer Robert P. Walker. I flew as a crew member with Bob (or "Pat" as he was known by many) ferrying various types of aircraft, including, B-17, B-24, B-26, A-28, C-74 and C-47. On occasion, due to pilot shortages I would assist the pilot as acting co-pilot. I also flew with Loris "Lo" Dorris and other pilots on taxi flights in B-17s named "Slap Happy" and "Paddle Foot."

During the period of June 13 through July 7, 1944, I was fortunate enough to have been a crew member ferrying war-weary B-17s back to the States from England. The flight plan was via Morocco, Africa, Central/South America, and the Caribbean. Upon my departure from New York, back to the ETO, I was issued an Elgin A-1 "hack" watch. I am pleased to say we are both still ticking.

*Left: Radio operator Bill White. The sign behind him reads, "E/M Ready Room, 310th Personnel Only." Center: Radio personnel at Le Bourget, 1944. Bill White is in the center. Right: Bill White working in the cargo door of a C-47.*

My most unusual mission was to Stockholm, Sweden, on U.S. Navy orders, wearing civilian clothing. As I remember, the crew spent the night at the Grand Hotel along with crew members from AXIS nations. I was also part of the taxi crew flying to Russia to pick up C-47 delivery crews.

One of my most memorable missions was the Christmas Eve flight to southern France to pick up support equipment and fuel for General Patton's counter-offensive in Belgium. We had to RON at Liege that night with "Buzz Bombs" going over and the battlefront nearby. Other memorable missions were air evacuation flights to German POW camps to pick up near-dead American military personnel.

In retrospect, the times spent with the 27th ATG are what memories are made of. My pilots and peers were all high quality people, and it was an honor to have served with them.

*B-17 taxi "Slap-Happy."*

**Bert Astrove, "The Scarsdale Comet":**

My family is from Scarsdale, NY. They were instrumental in raising funds to build several "Jugs" (P-47s) during the war. To my surprise, I was asked to deliver this P-47 out of Renfrew, Scotland, through Prestwick. At Prestwick, I asked the PR Officer to take some pictures so I could send them home. He did, I did, and it was printed in the local paper. Scarsdale Village published a book, *Scarsdale at War*, and this story was in it.

*Tow photos at right: Bert Astrove with the new P-47D "Scarsdale Comet."*

*Right: J.J. Canning by the 310th "Ferry Pilots Only" entrance.*

*Below: Wedding party of J.J., and Dorothy Canning. Left to right: Hilda Drake, Dorothy (Drake) Canning, John J. (J.J.) Canning, Barbara Drake, Vi Hall, Calvin A. Curtis. Hilda and Barbara are Dorothy's younger sisters. Vi Hall (Matron of Honor) was a married friend of Dorothy's. Photo was taken outside of St. Peter's Church, in Ashton-u-Lyne, Lancashire, England.*

**John J. Canning, pilot, 310th and 311th Ferrying Squadrons recalls a new P-51 delivery which ultimately changed his life:**

I checked out in P-51s on May 11, 1944. I already had more than 75 hours in P-47s by then. On 14 June, 1944, I had a chance to deliver a new P-51 to a unit at Steeple Morden (355th Fighter Group), Cambridgeshire. I had about eight hours in P-51s by then. When I got to Steeple Morden, I was informed that due to wind change, I would have to land on their short runway, which was considerably shorter than the one they had been using. This didn't bother me because I had landed P-47s on some very short runways. This is when I found out there is quite a difference in the flight characteristics of these two aircraft. Since it was a short runway, I brought it in on the approach nose high and with power on. When I crossed the end of the runway, I chopped the power off and expected to drop it on the runway in a perfect three point landing. It was precisely at this point I found out it didn't fly like a P-47! Instead of dropping straight down on the runway, the left wing dropped suddenly. I tried to correct this by kicking full right rudder while shoving on full power at the same time. I needed the power to pick up the left wing, but the torque caused by the burst of power caused the left wing tip to hit the ground. I knew I had a problem when, out of the corner of my eye, I saw about six feet of the left wing go sailing over my head and the stick was completely loose, as if it wasn't connected to anything. While this beautiful, brand new P-51 was cart wheeling down the runway, I remembered there were certain things I should be doing like shutting off my fuel supply and electrical systems. I was lucky because it landed right side up and didn't catch on fire.

When I returned to my base at Warton, I was grounded and told that I would need to pass a flight physical to get back on flying status. Our flight surgeon at the time checked my flight records and told me to go to town for a week and get drunk, then come back and take my physical. Due to the D-Day build up, I had flown a lot of hours in a relatively short time. Joyfully, I set off for Manchester, the nearest big city. After about three days of drinking and throwing up, I decided I better sober up, or I would never last a week! So that afternoon I went to a tea dance at the Ritz ballroom that changed my life forever.

It was that afternoon that I met a pretty little English girl. By the time the dance was over, I knew her name was Dorothy Drake, she lived in a suburb of Manchester called Dukinfield, worked in a munitions factory, and had lost a brother in the war. We enjoyed each other to the extent that thirteen months later, on July 14th, 1945, we were married.

By that time I had been transferred to Burtonwood. Three of my flying buddies were at the wedding. Calvin A Curtis was my best man, and Herman Estrada and Vincent Alexander were the other two.

At the time of this writing, J.J. and Dorothy have been married for 52 years. They have two sons and five grandchildren. (J.J. passed away in 1998. We will miss him and will always be grateful for his contribution to the 27th ATG Veteran's Organization. Happy Landings J.J.)

**Fay Brandis served as a pilot and executive officer of the 310th Ferrying Squadron:**

I do have a simple "diary" that I attempted to keep. I left NYC on November 24, 1942, on the *Queen Elizabeth* (1) and arrived in Greenock, Scotland, on November 30th, 1942. Then to Stone, England ... a "Replacement Center" ... December 11, 1942, I was sent to Burtonwood ... First flight was in a Bell Airacobra P-39 (P-400). We were called the Eighth Air Force Service Command ... on "detached service" with the Ferry Command. We had eleven pilots stay in this outfit. We then moved to Warton, January 19, 1943. Guess I flew the first of the "Taxi" airplanes which was a DeHaviland 89 "Dominie," a biplane. (Fay also flew many hours in the B-26 "taxi ship," "Demon Deacon"). Checked out in a P-47 Thunderbolt on Jan 24 1943. On January 30th, I was told that I would be going to Speke Airport (Liverpool) for a temporary base with six other pilots. Moved to Speke on February 8, 1943. I lived with a private family and I am still close friends with their son, Derek Lunt! Stayed with the Lunts until March 10th, but spent many days with them when I had the time. Then, back to BAD II (Warton) and was based there until I left for the States on June 29, 1945. Flew a B-24 home and arrived at Bradley Field, CT, on July 4, 1945.

**Joe Clemow, 310th Ferrying Squadron, "Our Trip from England to Poltava, Ukraine":**

A round trip from England to Poltava, Ukraine, took heavy bombers and long range fighters two or three days. However, it was eighteen days, from September 16 to October 3, 1944, and with more than 82 hours of flying time, for a 27th Air Transport Group crew to deliver a new C-47A #348258 equipped with long range-tanks in the cabin. The crew returned with a weary C-47A #223936, which had been heavily used by the Russian Air Force.

Cecil Pierce of Modesto, California, the command pilot; Joe Clemow of Billings, Montana, co-pilot; Joe Gilinsky, navigator; Howard Schimpf, radio operator; and Joe Ververka, flight engineer, were the crew, who left Warton for Grove and for St. Mawgan, September 17, 1944.

The next day our flight was out over the Atlantic Ocean, a safe distance from the German fighter planes based in France. Then, straight south,

*Left: Captain Fay Brandis. Center: Brandis and Stenglein by the board A/C Movement, Warton. Right: Brandis in a Link Trainer, Warton, 1944.*

*Delivery of a P-51D to Lt. Bill Quinn by Captain Fay Brandis at Little Walden Air Field, Essex, home of the 361st Fighter Group. Quinn and Brandis were high school class officers (Class of 1938), at Clinton, NY.*

*B-26 "Demon Deacon" flown by Fay Brandis.*

*"Demon Deacon" crew chief S/Sgt. Ray Dlouhy*

*Right: Sgt. Ray Dlouhy and Bob Schenebeck. Far right: Fay Brandis and Ray Dlouhy.*

until we could make a diagonal, safe course, to Gibraltar. A day of one of the longer flight times was 7+50 and, of course, we logged the airplane and pilot time as takeoff to touchdown – not block to block, as did the airline pilots, and later, as did the CAA by definition. Landing at Gibraltar appeared to be easy, as the runway looked VERY LONG. The British controlled THE ROCK and the flat ground from THE ROCK to the mainland of Spain. All of the flat ground was used as a cemetery until they needed an airport, so they moved enough graves to make a very narrow paved strip across the isthmus. Our wing tips were over graves as we landed, and there was a small turn-around space at the west end of the strip, with parking at the opposite end. With Ververka and Schimpf to take care of and service the plane, the rest of us went to the quarters in THE ROCK with the monkey pets. Can't recall, but I imagine we had prewar Scotch.

The next day was an easy one with all CAVU (ceiling and visibility unlimited) weather. We flew low to look at scenery and noticed huge, long-legged men riding donkeys. Flying lower we decided they were normal men on small burros. We landed at Castel Benito Airport in Tripoli. U.S. Air Transport Command (ATC) took care of us then, and on the rest of the trip to Teheran. They furnished us weather, route charts, airport maps, radio communication, and transport to and from their better hotels. The hotel in downtown Tripoli was average and satisfactory.

The next day was also easy CAVU with tail winds. We landed at Payne Field, Cairo, and laid over a day there to have ATC maintenance check the plane. We stayed at The National Hotel downtown, which was one of the nicest at that time and may still be one of the better ones as of 1995. We went to the nearby Pyramids and the Sphinx, where we rented a very short ride on uncomfortable camels. The natives had a tourist business kept alive by GIs, WAVES, and WACS.

September 22, we were briefed by ATC for the route and weather to Teheran. En route, Schimpf, our radio operator, got a message that Teheran Airport was closed because of a severe sandstorm which reduced the visibility below safe limits. We got out the ATC Manual of Airports and decided to land at Kermanshah, Persia, because it was supposed to have weather service, fuel, and accommodations. Upon landing at the dirt field, which had no hangar, we noticed a Persian Air Force plane parked there. It was about a 1929 biplane. Soon after we landed, some Persians arrived in an American built army truck and could speak no English. We got in the truck and they took us to the town – such as it was. The streets were dirt with sewage in the ditches alongside, and the hotel was horrible. After much attempting to talk to the locals we got out the ATC manual, which showed a British outpost in Kermanshah, so we had the truck driver take us to the outpost. It was not a large building, but had stone walls several feet thick with gun ports in the walls. The men spoke English, had decent food, but no extra beds, so we slept on the floor and were glad we weren't in the hotel.

The next morning, the British took us to the airport and Schimpf got the weather report for Teheran and an ATC clearance with his long-range radio. That was our easiest flight day with only 1+40 in the air. I can't recall the Teheran hotel or airport, as they were satisfactory but not outstanding.

To fly into Russia we took on board a Russian navigator, who sat in the co-pilot's seat, with no maps and merely pointed left, right, up or down the whole trip as he did not speak English. We also had a Russian radio operator who continuously tapped the telegraph key sending messages to someone. He also could not speak English, but kept himself busy the whole trip. The flight from Teheran to Poltava was over the high Caucasian Mountains and then across the part of Russia invaded by Germany. The Germans did not leave a fence post, a tree, or a building standing. The countryside

*Joe Clemow and Coleman at A-40, December, 1944.*

was devastated! After a 7+25 flight to Poltava, we flew food supplies to Mirgirad and Piryatin, other U.S. Air Corps areas nearby, with another hour and a half flying time.

The next day the extra fuel tanks from the cabin of the new C-47A were transferred to a C-47A, #223936, the Russians had been flying for a year or so. We were to take it back to Warton, Lancashire, for repair (or scrap). We had Ververka look it over very carefully and made a 50 minute test flight about the area on the 26th.

On the 27th, we took off for Teheran with a different Russian navigator and a different radio operator. After flying for three or four hours we computed the ETA (estimated time of arrival) for Teheran. The fuel flow was so great, we did not have enough, even with the extra fuel in the cabin. We got the message to the Russian navigator by indicating on the clock, "Teheran," and then, "benzene fini," for the time we would be out of fuel. He got the idea and indicated left turn. After some time, he had us circle what looked like any normal agriculture field. We weren't too eager to land there, but he insisted. The field had an underground barracks, with mess hall, aircraft maintenance shops, and fuel supply. We got fuel and a chicken dinner! Then an American built truck ride to the city of Makhachkala on the Caspian Sea where we went to a Russian movie in a small church. No one spoke English all the time we were on the ground. That was a 6+00 hour day of flight, plus the truck rides and movies.

The next was an easy 3+25 to Teheran where the ATC gang helped us purchase ten cases of Vodka in the thinnest glass bottles I've seen, but packed in adequate cases which got it all back to Warton. No weather or other problems to Cairo and Tripoli.

Since our departure from England, Southern France had been taken from the Germans, so we stopped at Tunis for fuel and flew on across the Mediterranean to Marseille, France. There we stayed in the Hotel de la Porte. My room had very little outside wall left, due to artillery shelling soon before, but the bed was wonderful.

The next day we went to Orly Airport (A-47) in Paris because the English weather wouldn't let us continue north. The next day was October 3, 1944, and we got back to Warton, where the vodka sold for a nice profit. Sabinske, Kutcher, and Dulick had lots of poker profits, so they could afford it, and we had an extraordinary experience!

**Joe Clemow also has vivid memories of flying for the generals of USSTAF – February to July 1945:**

In September, 1943, I arrived in England by convoy ship. After a few days at Stone with *Introduction to British Food and Customs*, I was assigned to the 310th Ferrying Squadron at Base Air Depot #2, Warton, Lancashire, flying mostly B-17s as well as B-24s, two engine bombers, fighters, and even Piper L-4s.

February 1945, I was ordered to report to Headquarters, United States Strategic Air Forces in Europe (USSTAF), St. Germain, France, where I was interviewed by Gen E. P. Curtis, Chief of Staff. I told him I did not want to take orders from a staff. He said "You will be flying General Spaatz's Twin Beechcraft C-45 and will take orders from me only." So I went to work then and there, and seven days later stopped in Warton to get my clothes. All war-long we traveled with maps, a change of underwear, shirt, and an eiderdown sleeping bag. (The sleeping bag and maps I still have).

I succeeded Bryce Smith, who married a Headquarters secretary. I got the job because I had flown 900 hours in Twin Beechcraft AT-11s training Bombardiers at Victorville, California, from September 1942 to July 1943. I kept the job by getting up for breakfast and never being late for work.

Tech Sergeant Harold Susen of San Angelo, TX, was transferred from the instrument shop at Villacoublay (A-42) and Toussus le Noble (A-46) to

*Pilot Joe Clemow with crew chief Harold Susen.*

*Joe Clemow and Harold Susen in the cockpit of General Spaatz's C-45. Note the water bottles added to each side of the doorway.*

*Sgt. Harold Susen at right wearing sun glasses.*

Loges Field, St. Germain, where the plane was based. He was mechanic-co-pilot, and not only maintained and cleaned the plane, but flew every trip. I soon checked him out to be able to land the plane in case of pilot incapacitation. I lived in a private home and ate in the Officer's Mess, which was also in a large old home. Harold lived in a nearby barracks and ate at the mess hall. Without his excellent work, my task would have been very difficult. Our passengers, mostly generals with World War I piloting experience, excepting some, like Doolittle, were much too old to be of help except for decisions.

17 March, we flew from Namur, Belgium (Y-47), to an airport in France (A-29) with Generals Spaatz, Vandenberg of the 9th Air Force, and Doolittle of the 8th. On that trip, Colonel Kimmel, Spaatz's B-17 chief pilot, acted as my co-pilot and we found the destination in foggy weather. Susen had to sit in a passenger seat, and the Generals swore him to secrecy, as they planned one of the big air raids of the war. Later that day we went to Orly, Paris (A-47), Reims (A-62), Loges, Bovingdon, England, and back to Loges. Only 3 hours and 30 minutes in the air of which 45 minutes was instrument time, during which we held altitude and heading for computed times to start a let down. Fortunately, we survived that type of flying.

21 March, we flew Colonel Hub Zemke from Reims to headquarters in St. Germain for interrogation. 22 March was our longest day of flight, with seven hours and a half from Loges to Cannes to Loges with Wesley Ruggles, Colonel Unger, and Miss Hood. Then we went to Boxted, England, with Colonel Zemke.

5 April, we left Loges early to pick up General Spaatz in Reims. There we fueled the plane and received a briefing for an airport in Germany. I was using a slit trench near our parked plane when General Spaatz's Mercedes Benz arrived. Hurriedly, I buttoned up and was surprised to see General Eisenhower with Spaatz. After they entered the plane I used the plane's wash bowl and got into the cockpit. After arriving over the briefed destination, we could see bomb craters and the Germans left it with many posts set in the runway. General Spaatz also saw the runway and came to the cockpit to say, "You can't land there Lieutenant." To which I said, "Day before yesterday we landed at an airport near Frankfurt, not far from here." Spaatz replied "Put us on the ground there and we can radio to determine where to go."

Soon after landing, a large German-made car arrived with an Infantry General, who said to me "Lieutenant, take your plane to the airport you were briefed to use." General Eisenhower said "General, the airport he was briefed for was unfit for a landing. You must show him the correct airport on his map." The car left, and we flew to a grass hospital strip at Darmstadt. Generals Marshall and Arnold had arrived there sometime before. They used Eisenhower's C-47 and Spaatz's B-25 planes for the last leg of their trip from the Pentagon to Europe. The grass strip was lined with small tents occupied by injured soldiers.

Before the scheduled afternoon departure, I was on board resting without my jacket when the generals arrived. With my right arm in the jacket, I gave them a left-handed salute as they got aboard. The occupants of the tents knew the Generals were there. On our takeoff, soldiers who could get out of their hospital beds stood alongside the runway strip and saluted as we roared past.

On the flight back to Reims, we called Luxembourg for weather along the route and they and Reims were below limits. Near our estimated time of arrival at Reims, we saw a railroad-highway-river intersection which is near the airport. We descended in one hole, saw the end of the runway, and received a clearance to land straight-in. We deplaned the generals, who had done more than their share of worrying. We refueled and took off for Loges Field, where the weather was such that we had no difficulty landing.

*Dorothy Davis and Patty Spaatz at Cannes. Sgt. Susen can be seen at the nose of the aircraft.*

17 April, we flew five American Red Cross women from Loges to their bases in Halle, Epperstadt, Eurfurt, Weimar, and Kolleda, where they operated doughnut dispensaries. At one of those airports we picked up RAF Wing Commander Douglas Bader. He had just been released from a German prison camp. The Generals at St. Germain were pleased that they could learn of his story. Before the war, he had lost both legs in an accident, but with two artificial limbs he had gone back to flying a Spitfire and been shot down. (Prior to being shot down, Bader scored 20 victories, 4 shared destroyed, and 11 damaged.)

During April, we flew twenty-five days, leaving very little time for Sgt. Susen to do any daily maintenance on the plane. Meals were often missed, but when at Loges, the mess hall would feed us at any hour – early or late. It was a busy time, but we enjoyed the hours and the flying.

**J.J. Canning, of the 310th, also had some contact with a few generals:**

Got to thinking about all the places one could eat while away from your home base. Food had always had a high priority with me, and my hut mates were always informed by me where I had eaten and how I rated them as to quality, quantity, etc. Once, when I returned to Burtonwood after a few days away, I was asked if I had eaten at the Cumberland Hotel in London. I wasn't even aware of an eating place there. About 10 days later I was in London and near the Cumberland Hotel, so at about noon I went to the Cumberland and inquired about a military mess. I was directed to the third floor and told that it would be directly in front of the elevator as I got off. I noticed as I entered the elevator that there were five other men in it and that they were all generals. When I got off at the third floor the

*310th pilot John J. Canning.*

Generals got off, also. Sure enough, they were going to lunch as well. The dining room wasn't too large, but it was very tastefully decorated. A uniformed little waitress seated my fellow elevator passengers, then she asked me who I was with. I told her I was by myself and just wanted to eat lunch. She said she had never seen a "Leftenant" there before, but said she had a seat for me with another officer who was by himself. The "other officer" was a lieutenant colonel and aide de camp to a general from Anzio. He was very sociable, and the food was very good. It turned out to be an Allied General officer's mess. There must have been forty or more officers there from several countries. When I got back to Burtonwood and told them where I had eaten, I don't think any of them believed me anyway.

**John McDowell also was a pilot in the 310th FS John shared a few vivid memories:**

"To me, it was remarkable that we never lost a "taxi" ship full of people. These taxi flights, I remember ...

About 30 of us had delivered B-26s to a new base. The war weary B-17 taxi went out of service, so a new B-24 was diverted to pick us up. I was the last to get aboard. Novak, the pilot, started to taxi, with me running on the ground and yelling in the bomb bay. I forced my body and legs through, but could not stand up, so I got to the little passageway next to the bobbing nose wheel and into the nose. After a wild turn onto the runway, we started the takeoff run. Shortly after rotation, the landing gear started up and #4 prop hit the ground, breaking the propeller gear case, which caused a heavy stream of oil. It did feather, and the quick landing was uneventful! From my vantage position I know what happened. I wonder if the crowd in the dark of the B-24 was aware of how close they came to death that day. There was no concern shown.

Another day, I was on a B-17, with a load going to Prestwick from Burtonwood to pick up B-24s. I was standing behind the co-pilot seat. We went into clouds, and I knew that we were below the level of the Scottish mountains. I pointed out the situation and suggested we turn around. This seemed to befuddle the pilot. He started a left descending turn, but went into an uncontrolled dive. I reached over the co-pilot's shoulder and pulled back on the control as the speed was over 200! 1st Lt. West reached over the pilot's shoulder to level the wing. We were then in the clear and proceeded around the mountains.

On one flight of a B-17, returning to Burtonwood from East Anglia, I was in the waist near a window dozing, when a different sound brought me to attention. I looked out the waist window and could see trees zipping by the wing tip. I then read the railroad station sign, "Tarporley," which was right on our usual course between the mountain and the barrage balloons over the railroad center at Crewel. About 30 seconds later we passed the area of very low dense clouds. I told Alvin New, the pilot, what I thought about that and he said, "I could see light ahead all the way."

B-17 #0631 was my favorite "taxi" machine. After VE day we were moving a large number of new B-17s out of England to Holzkirken, near Munich, Germany. I picked up about 40 crew members to return to Burtonwood. We were at 5,000 ft. in heavy clouds when I noticed turbulence building up. This plane was stripped of war equipment, so it cruised faster than normal. I reached for the throttles to reduce power and we were hit by lightening. The strike was over my head and through the radio station located under my seat. My reaction was to pull the throttles all off. The whole plane filled with smoke and there was dead silence. Then we broke out of the line front. We were over Karlsruhe. The radio operator had the trailing antenna out so the big lead weight and wire hit Germany. Who says the 310th didn't bomb the NAZI! That was the last flight of #0631. I have since met the pilot that flew it on its first flight. It was an F model and was the test bed for the G before being configured for passengers, and hence to the 310th as a taxi.

The C-87 was the passenger version of the B-24. We flew one which had been returned by the British, possibly the one that Churchill returned to England in after his famous meeting with Roosevelt. It was in poor condition. I had hydraulic failure and had to use the emergency mechanical gear let down system. Also, it continually overheated and burned out alternators. I decided it was too dangerous for me, although it was fun to

*John McDowell sitting on the fuselage of an early A-26 in England, 6 June 1945.*

*Part of a taxi load, Burtonwood. McDowell is at far left.*

*A view of Burtonwood.*

fly and comfortable for passengers. I was told years later by Ralph Jenks and Buzzy Barrett that they rode it down on fire one day, and after a few days, found the electrical short behind the oxygen tanks in the nose compartment. How close can you get?

One day my orders read: Take taxi to Langford Lodge Air Depot in Northern Ireland. Fly a B-24 to Manduria, Italy, and return by any available means.

The B-24 only had half levels of fuel in its tanks, but had 600 gallons in bomb bay ferrying tanks. It also didn't have wing deicers. On the flight, we had to climb higher to stay above the clouds. Just west of the Alps, only the tip of the Matterhorn was visible.

It was time to pump fuel from the bomb bay tank to the main four tanks. One was about empty. I sent my new engineer back to open the valve so I could turn on the transfer pump switch. Even though we had gone over this procedure before takeoff, he came back and said he was confused and was afraid because he may get air in the cross feed. In retrospect, I now realize he was suffering from hypoxia from the 2 hours over 12,000 feet. I was upset about the low fuel level in #1 tank, so I said, "You fly it." I went to the bomb bay valve and felt the nose go up and the wind noise go down, so I scrambled on all fours, back to the controls, and instructed him on how to read the artificial horizon. Back to the valve. It was tightly shut and safety wired. I couldn't get the wire off with my fingers, so I pulled out my knife and cut it. In haste, I also jabbed it into my knee! I still have a small scar.

At Manduria, we were diverted to another field farther down on the boot heel of Italy. We hitched a jeep ride into Bari where there was a much better chance of transportation and unlimited ice cream. I saw the sights of the ancient seaport. In the boat yard they were sawing a big log into boards. A big guy was in a trench underneath, and a little guy was pulling the saw back up.

After four days we were called and told that they were holding a British C-47 in takeoff position for us. The door slammed shut, and we started to roll. I noticed that the control locks were on, and I ran to the cockpit yelling the news! The pilot seemed to be more irate about waiting 20 minutes than the inconvenience of taxiing back for another T.O. attempt.

The new airplanes out of BAD 1 & 2 were almost flawless. I only had two unfortunate incidents. Both were in B-24s, and both happened on takeoff on the short NW runway, close to the hangars at Warton.

The first was an older model, with complicated, every way adjustable, green plush seats. On takeoff, shortly after rotation, the seat latch broke, allowing the seat to slide back a couple of feet. I didn't let go for a moment, and the nose pulled up too high. Luckily, my favorite flight engineer, E.C. Johnson, was in the right seat. I yelled, "Push the nose down, more – more." He did, and I unbuckled my seat belt, stood up, and enjoyed the climb out.

The other incident was at the same location. I heard a loud bang and whistling of wind on the right side. There was a 2 inch hole in the navigator's window. On landing, we found that a plastic door had come off the nose

*The old C-87 in a hangar at Burtonwood.*

*Burtonwood, McDowell's home for three years. Frosty days and freezing fog.*

turret and #3 prop hit it about 6 in. from the tip, leaving the thread imprint of the attachment bolt. That was the best seat for a passenger, because of the bubble window. We were lucky there was no passenger that day.

**John McDowell also recalled a new pilot arriving at the 310th, who wanted to fly P-47s. This anecdote provides a good illustration of the risks involved in flying high performance combat aircraft with little time for familiarization. This type of flying was required of ferry pilots on a daily basis:**

Oskar Heintz arrived at the 310th and mentioned that he was from Bickelton, WA. He had just finished his tour of 50 missions in B-24s, but was not ready to go back to the States. I asked him what he would like to do with us, and he expressed a strong desire to fly P-47s.

I gave him the manuals to read, and the next day asked him if he remembered what it was like to fly the AT-6. After a cockpit check to be sure he knew about the P-47, I saw him taxi out. I was then called to go to Speke Airport about 30 miles away. On return, I saw Oskar's plane upside down, short of the runway with the wheels pushed up into the wing.

I went out to the crash sight and could see where the rescue people had dug a hole under the smashed canopy, dirt filled the cockpit. I also saw his gasoline soaked A-2 jacket and took his personal notebook out. Then he was taken to the hospital.

When Oskar "came to," I asked him what happened. He said on the second final approach, the tower gave him a red light. He started to go around, then was given a green light, so he chopped the throttle and it fell like a pancake. He didn't remember anything until he woke up in the hospital. He thanked me for retrieving his address and notebook, and I said, "I'll see you in the morning." Next morning, I found he had been sent to another hospital.

My conscience has bothered me, because I didn't make him wait for some time in an AT-6.

Epilogue

After the war I tried to find him but had no luck, so I figured he didn't make it. In November of '96, I was in a multiple ham radio "ragchew," and one guy was in Bickelton. I asked him if he knew Oskar. Negative, but would ask old timers and report next day. He found R. Furguson, Oskar's buddy from CPT days. 80 year old Furguson knew about the incident and said that Oskar had many facial operations and a plate in his skull from the accident. He was well liked and worked for the land conservation department until his death in an auto accident returning from a retirement party on a foggy night in 1965.

I only knew Oskar for 3 days. Would have been nice to meet him again.

**Sometimes young pilots did not always use the best judgment, but then again, they didn't always get caught! John McDowell remembered one of those times:**

This was during the time when we were flying supplies over the German lines to Patton's army. I was given a C-47, along with my friend John Crawford, co-pilot, flight engineer, Johnson, and radio operator, Chalupsky.

This cargo was a load of canisters of fresh blood in ice buckets for the medics. When we landed, nobody wanted the blood, and we were diverted to other cow pastures, before finally being unloaded of the now iceless, and probable useless, load. Crawford was upset about this effort. On our return, we heard on "Radio Luxembourg" that Paris had been declared an open city. "Playboy" John said, "This is the opportunity of the war, lets join the party and RON in Paris."

*Flight engineer E.C. Johnson in the cockpit of a B-26.*

So we landed at Le Bourget, locked the airplane, and boarded an ancient, solid rubber tired bus, that took us to town at about 20 miles an hour. It was a great, city-wide party, and as we were the first Americans they had met, we were toasted with champagne, which had been hidden for this occasion.

In an alcoholic fog, I heard a rumble and saw a German tank, at high speed, going down the street. Hitler had ordered the army to hold Paris. That sobered me up. I found the RO and engineer, but John wanted to stay. I commandeered a car for transportation back to Le Bourget and returned to London's Hendon airport.

Next morning I was loaded with mail to be delivered to various places. Then I returned to Paris to find that John had taken over a German officer's apartment as per war rules. I flew 1st week, John the next, etc. We enjoyed the experience of free Paris!

**The Eiffel Tower was always a tempting target for young pilots. John was no exception:**

You probably noticed an unusual number of photos of the Eiffel tower in the pictures I sent to you. The reason, shortly after the fall of Paris, was that there were reports of fighters flying under it. I thought that was great!

*John McDowell at Cafe Du Paix the day after the "Krauts" ran – looking for Crawford.*

I wanted to look it over, in case the opportunity happened, I would be ready. A B-17 could fit, so no problem with a P-47. However, the authorities let it be known that cables would be strung if it didn't cease. A couple of weeks later, I had a P-47 delivery to a base about 50 miles NW of Paris, so I went to look it over. To my delight, I saw many P-47s circling it. I joined the circuit, and we all went through. I followed them for about thirty miles, then made my delivery. At one of the reunions, Smoky Callahan showed me a picture of the 310th Ferrying Squadron's, Villacoublay based, P-51 going through. That was after the war, and he was the 310th CO. He didn't tell me the consequences.

**Many pilots flew under the Eiffel Tower, but Bob Lawrence is one of the few who can actually prove it with his "certificate" from General Ott (see opposite page). (Unfortunately, some "ground pounder" got his tail number when he flew through.)**

**Hal Kinkade was a captain in Administration, at AAF #582 Warton. Hal recalled some interesting experiences with some ferry pilots:**

When Warton Administration resolved into a base-wide Military Administration Division, which encompassed all site headquarters and section administration personnel, I found my first job, from 3 December 1943 to 3 April 1944, was at Site 11 as executive officer, with a Major Faust, from Chicago. Site 11 housed the many pilots and personnel of the 310th Ferrying Squadron and the 87th Transport Squadron. This was a most interesting experience, especially in view of the events of Saturday, 4 December, my second day on site, when the officers held a party.

It seems that several enthusiastic members decided that 0100, Sunday AM was the appropriate time to hold a pistol firing match inside the pilot's barracks, using a circled door knob as a target. Because several members

*Left: Lt. Bob Lawrence in the cockpit of a P-38 "Lightning."*

*The Eiffel Tower – a tempting target!*

*Waiting for someone to fly under the Eiffel Tower.*

C O N F I D E N T I A L

5TH IND

201 - Lawrence Robert R. (O)
Headquarters, Central Air Depot Area (Prov), Air Technical Service Command in Europe, AAF 389 APO 744, U S Army, 17 March 1945.

TO: 2nd Lt Robert R. Lawrence, 0778848, AC, 325th Ferrying Squadron, APO 744, U S Army.

THRU: Commanding Officer, 302nd Transport Wing, APO 744, U S Army.

1. I have carefully considered the report of your misconduct in that on or about 27 September 1944 at Paris, France, you did wrongfully and in violation of General Order 90, Headquarters, ETO, 11 September 1944, operate and airplane below 3000 feet within the air space area above the City of Paris, France. Also that on said date you did wrongfully and in violation of Section 1, Paragraph 1, Flying Bulletin No. 8, Headquarters, United States Strategic Air Forces in Europe, 3 May 1944, operate an airplane in a reckless manner so as to endanger persons and property on the ground by flying low through the underpass of the Eiffel Tower.

2. Your conduct was most reprehensible and shows that you do not have the proper appreciation of the duties and responsibilites of an Officer of the U S Army. Such conduct was contrary to all fundamental principles of military discipline and cannot be condoned or tolerated in an Officer. I therefore reprimand you most severely for your unsoldierly conduct and hope that this reprimand will impress upon you the serious nature of your offense and cause you to conduct yourself in the future in a manner in keeping with your responsibilities as an Officer.

3. In addition to the foregoing reprimand I hereby direct and order that you be assessed the fine of $75.00. You are directed to pay such fine to your appropriate Finance Officer and to obtain therefrom a duplicate receipt, one of which you will send to this Headquarters.

4. You have the right to appeal from this punishment if you deem it unjust or disproportionate to the offense, which appeal, if made, should be by indorsement hereon and include a definite statement over your signature whether or not you desire to appeal from this punishment.

5. The Commanding Officer, through whom this correspondence is returned, having possession of your Officer's Qualification Record (WD:AGO Form 66-1 or 66-2) will enter thereon the punishment hereby imposed and will include in his indorsement a statement that such entry has been made, with a statement that the forfeiture has been paid, as evidenced by the above-mentioned copy of receipt, and will thereafter return the file through channels to this Headquarters.

I. W. OTT,
Brigadier General U. S. Army,
Commanding.

*The Eiffel Tower was not the only thing young pilots were tempted to fly under. This photograph, from Gordon Fisher, was captioned, "From the control tower at Warton – they cleared out the hangar for me to fly through. I didn't."*

were sleeping in their double bunks, along the line of fire, and because the said door fronted on a public road, certain authorities objected strongly to this performance. The result was a restriction to site, until the culprits came forth and eventual courts martial and fines, for five officers, who shall remain nameless.

Among several coincidences, or what-are-the-odds events, I found a note that reads, "3 Mar 1944 – a four-hour round trip, emergency flight, in a C-64A to Heston, London, for a NAAFI pickup." NAAFI was a supply source for certain club refreshments. My note says a Lt. McDowell was the pilot, and I was the unofficial co-pilot. This probably accounts for the reason we looked at each other searchingly, in 1988, when we became fellow committee members for the Seattle reunion, as we wondered where we might have met before.

**Dudley L. Willis, Pilot with the 312th, remembers a story he calls "The Night Fighter":**

Last night, I watched a TV documentary on the role of the British Air Command during the Battle of Britain. One of the statistics shown was that seven American pilots had participated and that one of these was killed. I knew one of the survivors, who was called "Alabama," and the following is a recount of how this came about. This is, of course, tempered by 50 years of forgetfulness and some selective recall – but none that I am conscious of.

Approximately ten of us ferry pilots in the 312th Ferrying Squadron were caught at Burtonwood by a historically heavy fog, which shut down all flying in the British Isles, from Langford Lodge in northern Ireland, on out past the White Cliffs of Dover. There was no place in a war to tolerate delays like this, and after two days the Burtonwood General (Ott?) told us to get on about our business as he could see for almost a mile out and probably for a hundred feet up.

For two days we resisted his orders, but we did follow his argument that we were chosen as old experienced pilots who could fly anything, anywhere, any time, and as a result of this, we were exempt from all flying regulations (and sometimes acted as though we were exempt from all regulations).

His orders did seem idiotic, as we were without any radio contact and would be moving too fast and too low to follow lap-held maps showing only general features. However, his threats of punishment were severe, so I told the group that I would go first but seek the first opportunity to land. I also told them that they should consider disobedience or follow my pattern and land at the first opportunity, as we were all confident that more than a tight circle around the field was impossible.

My plane was the first P-38 (J25) to hit the European Theater. I had two hours of cockpit time familiarization and had flown it the few minutes that it took to go from Langford Lodge in northern Ireland to Burtonwood, where it was checked over and returned in accordance with my notes. Perfect or not, it flew like a dream when compared with other P-38s, as it was the first model to have hydraulic booster controls and therefore no longer handled like a railroad freight engine.

I got into the air and rapidly decided to circle and land back on the same runway; then, three-quarters around I caught a glimpse of the river and decided to try another field approximately ten miles to the south. Needless to say, it never showed up, so I stayed on the water, under a couple of bridges, and simply followed the river for a long way. By then, I was hopelessly lost and had to follow holes in the fog, which zigzagged at random. Eventually, I hit the south coast and went out over water where I was below barrage balloons, which were pulled down almost onto the deck. Fortunately, there were no cross-snares, and I turned west to follow the coastline. From this position I got an excellent view of the cliffs and waved to people on small beaches, as I was probably flying at 20-50 feet. However, gasoline eventually ran low, and I made the decision to go up, turn inland, and parachute. No sooner was this decision made that I saw a break in the cliff and a runway lined up with it. Before I could actually think of what to do, I had swung in, dropped wheels, and landed.

Total shock lasted long enough for several lorries to get out to me and to have RAF pilots pulling me out and expressing amazement at my plane and how we "American Night Fighters" could handle such weather. By then, I was again conscious and had a guard put on the plane before I was carried in as a hero. Never did I tell them differently, and for the next two days of zero-ceiling, I was kept and partied by a British night fighter squadron who turned me over to a highly experienced pilot by the name of "Alabama." He had gone early to Canada, on into the Battle of Britain, and continued on as an experienced combat teacher.

I felt a little bewildered and ashamed not to tell him my true status, but I didn't. He would never have understood that I was not an experienced pilot who had only accidentally (or for convenience) been put into my group.

My squadron was made up of many who would not actually pass Army test:

1. A former General in the Mexican Air Force
2. A Hollywood stunt pilot
3. Several crop dusters
4. Several grandfathers and semi-cripples
5. A former major who had been court-martialed and made a "Permanent 2Lt."

(There was no precedent for his behavior and the military could not stand the exposure. The day after Pearl Harbor was hit, we sent all flyable U.S. based B-17s to help. We had only eleven. He took one of these, but found only confusion when he got there plus lack of respect for his rank. He then had his crew refuel his ship and took his airplane back home.)

**Donald W. Diehm served as a radio operator with the 312th Ferrying squadron. Don contributed the following story of a great family reunion in the ETO:**

I can relate a story that happened to me while on detached service with Lt. Harry Hall, Lt. Samberger, and Sgt. Larry Kelly. We were assigned to fly high priority material for General Ott, up in Compiégne, France, from Grove, England, to all over Europe. While there, I hurt myself and went back to Villacoublay to sick call. One night coming back from chow, I heard someone ask for a Sgt. Diehm. I turned around, and it was my brother Dennis, a T/Sgt. in the 26th Division, on a three day pass. How he found me is another story.

I also had another brother, Eddie, who was a S/Sgt. in the 439th Troop Carrier Group, and I happened to know where the group was stationed in France. I got a three day pass and went to the Red Cross in Paris, and they called my brother. I told him that Dennis was with me. He told his executive officer, and got a three day pass and a jeep!

We met at the Red Cross Club in Paris. I can say it was one hell of a party! We had not seen one another for three years. We had a picture taken and agreed not to tell our mother about the reunion until I had gotten the picture and sent it to her. She was one surprised mom!

*Sgt. Donald Diehm at 312th Communications.*

I went back to Compiegne and continued to fly for General Ott until the end of April 1945. In that time, we flew a total of 529.05 hours and had 362 landings and takeoffs.

We had very little time off during that period.

**Joe Cioffi was the Communications Chief of the 311th. He has special memories of "Static":**

When the 311th was at Langford Lodge (LLAD) in northern Ireland, the radio section acquired two dogs (Irish/Scottish Terriers) and named them Static and Chaser after the Radio Section, which was known as "Static Chasers." Chaser died a few days after we got the dogs, but Static was in good shape. We had him for the whole time we were in Europe, and he went everywhere we went. He had a lot of flying time and was very well liked by all of the squadrons.

When we were at Istres, he got into a chicken house of one of the French people and killed a few chickens. The attached letter (see page 166, and photos on page 167) from the Provost Marshal explains it all. The CO of the 311th received this letter, and before it got to me everyone that saw it in administration clipped some money to it to pay for the chickens. By the time I received it we had enough money to pay for all of them.

All of the French women who worked in the kitchen loved this dog and fed him daily.

After the war I took him home with me and he spent many years with my children, who loved him, and he just loved the children and watched over them. After 14 years we had to put him to rest.

**Jacques A. Gordon, of the 311th, answers the question, "WHO WERE THE MOJAKS ?":**

I have attended the last two 27th ATG reunions. At the small talk sessions in the hospitality room the mention of the Mojaks created some interest. Some squadron members thought we were a little different and wanted to hear our story. Different? I don't think so. We were a cross section of the American GI of the time. I promised the editor of "Ferry Tales," Joe Cioffi, that I would do a little story about our previous assignment, and although it is not a tale of the 27th Group, it is a story of some of its people.

In mid February 1944, a group of approximately forty-five enlisted men joined the 27th Air Transport Group. About 15 of them (radio operators and aerial engineers) were assigned to the 311 Ferrying Squadron at Maghaberry, in North Ireland.

I was a member of this group. We arrived from a replacement depot located at Crew, England. This was not our first assignment, however. Some had been in the ETO since July and with the rest of the group. At appropriate times we played hard, and a few got into trouble and were disciplined. Somehow we acquired the name "MOJAKS," and it endured until we returned home to the States in September, 1945.

In July 1941, the troop ship "American Legion" headed out into the North Atlantic on course to Iceland. On board were approximately 350 officers and men of the 33rd Pursuit Squadron, 8th Pursuit Group, and another 100 men from the 1st Air Base Squadron, 2nd Air Base Group, which was located at Mitchell Field, Long Island. Along the way, the aircraft carrier *Wasp* joined up with "the Legion." The Pursuit Squadron's thirty P-40C aircraft and three Stearman PT 17s had been lifted aboard in Norfolk, Virginia, and secured on deck in a "ready to fly" condition. The

OFFICE OF THE PROVOST MARSHAL
AY 17

APO 744
24th January 1945

SUBJECT: REPORT OF DAMAG TO CIVILIAN PROPERTY.

TO : Commanding Officer, AY 17, APO 744

1. Report is made of the destruction of six chickens on or about the 4th of January, 1945, the property of Lt. Bertin of the French Security of the Airdrome at Istres. The offender, as charged by Lt. Bertin and his wife, was the dog of Irish Terrier Stock answering to the name of "Static", owned by S/Sgt. Joseph V. Cioffi, 3 605110, 311th Ferrying Squadron.

2. This case was investigated by myself in the capacity of provost marshal. I was shown the five dead chickens, all allegedly egg layer, and each killed by the breaking of the spine. The sixth was not in evidence, having disappeared at the time of the incident, as stated to me by Me. Bertin. She stated that both she and her hubband had found the dog in the chicken pen chasing the chickens, and that they had seen him kill one of them.

3. I took the dog from the woman and had him identified by Sgt. Cioffi as his own. Sgt. Cioffi and I went with the dog to the house on the Cravon Site at Istres to see Me. Bertin. There we established that the dog had been seen to bite the chickens. It was arranged that Lt. Bertin would seek to replace the chickens and that the sergeant would pay the value of the five that had been found dead.

4. Lt. Bertin has this day reported to me that he has found chickens to his satisfaction in the local market at the value of 350 francs a head, total value 1750 francs for five chickens. He has priced the same type of chicken in Marseille and found that there they sell for 500 francs apiece.

5. It is recommended that this matter be settled by private arrangement as soon as possible.

Malcolm F. McKesson
MALCOLM F. MCKESSON
CAPTAIN CMP

Distribution:
1 copy to C.O., 311th Feryying Squadron
1 copy to file

*Left: Sgt. Albert Bak with "Static" and "Chaser." Center: Static. Right: Static (right) playing tug-o-war with Chips at Le Bourget. Chips died in October of 1944.*

ships arrived at Reykjavik, Iceland, on August 6. The troops disembarked, and the aircraft were flown from the deck of the *Wasp* by their Air Corps Pilots to our new base on shore.

We moved into Nissen huts, which had previously been occupied by the British. These were small metal, rounded structures that held about twelve men. They were banked with earth halfway up both sides for protection against weather and were heated with small coal burning stoves. They were illuminated by low wattage bare bulbs strung along the ceiling. No additional lights or outlets were permitted. A mess hall, latrine, ablutions hut, and an orderly room made up the rest of the sight. We built a large hut as a movie theater, and officers and men from all surrounding areas were invited to attend. This was home for the next two and one half years.

The airfield was only a few miles outside of Reykjavik. It had two paved runways approximately 5,000 feet long, which provided approaches from four directions. There was one large hangar which was shared by the Icelandic Air Service and the RAF. The RAF was equipped with Vickers Wellington bombers. The United States Navy and a small contingent of Norwegians occupied a site in the bay, off the end of the south runway. They operated PBY and PBM flying boat patrol bombers. Their mission was to provide North Atlantic convoys en route to England, Iceland, and Russia, with anti-submarine protection. They flew long daily patrols, and their presence became a comforting sight to convoys. Our small detachment was assigned a portion of the field at the end of the north runway. We had a small unheated hangar and some sandbag revetments to park our aircraft in. We and our thirty P-40s were charged with the air defense of the island, and it was a task indeed. The pilots settled into their routine of flying daily patrols. In addition to the routine patrols there were always three aircraft on full standby at the alert shack. This was a twenty-four hour assignment for pilots and ground crews. The engines of these aircraft were kept warm and the fuel tanks kept topped off. They could be airborne in a matter of minutes, if necessary.

Our commanding officer, Major Donald Hudson, and our engineering officer, Captain John Kelso, were pilots who had flown in WW I. Our senior non-commissioned officers were old soldiers with several enlistments to their credit. Most of them were married and had families back home. They knew their jobs well and kept us on the ball. Sightseeing was about all there was to do in Reykjavik. There were no bars that we could go to, there was a language barrier, and the people were not particularly friendly to soldiers. It took only a few trips to town to realize that there were almost as many troops in town as there were on the base, so we soon quit going in. Two days before Christmas in 1941, a second group known as "task force four" arrived. It was made up of new outfits, mostly infantry, and reinforcements for units already stationed on the island. We received an additional one hundred men and five officers.

The winter of '41-42 was a tough one for us. Our tired P-40 aircraft were replaced with Bell P-39 aircraft which had been shipped to us in crates. It took the entire winter working around the clock to assemble these aircraft in an unheated hangar, but the rewards were gratifying – we had a squadron of airplanes. The weather was very severe. We lost three pilots, Lt. Meeks, Lt. Patterson, and Lt. Hoffman, in snow squalls which moved in without warning. The International Airport, presently located at Keflevick, was originally know as Meeks Field, named in memory of our Lt. Meeks. It was built in 1943 by Navy Sea Bees and intended for use by the Air Transport Command. It has been improved many times before achieving its present day status. Lt. General Andrews and his entire B-24 crew were lost attempting to land at Reykjavik. They struck a mountain and became more bad weather casualties. The Navy lost some of their patrol bombers that were secured to their moorings in the bay during a severe storm. The winds were clocked at 132 miles per hour.

The Germans did not bomb us, but they did make frequent recon flights. These would trigger air raid alerts, and we had to get into our fox holes, which had been dug for us by the Infantry (not too willingly, I am sure). The Infantry also helped us bury drums of reserve aviation fuel in the hills. On August 15, 1942, we shot down a Focke-Wulf 200 bomber, and again in October, a Ju 88. Both aircraft were downed by Lt. Schaffer. He was flying the same aircraft on both occasions. Robert Millar, a member of our 27th Group, was the crew chief of that aircraft. Robert's commanding officers presented him and Lt. Schaffer with a fine pistol and holster each, which had been taken from the downed crewman. On another occasion, Millar ran onto the runway and stopped a RAF Hudson bomber that had started its takeoff roll. He had noticed that the rudder locks were in place. The station RAF commander honored him with a letter of commendation for his alertness and fast reaction.

The spring and summer of 1942 brought about many changes and set the pattern of things to come for the next year and a half. The weather grew milder, but definitely not short sleeve variety. The days grew longer, from approximately five hours of daylight in winter to almost twenty four in the summer. Iceland has no trees, and we missed the leaves and color that go along with springtime. Military activities were significantly increased. More ship convoys were going to Russia, and more ships were being sunk in spite of stepped up anti-sub patrols. Army Air Force bombers started arriving at our field, a squadron at a time – B-17, B-24, or Martin B-26 aircraft on their way to England. These were part of what was called the Bolero movement. They were not the replacement variety that we moved from Burtonwood or Warton. They were complete tactical units. We helped these crews service their aircraft, and gave them a good meal and a place to sleep. On the next day they were off to the UK. These flights continued as long as the weather along the Northern Route was favorable. The name Air Force had been given to the Air Corps and it was getting big. Big as it was, we knew some of the men that passed through, men we met at tech schools or served with at other bases.

The months of 1943 slipped by. Dull routines and the lack of furloughs were having an adverse effect on morale. In January 1944, we were told that we were being relieved and we prepared to move. We hoped it was home, but this was not to be, and we landed in the UK. Naturally we were disappointed, but the next best thing that could have happened to us was being assigned to the 27th Air Transport Group. The very nature of this group's mission afforded us freedoms and liberties seldom realized by enlisted personnel. We all drew flight assignments and got to travel extensively in England and later on the continent. There were friendly people to talk to, trains to go places on, pubs to buy beer, dances, and girls. Troops that came directly from the States had little appreciation for these things. They tended to make comparisons to what they had at home, and of course, there was no comparison. We, however, had found an outlet for our long suppressed frustrations and enjoyed it. Perhaps in that respect we seemed a little different.

**Franklyn Terry served as a radio operator with the 312th Ferrying Squadron. He chose to remember something other than flying:**

In 1945, after serving in the ETO for nearly two years, I was the happy recipient of a 10 day rest leave. I was flown to the French Riviera, where it took me a short time to settle in my room in a beautiful old hotel run by the Allied military. I was anticipating long days of rest and relaxation.

The day after I arrived I met a pretty 18 year old French girl and her mother on the beach adjacent to my hotel. With mother nearby, mademoiselle and I had a pleasant afternoon busily attempting to increase our language skills. Before making plans for a date the next day, I was informed by the girl that her mother would not let her go with me without the mother being in attendance. I guess she did not trust me, and I really couldn't blame her. I told the girl I liked her enough to have the mother join us, which she did. Every day she came with us. At no time did we do anything that might displease her. My reward came on the last day. My patience and persistence had paid off. Mother announced that she trusted me to be alone with her daughter. However, I now began to feel responsible to the mother as if she was my mother. How could I let her down?

On our last date, as soon as we were safely away from her mother's scrutiny, this sweet, innocent girl, who had to be protected from the Yankee airman on a daily basis, did everything but rape me. She was unable to be satisfied in her wild sexual passion. Who knows? Possibly the mother had become aware that her daughter did have to be protected, not from me, but from herself!

*R/O Franklyn Terry.*

**Kit Carson flew a combat tour as a B-17 pilot with the 351st Bomb Group and was ready to go home. However, he was to live his own Ferry Tale with the 312th Ferrying Squadron first:**

After I finished my 30 mission combat tour with the 351st Bomb Group, flying B-17s, I fully expected to head for the States and an instructor's job at some training base. It was a real low blow when they handed me my orders to put in a three month tour with the 312th Ferrying Squadron at Langford Lodge, in Northern Ireland.

Two days later I was picked up by a C-47 taxi ship, and after a six hour flight that included stops at a couple of other bases to pick up some more lucky ones, we were dumped on the tarmac at Langford Lodge on the shore of beautiful Lough Neigh, about twenty miles west of Belfast.

I was in a pretty foul mood when I reported to the 312th orderly room to turn in my orders and get my BOQ assignment. After being welcomed by the Squadron Commander, I felt a little better. He said I might get the chance to ferry several different types of combat aircraft to the units in England during my tour, but that mostly I would be delivering B-17s out of the repair depots at Warton and Burtonwood. After the interview, I commandeered a jeep and driver to take me to Base Operations to pick up the footlocker, B-4 bag, and duffel that contained all my worldly possessions and haul them to my BOQ Nissan hut. This was an open bay hut that contained ten double-decked bunks with open clothes racks along the walls for hanging uniforms. Since all the lower bunks were taken, I chose an upper (what else?). I didn't mind, as I never did like a lower bunk where you had to lie there looking up at the sagging mattress above you and banging your head on the upper bunk frame every time you sat up, sleepily forgetting that the upper was there.

It seemed to me that ferrying aircraft to combat groups in England should be pretty tame stuff after surviving 30 missions over France and Germany, with the German Luftwaffe and flak to put up with. I was to find out that ferry duty, as we were doing it, was as dangerous as combat; perhaps even more so.

I was really excited to find out that Tony LeVier, the famous racing and test pilot, was at Langford testing the P-38s that came out of the modification center after they were fitted with a new aileron boost system that improved their acrobatic capability. Every time he went up, he put on an air show for us, doing things with the twin-engined Lightning that seemed impossible to a bomber pilot like myself. I had always liked to see the P-38 as escort for our bombing missions because they were so easy to recognize as friendlies. The P-51s and P-47s could be mistaken for Me 109s and Fw 190s at a distance.

I soon found that ferrying aircraft was not a safe and sane existence. The 27th ATG lost several crews while I was there. Most of the losses were due to pilots flying aircraft with no training or experience in them, or trying to fly VFR in IFR weather. They would try to fly under a very low ceiling in poor visibility because they were afraid to fly instruments.

This was especially true of the service pilots with the group, who had little experience or training in instrument flying. This led to aircraft running into hills in rain or fog. Being unfamiliar with an aircraft led to fatal mistakes, like stalling out on final approach and crashing short of the runway, or flipping the wrong switch at the wrong time and inadvertently shutting off fuel to an engine. I had a few memorable and exciting flights with the 312th. The following are some of them:

I was sitting in the ready room at Squadron Ops on June 19, 1944. I was the only pilot in the squadron who wasn't either out on a trip or on pass. It was raining outside, and I was just feeling glad I wasn't flying that day. About that time, the dispatcher called my name. "Lieutenant Carson," he said, "There is a P-51 at Warton that needs to be delivered to Fowlmere. Grab your bag, pick up a seat-pack chute, and the driver will take you out to the taxi ship that is just now landing to pick you up."

"Hey, wait a minute!" I answered. "I'm a bomber pilot. I've never been checked out in a P-51."

"That ship has to be at Fowlmere this afternoon, Lieutenant," he snapped. "You're a pilot. You fly airplanes. That's an airplane, and you will fly it to Fowlmere, Sir! General Ott, the Group Commander, says so!"

Actually, I was thrilled with the idea of strapping a fighter to my rear end, so I didn't argue. I got on the C-47 when it taxied in and was soon on my way to Warton. When I got off the taxi ship on the Warton ramp, I was met by a lieutenant who took me across the ramp to where a sleek, brand-new P-51D was parked. I told him I had never flown one before.

"I'm just a maintenance officer," he told me. "I'm afraid I can't be much help to you, but I have listened to the pilots talk about the bird and I've run up the engine and taxied a few, so I'll show you what I can."

I went into Base Operations to file my flight plan and get my weather briefing. Imagine my surprise to find that the tech sergeant who briefed me on the weather was from my home town of Stonington, Illinois, a dinky burg with 1,300 population. After we had a short visit, he told me that my takeoff would be with a 500 foot ceiling and that the weather at Fowlmere would be about the same. I returned to the airplane to get ready for my first flight in a single engine aircraft since basic flying school.

The maintenance officer and crew chief gave me some help in doing my walk-around preflight check and assisted me in starting the engine. The only helpful hint they gave me was to watch out for torque on takeoff, set in four degrees of right rudder trim, and feed the throttle in rather slowly in order to compensate for torque with the rudder.

I taxied out, remembering to do "S" turns to clear the area in front of me, since I couldn't see over the engine. I received my takeoff clearance from the tower and took off, thrilled by the sensation of REALLY FLYING that you don't get a whole lot of in a four-engine bomber. The stubby wings of the Mustang were an unfamiliar sight to one used to 45 feet or so of wing and a couple of engines churning on each side.

I climbed through the overcast with no problem. I was a real good instrument pilot, as I had been a Link Instrument Trainer Instructor for two years as an enlisted man before I was accepted for Aviation Cadet training. I broke out on top of the overcast at about 7,000 feet and turned on my heading for Fowlmere. I wasn't sure what power setting to use for cruise, so I set up the standard B-17 fast cruise setting of 30 inches of mercury manifold pressure and 2,000-RPM on the prop.

I found out later that this was somewhat less than proper power setting for the P-51. I noticed that I was only cruising at about 165 mph and wondered why I wasn't going faster until I realized I had forgotten to raise the landing gear. I guess I was waiting for the co-pilot to do it. It took me a minute or two to locate the gear control handle, but, when I finally retracted the gear, the speed increased to about 200 mph.

I enjoyed the one hour hop to my destination. I toyed with the idea of trying some aerobatics, but it had been a long time since basic flying school, so I decided not to tempt fate. I was remembering Orville Oldham, a 351st pilot who transferred to a fighter outfit after finishing his bomber tour. He spun in and killed himself trying aerobatics in the Mustang before he had any training or experience in the aircraft to speak of.

When I reached Fowlmere and received landing clearance from the tower, I realized that I had no idea what approach speed to use, how much flap was required, or whether I should try to three-point land or land on the main wheels with the nose level. I asked the tower officer to answer a couple of these questions and told him this was my first flight in a Mustang. He was very helpful, and I set up my final approach with a bit more confidence. Halfway down final approach, I started searching for the flap handle and had to make a go-around while I got instructions from the snickering tower officer. This time I made my approach, and when I leveled out to put the wheels on the asphalt, I realized I was about ten feet too high. I was accustomed to seeing the runway from a bomber cockpit, and the perspective was somewhat different.

When the Mustang stalled, I kicked rudders to keep the wings level as we hit the runway pretty hard. It only bounced once, however, and settled in nicely. Heaving a sigh of relief that I was down safely without damage, I started to taxi to the parking ramp. Just as I turned off the runway onto the taxi strip, the engine quit cold. Somewhat nonplused, I called the tower and asked for a tractor and tow bar to pull me to the ramp. When I was finally parked, a maintenance officer hopped up on the wing and said, "What happened, Lieutenant?"

"I dunno," I answered. "Just as I turned off the runway, the engine quit. I made a pretty hard landing. Maybe I broke something."

"Nah," he said. "That wasn't a very hard landing. Which fuel tank were you using from?"

"There's more than one?" I asked. "I don't even know where the tank selector switch is."

"He took a look in the cockpit and said, "Ye Gods! You are on the fuselage tank! It only holds 75 gallons! How long were you in the air?"

I told him, and he figured I should have run out of fuel ten minutes before I landed. When I told him what cruise power setting I had used, he figured that was what saved my neck and the airplane. He said normal cruise was 34 inches and 2,200 RPM. I'll admit I felt a bit shaky when I thought of what would have happened if the engine had quit two or three minutes earlier than it did.

Another flight I remember was on the 26th of June. I was directed to fly a war-weary B-17 from Burtonwood to St. Mawgan, down in Cornwall. The ship was to be picked up by ATC pilots and flown back to the States from there. Due to the fact that the 312th was a bit short of pilots, we often flew without a co-pilot, using a flight engineer in the right seat instead. That was the case on this particular flight.

In the combat theater in those days, a preflight inspection was generally a walk around the airplane to make sure the tires were inflated, and the props were pulled through a few blades by hand to prevent liquid locks in the bottom cylinders of the Wright Cyclone radial engines. I performed this inspection along with the engineer, and we climbed aboard to takeoff for the one hour flight to St. Mawgan. As we climbed out after takeoff, we received a call from Burtonwood tower. "B-17 that just took off – be advised that you are siphoning fuel from all four wing tanks."

We looked out at the top of the wings and discovered that the filler caps were missing from all four tanks. The negative pressure on top of the wings was drawing out the fuel in four steady streams. To break the siphon, I pulled the aircraft up into a stall. This stopped the siphoning, and after recovering from the stall, I called the tower and advised them that we were returning to land. They came back with the information that we might as well continue to St. Mawgan, as the aircraft arrived at Burtonwood without caps, and there were no spares to be had. In other words, they wanted to shift the problem to the maintenance troops at St. Mawgan.

We continued the flight and landed at our destination. I made sure that the missing caps were entered on the aircraft Form 1A so that the next ferry pilot would at least be aware of the problem before he took off.

I think the ferry flight that gave me the most fun occurred on July 21st. On that date, several pilots from the 312th were sent to Snailwell, England, to pick up some A-20G aircraft that had been stored there when it was decided not to use them in the ETO. We were to bring them back to Langford Lodge, where they would be picked up by ATC pilots and flown to the North African Theater, where they would be deployed as fighter-bombers.

The Douglas A-20 "Boston" was first manufactured as a medium bomber, carrying two pilots and a bombardier, plus one turret gunner, as the crew. It had four forward firing .50 caliber machine guns in the nose, plus the twin .50s in the turret on top of the fuselage, just aft of the cockpit. The "G" model had been modified, having only a single seat for the pilot and the turret for the gunner. The pilot controlled forward firing 50s, and the modified aircraft was so maneuverable that it could hold its own in a dogfight.

When we arrived at Snailwell, there was one pilot in the bunch who had flown A-20s previously, so we gathered around him at one of the airplanes to get some instruction on the aircraft and how to fly it. He showed us the location of the various cockpit controls, briefed us on stall speeds, approach, and cruise power settings, and told us it was a very responsive airplane and very easy to fly. The only caution he gave us was to be sure to close the top cowl flaps for takeoff, as the open flaps would cause a severe tail buffet about the time one became airborne on takeoff.

Ferry pilots were pretty much on their own when they were on a trip. Group Headquarters didn't mind if you took a side trip, as long as you didn't abuse the privilege. I decided to drop in on my old bomb group at Polebrook for a visit. I found that flying the A-20 was a pure joy. It handled so easy and was so responsive. It was really more fun than the P-51, because it was so much easier for me to fly. I guess I felt more comfortable with more than one throttle in my hand anyway.

I landed at Polebrook just before lunch. A lot of the Group Staff, including the Group Commander, came out to see who was in the A-20 and why it was there. They all seemed glad to see me and the CO invited me to RON and have a good visit with the guys I knew who were still there. The operations officer asked me if I would check him out in the A-20 while I was there. I gave him the same checkout I had been given, and he climbed in the bird and took off. I told him that if anyone else wanted to fly it, they could be my guest, as long as each would pass on the pertinent info to the successive pilots. I then headed for the officer's club to get some lunch, after which I looked up some of my friends. At various times during the day, I saw the A-20 in the traffic pattern, and that night I heard it tooling around overhead when I went to bed after the Club closed. The next morning when I went to my airplane to depart for Ireland, I found that six pilots had flown it and had logged a total of almost 13 hours.

I was to make only two more ferry flights prior to my departure from the 312th on August 10th. The departure from Langford Lodge was a hair-raising tale in itself. There was a collection of 42 crew members gathered at Langford Lodge, trying to get transportation to England to be processed to leave for the States on the *Queen Elizabeth* out of Glasgow on the 13th of the month. We were all desperate to get over to the 12th RCD at Chorley to get processed in time to catch the ship. When a modified B-24 landed at the field to drop a load of freight, we cornered the pilot and begged him to fly us to Warton or Burtonwood. He agreed to do it if we could find room on the aircraft for 42 people and baggage.

The B-24 had been modified to carry cargo. Bomb racks and turrets had been removed, and the bomb-bay floored. After we had loaded 42 footlockers, 42 B-4 bags and 42, A-2 duffel bags in the fuselage, there wasn't room for passengers except on top of all that baggage. After twenty-five laid down on top of the baggage, seventeen of us crowded into the nose compartment that had been designed for two crewmen, the bombardier, and navigator. The turret and bomb sight had been removed, so there was only a navigator's table and a little bombardier's stool in the nose. We were crammed in there so tight that I was sitting on the bombardier stool with my nose against the plexiglass, staring at the short 6,000 foot runway with pine trees at the end. I can't imagine how much we were exceeding the weight and balance tolerances for the aircraft, and I was beginning to wonder if this was such a good idea. I certainly was wishing I was somewhere in the rear of the aircraft so I didn't have to sweat the takeoff so closely.

The pilot lined up on the runway, opened all four throttles, turned on the superchargers, and released the brakes. The ship seemed to waddle forward very slowly, and I was sure, as we started eating up the runway, that I would likely be eating pine needles if I lived through the crash I was sure was going to occur. The pilot held the ship down until we almost ran out of asphalt, then hauled back on the wheel, and I was sure I felt pine boughs scraping the bottom of the nose as we cleared the trees. He leveled out to gain a little more speed before starting to climb out and turn on a course to Burtonwood.

I said a thanksgiving prayer as we headed out over the Irish Sea and continued it 'till we passed the Isle of Man. So ended my tour in the ETO and my short duty stay with the 27th ATG.

**Howard Stillwell was a pilot in the 311th Ferrying Squadron with vivid memories of his World War II service. Here follows "A Pilot's Recollections" by Howard Stillwell:**

It might interest you to know that I returned from WWII to finish college and start teaching. I was recalled to active duty in 1951 and made a career out of the Air Force.

My best flying experience was in the 21st Troop Carrier Squadron in Tachikaua, Japan. I flew as a pilot, instructor pilot, operations officer, executive officer, and CO of the 21st TCS.

Other assignments included: Operations at Headquarters, United States Air Force, in the Pentagon; Headquarters, Pacific Air Forces, Hickman AFB, Hawaii; Air Force Representative to the Assistant Secretary of Defense, OSD, Pentagon; Vietnam, Air Force; ROTC professor at UCLA; and advisor to the Air Force Reserve, Hamilton AFB.

I accumulated 7,500 hours of accident free flying and retired in 1974. In civilian life I returned to college as a teacher and counselor.

**PRE-FLIGHT**

After a short stay with the 87th and 310th Squadrons in September and October of 1943 at Warton Airfield in England, I was assigned to the 311th Ferrying Squadron, 27th Air Transport Group (ATG), 302nd Transport Wing, 8th Air Force when it was formed in November of 1943 at Maghaberry Airfield, Ireland, not too far from Belfast. I later outlasted two reorganizations, which saw friends transferred to other 27th ATG units, and stayed with the 311th Squadron until I returned to the USA in August of 1945.

The experiences described in this work are typical of many of the 311th air crew members who stayed with the squadron for 22 months in both the ferry and transport missions.

### Part I Take Off and Fast Cruising
### AIRCRAFT FERRY OPERATIONS

"Flight Delivery of Any Aircraft, Anywhere, Anytime"

I believe this is an accurate description of the 311th mission as a ferrying squadron. However, I don't remember seeing an official 311th mission statement, and mine is based only on the experiences I had or knew about in 1943-45, while stationed in the European Theater of Operations (ETO) during World War II.

My flight logs show 299 flights totaling 550 hours delivering all types of USAAF fighters and bombers to the operational combat unit's bases. Usually we would pick up our delivery aircraft at one of the Air Depots at Warton and Burtonwood in England, Langford Lodge in Ireland, and Renfrew/Prestwick in Scotland. Most deliveries were to the 56 or so U.S. fighter/bomber bases in the East Anglia section of England.

Ferry flights were scheduled every day of the year. Bad weather was normal, but occasionally weather was impossible. Weather fronts queued up out in the North Atlantic Ocean just waiting their turn to roll across Great Britain.

Pilot Log Entry: 13 December 1943, Flew a P-38 from Maghaberry across Irish Sea near the Isle of Man, in almost 0-0 weather. As usual, flying on the deck trying to stay under the clouds, and just missed hitting the mast of a fishing boat. Later, in foul weather, one of our B-24 crews hit a hill on the Isle of Man and all were killed.

During the early days of ferry flights there were few or no navigational aids available to us. Consequently, most of the time we flew under the clouds, with one finger on a map, trying to stay on course. There were so many airdromes in East Anglia that if you lost an engine on the takeoff it was almost possible to just go straight ahead and land on the adjoining airfield. Very little formation flying was done because of the low altitudes flown, fighter aircraft speeds, and bad weather. Each pilot wanted to know exactly where he was at all times in case of separation. He could not keep his finger on his map while in formation.

*Four photos below: Crash damage to P-47 aircraft flown by Bert Astrove. Crash occurred at Darvel, Scotland. Right: Instrument panel of Astrove's P-47 after the crash. Note mud and debris.*

Speaking of weather, Bert Astrove was flying a P-47 from Renfrew, Scotland, to Warton Airfield in England in a big snowstorm on 13 November 1943. He became lost and started to circle when his estimated time of arrival (ETA) was up. Suddenly, a large black shape appeared dead ahead. He hauled back on the flight control stick and hit a mountain going up at a 30 degree angle. The P-47 skidded to a stop at the top of the mountain. (See crash report below).

He was bleeding, badly bruised, and was unable to raise anyone on his radio after he crashed. He then climbed out of the cockpit and put his borrowed parachute over his shoulder – he did not want to have to pay for it – and walked five miles to a farm in Kilmarock, Scotland.

The farmer thought he was a German aviator and called the police, who correctly identified him and took him to a hospital. He was then taken to Warton. There is a picture of a badly bruised Bert and his parachute in my photo album.

Flight Log Entries: No sweat with a single engine landing in a P-38 ... Lots of sweat when engine trouble caused emergency landing in a Martin B-26 on my first flight.

I took off from Renfrew in P-47 no. 5145 Nov. 16th, 1943, approxiamtely 1445 hours. I was to have joined f rmati on circling above field. I had climbed to about 8oo ft. , cirlced the airport, looking for the other aircraft. I couldn't see them for the heavy snow that was falling. The ceiling stardted to drop until it was about250 ft. I continued circling, trying to set down, but I couldn't locate the drome. I decided to go through and make the trip alone. I took up a 240 degree heading that would bring me out on the coast. I climbed to 2000 ft. and held that altitude for about five minutes. I had no contact with the ground at all. I was on instruments. I let down to 1500 ft. I could see wisps of the ground every now and the It was still snowing quite hard, making the visibility very poor. I was still on course, and by my ETA, I figured that I was near Prestwick. I let down to 1200 ft. It cleared suddenly. I had my pitch well for ard in case I had to give her the needle. Went thru another cloud. When I c me out of that one, a hill was directly in front of me, and not far off. I gave her the throttle, and pulled her sharply up in a right climbing turn. A high speed stall resulted, and she mushed into the hill. I switched off as somn as I was able and crawled out. The plane did not catch afire.

Aircraft check outs consisted of a local flight after a cockpit orientation, then start delivering aircraft. My first ferry trip, the day after checking out in the P-51, was a thriller because the airfield where I was to deliver the P-51 suddenly became foggy. Fortunately, after 3 passes a safe landing was made.

It was an exhilarating experience for a young pilot to check out in the P-47 aircraft with its awesome 2,000 horsepower engine.

My first twin engine time came in the fifth ever made Lockheed Lightning (P-38) that was given to us by the RAF. It was distinguished by both propellers rotating in the same direction, causing lots of torque on takeoff. The later P-38s were much better and easier to fly with the counter-rotating props.

In November of '43 the log book shows 24 aircraft deliveries of P-47s, P-51s, and P-38s. December of '43 entries reflect twenty-two P-38 and P-47 deliveries. I did not fly on Christmas, but did deliver a P-38 on my birthday, December 30th.

Pilots delivered aircraft to combat units in East Anglia, and as normal procedure, waited for the B-17 or Anson (British) "taxi" aircraft to pick them up. The ferry pilots were picked up at many different bases and returned to different home bases. This was a long process in a slow airplane, so it is probable a 1 hour 30 minute P-38 delivery would be followed by a 3-4 hour passenger ride to home base. Consequently, my 550 hours of ferry pilot time probably resulted in close to 800 hours of passenger time in the taxi ships. Sometimes the taxi ship would not show up, so it was a train ride to London with parachute slung over a shoulder. 27th ATG C-47 shuttle aircraft at Heston took us back to home base the next day. Taxi pilots logged flight time, passenger pilots logged anxiety time.

Blacked out London at night was sometimes lit up from the flames caused by German V-1 guided missile "Buzz Bombs" as they exploded in the city. The V-1s were powered by pulse jet engines that were timed to run out of fuel over the target area, then plunge to the ground and explode. The silence after the engine quit from lack of fuel was fearful, because you knew the bomb was coming soon. What you didn't know was how close to you it would hit. Later, the V-2, rocket powered bombs were not as bad psychologically because they traveled so fast. The only thing heard was the explosion, when they landed in the city without warning. Royal Air Force (RAF) aircraft defense against V-l Buzz Bombs seemed to be to try to shoot them down before they reached large population areas like London, or to fly close and use their aircraft's wing tip to lift up a Buzz Bomb wing to make it turn away from London.

While at Maghaberry I was a qualified first pilot of L-4, C-61, P-38, P-47, P-51, A-20, B-26, B-17, and B-24 aircraft all at the same time. Even though living conditions were rather primitive at Maghaberry, I was in a position all pilots dream about: flying the best aircraft the U.S. could produce, almost every day with no extra ground administrative duties to distract me. Just fly! Also adding to my high morale was my promotion to 1st Lt. by command of General Eisenhower.

Speaking of the weather, riding in the plexiglass nose of a taxi aircraft returning pilots to Maghaberry at the end of a long, wet, bad weather day caused some excitement. The pilot could not stop the taxi aircraft on the wet pavement before we went off the end of the runway. I saw what was coming and climbed out of the nose into the cockpit above. No one was hurt, that I can remember.

At Maghaberry Airdrome the 311th Commanding Officer was 1st Lt. (later Capt.) Gregory P. Thomas, and our Operations Officer was Captain John Howard. During our 5 months stay at Maghaberry my monthly form 5 flight records were signed by Assistant OPS Officer Lt. Morris McGhee, Lt. John Trostle, and Lt. Ira Sullivan.

On April 5, 1944, the 311th Squadron moved to Langford Lodge Air Depot (LLAD) near Belfast in northern Ireland. CO Captain Thomas was ordered away to fly missions for headquarters personnel. Living conditions improved considerably. Major John McDonald signed my two officer effectiveness reports as the 311th CO at Langford Lodge from 6 April to 17 August 1944. Captain John Howard was the Operations Officer, and his assistants who signed my form 5 monthly flight records were Lts. John McCormick, Morris McGhee, Ira Sullivan, and John Trostle. Captain Howard and Col. Leslie P. Arnold signed my instrument check ride forms during this period.

## ICELAND TRIP

On the 27th of April 1944 HQ 27th ATG, Operations Order #2 was published. It directed 311th pilots Lts. Stillwell, Coleman, Jenkins, Kellogg, and Petty to fly P-47D aircraft from Warton Airdrome, England, to Meeks Field, Iceland. Allen Jackson was placed on different orders for the trip. We, along with five 310th pilots, were to follow Capt. Fay Brandis flying a B-17, with a navigator on his aircraft.

Our first leg of the flight on 29 April was to Stornoway in the Orkney Islands NW of Scotland. Naturally the weather was bad, and a let down through the overcast was required. One 310th pilot lost the formation for a few minutes, but found the flight and landed safely at Stornoway.

The P-47 pilots' preflight included, "Don't get separated from the B-17. If you get lost and have to bail out over the freezing North Atlantic Ocean or ditch your P-47 in the water, you would only live for 20 minutes even in your dinghy."

After a two day delay for bad weather, we took off for Iceland. Lt. Coleman had to abort with generator trouble. We climbed up and down through a thick layer of clouds trying to find the altitude with the least headwinds.

Because most of us had very little fighter close formation time, it was exciting having a large number of P-47s trying to stay in tight formation on one B-17 through dense clouds. The pre-takeoff briefing about the icy waters helped. We did not look like today's Air Force F-16 Thunderbirds, but all P-47 Thunderbolts safely landed in Ceiling and Visibility Unlimited (CAVU) weather at Meeks Field, Iceland, 4 1/2 hours after takeoff.

We were told that this was the first east to west P-47 flight on the route. After a couple of days sightseeing in Iceland and a short flight to the Arctic Circle, Fay gave us a nice ride in the B-17 back to Ireland.

During May and June, for the first time my flights were more in bombers than in fighters. In June of 1944 many 311th personnel were transferred to the 312th squadron back at Maghaberry when the 312th mission changed from checking out pilots to ferrying aircraft.

One of the highlights of my stay at Langford Lodge was watching Lockheed Aircraft test pilot Tony LeVier put on a P-38 demonstration flight that left all normal pilots breathless. He was en route to the fighter bases to show the P-38's potential.

Of the 56 or so airfields in East Anglia, I delivered aircraft to 12 fighter bases and 29 bomber bases. Some of the ones with quaint names by aircraft type were: P-38 – Nutts Corner (1404 AAFBU), Kingscliffe (20th FG), Nuthampstead (398th BG), P-47 – Wattisham (479th FG), Kimbolton (379th BG), P-51 – Boxted (386th BG, 56th FG, and 5 Emergency Rescue Sq.) and my log says "Bag Puss," B-17 – Rattlesden (447th BG), Old Buckenham (453 BG), Polebrook (351st BG), Bassingbourne (91st BG), Deopham Green (452nd BG), B-24 – Hethel (389th BG), Horsham St. Faith (458th BG), Eye (490th BG) , B-26 – Greencastle (12 Combat Crew Replacement Center), St. Angelo A-20 – Little Walden (409th and 493 BG), and Stansted (344th BG).

For a while I kept track of the tail numbers of the fighters that I flew, and even now on my annual trip to the Reno Air Races, in September, I check P-51 and P-38 tail numbers to see if, by chance, I had flown one of them.

**USA TRIP**

After 11 months in the ETO, I was placed on orders to pilot a B-17F, with some secret modifications on it, back for analysis at Wright Patterson Army Air Field in Dayton, Ohio. Gordon Jenkins was co-pilot, Robert Schucker, engineer, and Colin Conley, radio operator. The navigator was not on our orders, and I believe he was from the Air Transport Command. We had one passenger, an Army colonel, who was along for an unknown reason.

We picked up our B-17 at Valley Airport in Wales and flew a short shake-down flight to St. Mawgan on the southwest tip of England.

On July 3, 1944, we flew at night over water to Marrakech, Morocco, in northwest Africa. The 4th of July was celebrated in Marrakech while some aircraft discrepancies were corrected. On 5 July our route of flight took us over the western Sahara Desert to Dakar, Senegal, on the western most point of Africa.

Our pre-takeoff briefing at Dakar covered forecast weather en route and at our destination, emergency procedures, and a warning to spray insecticide in the aircraft before landing in Brazil. Plus, do not open any doors or windows after landing until Brazilian inspectors boarded our aircraft.

The long 10 hour flight to Natal, Brazil, was routine except when the navigator wanted me to fly a search pattern to find a rock that was supposed to be sticking up out of the ocean in our general vicinity. In view of the long flight, our fuel conscious engineer and the fact we were picking up the radio beacon from Brazil, influenced our decision to not fly a search pattern. After landing on a very hot and humid day at Natal, which is near the Equator, it was extremely uncomfortable in the closed up aircraft. Our passenger opened a door and jumped out. I, as Aircraft Commander, was fined $50 as a result. We were given a day off at Natal and bought some fancy leather flying boots, and spent an afternoon swimming at a beautiful beach.

Our next leg to Belem, Brazil, was all bad weather. The following flight took us over the Amazon River and thunderstorm conditions that shook up the old war weary B-17 severely until we landed at Atkinson Field in what was then British Guinea. Boringuen Field, Puerto Rico, was the next stop, and then a 5 1/2 hour flight to Homestead Army Air Field in Florida brought us back to the USA.

A two day stop at Washington, D.C., was made to allow some Pentagon officials to inspect the modified B-17. On the 15th day of our trip we delivered our aircraft to Wright Patterson Air Base in Dayton, Ohio. Our total flight time was 52 1/2 hours, 9 hours at night and 11 hours in instrument conditions weather.

After two days at home on the west coast, I returned to the 311th at Langford Lodge, where I found my squadron flying C-47s.

C-47 OPERATIONS

Air Transport – Anything, Anywhere, Anytime

In retrospect, I see this title as our C-47 mission statement, and it is based on my approximately 710 flights and 1,043 flight hours as a 311th C-47 pilot from August of 1944 to August 5th of 1945.

ANYTHING

USA troops – USA wounded – Allied forces troops – German prisoners – gasoline for aircraft and tanks – ammunition – bombs – medical supplies – aircraft engines – aircraft parts – jeeps – VIPs.

*311th C-47 pilots Dick Seebers and Don Kogge.*

ANYWHERE

Austria – Belgium – Czechoslovakia – Corsica – Denmark – England – France – Germany – Holland – Italy – Luxembourg – Scotland – Sweden-Switzerland.

ANYTIME

Seven days a week

In July and August of 1944 the 311th Ferrying Squadron converted to flying C-47 air transport missions out of Langford Lodge Air Depot, but retained the "ferrying squadron" designation. The flight log reveals that the last part of August and the first part of September, I was TDY (temporary duty) to Heston Aerodrome flying airlift missions to and from Cherbourg, Breast, Rennes, Avranches, Thorney Isle, and Granville along the French Normandy coast and into Paris.

Unfortunately, I did not keep names of the pilots who flew with me in the multi-engine aircraft, until 1 January, 1945, at Istres.

Not remembered at all, but revealed in my records, was that I was a Flight Commander from August '44 to August of 1945. It did not seem to restrict my flying the last year, which averaged 88 flight hours and 65 landings per month.

The first week of September 1944 the 311th moved to Grove Airdrome, Berkshire, England, near the town of Wantage. Capt. Gregory P. Thomas reassumed command of the 311th as of 17 August '44 according to my records. Capt John Howard continued as Operations Officer.

September and October 1944 were high flight time days for the 311th. Most flights were hauling supplies into France and Belgium, and evacuating wounded U.S. troops. The flight log shows 187 flights and 264 hours flying time for me those busy two months. I flew every day except six during September and October.

The influx of new 311th pilots, including Dick Seebers, Dean Sheets, Art Ryan, Don Kogge, Lou Gale, and Wayne Preston helped us immediately. Their knowledge of the C-47 complimented the old timers' peculiar flying skills that had been developed overseas.

Before any discussion of individual C-47 flight experiences, I must give due credit to our flight engineers, radio operators, and maintenance personnel who were our unsung heroes. In 710 or so flights in the C-47 I did not have to abort one mission because of maintenance or parts and did not lose an engine or any aircraft systems.

*A 311th Gooney Bird taking off.*

*Radio operators of the 311th.*

Thinking about weather again, I will never forget one very foggy early morning takeoff at Grove. We got a clear-for-take-off green light from the control wagon at our end of the takeoff runway. Prior to attaining normal lift off speed a C-47 taxing toward us from the other end of the active runway suddenly appeared in the fog. We managed to jump over the approaching C-47 and stagger into a climb on instruments. A great airplane, good crew coordination, judicious use of flaps, and lots of luck helped our cause.

It turned out that my close friend, Tom Mostyn, was the pilot of the wrong way aircraft. Tom was killed later while flying a C-47 through a thunderstorm back in the USA.

FIDO (Fog Intensive Dispersal Of), was the name given to an experimental effort to improve takeoff and landing in foggy weather conditions. It was conducted on an East Anglia Aerodrome where fog conditions were common. The idea was to set on fire large drums of kerosene/gasoline dispersed along the sides of a fogged in runway. The heat generated was supposed to cause the fog to rise and thereby increase visibility with higher cloud/fog ceilings. It did help some, and I remember landing at that base. Mixing fire and aircraft gives any pilot an uneasy feeling.

More weather: It was an eerie feeling to hear sirens on our radio head sets while flying on instruments in the clouds. The siren sound indicated you were not staying in the safe corridor between tethered barrage balloons, while flying over English cities, that were intended to trap enemy bomber aircraft.

More weather: In the early 311th days, not only were the navigational aids inadequate for our needs, I believe there were no instrument flight rules (IFR) that we followed. Consequently, it was not unusual while flying in the clouds to fly into prop wash. That meant that shortly before you occupied that airspace, another unseen aircraft had been there just before you.

Weather again: Close calls were routine on our flights to forward airfields in France when we would let down through clouds on estimated positions. No aircraft would be near when we started down. However, upon breaking out underneath the clouds, we would find other aircraft, with the same destination, almost in formation with us.

Captain John Howard, OPS officer, signed my form 5 flight records while we were at Grove Airfield.

After two months of flying out of Grove Airfield, the 311th packed up and flew to our new home at Istres, just west of Marseilles, France. On the 11th of November 1944, the fight log shows a 3 hour and 45 minute flight to Istres Airfield.

I have a picture of the inside of my C-47 on that trip. We were completely full of maintenance men, flight engineers, baggage, pet dogs, mattresses, and all the possessions of everyone on board. It was our first trip to the area where there were high mountains nearby. Sadly, we lost Lt Ken Halverson and his crew on the flight when they hit, in bad weather, one of those mountains hidden in the clouds.

*Captain John Howard working at his desk.*

The Germans had occupied Istres until shortly before we arrived. They had left mine fields around the airfield, and one of our pilots was killed and another badly injured when they stepped on mines. Also, there was an abandoned ammunition storage area, and some of our personnel would let off steam by igniting and tossing flares around.

The Germans had moved out of some houses that we moved into next to the base. We were there during the coldest part of the year and could feel the icy blasts of air coming down from the Alps. The solution was to manufacture a gasoline drip stove to keep each room warm. I remember our Administrative Officer, Captain Palma, accidentally starting a fire in one room.

At Istres, the 311th was assigned, for operations control, to the 1st Tactical Air Force, 9th Air Force. Among other tasks, the 311th supported the U.S. 7th Army going north from southern France, according to the 302 Wing history. Flight records also indicated many trips to Bordeaux, Cognac, and Toulouse in support of French forces, I believe.

At Istres, Y-17, Captain, later Major Thomas continued as CO of the 311th with Captain John Howard and Capt Bob Decker as Operations Officer. They both certified my form 5 flight records while at Istres.

On January 5, 1945, I was assigned to fly a B-26 from Marseilles up to Warton, England. I had not flown a B-26 for over five months, and my co-pilot, Jack Evarts, was making his first flight in a B-26. He was impressed with the final approach and sink speeds. The next day, we were assigned to fly a B-24H from Warton to Marseilles, and then on to the island of Corsica. I had not flown a B-24 for six months.

On 4 January 1945, a 27th ATG travel order directed six 311th crews to ferry B-24s from Marseilles to Gioia, Italy. Some of our current 27th ATG personnel who made the trip included Richards, Bogdan, John Howard, Krautbauer, and Jim Iacono. From that date on to April, it was again all C-47 flying.

In January of 1945, Wayne Preston and I made an educational trip while airlifting passengers and cargo to Rome, Naples, Florence, and Pisa, Italy. We both still have pictures buzzing the Leaning Tower of Pisa and also while in a steep bank (well, maybe 45 degrees), circling the tower.

Istres weather report #1: Corin A. Lewis (Red) was the pilot of a C-47 that got caught in a thunderstorm over the Alps while airlifting two B-26 engines from Italy to Dijon, France. The engines were strapped down, but while the C-47 was upside down one broke loose and wedged itself on top of the other engine. It stuck there through more wild gyrations. Unbelievably, the C-47 was thrown out of the bottom of the storm into a canyon heading right down the Rhone River Valley, and Red recovered safely. However, it was rumored that his crew members requested transfers to ground duty after that experience.

Istres weather report #2: Took off on a freezing cold morning in a heavily loaded C-47. We climbed out, but passing through 1,500' the flight controls became frozen in place. It felt as though the ground control locks had been left on. Visually checking the controls we saw a thick layer of ice on them. We knew the text book solution was a temperature conversion, and the solution was to climb into the rain above. However, we tried using the flight control trim tabs and managed to fly almost flat turns around the pattern, and we used a long shallow final approach and landed successfully. The aircraft tail number was probably 038 or 354, as those were my favorite C-47s.

One afternoon (Christmas Eve, 1944) at Istres, intelligence reports indicated there could be an attack that night by German paratroopers. Our CO immediately had the 311th in battle gear – helmets, .45 caliber pistols, etc. Air crews had to sleep on the floors (it was freezing) of the C-47s and be ready to fly them out with a moment's notice. A young PFC engineer, Dillard "Red" Hyden, arrived at Istres at this time. Before he could even check in he was given a carbine and placed on all night sentry duty at a single man post on the isolated perimeter of the airfield. Fortunately for us all the German attack did not materialize. Later, Dillard was my engineer on a trip to Copenhagen, Denmark.

For the first ten days of February 1945 Wayne Preston and I were TDY to Grove, England, flying into Belgium and France and back through Chilbolton Airfield in East Anglia. After our return to Istres, we found that we were moving to A-42, Villacoublay Airfield, on the outskirts of Paris. We made the 311th's fourth move to our new airfield about 11 February, 1945. By this time weather had become less of a problem with the installation of many radio ranges and beacons as navigational aids throughout France and England.

Gregory P. Thomas, now a major, continued to be our CO at Villacoublay until the 23rd of March 1945, and Captain John Howard as Operations Officer. Bob Decker, Assistant OPS, signed my February and March '45 form 5 flight records, as did his assistant, 1st Lt. John Wickey, in April and May 1945.

*311th C-47s operating from a field in southern France.*

1st Lt. Allen Jackson, our consummate master of all weather flying conditions, gave me an instrument green card 4 hour flight check on the 10th of March '45. I don't think he let me out from under the hood except for touchdowns on a trip. Passing this test was a big deal. Green card holders could sign their own flight clearances, regardless of weather.

Remember those flight physical exams? The 6th of March 1945 was my 2nd and last while in the 311th. Both were given by Dr. Donald G. Stannus, Capt., Medical Corps, Senior Flight Surgeon. I'm the same height and weight now, but there are many changes to the rest of my body.

March and April were very busy C-47 months with lots of ammunition and gasoline as cargo, American wounded being air evacuated, and German prisoners flown to Bovingdon near London.

Excerpt from 27th ATG document April '45:

*Above and below: Damage sustained by C-47 in which Lt. Frazer was killed. (See Appendix I for details)*

"The 311th, in its operations, flew to advanced units so far ahead of intelligence reports that often pilots used maps from the *Stars and Stripes* to find enemy locations to avoid."

One unknown enemy location not avoided was a by-passed pocket of Germans where they had retaken the city of Boulogne. One day we were air evacuating wounded U.S. troops from an airstrip near the front battle lines back to a hospital in England. Flying in the clouds and approaching our estimated time for reaching the English Channel, I started a descent. We broke out of the clouds at about 1,000 feet, and shortly thereafter, started seeing tracer bullets close to us. We also saw and heard other anti-aircraft firing. Because of the wounded on board I could not take evasive action, but fortunately the "Ack Ack" only lasted a few seconds and we were not hit. Our Flight Nurse came running up to the pilots' area and said it sounded like someone was pounding on the cargo door.

Weather again: Capt Bob Decker and his C-47 crew flew into one of the front lines' grass, cow pasture airstrips. I had flown in and out earlier in fairly good weather. When Bob came in it was raining and the grass was slippery. The runway sloped down, and after his aircraft touched down he realized that he was at a speed where there wasn't room to takeoff again or stop on the bumpy wet grass.

(In March of 1945 Lt. Frazer of the 311th FS was killed when the left prop on his C-47 hit the ground as a result of a gear collapse or a blown tire. The prop broke loose from its mounting and spun into the cockpit.)

A thought about Lt. Frazer's death, when the left prop came through the pilot's seat, flashed through Bob's mind. With lots of good luck, feathering the left prop and unconventional procedures, he and his co-pilot managed a left ground loop and slid to a stop unscathed right next to some German prisoners he was to fly out back to England.

Bob became an Army Air Corps pilot after transferring from the Royal Canadian Air Force in England. He also was in the 311th from its first day until he went home in August of '45. He frequently worked as Operations Officer.

After less than 60 days at Villacoublay, the 311th packed up again in mid April 1945 and moved to A-46, Toussus Le Noble Air Field, in Paris. Again, many of our personnel were transferred to other 27th ATG flying squadrons.

The flight log showed a diversified mission for the 311th starting mid April '45. Seventeen flights in C-47s, some with generals as passengers, twenty-four flights in B-25Cs, eight flights in C-45s, one in a P-47, four in a P-38, one in a C-78, one in a T-6, and one in an L-4 Cub.

I have no recollection of why our missions suddenly changed to flying passengers around. I researched the Wing history and found that the 311th assumed the operation of a communications flight from A-46. That meant flying VIPs and providing flight time and transportation for staff officers at HQ, U.S. Strategic Air Forces and Air Service Command. There were 80 aircraft of 14 different types to fly.

(More of Howard Stillwell's recollections are found in Chapter 7 "The End of the War")

**Vincent Alexander, pilot with the 310th, remembers the trip to Casablanca:**

One of the most interesting and fun assignments of pilots in the 27th Air Transport Group during the later days of World War II involved the pick up of fighters in Africa with a destination in England.

On or about April 25, 1945, a contingent of 310th and 311th ferry pilots were flown via a B-17 taxi ship from Burtonwood to Casablanca. Our assignment – pick up fighters at Casablanca and fly them to England. We were told that these fighters had been on a carrier which, although damaged by a U-Boat at sea, had been able to dock at Casablanca and unload its cargo. Subsequently, the fighters were readied for flight and orders cut for their delivery to England.

*Lt. Vincent Alexander on the wing of a P-38.*

*Lts. Vincent Alexander and Herman Estrada at Algiers.*

Our brief stay in Casablanca afforded some time for sightseeing activities. We were impressed by some of the architecture, but also by the number of maimed and disfigured natives gathered in park-like areas of the city.

On April 26, 1945, we flew our assigned fighters to Algiers. The flight over rugged terrain, sometimes obscured by thick foreboding looking sand storms, was made without incident or loss.

For almost three full days, we remained grounded at Algiers because of so called poor weather, which, of course, looked better than many flying days in England and on the continent. We used the respite for sightseeing, relaxation, and purchasing leather goods for the folks back home.

Finally, on April 29, 1945, we were cleared for the flight back to England. Like many others, this pilot's P-47 had a limited range because of the absence of any external fuel tanks. Consequently, several pilots landed at Sardinia, a British controlled air base, for fuel. Across the rest of the Mediterranean Sea, either in groups or alone, we flew to Marseilles. After an overnight stay at Marseilles, informal groups of ferry pilots took off for Paris, and after refueling, climbed over a snowstorm in the area and landed safely at Burtonwood.

**PFC Dillard T. "Red" Hyden came to the 311th at Istres, Christmas Eve, 1944. His first night was spent on Guard duty, awaiting a German paratroop attack, which fortunately never came. (See Chapter 5 on "the Battle of the Bulge" for Red's account of that night) After this exciting start with the squadron, Red began to settle into the day to day routine:**

Since I had not been assigned a job, I wandered around and helped anyone who could use an extra hand – mostly on maintenance projects.

As I became better acquainted with the crews, I was able to make a lot of trips with them and I learned a lot. On some trips, we were asked about tail wheel shear pins. I guess landing in makeshift grass fields had taken their toll.

I told Lt. Brown I had training as an aircraft machinist, and I could make the shear pins if we could get the materials and equipment. He wanted to know where we could get them. I had read in *Stars and Stripes* that the Army had cleared Frankfurt and told him that we should be able to find a repair depot in the area.

"Get a crew together and see what you can find," he said.

This surprised me. My first job assignment was for me, a private first class, to round up a crew and airplane to find what I needed to make shear pins. To my knowledge, no one questioned my request. I found out later that Grove Air Field, in England, had zero stock, and we had a couple of planes that needed them.

The Corps of Engineers was just finishing a steel mat runway when we arrived at Frankfurt, and approved our landing. We found an immense repair depot filled with equipment. The problem was finding something small enough for us to carry. We located a small lathe, tools, and aluminum bar stock, and brought them back with us to Istres.

I don't remember the names of the crew members or the name of the electrician who did the necessary wiring. We set up the little shop in a small shed behind the bombed-out hangar closest to the 311th Engineering Office.

Since I was so new to the 311th, I don't know of anyone except the crew who hauled the equipment who even knew about this small operation, but if anyone in Europe needed a shear pin, I gave them one or two. I have a picture that someone made showing me working with a lathe, and that's all I can offer as proof of this. Someone had to take the picture, and I would like to hear from anyone involved.

A few weeks later, I asked Lt. Brown if I could be a flight engineer. He said to make arrangements with the medic. The medic (wish I could remember his name) said the flight surgeon would arrive the next day and I could get in line.

But there was a problem. I had already been turned down as a Cadet because I was color blind. Sure enough, the medic handed me the color blind book, and I could only pick out one of the numbers.

The medic had an idea – using a yarn test instead. He pulled out the box of different colored balls of yarn and hid the ones I couldn't identify.

The next day, the first thing the surgeon asked for was the color blind book. The medic said he hadn't seen it since the surgeon's last visit and assumed he had taken it with him. The surgeon then asked for the yarn test, and I passed with flying colors, so to speak.

My next liquor ration went to the medic.

*S/Sgt. Korecerk and D.T. "Red" Hyden.*

*Red Hyden hard at work making much needed C-47 shear pins.*

*311th FS engineering building.*

# Chapter 4

# The Diaries

Personal diaries present an interesting window into the thoughts and minds of individuals in a certain period of time. Presented here are excerpts from the diaries of two men, both in the 311th Squadron, one an enlisted man, the other, an officer. The 311th is an interesting squadron, in that it started as a Ferrying Squadron, and by 1944 was functioning frequently as a transport squadron.

Richard J. Mollwitz served as a radio operator with the 311th Ferrying Squadron, from November 1943 to October 1945. "Molly" kept a daily journal of his time with the 311th, which provides great insight into the life of a young airman. Many men of the 27th ATG shared similar experiences.

There are many entries deleted in this work which were repetitive "easy days." This might sound as if these airmen had it pretty soft, but actually, the weather in England, Ireland, and Scotland often caused "no flying days," so they "goofed off." This resulted in boredom, which was often harder on morale than flying. Generally, barracks type living was pretty good for the 27th ATG.

There are many comments on drinking wine and beer. The men were young, and for the most part, handled it well. They did fly on occasion with "short sleep," and perhaps some hangovers, but it did not cause crack ups. There are also comments on seeing many movies. These were not in theaters, per se, but in mess halls, day rooms, etc.

The excerpts from the diary are reproduced with minimal editing. Names have been changed or deleted in some cases, where appropriate. The journal picks up in November of 1943, with Molly on board the Queen Mary bound for the ETO.

*Monday, November 1:* Up at around 6:15 and down to the galley for KP. I'm getting to smell like a regular coffee pot. The stuff is spilled all over my fatigues and has probably permeated my skin (sounds good, eh). They passed out $5, partial pay, to me at noon, and I also received a days supply of k-rations for use aboard the train. Most of the fellows will leave the boat sometime tomorrow, as we will pull in early in the morning. Our bunch has to stay aboard for another day and take care of the KP. Really was nice outside today, water was calm and blue as turquoise. I took a salt water bath and so to bed, as we have to be up at 4:30 for KP. Didn't get to sleep as our entire room was awake until about 1:00. A lot of horseplay, etc.

*Tuesday, November 2: 7th DAY AT SEA:* Felt like I had a hangover this morning, since I only had a few hours of sleep. Woke up at 4:15 with a bit of corny music over the PA system, and down to the galley once more. Up to the room for a bit of sleep at 9:30, and then down to work for the noon meal. At this time we were passing through the Fifth of Clyde and got a glimpse of the coast line of Scotland, our first sight of land in a week. By 1:00 our ship had anchored near the fishing city of Gour(?). The roadstead has quite a few ships in it, including some warships (aircraft carriers). Also saw a Short Sunderland flying boat. Went back to serve an evening meal at 3:30 and finally finished the day at 7:00. Seems as though our outfit will go to a replacement center, but nothing is definite yet. A few of the troops got off today (via ferry to the shore), and the rest, including us, will leave tomorrow.

*Wednesday, November 3:* Got up at 6:00 to work KP and then down again at noon. Served the last two sitting and was done for the day. Made some sandwiches, said "goodbye" to Rollie, and then to the room to pack up. So, at 5:00 we finally left the good ole' Queen Mary and got aboard a ferry which took us ashore. That's the first land my feet had touched for a week. We boarded an English train (six in a compartment), had some coffee and doughnuts courtesy of the Red Cross, and took off for our new camp. All of us got quite a kick out of the landscape, houses, and the kids who yelled and waved at the train. Our compartment played cards and chewed the fat till the wee hours. Got a few fitful hours of sleep, but we couldn't stretch out. One stop at 11:00 for more coffee.

*Thursday, November 4: LYDIA PARK:* Stopped at 8:00 this morning and got out of the train once more for tea and cookies. Started up once more and looked over the scenery, including a few bombed cities. Went through Bristol, and around 11:00 we ended up in Trowbridge. I was on baggage detail, and after unloading, I piled on the rear of the truck. We drove about 30 miles through a lot of little towns, around curving roads and picturesque waysides. After a long ride the truck pulled into one of the most dismal camps I have seen in a long time. Tin huts, mud, strict discipline, and a brand new camp (opened last Sunday) is what we're in. Sleeping on three boards raised off the ground and a straw "tick." Barracks are one story, cement floor, and the blackout is enforced at night. Don't think that we'll stay here very long, and all of us will get out as replacements. No squadron stuff.

*Friday, November 5:* Woke up about 7:00 and made the fire, as no one had kept it going (there's 12 men in our side of the barracks). Went over to eat breakfast and then back on the bunk for a short nap. Had to fall out for a barracks cleaning detail in the morning, and we swept out a couple of empty huts. Had another detail, shoveling coal in the afternoon, but I managed to get out of most of it. Finally got the hot water system in the latrine working, and I took my first shower in quite a while. It was a bit clumsy, as the hot water wasn't plentiful and it had a chain faucet release, yet it felt good. Heard of a movie over at the Post Theater (hardly the comforts of Topeka!), so I went over there during the evening and saw "Priorities on Parade." The day's weather was rumored to be an example of the best, but it certainly was foggy. There's planes flying over this place every day, and they aren't on training flights, either.

*Saturday, November 6:* Took it easy all day for a change. Got up around 7:15, washed, and just made it to chow hall. Was to be some sort of an inspection in the morning, so we got the place all cleaned up, and though it looked pretty good, no one came around. We loafed and played cards all day since there was nothing else to do. Really was a nice day, too, the first time I've seen the sun shine since I've been in Great Britain, Scotland included. Wrote a letter to the folks, but won't be able to mail it until tomorrow. Washed a few underclothes and then to letter writing again. Getting kind of used to this camp now, although I'd still rather be settled permanently. Looks as though we might be here for quite a while. There's also the chance of taking a daily five mile hike to look forward to.

*Sunday, November 7:* Rather a dull day, and my cold made it worse. Woke up at 5:30 to make the fire and then up again for chow. Some of the Catholic boys went into church on a convoy, but I read my Bible a bit. Incidentally, we had quite a display last time of searchlights and flares. My guess was that some town on the French coast was being bombed. 'Course, everyone had their own opinions.

Was rather disgusted most of the day 'cause I lost my pipe, the censor returned two of my letters, and my head felt pretty bad from the cold. Really wish I was out of this camp and working at some field. I'm getting kind of sick of replacement centers, being a casual, and just drifting around. I wanted to go overseas all right, but I didn't expect to be a replacement. Took in "That Uncertain Feeling" at the Post Theater in the afternoon.

*Wednesday, November 10:* Looks as though our inactivity is going to be ended, 'cause a supervised day is going to be put into effect. I had another "busy" day doing nothing. Paid 2 shillings (10 dollars) for seven packs of cigarettes, 2 bars of candy, one pack of gum, two packs of matches, and a pack of cookies, which was my first ration. The PX is supposed to open regularly now, which will help things a little. Had a couple of colonels come around on an inspection, too. Hope they noticed some of the conditions.

*Thursday, November 11:* Got a break for the first time today. At 10:00, Red, Wirth, and I went into Bath on a truck convoy. Took us till 12:45 to make the trip, and so we only spent two hours in the town. Was a heck of a lot of fun, though, and I hope to go to town again soon. Looked the place over pretty well, had my first glass of English beer, bought a few items, and had a good time. The people were pretty swell to us, and the girl in a confectioner's shop even gave me her ration point to buy some candy. The town itself has been bombed a good deal, although I didn't see much evidence of it. As usual, there were a few drunks in the crowd, although we only spent two hours in town.

Full moon out at night and beautifully clear. Went over to the theater and saw "Meet the Stewarts." Not too bad.

*311th radio operator Richard "Molly" Mollwitz at Maghaberry Northern Ireland, April, 1944.*

*Friday, November 12:* Really got something to eat at breakfast this morning, and then loafed around. Screwed off of the hike in the afternoon and decided to go into town at night with Snyder, Rick, and Fredsell. It was just like going AWOL, since we had to go across the field, sneak past the guards, etc. We hit a pub in the village of Purton and had a pretty good time drinking beer and talking to the English fellows. It was a nice clear night, so we didn't mind the walk of three miles or so. Got back to the camp about 11:00.

*Saturday, November 13:* Another day. Took in "Eyes in the Night" at the theater in the afternoon. Got some doughnuts and coffee at the Red Cross truck that comes around. Decided to go to town again at night even though it was dark as pitch. Stopped at the Angel Hotel again, but it was too crowded to stay there. Same two English fellows were back, and they took us to the Manor Arms and we had a room to ourselves complete with a fireplace and all. Quite a few more fellows came in, and we sang and drank beer till 10:00. Fredsell and I nearly got caught by a guard while coming through the fence, but he evidently was a "good Joe" and didn't stop us.

*Monday, November 15:* Days certainly are going fast. Took in "My Heart Belongs to Daddy" at the theater in the afternoon and then got my weekly rations from the PX for 3s, 6d. Passes for Swindon were to be given out for the first time tonight, and I intended going in with Rick and Snyder, but it seems that a few cases of mumps have occurred and the entire camp has been quarantined. That's kind of rough, since today they decided to start passes regularly. I'm rather broke, though, so it won't make much difference. Doesn't really seem like we're in a combat zone here, with nothing to do. Darn, but I certainly hope they send me to a field where there's some action soon.

*Tuesday, November 16:* Yeah, I thought it was too good to be true. I didn't like the inaction, so now we've got just the opposite. They moved both sides of our barracks out today and we are now in block 8, all in one room, in a bldg. that looks like it was designed to be a hospital. The new set-up involves guard duty, KP, calisthenics, drill, and hikes. The orderly room has made up a supervised day for us, and this time I imagine it will go into effect. Oh, for the blissful days of Topeka!

*Wednesday, November 17:* First day in the new barracks, and they woke us up at 5:45 (the ice had to be broken off me!). Didn't do anything till 7:30 chow time. After chow we policed the barracks, did a little close order drill, and then were supposed to have some sports. I washed my clothes instead. Took a hike in the afternoon to within a couple of miles of Swindon. Passed the Lydia Park searchlight battery, anti-aircraft gun emplacements, and the surrounding camp. Back to camp just in time for coffee and doughnuts from the Red Cross clubmobile. Had our first mail call in 24 days, and I picked up one letter. Hope that it keeps on rolling in now. Wore my "longies" to bed and was nice and warm all night.

*Thursday, November 18:* Saw a British training film on spies which was pretty good. Could have gone into Swindon at night, but only a shilling and six pence to my name. Picked up six letters in a late mail call and that made me feel pretty good.

*Saturday, November 20:* Up at 6:30 this morning, and the rest of the barracks were to stand an inspection, but instead we fell out for a shipping list. Over 200 fellows are to leave in the next day or so, including Red Ellis. Hate to see him leave without us 'cause he's a good boy. Went over to the guard house and pulled the third shift. My post is the entrance to the motor pool, checking the passes of the incoming trucks. Stood the 4-6 stretch so far and nearly froze my feet, although the rest of my body was warm. Some of the boys were paid tonight, but I think I'll wait til tomorrow. Got a bit rugged on the 10-12 shift, foggy and lonesome.

*Sunday, November 21:* Sweat out the relief on the 4-6 shift with more fog, etc. That guard duty is certainly a thankless job. Watched the crap game in the barracks awhile and then went on the final 10-12 shift. Was relieved to go over and get paid, and I received £8.4. Was going to screw off again, but decided differently and went back on guard to finish up.

*Monday, November 22:* Up at 6:30 or so and then to early chow. Usual dull morning with rain and fog. Got my PX rations and also bought part of Wirth's. Saw the USO camp show over at the post theater and it was really good. Had a couple of fairly nice looking American girls in it, too. Wrote a few letters at night and then hit the hay. If this life keeps up, I will have forgotten everything I know about radio in no time at all. Keep thinking about how nice Topeka was compared with this. Certainly no glamour over here, but I asked for it.

*Wednesday, November 24:* Damn, tomorrow is Thanksgiving and what do I do but pull guard duty. The other Cpls. got KP, but not me. More shipments are being made up every day, so I ought to get noticed pretty soon. The Red Cross clubmobile came around and I got my usual doughnuts. Saw "The Mayor of 44th Street" at the theater with Wirth and then to bed. That guard duty really makes me mad, 'cause I wanted to go to church tomorrow morning.

*Thursday, November 25:* My second Thanksgiving away from home and my first on foreign soil. Didn't get up till 7:30 and so I missed breakfast. Loafed around awhile and then decided to go to church despite guard duty. Went over to the old church with Snyder in a formation and had a nice service by the chaplain, conducted almost like ours at home. He must have been Lutheran, also. Got to the guardhouse at 11:30 and was assigned my same post, #7, on the second relief. Ate my Thanksgiving dinner with the guards, and it was a good meal despite the small amount of meat (turkey and pork). Learned that the rest of the complement of men on the base will ship to Trowbridge tomorrow. Stood the 2-4 shift and then over to the barracks to start packing. Really got soared by the OD on the 8-10 shift as I halted him and he said, "two soldiers going into town." I let him go on without further ado, and he chewed me royally, threatened to stick me in the guard house, etc. He came back a little later and I halted aim properly, so I think he let it go at that (I hope).

*Friday, November 26: TROWBRIDGE:* Stood the 2-4 shift and nearly froze my feet, reported for duty again at 7:15 and found that all the guards had been relieved, so I finished packing and helped clean the barracks. Got on the trucks about 10:00, and after a rather long, cold ride we arrived at this camp. It's even more dismal than the last one, although quite a bit larger. The roads are muddy as hell, the latrine divided into two bldgs for washing and the other for nature's visitations. Both look like they'll fall apart. The one good note is our 7 man hut. It's got GI cots, which isn't bad, and we have a locker to hang our clothes in. After a lot of fuss, we've got it looking pretty homey. Was also issued two more blankets, since I turned in my others.

*Saturday, November 27:* Got up this morning at 10:30, almost too late for noon chow (missed breakfast). Learned that some fellows had shipped out already last night. Decided to takeoff for town in the afternoon. The Sgt. in the barracks wanted to go with me. I got dressed, and at around 3:00 we went down the road into town. Really was a lot of fun in Trowbridge, 'cause there weren't many GIs in at that time. We bought a lot of things, visited a canteen, and then saw a show. Got out of the movie just in time to drink some beer as the pubs had opened. Met a really attractive blond WAAF in the George Hotel and was with her part of the evening. Went to a dance with her, but didn't go in 'cause I had my coat at the canteen and that's where I lost contact with her. She was at the pub again looking for me, but I didn't know it until later on. Pulled into camp about 11:00, despite losing our way in the black out.

*Wednesday, December 1:* Up in time for breakfast and then signed the payroll. Then in came a fellow who said I was wanted as a runner. I told him that I just got off of guard duty and he came back 3 different times, the last time with a direct written order. So I went up to see what it was about and I got a job as runner for Regimental HQ. They made me run, too, with messages for all over the base. Got through at 5:00 and then went into town with Kenimer and Wirth. Boy, we really beered it up, too. All of us were feeling pretty high, 'cause we must have had about 10 or 12 pints apiece. Had a good time, though, and pulled into camp at about 10:45 or so.

*Thursday, December 2:* Well, tomorrow will be a big day, 'cause I just found out that a number of us are shipping, including Rick and Snyder. Have to carry a full field pack, so we must have a pretty long trip ahead of us. Hope that this will be a permanent base, 'cause I'm rather tired of moving around.

*Friday, December 3:* Woke up at 5:00 and started to get ready for shipping. Time flew by pretty fast, and all of a sudden I had to grab all my things, draw my C rations, and get up to the circle. Then we waited around and finally got a truck ride to Trowbridge. From there we caught a train, which finally took us to London. Had a layover there, so we ate at the YMCA canteen in the station and then caught another train for Scotland. (My sight of London was limited to about a mile ride in a truck when we changed stations. Saw the barrage balloons overhead and a few bombed areas.) We were crowded, six men into a compartment, for the second ride, so I didn't get much sleep during the night. Passed through a lot more towns, but it was too dark to see anything. So far I'm still with Rick and Snyder, and rumors say we are going to Northern Ireland.

*Saturday, December 4: Maghaberry – Northern Ireland:* They got us out of our compartments at 6:00 this morning and found that we were in Stamare Harbor on the west coast of Scotland. Waited around quite awhile until we got organized, and then boarded a small packet "Princess Margaret" for Ireland. Had a nice ride, too, not more than two hours or so in length. Landed at Lerne Harbor and boarded another train for Belfast (nice looking town). GI trucks took us to another station, and we got our final train ride to this camp. From the looks of it, this will be a permanent set-up and on the all-right side. The camp is brand new, had a landing field, and I think I'll be able to go to work up on the line. Had a good supper, took a shower, and now to bed. We'll see what the morning will bring.

*Sunday, December 5:* Went over to a good breakfast for once and then took a long walk up the road to the field and hangars for an "interview." Lot of radio men around, so tomorrow they say we'll get organized. Pretty big flying field up there with all sorts of planes. Saw some -17s, a Spitfire, P-39, etc. Didn't do much the rest of the day, although the rumors are flying around about flying and stuff since we are now in the 311th Ferrying Squadron.

*Monday, December 6:* There's a Stirling assembly plant nearby, and we went through a Short Stirling and also a Wellington. Quite different from our planes.

*Sunday, December 12:* Up and at 'em! Worked on a P-39 most of the morning installing the crystals in a VHF. Was pretty interesting, too, since I never worked with that type of ship (fighter) before.

Had a squadron meeting at night over at the service club and met our new CO, Capt. Thomas. Learned a little bit about the squadron, and then had to listen to the articles of war. Hope to get in a little flying tomorrow since most of the fellows will be in school.

*Monday, December 13:* Roll call and then up on the line alone, 'cause Rick has an off day. The fellows got ready for the trip to school and finally left about noon by truck. I was assigned two planes to work on in the morning, but couldn't find them, so I let it go. In the afternoon there was hardly anyone up on the line. I went over to another bldg. and looked over a ground station that had been set up. Took off at 4:00 and back to the barracks.

*Wednesday, December 15:* Helped finish setting up the ground station today, although I didn't do too much work. The station works OK and will probably go into operation tomorrow. The 522 and command sets have to be set up, and then we'll be pretty well organized. Incidentally, Friis is a pretty good man. He and Rick are doing most of the work up there. Got a new man in our barracks, but I think he'll only be here for awhile.

*Friday, December 17:* Same old roll call and then to work. Helped Rick finish the mock-up of the command and liaison sets and then went down at 3:00 to be paid. Certainly was a miserable day, raining most of the time. Had a little Irish kid over at the barracks most of the night, and I think we're going to work up a deal with him for exchanging cigarettes for fresh eggs. Cadell gave him a haircut, and we had quite a time with him.

*Saturday, December 18:* Made out two money orders, $25 each for Mom and Dad, but won't be able to pick them up until tomorrow. Spent a good

*Molly at Maghaberry wearing an English made, enlisted, ETO jacket he referred to as the British version of the "Ike" jacket.*

day of loafing up on the line. It was another day of rain and wind and generally pretty poor weather. Bought some cheese and bread from devious places and intended having a feed, but postponed it awhile. Went to bed early, as I've got a damn cold. Didn't stay in though, 'cause the kid came back with eggs and we had a bit of a snack. Boiled eggs, bread, cheese, and "pop."

*Sunday, December 19:* Had our last roll call this morning – thank goodness. Put in my longest day of work – til 5:45, setting up the code table, transformer, and oscillator. Getting the place looking pretty good.

The kid brought in two live chickens for us, and what a panic they caused. No one wanted to kill them, so the kid finally strangled one, and Slim cut the head off the other. Snyder, Rick, and I went over to the all-girl show at the Service Club and then had a beer at the NCO. The barracks looked like a mess when we came back. Ate a couple of boiled eggs and a cheese sandwich and so to bed.

*Monday, December 20:* Finished wiring up the code table, and it works pretty good. The rest of the boys came back from school, and we certainly have a mess of fellows up there, no one doing anything, of course.

*Tuesday, December 21:* Up for chow and then a shower while I was down that way. Got dressed and went into town with Rick, Snyder, Fred, and Bill. Caught a ride into Belfast on a GI truck, which brought us in at noon. Visited quite a few pubs and drank a bit of wine and beer. Also did a lot of shopping – bought a map, diary for '44, and some fancy embroidered handkerchiefs (without ration stamps). Saw quite a bit of Belfast just by walking around. Caught the 9:35 train back – was drizzling, so that provided a nice gloomy end to the day.

*Wednesday, December 22:* Finished rewiring the code table today as the other "shorted out." The old set-up was no good since they brought in another type of oscillator. Even worked overtime when all of the other fellows had left. Hung up the wreaths we bought yesterday, on the two doors of the barracks, adding a touch of Christmas to the place.

*Thursday, December 23:* Spent most of the day up on the line by taking and sending code, trying to pick up my speed once more. Went out to the dispersal area in the noon to see what we could find in the new B-17s. Picked up a wrench, and then Rick and I helped the radio operator get set up as it was his first flight. Really pitiful how little he knew about it. Quite a bit of flying going on, but I haven't seemed to get on any flights.

*Friday, December 24:* Usual day with nothing much to do. Went to the Squadron party over at the Service Club at night with Rick and Snyder, and it was quite a rat race. I was never so disgusted in my life – especially since it was Christmas Eve. They didn't have enough beer, and the general run of women seemed pretty horny. I went home early – around 10:15, with a day of KP to look forward to tomorrow.

*Saturday, December 25:* Wasn't it Scrooge who said, "Merry Christmas – Bah! Humbug!"? This Merry Christmas morning I was awakened at 5:30 for KP, and by 6:00 had my hands in the pots and pans water at the officer's mess. Didn't work any too hard all day, but it was a holiday for the rest of the camp. Ate enough turkey and trimmings to stuff a horse, so that was one consolation. Also swiped a cup of egg nog – my Christmas drink.

*Sunday, December 26:* Had to be up on the line early, so I got up there around 8:15 and none of the others were there. Listened to a little pep talk by our new Communications Officer and then started setting up the VHF in the ground station. Finally got it finished at 5:00, and it's all set.

*Monday, December 27: CLUNTOE, Northern Ireland. (Special radio school):* Got all my things together this morning and finished packing my knapsack. Walked up to the line, and at 10:00 or so we piled into a truck (19 of us) and took off for school. Wasn't a bad ride, and we arrived at Cluntoe just in time for noon chow. They didn't have any notice of our coming, consequently – we had to get them on the ball – we checked out blankets and then went over to the barracks. Rick and I are in one along with 4 other fellows. This camp here is very similar to Maghaberry, stretched out and all. There's an air field on it, and we'll probably go to school some place near the line. It's muddy as all get out around here, no coal for the stove in this refrigerator we call a barracks, but I think I can last out for six days. They've got a nice Red Cross Service Club on the post, so I may spend quite a bit of time there.

*Tuesday, December 28:* Woke up at 6:30 and after my morning ablutions and chow we were taken down to a building near the line. So, in a very informal atmosphere, an intelligence officer gave us a lecture on security and a little history of Ireland, and that was followed by a class in aircraft recognition given by another officer. They gave us a little better than an hour off for lunch and then back again, finishing up on aircraft and starting in on surface vessels. We ended the day with a short exam, and I think I learned quite a bit. Both officers seemed to know what they were talking about, and the lectures proved to be very interesting.

*Wednesday, December 29:* Went up to the radio room this morning, and our instructors are almost all "25 mission" combat men, really a good bunch of Joes. Had two lectures during the day, one on MF/DF and one on HF/DF organization. They were a little confusing, but time will help to smooth that out. Code class was started in the afternoon with a tape-run oscillator (variable speed). I didn't do so hot, but they held a special one and a half hour class at night and I started to pick it up a little better. Most of these combat men are sweating out 90 days, and then their return to the States. Seems as though they're a bit on the nervous side, which would be natural after going through 25 combat missions.

*Thursday, December 30:* School again today, and we started with a couple more lectures on procedure and beacons. Went through an equipment lec-

*This photo in Molly's album was captioned "Heading for 'The Red X', Belfast, Northern Ireland."*

ture in the noon and looked over a really swell mock set-up. Most of the equipment had plexiglass cases so that you could see the entire "works" inside. It certainly would have made our mock up at Maghaberry look sick. Took code to finish up the afternoon. I passed 16 wpm on a code check, so that means I'll get by the course on that scare. Would kind of like to pass 20, though. Took a shower at night and then recopied my notes.

*Friday, December 31:* Went into the Harwell box trainers this morning on a simulated flight. It was darn good training, too, 'cause we had to tune up, ask for frequency checks, QDMs, fixes, change frequencies, etc. It took me about three hours to get through with my flight. Your highest possible score was 40, and I received 33, so I did fairly well.

Took code all afternoon, and the instructor passed me on 18 wpm, which was more or less of a gift. I think I could pass it again, though, therefore my conscience won't bother me.

Tonight is New Year's Eve, my second while in the army. It's quite a difference from last year's, too. All the boys in our barracks stayed in – didn't even inquire whether passes were available.

All the big shots say that the war with Germany will culminate in 1944. It doesn't seem to concern me very much any more, perhaps because there's still a war in the Pacific to take care of. Can't say that I care much for the ETO, so a change of climate might help some. Home would look pretty good right now, but I'm afraid that I won't see it for quite some time. With that pessimistic outlook on life, I leave 1943 and enter 1944.

**January 1944**

*January 1, Saturday:* First day of the new year and also the first in this diary. Got up in time for breakfast and then laid around most of the day as there wasn't any school. Had a pretty fair turkey dinner at noon, and then washed up some of my clothes. Spent the rest of the afternoon over at the Red Cross listening to short wave broadcasts from the U.S. I also played a little ping-pong. Took in "Johnny Come Lately" at the evening show, even though it was for the second time. I guess this was hardly a momentous day, considering it was the first of the new year, but then, who cares?

*Sunday 2:* Last day of school (I hope), and so we had a general review in the morning and then the final exam. I thought it was pretty easy and did OK. I am supposed to spend a little more time in the Harwell box trainer, but it didn't pan out, oh well. Later on, I learned that my total mark was 88%, third highest out of the 19 in our class.

*Monday 3: Back to Maghaberry, Northern Ireland:* Last day of school, and we had code practice in the morning. I passed 20 W.P.M., but it was more or less a gift of the instructor. Had a class on map reading and primary navigation in the afternoon which proved rather interesting. Took a little more code, and we were finally dismissed at 4:00. I "graduated" as a First Operator.

Got our clearance papers and left camp around 7:00 via bus. I rode in the cab and had a nice trip back. Maghaberry looked pretty darn good. Learned that my "B" bag had arrived – oh, happy days! Also received a pair of GI glasses which I had ordered back at Topeka. Lots of flying going on here, too – here I come!

*Thursday 6:* Nearly got a flight this morning as second operator with Ekalo, but the taxi ship was too crowded. At that rate I'll never get checked out. I sat around the ground station and copied call signs all day. Went up to the control tower for awhile and looked over their set-up, which is OK. Kinda wish something would happen up on that line, 'cause it's darn boring. You either fly or just sit around.

Doc came over at night and we had a little bull session. The card about the death of Sloboda set me to thinking quite a bit about him. Two new men in the barracks now which is rather crowded.

*Friday 7:* Went out to two B-17s while it was still dark and preflighted them. Spent most of the morning out there and then came in and worked on the mock-up of the command set. We've got a battery for power, but can't seem to get the thing working right. Took us all day, and we still didn't accomplish anything.

*Saturday 8:* Up at 5:15, and I was the first KP over at the officer's mess. I was supposed to work in the supply room, so I kept out of everybody's way the entire day and did as little work as possible. Cleaned up and restacked the shelves and that was about all. We finally got through at around 7:45, and my legs were pretty tired. Really was "browned off" when I got back to the barracks, 'cause I found out that Rick and Levin went on a flight down to England. If it hadn't been for KP I would have been on that ship. Good night, Diary!

*Tuesday 11:* Worked on the co-pilot's mic switch on a -17 all morning which was "snafued." Couldn't get a new button, so we put in a press-to-talk and left it at that. Turned carbine in today.

*Wednesday 12:* Yes, I was supposed to have this day off, but instead it was spent down at the hospital in taking a physical exam for flying status. It was a complete exam from head to toe. I passed it OK. I guess now, I think, that I can get on flying status.

*Thursday 13:* Raining again today for a change, so despite the fact that a lot of flights were scheduled, none went up. I loafed around all morning while the other fellows had code practice, and then goofed off. Turned in my shoes for repair.

*Friday 14:* Headed for town on the 9:10 train with Rick and spent the entire day in town. Picked up my watch from the repair shop, tried to get my pen fixed, and ended up buying a British pen. Wandered around the various shops, ate dinner at two different cafes, and then took in a movie, "The Life of Colonel Blimp," which was pretty fair. Had supper and then drank beer the rest of the evening. Found a nice pub with a private room, so it was a real pleasure to drink there.

*"Raunchy Radio Operators, 1944" – Al, Spot, Sandy, and Molly.*

Pulled into camp around 10:30 and learned that I have KP again tomorrow. Am I a basic (521)?

*Saturday 15:* Six days rest and here I am the "pride of the kitchen" again! This damn KP is really coming up often. Levin and I entered the portals of the mess hall around 6:00 and got a job in the dining room. We managed to keep the place clean and be busy at the same time, with the minimum amount of effort. At supper time they changed us over to pots and pans and we finished up the day on them. ( it was our hardest work, too!)

*Sunday 16:* Heads up! My first flight in the ETO, originally scheduled for Renfrew and then changed to Prestwick. Poor weather, plus the fact that Mike and I couldn't get a QDM, got us lost, and we stayed that way for an hour or so. Really was nip and tuck for a while, and might have cost us our lives since we were over the Atlantic and low on gas. The pilot finally found his way and we returned to Maghaberry.

Took off again in the afternoon on a short hop to Cluntoe and back, same ship and pilot. All in all I got in quite a bit of timing practice and also a bit of operating. Quite an eventful day and one I won't forget.

*Monday 17:* CQ woke us up at 5:30 and we had our monthly physical exam in the day room. Mike and I were supposed to make a return flight to Cluntoe, but it didn't go through. Consequently, I spent a very dull day. Intended working on the snafued equipment in #5887, and only made a half-hearted attempt at it since I wasn't in a working mood.

*Tuesday 18:* Found out today that a number of the boys are shipping to Prestwick, Scotland, tomorrow on DS. They'll be there quite awhile in a detachment which will still be connected with the 311th. Ekalo, Levin, Ryan, and Cowley will leave from our barracks. That means that Rick and I will probably get checked out as operators pretty soon.

*Friday 21:* Galarza and I were right on the beam this morning and preflighted a couple of -17's. I couldn't seem to latch on to a first operator, so no flight despite the fact that there were quite a few. Worked the ground station almost all day, which helped me to brush up on procedure and Q sigs. Saw a flight of about 20 C-47s land (hospital ships), and a bunch of ambulances came out to load them – 40 or better. Who said there weren't any casualties in this war?! They took the patients to England, and then I suppose they'll start for home. The war is over for them.

*Saturday 22:* At this rate I'll never get checked out. Once more I was assigned on a flight, this time with Sheppard on the taxi ship, and then stayed on the ground 'cause it was overloaded. So I stayed around the ground station all day and worked a few planes. Rick was supposed to go up, also, and his flight was canceled.

I'm getting kind of disgusted with this loafing. Once I'm checked out I'll be a little more satisfied.

*Tuesday 25:* More bad weather, rain and sleet. Went over to the ready room and listened to a British navigator give a lecture for the entire morning. Almost a review of the Cluntoe school, but still rather interesting.

Had to go down to the hospital in the afternoon for a gas mask-eye glass exam (I don't need any) and then up on the line for awhile. Sat around per usual and then down to the barracks. Chop-Chop came in from Warton at night on a C-87 and we had a bit of a bull session. He seems to have a good deal – I almost envy him.

*Thursday 27:* Well, today I got in a helluva lot of flying! Went over to Langford Lodge by truck and then went up with McLean. We took a ship down to Knetishall in north eastern England. Rough weather in the 1 3/4 hour ride down, and I got a bad case of air sickness – wasn't much help – just laid around.

We got down there about 12:45, ate at the combat crew mess, and then went aboard the taxi ship. It made one stop at a fighter base to pick up some pursuit pilots and then continued. Bucked a head wind all the way, so it took up about 4 hours to get back. I had a heck of a headache – missed supper and then laid down awhile to get rid of it. Up again at 8:00 – back to bed at 10:15.

*Friday 28:* Quite an epidemic of diarrhea in camp last night, but I missed out on it. On pass today so I did a few odd jobs around the barracks. Got cleaned up at noon, and Rick, Freddie, and I went into Lisburn on the train. Ate dinner, walked around a bit, and then caught a bus into Belfast. Bought a few handkerchiefs, ate again, and then took in a movie. It was the usual day of very little to do and a lot of time to do it in. Saw some darn nice looking waitresses in one restaurant, so I might look into the matter at a future date. Got back to camp around 10:30 and was greeted with a nice stack of mail.

*Saturday 29:* Back to work again, or is it work? Rick had his first flight alone and went over to Prestwick in a B-26. I spent the usual day of doing nothing. Sat around the ground station awhile and then took off.

Got kicked out of the ground station in the noon because they only wanted the regular men there. I went over to the waiting room, wrote a letter, and so back to the barracks at a little after three.

Saw the orders that made Friis acting Sgt. He deserves it. Hope that I get checked out soon, 'cause I'm anxious to see whether I can overcome that last case of air sickness.

*Sunday 30:* Watched a Spit and a -38 play around in the sky a bit (you can see I'm a busy lad!) and then took off once more.

*Monday 31:* Nearly got checked out this morning as Gulden and I were going over to Prestwick in Feb. However, it was a 321st ship and they stuck their operator on it. So once more I sat on the ground.

Got a swell package from home today. Including leather gloves and a box of candied fruit. Rick got back today, too. (General Doolittle on the base)

*"Rick" and Gulden – Oscar Richter and Eldon Gulden, Paris, 1944.*

**February 1944**

*Tuesday 1:* Took code all morning at the Link Trainer and then stayed down at lunch time for payroll. Back up on the line for awhile and helped put up some more guide wires on the antenna posts. Had to go back down for retreat at 4:00, and we marched to the HQ for the occasion.

*Wednesday 2:* Over to the code room in the morning and fooled around there till noon chow. Right back again afterwards and thus managed to waste away the day. Rick told me that he talked to the office staff and got me straightened out once more. They say that I'll be checked out this week – damn, I hope so. All I've been doing is sitting around, which isn't gratifying to my conscience. After all, I should earn the money the Army is paying me!

*Friday 4:* Rather desultory weather today, cold, windy, and intermittent flurries of snow. Rick got a flight in the morning, but I sat around per usual. Five operators were taken up on a local flight in the afternoon, including me. We were supposed to go to Londonderry and possibly be checked out en route. However, we no more than got in the air when the right wing gas cap loosened up and started to spill gas. Lt. Howard brought the ship down in a hurry and didn't take it up again. We were in the air about 10 minutes – quite a flight.

*Monday 7:* Well, today I finally got a break. They needed an operator pretty badly this morning, so I went over to Reimer and asked him if I could go. He said OK – I took the taxi to L3Q, picked up a ship, flew down to Deenthorpe. I was all on my own and can't say that I helped out the pilot very much. My QDMs were slightly tardy, but it was good experience. Alm was the pilot, so that meant I had an easy time of it. Caught the taxi ship back to Maghaberry and arrived at 7:00. Quite a day!

*Tuesday 8:* Turned in my Recon card this morning and was assigned another flight. Over to LLAD in a truck and took off, with Alm as pilot again. Accomplished a little more with the DF, although it didn't mean anything to the guy who flies the ship. I'll have to gain a little more confidence in myself first before I consider myself a decent operator. Heard Alm calling "Darky" for QDM, which didn't boost my "morale" any. Landed at Great Ashfield, didn't even stop for lunch, and caught the B-24 taxi ship back to Maghaberry, arriving at 5:00. Another busy day ended.

*Wednesday 9:* Lots of flights again, but I wasn't assigned any. Kind of tired and glad I didn't go up. Spent the day over in the code room writing letters and checking up on my list of call signs. Received a package from home with 24 candy bars, 14 rolls of Life Savers, and 15 packages of gum. Darn, but it was swell to get a box like that. I passed out a bar to each of the fellows in the hut and that still leaves some left for me.

*Thursday 10:* Only a few flights this morning, but I was told to stay around. Around 9:30, four more operators were needed, so we boarded a truck for LLAD. Had a couple of combat men (25 missions) for pilots, so we had a good trip. Landed at Molesworth for chow and the wind blew us off the runway. Didn't have much to do along the DF line, 'cause I had the wrong freq. Took off in the afternoon and "landed" at Podington, ten miles away. Rough pancake too, 'cause of the strong cross wind, off the runway into the mud. Caught the taxi ship back to NYZA.

*Friday 11:* Another busy day. Got up on the line and was assigned a flight. Took a taxi ship over to LLAD and took off around 11:00. My operating worked perfect, and I got QDMs from four different stations. Nice flying weather, so I had a darn good 2 1/2 hours. Didn't even have time for lunch again at Framlingham – just got in the taxi ship. Picked up a steak sandwich at Poddington and ate it en route. Just got there in time, 'cause a mission was coming in from "deep in the heart of." Heard they hit Frankfurt – can't say for sure. Got back around 6:00 – another bit of time in. Am on flying status as of yesterday.

*Sunday 13:* Had quite a lecture given to us this morning on the set up and future of our communications section. Got to understand a few things. A lot of flights were scheduled, but poor weather held them down. Just after lunch, around 2:00, a call came in for five operators. So I was in a bunch that flew over to LLAD in a taxi ship. Got all set to takeoff for Snetterton Heath and the flights were canceled (weather had closed in again). Back to Maghaberry by truck in time for evening chow.

*Monday 14:* Started out with bad weather today, but the call came through in the afternoon for operators and out we went. Took a taxi over to LLAD and then flew our ship over to Maghaberry since that was as far as weather permitted. Took off for noon chow and then was paged over the Tanoy as our ship was due to takeoff. Flew over to Warton and stayed there all night in the transient barracks.

Met Chop-Chop, so we went into a nearby town and drank a little beer. Went back to my steam-heated barracks and had a nice night's sleep.

*Tuesday 15:* Up in time for morning chow and then loafed around the rec hall waiting for our pilots. They didn't show up until after noon. We took off again and delivered our plane to Chelveston. We're supposed to stay there that night and then catch a train into London the next morning. Ate over at the combat mess, and then the loudspeaker announced that we were to call flight control. The taxi ship had come in, so we caught it and got as far as Warton again. Made a night landing there and stayed once more in the transient barracks.

*Wednesday 16:* Another good night sleep even though I have a bad cold. Down to operations, and the taxi ship took off and brought us into Maghaberry just before noon. Had time for chow and then they came down to the barracks and told me I was on flight. High-tailed it up to the line and was stuck on a bus for LLAD. The weather closed in again, and at the same time we ran off the taxi-ship. Finally got pulled out and took the plane over to Maghaberry.

*Thursday 17:* They came in for me this morning, but I got out of KP because of switching beds. Went up on the line and took my ship out as was expected, but only as far as Warton since the weather was poor further on. We stayed there again, and I went into Blackpool at night with Chop-Chop. Drank a little beer and was offered a chance to stay at a rooming house, but I declined. Caught a taxi back to camp and left Chop-Chop, who was a bit mad. Guess he was a little "eager."

*Friday 18:* Left Warton this morning and ran into some bad weather near Lichfield. Poor visibility and snow storms. I managed to be of a little help, and we landed at Ridgewell.

Caught the train into London, transferred to the subway, and then got a room at the Columbia Red Cross. Ate at a Maison and Lyons restaurant, saw a show, drank a little beer and so to bed. Was woke up at 1:15 by the ack-ack guns and looked out the window at my first air-raid. Heard the Jerry planes overhead – lots of excitement.

*Saturday 19:* Up at around 9:00 after a good night's sleep between clean white sheets. Had a big breakfast over at the restaurant and then went over to the Ferry Service. Rode out to Heston on a GI bus and passed by a few buses that were casualties of last night's raid. Caught the afternoon shuttle which stopped at Burtonwood, Warton, and then Langford. We're there just in time to get a flight back to Maghaberry and pulled in around 6:00.

Really is nice to sleep in my own bed tonight, but I'll probably be out on another flight come the morrow. "Rugged this ETO."

*Sunday 20:* Another day in this "rugged" ETO! Up on the line and tho the weather here was damn poor it was OK in England. Over to Langford in a truck and then on the go again. Lots of ships out so the stations were busy as hell. I had a pretty good day – flew with Lake who is an "all right Joe." Didn't have an engineer, really didn't need any. Landed at Horham, ate lunch, and then caught the -24 taxi ship back, flown by the 321st.

*Monday 21:* Started out on another flight this morning and delivered a ship to Burtonwood. Was supposed to pickup another ship there and continue on to England. However, one ship had left and the other developed command set trouble, which I couldn't seem to fix. Left the ship to sit there and caught a C-47 back to Maghaberry.

Pleasant situation awaited me cause I'm on KP tomorrow even tho it's my off day. Damn that makes me mad. To top it off, the official flying status list with my name on it came out today – "I've had it!"

*Tuesday 22:* CQ woke me up at 5:30, and I was over to EM's mess by 6:00. Was assigned to the kitchen and worked in there all day. Took a little time off to get my rations and went down to the barracks for about 15 minutes. Didn't "strain" myself all day – scrubbed the floors a bit and that's about all. Had to GI one dining room before we left at night, so we didn't get thru until 7:30.

*Thursday 24:* Up on the line and assigned to a flight for a change! Over to Langford on a taxi ship, and after the usual preliminaries we took off. Encountered a little fog near Harwarden and took another crack at it. Landed at Ridgewell, ate dinner there, and then made the trip back to Maghaberry in the 321st Lib. (After a number of stops). That certainly is a cold ship to ride in.

*Friday 25:* Didn't have a flight today, so Cioffi gave me the day off. Went back to the barracks, did a little washing, sewed an insignia on my blouse, and generally loafed around. Went over to the day room in the afternoon to write a letter, listened to the music for awhile, and then back to the barracks for a short nap. Mailed a package home and also picked up a pair of arctics at supply.

*Saturday 26:* Thought I wouldn't go up today, but more ships were assigned and so over to Langford in a C-47 taxi. It started to snow, therefore we were only cleared to Maghaberry and brought our ship there. Really had a heck of a snow storm all day, although it was fairly warm and it didn't stay on the ground.

*Sunday 27:* Had my same ship again today and we spent most of the morning cleaning the ice off of the wings. Ice on the runway kept us from taking off. After noon chow we took off and started to go to our destination. Was a little too thick just this side of Lichfield, so we turned back and sat down at Warton.

Had quite a few boys RON there – Rick and I went into "The Plough" and had a few beers. Quite a busy place. Back to the transient barracks, and so to bed.

*Monday 28:* Up in time for breakfast and then down to operations. The weather had cleared up, so off we went and had a pretty good ride all the way down. Had a helluva headache though – guess it must have been the beer from last night.

Landed at Horham and started "sweating out" the taxi ship. Watched an "operational" takeoff and return, just a milk run. The taxi ship didn't show up after all our waiting, so we're going to catch the shuttle out of London tomorrow (if we get there). Our pilot and co-pilot kind of left us on our own, so we got ourselves a bunk and hope to get a train tomorrow. I'm not going to worry about getting there on time, though.

*Tuesday 29:* Woke up at 7:00 and hurried around to catch a 7:30 truck to Diss. Didn't eat breakfast, but caught our train all right and at Ipswich, changed to the dining car where we ate breakfast. Met an elderly couple there who offered to show us a bit of London, so we accepted. He hired a cab and showed us Whitehall, Big Ben, changing of the guard at Buckingham Palace, Piccadilly, St. Paul's, Westminster Abbey, and then dropped us at Audley St. The afternoon shuttle was full, so we got a room over at the Victory Red Cross. Spent the day in walking around, seeing a show and dodging MPs. Back to the Red Cross for a shower and so to bed, as we have to be up early tomorrow.

**March 1944**

*Wednesday 1:* Jerry was over in light force last night, but hardly enough to disturb our sleep. We're awakened at 6:00, went down to the snack bar for toast and coffee, and then walked over to the ATG office. Had the usual monotonous ride to the shuttle, although there were two brigadiers along. Got a truck ride out of Langford to Maghaberry, just in time for noon chow.

Today was supposedly my day off, so Cioffi gave me the rest of the afternoon. Didn't feel any too sharp – took a shower and laid down for awhile. Went to the show at the service club at night – "China Girl" – and then to bed. Snowing outside again and rather cold.

*Friday 3:* Out again on a flight – my first one for March. Originally scheduled to go to Thurliegh, but we changed to Framlingham. Took off in a bit of a snowstorm, but had good visibility over England and didn't have to work hardly at all. Started sweating out the taxi ship along with another crew, but it never showed up. So our pilot hunted up a place to sleep for us and we went down to the barracks in which there were only two fellows – the rest had been shot down. The bed I slept in was still made – hadn't been touched since the fellow had slept in it. Rather a morbid and ghoulish thought. One of the boys was awakened at 3:00 in the morning for another mission.

*Saturday 4:* Woke up around 8:00 – just in time to catch morning chow. Helped clean up the barracks a bit, and then loafed around awaiting a call from our pilot. Picked up a few rations from PX (gratis of card) and then intended going to the show, but a taxi ship was due to come in. We hurried up to flight control and met four more of our crews there who had just brought ships in. When the C-47 taxi came in, it was filled up in no time at all, and a number of us were left behind, including Spot, Rick, and myself. Spat and I went back to our original barracks and then met Rick and Sierak at evening chow. Took in the show and then over to "Ye Ol' Bitching Post" for a bit of beer drinking – so to bed.

*Sunday 5:* Well, once more "I've had it," and on such a beautiful day. We ambled up to the control tower around 11:00 and were told to eat chow and come back at 1:00. So, what happens but a C-47 comes in at 12:30, picks everyone else up and takes off without us. We were just walking up the road to FC when we saw the ship clear the runway. That left us rather doubtful as to what to do, so we stuck a putt-putt on an old ship, and called into Maghaberry for orders. "Wait for the taxi" was our only reply. Stuck around the tower all afternoon and then went down to Rick's barracks to sleep as they expected new crews in our old hut. Have to wait and see what 'morrow brings.

*Monday 6:* Just waited around the control tower all day, but still no taxi ship. Called into B3M and received the same answer as yesterday. Watched the ships return from the raid on Berlin and then went down to find a place to sleep once more. Stuck our stuff in Frank's barracks again, had a few beers, and when we came back, a new crew had moved into the hut. So we had to find a new bed, and the 1st Sgt. stuck us in a vacated hut where the crews had gone to the "flack home." So to bed for another night at Framlingham.

*Tuesday 7:* As usual, we got up for breakfast and then went up to the control tower for a change. Down for noon chow and on the way back we saw a silver ship landing, which proved to be for us. The ship took us to Cheddington, where we switched to an old crate. It, in turn, stopped at Glatton and Deenthorpe. No key on the thing, so I fooled around getting QDMs by using a hand mike. Landed at around 7:00, and it certainly felt good to get back to Maghaberry once more. Learned that a B-26 had cracked up here a few days ago, and the dead included an engineer I knew.

*Saturday 11:* Assigned to the same pilot and ship as yesterday, but doubtful weather kept us from taking off for awhile. Encountered quite a thick fog over the Irish Sea, started to go over it, and then flew underneath. All the stations were busy, so my DF was any too frequent.

Landed at Glatton at noon and didn't have much to eat for noon chow. Watched a B-29 land there, and it certainly is a beautiful ship. Smooth contours, lotta guns. We're picked up by a C-47 and didn't get to Maghaberry till dark after a 3 hour ride. I had a helluva headache, so I hit the sack early and got a good night's sleep.

*Monday 13:* Woke up at 6:00 by "reveille" over the Tanoy system and then outside for roll call – "shades of basic training!"

Very few flights today, so I just loafed around. Watched a couple of the card games and then back to the barracks early. Went over to the day room to write letters again at night, and got a few more finished. In due time I ought to be caught up once more. Lots of rumors flying around about the sqdn. moving or possibly just the flying crews. My personal opinion is that we'll end up in India. How about that?

*Thursday 16:* Out on flight today, although we didn't get started till noon as LLAD was closed in with fog. Took off at 12 sharp and had a nice trip down to Thorpe Abbots. The visibility wasn't any too good, but none of the stations were busy and I had an easy time of operating. Stuck Rydzynki's name on the form as he needed the time.

Landed around 2:30, ate dinner, waited until the mission returned, and then started the return trip in a -17 taxi ship. Beautiful flying weather all the way back – really a swell day.

No coal again, so the hut is like an ice-box. Guess I'll have to get in my bunk again.

*Sunday 19:* No reveille this morning – didn't you know? Sunday is a day of rest! Up on the line and assigned a flight with Lt. Davis. Went off the taxi strip into the mud at LLAD, so we got a late start. Made it in good time down to Thorpe Abbots. Missed chow 'cause the taxi ship was there already. After a couple of stops, we were dropped off at Chelveston. We're supposed to take an old -17G over to Burtonwood, but it didn't have decent brakes. Decided to RON here along with another crew of ours whose ship had the same trouble. So I ate chow, played a little ping-pong over at the Aero Club waiting for word from my pilot, and then took off on my own to the same hut Briesacher was in. A mattress cover, four timely blankets, and a good fire. (Yawn)

*Monday 20:* Had a good night's sleep, but was awakened early. Over to the combat mess for a pick-up to the line with Briesacher and Nick and watched the mission takeoff. Our ship was taxied out and still had the brake trouble, so we let it sit. Finally took off around 11:30. Landed at Burtonwood and took off again immediately in a C-47 bound for LLAD. Ate chow there and then got a truck ride back to dear ol' Maghaberry.

*Tuesday 21:* Ho-hum – roll call, breakfast, and up on the line by 7:30. Quite a few flights again, but I didn't care about going up as I had flown yesterday. Spent a rather boring day sitting around the ready room. A couple of more flights in the afternoon and Lt. Reimer did a little "chewing" cause there weren't more volunteers to take them! Made us police up the area and clean up the place. Temperamental – tsk, tsk.

*Wednesday 22:* Started out early this morning since the buses aren't running anymore and I had to walk up on the line. Assigned a flight down to Poddington. Had a little engine and XMTR trouble, so we didn't takeoff from Langford til afternoon chow.

Flew at around 5,000 ft., really beautiful up there. Smooth riding, good reception on your receiver, and you avoid the bad weather. Had a perfect trip and arrived just in time to be picked up by a C-47. Back at Maghaberry a little after 6, we saw the wreckage of an airplane that cracked up on the field. Killed the pilot, a 321st man, and burnt the ship up completely. That's the first real aftermath of a crack up that I've seen, and it isn't a pleasant sight.

*Thursday 23:* Walked up on the line once more and picked up my flimsy for another flight. Over to Langford and had a pretty good flight down to Ridgewell. The stations were rather busy, but I managed to get a couple of "QDMs." Ate down there, and then got on the C-47 taxi. Stopped at Kimbolton, Poddington, and so to Maghaberry. Flew rather high, too, quite a contrast to the hedge hopping of yesterday's taxi ride.

*Friday 24:* Caught a 7:15 truck up to the line and up on flight once more. Went down to Rattlesden this time, with Lt. Davis again. Had a good trip, as the stations I worked weren't very busy. The C-47 was waiting for us, so we ate and took off again. Made three more stops and got back to B3M at 5:30. Beautiful spring day here. I borrowed a bike, and Taylor and I went out for a quick ride. Finally ended up in Ballanderry, where I saw Rudy Einwald.

*Sunday 26:* Out on flight once more just for a change. Beautiful day, so I didn't have to work very hard. Landed at Deopham Green and ate chow there. The C-47 picked us up and we went over to Sculthope. Got another ship there which was flown to Langford Lodge. Caught a ride in a weapons carrier to this base, and so the end of another day. Getting to be quite a routine, this flying stuff, and at times almost monotonous.

*Monday 27:* Had to listen to a sex lecture and reading of the articles of war at 6:30 over at the service club, and then we had a little bitch session about squadron affairs. Didn't get out until nearly 9:00, so that spoiled the entire evening.

*Wednesday 29:* Was assigned a -17 today, but changed with another operator and was to take a B-24 instead. Flew over to Warton in the C-47 and found out that the weather was bad and so we RONed there.

Went into Blackpool at night, saw a show, ate dinner, and then started to drink a little beer. Met a couple of girls, but there were three fellows, so we decided to leave them – I walked home with one, and after a little romancing, I missed my train. Had to take a taxi back to Warton, costing me 35 shillings. Once a fool, always a fool! Even had to walk a mile besides. Got to bed around 2:00.

*Thursday 30:* Up early this morning, turned my blankets in, ate chow, etc. and then up on the line. Didn't waste any time, so we went right to our ship. So it was my first crack at operating on a B-24 in the ETO. Awful cramped quarters and all, and I only worked two stations. Rather busy, so I just enjoyed the ride. Hit 240 mph at one time.

Ate lunch down there and then were picked up by the C-47 taxi. Finally got back to Maghaberry at 7:15. Had some good letters waiting for me which put me in high spirits.

**April 1944**

*Saturday 1:* Had a big rush job just before noon today and 20 operators were needed. We went down to early chow and were back at 12:15. Two truck loads went over to Langford, and they were pretty busy with all the ships taking off. We circled awhile, checking #1 engine, and then hit the road. Fair trip down to Great Ashfield, poor weather, so we flew around 8,000. Were picked up immediately by the -17 taxi and made it back to B3M in record time, approximately 1 1/2 hours. Learned I am on KP tomorrow, which is a pleasant thought to look forward to.

*Sunday 2:* Cioffi (CQ) shined a flashlight in my face this morning at 4:00, and with a cheerful, "yes, I know," I started my day of KP. Over to the "sweat shop" and got the job of peeling spuds with Gorecki. We must have used up ten sacks, and thought we'd get off early. However, I learned that I'm one of 5 crews on DS to Langford and will probably ship out tomorrow, so I screwed off around 6:15. The mess sergeant didn't like it too well, though. No one seems to know much about this shipping deal, so I'll have to wait until tomorrow. My off day – I've had it!

*Monday 3:* Stayed in bed and then ate a late breakfast. Got half-way packed and then learned I wasn't to ship today (at least according to the first sergeant). So I went into Belfast with Chappie, it being my off day. We did a heck of a lot of walking, saw and saw, and drank a few beers.

Saw a lot of Belfast, but the town didn't hold our interest very long and we caught an early train back to camp. Bad weather has held up the deliveries lately, so I haven't been missing out on any flying.

*Tuesday 4:* Poor weather again today so, although I was given a ship in the morning, none went up. Sat around the mechanics room all day and wrote letters. Along about 3:30 the weather cleared up and two of us were sent over for a possible flight. Spot "had it," so I went down to get cleaned up for the Sqdn. party.

We walked over to the Service Club early and started imbibing the brew. It was quite a drunken brawl, but everyone seemed to have a good time. I met a tall blonde, but didn't make a move. Was very "gallant," and walked a girl halfway home around 1:00.

*Thursday 6:* Weather cleared up today, and the radio operators' vacation was over. Twenty-eight ships were delivered, and I had a good pilot who didn't need any work done. Waited around at Ridgewell along with 10 other crews till a C-47 finally picked us up at 6:30. (Had ice cream for supper there, too). The ride back brought us into Ireland at 9:00.

Had an air raid alert tonight, as did Belfast. Might have been practice or just a scare. Got a package from home today with my garrison cap, wings, magazines, and candy bars. Darn nice box!

*Sunday 9:* Happy Easter! Was supposed to take a ship from this base, but it was postponed until the afternoon because of bad weather. Went down to the Protestant services at the Service Club at 11:15, although they were rather unimpressive since we didn't have any hymnals or an organist.

My pilot had me paged over the Tanoy at lunch time, and I left my dessert in order to get up to the tower. Delivered our ship to Molesworth, and the C-47 picked us up after a little wait. We got back here at 8:00 or so, and after a pick-up meal, took a shower – and then time to hit the hay.

*Monday 10:* Another slow morning with little action. I didn't have a hop assigned – just loafed. In the afternoon I went down to the hangar and helped Irwin strip the radio equipment from a P-38 that's being junked. Really a lot of work to get at the stuff, and we didn't get through till 4:30. I drove a jeep down to pick up the parts and took off for supper.

*Tuesday 11:* Stayed in bed till about 10:00 sleeping off the effects of last night's ale. Stayed around camp all day even though I was on pass. Washed my OD pants and pressed them, plus burning a hole in my blanket. Kind of wasted the day, but I didn't have any clothes to wear to town anyway.

*Wednesday 12:* Lot of talk going around about the invasion, but nothing concrete. Rick spoke of seeing a 500 truck troop convoy on the highway. The "Fighting 311th" will probably stay here, though!

*Thursday 13:* Lot of ships went up again today and the entire outfit was busy. Had a "smashing" trip down to Bury St. Edmunds. We buzzed England for about a half hour, the trees were higher than us at one time. Saw three girls on a lane, so Lewis made a 180° and came down in a swipe at them. Just like a roller coaster ride, and I got quite a kick out of it. Didn't have to do much DF work.

Sweated out a C-47 taxi which stopped at Wattisham, Honington, and then Burtonwood. Ate supper there, then dropped a civilian at LLAD, and so back here at 8:30. Another day finished.

*Friday 14:* Started out to be a slow day again, and I didn't do much all morning. I had just settled down to an afternoon of letter writing, when in comes a request for three operators. I took Galarza with me and we had a pretty fair trip. Good weather in the Midlands, and we landed around supper time. Had a -17 taxi waiting for us, and so back we went, arriving here at 9:00. Had chow, took a shower, and then hit the sack. Really tired and wasn't in bed till 11:00 or so.

*Saturday 15:* Sat around for awhile this morning and got grabbed for a detail over at base HQ – cleaning up the place. Went back up to the line at noon and didn't have long to wait before I was assigned a flight over to Nutts Corner, and we took a -24 out of there over to Warton. Once again a -17 taxi was waiting for us and back we came. Left my log book in a ship over there, so I'll have to try and get it back.

*Monday 17:* Got an early start out of Warton this morning and I had "receiver" troubles. The weather was poor again and we stooged around till we finally hit Deenthorpe. Landed, and because of the receiver, I didn't know whether a taxi would come for us or not. Tried calling B3M from on the ground, but didn't have any luck. Couldn't go into London because we didn't have decent clothes. Met Steve Poklemba (Topeka) in the Red Cross, and we had quite a bull session about old times and stuff. RONed at DIT and slept in a combat crew barracks.

*Tuesday 18:* Up in time for breakfast and spent the morning at the Aero Club. Went up to the tower at noon, and we managed to get a ride from a C-47 which took us into Burtonwood. Couldn't seem to find a ship going to Ireland, so we stayed at BAD for the night.

Slept down at Bruche hall in a steam heated two man room – pretty good deal. Wanted to go into nearby Warrington for awhile, but it was too late, plus a little matter of no ODs to wear.

*Wednesday 19:* McMahan (my pilot) asked me if I was "eager" 'cause he found another delivery to make and our co-pilot had decided to sweat out a ride back to Ireland. So we took off at noon with myself as co-pilot and Weaver as RO. I didn't help out any too much but learned a heck of a lot. We flew the beacons all the way down to Deopham Green. I got in about twenty minutes of stick time – how about that?

Got picked up by the 310th taxi and made it into Warton again. RONed there – slept in McKenzie's barracks. (no more Nissen hut!)

*Thursday 20:* Intended catching the shuttle out of here this morning, but our pilot found a UC-64 that was to be delivered to Maghaberry and we made the trip in that. Flew up the coast to Scotland and crossed to Ireland over a narrow strip of water. Flew over a 50 ship convoy plus two aircraft carriers (Seafire aircraft – the RNAS version of the Spitfire). Pulled into this place at noon after a rough ride.

Learned that the detachment was over at LLAD and I'm in it, so I started to pack up.

*Friday 21:* Ripped up my bed, packed my bags, and then went up on the line to see about my orders. Learned that the deal has been canceled once more, so I sat around the entire day.

Unpacked my bags once more (the second time this month) and flubbed my dub the rest of the day. Took in the early evening show with the boys and then over to the Red Cross to fry a couple of eggs. Another day – another $3(?).

*Saturday 22:* Was assigned a -24 this morning and then had it taken away from me. They still think something might come of this LLAD deal. I loafed around all day and then around 4:00 a call came in for a couple of operators. I asked for one of them and we took it off from B3M.

Got down to Bury St. Edmunds pretty late, and so our crew and two others RONed there. Watched the mission land after dark and while in bed, heard the sirens going 'cause of Jerry intruders. – Nice clean hut, although those Limey blankets are a little rough.

*Sunday 23:* Didn't get up until 9:30, washed up, and then wandered over to the tower. Sat around and sat down to noon chow. Called in the B3M on the ground, and a C-47 picked us up a little later. Made a stop at Warton and finally arrived here at 6:00.

Had a few beers over at the new bar they set up at the Service Club, and after a shower I felt all-right with the world once more. All the boys went to the show, but I stayed in, writing letters.

*Monday 24:* Nothing doing in the way of planes this morning, so I spent a day of "puttering." Worked on my plexiglass heart, which absorbed a lot of time. Also knocked apart a box and am going to have the carpenter build me a foot locker (I hope).

*Tuesday 25:* The KP kid had his opportunity again today, and I worked over at the officer's mess. Got in quite a bit of "flying time" on the clipper, too. Wasn't such a rugged day, though, 'cause I was relieved at 7:00 by the night KPs. Shot the breeze with some of the Irish girls working there, but most of them are short on both looks and intelligence.

The latest news has it that the 311th will move over to LLAD tomorrow, lock, stock, and barrel. This will make the third time I packed in two weeks – hope something comes of it.

*Wednesday 26:* Spent just about my busiest day in the Army today. Took a -24 over to Warton in the morning, then transferred it over to Burtonwood in the afternoon. Got a ride back to Warton in a -17 around 7:00 and missed supper. (Ate K-rations while going over) Took another -24 out of Warton over to Burtonwood – acting as flight engineer – RO (with the flight engineer as co-pilot.)

We had a -17 to deliver to LLAD, but my pilot took it and a couple of other crews to B3M. I let another fellow operate all the way back – Here it is, nearly 12, and I haven't washed up yet. Certainly was a busy day for the 311th "Limited."

*Friday 28:* Off again for another full day. Delivered our ship and after lunch, we took another ship back to Langford with me as co-pilot. Didn't fly the ship at all, but was more or less a passenger. We were taxiing over at LLAD and I put the brakes on before the ship had stopped and nearly nosed it over: Got hell from my pilot, too, but no harm done.

*Sunday 30:* On Sqdn detail today so up to the line and the utilities office. No one showed around to take charge of us until 10:00. Consequently, I got my foot locker from Ed and took it up to the shop to be painted. Delivered one truckload of coal during the morning and that constituted my day's work.

**May 1944**

*Monday 1:* Nothing much doing in the morning, so I fooled around in the maintenance room, painted my foot locker and all. The Tanoy announced that we were to be up on the line early after noon chow, and so eleven crews were sent down to Nuthampstead. Only five crews got ships, however, and I was one of them. Flew all the way across England, the Irish Sea, and Ireland about 50 ft. off the ground. Strictly a buzz job.

*Tuesday 2:* Another day and this time I made a trip down to Deopham Green. My pilot was flying a buncher beacon, and consequently told me that my QDMs from Watton were coming from Germany. I challenged the station, proving that they were OK. He got out over the channel a bit, but the visibility was good and we weren't lost. He then flew in on my QDMs and found out later that the beacons had been off. (Snafu)

Caught a C-47 over to Bassingbourne where we were to pick up another ship, but weather prevented getting any further and we RONed there. Slept in a Nissen hut with a couple of other crews. Took in the post theater and then to bed.

*Wednesday 3:* Missed breakfast and then hung around the tower waiting for our pilot. Went out to our ship, ran it up, and then went to noon chow. Got back just in time to get in the ship as we were all set out to go. Got a ride from Burtonwood over to Warton in a B-26, and then down to Valley in a C-47. Took a ship out of Valley to LLAD and then got a -17 ride back to B3M. The taxi ran off the runway here and pranged the ship pretty good. We almost "had it." Found out that I made "buck sgt." as of the 1st of May.

*Saturday 6:* Started out from Maghaberry this morning as our ship was there. Went down to Staverston, which is a RAF field, and let off a passenger. Australians swarmed all over the ship as it was the first -17 they had ever seen. Got quite a kick out of them and their remarks about our "smashing kite."

We were taken over to Nutts Corner again and took another ship out of there to LLAD. I flubbed around the entire day as a passenger 'cause the pilot did the navigation. Came back to Maghaberry only to learn that we will leave for Langford on Monday.

*Sunday 7:* "And on the Sabbath He rested." Joe came in with the usual stack of flimsies this morning and out we went once more. I got a good pilot, plus good weather, and therefore enjoyed the ride. Ate at Poddington and again rode over to NH in the taxi. Watched their first operational come in (3x) and then waited around while they serviced our ship. "Sich a deel."

Finally took off (as "passenger") again and got into Langford around 7:30. Everything was closed up, but we "chartered" a command car and made a fast trip over to Maghaberry. Had the rest of my eggs fried at the Red X and then started to pack up.

*Monday 8: LANGFORD LODGE, Northern Ireland:* Finished packing up this morning and went up on the line around 7:30. Was given a flimsy and told to report over to LLAD and that the shipping of my bags would be taken care of. Sat around operations a while, looked over hangar 8, and then moseyed over to site 3 just in time to help unload the bags and get myself a good bunk. (inner spring mattress!)

Worked on various details in the afternoon and got to look over the place. Really a swell set-up with steam-heated barracks (all radio together), nice showers – and oh, those soft mattresses! Darned glad I moved over to the base, but I'm not sure how long we'll be here. -India-

*Tuesday 9:* Breakfast in the new mess hall this morning and then we sat around the barracks most of the morning. It was raining pretty hard when a call came in for radio ops and out we went. Had a taxi ride down to Halesworth and took a -24 out of there to Warton. We were eager, so we got another ship going back to the same place.

Started out rather late and RONed at Old Buckingham along with some other crews. Had late chow, checked out some blankets, and got to bed around 1:00. Quite a busy day.

*Wednesday 10:* Up at 7:00 and over to combat mess for hot cakes. Walked up to the tower, got a jeep ride for some verification tables, and off we went for Halesworth with the other crews as passengers.

Picked up more ships there, and I had radio troubles again. Pulled into Warton around 1:30, and decided to catch the 321st taxi back to LLAD. Wanted to get a hair-cut, but it was too late. Lot of things going on around here such as heavy on the KP, busting a couple of fellows, etc. Looks like it might be rough for awhile, but then, this is only a "POE!"

*Thursday 11:* Managed to dodge a flight all day 'cause I had a bit of a cold, and besides, I'm 20 years old today. Started to write letters in the afternoon and was too tired, so I adjourned to the sack for a cat nap. Just got back from evening chow and I was given a flight.

So I made an uneventful trip down to Grafton Underwood. Another crew was with us, so all of us decided to go into Kettering. Walked half-way and then got a ride from a civilian. By the time we got in, it was 11:00 and all the places were closed up. Finally managed to get a bed at the Red Cross, and I stuck my 6 ft into a 5 1/2 ft bed.

*Saturday 13:* Started out with a -24 ride from Nutts to Warton in the morning, and then took another -24 out of there without even stopping for noon chow. My bunch consisted of K-rations "palatable but hardly sustaining." Caught a taxi to Burtonwood and had supper there. Delivered our third Lib of the day to North Pickenham and landed in a rain storm and fog. Almost decided to take another ship out of there, but waited for the taxi instead. Took off around 9:30 and finally made a night landing at Maghaberry at 12:30 (my first night landing). A weapons carrier took us over to Langford, and we go to bed at 3:00.

*Sunday 14:* Didn't get up till around noon and managed to keep out of harm's way the entire day, so I didn't get a flight. The afternoon passed quickly, and after a shower I took in the show at Projma Hall with the boys. Darn nice theater there. (It was built for the LOC civilians) The more I see of this camp, the better I like it. Only hope we stay here long enough to really enjoy things. The bunch of fellows in the barracks are OK, and we have a barrel of fun. Heard a few rumors about ships going back to the states, and also a taxi ship to Iceland. Both sound good, but ...

*Wednesday 17:* Received a Parker pencil from home in a pkg. – walked down to site #4 for evening chow. Wrote letters all evening and then went over for a shower. Had a bit of a bull session with the fellows – Gabby says the invasion will be on the 21st, 3:30 in the morning?

*Friday 19:* A lot of ships out again today. I flew with Garrard and acted as taxi for two crews, after which we delivered our ride. Picked up an old ship down there and took it back to Burtonwood. Had a pretty good time with my pilot as he's a good Joe.

Arrived back here on a C-47 around 8:30, ate chow, and after a nice shower I think I'll go to bed. Rather a long day – logged five hours. I'm kind of tired and would just as soon loaf around tomorrow. Wonder how many ships have to be moved?

*LLAD July, 1944 – First row: Andrew Garabedian, Everett Sheppard, Harry Weinshank. Second row: Dick Mollwitz, Joe Cioffi. Back row: Al Bak.*

*Saturday 20:* Took in early chow and also the early show "Government Girl" with the fellows. Spot and I played a few games of ping-pong at the pilot's ready room after the show and split even – three apiece. Nothing much else doing, so cleaned up a little around my bunk for tomorrow's "big" inspection.

*Sunday 21:* Didn't go up in the morning, so back to the barracks to clean up a bit. The barracks looked pretty good, although "I.G." found faults. Took a taxi ride down to Valley in the afternoon and then had a short trip in a Lib out of Valley to Warton. We're supposed to go back to LLAD, but my pilot had to deliver another Lib and out we went.

We were picked up again, but by the -17 taxi and started back. It was pretty late, 12:15 to be exact, when we landed at Nutts Corner. A couple of weapons carriers took us back to base and we ate our "supper" at that time (chicken at that – I never had it so good!)

*Monday 22:* Slept all morning and got up in time for noon chow. No more than got back to the barracks when Joe came in and got some fellows for flights, including myself. Just a routine Fort delivery, but once again we got a late start for the return trip and the taxi didn't land til around ten. Course, almost all the crews came in late, so we couldn't bitch.

*"Gabby" – Andrew Garabedian at LLAD.*

*Wednesday 24:* Had a beautiful flight today as I sat up in the nose during the entire trip. Flew down to Oxford in southern England where we buzzed a nurse's camp a couple of times and then delivered the ship. Nice weather all the way.

Ate noon chow and then a C-47 picked us up and we got back around 5:00. Had a bit of a bull session with Spot during the evening and then put him to bed as he was a bit "unstable." The rumor factory is still turning out it's products, ranging from participating in the invasion to the carrying of gas masks and side arms in flight. Something better break soon.

*Thursday 25:* Gabby and I spent the afternoon (with Joe's permission) washing our clothes in 100 octane. I went over to the maintenance shop in evening, pressed my shirts and pants, and so I'm all set to go to town tomorrow, if I should decide so.

*Friday 26:* My off day, and after the due preparations I caught a bus into "Belshaft," along with Mutone. We did a little shopping plus quite a bit of walking. Took in a pretty good show and then a fair piece of steak for supper. We started to make the rounds of the pubs, having a beer here and there, and had quite a good time. Met some of the rest of the boys in town, also.

*Saturday 27:* Had to fall out at 6:30 to police the area – how about that? Felt rather rugged this morning, but was assigned a flight and off I went. Had a good trip and met John Connor again down at Chelveston. We had a heck of a good bull session, and I hope to see 'em again. They're carrying side arms, helmets, and gas masks down at that base.

*Sunday 28:* Joe came in with another -24 flight in the evening, so I, being eager, said I'd take it. Got a ride in a UC-64 over to Maghaberry, but the ship wasn't there and back we came. The darn ship ground looped on the runway but didn't wreck anything.

Monday 29*:* A beautiful day in Northern Ireland, and with nothing to do, I played a little softball. Along about noon a bunch of movements came up, and I went out right after lunch. Just a routine -17 delivery across the Irish Sea.

Got stuck over at Burtonwood since my pilot took off, so I rode down on another delivery with Mutone. Sat in the nose and read a map all the way down. The brakes failed to work while taxing, and we went off the perimeter track into a wheelbarrow, sand pile, etc.. Not too much damage to the ship. The taxi picked us up and we got back around 10:00 or so. – Saw "Mild and Bitter" and "Bingo Buster" – 100 mission B-26s down at the hangars.

*Wednesday 31:* The merry whistle of the C.Q. awakened me from my peaceful slumber at 6:00, and since they unlocked "ablutions" I managed to freshen up a bit. Turned in our blankets, had chow, and then the officers picked us up. Rode back on the freight run out of Alconbury with only one stop at BAD.

Picked up my pay and spent most of the afternoon washing up some clothes. Wrote letters during the evening plus the usual bull session. Latrineogram: We're being sent to gunnery school – the latest news is that the pilots are going to be trained on fighters and B-26s and the 312th will take over the heavy stuff – Looks as though we'll be flying in a "hot" airplane.

*Famous B-26 "Mild and Bitter." Dick mentions this airplane in his diary on May 29, 1944.*

**June 1944**

*Thursday 1:* Nothing much doing on the flying side this morning as the 312th is supposed to have taken over officially. I went down to the dentist again and was chewed out a bit for missing my other appointment. So he looked me over, and I have to come in again next Tuesday.

Started to make a pair of plexiglass wings to absorb my time and spent the afternoon on them. Went to a movie in the mess hall during the evening with the boys and then had a bit of a bull session back in the barracks with Spot, who was "high" again. The usual clowning around, and it ended when he took my helmet off my bed and started to "obey the call of nature" in it. I chucked him out of the barracks and was plenty browned off.

*Friday 2:* Yes, the 312th has taken over, but four of our operators spent the entire day working with them (myself included). I got over to Burtonwood, wandered around aimlessly, missed chow, and then made another delivery while the 312th boys, who need the experience, rode back in the taxi ship.

Naturally, things happened while we were gone. Besides reveille which started this morning, a certain group are going to be extensively trained as COMMANDOS. – The fightin' 311th!?

*Saturday 3:* Heard about a new -17 that cracked up on the mountainside just outside of Belfast – entire crew killed. Just came over, too.

*Sunday 4:* Started sweating out some -24 deliveries from the morning on, and since it was raining to beat the band we saw "Pacific Penderous" in the ready room. Weather cleared up slightly so we started, I being an instructor with a 312th student.

Didn't work at all – let the student do everything, and then we ran into a mess of fog over the Irish sea. The pilot got eager and nervous, so I took over, sent out "OP," and got a series into Squires Gate. (I don't like to get lost – that sea looked kind of cold) A fort took us back to LLAD, and I pulled in around 9:30.

*Monday 5:* Roll call and then a nice little trot around the block to freshen up. Saw "Mutiny on the Bounty" in the ready room and then assigned a flight as instructor again. We rode over to Warton in a -24 in the afternoon, and a couple of us got kind of disgusted about going down to East Anglia

– so we hopped a ride on a Lib with Robbie back to LLAD. I rode along as engineer and got quite a workout.

Wrote a letter during the evening and even had trouble getting that one off. – Latrineogram: the 27th ATG is taking over some converted -17s and is going to run a mail and transport service between Gibraltar and India. Good luck!

*Tuesday 6:* D DAY!!: Didn't go up today 'cause of my dentist appointment, and I was sitting around operations when the news of the invasion was spread around. I listened to the radio "alert" to the conquered countries and also a propaganda announcement from Berlin. Lot of excitement going around and everyone glued to the radios.

Signed up on an aerial gunnery list – hope I'll go to it.

*Wednesday 7:* Reveille and calisthenics – what a good and healthy soldier. Went up on a hop as instructor again, but I rode in the nose almost the entire trip. Wanted to see some of the invasion excitement down in England, but there was nothing to see. Weather was poor so there wasn't much activity for the heavy ships.

Rode a five hour trip back on the taxi ship which made five stops. Even so, we pulled in just in time for evening chow. Wrote a letter during the evening plus a little wrestling and horse play, Gabby being the recipient for the most part!

*Thursday 8:* Nothing doing till the afternoon when I got a taxi ride down to Valley and then took a -17 up to Burtonwood. Bad weather again, but an order came out that we were supposed to observe radio silence as much as possible. Even though we could see enough for pilotage, the pilot couldn't find the place and I had to work Spike. Finally found it after an hour and a half of flying.

BAD was practically socked in when we left after receiving a report of favorable weather at LLAD. Pulled in around 10:00.

*Friday 9:* Heard that we've had a -24 lost since yesterday afternoon and it had a four man crew of the 312th aboard it. Latest rumors tonight say that the wreckage was found on the Isle of Man and everyone was killed. Certainly hope it isn't true, as I knew the radio op and pilot.

*Saturday 10:* Most of the boys were off today (commandos), so the waiting room was kind of empty. I didn't do anything all morning, but as expected I was assigned a flight in the afternoon.

Rode over to Warton in a -24 taxi, but the deliveries didn't pan out and we waited around to see if there would be any developments. Ate evening chow and then rode back to LLAD. Took a look at Lennox's plane over the Isle of Man and it certainly was messed up. Hardly anything left of it.

*Sunday 11:* A day of rest for me. Helped Gulden in a bit of carpentry in the morning – a bit of drizzle going on. Took off around eleven for chow down at site #4, the usual "chicken, ice cream, and Coke!"

Afternoon was slack, also, so after a vain attempt to drum up a baseball game, Gabby and I went over to a matinee show in the mess hall. Time to knock off "work" when we got out. Went to chow early and then worked down to Projma Hall to see "Best Foot Forward." Two movies in a day is enough – wrote a letter home and that ended another day. Off tomorrow, perhaps I'll make a mission to "Belshaft."

*Wednesday 14:* Started to loaf away the morning and then got a lone -17 delivery down to East Anglia. Had a good trip as the air was free. The

*"Gabby", "Chicago", and "Bob" – Andrew Garabedian, Al Bak, and Robert Brentlinger, Northern Ireland, 1944.*

pilots decided to take their off day down there, and I was told to wait for the taxi ship. Didn't think a ship would show up, but it finally did in the late afternoon. If it wouldn't have come in, I was going to takeoff for London on my own.

*Friday 16:* Took off on a bike down to the LOC PX this morning and bought myself a couple of khaki shirts as the first business of the day. Came back and moved my belongings into Hut 307 as we're having a bit of a moving.

Spent the afternoon in rearranging things, and after a shower and early chow, I started my stretch as CQ. Nice dance going on in the sight theater, too, with women running around and all. Kind of like to see what's cooking, but – Writing letters for fare-the-well right now. Got pretty tired later on, and right now I can barely keep my eyes open.

*Sunday 18:* Lotta exercise today. Pitched about fourteen innings of softball in the morning, plus another game in the afternoon against the officers. Ah, really tired!

*Monday 19:* Flock of ships delivered today. I had a trip over to Burtonwood (listened to the compass music), and then after noon chow, we delivered another ship down to East Anglia. I flew along as co-pilot and had a nice trip. Taxi picked us up and we hit LLAD about 6:45. I had a nice nap all the way back.

The newest rumor has it that we will move to Grove on Wednesday – also sergeants are going to pull KP. The first is OK by me, but I don't care much for that second ... Off day tomorrow, so I think I'll go to town with Gabby.

*Tuesday 20:* Off day – slept till 10 or so and then got cleaned up for town. Gabby and I walked down to the gate and got a ride into "Belshaft" with a major. We took care of all our business, looking over the proofs of my pictures, etc., had chow at the Abercorn, saw a show and wandered around a good deal. Walked down to the docks and looked over the piers, etc.

Met a couple of the boys and got to drinking beer again. So I didn't get a train till late – prided myself on being the only awake and sober person in the compartment on the way back.

*Friday 23:* Heard a pretty good rumor tonight about a "special mission" of eight crews going out. I'm supposed to be one of them. Didn't do much all

*Portrait of Richard Mollwitz taken in Belfast.*

*"Gabby" and "Brent", Andrew Garabedian and Robert Brentlinger, LLAD.*

*"Sharkey" – Walter Sierak, LLAD.*

*Molly and Pete Genovese, LLAD, 1944.*

*Molly and Willy Lulf, LLAD, 1944.*

*S/Sgt. Robert Brentlinger.*

day again except diddle around in the maintenance shop. Saw a movie in the ready room in the afternoon, that's about all. Received my second package from home.

Yesterday's rumor has been substantiated quite a bit, and the latest development is the taking of yellow fever shots tomorrow morning. The conceptions of where we are going are really varied – Russia, the states, Africa, France, or just in the UK. It beats me, 'cause it's hardly a "picked" outfit. I'm really curious. At any rate, it looks as though the outfit is getting ready to move.

*Sunday 25:* Well, the big deal is on. I've talked, ate, and slept the "trip" today. It's unanimously considered that we're going to the States. Four crews are leaving tomorrow morning, and it's supposed to be the southern route via Africa, Brazil, and Florida. I'm kind of excited, apprehensive, and what not all rolled into one. It's about the biggest thing that's ever happened to me. I still have to get a yellow fever shot, though, and I'm scared that a lack of that might screw me up.

*Monday 26:* All the fellows on the first flight packed and got organized today for their first trip, but somehow they didn't get started. I was supposed to fly over to Blackpool in the afternoon to get my yellow fever shot, and that too was postponed till the morning. The excitement is still riding high, although the undercurrent of pessimism persists in "last minute cancellations."

Well, here it is the end of the day and the first four crews are still here. My mind is working overtime as to whether I'll really get to go, what kind of a trip it would be ... Holding thumbs!

*Tuesday 27:* Over to the flight surgeon's office early this morning and finally got a ride over to Warton in a C-47. We had noon chow and then went out to Blackpool in an ambulance. Spent a free hour walking around the beach, pier, and looking over the place. Guess it was a resort city during peace time, being right on the Irish Sea.

A RAF officer gave us the yellow fever shot – right off the ice, and it burned like hell. Rode back to Warton and had a devil of a time getting a ride to LLAD, but finally caught the shuttle. The first crews still haven't left. I wonder what the story is ...The latest rumor has it that our outfit is being turned into an "Air Transport Sqdn."

*Wednesday 28:* Am off today, but didn't go to town because of this "States" deal. So I just sat around all day wasting time. Nothing definite has come out yet – it's all still pending.

*Thursday 29:* Another day and still the first crews haven't left for the states. I've just about given up all hope, even though those five might leave. The chief reason for that is because I found out that I'm one of 19 men who will be in the 311th Air Transport Sqdn. We start the freight runs this Saturday, supposedly between France and England. That evidently involves moving down near London someplace, or at least to England.

Took in the early show at "Pajama" Hall in the evening – "Cover Girl" and strictly class B. Authoritative sources say that the first five crews leave tomorrow, and if we go at all, it won't be until they get back.

*Friday 30:* Pay call this morning and rather timely since I was flat busted. Paid off a few debts and loafed around the entire day. Saw "A Guy Named Joe" – a darned good pic. Three of the crews finally left for the states – the other two should leave soon. They say 312th is going to take some back, too – I guess I've had it.

**July 1944**

*Saturday 1:* Asked for a flight today, and though bad weather held us up during the morning we finally got off from Nutts Corner in the afternoon. Just an ordinary -25 delivery to Warton – nothing exciting. Fooled around with trailing wire a bit. Back to LLAD on the taxi around 6:30.

Bunch of fellows shipping out tomorrow. Looks as though the sqdn is being cut down. We're supposed to have gone into operation as an Air Transport Sqdn. today, but the C-47s aren't ready yet. I'd like to get going to see what France looks like. Have it pretty soft here yet we can be doing a better and bigger job.

*Sunday 2:* An entire day of rain, and though I could have gotten in some sack time if I wanted to, I didn't feel so inclined. Had every intention of going to church and missed out 'cause I saw "Lady in the Dark" in the ready room (rather a weak-willed character I am).

Messed around in the maintenance room all afternoon working on my dagger, but didn't get very far with it – lack of tools and equipment.

*Monday 3:* Did a little work this morning as Sheppard sent Gabby and I out to replace a couple of antennas on one of our B-26s. Took all morning to do it – brought back memories of the work at Topeka.

Nothing doing in the afternoon – took a little code and then screwed off. Washed some clothes and had a short nap. Pretty soft – Spotanski left for the States today (or at least England), so that makes four crews gone. There's slight hopes for the other six, but I'm rather pessimistic about my chances.

*Tuesday 4:* Just had a short delivery today, and we took a ship from Valley to Warton. Got off late 'cause there were a lot of new ships coming in making instrument let down through the overcast. Saw Spot, who is all set to make the big trip, leaving tonight.

Got back to LLAD around 6:30 – a long day just to log an hour of log-time. Made me feel kind of funny to see Spot all ready to make his trip. Sort of revives hopes – after all, we were given the hope of going home, and that's quite a castle to fall down all at once. Had a bit of a fireworks display before we went to bed – shooting off pistol flares.

*Wednesday 5:* Worked on my ornamental dagger all day as the weather prevented flying during the morning. Lot of deliveries in the afternoon, but I didn't get any. Went out with Gabby later on to work on the command set troubles of a -26, and by the time we got through, the "working day" was over.

Went over to the shop in the evening to finish up my dagger and then wandered over to the orderly room to try and write a few letters. Have cuts all over my hands, so I didn't have much success.

*Monday 10:* Just like old times today. Got a bunch of 311th crews together to take some B-26s out of Nutts Corner, but CFC was SNAFU and we took C-47s to Burtonwood. Made three approaches on our landing 'cause weren't sure the wheels were locked.

Had a ride down to Stansted in the afternoon to supposedly deliver some -26s to LLAD. They wouldn't release the ships, though, so it was a useless ride. Got back around 7:00 or so with a lot of flying behind me but only two hours logged. Learned that ten crews are supposed to go over to Warton tomorrow and pick up our C-47s.

*Tuesday 11:* Started out rather early on a C-47 to Warton as part of 10 crews which were to bring back our ships. Landed at Burtonwood instead, ate lunch (?) and then got a ride in a C-87 over to Warton. As usual no one knew anything.

So Gabby and I got cleaned up and went into "Cess" Pool. Did a bit of beer drinking out on the North Pier and all over. Met a couple of girls and had a little romancin', that's about all. Got a taxi cab ride all the way back to Warton, right up to site 11. Not a bad evening.

*Wednesday 12:* Up around 7:30 for a breakfast of one fresh egg – even then we were late for chow. Went down to the line, picked up my A-2 jacket and flying coveralls, and then waited around the entire morning. Went down for noon chow where we learned that only a few men were needed. So, grabbed a -24 ride to LLAD – flew at 8,000 above thick stuff and after a prolonged ride we let down at Andreas on the Isle of Man (short runway, nearly burnt out the brakes). Decided not to return that night, so we took a bus into Ramsey and then caught the electric train to Douglas. Really had a nice time in town – a little drinking, romancing, and a good bed. – Grandmother died today at 2:15PM after a brief illness.

*Thursday 13:* Up around 7:30 and had a good breakfast. Walked along the waterfront, past the Royal Navy hotels, the internee camp, and then caught the electric train to Ramsey. The weather was pretty bad so we called Andreas to check whether we were leaving. No one knew anything about takeoff – therefore we walked around town a bit, ate lunch, and then took a bus into the field.

Took off in the afternoon although it was sweated out a bit because of the short runway. Landed here at LLAD around 4:30. Rumor hath it that another crew will leave for the States tomorrow. The engineers came back from Warton, and some of them are filling up our barracks.

*Saturday 15:* Went down to hangar 111 in the evening and saw Joe Louis put on an exhibition with Thompson. Not much excitement – thought the prelims in which two colored welterweights boxed two Limeys were much better. A little tired now – a shower and then to bed. Had to get out of bed to pull an acceptance on my new C-47. Got finished around 2:00.

*Sunday 16:* Well, the days of loafing are gone forever. Sweated out a hop in my ship all morning, but didn't takeoff till noon. A freight run to Honington, Warton, and then here. Made a couple of dial settings, gave the equipment a good workout, and put in six good hours of flying. I imagine that this freight run is going to get rather tiresome, 'cause there's certainly a lot of work to be done in England. I finally got back here at LLAD at 9:00. Our ship was hardly unloaded before they loaded it again for tomorrow morning. How about that?

*Monday 17:* Up at 6:30 this morning, had a short meeting over at the shop and then went down to the ship. Stuck around there until the pilots came out, and since we were all loaded up, we took right off. Had a long trip down to a Navy base – steak and fresh eggs for chow and then back over to Toome and then back to LLAD around 6:30. We're supposed to take another trip after supper, but it was canceled. Kind of glad of that, too.

*Tuesday 18:* Didn't fly today as Gorecki took my place. So I worked in the ground station most of the day. Was on the key awhile and got a little practice. At times they really keep an operator busy.

Worked in there till supper time – then my ship went out again so I went out with it. We got banged around a bit in a jeep accident going down to the line, but no one seriously hurt. Had a quick trip over to BAD and back and got to bed rather late, since we didn't start till after supper.

*Wednesday 19:* Up early this morning, and though we were ready, got a rather late start. Made quite a few hops plus a long one from Honington to Prestwick. The weather wasn't any too good up there, either, plus the fact that we had ten passengers. We were at a Limey mess for noon chow – ate with the Flying Sgts. and I don't know how they stand it. Got a little chewing from the flying control officer at PWK for some improper use of WT (or he said). Finally arrived back at LLAD around 10 at night. Logged nearly ten hours for the day. Incidentally, we changed barracks again today and Gabby had to move my stuff for me.

*Sunday 23:* Up and at 'em! Just a routine trip today down to Staverton. One in the morning and one in the afternoon. Checked in at BAD before crossing the Irish Sea in the evening and got back here around 6:00. Had trailing wire troubles again and had to rip up the floor boards once more. The reel slipped off of the axle, so I had to rewind the reel and also put on another weight. Didn't get through with the job until quite late, so after eating late chow and a shower, I hit the sack.

*Monday 24:* Off day, so I slept late and after getting cleaned up and having noon chow, Gabby, Chappie, and I went to town. Rode in on a '42 Chevrolet sedan (LOC) pretty darn nice. After a number of beers and a little Scotch we decided to go out to Bellevue Park. Met a couple of girls out there and took them home, but they weren't so much. Caught the 12:15 train back to camp and was pretty sleepy when I hit the sack.

*Tuesday 25:* Got up a little late this morning and got down to the ship almost the same time as the pilot. Made about a dozen stops serving as a taxi ship for the detachment up in Prestwick. We were kept busy, but didn't log any too much time. Ran into a little bad weather coming back, but we made it into LLAD OK. Got hauled out again to pull a 100 hour inspection on my ship, and since it was in the hangar, there wasn't much I could do about it. So I postponed it till tomorrow night.

*Friday 28:* Got down to the line this morning only to learn that we wouldn't go out till 1:00. Went back to the sight only to be called back again and out we went. Served as a taxi for the fighter pilots working out of Prestwick and got quite a bit of flying in. Kept us going all day, and it was nearly dark when we got back to LLAD around 11:00. Ate supper on the ship – just K-rations.

Took our big soft LOC sacks away from us today. We now have biscuits once more and steel cots. P-poor..

*Sunday 30:* We were a taxi ship again today and, as usual, things were pretty well mixed up. We flubbed around Warton and BAD and then made a trip down to the Midlands to pick up one man. We returned to Warton and went straight to LLAD.

Had to work on my ship when I got back and didn't get through until around 1:30. Had half the floorboards ripped up and all. Really a job to remove the radio compass and all that just to replace a tube. Off tomorrow, so I didn't worry about getting in late.

**August 1944**

*Tuesday 1:* Slept rather late this morning cause it was my off day. After due preparations, Gabby and I went into Belfast in the afternoon. Rode in on a weapons carrier – nice rough ride. A Limey civilian drove it and naturally took care since it was U.S. property!

Really spent a rough time in town. Took care of my shopping, had a steak, and then a few beers. Boy, those people certainly know how a Yank spends his money right after pay day. We got rid of our share – always seems to be someone to buy a drink for, etc. We caught the 11:00 bus back to camp and got in around twelve. Flying tomorrow again.

*Wednesday 2:* Was down at the line till 11:20 this morning waiting for the pilots and then they finally showed up. Went over to BAD where we ate and then delivered our load. Pretty bad weather all over the midlands. Missed supper, but ate at LLAD after we pulled in around 8:30. Shot the bull in the barracks awhile and by that time I was tired enough to hit the hay. Don't have any ambition what so ever after a day of flying, can't even write a letter.

*Thursday 3:* My pilot went down to Heston on DS today, and in return we got one of their boys. Went local in the morning and worked my behind off. Then in the afternoon we flew above the overcast and I had to keep that set going. All in all, I got six series of QDMs – where did he go to flying school?

*Sunday 6:* On flight again today with a couple of good Joes as pilot and co-pilot. We made two trips down to Staverton and back, no excitement, just routine flying. Like to fly that way 'cause you're not bothered with a lot of work. We got back to LLAD early – around 6:30. I helped Rick and Gabby start a 100 hour insp. on their ship, and then took off for the sight as I'm on schedule again tomorrow.

*Wednesday 9:* Really my off day, but I had to fly for Mendelsohn and in the end I was glad I did. Made a few short trips and got back to LLAD at 4:00 where we found out that our ship is going to Heston and then France. Drew a .45 out of supply and got a few things together and off we went. Got down to Heston, watched them paint invasion stripes on our ship, and took off for London.

Weinshank and I stayed at the Mostyn Club, though of course, we had a brief excursion out into the night life first. The Piccadilly Commandos were out in full force as usual. Got to bed around 1:00, although the "buzz bomb" alerts woke me up a couple of times.

*Thursday 10:* Left a call for 6:00, so up we were and had a "bit" of a breakfast (coffee and toast) in the Mostyn Club. Walked over to N. Audley where we met the pilots and inveigled a ride on the bus out of Heston. We were scheduled for a freight run and got as far as Wattisham, but they recalled us. Saw Generals Spaatz and Royce at ATG HQ – big show. We loaded up with passengers – 23 of them and away we went. All the ships went on their own. Got quite a thrill out of crossing the channel, seeing Pte. Barfleur, Cherbourg, and its harbor, the landing strips, shell craters, etc. Landed on a field near the harbor (A23-E) and was on the ground exactly 7 minutes. Back to Heston and helped my crew chief pull an inspection on our ship. Finally decided to sleep in our ships. Back to Heston and into my sleeping bag on the floor of 046.

*Friday 11:* Woke up around 7:00 this morning, "made my bed," and then walked across the field to operations, learned that we wouldn't make another run to France today, but had a freight run into the UK instead. This is my third straight day of flying, but I don't mind it so much. Ran into quite a bit of bad weather, but naturally, we got through. That C-47 certainly is an all weather ship.

*Sunday 13:* Didn't think we were making the Cherbourg run today, but found out differently when I got down to the ship. So we flew down to Heston, and even though it was still early we went back to LLAD.

Arrived here only to learn that we were due to go out on DS for a week. Finally got it straightened out that we'll start out early tomorrow morning, taking about half the personnel of the outfit.

*Monday 14:* Roughly awakened by the CQ this morning at 4:00. The DS fellows got their things together and we took off at 6:05. Had a nice trip down to Heston, flying just as the sun came up. The usual confusion reigned down at Heston, and after due deliberation we found out that we're due to make a mission. All the extra men were sent back to LLAD – only a R/O, engineer, and pilot were left with the ship. We flew to Cottesmore, then to Barkston Heath, which is a Troop Carrier base. Saw a company of paratroops at Cottes, but they weren't for us. Got a bed in the transient barracks.

*Tuesday 15:* Only one up this morning, went to chow and then didn't do anything but sit around the ship all day. In the afternoon the engineers flew back to LLAD to pick up Para-racks and all the necessary equipment as we will be in on a para-drop mission. We're officially attached to the 16th TCS on DS – The other ships are with the other outfits on the base. Got a bed down in their sight along with Shep and Bob.

*Wednesday 16:* Went over to the 14th TC communications this morning. Learned a little about the operating procedure and facilities of this group. Attended a briefing by the intel. officer as to possibilities of escape after capture. Went to another briefing in the afternoon pertaining to the use of radio on the mission – had a false alarm 3:00 – got all my stuff out in the ship and then it was scrubbed. So I wandered back to the transient barracks and spent the evening there.

*Thursday 17:* Spent the entire day laying around the transient barracks. Went over to another briefing in the afternoon which was identical to the radio briefing of yesterday. Still nothing happened. At 5:30 we were in the post theater listening to the story of a P-38 pilot who escaped from France. At the end of the meeting we were told that everything had been canceled. It was quite a let down – probably my only chance at combat.

We got all our things together and managed to takeoff at 7:30. So back to LLAD once more.

**September 1944**

*Saturday 9: GROVE, ENGLAND:* Over to France again today – dropped off our load of tires and then went to Le Bourget, Paris, to pick up the litter patients. That was really a beautiful field at one time.

*Wednesday 27:* Going to break my silence here and see if I can continue these daily notations again. I've been too darn busy lately that I just left this diary as is. Making trips to France almost every day now and have been for the past month. Seems to have changed my entire character – become nervous, irritable, and short-tempered. Perhaps starting to write again will serve as an outlet.

Made two trips over today, and since we missed lunch we got back rather early – 6:00 or so. Spent the usual restless evening around the barracks, took a shower, and then "flubbed away" the time. Couldn't seem to get settled enough to write a letter.

*Thursday 28:* Made a little mistake in dates yesterday and wrote on the wrong date. The usual two trips to France today, moving the 9th AF over there. Man, that certainly is a job with all those bases to be moved. Getting to be like a regular civilian working day – up at 6:30, takeoff at eight and back some time in the evening. Piling up a record amount of time this month, but so have all the fellows. Just got tomorrow's schedule – Get'er in the blue again!

*Friday 29:* Not too good weather today. Ceiling low enough to bump your head on, but we made two trips anyways. Missed breakfast 'cause there was too long a line to sweat out, and also lunch 'cause we were flying – never gain any weight that way!

More rumors going around that sqdn. is losing ships and also gaining some. Wished they'd make up their minds. Haven't heard any more about moving to France, either. Oh, well. I'd be willing to spend the winter here in the Grove. A pup tent is mighty cold, even in France!

*Saturday 30:* There's a hot rumor floating around that a number of the old boys, including myself, are going to be shipped out. That would be just the fitting climax of all that has happened during the last month. Logged 135 hours, which is pretty good. On the ground seven days of the month.

*Richard Mollwitz in flight clothing at Grove, England.*

**October 1944**

*Monday 2:* Early takeoff this morning – airborne around twenty minutes to eight. Two trips of 9th AF personnel, missed lunch as usual and then back early at four. Slept most of the time 'cause I've developed a head cold and feel kind of miserable.

*Tuesday 3:* Two new pilots on the ship today, didn't know either of them. Took a load of AOG stuff out of Grove to Villacoublay and then back to this place. Ate noon chow here and were all set to take another load over when the tower told us the far shore was socked in. So I was off around 3:00.

*Wednesday 4:* Same pilots as yesterday – pretty good Joes. Made one trip in the morning and back to Grove for lunch. Took them quite a while to get us loaded again, so they decided not to make the second trip – would have returned too late, I guess. So that left me off rather early.

*Thursday 5:* Well, my Cardinals came out on top again – really shouldn't say again, 'cause they lost the opener. That makes one apiece now.

*Friday 6:* Again we were held up for awhile this morning, but took off at nine. Made our one trip, but since we had an evac team we had to go to A-90 to pick up patients.

Felt terrible all day 'cause of a bad cold. Really shouldn't have been flying. Got back at supper time, and after a shower and a trip to the dispensary for some aspirin, I crawled in the sack. Listened to the series game while in bed – lost another five shillings on the pool.

*Left: The perimeter track at Grove. Below left: Control tower, Grove. Below: C-47s at Grove.*

*Sunday 8:* All indications point to the fact that we'll ship to France within the next couple of days. Afraid that I'm going to lose #046, too. Going to have all "Bs" in the outfit for high altitude and short takeoff work. "They say" we might be sent to Marseilles. French Riviera, here I come!

*Monday 9:* Been assigned a new ship, #491, which I'll probably start flying tomorrow. Really is a wreck, too, from what I hear, the entire compass receiver is missing – how about that. To top it off, I've got a "hand job" of a pilot tomorrow. Why does everything happen to me?

*Tuesday 10:* Thick ground fog held us up all morning. Went out to the ship at noon and looked it over. Not a bad "kite," although they shipped out a lot of accessories. The pilot came out around one, found out there was no radio compass in the ship, and so refused to fly it.

That meant I had the rest of the afternoon off. Back to the site, wrote a letter, and took it easy. Went down to the shop in the evening and started to re-equip #491 with some of the items missing. Also brought my footlocker down for shipment with the communications equipment.

*Wednesday 11:* Once again the weather wasn't any too good. However, we took our load over to A-42 and learned that Grove had almost closed in. That was a good excuse to RON, so we closed up the ship and into "Paree."

Spent a rather quiet evening, although a couple of MPs took us down to the Provost Marshall. They didn't seem to care for the absence of the engineer's pass or my reference to "CS." Rode back in a "pick-up" wagon and spent some time in the Red Cross talking to some girls who spoke English. Had quite a time with them.

*Friday 13:* Up and at 'em. A trip over to A-42 as usual and then waited most of the morning to get unloaded. Made a couple other jaunts around France. Ate noon chow over there, and we wasted enough time so that we wouldn't have to make a second trip.

Came back to Grove in the midst of a rain storm – quite a gale. Received my GI watch from Tech Supply – scratched the crystal already. Not much doing in the evening. Irvin came in from Warton, and we talked things over a bit.

*Monday 16:* Raining this morning – everything canceled. No one knew what was cooking most of the day. We finally took off for A-40 at 2:30. Had a few slight hopes of RONing, but this new pilot of mine doesn't seem to worry about bad weather or late flying. Back here just before it got dark – another long day of doing nothing.

Rumors are rather cold about shipping – looks as though we may spend the winter here at Grove. Not much to look forward to.

*Tuesday 17:* Early takeoff this morning, picked up a load at BAD and then went over to the far shore. Learned there was a "front" back in England, but we started for Grove anyways. Ran into the worst weather I've flown in since I've been in the UK. Pretty bad all over southern England. I called for weather reports from four different places – all bad. Getting rather low on gas, so we finally sat down at Northolt.

No transient accommodations there, so we took a tube into London, booked in at Rainbow Corners, and got a bed at the Milestone Club. Nice place, too.

*Thursday 19:* Started to go out on #491 as usual this morning, but it turned up with a bad tire. Started to have it changed, but it took quite a bit of time so they changed the crew to another ship. Flew #5 instead which had a load on already. Just one trip, fooled around at 9,000 ft over France awhile and then back here.

*A Gooney Bird somewhere over England.*

Traded my A-2 jacket in for a new one – then had a bit of a champagne party back in the barracks since Al brought in a case from Reims. Right now I have half a buzz on. Think I'll wash up and hit the sack.

*Saturday 21:* Again a day of poor weather, but not bad enough to hold us up since I was with Stillwell. Flew on instruments all day, made two let downs on the radio ranges – he's really a darn good pilot. Just one trip and back here in the early afternoon.

The 321st lost a ship today – hit a small mountain near Stansted. Five men killed including "Willy" Lulf, one of the swellest fellows I've met over here. He intended living in Shorewood after the war was over since he married Ruthe Breese who lives about two blocks away from me. Just can't seem to realize that Willy got it.

*Wednesday 25:* Awakened this morning to the blithe strains of a whistle followed by a "bugle blown reveille." Ate chow with the boys who were leaving, and then caught a ride to the center of town. Met the pilot there and rode out to the base.

Took some captured German material over to Chipping Ongar and then home once more. Had a bit of a champagne party in the barracks at night – hardly got a buzz on, though. Finally took a shower and went to bed. Had a good look at the famed Reims cathedral this morning – minus its Rose window, which has been stored away 'cause of the war.

*Thursday 26:* Supposed to open up the ground station at 6:30 this morning for a weather ship, but the fog was too thick to takeoff. Went down rather early anyway 'cause my ship was grounded for a 100 hour. The tube tester was packed up, so I couldn't pull much of an inspection. Cleaned off the antennas, etc. Relieved the ground station operator during chow time and sat around shop most of the day.

Quite a few of the boys RONed tonight 'cause of the weather.

*Friday 27:* Really beautiful weather here this morning, CAVU, but as luck would have it, it was really socked in on the far shore. Waited out in the ship for awhile and then came into operations. We all sat around the shop the entire day just waiting for something to break. Finally had everything canceled around 3:30 and we took off.

*Sunday 29:* Woke up in that nice cold Nissen hut this morning – managed to wash up a bit and get over to chow. Caught a truck ride down to the line and then waited around all morning for the pilot. Talked to a few of the old Prestwick boys who are now stationed there at BAD. Finally took off at around 2:00, delivered our load and made it back to Grove. Last ship in the outfit to land – almost dark, and then we had to run into a squall of bad weather just before the field.

Learned that I made S/Sgt. today – they certainly are indiscriminate in the way they pass out ratings!

*Monday 30:* Nice weather this morning for a change – clear and cold. Flew up to Warton where we picked up a load and from there took it over to Paris. Returned to Grove from there, but the day was spent by then, it being late afternoon.
Couple ships going up to Iceland tomorrow – Bak and Galarza were the lucky boys. Be a nice deal for them 'cause they've got American beer up there. I've had quite a few breaks in the outfit, so I can't kick.

*"Spot" in the sack, at Grove – Anthony Spotanski.*

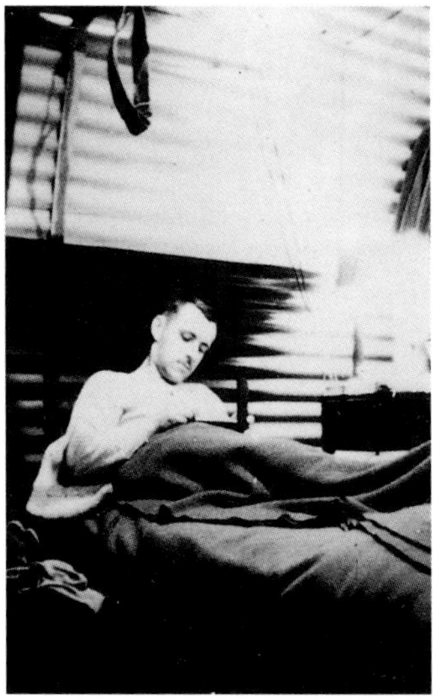

**November 1944**

*Wednesday 1:* Changed ships with Weinshank this morning 'cause I didn't care for my pilot – then what happens but his ship turns out to be the weather ship. Took off around 8:10 and really worked my behind off sending in the various reports. Thought I'd get a break and be back early, but no such luck. Went right up to Warton after the trip to the far shore, and picked up another load. Ate a combination lunch and supper at site #13 – really a swell mess hall there.

Came in just around dusk before the ground fog started to settle in. Latest rumor is that we'll move to Chartres in France on the 7th.

*Thursday 2:* Flew Weinshank's ship again today as he RONed with mine last night. Delivered a load to Le Bourget after a rather late start in the morning and got back to Grove around 2:30. They intended sending us up to BAD, but by the time we ate, enough time was wasted so that we couldn't make the trip without RONing. Managed to talk our way out of it and was through for the day.

The outfit is supposed to be alerted, which means we'll move darn soon. Washed a few clothes tonight and repacked my foot locker preparatory to shipping. Might as well get organized, 'cause I think it's for keeps this time.

*Friday 3:* Over to Greenham Common this morning to pick up a load of medical supplies and from there to Le Bourget. That Paris field is really a mass of mud – you have to taxi a plane as if it were a heavy tank in order not to get stuck.

*Monday 6:* Our ship was held in readiness all morning for a call from Northolt and nothing came up. So I worked in the ground station off and on to help out Weinshank. In the afternoon they sent us out on a useless trip to A-23 to try and pick up a jeep trailer.

Well, the big deal is on and the outfit is scheduled to move tomorrow. The ships are being loaded up right now. All the personal belongings are packed up, and we'll bring the bags on the ship sometime tonight. Scheduled for a 6:00 takeoff tomorrow morning. Went out in the rear of a 6x6 during a pouring rain around 11:30 to load my bags on my ship. Really got soaking wet.

*Tuesday 7:* Up at 4:45 this morning and took off at 6:50 bound for Marseilles. As luck would have it, I had liaison XMTR troubles and we got good and lost. Flew for five and one half hours, once at an altitude of 14,000 and finally set down at A-54. The pilot blamed most of the troubles on the XMTR, and since the weather was in a sad state, we RONed.

*Wednesday 8:* Some GI blowing his brains out on a bugle woke us up this morning. The engineer and I went right out to the ship, and a little while later the pilot came out just to tell us that we were due to stay another day. Bad weather again, I guess. Went back to the apartment, and in the afternoon in the midst of a pouring rain, Myers (pilot) told us to go out and work on the ship. So I took another radio man and flubbed away the entire afternoon out there.

Back to the apartment again in the evening. Went over to a movie in the evening and then in the sleeping bag once more.

*Thursday 9:* Beautiful weather this morning – good enough for Myers to takeoff, so back to Grove.

We went along with the 16 passengers who were originally bound for Marseilles. Got back here around noon and then flew as co-pilot over to Membury with Garrard. Worked on the set again all afternoon along with some TC boys and then put in a new liaison set for me.

*Heavily damaged Le Bourget Air Field, Paris.*

Views of Istres Air Field, in southern France.

*Friday 10:* An early start again this morning – had to catch a truck ride over to sight #8 in order to eat breakfast. Went to the ship right from there – takeoff at 7:30. Flew with Lt. Paulic who was OK. Worked a couple of French stations over there, the operators are plenty fast. Good weather, though, and we had a good trip. Got a good look at some of the high mountains down there.

Got unloaded right away and back to Grove once more. My first look at Marseilles wasn't very impressive – Quite a wind blowing a fine red dust around, no trees on a big open plain, and nothing much to meet, though. Back here in the late afternoon. Still no news of Soup – looks bad. We lost a ship on takeoff here today, but no one was hurt.

*Saturday 11: ISTRES FIELD, outside of Marseilles, France:* Up at 5:00 this morning with takeoff around 9:00. Flight checked my new XTMR – works OK. Got down to Istres just past noon. Found the mess hall just by walking around. Lots of bldgs. on the field, but most of them are pretty well demolished. For the present we're quartered in the rooms of an apartment or French army barracks. They're in sorry shape, but after cleaning up a bit, the rooms aren't so bad. The officers are living in our sight – we're supposed to move up there in a week or so. Much better deal up there 'cause it's in town, nice houses, etc. Don't imagine there'll be much doing around here for awhile.

*Monday 13:* No flying again today – had a meeting of all the communications personnel and various assignments were made. I worked on my ship most of the day. Stuck a new radio compass in and did a lot of tinkering in general. Took another crack at fixing a stove in our room with the usual smoke. No more candles for the lamp (not even a hint of electricity). Chow lines still long, most of the fellows heading for town right away in the evening. "Whore House" right outside one of the gates and well patronized. Gab brought in a couple of bottles of wine later on for a night cap.

*Tuesday 14:* Detailed to the wire laying this morning and we put telephones in the mess hall and dispensary. We were done rather early, as part of the job had been taken care of yesterday.

Went into Istres in the afternoon. Took a "douche" in the public bath house – cost 7 francs, warm water plus a new experience. Walked around the town a bit – a typical small French town – not much doing, quite a bit of fruit for sale (in comparison to England). Still have hopes of being quartered in the apartments or at the sight.

Two officers were fooling around in a field today – one tripped a wire on a land mine – result: one dead, one injured. Soup's ship has been given up as missing – perhaps they landed in Spain or Switzerland.

*Thursday 16:* Nothing doing yet today, although my ship has been loaded with belly tanks since noon. The ships will probably go out tomorrow morning. I played around in the maintenance shop most of the day. Washed a couple pairs of pants out in gasoline.

*Saturday 18:* Rumors going around that we will be carrying gas up to the front lines for the big offensive that is taking place. Haven't heard any news for so long that I hardly know there's a war going on. Guess they're starting a "big push" or something. Ace came back from Paris after RONing.

*Sunday 19:* Big deal today. Took off in the morning for Naples, Italy, supposedly to pick up some gas. Flew over Corsica, Elba, Rome, and it was really a nice trip. Landed at Capadochino, ate noon chow there, and came right back to Marseilles as the entire trip was snafu. Had a couple of good pilots so we had a good time. Got back rather late as it was after 1800 and kind of dark. I put on a trailing wire fish and reel, ate a bite, and then went right to the sack. Kind of tired, I guess.

*Monday 20:* Still sound asleep when Brent woke me up this morning. Took off in the other direction for a change – had a freight run up to Cognac near Bordeaux. Rather an uneventful trip, although it was over new territory. Ate lunch at a French air crew mess – what a time. Opened with oysters in the shell – if you could open them. Meal was fair, though, and we got filled up anyway. They say there is still a pocket of Krauts holding out in Bordeaux.

*Tuesday 21:* Thought I was going to fly again today, but they stuck me in the ground station instead. So I tore my hair over the "calls" most of the day. The traffic was pretty well ended by the afternoon, though.

*Thursday 23:* Thanksgiving today, but our ship had a long schedule. Left engine acted up, and for awhile I had hopes of eating dinner at Istres, but no soap. Took off for Cherbourg, and my Thanksgiving dinner was a can of meat and beans on the plane. After the long ride up to A-23 we found there was no food up there. Hopped over to Le Bourget to gas up and decided to RON there.

Had just about all the turkey we wanted that evening at the 10th AD 'cause we brown-nosed the mess sergeant. Saw "Four Jills in a Jeep" while we were there and then went over to a cafe for a few wines. Visited the 321st boys for a little bull session, and then to my cold bed in the apartments. No sleeping bag – really froze.

*Friday 24:* Up and on a truck over to the chow hall. Preflighted the ship and then waited for the pilot. He finally came around in the noon, and we found out that there was bad weather along the route. Engineer and I decided to go into town rather than sleep in that ice box again. Hitchhiked all the way in, got a hotel room, and then out into the city. Took in two acts of a French play – couldn't make anything of it, though, and then hit a few bars. Cognac and beer with a couple of infantry men was the order of the rest of the evening. Back to the hotel for a good night's sleep – strictly a good boy.

*Left: Eldor Guldan at Istres. Right: "Matz" and "Ace" – Harry Weinshank and Ray Lockhardt at Istres.*

*Sunday 26:* Had a flat tail wheel first thing this morning so I helped the engineer change it. Finally took off at ten and made a trip to Cognac with nine, five hundred pound bombs. Beautiful weather all the way, so I had a nice lazy time.

*Monday 27:* Early takeoff this morning, and though it was CAVU most of the way, we ran into a little bad weather and turned back as did most of the other ships. Supposed to go out again in the afternoon, but #491 developed a cut in the right tire – the fourth straight day with troubles. That meant no more flying for the day. Took a shower in the village and up to the bungalow. Ate early chow and went to a movie in town, which got as far as the first reel due to a projector break down.

*Tuesday 28:* Early takeoff this morning – nothing was wrong with the ship for once. A quick trip over to Cognac, CAVU most of the way. Got back just after noon and they loaded us up again. Thought for sure we were going to have to make a second trip and either RON or get back late. Luck was with us, though, and we had the afternoon off. Went up to the sight and worked around the bungalow a bit – filled in the slit trench and cleaned up the yard a bit. Smitty brought in two cases of cognac in the evening and we all had a good time.

*Wednesday 29:* Strictly a paddle-foot today. Rick and I are now supposedly in charge of the maintenance shop to start a new regime. Probably lose my ship and rotate flying Rick's ship. We worked in the shop all day, set up a shelf, and generally started arranging things. Heck of a lot of work to be done before the place is running according to my liking.

Had one stickler of a job – Rick was working on it for the most part and we didn't get through until 8:00 at night. Going to fly #390 tomorrow while Rick will work in the shop.

*Thursday 30:* Flew Rick's ship for the first time this morning – it's a pretty good kite. Took off in mid morning with a load for A-96, but landed at A-54 to get rid of a couple of passengers. Couldn't continue on though 'cause the weather was bad, so we RONed.

Went into Paris around 5:30 and spent quite a bit of time hunting for a hotel room. Bought a transformer, some perfume, and used up a couple of hours talking to a woman who spoke English very well. Coffee and doughnuts at the Red Cross and then a night cap at a cafe near the hotel.

**December 1944**

*Friday 1:* Up at 6:30 and caught the 7:30 bus out to A-54. Arrived plenty early and found out that the weather would probably be bad for two days. I called in for instructions and was told to "sweat it out." So we had dinner over at the 10th and then into town again. Saw a few of the sights this time – Church of Madeline, Champs Elysees, Arc de Triumphe, Eiffel Tower – put in quite a bit of walking. Saw a French movie in the evening and then over to the Red Cross. Met a very nice girl – walked home with her (down to the arc again) and finally back to the hotel around 1:00.

*Saturday 2:* Caught the 8:30 bus this morning 'cause we weren't quite so eager. Out to the field and took off around 10:00 bound for A-96. Delivered our load there, and then once more to Le Bourget to RON for the third night. Had to wait for some passengers for the next day.

Into "Paree," the usual hotel hunting, supper at the Red Cross and also a free movie. Spent the entire evening there, hoping to meet Nick again, but no luck. So I wandered back to the hotel and hit the sack.

*Sunday 3:* Finally went back to Istres. Rather an uneventful trip – good weather most of the way. Back around noon and right into town for a shower – man, I needed it.

Bunch of the boys from the ferrying group came down here today – Burkhardt was among them, and a lot of the other boys who used to be in 311th. Some of them slept in our barracks – quite a time.

*Tuesday 5:* Flying again today with a trip up to A-96 – uneventful except I missed dinner. Started back home and got diverted to Rama Touelli from which we are moving a fighter outfit. It's a bit of a dirt field that was used in the invasion of southern France, and the runway is so short you can spit from one end to the other. I imagine we'll spend some time moving that outfit now.

Back to Y-17 (Istres) around 3:15, and I went right into town for a shower.

*Wednesday 6:* Maintenance shop for me again today. Tried to build a box to ship a bottle of cognac home, but I made it too small. Worked the entire afternoon on a repair job on a ship, and though that part of it was fixed, there still was a bug in it. I finally quit on the job and "Henry" (Galarza) went to work on it.

Got my first pay check in French money, picked up my "limited" rations, and also learned that I'm due to leave on 10 days of DS to Burtonwood as soon as possible. Borrowed Weinshank's B-4 bag and got all packed up – the first leg being to Paris to pick up my orders.

*Friday 8:* Caught the shuttle trip up to Paris this morning – started things off right by breaking a bottle of wine in my B-4 bag. Quite a mess, but I saved the other two. Got into A-54 about 1:00 and found out that my orders had been sent down to Istres. Snafu as usual, so I took off for the Pigalle section for a bit of night clubbing. Took in the floor show at the Bal Tabarin, a little dancing at another place, and drank "beau coup" champagne. Spent numerous francs and had an edge on when I got back to the hotel.

*Saturday 9:* Gosh, that soft bed felt so good this morning, but I had to catch the early bus out to the field. Met Spot out there, and after a lot of talking I got put on the manifest of his ship, without any travel orders, and flew to Grove. Spot was half tight all the way.

*Sunday 10:* Carried my B-4 bag halfway up to the line this morning before I got a lift again. I had to talk a lot since they wouldn't give me a ride to BAD unless I was manifested. Terrible weather all the way up, and we landed in a snow storm – could barely see the field. Got myself organized a bit with a phone call and went over to the radar shop. Found out a little about the school and all and then went down to the sight where the other fellows are. BAD is the same as ever – cold Nissen huts, fog, mud, and dampness. To top it off, someone swiped my B-11 jacket while I was at chow. Really browned me off. Went over to the Red Cross in the evening for awhile and then to bed.

*Monday 11:* First day of school, and we had to march down in a formation. Started right in on the stuff, and the S/Sgt. teaching us seems to know his onions. The bldg. we're in is just like a big factory with men doing their regular jobs everyday. Most of this radar stuff is still rather secret, so I'll let it go at that.

Off at noon for chow and off for the day around five. Back to the sight in formation – strictly GI, you know. Still no trace of my B-11 – guess I've had it. A couple of Cokes at the Red Cross and to the sack.

*Tuesday 12:* School again today and more schematic drawings – hope I know something about radar by the time all this is finished. Ate down at sight 3 at noon and then back once more. We were off for a couple of hours in the noon so I went over to Tinker Hall to see if I could exchange my watch. No soap, though, so I made the trip over to the other side of the field for nothing. Left school early 'cause the instructor didn't show up.

*Wednesday 13:* School days, school days! More circuits and stuff. Learned that we'd be off tomorrow since the instructor has a day off. Zero – zero weather today – fog was really thick. Shore and I cleaned up after supper and took a bus into Warrington. We just missed the train to Manchester – took one to Liverpool instead.

Got booked for a bed at the Red Cross in Liverpool, and my first impression is that it's really a rough town. Went into one old bawdy pub that looked like it should have been placed down on the water front. Plenty of women around – I went to bed instead.

*Thursday 14:* Glenn Miller left Madingly/Twinwood Farm outside of London – Lost in Channel.

*Saturday 16:* Called the control tower this morning to see if anything was being cleared for Grove or the far shore, but no soap. That meant another day of loafing around – I'm trying to read "Gone With the Wind."

*Monday 18:* Still didn't know just where we were at this morning. Finally got a lift from a 325th ship over to A-54, but had to circle for quite awhile again. Ate over at the 312th mess and then started sweating out the "shuttle." It came in around 4:00, too late to return, and by that time I was all dressed up to go to town.

Had a heck of a time getting a hotel – they all were "complete." My "Have you a chambre'?" in French really got a work out. Spent the entire evening over at Rainbow Corners and met Nick and Nicky once more. Walked down to the arc with them once more and (repetitious) who was it that said "Man is a fool for a pretty face?" It's a very pretty face, though!!

*Wednesday 20:* The new "last push" offensive the Germans started has caused a bit of to do since there's supposed to be some "Allemand" parachutists around. Most of the boys are packing their .45s into town. Some Frenchmen even say that the Krauts will be back in Paris by Christmas. How about that?

*Friday 22:* Latest order is that we'll wear our side arms at all times 'cause of the paratroop scare. I don't have to worry since my .45 was swiped long ago. The usual barracks bull session in the evening. Had some of that American bottle beer we got on our last rations.

*Sunday 24:* Flew on another fellow's ship today, just to get up in the air. Took Sierak along and let him work all day. Just ordinary bomb runs – almost thought we'd have to spend Christmas eve at Dijon, but we got out in time. Came back here to learn that we were in "imminent" danger of attack – the entire sqdn. has been called out for guard duty with guns, helmets, etc. The ships are parked on the dirt and surrounded by B-26s, each one with nose or tail guns loaded and manned. Guards were posted all over, but I was up at communications most of the evening. Around 75 C-47s landed around 12:00 – all the ships in the group are here for a big deal tomorrow. Finally got to bed at 2:30, as I have to fly tomorrow. Quite a Christmas eve.

*Monday 25:* Up at 6:00 this morning, but didn't takeoff till 9 or so. Our load was infantry, fresh from the states, no rifles or equipment. We flew them up near Verdun – had to circle for about an hour waiting to land. We dumped them off and got right out of there again.

Got back for my Christmas dinner anyway, and it was OK. They didn't want us to stand guard duty tonight, but the entire sqdn. was supposed to sleep in the hangar instead, on the alert. I got disgusted with the whole affair and crawled in my sack. Gabby and Al locked the doors, turned out all the lights, and did likewise.

*Tuesday 26:* Flying again this morning. Got up around 7:45, and made it out to the ship in time, although I missed breakfast. Flew up to Dijon to pick up a load and didn't get out of there until late in the afternoon. We ate dinner in town at "GI Joes" – had a good steak, small as it was. Got a little look-see at the town and then out to the ship once more. We finally got loaded, and instead of delivering it, we went back to Y-17

The alert was still on, so I had to sleep up on the line with the others. Made my bed in the shop along with eight others – Gab slept on the bench top, I was almost on the floor on a stretcher. Had a scare when a rumor came through that "they're bombing Marseilles and headed this way!"

*Wednesday 27:* They lifted the alert at night, or at least we can sleep in the apartment once more. The guard is still heavy and all, but I guess the scare is over. Had us going for awhile last night – wasn't sure what was up.

*Thursday 28:* Ship flew local today, so both Rick and I were in the maintenance shop. Worked on the command set mock-up most of the time as we've got a 24 volt power source now. Puttered away on that plus a few odd jobs on the ships.

Heard again today that the ATC boys are due to return to Prestwick next month. Just as soon see them go as it would cut down the number of ships.

*Saturday 30:* "Slept in" this morning, that is, until around nine or so. Then down to the shop – the ship was flying local again. Didn't do much all morning, and then in the afternoon we found out four B-26s had to be checked over since they're leaving for England tomorrow. Every one of them had some sort of trouble, and we didn't get through until 6:00. Ate chow and then up to the sight to a meeting of all communications. Harry brought home the "bacon" once more and we had steaks – "a bit of all right."

*Sunday 31:* One heck of a wind blowing all day – close to fifty miles an hour. Kept the ships grounded and the shop full of smoke. Worked on an interphone job in the morning and finally got that fixed.

In the afternoon Rick and I started in on the 4th B-26 which had to be preflighted. Had putt-putt troubles and couldn't seem to get one that worked. Once we had the power, it only took a second to check the equipment over. Well, here it is New Year's Eve, my second in the ETO, and third away from home. Come along way from my civilian days, and there's probably a long road still ahead of me.

**January 1945**

*Monday 1:* Wow, did I feel rough this morning! I put three drunks to bed last night and crawled in mine unassisted, then this morning I was the only one of the bunch that felt sick. Laid around the shop all morning and then everyone was excused. Couldn't even eat noon chow, but crawled right into the sack. A couple of hours sleep fixed me up swell, and I was able to eat the evening meal. Rather a poor way to bring in the new year, but I don't think that mine was the only big head in this world today. We certainly killed enough bottles last night.

*Friday 12:* Those darn old-fashioned "eggs in the shell" for breakfast again this morning. Been having them rather often lately. In the shop all day with little or no work to do. Rick went up to BAD with #390 in the morning, so that means I won't do any flying for nearly a week. What gripes me though is that there's going to be a limitation of men on flying status, which will probably put us on every other month. "Cest le guerre!" (plus quite a loss in dough)

Took in the play "Junior Miss" at the theater in the evening. The cast was very good, and I got a big bang out of it. They say that a few actors from the original Broadway cast were in this performance.

*Saturday 13:* Another day in the shop – almost all the ships are up in England now, so that doesn't leave much for us to do. About all we do is sit around and keep the fire going. Guess there's no business down here so they send the ships up to BAD. Rumors are rife about moving up to Paris and all, but as usual, it's all indefinite.

Sat around all evening again and only got one letter written 'cause we had a bit of a bull session. Oh yes, Weinshank broke our sink just for a little excitement, and so I think I'll go back to washing out of a helmet.

*Sunday 14:* Some more of the new fellows are shipping to the 320th tomorrow, which will further cut down the sqdn. Think I'll try to go to the dentist in Marseilles tomorrow if the ambulance goes in. Like to have my teeth looked over.

*Monday 15:* Signed the sick book this morning and then rode into Marseilles in the ambulance. Roads were crowded with trucks and we didn't get in till almost noon. Ate chow with the medics and then went over to the dentist. He took care of us right away, and I had two or three cavities filled. We stayed in town all afternoon, so I had about two hours to myself. Wandered around town, bought an electric heater, and then caught the ambulance back to camp.

*January 17:* Took off around 5:00 and intended coming back for the last ship, but didn't bother to. Hurried in for a shower right after chow and then attended a sqdn. meeting in the mess hall. The usual periodic talk on VD plus a "short arm" – in the mess hall of all places! What the hell is this army coming to?

*Thursday 18:* Took off at 5:45, even though Harry's ship was the last in and it had troubles. Went to the evening show, a "whodunit mystery." Also poured out my troubles to Joe about the shop. Really getting tired of it and would like to have a ship of my own once more and do some flying. If I thought it would do some good, I'd ask to be relieved, but I don't think that would help. C'est la guerre!

*Friday 19:* Up on the line at 7:30 this morning as I had to help Harry fix the T/W on his ship. Then later on the RO of a transient VIP came in, and I spent a good bit of time working on his ship.

Started to put the old XMTR back into #308 in the afternoon and went up for a short hop with the CO and another major. They had a cable on the glider tow and buzzed the mine fields trying to detonate them. The cable broke off too soon for any results, though.

*Saturday 20:* Flying again today, and it was a trip up to England. Gassed up at Marignane and off we went. Ran into quite a bit of bad weather on the way up, but made the trip OK and landed at Stoke Orchard, a grass RAF field. Ate chow over at the flying crew mess – as usual we weren't expected and had to wait for a load. Managed to acquire a few lbs of freight and then flew over to Grove to RON, intending to return for the rest in the morning. The crews of the other ships went into Cheltenham.

Had to wait around at Grove to gas up the ship before we left it, and then I had command set troubles, so we missed chow entirely. Meandered down to the 325th sight for a bed, had a beer at a nearby pub with Spot, and then walked into Wantage for fish and chips. It started to snow just to spoil the evening a bit more.

*Tuesday 30:* Beau coup fatigue this morning. No sleep at all or anything to sleep on, for that matter. We got that familiar "80" bus into town, had a snack, met Taylor, and over to the train station. The snow had turned into slush and the streets were a mess. Met the pilots on the train, and in due course we were out at BAD once more.

Well, it seems that the ship now needs an engine change as they can't seem to fix that left one. We inveigled the PX officer out of another week's rations and struck out for dear ole' Manchester. Met a nice WAC on the train – after I had a shower and a hair cut, the three of us took Miss Pat Brogan out. She had to get back to BAD, so we had exactly two drinks, plus a lot of talk, at the Queens, and then she left.

Another snack at the club before bed time and at little discussion. Oh so intellectual – with one of the volunteers, on history, evolution, and what have you.

*Wednesday 31:* Had breakfast at the ARC and dropped in to see our pilots over at their place to find out the score. Neither of them seem eager, which means our departure is very indefinite. We decided to go to a show, and the boys, Max and Taylor, figured we ought to keep the vague sort of date we made with the "historian" last night. They met her at the library, I went to the cinema alone – "Kismet" – and they came in and sat alongside of me. Took leave of them and back to our hangout once more, the Red Cross. I decided to spend a quiet evening for once, so I went up to the writing room to try and catch up on this thing. Intended heading for the dorm rather early and do a bit of laundry if I can dry the stuff out.

**February 1945**

*Sunday 4:* Up to get at those fresh eggs this morning, even though I was plenty tired. Went down to the line and the almost empty shop. Only three ships are left down here – the rest are all on DS to various outfits, so that leaves us very little to do. Helped pack up some more of the stuff as we're due to move to A-42 any day now. The outfit was alerted once already, and then everything was supposedly canceled til the eleventh of this month. Gosh, I hate to move again, yet that's what's going to happen.

*311th C-47 over heavy fog.*

*Wednesday 7:* Took my time getting down to the line again this morning. Played around with a few of 45 husky dogs they brought in on a C-54 that landed here last night. Really beautiful dogs – bound for the northern front, supposedly. Wrote a letter in the office in the morning. Looked through the C-54, the first one I've ever been in, and it's one sweet ship.

*Friday 9:* Nothing much doing again. ATC has sent over an advance party and they're starting to clear up a lot of stuff. Saw "An American Romance" in the evening and stayed over afterwards for a talk by the CO. Just the usual pep talk about moving up to A-42. Said we did a good job and all down here.

*Saturday 10:* Had to clean up the place again this morning, so I didn't get down to the line till around 9:00. ATC brought over a generator today plus some more men. They really go about things in a big way. Took off around 4:00 for a shower up at the sight. Rick and Weinshank came back tonight – had a pretty good time.

*Sunday 11:* Up early as I am flying today. Had the shuttle run with Stillwell and Decker on my old ship #491. Seemed just like old times. Just an ordinary hop up to A-42 where we dropped off a jeep and trailer. As muddy as ever – I'm certainly going to hate that place.

Over to A-54 in the afternoon and decided to RON 'cause of weather and stuff. I didn't feel much like going into town the way I was dressed, so the engineer and I decided to stay over at the transient quarters. Met Doc Snyder at chow, went to the 321st movie with them, and then out for a few wines at a local cafe. That took care of the evening.

*Monday 12:* Got my radio poop and in the tower learned that #314 cracked up in England yesterday, killing the entire crew, including Smitty, Carson, and Norris. That was quite a blow to us.

Had a beautiful trip down to Y-17, flew around 9,000 and came right into CAVU down here. Helped pack up Smitty's stuff in the afternoon, got my rations, took a shower and stuff. Saw the evening show which was pretty good – "Thousands Cheer" – a musical.

*Tuesday 13:* I packed up a few of the tool kits and now there isn't much more to do. I brown-nosed myself in for flight tomorrow. Going to fly

*A group of 311th radio operators at Villacoublay.*

*A C-47 of the 306th Troop Carrier Squadron, (7H), 442 TCG, on the tarmac at Villacoublay.*

#308 tomorrow and see what makes that ship tick. Have had a lotta troubles with it lately. The fellows had a woman in the rooms tonight, but not for me.

*Wednesday 14:* Flying today, so I was up early and then down to RAF briefing. Believe it or not, the field was socked in for a couple of hours due to a heavy ground fog. It cleared up around 10:00 and away we went. Flew in #308 up to A-64 with good weather all the way. Had a heck of a time unloading the ship 'cause the boxes weighed so darn much.

Took right off again and back to the sunny Riviera. Most of the ships and crews have come back already, so we'll probably start moving tomorrow. Gabby hasn't returned yet, but it seems good to see the boys again. The same old French gal was up in the rooms tonight, and she had "beau coup" customers. I went to bed and slept good despite the noise.

*Thursday 15:* They gave me a break, so I'm flying two days in a row. The sqdn. started moving out in earnest today as most of the ships are back. Took a load up to A-42 and there was really swell weather up there for once. The mud was still present, but the field looks a lot better with the sun shining on it. Ate chow there at the transient mess and came right back to Y-17. Didn't have a chance to see what our quarters will be like as we didn't have the time.

*Saturday 17:* Flew #308 again today and had a couple of good Joes as pilots. Music all the way up, although we had about a 300 ft ceiling to land underneath. Landed up there and a couple of us decided to walk over to the transient mess. Quite a walk, but at least we had chow, which is more than the other fellows had. Got rid of our load of bicycles. Started to taxi out for takeoff, but what happens but a flat tire. Finally got it fixed and we were the last ship to return back to base. Came in around 1800, had chow down at the officer's mess where we now eat, and then to a movie.

*Sunday 18:* More moving again with me on #308 once more. Sweated out bad weather for awhile in the morning, both here and A-42. Got off a little later than usual and had just an ordinary trip up there. Got a jeep ride down to our sight which is about four miles from the field. Looked the place over a little, but didn't have time to see exactly where I'm staying. The set-up is pretty fair – perhaps even as good as the one we had down at Istres. We took right off again and so back to Y-17 around 5:00. Wanted to take a shower, but the machine had been taken out. Took in "Greenwich Village" in the evening and then to bed.

*Monday 19: VILLACOUBLAY (A-42):* Well, today was the last trip out of Y-17. We had to wait for the weather to clear up at A-42 until a little afternoon. Had to eat up the ship's rations 'cause the mess hall was all packed up. Took off a little after 12:00, a quick flight up here, and then unloaded the ship in a hurry. Put all our stuff in a weapons carrier for the sight.

We're staying in houses of the village of Viroflay about four miles from the field. I'm living on the first floor, in the living room of a three story house. It's a pretty nice set up, the chow hall only a block away.

*Wednesday 21:* Out to the maintenance shop early this morning and we started right in building shelves for the equipment. Worked steady all morning and then back to the sight for chow. Didn't go down in the afternoon 'cause I had to make out another report on the equipment in all of the ships. Got a haircut later on and screwed off the rest of the time.

The newest bit of c/s to hit us is guard duty – five men each night and reveille every morning, starting tomorrow at 6:15. Ouch!! That's what happens when we get back with "Group" once more. Oh well, the rumors say we'll be home within three months.

*Sunday 25:* Up very early this morning – took the jeep out to the field and stuck another command receiver on #491. Took the jeep back and hung around the ground station awhile. Had the jeep later on and kept it the rest of the morning while down at the shop. Puttered around as usual all day. Rick came in on #390 in the afternoon with a lot of equipment, which puts the shop back on its feet. Took care of a couple other jobs and came down to supper around 6:00.

The latest rumor is that we're going to be used over here as the army of occupation – doing air transport work as usual. How about that?

*Tuesday 27:* The latest rotation plan is at least two years overseas with 1,500 hours. Check that! Also heard that we have acquired another battle star for our ETO ribbon.

**March 1945**

*Thursday 7:* Another day of flying. Got an early start, over to A-54 to pick up litter patients and then to England. We made good time and ate noon chow at Cheddington. All set to leave with a load of passengers and the ship developed some trouble in the exhaust stack of the right engine. So we kicked the passengers off, fixed it up, and came back to A-42 to get it repaired better.

*Friday 8:* Rode down to the dispensary this morning and took my 64, flight physical. Thought I might have a little trouble with my eyes, but I knew the medic giving the test. Spent most of the morning there – got a ride back in Gen. Smith's Packard. (Gen. Smith wasn't in it!)

Started out a soldier's deposit account today with $40. It's a good way of saving my extra money.

*Sunday 11:* Flying again today on #390 – had the "Mice" as pilots. Just routine trips – wounded out of A-54 – at chow at Grove and then took a load of medical supplies out of Greenham Common. Didn't deliver it, but came right back to A-42.

Sweated out a ride back to the sight and picked up the leavings of supper per usual. Just a regular day with nothing new happening.

*Friday 30:* #358 blew a tire on takeoff at A-98 today and cracked up. The prop came through the left side and injured Lt. Frazer. He died during the night. The rest of the crew was unhurt.

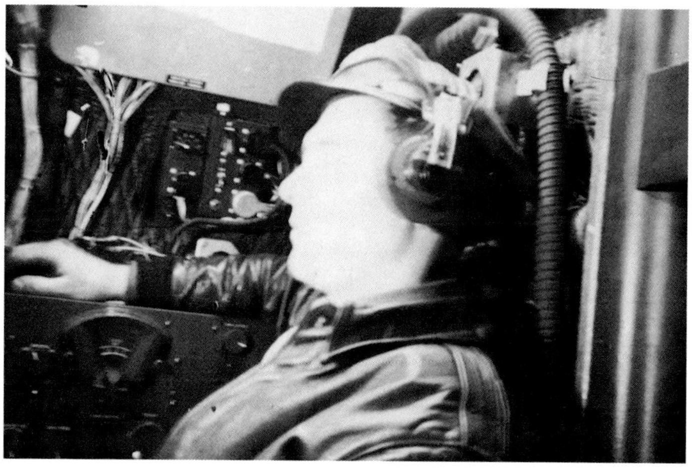

*"Fung" at his post – radio position in a C-47.*

**April 1945**

*Monday 9: A-46:* Took Al and Fung down to Air Traffic this morning to catch their plane and then terminated my tour of CQ about 7:30. Washed up and crawled right into the sack and slept till noon, at which time my buddies woke me up for chow.

Just loafed around the rest of the day, although the other fellows were helping to move over to A-46. Personnel moved over today, and some of the other sections started to move.

*Sunday 15:* Over to breakfast again – man, that's a rough ride over to A-46. Learned that inspections had to be pulled on two C-53s and it kind of browned me off, since no one knows what the score is yet. Rumor has it that the rest of the operators will be transferred to some more of the outfits in the wing. Kind of hope so, 'cause I'd like to be doing a little flying.

*"Back from chow" – Oscar Richter, Eldor Gulden, Al Bak, Andrew Garabedian, and Robert Spudis, Viroflay, Villacoublay, Paris.*

*Wednesday 18:* Another one of those "Hex" days for me. Came back to the sight after noon chow and I discovered that I lost my wallet out of the rear pocket of my fatigues. The wallet itself is worth $20, and contained 5 one pound notes, 100 lire, a $20 bill and about 3,500 francs. That, plus my pay book, shot record, ration card, 121 form, etc. Man, that was a heck of a loss to take. I searched the road, figuring it had bounced off the truck, but no luck. Notified the MPs and all, so I'll have to wait and see.

Nose wheel on an A-20 collapsed on landing at the field today. Messed up the nose a bit, but no one was hurt.

*Thursday 19:* A-46 for breakfast once more and then the usual loafing around all morning – still nothing much to do over there. Had a new pay book, shot-record, and form 121 made out in the afternoon, and then around 4:30 I received a call that someone had found my wallet. Had supper and then checked it to a medical detachment in Buc, and there it was. Seems that a little French kid found the wallet in the road and turned it into them, intact. Couldn't find him to give him a reward, so I'm going to try again tomorrow. Man, I was really thankful to get that thing back again.

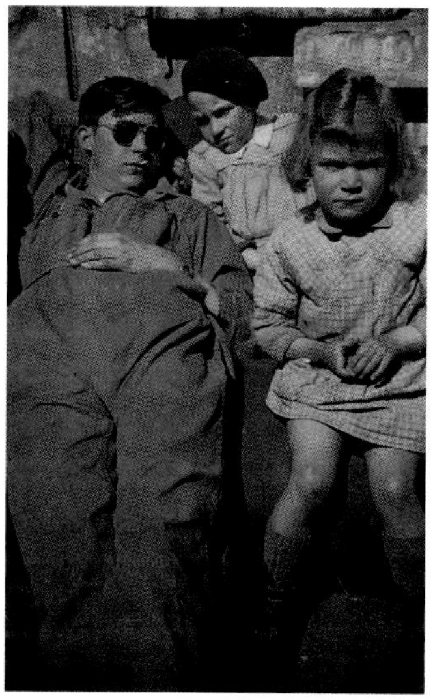

*Taken outside of the "maison" (house) in the town of Viroflay, Paris (A-42). The small boy and young lady were from a nearby residence. Dick Mollwitz made friends with them in elementary French and saw them almost every day.*

These are some of the last entries for 1945.

It should be noted that Richard Mollwitz only logged 10 hours of flying time for the month of April. He was able to log 60 hours in May, 30 hours in June, 106 hours in July, 93 hours for August, and in September, Richard logged 146 hours of flying time.

And so ends the diary of Richard Mollwitz with approximately 1,200 hours flight time logged in the ETO.

*Douglas A-20 "Havoc" with collapsed nose gear.*

*311th FS radio operators at A-42, Villacoublay, Paris.*

**Richard H. "Dick" Seebers served as a "Gooney Bird" pilot with the 311th and the 321st Squadrons. Dick stayed on with the USAF and flew B-47s, B-52s, and retired as a Lt. Colonel. He was kind enough to share his diary of the time he spent in the 27th ATG. Although not extremely detailed, Dick Seebers' diary does provide the reader a contemporary record of daily activities, which is typical of many C-47 pilots in the 27th during the '44-'45 period. Dick's diary picks up as he prepares to go overseas.**

SERVICE RECORD – TRANSFERS

| | |
|---|---|
| April 1943 | Fresno, California – Reno, Nevada |
| July 1943 | Reno, Nevada – Santa Ana, California |
| October 1943 | Santa Ana, California – Wickenburg, Arizona |
| December 1943 | Wickenburg, Arizona – Minter Field, California |
| February 1944 | Minter Field, California – Pecos, Texas |
| April 1944 | Pecos, Texas – Alliance, Nebraska |
| August 1944 | Alliance, Nebraska – Ft. Wayne, Indiana |
| September 1944 | Ft. Wayne, Indiana – Grove, England |
| November 1944 | Grove, England – Istres, France |
| February 1945 | Istres, France – Paris, France |
| April 1945 | 311th Ferrying Squadron – 321st Air Transport Sqdn. |

**FIRST TIME UNDER FIRE**

*November 19, 1944*: Off the coast of France, north of Nice. We must have drifted over the wrong side of the lines.

**CALENDAR 1944**

*August 20, Sunday*: Left home and arrived at Baer Field – Staging area. Assigned to BOQ. Talked with the fellows and heard the rumors.

*August 21, Monday*: Started processing and collected travel pay. Went to show in the evening.

*August 22, Tuesday:* Went to school all day and had a few tests.

*August 23, Wednesday:* Had another day of school and tests. Had interesting lecture on escape. Went into town at night. Called home.

*August 24, Thursday:* We had nothing scheduled all day. Played a game of ball with the enlisted men and beat them – retreat. Went to show.

*August 25, Friday:* Had to pass my blinker check this morning. Nothing the rest of the day till retreat. Big parade. Show in the evening. Some of the crews will be alerted tomorrow.

*August 26, Saturday:* Nothing to do today. All the boys up to crew 168 went through supply. Went into town again.

*August 27, Sunday:* The boys left this morning for Maine. The weather is cold and wet. Nothing to do. Open post from 1400 to 0030. Couldn't get train connections home.

*August 28, Monday:* We went through Supply today. They packed our clothes and issued us a plane, guns, and flying clothes. We leave for our POE early tomorrow.

*August 30, Wednesday:* We left Baer Field this morning. Buzzed the cottage and home, also the navigator's home in NY. Arrived at Bangor, Maine – processed and briefed on the trip to Goose Bay. Was appointed censor for our crew. Swell field – Dow Field.

*September 1, Friday:* Got paid early this morning and then left for Goose Bay, Labrador. Very nice field. Had a good trip. We have a good navigator. I made a good landing.

*Right: Lt. Richard "Dick" Seebers.*

*September 2, Saturday:* Was briefed early this morning and left for Greenland. First time out of North America. This is wild country. I would sure hate to be stationed here (BW-1). Saw a lot of icebergs. We were briefed for our trip to Iceland tomorrow. Runway started at water's edge and went up.

*September 3, Sunday:* We left Greenland this morning. Flew over "ice cap" and on to Iceland. Very barren country. Fighter base, P-47s are next door. Town, also. Terrible base – ready for war. Red Cross had a club for us – coffee and doughnuts at 8:30.

*September 4, Monday:* Were briefed this morning for flight to UK. Bad weather ahead. Flight was called off. The A-20 and 26s left, however. We went to show and hung around the O club all day. Met Wockenfuse, co-pilot on a 17.

*September 5, Tuesday:* Left today for the UK. Everything swell till after we hit the coast. Bad weather. Saw a sub and other boats. Our destination was closed (Nutts Corner, Northern Ireland). Went to Prestwick, Scotland, after wandering around in the soup. Quite a mess. No altitudes were assigned. Finally got in, though. Officers club in a big old house on a big and pretty estate.

*September 6, Wednesday:* Were alerted most of the day. Left at 1800 for Warton, England, a short hop. Four of us followed 17s into the field. Weather was bad all the way. We took three passes to find the runway. A good field. Many P-51s and some 38s. We stayed at a very nice camp.

*September 8, Friday:* Left Warton and flew formation to Grove. Saw and heard my first balloon barrage. Lousy field here. Our group had just moved in and everything is a mess. I don't think I'm going to like the food and housing here.

*September 9, Saturday:* Didn't do much today. A couple of the boys rode CP over to France. Had a lecture on the UK and France. After moving twice, we finally got settled in our barracks. Our navigators got four days leave to go to London.

*September 11, Monday:* Still no flying. Went over and collected $70 per diem. Helped the captain move offices. Shot some baskets in the gym. Show in the evening, "Joe E. Brown." Walked into Wantage.

*September 12, Tuesday:* Started flying today with Lt. Sico. We went to France – St. Dizier (A-64), with gas. Also saw Paris (Eiffel Tower). Then flew around southwestern England. Later flew to Langford Lodge near Belfast, Ireland, and then returned. Saw some real evidence of the war via our bombings. 9:45 hours

*September 13, Wednesday:* Flew again. Late start because of the fog. Went to Heston (in London). Saw Bill Russell. Then went to Le Mans, France (A-35), with passengers. Then on to A-52 near Chartres and then to A-13 near Bayeux. Saw much of France, the original landings on the coast. Talked with some of the French boys. Gave them some candy drops and received some apples. I like France better than England. Got my rations. Saw some prisoners at Heston. 5:45 hours

*September 14, Thursday:* To France again. We went to A-13 again below the overcast. Saw a great deal more of the results of the war. Saw lots of supplies and troops. Made another trip to A-23 at Cherbourg. Flew over port and harbor. Stopped at Heston on the way back with mail and had a Coke. Hauled passengers on these hops. Saw "DuBarry was a Lady." 5:45 hours

*Dick Seebers' home in England, Grove, Fall, 1944.*

*September 15, Friday:* Bad weather, so we took off late. We went to A-25, A-23, A-35, and A-42 (Paris). We had to RON in Paris. The field was a wreck. Many wrecked Ju 88s were there. We couldn't get any food.

We hitch-hiked into town. Got a ride on a big truck loaded with TNT. All the people waved at us and made a 'V' with their fingers. We ended up riding in General Tedder's car. We had quite a time walking around. The army gave us a hotel room. We didn't like it, so we got one ourselves. What a place! All the people ride bikes. Never seen so many bikes in my life. The buildings are pretty nice – so are the girls. Lights aren't on much and no food. 3:50 hours

*September 17, Sunday:* Went to Warmwell and got gas and took it to A-76 near Germany. Returned to Zeals and got belly tanks, but couldn't get gas to go to A-62. Flew with Lt. Bachelor. Saw the Horsa gliders for the mission in Holland. Some of the boys were up to the front lines east of Verdun to evacuate wounded. The boys from Heston moved here. 5:40 hours

*September 19, Tuesday:* Took some belly tanks to A-62 near Reims. Then picked up 28 wounded at A-85 in Belgium and took them to A-25. Went to Warmwell and got gas and returned home. 5:50 hours

*Dick Mollwitz, Everitt Sheppard, and Al Bak, while on a medical evacuation mission, in Belgium.*

*September 20, Wednesday:* Another day off. Did a few odds and ends. Got a navigation kit. Took my new pants into town to be shortened. Went to a French class and movie. Had a visit with Price.

*September 21, Thursday:* Flew with Capt. Jarvis. Went to Heston about noon time (bad weather) and took some passengers to A-81. Then went to A-85 and picked up 28 wounded for A-54. RONed at Paris and had a big time. They wouldn't let the nurse in town. 4:15 hours

*September 22, Friday:* Looked at perfume this morning (we just had an air raid alert). Left at noon (bad weather) and took 24 wounded Jerries on stretchers to A-25. Then returned to Grove. Flew over to Weatherfield late this afternoon and RONed. 3:30 hours

*September 23, Saturday:* We moved the A-20 base to Weatherfield to A-55 (south of Paris). We made two trips. Saw the TCC go over with gliders. Stayed at Andrews Field. B-26 base at night. 8:20 hours.

*September 27, Wednesday:* Went to A-60, Great Dunmow, A-60, Gosfield, and Grove. Moved another B-26 base. 6:40 hours

*September 29, Friday:* Made two trips from Andrews to A-61. We RONed in Paris again. Had a big time. Met a beautiful girl there – Swiss. 5:10 hours

*September 30, Saturday:* Flew to East Anglia, but no one needed us, so returned to Grove. Flew to A-42 and RONed at A-47. Walked all over Paris and finally found Souses house – too late at night. 4:15 hours

*October 1, Sunday:* Sat around the Red Cross club and ate doughnuts and drank coffee and juice while the RO played the piano. Took off for Matching and they sent us to Grove. Got paid $112. 2:10 hours

*October 2, Monday:* Had my checks today. Guess I'm a first pilot now. Wrote three letters tonight. 1:55 hours

*October 3, Tuesday:* Rode with Robbie today and split the time. Made one smooth landing. Went to A-58 and back to Grove. Then to Chipping Ongar and home. Found out that Bob Prior is at A-58. He wasn't there today. 5:35 total hours – 2:50 first pilot hours

*October 4, Wednesday:* Flew with Robbie. Went to A-42 and A-54. Took patients to Member. 4:15 – 2:05

*October 5, Thursday:* Went into London with Bill Canaan. Bought some things. Found a good place to eat.

*October 6, Friday:* Flew with Swank. Went to A-42 and A-54. Took patients to Ramsbury. Got my first letter from home. 4:10 hours

*October 7, Saturday:* Flew with Frazer. Went to A-42, A-54, and Ramsbury. Found out that Hawser and Buikema are there. Didn't see them. Heard they had the Air Medal, three OLC, and Presidential Citation. 4:25 – 2:10

*October 9, Monday:* Wasn't scheduled, but was up before I found out. The boys were grounded till afternoon. Took some laundry in town. Mailed package of perfume home. Saw clipping in "Stars and Stripes" about Urban Drew. (A friend of Dick's from school, who was a P-51 Ace, and the first American to shoot down a Me-262 jet.)

*F/O Jim Leverick at A-54 Le Bourget Field, October 1944.*

*F/O Jim Leverick.*

*October 10, Tuesday:* Wasn't scheduled again today. Signed pay-roll again today and met Dan Davis (squadron Capt. at Santa Ana), co-pilot on C-47, came over with ATC.

*October 11, Wednesday:* Flew with Robbie. Went to A-42 and back. Bad weather. Got two letters from home. Read a book. 4:25 – 2:15

*October 14, Saturday:* Flew with Ryan. Went to Burtonwood to pick up a load (got some sleeping bags, too). Went to A-62 and then home. Got a letter today. 5:45 – 2:45

*October 15, Sunday:* Was on stand-by today. Didn't fly. Had my parachute taken off my 121. Went to a show in town. Read a book.

*October 16, Monday:* Didn't get off till 1530. Went to A-42. Stayed in Paris. Met Jack Lowe from Redford in mess hall. Flew with Kogge. 1:45 as 1st pilot

*October 17, Tuesday:* Returned to Grove. Left a Lt.Col. off at Greenham Common. Bad weather. Finished another book. Finally got my Ballot.

*October 18, Wednesday:* Flew with Kogge. Got stuck in the mud here at Grove. Went to Northolt and A-46. Two bad landings. 4:15 – 2:15

*October 19, Thursday:* Went to Warton to pick up a load. Got an A-2 jacket. Went to A-42. RON and went to the Lido Club. 4:00 – 2:00

*October 20, Friday:* Sat around the field all morning. Bad weather so went back into town. Went shopping. Met Buikema and Barkmeyer. Got checked out on the Metro.

*October 21, Saturday:* Went out to field and sat around till 1600. About twenty ships in today. Bad weather. Met Robbie, Malaby, Meyers, Saunders, and Evarts. Went to see a show at Olympia. Then we all went to Ciros.

*October 22, Sunday:* Sat around till noon and finally took off. Weather not too good over the channel and UK. Flak was here to see Robbie. Some of my back mail was here – 10 letters. 2:00 – 1:00

*October 24, Tuesday:* Went to Seighford to pick up a load. Weather stinko. Went to A-54. Wrecked the aileron when the plane skidded around at the end of the grassy, muddy runway. RONed in Paris with Leverick, co-pilot. Red Cross got us a room.

*October 27, Friday:* Weather stinko – didn't go out to field. Tried to get a ride to A-42. Met a fellow from Detroit (Patty).

*October 28, Saturday:* Went out to field early. A beautiful day. Aileron came. I went back to Grove. More mail here. Took a shower and shaved. New boy in the barracks from Boston (B-24 pilot).

*October 29, Sunday:* Flew with Sheets (Michigan Boy). Went to Stansted and picked up some tires. Went to A-60 and ate. Then to A-61 and got rid of the tires. Back to Grove and show at night.

*October 30, Monday:* Went to Hixon and picked up some passengers. Took them to A-54. Then home. New boy for co-pilot.

*October 31, Tuesday:* Weather stinko. Got paid. Went to A-62. Preston C.P. RON. Went into Reims.

*November 1, Wednesday:* Left at noon for Grove. Landed and then went to Burtonwood – RONed and went to a show.

*November 2, Thursday:* Took off at noon for A-42. Hit a wire with a wing tip. Got stuck in the mud. Finally got home. One letter waiting for me.

*November 3, Friday:* Was on the alert list. Slept in. Had an hour of link training. Went to a show in town. Got my footlocker.

*November 4, Saturday:* Alert again. Another hour of link. Got letters from Marg (3) Cliff, and Edna. Listened to Navy-Notre Dame game.

*November 5, Sunday:* Was supposed to fly but ship wasn't loaded. They finally canceled the trip.

*November 6, Monday:* Day off. Slept in and laid around the barracks most of the day. Got briefed at night for our moving to Marseille.

*November 7, Tuesday:* Got up at 5:00 in order to make an early take-off. Our ship was U/S. Sat around the ready-room most of the day. Sixteen ships went to Marseille. One ship has not been heard from.

*Airfield storage area in France, probably Istres.*

*November 10, Friday:* Early takeoff for Marseille. Good trip – 3:30 hours for trip down and 4:30 for the trip back. Good field but windy as heck. Had a lot of fun on the way back.

*November 11, Saturday:* We got up early again and left Grove for good. Windy here again. Found our barracks and got settled a bit. When we get this place fixed up it will be a good deal. 3:45 as co-pilot

*November 14, Tuesday:* Robbie was killed today and Bill Keenan injured when they walked on a land mine while hunting. Bill was hit in the leg, hip, and chest.

*November 15, Wednesday:* I packed Robbie's clothes and locked them up. Bill Robinson dropped in and stayed with me over night. He's stationed right next to Grove in TCC.

*November 16, Thursday:* Went to see Bill in the hospital. I fainted there. Went to Marseille and bought some shirts and got my pictures.

*November 17, Friday:* Ship wasn't loaded so I didn't fly. Packed Bill's clothes and cleaned mine in gas. Changed my allotment to $200.

*November 19, Sunday:* Went on a sight-seeing tour of Italy. Was supposed to pick up gas at Naples. Saw Corsica, Rome, Anzio, Naples, and Pisa. Got shot at near Nice by the Jerries. Landed after dark. Flew co-pilot for Garrard. 8:35.

*Old operations/pilot's ready room, at Istres.*

*New Operations, at Istres.*

*November 20, Monday:* Was scheduled to fly but ship wasn't loaded. Bad weather in the afternoon. Turned in Robbie's flying clothes.

*November 21, Tuesday:* Went to Dijon. Had to wait a few hours to be unloaded. We finally had to do it ourselves.

*November 22, Wednesday:* Slept in. Went down to hospital to see Bill. Took his clothes. Got back late and had a letter from Marg waiting. Also one from church and Temp APO and from cliff. All old.

*November 23, Thursday:* Was supposed to go to A-23 and A-64 with Gale. We started out but came back because of the bad weather at destination. Got a haircut by a female barber. Had turkey.

*November 25, Saturday:* Wasn't scheduled to fly. Cleaned a pair of pinks with gas. Started reading "King's Row." Took a shower.

*November 26, Sunday:* Went to Marseille with Gale. Saw Bill in the afternoon. Went to the opera at night.

*November 27, Monday:* Walked around town. Went to the PX. Came back in the afternoon. Went to an American movie at night. Saw a reel of "Janie." Projector broke.

*C-47s on the field in southern France.*

*November 28, Tuesday:* Flew with Gale to Cognac. Took a shower and finished "Kings Row."

*November 29, Wednesday:* Took off for Cognac. Weather O-O. We came back. Wrote letters in the afternoon. Got seven letters today.

*November 30, Thursday:* Went to Cognac. Malaby was my co-pilot. Started to read "A Tree Grows in Brooklyn."

*December 1, Friday:* Went to Cognac. Had to circle field for an hour till the ground fog dissipated. Had a big, old rat-race.

*December 2, Saturday:* Went to Cognac. Finished "A Tree." Heard Army-Navy game. I picked Army.

*December 3, Sunday:* Something new – went to Cognac with DeJougne. Had a fire. One of our little villas burnt down.

*December 4, Monday:* Was on alert. Didn't fly. Wrote quite a few letters.

*December 5, Tuesday:* Went to Cognac (the southern route) with Hawkins. Had to wait till he got 15 cases of cognac. Then to Ramatuelle. What a place. Full day.

*Ralph "Robbie" Robinson, 311th Pilot, killed by a land mine on November 14, 1944.*

*C-47 in the air November, 1944.*

*December 6, Wednesday:* Scheduled for A-96 but weather stinko. Wrote some letters. Had a second letter returned by the censor. Better watch out. Got paid $62.

*December 7, Thursday:* Three years later. (Pearl Harbor). Went to A-96 with Hawkins. Had a rough time coming back. Went up to 17,200 ft. The field was socked in for a change.

*December 9, Saturday:* Good weather. Went to Cognac with Kennedy. Letter from home and Scout troop. 3rd letter returned by censor. Got the Paris shuttle tomorrow. Got a hair cut.

*December 10, Sunday:* Took the shuttle to Dijon, Y-31, and A-54. Flew on the deck to Y-31. Let down on the beam at Paris – 200 ft. ceiling. Met Danny Sherman, Bill Russell, and a friend of Robbies. The big building at A-54 is fixed up pretty nice. Field in a terrible mess.

*December 12, Tuesday:* Got lost going to Cognac. The congressional tour landed here in C-54s. Wrote some letters and got two.

*December 15, Friday:* Went to Cognac. Weather not too good. Played football in the afternoon. No mail.

*December 17, Sunday:* Went to Cognac with Sheets. Then to Toulouse. Got eight letters. Saw "The Amazing Mrs. Holiday" – pretty good. Got a letter from Mrs. Moore telling that Norm was missing in action.

*December 19, Tuesday:* Scheduled for Dijon and Cognac. One ship U/S. Took off and was back in half an hour. Weather on the deck. Got our Christmas rations. Gave my beer to Malaby. Saw "North Star." Got a package.

*December 22, Friday:* Slept in. Took a shower and wrote a letter. Got a card and letter from Marg. Plenty cold today. Another fire – we carry guns 24 hours a day.

*December 23, Saturday:* An alert – didn't fly. Slept and read. Got a package. Heard that paratroopers landed at Lyon.

*December 24, Sunday:* Went to Y-5 and then Dijon. Came back to base and found we were alerted. Rumors of breakthroughs and paratroops. Sat up half the night ready to fight. Big mission tomorrow.

*December 25, Monday:* Christmas – didn't fly. Slept most of the afternoon. Had turkey at night. Slept down at operations all night. Rest of the boys flew infantry replacements up to the front. They were young, green, and had just landed in France. Poor boys.

*December 26, Tuesday:* Went to Dijon. Waited most of the day for a load. Went in town. Got cards from Edna and Gentiles. Have to sleep in op's again. Saw a terrible movie in a wrecked hangar. Saw ack – ack.

*December 27, Wednesday:* Went to Dijon but couldn't get in. Took a shower. No mail. The alert is off. I guess all the rumors were false. We're through playing soldier.

*December 31, Sunday:* Saw Bill – he's doing very good. Ready to go home. Went to a movie. Had a couple of drinks at the club. This has been quite a year.

*Lt. Lewis Gale in the cockpit of a C-47 November, 1944.*

*A Gooney Bird on top.*

**1945**

*January 1, Monday:* Too windy – no flying. Got paid and went to the Riviera Bowl in Marseille. Saw "Going My Way." Got two letters.

*January 3, Wednesday:* No place to go and the ship U/S, so I didn't fly. Took a shower and went over to Marignane to get a haircut. big party at night.

*January 7, Sunday:* Took off in the afternoon for BAD. Got as far as Paris. RON.

*January 8, Monday:* Lost a blower on take-off. Had group work on engine. Met Russell and Price.

*January 9, Tuesday:* Went into town with Russell and had a big time. Met Paulette.

*January 13, Saturday:* Bad plugs in morning. Finally got off for BAD. RONed there.

*January 14, Sunday:* Not loaded. Went into Manchester with gang.

*January 15, Monday:* Got off in afternoon and finally got home. Had about 8 packages and 5 letters waiting.

*January 16, Tuesday:* Went to Marignane and A-64. Came home and straightened my room and footlocker.

*January 17, Wednesday:* On alert – didn't fly. Boys got home from Cannes.

*January 19, Friday:* Went to BAD with Gale. Stopped at Altermaster. Went into Manchester.

*January 20, Saturday:* Runways U/S. Talked with Don Cohoe. Went back into Manchester. Saw a show.

*January 21, Sunday:* Finally got off. Went to A-64 and home – got in after dark.

*January 25, Thursday:* Went to Naples with Gale. Met Curt Yates. Got home late. Flack house tomorrow.

*January 26, Friday:* They wouldn't let us land at Cannes. Rumors of us moving to A-42. Wrote some letters. A bunch of Russians came in today – civilians.

*January 27, Saturday:* We are moving to A-42. Flack house is out. Packed my clothes. Party at night and General Marshall came in.

*January 29, Monday:* Move to A-42 called off. We are going on DS to 54 and Grove. Didn't do anything.

*February 1, Thursday:* Slept in. Left for Paris DS to 86th. Visited Malady.

*February 2, Friday:* Took off in the afternoon for Biggin Hill with the mail. We then RONed at Little Walden. Went into Cambridge to Red Cross. Called Snuffy – he has gone home.

*February 3, Saturday:* Moved a P-51 base to A-84 in Belgium. It was the outfit that Urban Drew belonged to. They say he was the hottest pilot there. Back to A-54.

*February 4, Sunday:* Took evacs to Membury. Late takeoff and went to Little Walden – no load. RONed at Grove. Stayed with Price and Russell.

*February 5, Monday:* Back to A-54 in the afternoon. Went in town to see Bob Hope's new picture.

*February 6, Tuesday:* On sick list. Went in town and got a haircut, took a R.C. tour of Paris, and bought a blouse.

*February 8, Thursday:* Went to Membury with evacs. Weather Stinko!! Let down over London 100 foot ceiling at Membury. RONed and met Ed Zoebb to which he put me up.

*February 11, Sunday:* Went to Grove with the evacs. Weathered in. Stayed with Price and Russell.

*George King on a field in southern France while playing a little football.*

*311th Squadron billet in Viroflay, Paris while stationed at Villacoublay.*

*February 12, Monday:* Weathered in. Found out that one of our planes hit a hill – seven killed.

*February 13, Tuesday:* Late start today. Went to A-81 and A-54. Going home tomorrow, I hope.

*February 14, Wednesday:* Came home today and glad to be back. Beautiful down here. Football game in the afternoon. Show at night.

*February 15, Thursday:* Moved the 10th Air Depot Squadron to A-54. Movie and stage show at night.

*February 16, Friday:* Started moving to A-42. Football in the afternoon

*Right: C-47 taking off from the grass field at Le Bourget.*

*February 17, Saturday:* To A-42 again. Flew co-pilot with a major. Back with Sheets. Got 28 letters and 3 packages.

*February 19, Monday:* Final move to A-42. Billets not so good. Good transportation into Paris. Living next to SHAEF HQ in Viroflay.

*February 20, Tuesday:* Started to play football but had to go to A-82 for passengers to Pisa. Stayed with night fighter bunch and saw a good movie.

*February 22, Thursday:* Returned to A-42. Unpacked some of my things. Drew names for some battle jackets. Somebody took some things from the room.

*February 23, Friday:* Played football in the morning. Put a lock on the door. Late takeoff at 1:00 because of weather. Went to A-54 for evacs and had to RON at Ford. Went into Brighton with nurse.

*February 26, Monday:* Was on alert. Took my laundry over. Went into town. Found out where the gym is, took my blouse in, and mailed home my film and mother's day flowers. Basketball at night.

*February 27, Tuesday:* Finally got off in the afternoon for A-41, Chilbolton, and Metfield.

*February 28, Wednesday:* Bad weather – didn't fly. Lost to the 321st. 46-35.

*March 1, Thursday:* Went to A-54 but didn't take evacs. Went to Honington and B-53. Won by forfeit.

*March 4, Sunday:* Went to A-54, Chilbolton, Horsham St. Faith, but couldn't get in A-81. Returned to A-42. Had a birthday cake and then a party at night.

*March 5, Monday:* Went to A-87, Grove, Y-35, and home. Show at night.

*March 7, Wednesday:* Went to Seething, Honington, B-53 and then home. Got shot at over Dungeness.

*March 9, Friday:* Went to B-53, then let DeJonge off at B-55, Grove, Y-35 and then home.

*March 10, Saturday:* Ship U/S. Got a sleeping bag. Went in town to get battle jacket but the store was closed. Game at night but we lost.

*March 14, Wednesday:* Went to Standsted, Greenham Common and home by 1:30. Went in town for jacket – still not ready. Group party at night – Glenn Miller's band. Col. Cochran and 2 star General there. Swell party.

*March 15, Thursday:* Had day off – slept in and then turned in some stuff at Tech Supply. Had a Coke in the PX. Went to see Paulette at night. Baseball game after supper.

*March 16, Friday:* Left for Cannes in afternoon, a beautiful place. Checked in at the Martineze. Took a hot bath.

*March 24, Saturday:* Ship U/S. Took laundry and film over. Show in town at night.

*Lt. Richard H. Seebers.*

*Dick Seebers with one of three best friends from Detroit, P-47 pilot John DeForge. Dick is wearing the battle jacket he had made in France.*

*March 25, Sunday:* Ship U/S. Went back to bed till noon. Got more mail and wrote some letters. Party at night.

*March 26, Monday:* Went to Y-42, A-93, Grove, A-93 and then home. Movie at night.

*March 27, Tuesday:* Day off so went into town. Saw a movie and picked up battle jacket.

*March 29, Thursday:* Bad weather. Took off in the afternoon. Went to A-96 and back.

*March 30, Friday:* Went to Stansted, Hixon, and back to A-42. Frazer cracked up at A-98.

*March 31, Saturday:* Went to A-81, Grove, Y-42, and then home. Frazer died today.

And so ends Dick Seebers' diary.

## *Chapter 5*

# Christmas 1944: The 27th ATG in the "Battle of the Bulge"

The 27th ATG flew in the worst of weather conditions, when flying was extremely dangerous, and performed a vital role in aiding the Allied victory. Much of the time, however, they were behind the scenes. On Christmas Eve 1944, the 27th ATG was called on in an emergency situation with "The Battle of the Bulge" to perform a critical mission, which made those who participated feel like they were "part of the action," and ultimately earned the 302nd Wing a commendation from Lt. General Carl Spaatz. The following short article from *Stars and Stripes* explains the mission.

**"Tankers Are Sped To Bulge by Air At-Peak of Battle"**
Hundreds of badly-needed tank mechanics and technicians were flown from rear areas to airfields in the bulge battle zone in less than a day after a rush call had been sent out for them at the height of the Nazi counter-offensive, USSTAF disclosed yesterday.
The disclosure was made in a commendation given to the Air Service Command's 302nd Transport Wing by Lt Gen. Carl Spaatz, USSTAF Chief. The commendation said that 100 planes of the 302nd flew from bases in England and France to a rear-area field on the Continent, picked up the men, and sped them up to the Third Army on Christmas Day, less than 20 hours after the operation began.

**The following release from 302nd Wing contains a copy of the commendation from Lt. General Spaatz:**

HEADQUARTERS
UNITED STATES STRATEGIC AIR FORCES IN EUROPE
IMMEDIATE RELEASE 23 January 1945
302nd Transport Wing Command for Emergency Operations During German Counter Offensive

A commendation by Lt. Gen. Carl Spaatz, Commanding General of the U.S. Strategic Air Forces in Europe, disclosed today that the Air Service Command's 302nd Transport Wing flew highly-trained ground troops to advance airfields in record time during the German counter offensive.

The story begins at 1630 hours on the afternoon of December 24th, when the Transport Wing was alerted. Squadron radios crackled with instructions. Planes already in the air with various military cargoes were recalled to their home bases and told to unload and stand by.

An hour later word was flashed that 100 planes were to proceed from bases in England and France to a continental airfield that must remain unnamed for the time being. There they were to pick up hundreds of tank mechanics and technicians and fly them to advance airfields in the battle area where General Patton's Third Army was fighting.

Freight men tugged and sweated to unload the big Douglas transports of their cargoes. Airplane engine specialists, radio mechanics, and other ground crew men swarmed over the C-47s, giving them a last-minute check before taking off. It was a race against time and the weather, for fog was fast threatening to close at least one base.

The first of the transports took off at 2030 hours on Christmas Eve. By 2200 hours the whole armada was on its way and several hundred Air Corps men spent their Christmas in the air. Meanwhile, at the destination airfield, where the highly-trained troops were to be loaded, a whole squadron sprang into action. Forty thousand gallons of gasoline had to be trucked from nearby supply dumps. Clerks, cooks, and carpenters all pitched in to do the job. Flying Control corralled extra jeeps and put them on tap to direct aircraft to dispersal areas.

The moon was riding high in the sky that night when the airliners began to arrive. Smoothly and precisely, they landed and pulled into parking areas to which they were directed by radio, signal lights, and jeeps.

Ground crews went to work on the planes almost as soon as the props stopped spinning. Gas trucks drew alongside and replenished spent fuel supplies.

By 0800 – that was Christmas morning – the servicing was completed, just as the tank men began to arrive. Twenty minutes later the first plane, with its cargo of men, raced down the runway, nosed into the air, and headed for the battle front. From then until 1430 hours Douglas transports took off in a steady stream on the troop-carrying assignment. Some of the planes even managed to get in a second trip to the front that day.

Before noon the vitally needed tank mechanics and specialists were pouring out of the C-47s onto an airfield within earshot of an artillery duel along the Western Front.

The whole troop transport operation was completed in less than 24 hours. Not a man nor a plane was lost.

General Spaatz's commendation reads:

> "With great satisfaction I desire to commend the Air Service Command and the 302nd Transport Wing. In particular, the effective

*A C-47 of the 321st ATS in the air.*

manner in which they met an emergency on December 24th in transporting troops from Istres to ________. (Destination was classified. The planes landed at a forward airstrip at Verdun)

The late hour when this project was received, the collection and dispatching of the aircraft, and the accomplishment of the mission in minimum time reveals a high degree of organization and management. The manner in which this mission was performed reflects not only on the Air Service Command, but the Air Forces in Europe at large.

The 302nd Transport Wing is commanded by Colonel Martin A. Bateman, of Camden, S.C."

**Howard Stillwell of the 311th made the following comments concerning this mission:**

Christmas of 1944 will not be forgotten by any member of the 311th or the rest of the squadrons in the 27th ATG. All C-47 squadrons gathered at Istres the night of 24 December. Starting about 0600 on Christmas, flights were made to airfields in the area of the "Battle of the Bulge" where General Patton's 3rd Army was fighting. Troops were carried to join the 3rd Army. Some of our crews made two trips, each lasting about 4 1/2 hours. I landed at Verdun. The replacements on our aircraft looked like young kids, 17-18 years old. Captain Decker had a large responsibility as the OPS Officer in charge.

**Joe D. Maguire, C-47 pilot of the 321st Transport Squadron, remembers the events of December 24, 1944:**

"The morning of December 24, 1944, I flew to Belgium and returned in the afternoon to our base at Le Bourget in Paris. Everyone in the squad-

*A 321st TS C-47 in the snow at the time of "the Bulge."*

ron was looking forward to a Christmas Eve celebration. Rumors were flying that we would get turkey and dressing with all the trimmings, which was a dream come true after weeks of powdered eggs, spam, and K rations.

As usual, a truck pulled up to the airplane to take us to our quarters. As I climbed into the truck, I noticed a small spotter type aircraft with what appeared to be Santa Claus on board. He was tossing sacks of fruit and candy out to the school children, who had gathered from the neighborhoods around the air field. Our headquarters were in a school house that had been occupied by the Luftwaffe. As the truck approached the building, here came Santa behind us, who was still tossing out gift sacks to the kids running along beside the truck. I suppose he was the same Santa that had been in the airplane. The sacks of candy and fruit came from military personnel who had donated it from their rations. Seeing those happy little faces made it all worth while.

We went on to our living quarters and started to get cleaned up for our Christmas Eve celebration. Someone had found a tree which was decorated with various and sundry things. It wasn't home, but a lot better than nothing. We knew it was Christmas Eve. Darkness had set in, and our appetites and expectations were growing, but alas, it was not to be.

We were given strong black coffee and told to get back in our flying gear. Orders came down from higher command that we were to fly down to Istres near Marseilles in Southern France to pick up badly needed tank personnel and fly them up to advance airfields near the Battle of the Bulge area. We flew down the Rhone Valley to the Mediterranean and tried to get some sleep in our airplanes until daylight. At early dawn, we could hear and see large trucks filled with hundreds of young soldiers who had just gotten off of ships from the States. We were going to take them to help turn the tide at "The Bulge." We flew our load of young soldiers up to an airfield near Verdun, which was close to all the action at the front.

I have been a Christian believer since I was 12 years old and I recall thinking, what a way to celebrate the birth of the Christ Child Jesus. I wondered why is all this war and "Battle of the Bulge" happening? My feelings for those young men and for all the ground troops were of great concern and sadness.

We returned to base, late afternoon, Christmas Day, very tired. I laid on my bunk thinking and thanking God for the dependable old "Gooney Bird" and for my safe return. Once again my thoughts turned to the Christ Child and the fact that there was hope! I soon dropped off into a deep sleep.

One of my most poignant memories of the war occurred about a week or so later, when I flew back up to the Bulge area on a medevac flight. My plane was loaded with litter patients, and I was walking up the aisle to the cockpit between them. A young soldier with his face heavily bandaged reached out and touched me and said, "Hey Lieutenant, you flew me up here." This memory, to this day, arouses deep and strong emotions.

**Lt. Joe Stevens was on the Christmas Eve mission, also. He remembers it as follows:**

On the 24th of December, I had made one flight of 2 hours and 40 minutes, and was looking forward to Christmas Eve celebration. Since we had already flown our mission we thought we were through for the day. Some of us had started the celebration by partaking of the usual "Christmas cheer," when word came down that we were to report to base operations. We were given a briefing and sent back to our billets to get our gear. We were also given strong black coffee.

We departed Le Bourget around 2030 hours, headed for Istres, near Marseilles. My log book shows the flight was 3 hours and 10 minutes, with 1 hour of instrument flying.

*Two enlisted men of the 320th TS at the time of the Bulge. The man at right is crew chief Marvin Diehl.*

*Left: Lt. Joe D. Maguire at Le Bourget around the time of "the Bulge" mission. Right: One of three portraits sent home to family by Joe Maguire, Christmas, 1944. Photograph was taken in Paris.*

After landing at Istres, the aircraft was refueled. We remained on the aircraft and tried to get some sleep. Shortly after dawn, our airplane was loaded with young replacement troops for the "Battle of the Bulge." We flew our replacements to a field within range of the heavy artillery.

While on the flight back to Paris, I recalled how fortunate I was to be a pilot and to be returning to a nice shelter and warm food. I never envied the soldiers in the field having to eat C rations and sleeping on the ground. Instead, I developed a new respect for their kind.

**Charles H. Harbaugh, Jr., was a Pilot in the 87th TS at Grove at the time of the Bulge:**

On Christmas Eve, we had dressed in pinks and all, and had just gone out the door, to walk to town to church, when the orderly came and said we were going flying. We laughed at him. As all can remember, the fog was near zero-zero. But fly we did. I couldn't see the runway from the cockpit,

*Lt. Joe Stevens by a Gooney Bird in the snow, winter 1944-45. Note the B-26 in the background.*

*87th TS pilot Charles H. Harbaugh, Jr. by the wing of a C-47.*

but put 45 inches on it, let off the brake, and made it. Fog was only 200 feet thick, and then off to Istres, arriving about 3:30 am. I slept well on the flat part of the floor, by the door, but the rest slept on the litters and said they had a terrible night. I suppose about 6:00 AM, here came the tractor-trailers with the troops we were to haul. The enlisted men had no rifles. The few officers were 2nd Lts., and they only had side arms. So load we did and off to a strip near Verdun, at the front lines. They were to join the Third Army. I told our guests they could come up front, and one, in particular, did. Standing between us, looking at bars on both of our shoulders, he said, "Hey driver, where are we going?" I turned around, looked at him, and said, "Sonny (he was probably much older than me), how long have you been in the Army?" Answer: "Six weeks." I really felt sorry for those guys, being dumped in a combat area after six weeks in the Army. We made the trip without incident, although I have thought since I should have gone up the river at low altitude. I elected to go at altitude. If we would have been attacked, we would have dived into Switzerland. We went straight back to Grove, and all returned safely. Ray says he made two trips from Istres. A Christmas Eve – not to be forgotten – in 1944.

**Not everyone was in the air that night. Les Veit has quite different memories:**

Due to the shipping orders transferring me to an outfit that it turned out later did not need me or want me, I missed the largest airlift operation of the war. When I heard what was up, and knowing the 86th was now short handed due to transfers, I volunteered to crew my old plane. I was told no way! You now belong to someone else, and if we got you killed, we would have a tough time explaining it to them.

So Chick, two others, and myself, sat out Christmas Eve, 1944, playing black jack and drinking champagne from our mess cups, while the rest of our unit joined in the most massive airlift ever. Fresh troops were flown from Marseille to the front. Patton was in most desperate need of tank repair specialists, so the Air Force got them to him. Some of them went from the ship to the airfield to the front. No time to enjoy the night life of Marseille. Oh yes, we did finish off two magnums of champagne, just about the time it finished us off. My bunk flew all around the room that night. I just held on for dear life!

**Private First Class, Dillard T. Hyden (better known as "Red"), arrived at Istres from Le Bourget for assignment to the 311th, Christmas Eve, 1944 – a day that he could not remember until the 1995, 27th ATG reunion in Denver:**

I arrived at Istres from Le Bourget late in the day, to be greeted by Lt. Brown and Staff Sgt. Fesler. I presented my orders to the lieutenant. As he scanned them, he looked up at me. I was carrying a .30 caliber carbine, and he asked if I had ammo for it.

"No, sir," I replied. He responded that a gun without ammo was worthless. He turned to Sgt. Fesler, ordered him to stow my bags in the orderly room, and issued a .45 automatic and ammo for the carbine.

He turned his attention back to me and said they were expecting a German paratrooper invasion. Everyone was on guard duty, me, the pilots, and crew members.

After a cold meal, I took my place on guard. By this time it was almost dark.

Sgt. Fesler drove the jeep down a lonely road bordering the airport that was partially covered in grass and looked like it hadn't been used in months. He left me there about a mile from the gate and suggested I get in the ditch under a tree with branches almost touching the ground. My orders: Shoot anything that comes up the road.

I really believed I was in for a night of bad trouble. Sgt. Fesler said he'd be back for me the next morning. I jumped in the ditch and was fairly well camouflaged by the dangling limbs.

Some time during the night, I heard someone (or something) walking toward me. The noise would stop for a minute or so, then return – closer and louder. I've never been that nervous in my life. But having been reared in a farming environment, I finally recognized the steps as those of a cow. That cow will never know how close she came to being hamburger.

After that, all was quiet until the planes started warming up for the takeoff just before daybreak.

I expected someone to come for me soon. Sixteen hours had passed, my canteen was empty, and I had no food. About 10:30 a.m., I was driven to the mess hall for an 11 a.m. breakfast. I slept all day, and barely made it to the mess hall for dinner at 6:30 p.m.

The next morning I was late for breakfast, and everyone was gone. Forty-eight hours after I had arrived, I finally found out that a big push was being made at the Battle of the Bulge. The flight crews had slept with their planes, which were loaded with troops.

A lot of things had happened since I had left Le Bourget. I had not seen a calendar in months. There were no religious activities, and absolutely nothing to remind me of the date.

I still have a hard time believing that first night on sentry duty was Christmas Eve. Guess my memory isn't what it used to be – 52 years later!

**Richard "Molly" Mollwitz, R/O in the 311th, made the following notations in his diary on December 24 & 25:**

*Sunday 24*: Flew on another fellow's ship today, just to get up in the air. Took Sierak along and let him work all day. Just ordinary bomb runs – almost thought we'd have to spend Christmas Eve at Dijon, but we got out in time. Came back here to learn that we were in "imminent" danger of attack – the entire sqdn. has been called out for guard duty with guns, helmets, etc. The ships are parked on the dirt and surrounded by B-26s, each one with nose or tail guns loaded and manned. Guards were posted all over, but I was up at communications most of the evening. Around 75 C-47s landed around 12:00 – all the ships in the group are here for a big deal tomorrow. Finally got to bed at 2:30 as I have to fly tomorrow. Quite a Christmas eve.

*Monday 25*: Up at 6:00 this morning, but didn't takeoff till 9 or so. Our load was Infantry, fresh from the States, no rifles or equipment. We flew them up near Verdun – had to circle for about an hour waiting to land. We dumped them off and got right out of there again.

Got back for my Christmas dinner anyway, and it was OK. They didn't want us to stand guard duty tonight, but the entire sqdn. was supposed to sleep in the hangar instead, on the alert. I got disgusted with the whole affair and crawled in my sack. Gabby and Al locked the doors, turned out all the lights, and did likewise.

**One of the pilots in the group who prefers to remain anonymous contributed the following:**

Movies have been made and books written about the "Battle of the Bulge." I was part of that battle and was awarded the Air Medal, more or less as a result of those flights. It is unfortunate more medals were not awarded to our pilots. Their flying was equally hazardous, and the ratio of casualties higher than many highly decorated combat units. My Air Medal was the only decoration I recall in our whole group. It came about thusly. Weather was a dominate factor in the success of the Germans during the Bulge. Continual low clouds and fog prevented our air support from being effective. For 54 mornings in a row, I made predawn takeoffs in a C-47 with only a radio operator along. I flew dead reckoning (compass and clock) to the area of the Bulge, making let downs to observe weather conditions and radio the observations to Fighter H.Q. I would try to get a positive ceiling and visibility reading and get the hell out. At times, we would break out of the clouds only 100 feet above tree tops. My radio operator's hands on the Morse Key were not too steady on those occasions. But, we survived. The day the weather broke open and we radioed a good report was a thrill. We flew back like flying into a swarm of bees. It seemed as if every fighter and bomber in the U.S. Air Force and RAF were coming to attack the Germans. The ending of the Battle of the Bulge began that day, and I for one was greatly relieved. I was tired.

**One of the radio programs of the day was "Top of the Evening," with Ted Malone. Malone did a two day show in February of 1945 on the 27th ATG. Here follows an excerpt from that show describing the Christmas Eve mission:**

**WESTINGHOUSE PRESENTS**
**"TOP OF THE EVENING"**
**TED MALONE SPEAKING FROM OVERSEAS**
**FEBRUARY 21, 1945**

*ANNOUNCER*: The story of Hitler's Christmas sock – that turned out to be a SOCK-O instead, is one of the great stories brought us by Ted Malone. And it's deeds like that which must soon bring victory ... and with it an age of peace ...

*MALONE*: Christmas Eve at the 27th Air Transport Group base, like Christmas Eve most places, the fellows were planning on celebrating with a party, but late that afternoon a message came in that changed everything. Colonel Feldman was asked if the 27th could possibly furnish planes to fly an Army across the Continent to stop the Rundstedt breakthrough. This was like asking a Sabetha, Kansas, boy to go to the World's Fair. Not that he got excited – I never saw the colonel excited over anything, except maybe Gooney Birds – but this was a challenge. Most of the planes were out on missions. The pilots were scattered, but Colonel Feldman knew that the 27th had been asked because other organizations were not prepared. So, regardless of difficulties, the assignment was accepted.

Colonel Feldman and Covalt walked into Major Bennet's office and, as casually as though they were delivering a Christmas card, they tossed the order on the operations desk. Bennet read it, looked up, amused. "What's the gag? I don't get it."

Colonel Feldman grinned. "Major" he said, "How soon do you figure all our planes will be back at the field here?"

And, mimicking his C.O.'s casual mood, looking out at the snow-covered fields and threatening skies, "Oh, most of them should be back in a couple of days if the weather breaks."

Feldman stroked his chin thoughtfully. "It won't be easy then, to get them back in a couple of hours, regardless of weather?"

Bennet's eyes twinkled. "No, that wouldn't be easy, especially since the weather is particularly "regardless" tonight."

"It's bad, so is the situation up around the Ardennes Forest," the Colonel countered.

Suddenly, Major Bennet became deadly serious. "Is this straight stuff? Do they really want us to move our Army tonight?"

"They're depending on the 27th to do it," Colonel Feldman said quietly. "I guess they figured that if anybody could, we could, and I told them we would. What do you think?"

For answer, Major Bennet was already on the phone. He got in touch with each Squadron C.O.; instructed them to check every plane, pilot, and crew available on the field, and report back immediately.

Within a quarter of an hour, ground crews were out sweeping snow off the wings of ships; fuel trucks were filling planes with 100 octane gas; pilots were excusing themselves from Christmas Eve dinner parties and climbing into trucks filled with pilots buzzing with questions. "What's up? What happened? What's the idea of canceling passes on Christmas Eve?" Surely nobody was expecting them to fly before morning, and why rush them in from dinner?

At the same time, planes of the 27th ATG closed up for the night at fields all over the continent were being opened and the motors warmed up for attempted flights back to the base, if they could possibly get through.

"What happened?"

"Well, the 27th Air Transport Group did it, of course," Colonel Feldman told me. "Bennet got the planes back, checked and refueled. They took off for a field in southern France where a whole army was waiting. It was the first night flight the pilots had ever made over France. They went to strange fields they had never landed on, picked up heavy loads, flew them back through the dark to a field near the Rundstedt bulge – and while I can't tell how many planes took the thousands of men, I can say there were enough so that it was generally assumed that there would be some accidents, which in an operation of this kind could hardly be avoided.

But there were no accidents at all. Every ship flew safely through the snow and sleet and delivered its load on schedule, and Christmas Morn a whole new Army stopped the Nazis dead in their tracks.

# Chapter 6

# The Secret Missions to Sweden

Some of the more unusual USAAF missions of WWII were carried out by detachments from squadrons of the 27th ATG, under the command of Colonel Bernt Balchen. For more than six months, USAAF men operated from a secret base at Lulea, Sweden, supplying forces in German occupied Norway.

I first heard of this operation at the 27th ATG reunion in 1994, and was immediately fascinated with the fact that this unit was involved in a clandestine operation which certainly stretched the neutrality of Sweden!

The last night of the reunion, there was a banquet. By chance, I sat down at the same table with Mr. and Mrs. Robert C. Merritt, who through the course of the evening's conversation told me he was on the mission and had some information he would share with me. Bob was kind enough to follow up by sending me what he had, which ultimately led me to other group members who were also on the mission. Their story is one of the most unique tales of WWII.

**Robert C. Merritt was a pilot with the 86th TS, 27th ATG. His recollections of the Swedish mission are as follows:**

Our trip to Sweden began by outfitting at an Air Force base at Metfield, England. From there we went to Leuchars, in Scotland. Then we flew individually, at night, across German occupied Norway to an instrument approach to Bromma airport in Stockholm, arriving on the 23rd of December, 1944. At Stockholm we were provided with Swedish visas and civilian clothes – presumably this was to be a top secret operation. However, when we flew we were in uniform, and of course the planes carried USAAF markings. Unfortunately, German propaganda radio announced our presence, what we were going to do, and that some Ju 88s were waiting for us. We found out later that these Ju 88s were stationed at Bodo, the Norwegian town we later visited. We proceeded to Kallax, a Swedish Air Force base near Lulea, Sweden, on December 30, 1944, where we were to be based.

In general, our original purpose in Sweden and Norway was to transport a group of Norwegian doctors and nurses to Kirkenes on the northern tip of Norway, to assist the local residents. These people were literally living in caves at the time, since there had been considerable fighting there between the Germans, Russians, and the Norwegians, and not much was left of the town or of the whole area. At the time we arrived, the area and the airstrip were Russian controlled. The doctors and nurses, and later on the Norwegian soldiers were a story in themselves in that most had escaped across the border into Sweden by one means or another. The soldiers had been allowed to form into a so-called "Police Force" by the Swedes.

Later on our activities varied greatly, including transporting Norwegian soldiers, all kinds of aid, food, lumber, skis, etc., to the soldiers, as well as to the Laplanders living in the northern area. We assisted in paratrooper training for some of the soldiers and dropped a number of them. A couple of us had experience with this in Troop Carrier before coming to the 27th ATG. We dropped hay to horses and to the Reindeer herds belonging to the Laplanders, and made paper parachute drops with many of the supplies. From my plane we made one trip to drop radio repair parts to a Swedish border outpost, and on another, made a parachute drop of two doctors and a nurse to assist Norwegian soldiers injured in a land mine explosion. As I recall, our crews each flew about 30 of these so-called missions during the six month period. Bad weather caused many delays with temperatures as low as 40 below zero.

As a matter of interest, all of our crews were trained by the Swedes in cross-country skiing, and we carried survival backpacks and skis in the planes, in case of emergency landing in difficult, isolated country, of which there was plenty. We were all quartered in Swedish barracks and ate with the Swedes in their mess halls.

**John J. Schneider, Jr., a pilot in the 321st Squadron, has very vivid memories of those cold missions in Sweden:**

For six or nine months, no one except Washington and (Norwegian-American Colonel) Bernt Balchen knew where we were. The big problem was not the enemy, but the weather. You could freeze to death in seconds. The average temperature was 40 degrees below zero. We couldn't walk fast, or the cold air would freeze our lungs. We looked after each other to make sure that no one had frostbite, because if we did, we wouldn't have felt it. As safety measures, the crews learned how to build ice houses – similar to igloos – out of snow. We also learned how to ski, in case we were shot down. We were fortunate that the emergency measures were never needed. We were shot at many times, but we were lucky. One tactic, flying low – 100 feet above the ground, proved successful in escaping detection by German radar. When we left France we were told it would be a 30 day operation. When we flew a plane into Scotland, we still didn't know about it. On the way out from Scotland, we opened our orders in the planes. For the next six months we operated out of secret quarters in Sweden, which was officially neutral, but was nevertheless supportive of the Allied cause. No one, other than the military intelligence in Washington, knew of the location.

*A Gooney Bird buttoned up to fight the brutal cold in Sweden.*

*(The following story by Joe Ellis was originally published in the "Friends Journal" of the Air Force Museum Foundation and appears with their permission)*

**Combat Airlift From Neutral Sweden**
by John A. (Joe) Ellis

*Joe Ellis enlisted in the Army Air Corps in 1942 from his home in Delta, Colorado. After training as a radio operator, he was assigned to a troop carrier group, which deployed to England in August, 1943. Due to weather and circumstances, his crew and aircraft were detached from the main body of the group. Sgt. Ellis found himself an aerial gunner after a very short qualification course, and he flew a tour as a gunner with the "Bloody 100th" Bomb Group. He returned to his primary duty as radio operator, eventually going to the 86th Squadron of the 27th Air Transport Group at Hendon, north of London. This organization moved supplies and equipment within the U.K., eventually supporting the Normandy invasion in June of 1944. The 86th moved to Le Bourget Field, outside Paris, and we pick up this unique story in late 1944.*

*December 1944*: I was stationed at Le Bourget Field outside Paris with the 86th Transport Squadron. We had moved there from Hendon Airfield in northern London. On the fourth day of the invasion of Normandy, Patton's tanks pushed the gliders to the side on a grass field north of Carentan, France, and we flew plasma and morphine to the 82nd and 101st Airborne Divisions, carrying wounded back to England. After Patton bypassed Paris and headed for Germany, we followed with gas in five-gallon jerry cans that we threw out in the fields, so we could install litters, and returned to England with wounded. I did not know at the time, but the 86th would later help supply troops during the Battle of the Bulge.

On December 6, 1944, we were told that five planes and crews from the 86th would join five others to take part in a secret mission. We flew to

*This picture was taken at Metfield, England prior to departure for Sweden. This was Robert Merritt's crew. Left to right: 1st Lt. William M. Murphy, navigator, (Temporarily assigned from 1406th AAF Base Unit, EURDATC), 1st Lt. Robert C. Merritt, pilot, 86th TS, 1st Lt. Sydney M. Wood, Jr., co-pilot, 86th TS, S/Sgt. John C. Rudzonis, R/O, 86th TS, S/Sgt. Benjamin W. Benson, flight engineer, 86th TS.*

*Right: A Swedish Air Lines DC-3*

Aerial view of Kirkenes, Norway, late 1944.

Air drop zone on a frozen lake in northern Norway. Supply drops were made to Norwegian troops with paper parachutes.

Norwegian paratroopers on board a 27th ATG C-47.

Inside a Gooney Bird looking back toward the cargo door, after a supply mission.

John Schneider in Lulea, Sweden.

27th ATG flyers try out their igloo which they learned to make as an emergency precaution.

*Left: Vic Boynton, Albert Rydznski, and John Reiggle at Lulea, 1945. Right: Schneider's crew, from the 321st TS: M/Sgt. Melvin L. Torry, flight engineer, Captain Jesse Wingard, navigator, (1406th AAF BU), 1st Lt. John Schneider, Jr., pilot, 2nd Lt. Norman C. Bishop, co-pilot, Sgt. George H. Rottner, R/O.*

Metfield, England, where we stayed about five days in a hangar, under tight security, with orders not to leave the building and to talk to no one. At one of our meetings, I met Bernt Balchen for the first time. All he told us was that we were going to Sweden, and he would tell us more when we arrived. We received a crash course in Swedish, and instructions on how to conduct ourselves during our stay in a neutral country. Balchen, the famous Arctic flyer, had dual citizenship in Norway (his native country) and in the United States, where he was an Air Force Colonel serving as Air Attaché to Sweden at the embassy. I think the reason he held that position was to give him permission to come and go from Sweden without problems. One evening after dark, we took off from Metfield, and following a course across the lower part of German occupied Norway, we flew to Bromma, outside Stockholm.

We had operated under blackout for so long we were not used to all the bright lights of Stockholm and Bromma Field. At Bromma, we were loaded into buses with covered windows and transported to a large department store after closing hours, where we received civilian clothes. From there we went to a resort outside Stockholm. The next day we returned to Bromma and flew north to the Swedish air base of Kallax, near Boden, and a few miles from Lulea, which is at the north end of the Gulf of Bothnia and north of the Arctic Circle. To our north we were separated from German occupied Norway by Lapland.

At Kallax, we found out what had happened in the past in the area and what they had planned for us. Colonel Balchen had been flying ball bearings from Sweden to England in B-24s painted black, and he later smuggled interned flight crews from Vasteras, Sweden, back to their units. Balchen told us that the airmen did not want to leave their plush life of steak, eggs, pilsner, cognac, and beautiful flickas, but he had to return them before there were more airmen in Sweden than in the U.K. As for our part, we would fly supplies to the Norwegian underground.

There was talk about painting out the Air Force emblems on our planes. At that time the Swedish government was leaning our way more than to Germany, so we left them alone. Colonel Balchen said it didn't matter, as the Germans knew by then what we were up to. We wore our uniforms on

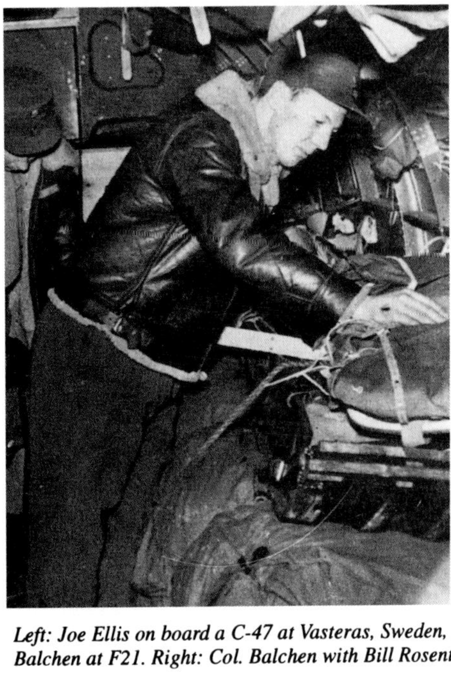

*Left: Joe Ellis on board a C-47 at Vasteras, Sweden, December, 1944. Sgt. Albert Lai is in the background. Center: Swedish AF Officer Gosta von Porat with Col. Bernt Balchen at F21. Right: Col. Balchen with Bill Rosenthal in the cargo door of a C-47 at Vasteras, Sweden.*

base at Kallax and "civvies" in Lulea and Pitea. On missions we wore flying suits without emblems or rank. We carried civilian passports.

We could go into Lulea when we were not scheduled to fly. We would call a taxi to come out from town and pick us up at the front gate. Due to the shortage of gasoline, these taxis were powered, or I should say under-powered, by charcoal burners bolted to the rear. When you came to a hill, the passengers had to get out and push.

In the summer we could take the ferry across the fjord (it was cheaper than a taxi, but it was a long wait), but in winter the fjord froze and the taxis drove straight across to pick us up. It was quite a bit shorter than the road around the fjord. Colonel Balchen had instructed us in cross-country skiing, both for physical fitness and survival in case we were forced down. We could ski down a slope into Lulea, but it was difficult to herringbone home after a few pilsners at our favorite watering hole, the Stad Hotel. We made several friends in Lulea, including a barber, Stig Eriksson, and his wife, Asta. On April 2, 1945, my 22nd birthday, I was restricted to the base for being tardy, and Stig and Asta, along with other Swedish friends, came to the front gate at Kallax with my birthday present, a metal etching of their church in Lulea. It still hangs on the wall of my bedroom. Later that month, Al Lai and I attended funeral services in that church for Asta Eriksson, after she was killed at a railroad crossing in Lulea. With Colonel Balchen's permission, we wore our full uniforms into Lulea for the first time.

The five C-47s from the 86th still had our group emblem on the nose. It was a large orange circle with Sad Sack carrying a pack on his back. A Bing Crosby movie was showing in Lulea, so we painted the words "VANDRA MIN VAG" under Sad Sack (Swedish for "GOING MY WAY"). The entire group did not return to Stockholm together until we left the country, but individual planes went back and forth, usually with Colonel Balchen and Colonel Dahl, who was the head of the Norwegian underground, on board. It was strange to sit in the plane at Bromma and watch German planes from Berlin land, unload, and return to Berlin. I took three such trips, with Colonel Balchen, Captain Charles G. "Pappy" Holliman, Colonel Dahl, Alex Dobrowen (interpreter), Crew Chief Joe Gasselein, and two or three others I did not know. I was on these flights because their regular radio operator, Bill Rosenthal, was sick. One was on Christmas Day when a Swedish princess had us to lunch at the palace, where 80 plus year old King Gustav made a brief appearance. He just dropped in on his way to play tennis.

*Staff from the military hospital boarding a C-47 of the 27th ATG at Kallax.*

*Chief for F1, Vasteras, Gustav-Adolf Westring, Col. Balchen, and Dr. Harry Soderman, Chief of the Criminal Institute in Sweden (SKA), Vasteras, Sweden.*

*Norwegian troops board a 27th ATG C-47 at Kallax, for transportation to northern Norway.*

On one trip down, we stayed at the Grand Hotel, which was across the river from the King's palace. The Grand and nearby Bern's restaurant were always loaded with members of all the foreign delegations located in the same square. These included Germany and Japan. All the countries, including the United States, had spies all over the place. We had a time or two when members of the German delegation would try to get us in a fight so that we would have to leave the country. They learned the phrase "You're a dirty bastard" just for that purpose, but we laughed it off and said "You're a dirty bastard, too." They didn't do anything, because they didn't want to be kicked out of Sweden, either.

My other trip to Stockholm was after VE Day when Colonel Dahl presented me with a dagger with my name on the thumb plate. The rest of our crew members were to get their daggers later. The story was that the presentation was made on behalf of King Haakon of Norway for our mission of flying a doctor and nurse into occupied Norway to operate on members of the Norwegian underground. Possibly the presentation was a publicity stunt – our crew chief, Floyd Schultz, said it was. I talked to my pilot, Leonard Callaway, recently and asked him if he received his knife, and he didn't know anything about it. He asked me if I still had the silver spoon that we received when we flew to Oslo, Norway, to join the celebration of King Haakon's return from exile. I told Cal I didn't remember the spoon.

*Lt. Leonard Callaway with 86th TS C-47, "Vandra Min Vag" (Going My Way), Lulea, Sweden 1944.*

So I got a knife, Callaway got a spoon, perhaps somewhere an airman got a fork.

I was told that both the doctor and the nurse had never flown before, let alone bailed out, but you wouldn't know it to watch them. Later they skied back to Lapland, where we picked them up from a landing strip where enough snow had been removed by Laplanders and reindeer so our wheels would have two strips to run in. After we unloaded supplies that the Laplanders would smuggle into Norway to the underground, we were pulled backwards by people and reindeer teams to the point where we touched down. With the doctor and nurse on board, Lt. Callaway set the brakes until we were pulling 31 inches of mercury, lowered the flaps, released the brakes, and tried to follow the tracks long enough to literally jump out of the snow and get airborne so we could return to Kallax.

All of Norway was occupied by Germany, with the exception of the northern tip of the country in a community called Kirkenes. Kirkenes was very important to the war effort for both sides, because like the Russian port of Murmansk to the east, a nearby harbor was open all year due to the warm water currents. We flew supplies into Kirkenes during the colder months, but if the war would have continued, supplies would have come by ship from Murmansk.

Our plane was only under attack one time by enemy aircraft when we were returning to Sweden. A Ju 88 made several passes at us, but our troop carrier training came in handy, as Lt. Callaway put us on the deck. Each time the Ju 88 would fly alongside and start shooting, he would turn into them and force them to turn away and climb. I got on the key and informed Kallax of the attack, but they would only fly to the Norwegian border and not cross over. Fortunately for us, the Germans would not cross over into neutral Sweden, so we were OK to return to Kallax. We later flew to Kemi, Finland, with Colonel Balchen to verify that it had been a Finnish Ju 88, which didn't want us to fly over their airspace.

Kirkenes was eventually overrun by the German occupational forces who wanted the supply port. When they took it, they killed most of the people in the town and set fire to a large coal mine that was still burning when we arrived. The Russian Army took Kirkenes back in the fall of 1944. They slaughtered most of the German soldiers, covered them with snow, and when spring came, piled them up and burned them. The Germans had laid mines in an area south of town with shoe box mines. They were made of wood, so the detectors couldn't find them. Then they destroyed the location maps. The Russians used the lucky German prisoners to "de-mine" the area by tying their arms together and marching them through the fields. We were uneasy when around the Russians at Kirkenes. Colonel Balchen didn't like them, didn't trust them, and told us not to drink enough vodka to loosen our tongues. So we didn't trust them, either. We continued to drop supplies and personnel into Norway and stockpile supplies at Kallax for future use of the Norwegian Army, then training to return to their homeland.

At Kallax during the last few months of the war in Europe, you would see Swedes, Norwegians, Fins, and Americans. The Russians stayed in Kirkenes. Our interpreter was a member of the Norwegian Home Guard

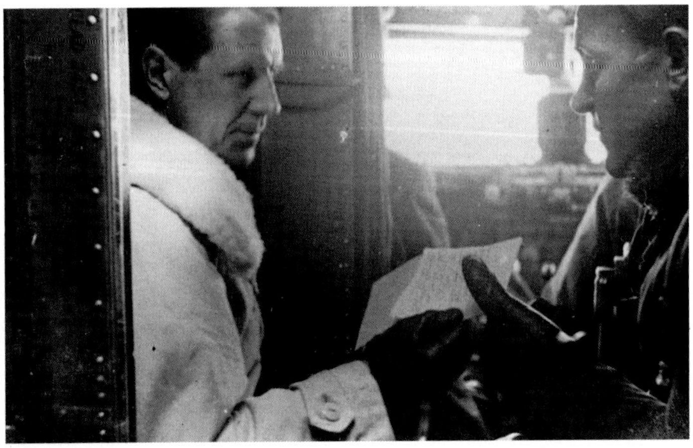

*Left: Col. Dahl, Head of Norwegian Resistance, on board a 27th ATG aircraft. Right: Lt. Callaway and S/Sgt. Ellis examine a downed Me 109 at Bodo, Norway, VE Day.*

*Left: Vic Boynton with Russian soldiers Kirkenes, Norway, late 1944 or early 1945. Right: Alex Dobrowen (Norwegian interpreter), S/Sgt. Ellis, a Finnish radio operator, and a Swedish airman at Lulea, Sweden, 1944.*

training at Kallax. Alex Dobrowen had fled to Sweden during the German invasion of his country, taking his father with him. His father was a famous symphony conductor in Oslo before the war and continued to conduct in Stockholm. Alex could speak all of the Scandinavian languages, English, and Russian. Alex became very close with the Americans at Kallax, and soon his English changed from European to GI. After I returned to the U.S. and civilian life, I received a letter from Alex. He was in Paris and was learning to speak French. He said that Balchen was back in Norway, had remarried, and was in charge of the airlines there.

At times one plane would go on a mission, other times two or three would go. On occasions when all ten went, Colonel Balchen would close the briefing by stating with his Norwegian accent, "VE VILL GO TOGETTER." Such were our orders the early hours of VE day, when nine of our ten planes, loaded with Norwegian Home Guard troops, "vent togetter" to Bodo, Norway. Plane No. 247, with Capt Posie Clinton, 1st Lt Bennett Robertson, my best buddy Radio Operator, S/Sgt Al Lai, and Crew Chief, M/Sgt Irvin Levy, were still in Kirkenes, having lived with the Russians for 30 days while they installed a new engine. They were the real heroes of this mission. They had very little daylight, sub-zero weather, and bad living conditions, but the vodka kept them going. When we landed at Bodo, the Germans were still armed and guarding the gates. They gave us a salute as we left the field to go into town for a parade. The Norwegians brought out the flags that they had saved for this day, and it was quite a sight. We made several more flights from Kallax to Bodo, transporting the Norwegian Home Guard back to their homeland, and after a short stop at Bromma in Stockholm, we returned to Le Bourget field in Paris and the 86th after our seven and one-half month journey north.

*Armed German soldiers at the entrance to the airfield, Bodo, Norway, on VE Day.*

**Colonel Bernt Balchen:**

Mr. Ellis mentions Col. Bernt Balchen several times in his preceding article. Anyone interested in learning more about Col. Balchen should view the special exhibit on the man at the AF Museum. The exhibit is located in the Air Force Museum's Modern Flight Hangar.

Col. Balchen is recognized by many as America's greatest Arctic expert of modern times. He was born in Norway, fought for Finland against the Russians in WWI, and was later a pilot of the Norwegian Naval Air Force. He ferried aircraft for the British in WWII and later joined the U.S. Army Air Force. Assigned to Greenland, he led many spectacular rescue missions, saving the lives of numerous U.S. flyers.

*The harbor at Bodo, Norway, VE Day. The vehicle in the foreground is the German equivalent of the American Jeep – the VW Kubelwagen. Kriegsmarine sailors can be seen on the boat, behind.*

*VE Day plus one, Bodo, Norway. Ten aircraft flew into Bodo with food.*

*Col. Balchen with officers and E/Ms of the 27th ATG on the secret mission to Sweden. Photo was taken at F 21.*

*Swedish/American brotherhood at the victory celebration at Kallax, 7 May, 1945. Note several men have switched uniform coats.*

*Swedish and American officers at the celebration dinner at Kallax, 7 May, 1945.*

*Col. Balchen in conversation with Gosta von Porat at the mess at F 21. The man on the right is Bjorn Rorholt an English trained radio man.*

Balchen was recalled by the USAF in 1948 when he served as commander of the 10th Rescue Squadron in Alaska.

He retired in 1956 and died in 1973.

**The following story of the secret mission in Sweden was published June 4, 1945, in the Swedish newspaper *Aftonblodet*. It was written by field correspondent Hans Abrahamson. It is reprinted here with permission of *Aftonblodet*. It was translated into English by 27th ATG member, 1st Lt. Bennet E. Robertson:**

Bodo, North Norway – Secrecy is no longer necessary, and many remarkable incidents are coming to light. Who, for example, had the least suspicion that at Lulea, during the last few months of the war, Sweden was definitely off side in her neutrality and went over to the Allied side. Since the beginning of this year, ten Dakota (C-47) planes, 33 American officers, and 35 enlisted men have been based at F-21, in Kallax, just outside of Lulea. During the last three months of the war, these forces were in the air approximately 5,000 hours, regardless of snow and polar darkness. The planes flew food, medicine, arms, and even barracks and many other things over the mountains to the Norwegian home front in northernmost Norway. They have transported 1,000 fully equipped and trained soldiers to the Kirkenes area with great secrecy, but there is much that can be told now.

Aftonbladet's field correspondent, together with the polar flier and Norwegian-American Colonel, Bernt Balchen, today undertook a 1,200 mile trip over the ravaged Scandinavian territory in a Dakota plane. During the first two hours, we flew west from Lulea to Bodo, just inside the Lofoten Islands on the Norwegian coast.

2,500 Norwegian soldiers, during the spring months, drove the Germans over two hundred miles back from Tana fjord to the territory around Alta fjord, far in the North. This had gone unnoticed. When Colonel Balchen told us of this, there was indignation in his voice, and he asked us why there had not been a single word said about the Norwegian's only field attempt during the five years of occupation. His own opinion was that in Oslo, the men who had fought in the northernmost part of Norway, carrying on a regular campaign against the German arctic troops and had driven them back, had been forgotten. They drove forward kilometer after kilometer and drove the Germans before them, advancing over two hundred miles before news of the peace reached the mountain plateaus.

I am sitting in the Dakota plane, "Vandra min Vag," together with Norwegian boys and Col. Bernt Balchen, the world's most unconventional officer and Byrd's pilot from the South Pole. Now the machine is flying over wilder and wilder territory up near Kalen. We are on the way to Bodo, in the midst of the furthermost Lofoten Islands. Bodo is the large flying field from which Swedish Red Cross personnel will go to a hospital in Fauske to take care of 400 sick Russians, going there by the ten American planes. The rugged Swedish territory and scenery was forgotten as one of the world's most popular and most traveled. We wanted to hear about his

*Gooney Birds of the 86th and 321st squadrons on the Swedish missions.*

experiences in Greenland during the war's first phases, when the German bases were only some minutes' flying time from that northerly land. We were lucky to hear from him himself, the unpublicized experiences and other wartime happenings in which neutral Sweden has actually taken part. For the first time during the war, Swedes know that they can be really proud of their "neutrality." More has happened here than we ourselves knew.

As early as New Year's Eve, the Königsberg radio warned that they knew that Colonel Balchen planned operations from Swedish territory, and when the transportation of food and troops to Kirkenes began, radio personnel heard clear and definite warnings from the German stations.

11 January, 1945, the first plane landed at Kirkenes. Since then, the ten American planes have flown over 5,000 hours over the war theater in the far North. In south Norway, they were shot at sometimes, but were never hit. In north Norway, the planes were difficult targets to hit as they flew very low, at about 200 feet or less, to deliver their cargoes. They did not dare go through the clouds, for danger of collision with the mountains. They could not use radio aids because the enemy could easily have detected them. Bernt Balchen's men took unheard of risks, and the Swedish Air Forces in Kallax also had something to fear, for it is unbelievable that the Germans did not know that an enemy base was located in neutral Sweden.

Exact figures as to how many loads and people have been carried to Norway by Balchen and his Dakotas since the first trip on January 11 are not available. A Yankee soldier from Kentucky guessed about one million, five hundred thousand pounds or more. Balchen said that his men had flown over 52 tons of provisions to Bodo the night of 13-14 of May, and Bodo was the first such airfield put into use after the war. In that one night, all the planes made three round trips.

During January the weather was hopeless, and the planes could not make more than three trips to Russian occupied Kirkenes. In February, trouble came for the Americans in the form of snowstorms. They flew to Kirkenes with loads of Norwegian soldiers. Balchen taught his men Swedish, and also saw to it that they should learn to ski and live in the Arctic climate.

During March the Norwegian forces drove forward to Porsanger fjord up near the north Cape. The Germans left the airfield at Banak devastated, but the Americans repaired it. They were soon landing there, and Norwegian headquarters were established in Skaganvaare.

By the end of March, the difficulties were less and Balchen's planes flew on a time table schedule over Norway, taking food, ammunition, medicine, and radios, dropping them to the Norwegian soldiers by means of paper parachutes. When the staff at Skaganvaare suddenly ordered twenty tons of supplies, the difficulties were many, but the only consideration was that they were needed and they were flown there immediately. When Balchen's men were landing at Banak, the German forward positions were on the other side of the fjord.

In the interior of Finnmark lay Kautokeino, the fifth airfield in Finnmark. All the area there was so thoroughly mined that landing was impossible. It was there on May 1 that thirty-one Norwegian soldiers were injured in a mine explosion. Nine were still alive that evening, and Balchen ordered two Norwegian doctors and a nurse to come from Stockholm on the ABA plane, but he did not wait and that night, obtained a doctor from the Boden hospital, T. Tornburn, to go by plane with medical supplies. Radio contact was attempted with the ground, and they waited for the light signal telling if the unprepared Swedish doctor should jump. Dr. Tornburn put on his parachute and decided to take the chance, but the signal then came and it was no. Eight o'clock, the evening after, the two Norwegian doctors and the nurse jumped. A complete surgical unit was dropped from another plane, and two hours later, the operations were going on in the church. The next day, two Swedish planes took the wounded to Kiruna, and the Americans brought them from there to Boden. It was without doubt the nine men owe their lives to this prompt action. The first landing at Kautokeino was made on April 11, where there was a radio station on the ice.

*Forty-below zero operations required heaters to prevent the engine oil from freezing up.*

The Norwegian troops in Norway were isolated from the outer world and had no effective transport system. Both fjords and roads were systematically mined by the Germans. All operations depended on supplies brought by the American planes in Sweden. The loading at Lulea was done by Norwegian soldiers who can still be seen around the Swedish base at Kallax. Ground radio was handled by personnel of F21. After VE day, they received help from the Germans with both weather reports and radio service when the American planes visited their fields. Berdofors voluntarily called and asked if weather reports were wanted at Lulea! While we are talking about the mixture of languages and uniforms in Kallax where Swedish flyers mix with Americans and Norwegians, the colonel told of an incident which happened the day after the peace. The home front in Oslo sent a telegram to an American officer who was born in Norway. The telegram went through Luftwaffe channels to the neutral Swedish Airfield, with an inquiry if the American officer wanted to confer in Oslo now that the war was over. The man who was requested in this unusual way was Balchen himself. He wanted to go, but duty in northern Norway prevented him.

*Swedish airmen gassing up a C-47.*

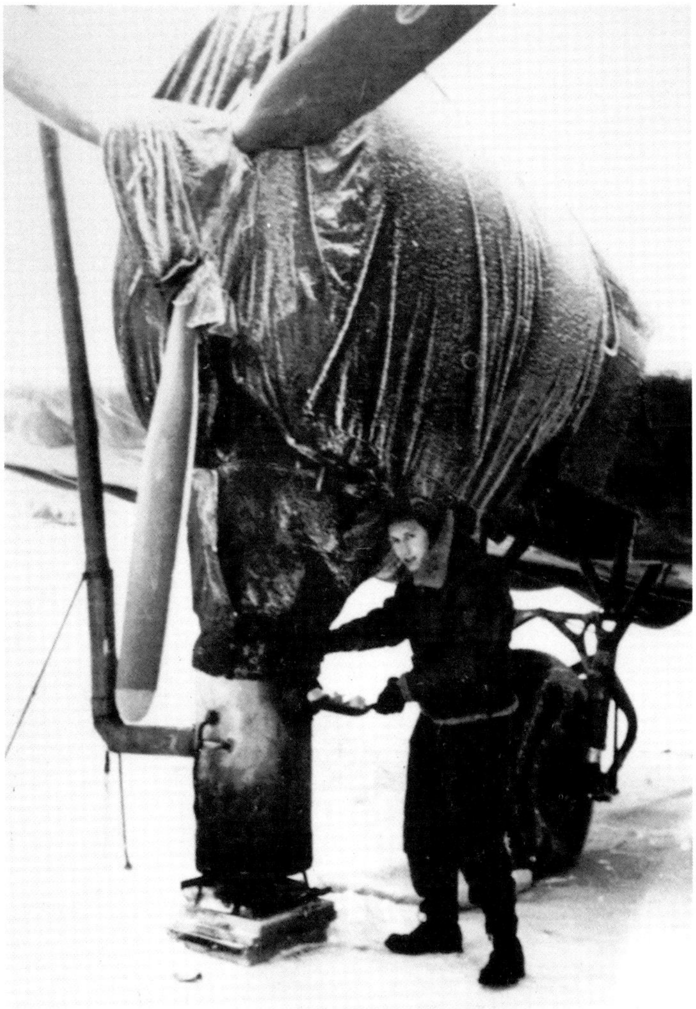

*Left: S/Sgt. Albert Rydzynski firing up the heaters. Right: John McAlpine servicing a C-47.*

THE WEST POWERS INVASION OF NORWAY CAME IN JANUARY

Speaking of Norwegians in the North, wasn't it the Colonel who discovered the concealed Tirpitz (German battleship)? "Yes, but that was in November, 1944, when I flew over the Alta fjord in a Liberator. They later took her to Tromso, where she tried to make her escape. But that was no achievement," Balchen said.

The day after capitulation, the question was asked in Oslo how the home front forces, which had grown like mushrooms out of the Oslo ground, had received weapons from across the border. The answer is this: Colonel Balchen and his men flew over their guns and ammunition. From these planes, the American magazine "Life" was distributed so quickly that it could be seen on Oslo tables the day it was published. The magazine was printed ten days in advance and flown to Balchen from America, completely deceiving the Gestapo.

Now what does the Colonel have to say about the western Allies landing in Norway? "Well, I say reporters are not right when they state that the first Allies came to Oslo on 10 May. It is more accurate to say that the first landing was 11 January when I landed with my American boys in Kirkenes."

The following two pages show the original orders showing the aircraft and crews that were on the Sweden missions.

R E S T R I C T E D

HEADQUARTERS
1409th AAF BASE UNIT
EUROPEAN DIVISION AIR TRANSPORT COMMAND
APO 741 U. S. ARMY

OPERATIONS ORDER 22 December 1944

NUMBER 22

1. PAC in Operations Memorandum No. 80-5, Sta 1, Hq, EWATC, subject "Operations Orders", dtd 5 April 44, and VOCG EURDATC, and 1st Ind fr CG, Hq, EURDATC, 1400th AAF BU, APO 741, file number 300.4 dtd 28 Sept 44. The following O & EM orgz indicated WP in acft assigned to orgz indicated o/a 22 Dec 44 fr Hq, 1409th AAF BU, EURDATC to Operating Location 1409-1 J, via the best available air route for the purpose of accomplishing a special mission, reporting upon arrival thereat to Col Bernt Balchen, for further instructions. Upon completion of such mission the crews concerned will return with acft to their proper sta.

C-47A 43-48245 27th T Gp, 86th T Sq

| | | | | | |
|---|---|---|---|---|---|
| 1st Lt | HARLOW A MARSH | 0-438830 | AC | Plt | 27th T Gp, 86th T Sq |
| 1st Lt | ROY F. ALLEMEIER | 0-802691 | AC | Co-Plt | 27th T Gp, 86th T Sq |
| 1st Lt | DEMPSEY J. DUPRIE | 0-794784 | AC | Nav | 1406th AAF BU, EURDATC |
| S/Sgt | Richard C. Stone | 11015406 | AC | Rad Opr | 27th T Gp, 86th T Sq |
| S/Sgt | Wilbur L. Cowley | 11013417 | AC | Eng | 27th T Gp, 86th T Sq |

C-47A 42-48958 27th T Gp, 86th T Sq

| | | | | | |
|---|---|---|---|---|---|
| 1st Lt | ROBERT C. MERRITT | 0-666411 | AC | Plt | 27th T Gp, 86th T Sq |
| 2nd Lt | SYDNEY M. WOOD, Jr | 0-720373 | AC | Co-Plt | 27th T Gp, 86th T Sq |
| 1st Lt | WILLIAM M. MURPHY | 0-794846 | AC | Nav | 1406th AAF BU, EURDATC |
| S/Sgt | John C. Rudzonis | 13038851 | AC | Rad Opr | 27th T Gp, 86th T Sq |
| S/Sgt | Benjamin W. Benson | 38173868 | AC | Eng | 27th T Gp, 86th T Sq |

C-47A 43-48247 27th T Gp, 86th T Sq

| | | | | | |
|---|---|---|---|---|---|
| Capt | ROSIE M. CLINTON | 0-481869 | AC | Plt | 27th T Gp, 86th T Sq |
| 1st Lt | BENNETT E. ROBERTSON | 0-437674 | AC | Co-Plt | 27th T Gp, 86th T Sq |
| 1st Lt | MAURICE P. SALIMAN | 0-696151 | AC | Nav | 458th Bomb Gp |
| S/Sgt | Albert Lai | 39610696 | AC | Rad Opr | 27th T Gp, 86th T Sq |
| M/Sgt | Irwin J. Levy | 12035905 | AC | Eng | 27th T Gq, 86th T Sq |

C-47A 43-47987 27th T Gp, 321st T Sq

| | | | | | |
|---|---|---|---|---|---|
| 1st Lt | LEONARD C. CALLAWAY | 0-465415 | AC | Plt | 27th T Gp, 86th T Sq |
| 1st Lt | WILLIAM J. OTTS | 0-529300 | AC | Co-Plt | 27th T Gp, 86th T Sq |
| 1st Lt | CHANDLER R. ROYAL | 0-712912 | AC | Nav | 96th Bomb Gp |
| S/Sgt | John H. Ellis | 17090460 | AC | Rad Opr | 27th T Gp, 86th T Sq |
| M/Sgt | Floyd J. Shultz | 16014358 | AC | Eng | 27th T Gp, 86th T Sq |

C-47A 43-48248 27th T Gp, 321st T Sq

| | | | | | |
|---|---|---|---|---|---|
| 1st Lt | JOHN J. SCHNIEDER | 0-675626 | AC | Plt | 27th T Gp, 321st T Sq |
| 2nd Lt | NORMAN C. BISHOP | 0-765910 | AC | Co-Plt | 27th T Gp, 321st T Sq |
| Capt | JESSE O. WINGARD | 0-792513 | AC | Nav | 1406th AAF BU, EURDATC |
| Sgt | George H. Rottner | 32634411 | AC | Rad Opr | 27th T Gp, 321st T Sq |
| M/Sgt | Melvin L. Torry | 33082536 | AC | Eng | 27th T Gp, 321st T Sq |

C-47A 43-48252 27th T Gp, 321st T Sq

| | | | | | |
|---|---|---|---|---|---|
| 1st Lt | THOMAS C. WAHRMUND | 0-664702 | AC | Plt | 27th T Gp, 321st T Sq |
| 2nd Lt | MARSHALL T. MESSELT | 0-775961 | AC | Co-Plt | 27th T Gp, 321st T Sq |
| 1st Lt | HENRY R. BURKARDT | 0-807136 | AC | Nav | 1409th AAF BU, EURDATC |
| Sgt | Samuel B. Alexander | 13011332 | AC | Rad Opr | 27th T Gp, 321st T Sq |
| M/Sgt | Willis D. Whipple | 36303055 | AC | Eng | 27th T Gp, 321st T Sq |

- 1 -

R E S T R I C T E D

Operations Order No. 22. Hq, 1409th AAF BU, EURDATC, 22 Dec 44. Cont'd.

C-47A 43-48262 27th T Gp, 321st T Sq

| | | | | | |
|---|---|---|---|---|---|
| 1st Lt | TROY W. NEWSOME | 0-496122 | AC | Plt | 27th T Gp, 321st T Sq |
| 2nd Lt | RICHARD TAYLOR | 0-775647 | AC | Co-Plt | 27th T Gp, 321st T Sq |
| 1st Lt | ROBERT A. LARSON | 0-800131 | AC | Nav | 1403rd AAF BU, EURDATC |
| Sgt | Arthur H. Krafft | 19167481 | AC | Rad Opr | 27th T Gp, 321st T Sq |
| S/Sgt | Joseph A. Karsak | 16047301 | AC | Eng | 27th T Gp, 321st T Sq |

C-47A 43-48351 27th T Gp, 321st T Sq

| | | | | | |
|---|---|---|---|---|---|
| 2nd Lt | JOHN W. ABERCROMBIE | 0-530855 | AC | Plt | 27th T Gp, 312th F Sq |
| 1st Lt | JACKSON B. EVANS | 0-503551 | AC | Co-Plt | 27th T Gp, 312th F Sq |
| 1st Lt | LEROY LAWSON, Jr | 0-807253 | AC | Nav | 1411th AAF BU, EURDATC |
| Sgt | John A. Reiggle | 33011786 | AC | Rad Opr | 27th T Gp, 312th F Sq |
| Cpl | Victor J. Boynton, Jr | 37504063 | AC | Eng | 27th T Gp, 312th F Sq |

C-47A 42-93703 27th T Gp, 321st T Sq

| | | | | | |
|---|---|---|---|---|---|
| 2nd Lt | JOSEPH J. LUKE | 0-687972 | AC | Plt | 27th T Gp, 312th F Sq |
| 2nd Lt | PHILLIP M. CLINTON | 0-681022 | AC | Co-Plt | 27th T Gp, 312th F Sq |
| 1st Lt | ROBERT L. PRIDDY | 0-390297 | AC | Nav | 1406th AAF BU, EURDATC |
| S/Sgt | Albert J. Rydzynski | 32551314 | AC | Rad Opr | 27th T Gp, 312th F Sq |
| Cpl | John A. McAlpine | 39031725 | AC | Eng | 27th T Gp, 312th F Sq |

PAC ltr, Hq ETOUSA, File AG 245 MTH, dtd 14 Oct 44, per diem of $7.00 per day for period of travel and temp dy is atzd. A deduction of $4.00 per day will be made when Govt qrs are furn. (Auth: Ltr CG, Hq EURDATC, dtd 18 Sept 44)
60-133 P 432-02 A 212/50425.

By order of Lieutenant Colonel WARD:

DAVID H. SCHREINER,
Captain, Air Corps,
Dir of Operations.

OFFICIAL:

David H. Schreiner
DAVID H. SCHREINER,
Captain, Air Corps,
Dir of Operations.

# Chapter 7

# Medical Evacuation Missions, Flight Nurses and POWs

Many different types of missions were performed by the 27th ATG in WWII. Some of the most stressful, yet rewarding missions were the medical evacuation missions, or "Medevac" flights. C-47 aircraft were flown to front line areas where they were loaded with litter patients and flown to hospitals back in England, Scotland, or France. On these flights, a flight nurse and often a medical technician were a critical part of the air crew. In the February 20, 1945, broadcast of "Top of the Evening," Ted Malone did a story on these operations and interviewed flight nurses working with the 27th ATG:

**WESTINGHOUSE PRESENTS**
**"TOP OF THE EVENING"**
**TED MALONE SPEAKING FROM OVERSEAS**
**FEBRUARY 20, 1945**

*MALONE*: I have talked to a great number of wounded boys recently, and they have all told me that the company aid men, the combat medics who go along with them on every patrol and every advance, are there beside them administering first aid almost as they fall. And, minutes later, carried on litters if necessary, they start back to the field aid station, the "evac" hospitals, and eventually the general hospitals in France and England.

A week with the 27th Air Transport Group based here in France has given me a good chance to see some of the operations that keep this mercy channel of the war machine functioning.

The first morning, Captain Vernon Smith of Mobile, Alabama, introduced me to a Squadron CO – Major James H. Lyons from McAllen, Texas. He arranged for me to fly a supply mission to Belgium to return with wounded. It was snowing briskly, and we were delayed a few minutes, during which time I had time to get acquainted with the young major. Snow doesn't bother him. He was flying Army planes to the West Coast three days after the Japs struck Pearl Harbor in 1941. He flew P-40 Fighter ships to Alaska that winter and was stationed there a while, but I think the assignment which Major Lyons is most proud of is a special job hauling wounded boys from the front lines back to hospitals in France and England.

The minute the snow let up, he called the tower for clearance and sent me out to the plane. The ship was loaded with blood plasma and medical supplies needed badly, and there were wounded to be brought back, so everybody was ready to takeoff when we scrambled aboard. "Scrambled" is the right word. Try climbing from a snow-covered jeep into an icy plane, with roaring engines blowing your coat off your back – and you're "scrambling."

The pilot was Lieutenant L. H. Sanborn, of Merced, California. He was a radio announcer on KYOS back in 1938. He has been in the Army three years, overseas only six months. "But that's a long time," Sandy says, "when you have a two-year-old girl home waiting." And a lot has happened in that six months, I can add.

One of the longest thirty seconds I ever waited through ticked off down a runway near Bastogne one day when Sandy's tire blew out as they landed – and just to make it worse, the next couple of days, while they waited for a new tire, the Nazis almost captured the flying field.

The co-pilot was Lieutenant Dick Ramer of Peru, Indiana. He has been in the Army three years, overseas nineteen months, and he has had his moments, too: once, when he found himself in a formation of Nazi fighter ships coming over to strafe British barrage balloons; and another time, when his entire electrical system went out on the ship. He tried to come in blind with no colors – colors of the day – no anything. He almost came in by parachute that time, but they made it.

Sergeants Emil Welsh and Fred Beck were engineer and radio operator – and Welsh had a story that amused the rest, but scared me, I'll admit. His plane was lost; the clouds were almost on the ground; the pilot had gone down on the deck to follow a railroad track, assuming it would lead them to some town that they could find on the maps! They followed the railroad track all right, but suddenly it went into a tunnel in the side of a hill and the pilot had to tip the plane right back up on its tail to keep from flying into the side of the mountain concealed by the clouds. Flying sounds easy, and fun. And it is – when nothing happens.

The snow was almost a foot deep over the field. The runway had been swept and salted, but there was still plenty of ice. We got off all right, however, reached our destination – another field up in Belgium – got down safely as the truck rolled up to unload our supplies. We ate lunch in some captured Nazi barracks. While we were there, a couple of buzz bombs sailed over to hurry us up. But they kept on going out of sight, so we relaxed to finish and returned to the ship. At last, the wounded men went aboard. Two hours later we were back at the field from which we started, and our load of wounded was carefully packed in ambulances on the way to hospitals.

*MALONE*: Every one of the planes of the 27th Air Transport Group that brings back wounded carries a nurse or a medic to take care of the injured aboard the ship. And what stories they'll be able to tell when they get home.

Of course, they're usually like Lieutenant Evangeline Comeau at first, and insist nothing ever happened to them. Lieutenant Comeau is from Omaha. She has been overseas a year. "Nothing much has happened," she said. Oh, at first they slept in tents and sudden rains floated their shoes away, but that wasn't anything. One time a field gave them the wrong heading, or somebody put it down wrong, and they found themselves flying over Germany unarmed. They discovered it when the Nazis began shooting, but they got back – so there wasn't anything to it.

Right after D-Day, when the Nazi fighters were strafing the strips where they flew in for wounded, they had to work pretty fast, but they always got out. Work pretty fast unloading supplies and loading on patients.

"How long did it take?"

Well, everybody helped, and once they emptied all the freight out of the planes and loaded twenty-four patients on litters and took off in eighteen minutes.

"Eighteen minutes?"

"And not one minute too soon, either, because as we took off one end of the field, the Nazi fighters started tearing into the other.

"But nothing ever happens, huh?"

Lieutenant Allen W. Plutz is married. She used to live on Long Island. Her husband was in the Army, but recently received a medical discharge, so now he's home and she's carrying on the battle. Mrs. Plutz, as the girls affectionately call the blond young nurse, says the only time she was really scared was when they were taking a load of patients to England once and an engine went out over the Channel. Here she was with twenty-four patients in casts and bandages, and the word came from the pilot to prepare to ditch. That means to prepare to land in the rolling, rocking, choppy English Channel. Of course, there are rubber life rafts and life jackets, but the problem of getting twenty-four patients out of a plane and landing them and loading them into rubber rafts before the plane goes under is really something to think about.

Mrs. Plutz didn't stop to worry. She just began to prepare to ditch. Fortunately, the plane made the English coast with its one remaining motor, and they didn't have to ditch. But to say they were worried puts it mildly. I guess it's like Barbara Edell, from Long Beach, California, said. ''When things really do happen, there usually isn't much warning."'

Lieutenant Edell owes her life to the pure chance of climbing out one side of a jeep. Two planes were leaving with wounded one afternoon when the two nurses rode out to the field in a jeep. Each casually walked toward the plane nearest the side where she alighted. The two planes flew in formation most of the way to the base, when, suddenly, a storm closed in. There was nothing to do but to try to get down, but before they could contact the field it all happened. One pilot suddenly saw grass almost under his wheels, and literally stood his plane on its tail in a vertical climb.

The other ship? Well, it was too late for that one, and it smashed flat against the mountain. This was almost a year ago, but Lieutenant Edell told it almost as if it happened yesterday. It's hard to forget some things.

Lieutenant Dora Large from Harlan County, Kentucky, supported the suggestion that there isn't any warning when things really happen. She has been in the Army four years, overseas three years. That's right, three years. She went to Iceland in September, 1941.

Her most dramatic experience came New Year's Day, when nothing at all happened to her plane. Oh, they made an emergency landing at a bomber base because of engine trouble, but that was taking care. And they were waiting to takeoff when a B-26 Marauder Bomber started to takeoff with a load of bombs and caught fire. The firemen and ground crew got three men out of the bomber when it exploded. Lieutenant Large will never forget the sight of that tragedy when they came over to her ship and asked her to come help.

*Flight nurses relaxing at Grove.*

*Flight Nurses chatting with enlisted men at Grove.*

The Chief of the air "evac" nurses attached to the 27th Air Transport Group is Captain Marybelle K. Fraser, of Pinole, California. Seven years ago she toured Europe on a bicycle. It was a different world. Although she is still very young, she spent four years in Hawaii as a nurse on a sugar plantation, one in South America – besides her three years in the Army.

The only story I could get from her deserves a whole program in itself – but so little of it can be told, I can compress it into a minute.

The only way to get supplies in to, and the wounded out from, some of the garrisons trapped by counter-attack is by air. A number of planes that have gone in on such operations haven't come back. Some have been shot down and crashed with their supplies and the crews bailed out. But one ship carried a nurse from this squadron, and that ship never returned. Later, the wreckage was found, burned and twisted, and some place in the wreck and ashes someone found a pair of shoes corresponding to the nurse's size. They were her shoes.

Some time later, in the tent chapel on the edge of the field, the nurses held a memorial service for their comrade who had not come back. Each one told stories she remembered. One mentioned her loyalty; another friendliness, courage. They even told about how neat and careful she was, how wistfully feminine. She would never go to dinner until she had combed her hair just so. One time when the plane had been forced down on a field away from the base because of bad weather, she was so put out because she had no bobby pins!

It was the kind of a memorial service any girl would be proud to have – simple, unaffected, and sincere. They even sang one of her favorite songs to close the service. They thought she would have liked it that way.

Then Captain Fraser told me the rest of the story. The next morning, a letter came from Reba S. Whittle, prisoner of war in Germany. The nurse. She was a prisoner of war. The shoes had been an extra pair she had always carried in the ship.

Lieutenant Whittle is a prisoner of war somewhere in Germany, and one line in her note reminiscent of the memorial service I must quote to you verbatim. She is the only girl at the prison camp, she confided to the nurses – and apparently togged out in overalls or still in her nurse's slacks, she writes, "They finally got me a little lipstick to make me feel a little more feminine."

This is Ted Malone overseas, wishing you "Top of the Evening," and returning you to New York and Westinghouse. *THIS IS THE BLUE NETWORK*

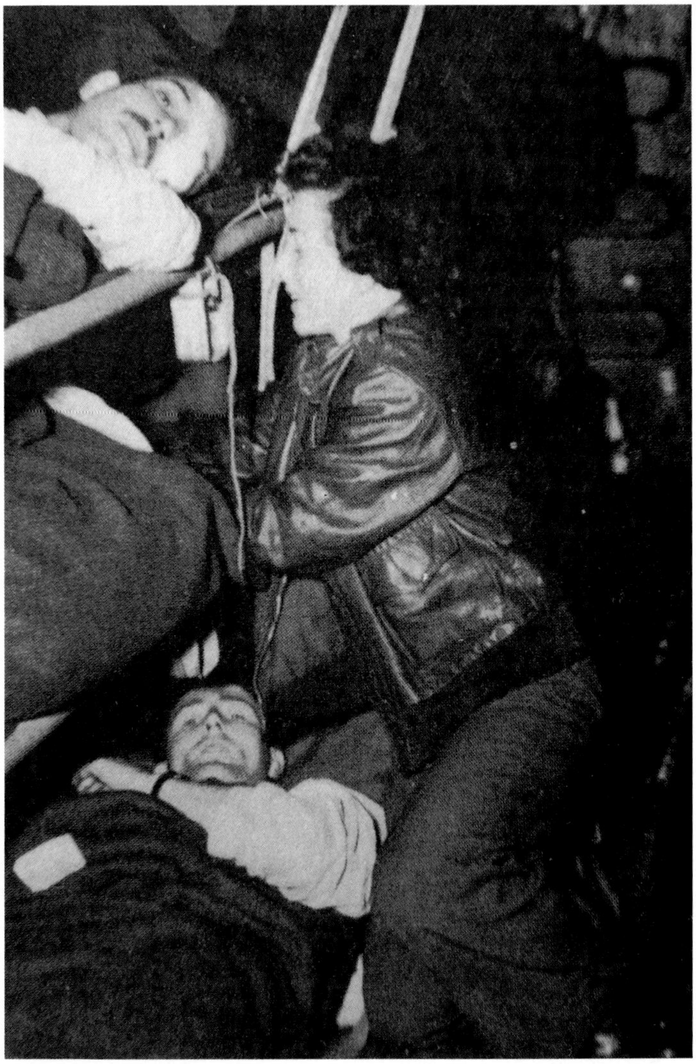

*A flight nurse tending to patients on board a C-47.*

**Reba Whittle did indeed survive the crash and became a POW – the only female POW in the ETO! Her story is quite unique, and we are extremely fortunate to have her diary which records those events:**

**Diary of Reba Tobiason Whittle:**

Wednesday, Sept. 27, 1944, as I left England, with big intentions of returning, and going to London on my day off, starting Thursday, Sept. 28.

Was sleeping quite soundly in the back of our hospital plane until suddenly awakened by terrific sounds of guns and crackling of the plane as if it had gone into bits. For a few moments I hardly knew what to think. Can assure no one had a more startled expression and sensation. Suddenly looked at my surgical tech opposite me with blood flowing from his left leg. The noise by this time seemed to be much worse. But to see the left engine blazing away – is simply more than I can express – But never thought I would land on the ground again in one piece. My prayers were used and quick.

Started to scream and cry as most women would – but Sgt. Hill consoled me and assured it wouldn't help – at that time I realized it would be of no value or benefit, and he had been injured and should be the one crying. About that time he was hit in the left arm, as I had my head on his left shoulder.

Minutes definitely didn't seem short, but hours, and as to how long this went on – I certainly have no idea myself. Suddenly we hit the ground, splash – myself landing in the navigator's compartment, head first. The

*Lt. Delick lets a flight nurse fly the plane from the co-pilot's chair of a C-47.*

*Left: Lt. Joe Maguire and a flight nurse who was on his crew for a while. Right: Flight nurse Reba Whittle. This photo was taken after she was captured. Note her head wound which occurred when the C-47 she was in was shot down and crash landed.*

ship was nearly blazing and holes every place – some large enough to crawl through back in the fuselage. Noticed the others crawling out the top hatch – so immediately went zooming out – 3 out before I – the pilot last – who fell as if he had been badly wounded. One man never came out.

Immediately we saw soldiers not many yards away. At first we thought they were British soldiers. Second glance we recognized they were German Gls. This feeling is one I never dreamed of having, but thought, we've had it, chump. The first thought in my mind – my boyfriend, and he would be waiting back at my quarters that evening. But how thankful and grateful to be alive.

They took a glance with their guns pointing and immediately one took out a bandage and put around my head as it was bleeding. The surprised look on their faces when they saw a woman was amazing. But they bandaged us and away we marched, our ship still burning. The firing and the sounds were terrific. This is where I actually thought of my training that we had back in Louisville, as I really wanted to hug the ground – But the German soldiers only laughed and motioned they were above my head. But to say the least felt sure they were coming for us.

They took us to a small village, rather a couple of old houses, and there we sat on the ground until an officer came, and I suppose they had a discussion of some sort by the sounds of the conversation – not understanding German, couldn't say.

After a while sitting there some guards marched us to a small town about 3/4 or a mile when we went into a dark dungeon cellar which really looked very spooky and smelled very bad. There a Dr. came in – had small candles for light and looked each of us over. Only one was really wounded. That being my Sgt. They gave him some medication, so we thought, and they rebandaged the three of us, who had slight wounds, and accidentally cut part of my hair when cutting the bandage.

Here they took our personal belongings, such as passes and money – rank and name.

The name of the village – sign Aachen – 4 Kilometers – have no idea, but it had been practically evacuated, saw only a couple of civilians and occasionally army vehicles and soldiers running around. Naturally all glaring at us – babbling something which none of us knew what they saying.

Off again – naturally walking – which had to be very slow on the account of Sgt. Hill's wounded leg. As we walked along the street of the village a German Soldier came up and yanked my Air Corp patch off my shoulder and threw it down, saying something. Why I don't know unless it was hanging loose, as I was the only one who he took it off of.

Think it took us about an hour, and considered it about 2 or 3 miles – that I couldn't be sure, but seemed like miles. Here we came to a neat brick house which at first seemed nice, as the firing still whistled.

They marched us in where 4 or 5 German officers sat in this office. There we stood like dummies and they gave us terrific glares. They showed us immediately out into another room where the guard gave the Sgt. a glass of wine. Before he had time to complete his wine they pushed us outside. There we sat on the ground – shivering as it was rather cold with no coats and the shock and scare. We had to sit outside there for some time – until a queer looking truck came up, and they motioned for us to get in.

The truck was full of junk, but seemed good and at least out of the wind. Never a word between the guards and us as neither could understand. So motion system was well carried on.

This time we arrived in a larger village and taken through a stall or barn connected with a house. There they put us in the barn – Lay on the floor, and shortly came a German officer who interrogated us one by one. A guard gave us some pears, which tasted very good, as we had nothing to eat all day. Some time passed, and the German officer, who spoke very good English, took us into the kitchen of this house where we had black German coffee, black bread, and butter. Seemed heavenly to have a bit to eat and be a little warm. During this time several more German officers came in and looked at our passes they had already collected from us. Each and every one taking a good glare and saying "Swester," which means nurse, and a very startled look. Don't know how monkeys feel in the zoo with so many people looking at them, but thought I must know by now.

This German family was eating their meal later, so a very kind old German woman who had talked to me continuously and naturally I couldn't understand a word she said gave me a cup of hot soup. Was afraid to eat it at first, but she insisted so I did. As she kept looking at me with such a sympathetic look and my judgment was she knew I was leery of drinking the soup so she got some sauce to season it. Still shook my head, so she tasted it and said good. Drank and ate. It was very good. Before I completed it they were after us again.

As we walked out, the entire family bid us farewell and shook hands. Was happy to see the bus for at least it was closed in and it was rather cold. My Sgt. and I sat in one seat. I know he was in pain as it showed. But he was too much of a man and gentleman to admit it. This ride was about 40 minutes. It was very dark, and occasionally we would pass a vehicle on the dark road and see horses and wagons moving on.

We arrived at a huge looking place surrounded by very high metal fence and a guard at the gate to let us in. All seeming very suspicious to me. We did as ordered – out and up those dark steps, naturally our guards still with us, and into an office where German officers were sitting. Very little said as no one could speak English. In came a huge container of cold stewed potatoes, which they sat in front of us. Not being very hungry after eating bread and butter only a short time before, those potatoes just wouldn't go down. Naturally we knew not what next – but they motioned for us to follow again. Up more stairs into a dirty room. They pointed to a straw mattress on the floor, then to me. Joining room was 2 double deck beds for the 4 fellows. Out they went and locked the outside door.

Was so scared and the thoughts of being in the first room alone next to the outside door was worse. So I got my mattress and pulled it into the others' room. There the five of us attempted to sleep but little was done. First comes the interruption asking usual questions. The air raid alarm came and he said, "Well, too bad – you know you might be bombed by your own people," and out he went. This night was the longest I ever spent. A continuous tapping went on all night. Each time I dozed this would awaken me. Then the horrors of what next went on and on.

Next A.M. they came in gave us cold black German coffee, black bread, and margarine. We ate what we could as we were hungry and knew not when we might eat again. After this we sat in this room for a long time, a guard with us. The fellows drew a circle and pitched coins to pass the time, and we gazed out the window. Time went very slowly.

At eleven we left again. This time in an old truck on top of wood chips. Seems we went such queer ways and so slow. But the truck ran on wood chips that we were carrying, so I found out later. So that explained the slowness, and the driver was always killing his engine.

Stopped in several villages for what I don't know. Once an old man very well dressed came up and asked "Americans?" and spoke very good English. He talked to us about 10 minutes. But each time he saw a German officer he would pretend he was leaving. He also wished us good luck. People all gaped at us as they do all POWs, but another glance came when they saw a woman. Guess many have wondered just what I was.

Next stop was a German hospital where they unloaded the wood. A German officer took us in where more questions were asked – and just what I was. A Dr. came in and looked all over and asked me questions of being a nurse. Shook his head saying "Too bad having a woman, as you are the first one and no one knows exactly what to do."

Sisters brought us in a bowl of hot sauerkraut mixture and slim slices of black bread, which tasted very good as it was hot and very clean. As soon as we had completed, we were out in the yard to wait for the truck to be finished unloading. People were looking from all windows and every place at us. The sisters got me a chair and I was shivering. So was everyone else. A sister from both sides came with a tray of coffee and soups, one had cream in it, so the other said that was best. It was good and helped the shivering. They also brought me an old overcoat which felt wonderful.

Soon we were off again, plus a few German soldiers and an officer this time to Köln-Sums. It took us a very long time. They had loaded empty crates on. Then we stopped at a fruit orchard where they loaded the crates and bags with apples and pears. Wasn't bad as we certainly ate enough of them. They let them off different places and also took the officer some place in Köln. Seems we went in circles in the city before getting to the airfield. The city was very badly damaged. Could hardly see a house or building that wasn't torn up. Something was still burning as a raid had been just a few hours before we arrived.

At Köln they gave me a room alone – called me out first. Naturally I didn't know what was going on and I definitely didn't want to be alone. This is when I really first let down and cried. They couldn't figure out what was wrong with me. So I asked for my Surg. Tec. to be put in there with me. Felt much better when he came in, but couldn't stop crying for quite a while.

Later a Dr. came in and looked each and everyone over. No one really needed anything but Sgt. Hill, but the Dr. was very good to all and put fresh dressings on.

Went to bed – all we took off was shoes and I neatly slept after I finally got to sleep between air raid alarms. Naturally every move the guard made seemed to awaken me, but did rest. Next morning as usual cold coffee and black bread, more alarms, etc.

About 10 AM they came after me first where I was taken about a block and a half into one office then into another where about 6-8 officers were. They all rose and greeted me. Again many questions were asked of me. They also said what a pity for them to have an American nurse and tried to assure me I would be back very shortly. The shock and everything had me very upset and tears were hard to hold back – a few started down my cheek and they thought someone must have been brutal to me so they asked that. Then they asked if I had had enough of it. So I said, "Yes, enough black bread and cold coffee."

Then he took me into another office where I sat down and he offered me a cigarette. I took it as I had none. When I stopped crying, he brought the others of the crew into this office and asked them a few questions. It was beyond me why they took me before all the other officers.

Here is when they took everything from us, such as pictures, pencils, and what had already been taken and we signed for it. They told us we would leave that evening by train for Frankfurt. First start of any POW. Also said the reason of night traveling, it was safer.

That day at noon they gave us a very good and hot meal. Nothing like at home, but was good in comparison. During our stay another American officer was there, too. They wouldn't let him talk to us until we all left for the train and he came, too.

About 5:30 or 6 late evening, we walked with the officer who escorted us to a trolley then to the train. Fortunately the train was in, so we got in as the officer said, out of the cold.

The station seemed rather beaten up. He pointed out the huge castle to me and it looked very beautiful of what I could see in the darkness. Traveled all night.

At approximately 2 AM, we stopped to change trains and had a 2 or 3 hour wait. So he takes us down into a cellar looking place at the station where about 8 or 10 more American boys and a British boy were. It was very dirty and dingy looking, but was warm and out of the cold. Some of these boys had been at a hospital so they had Red Cross parcels. So we had a bite to eat which was thoroughly enjoyed. The best of all were the cigarettes.

At approximately 5 AM the entire group of us went up to get on our train. Never saw them again until we got to our destination, which was Frankfurt. There we got off and got on a trolley which went very near the Stalag or POW camp. They march us all up to the camp where we all stood outside in a sort of formation.

Immediately they took the 6 of us in. Only a few minutes after we were inside they asked me to go with one of them, which I naturally did not knowing what would happen. Those were sad moments as I left the only people I knew and knew quite well I would never see them – but that was there. They took me to a room about 8x8 ft., motioned for me to enter, and closed the door. Well that was a cell, and I was locked in proper. Extremely depressing. The more I thought of being in a cell and wondering what would happen next, I became terrified and started crying. Felt more like screaming, and a perfect wonder I didn't.

Although I actually didn't start crying until a guard opened the door and slammed a black sandwich on the table, which really sounded like a chunk of wood. Felt just like a child. I wanted to throw it back and do wish I could have.

The place was dirty, but at least the warmest place we had been, and I was so tired and filthy myself.

Two German officers came in and just to look at them made me cry more. Think who ever it might have been to come in, the same thing would have happened.

Took my name and said how sorry they were to have to have a nurse as a POW as they had no facilities at all. Asked some questions and said I would go to a hospital nearby and they had a few of our boys there. A guard and officer went with me. They gave me a blanket to wrap around me as it was very cool. Had to walk about 15 minutes, and it seemed way up in the woods.

Arrived through locked gates, of course, and into a large area which was very beautiful. Nice lawn, flowers, and very nice looking buildings under those huge trees. Sat me in a small hall, gave me coffee, black bread as usual, and butter. It did taste good.

A German Sister was getting my room ready and one glance they said I could have a bath first if I desired. Naturally that did sound wonderful, but for same reason tears would keep coming. When they took me into the room I felt more or less lost. No clothes except what I had on and had had on since I left 4 days past. Guess I just felt sorry for myself.

In came a gentleman first I thought an American, but was British with an American R C Capture kit. In it were men's shorts, socks, and what have you – cigarettes, gum. All looked good as that was all the clothes available. Then he brought me a pair of men's trousers.

He left, and a German orderly locked my door, then I suddenly got hysterical. A German Sister came in to try and console me, but couldn't speak a bit of English. She was such a sweet old soul. After my cry had calmed – the German Dr. had been in – went to take my bath still crying.

*Reba Whittle with RAF men at the British POW hospital.*

Asked for a wash cloth in my motion language and the maid who was mopping thought I was afraid the tub wasn't clean and got some disinfectant and started letting the $H_2O$ out of the tub. Then the Sister came with the wash rag. Now it seems funny, but certainly not then.

My room was very comfortable with a large comforter, curtains, and it was spotless, overlooking a big garden. The Sister brought me flowers, fruit, and gave me 6 bobby pins.

I ate with a Capt. Stuffan and WO Stanley, who worked there. They took me for walks within the area morning and evening.

The surprised looks of some of our boys to see me was amazing. And they all treated me swell.

The morning of Oct. 6, 1944, left with a German Officer for Obermassfield – left at 9 AM and arrived about 7:15 PM. Had a box lunch along the way. Naturally everyone would gaze to see a woman POW with a guard. But that didn't bother me much – was wondering what would happen to me. Felt sure I was going to find news on me returning home.

This was a British and American hospital run by British Dr. Maj. Sherman. The SBO (Senior British Officer) met me and was extremely nice to me. But he was extremely overworked and over crowded and his problem was to find a place big enough for me to sleep as they had all men. So he placed me in an examination room to sleep.

Helped the Maj. with some Dip. shots in his dispensary, and he also started me on my shots.

Next A.M. ate in the so called mess combination living quarters for some of the Doctors. Later the Maj. takes me for a tour over the hospital. All the boys seeming very glad to see an American nurse, plus being greatly surprised and all anxious to hear how I was taken.

Shall never forget one of our boys by the name of Davis from Dallas who had lost his right arm. His kind words and hospitality were really appreciated. Then to see how he made himself so useful after having an arm off was remarkable.

All the hospital staff were very good, but I especially liked Maj. Sherman. I can never express my full thanks to him. About noon he came and told me I would go to Meiningen as they had several bus loads of patients going. So I left for my new place again. By this time I was wondering if I would even stay there. But never the less obeyed as they definitely had no place for a girl there.

With the load of patients, arrived at this place about 4:30 PM. A very large building which used to be an old concert hall. A few barracks scattered in the yard behind the barbed wire. Many fellows out in the yard.

A British sanitater who came with us presented me to a Scottish Capt. by name of Bill Havrie, who then took me where the 6 of them stayed, introducing me to them and the SBO by the name of Capt. Wooding.

He was especially nice and said a room was being made ready for me. I was so happy to meet Maj. Evans from Tenn. in charge of all clothing. He said if ever he could be of any help to be sure and call on him. I felt as if I could always look on him, as a guardian.

My room was on 4th floor and I was the only person on that floor. They put little scanty curtains and fixed my room up as nice as possible, which was very comfortable. Their orderly took care of me as well, and awakened me each morning and brought my washing $H_2O$.

Sunday Oct. 8 – my first walk in the mountains. We were allowed walks with a guard so many hours a week. Thoroughly enjoyed this, but not being used to walking was extremely tiring. The country was perfectly beautiful.

Capt. Laurie took me around the entire hospital to see all the boys. Was greeted cordially by all, but naturally I felt very out of place being among over 500 men.

That night the boys had a concert which they had to alter considerably in order to have a woman present and thoroughly appreciated them making the arrangements. The show was very good, had different skits, songs. Was very hard to understand the British and Scottish boys, and usually all our boys would yell out translation.

They had made up a song to John Brown about the staff in which I noticed had one about me since I was considered a part of their staff. All were very cute. They had some very talented boys.

Monday Oct. 9 – I started to work in the Massage room. Mainly on burn cases by supervision of Lt. Sinclair, a Scottish man, who was one of my favorites. This helped pass my time and gave me something to do each day. Had my own patients and enjoyed talking to them. Most were USAs, which pleased me.

This hospital was one where patients came after so long as very sick ones to get legs and PT, called a rehabilitation center. The work was perfectly marvelous these 2 Scottish men did ... leg joints all movable and teaching the boys with artificial legs to walk. They had a big gym. Capt. Laurie gave all his exercises to these boys in casts with legs off.

All his machines and exercise apparatus had been made by them with British materials. No help from the Germans.

They had a leg shop where 3 boys worked every day making legs which were certainly excellent considering they were made out of whatever they could get. And to think this boy had never done this in civilian life.

Several occasions the officers invited me to their private messes to have evening tea. They would save until they had sufficient ingredients and make a cake or a sort of pie, which were very good. Food wasn't much as a rule, but never went hungry.

The German rations to POWs were very little, but again the Red Cross comes in. The American, British, and Canadian all sent R.C. food parcels, which actually saved many from going hungry. At first we were on full parcels, but shortly after I arrived everyone went on half, which made it a little less. But most foods were CHO starch, so no one lost much weight.

Never got over my feeling out of place and I stuck to my room most of the time, especially after I moved one floor down to a very long room with a stove in it.

Captain Laurie had three pictures framed for me. Curtains were made. I had a bedside table, a table and a tiny cupboard in my room. Only room to get around – but quite comfortable. Captain Laurie also made me an easy chair.

They all actually were too good to me. Always trying to get or make me something to be more comfortable or make me happy. One fellow gave me a small bag which had an old white shirt and some hankies in it.

A South African gave me a lovely bottle of perfume which he had carried through Sicily and Italy and as a POW for four years. He was very timid and shy as he gave it to Major Evans the Supply Officer to give to me.

Some of the boys made little what nots for me. Some sent them up but wouldn't give their names. Usually found out later and thanked them, as I certainly appreciated each and every one.

After about four weeks with no lipstick, Major Sherman sent some over. Again this was stuff from home sent to the boys in dramatic supply. Wasn't what I would buy back home, but I think I was more proud of it than any expensive brand I always buy, as my lipstick was my only feminine thing. It was too bad I didn't get out of the airplane with my jacket, as I even had nail polish in my pocket.

The German Officer in charge got his wife to get me some more bobbie pins and curlers, so I took great pride with my hair.

The $H_2O$ was very hard and it made my hair sticky and gummy. Was a terrible mess until I caught more $H_2O$ to wash it in. That solved the problem and made a great difference.

Was allowed a bath once a week, and that day was always enjoyed. Then the trouble was of it being warm. Was much luckier than the boys. The orderly brought me a pitcher of warm water at night and mornings so I could have a sponge bath twice a day in my room.

Did my own washing in my room of towels, pajamas – only had two of each. But this always passed some time, therefore more or less enjoyable.

Passing time was the great problem. My mornings were OK as I worked, but afternoons and evenings sometimes seemed like days. Tried reading as they had a fair size library, but my mind just couldn't stay on a book. Tried drawing, painting, embroidery, knitting, making little animals.

During my stay the Swiss Board came by to see boys who were to be repatriated. All amputations automatically would, and others went before the board. I didn't see this board, but about four weeks later, the Swiss Welfare Commission came by and they were to see me.

Was so in hopes they would have some news on me. They were very nice to talk to, but knew little about my case and said it was so unique. Naturally I was quite disappointed, not being able to gain any news of what would be done. They said it was all held up on my government's reply with a decision on what they wanted to do. They promised to gather all information available from our embassy when they returned to Switzerland, and also see what the German government had to say in Berlin.

One of my surprises was on November 23rd when I had a message from an old friend I had known back in San Antonio when he was a cadet, and I, a student nurse. Not many people around now I had known previously, therefore it really cheered me up.

The message was sent by another officer who thought my name slightly familiar. When he saw me, he remembered we came to England on the same boat – had even played cards and seen a show together. He had run around on the boat with a good friend of mine. Also knew many of the girls from my squadron. I thoroughly enjoyed talking with him, and he also the same.

To me it seemed I had known the boy all my life. After two months of seeing so many of our boys and never one I had known previously.

**Reba Whittle's diary ends here, but she did go on to be repatriated to the United States. When she returned to San Antonio she was interviewed on the radio program "Army Hour." Her story concludes with a transcript of that broadcast:**

**Army hour pickup**
**WOAI, San Antonio**
**Sunday, 25 February**
**Broadcast Time: 3:22 pm**
**Overall Time: 5 min.**

*Lt. Reba E. Whittle, Air Evacuation Nurse, Former German Prisoner of War (on cue "To meet Lt. Whittle, the Army Hour takes you to San Antonio, Texas")*

*Announcer*: Here in San Antonio, Lieutenant Whittle is at home. She was born in neighboring Rock Springs, Texas, and her parents live there. It's good to be home, I'll bet, Lieutenant Whittle.

*Lt. Whittle*: Yes, it certainly is! There were times when I thought I might never see Texas again. I've been in the Army Nurse Corps since my graduation from nurses' training in June of 1941, and in the European Theater of Operations since January of 1944. That's a long time.

*Announcer*: Were you a flight evacuation nurse all that time?

*Lt. Whittle*: I was assigned to hospital planes all the time I was in Europe. We made flights to Scotland, Ireland, Belgium, Holland, and France. Our real work started on D-day. That day, and every day and night afterwards, we'd fly across to the battle front, pick up a load of wounded, and bring them back again. Many times we made two evacuation flights a day – we'd fly from England to an airstrip just behind the front lines, load quickly, and fly back. Then we would unload our casualties and go back for another load. There was always a shortage of nurses, but we did the best we could. Every time we'd get feeling sorry for ourselves, we'd look at the wounded. That's the best cure I know for aches, pains, and lack of sleep.

*Announcer*: You were on such a mission when you were shot down?

*Lt. Whittle*: That's right, but we were lucky. We were on the way over to pick up a load and we didn't have any wounded aboard. There was just the plane crew, my medical technician, and myself – six, in all. It was in September, and we'd made so many flights by that time we thought nothing of flying over enemy territory. The plane was a C-47 – exactly like the ones flying the commercial airlines here – but remodeled to take care of litters.

*Announcer*: And what happened?

*Lt. Whittle*: We were caught in the flak. Everything seemed to happen at once – so fast that I didn't know what was going on at first. Then the plane caught fire, and I was sure we'd never get down alive. But the pilot was good, and brought us down in a big turnip field.

*Announcer*: Were you injured?

*Lt. Whittle*: Luckily, no one was seriously injured. I got some scratches and twisted my back, but my most serious injury was a big bump on my head. My medical technician was hurt more seriously, and I was able to help him out of the plane before the fire reached us. All six of us walked away from the plane. I'll never forget standing in the middle of that big turnip field with the C-47 burning behind us, realizing that we were in the midst of the enemy.

*Announcer*: How long did you have to stand there?

*Lt. Whittle*: Only a minute, really, although it seemed more. Some German soldiers had seen the plane fall, and came out to take us prisoner. You should have seen their faces when they saw me!

*Announcer*: What did they say?

*Lt. Whittle*: I haven't any idea! They didn't speak English, and we didn't speak German, so conversation was little strained for a while. They thought I was the pilot – it took a long time to convince them that nurses really fly in American hospital planes! And then they didn't know what to do with me!

*Announcer*: How's that?

*Lt. Whittle*: Apparently they'd never taken a woman prisoner before and

*Photo of Lt. Whittle from her hometown paper after she returned to the States.*

**LIEUT. REBA Z. WHITTLE**
**To relate experiences.**

they didn't have any facilities for keeping me. I'm sure I was the greatest nuisance they ever had! They put me in a prisoner-of-war hospital, and I volunteered to do nursing duty for the other prisoners – they were Americans and British, mostly. But I kept annoying the Germans.

*Announcer*: Annoying them?

*Lt. Whittle*: They couldn't figure out what to do with me, and I helped them wonder. I kept quoting the Geneva convention to them – the part about proper segregation of the sexes among prisoners of war – and the more I quoted, the more confused they got. They moved me to three different camps, and finally, in desperation, they repatriated me. I'll always think they breathed a great sigh of relief to get rid of me!

*Announcer*: And you came home on leave to Texas.

*Lt. Whittle*: That's right. It's been awfully nice, but I'm getting anxious to be back on duty. I've seen how short-handed our hospitals are – both here and in the theaters – and I've flown with the wounded. That's a wonderful experience, and I want more of it.

*Announcer*: You must have seen hundreds of American wounded on your flights from the battle fronts to England. What would you say the men wanted most?

*Lt. Whittle*: It sounds a little strange, I know, but it wasn't medicine – not even medicine to deaden the pain. It was the sight of an honest-to-goodness American girl waiting for them at the door of the plane that seemed to mean most. You could tell by the expressions on their faces when they saw us. They want someone to smile at them, light a cigarette for them, and tell them they're going to be all right. Professional training is fine and essential, but the mere fact that army nurses are American women is pretty important, too.

*Announcer*: And that, of course, is where the hospital technicians of the Women's Army Corps come in.

*Lt. Whittle*: That's right. To me, that's the ideal assignment for the woman who wants to do her part and who doesn't have professional nurses training. WAC hospital technicians cannot replace nurses. But they are doing a wonderful job in Army general hospitals, alleviating the shortages in skilled personnel. If every American woman could see how much work there is to do – how much good their sisters in service are doing both in the Army Nurse Corps and in the WAC – there wouldn't be any shortages. It's a great privilege to me, to have served as little as I did in helping those wounded men. Actually, I have only one brother, but after my experiences in Europe, I feel I have thousands. My heart and prayers are with them always.

*Announcer*: From San Antonio, Texas, the Army Hour returns to New York.

**Sgt. Harold Bonser was the flight engineer on that trip with Reba Whittle. Bonser was wounded in that action and did not receive the**

**Purple Heart as he was entitled. As historian of the 27th ATG, Marvin Diehl helped Sgt. Bonser receive the medal. This is the story of how that was achieved, in Marvin's own words:**

Searching for evidence for the Purple Heart for Sgt. Harold Bonser was my greatest achievement and satisfaction as the Historian of the 27th ATG It all started when I met Harold at my place almost two years ago.

I did not know Harold in civilian life, but I did know his sister, as she went to the same high school as I did. After the war I worked for her when she built a new home.

I wrote to Harold soon after I joined the 27th ATG association, as he was about fifty miles from my place. He told me he had been a POW, and was in the 310 Ferrying Squadron when they were shot down by small arms fire and flak, but he never talked much about it.

Later I talked to his sister Mary, and she told me a little about it. Harold never received the Purple Heart, although he had been wounded. Something did not seem right to me, so I wrote a letter to Harold, who had moved from Pennsylvania to Crossville, Tennessee.

Harold told me that he did not get the Purple Heart and he was a prisoner of war for seven months, but his discharge does not say anything about it. He told me that everyone on the C-47 was wounded pretty badly, but he only had minor injuries and didn't mention it, because others needed help more than he did. He was treated at the crash site and later by the Germans.

The shooting down of the C-47 started when they left England and went to Le Bourget, Paris, France, for litter patients. Upon arriving at Paris there weren't any patients there, but they could pick some up near Liege, Belgium, which was almost at the front lines.

The pilot would not go unless the whole crew agreed to go. They didn't want to go back empty, but they all voted to go. The crew was as follows: 1st Lt. Ralph T. Parker, Jr. (pilot); 2nd Lt. David L. Forbes (co-pilot); 2nd Lt. Reba S. Whittle (flight nurse); T-5 Jonathan Hill (medical technician); Sgt. Harold R. Bonser (flight engineer); and Cpl. Chester D. Bright (radio operator).

Upon arriving near Aachen, Germany, they were about three miles over enemy front lines when small arms fire and flak hit the C-47, which caught on fire at four places.

The pilot instructed Sgt. Bonser to open the escape hatch in the crew compartment. The pilot said he would make a crash landing in the turnip patch, because they were only about three hundred meters above the ground (about 1,500 feet). They barely missed a large smoke stack, but the landing was a good one.

They all got out of the C-47 and gathered near the airplane as the pilot had instructed.

The pilot stated that Cpl. Chester Bright was in his seat in the crew compartment, but a quick glance before the crash, he was not there any more and a large hole was there from flak. He also stated that he was the last one to leave.

The pilot gave a quick check in the cargo compartment and saw nobody in the aircraft. Some thought Bright bailed out without a parachute. Later it was confirmed that his charred remains were buried there and he still rests there. There is more to this, but I must get back to the Purple Heart for Sgt. Bonser.

After I gathered all the information, I sent it, with a request for the Air Medal, and to correct his discharge to General Eade. Sgt. Bonser received his Air Medal, although the Purple Heart review board did not think he received his wound by enemy action.

I was sitting at my desk and going over some papers when I saw a package I had received after I had sent for the Air Medal and request for the Purple Heart. I opened it, and the diary of Lt. Reba Whittle was inside.

I read her story of the crash, since she had been the only woman the Germans held as prisoner of war. She spent four months as a POW (because the Germans didn't know what to do with her). It was too much to keep a woman, so she was exchanged for German POWs that we held.

In her diary she told about how she was treating T/5 Hill (medic) for small wounds in the arms and legs as the C-47 hit the ground. She slid across the cargo floor into the crew compartment, and her wound was a large cut across the face, for which she received the Air Medal and the Purple Heart.

I kept wondering why she had gotten the Purple Heart and Sgt. Bonser had not. All the survivors of the crash were treated, and records show WIA behind each name.

With the pilot's report of the crash, Lt. Reba Whittle's diary, the report from overseas on treating WIA, Sgt Bonser's personal report, and the Government crash report, I again asked General Eade why this did not qualify Sgt. Bonser as being hurt from enemy action as records show. If Lt. Reba Whittle received the medal, why hadn't Sgt. Bonser?

General Eade, upon receiving all material on Sgt Bonser, studied it and again sent it to the Purple Heart review board. He later called me and asked if Sgt. Bonser heard anything in the last year about his Purple Heart medal or the correction of his discharge.

I called Harold and he said he hadn't heard anything since he received the Air Medal. General Eade went to work again for his fellow member of the 27th ATG. It was not very long after that General Eade called me again and said that Harold had received the Purple Heart. I asked if I could tell him.

Before twenty-four hours had passed Sgt. Harold Bonser called me to say he got the Purple Heart in the mail and he wanted to thank me. He is very proud of it.

*Chapter 8*

# The End of the War in Europe

**Howard Stillwell, 311th FS pilot, recalls the days after VE Day**

**VIP Flights:**

A little while after Victory in Europe (VE day) in May 1945, Bob Decker, Tom Powers (Pappy), flight engineer, and I were fortunate to receive orders to fly General Carl Spaatz, the Commanding General of the U.S. Strategic Air Forces in Europe, and Mr. Lovett, who was U.S. Secretary of War, I believe, on a five day trip to Germany, Austria, and Czechoslovakia. General Curtis and staff members were also on board. We picked up the VIPs in Paris and took them to Frankfurt, Germany, the first day. This was our first flight in Class A uniforms.

We had a special C-47 model (tail #979) that had a complete set of flight instruments mounted in a panel in the passenger compartment. A worried staff officer came up to the cockpit a couple of times wanting to know exactly where we were and asked if we knew we had to make good our estimated time of arrival (ETA). I had the feeling I was taking a check ride with more than one passenger who had probably been a military pilot before I was born. When we had to go on the gauges for an hour because of the weather, someone came up front with us to watch. We evidently passed the "check ride" OK, because we received some "good flight" remarks.

It was not an easy airplane to fly because of a jeep that was loaded and chained on board just inside the rear cargo door. That jeep and the special cabin configuration gave us an uncomfortable, tail heavy, weight and balance situation. However, because a staff car for the VIPs always met the aircraft, our crew used the jeep extensively. The next day Salzburg, Austria, and Berchtesgaden were visited with an overnight stay at Frankfurt.

The third day itinerary was to Pilsen, Czechoslovakia, where the large Czech armament center was located and there was a German prisoner of war camp. Our flight crew had an interesting time checking out a field full of German Stuka dive bombers. Then on to Weimar, Germany, where the infamous Buchenwald Prison camp was on the outskirts of the city

Somewhere on the trip I think General Spaatz was going to transfer to a B-17 he was originally scheduled to take. Bob, Pappy, and I were to continue with staff members and "our" jeep. (I do not remember whether this happened or not.) The next day Nordhausen was visited. This was where the German V2 rocket powered bomb was assembled, and Bob, Pappy, and I appreciated seeing them first hand instead of just hearing them explode in London. Then it was back to Frankfurt and to Paris on the 5th day.

About a month after VE day I had the famous cowboy, Tim McCoy, as my passenger on a B-25 trip. We took Army Col. McCoy to Nuremberg and Munich, where he was going to set up rodeos for the troops waiting to go home to the USA.

On June 5th Bob Decker and I flew members of the Press to Berlin where peace treaty discussions were happening.

You might recall the Russians were allowed to occupy Berlin first. It was interesting to mingle with and try to talk to the Russian men and women troops. There were parades and VIPs everywhere. We did talk to some English soldiers there with their General Montgomery. The Russians gave us a jeep and driver to tour Berlin.

June '45 flying was all C-47s again, with only a few flights in P-38s and B-25s. On one B-25 trip our maintenance officer, Lt. Brown, went along as my co-pilot. Bob Decker and I made two B-25 trips to Biarritz, France, on the border of Spain. Each time we picked up passengers in civilian clothes who did not talk to us. Assuming their secrecy was required, we just took them to Paris as directed.

*Loading a Jeep into a C-47.*

My flight records show that the 311th operations moved back to A-42, Villacoublay, Paris, on 3 July 1945. This was the fifth relocation for the 311th.

Major James Lyons had assumed the 311th CO title in March of '45, and retained it through my departure, August 5, 1945. John Howard continued as OPS Officer, and shortly after I left, he assumed command of the 311th. He had been an outstanding OPs Officer since the 311th was formed, and was a fully qualified, outstanding choice to be the CO of our flying squadron. Lt. Corin A. Lewis (Red) signed my flight records for June, July, and August of 1945.

June and July 1945 were busy months with 208 hours flown to many interesting places. Austria and Hitler's Eagles' Nest retreat, the French Riviera again, Naples, Italy, Denmark, Sweden, many different cities in France, Germany, Belgium, and all over England again. I did get a chance to fly a captured German aircraft, the Fieseler Storch. It took off and landed at about 35 mph. I spent an hour of slow, leisurely sight seeing over Paris and suburbs. (And no John Howard and Bob Decker, I did not fly under the Eiffel Tower in *this* aircraft).

Flight records show five C-47 and six B-25 flights with flight engineers as co-pilots. I don't know why unless most of our pilots had transferred to other squadrons.

Earl Carroll, attorney/pilot in that order, was my co-pilot on a C-47 trip to London where he said he had business. Earl was a close friend who lived near in California. Remembering some of his flying escapades, I flew the aircraft. Earl defied the flyers' credo, "There are old pilots and bold pilots, but no old bold pilots." As an attorney Earl helped some members of the 27th ATG, and later became famous as Krupp's attorney during the Nuremburg Trials.

During the relaxed time after VE day we had a P-38 aircraft with a very small "piggy back" rear seat installed. One flight I flew a six foot tall news reporter from Paris to London. We had to pry him out of the seat after I landed, and he couldn't straighten up. However, he made his deadline and thanked me for the fast transportation.

A college friend of mine who was a foot soldier in the Army came by and enjoyed (?) seeing the ground from the back seat of the P-38 fighter.

My last rear seat rider was Hensen, one of our maintenance men, who had worked on the P-38 and wanted to experience the results of his efforts. A little aerobatics satisfied both of us during my last flight in the P-38, my favorite aircraft.

## FINAL APPROACH AND LANDING

On 2 August I flew to Nice on the French Riviera and Naples, Italy. The next day I flew to Frankfurt, Germany, Berlin, Frankfurt, and back to Paris. My flying in the 311th squadron was finished.

So, at the start of my 24th months in the European Theater of Operations and 1,009 flights, 1,593 hours of pilot time in 15 different aircraft, on four continents, and twenty-six countries, I had finished my WWII flying without injury or accident.

**Red Hyden recalls his time as a flight engineer at the war's end:**

The end of the war was the beginning of my most enjoyable time with the 311th. The day after the war in Europe was over, I flew to Denmark with pilot, Howard Stillwell, and several medical personnel. If I remember correctly, we landed at Viborg, taxied up to a small building near the tower, and German soldiers came out to greet us. The English had taken charge, but German soldiers were still operating the airport. I don't know about Howard, but I was a little nervous when the German sergeants appeared.

The next day we flew to Copenhagen and enjoyed ourselves. I have pictures of the crew with Tivolie Gardens in the background. I don't remember spending but one day there before flying back to Paris the next.

*A captured German Fieseler Fi-156 "Storch" in American markings.*

I believe it was the third day after the Armistice when my plane made another very enjoyable flight to Stockholm. The pilot was Lt. Gordon Jenkins, co-pilot, 2nd Lt. Norman Johnson, R/O, T/Sgt. Frederick M. Roberts, engineer, Pfc. Dillard Hyden, assistant engineer, and Elliotte Holland. Elliotte had a broken arm and was listed as assistant engineer. That evening, Holland and I went one direction. I don't know where the rest of the crew went, but I'll bet they didn't enjoy their evening any more than we did.

We left the hotel and found a place to eat. As we were trying to translate the menu outside the entrance door, a young lady approached and said, "Excuse me, are you Americans?"

We answered, "yes," and she said, "Please talk to me." She wanted to practice her English.

Her English was better than ours, and she ordered dinner and talked to us while we were eating. The meal and conversation were both first rate. The young lady explained that she had been born in Brooklyn, and her family moved to Sweden when she was 9 years old. She had few opportunities now to speak our language.

*Day one after VE Day, this crew transported 25 medical personnel to Denmark. Left to right: Captain Howard Stillwell, pilot, Lt. Marion, co-pilot, Cpl. Dillard "Red" Hyden, flight engineer, S/Sgt. Korecerk, flight engineer, Sgt. Gulden, R/O.*

As we finished our meal, she asked if we would like to go to a nice place with good live music, drinks, and dancing. We quickly agreed.

We walked eight or ten blocks to the club, and she explained to the doorman that we were on the first U.S. plane to arrive in Stockholm since before the war. You would have thought we were celebrities – we had it made from then on.

Good tables, free food, drinks, dancing ... even the band leader visited with us. He said they could play and sing most of our American music, and asked us to make requests (although he pointed out they might not have yet learned some of the latest songs). He said to just let him know if there was anything we needed.

Our table might as well have had a spotlight on it, because it became the center of attention for the evening. I have never experienced a welcome like this. I don't remember when we got back to the hotel, but it seemed like there was time for just a short nap before time to go.

We didn't see her again, and she didn't give us her address so that we could correspond. I've wished we could have had more time.

It was indeed a night to remember.

**After VE Day, Joe Stevens of the 321st TS was assigned to fly General Collins:**

After VE Day, I was assigned to fly General Lawton Collins wherever the General desired to go. We made flights to London, Ireland, and Scotland.

When flying over the continent, the General liked to sit in the copilot's seat and point out places where various battles had occurred.

While I was flying the General, my fellow pilots back at Squadron volunteered to go to the South Pacific, and they didn't want to leave me behind, so they volunteered me to join them! It turned out for the best, however, as the war in the Pacific ended while we were en route to Marseilles to board ship. We returned to the States in August of 1945.

I live in a small town in northern Idaho – population about 32,000. I became acquainted with a Jerry Collins through my church. After knowing Jerry for several years, I found out that General Collins was his father. Jerry is a retired Army Colonel. Small World!

**310th pilot John McDowell well remembers his "worst flight" occurring after the end of hostilities:**

After VE day we were busy returning B-26s to Burtonwood to be scrapped. Somebody had landed three on the small grass field called Friston on the edge of the White Cliffs of Dover about 10 miles east of Brighton.

Three crews, that is, three pilots and three flight engineers, were dropped off there to ferry them to Burtonwood. All of them were patched and warn out.

Mine checked out OK, but I was told years later by John Crawford that after five days of work, the others were left as unflyable.

On takeoff the right engine broke apart and almost tore loose before it could be feathered. Due to the 150 ft. cliff I was able to get it under control and climbing into the overcast (no small feat in a Marauder).

I turned to true north heading for Stansted Airport where we had been an hour earlier, and it was open. In dense, snowy clouds, I saw only the tail of a British C-47 flash a few feet directly in front of me. My engineer also saw it. He was standing between the seats and turned white! He decided he had better sit down, but had to remove his 30 lb. satchel of tools that was strapped in the seat.

*John McDowell and engineer Johnson on autopilot in a B-26 in the clouds.*

*Left: John McDowell in the cockpit of B-26 "Bunny's Honey" at Stansted, England after the worst incident of his flying days. Center: Flight engineer Bush on the tail of "war weary" B-26 #295875. Right: John McDowell on the tail of "Bunny's Honey" after staggering into Standsted having lost an engine on takeoff from Friston.*

He threw the tools over the back of the seat, where a crudely made escape hatch had been constructed. Out went the hatch and tools. I estimate we were then over London's east end dock area. The noise of the fresh air was welcome.

Landing was uneventful, except for the ire of the lone Major who was trying to close the field so he could go home.

**Donald M. Clark joined the 27th ATG, as a pilot, after the war in Europe was over. His narrative begins in August of 1945 with his transfer from Troop Carrier.**

We low point men were shipped to Paris in August, to the 27th ATG. After we were there for a while, with not much to do, I went to Operations and asked for something to do. That is when I met Captain George Eade (later General George J. Eade, USAF).

He put me back to work. In September, he transferred me to Headquarters Squadron, and from that day forward, it was a real learning experience. I found that experience with George Eade very helpful when I was in business for myself several years later. Thanks to his no nonsense approach to responsibility, and dedication to the job at hand, it rubbed off on one.

In March of 1946, we all transferred to Orly Field. EATS (European Air Transport Service) had expanded into a regular scheduled air lines. We, in Operations, were having a hard time keeping the boys from Munich in their planes so they could keep their schedule and return to Munich on time. We had to put a crew on to check their airplanes and make sure they were OK to fly. They were coming up with all kinds of excuses to RON in Paris – mags, lights, you name it! It became so bad that I had to leave my jacket in a back office so they would not know what my rank was when I ordered them back into their planes to return to Munich. I know I would have had a harder time if they had known my real rank.

Lt. Jenkin Stenerson was also in Operations under Captain Eade. Things got a little dull once in a while, and someone had left a C-45 on the ramp. I said to Jenkin, out of fun, "I'll flip you to see who checks out who in that C-45." To my surprise, Stenerson said, "OK." So we flipped, and I won. Stenerson checked me out, and vice versa. We both sat in the cockpit, figuring everything out, and away we went! A UC-78 "check" followed, and then Captain Eade found out. Well, things happened quick, and we got an ass chewing that I remember to this day. It was good that he found out, because I always wanted to fly a C-54. With ATC landing at Orly all the time, it probably was next on my agenda.

Later, Major James R. Lyons replaced Eade. On May 27, a F-5B (photo recon P-38) landed. I got checked out by the pilot and logged 2 hours flight time. The most stupid trick I pulled was on June 11, 1946. Major Lyons asked me to find someone who was checked out in the AT-6. HQ had called for us to deliver a C-45F to an RAF outfit in England, and fly an AT-6 back to Wiesbaden, Germany. I told the Major I could go, and he said, "OK." (I did not tell him I was checked out in the "6." I only told him I could go.) According to my Form 5, it took 2:15 to go and 1:30 to return. It was late in the day, so I returned to Orly. Upon arriving in England, I had told the RAF pilot to give me a cockpit check, because it had been quite a while since I had flown a single engine plane. He did, and away I went. I arrived back at Orly and told Major Lyons it would be good for morale to keep the AT-6 around for awhile. He said, "OK, take me up first." (Here I had 1:30 cross country time.) Up we went, for 50 minutes. We rolled and looped, and he really had a ball. That was one of the few times I saw him smile. When I landed, he said, "Don, line up some of the boys and check them out." (I then had 2 hours, 20 minutes.) Weather closed in on the 13th and 14th of June, and on the 15th, I checked out the first of many who had signed up with a 1:15 flight, plus 2 landings. When we landed, there was a pilot from

*Jenkin Stenerson and Donald Clark waiting for a bus outside the gate at Orly Field, May, 1946.*

Headquarters, and he said, "HQ is not too happy with what has happened." That ended my career in the AT-6, with a total of 4:35 IP and pilot time. Probably my Air Corps career would have been gone if I were of higher rank, but it had ended before this anyway.

In late Spring of 1946, EATS had grounded all flight officer pilots who would not accept the rank of 2nd Lt. In order to be promoted you had to sign up for one more year plus your original. That would have made me eligible to come home in June, 1948. There was one person in our squadron that accepted the promotion. After two days, they had to reinstate all of us, because they did not have enough first Pilots in EATS to operate.

We had a Lt. Colonel as our CO who made it a point to greet USO shows that arrived at Orly. I used to fly with the Colonel, on his four hour monthly flights in our "VIP" C-47. He called one day and asked that I hold the VIP plane for a certain day and that I go with him on this flight to Frankfurt. "Have the plane at the gate at 0800." So we taxied up, got out, and waited. It was put down as a training flight. So here comes the Colonel and a lady in a white fur coat. When they got up to the plane, he introduced her as _______, a well known movie star at the time. We boarded, and after takeoff he took off for the back. He said to call him 10 minutes out of Eschborn. We did, landed, discharged our cargo, and returned to Orly. When we got back to Orly he said, "Now you set up another training flight and be in Eschborn at 9AM. I will not go with you, but being you are on a cross country training flight, stop and pick up Ms. _______ and bring her back to Paris for the weekend – and make sure your crew is discreet." Being only a high school graduate and a farm boy to boot, I had to ask someone what it meant. I asked Major Tom Clark, who had joined Operations. He said, "It means to keep your mouth shut." Major Clark (no relation) had headed a squadron in the States during the war, flying navigator trainees around. I was given the task of checking him out in the C-47. He wanted to know what was going on. I said, "Can you be discreet on a mission." He said, "Yes." When his face lit up, I assume he thought he was going on an OSS mission or something. This country boy didn't like the way things were shaping up – so a little rank in the right seat might be a good hedge if something goes wrong. After we left Orly the next morning, I told him where we were going and my orders were to be discreet, etc. We landed and waited all day until 4PM, and she never showed up, so back to Orly we came. The Colonel met the plane and said, "Where in the God have you been? Where is she?" We said, "She didn't show up, and we are not allowed to fly after dark, so we had to return." That was the last of several training flights that I had taken part in.

On a Sunday night, I was on duty at Operations. It was raining, blowing, and Orly was below minimums. About 6PM, a call came in from HQ to fly a brain surgeon to Brussels at once. A nurse had been seriously injured in a jeep accident. No one was available on Sunday night, so by the time the doctor arrived at Orly, from Paris, I had gathered a co-pilot. Orly was closed. Brussels had 1,000' cloud ceiling and 2 miles visibility, but we were ordered to go. When we arrived at Brussels, the weather had gone to 1,500' and 2 miles. A normal let down was made. The doctor was met, and I found out later that the nurse's life had been saved. That is one flight I remember with some pride. I am glad I was able to help.

That story was written up for publication in *Stars and Stripes*, but gave no credit to the 27th ATG. Everyone probably thought ATC did the job.

**Werner E. Koethe recalls VE Day:**

I was a young 2nd Lieutenant fresh from the Army Air Forces Technical Training School arriving in Liverpool October 1943. My first assignment at BAD #1 was relatively short, and I was then transferred to the 311th Ferrying Squadron while it was in Langford Lodge and still a ferrying squadron. Shortly thereafter, we were assigned C-47s and became a transport squadron. Our mission was to provide air transport in support of the invasion of Europe as so ably described by Howard Stillwell in "A Pilot's Recollections." (Included in Chapter 3 of this work.) We had the best pilots, air crews, and ground crews that anyone could wish for. I am proud to have been associated with them.

One of my assignments was to get our vehicles and ground equipment from Grove, England, to Paris and ultimately to Istres. Miraculously, we made it with all vehicles and personnel accounted for.

In March of 1945 I was placed on TDY along with another officer and 29 enlisted men and returned to England where we boarded an unarmed B-24 and were flown to Stockholm, Sweden. There we were placed under the command of Colonel Bernt Balchen to provide aircraft maintenance for his squadron of C-47s that were flying into Norway from Lulea. That's where I was on VE Day.

**Many men of the 27th were involved in transporting former POWs out of Germany and other locations, near the end of the war and after hostilities ceased. Joe Maguire, a pilot of the 321st TS, remembers one of those trips:**

At the end of the war we flew several loads of POWs out of camps in Germany. I guess I will always be impressed by the dignity displayed by a Scottish officer in charge of one group I picked up. This man was very emaciated – literally skin and bones, but he looked as sharp as he possibly could and was wearing his kilt. He approached me, popped his heels, and gave me a proper British type salute. After I returned it, he offered me a cigarette, which was probably about all he had in the world at that time. After all he had been through it was almost like nothing ever happened. After a while we had a chance to talk, and he began to tell me of his family, which he had not seen in five years.

*Lt. Joe D. Maguire, 321st TS.*

**Gordon Fisher served as a pilot in the 310th, 312th, and 321st squadrons. His last assignment in the 27th was as the CO of the 321st. At the time he wrote the following letter home, he was in the 312th Ferrying Squadron. Gordy's parents turned the letter over to their hometown newspaper, the *Waukesha Dailey Freeman*, which published it on May 1, 1945. Parts of this letter are quite disturbing:**

I have seen what I am fighting for. I wish all could see it, gory and brutal as it is. Death and murder on the battlefield and in the air are a normal course of war. Death and murder at Buchenwald Prison Camp is a compact illustration of the warped, inhuman Nazi mind. It is here our enemies, the pride and joy of our enemies, are taught the technique of mass murder; here the fanatical Hitler Youth develop the supermen complex which leads them to enjoy the agony and pain of their believed inferiors. How can we handle a people, or can we call them people, who have caused and enjoyed the misery and suffering of our fellow men. The tales I am relating in the following will clearly illustrate the madness and sadism of the Hitler regime.

I was fortunate to be able to fly a group of newspaper and magazine correspondents, including Marguerite Higgens, Margaret Bourke-White,

*Aerial view of a concentration camp near Dresden.*

Lee Miller, and Percy Knauth to Weimar, captured three days before. From here the group would circulate to nearby interesting points, gathering information and pictures for articles. It didn't take long to gather such information. We were met at the landing strip by Colonel Max Boyd, commanding officer of the touring party, anxiously awaiting our arrival. A few short sentences explained his anxiety. Nearby was the famous political prison camp of Buchenwald. Here rumor has it that 2,000 people were put to death every month. We had the chance to visit and interrogate the remaining prisoners. Three days before the 600 "SS" guards had left, taking with them 35,000 prisoners, most of whom were Russians. That left 21,000 quartered in an area smaller than that occupied by Waukesha's three high school buildings. That would make conditions more than crowded. Crowded could be uncomfortably close.

Conditions at Buchenwald were unlivably close. Dead and dying were stacked and packed in the too few buildings. Some dead were piled outside the crematorium, the first object of our tour. "Some" refers to a stack of naked skeletons of 100 or more Poles, Russians, Czechs, French, Belgians, British, and even representatives of our own Air Force, plus a wagon load of another couple of hundred bodies. The stench of death and blood hung around the rotting blue and gray corpses – like fog over London. Too much even to gag one were the odors that erupted from fathers, mothers, brothers, sisters, and children of still living prisoners who shuffled around us, mumbling praise and thanks for the liberation. What did we accomplish by liberating the dead? They only became free when they were killed. A small Jewish Czech of 9 years, 3 of them spent at Buchenwald, tugged at my sleeve. Then crawling to a corner of the bloody, stiff pile he grabbed the cold fingers of a young woman muttering "Mein Mutter."

I couldn't tell whether he was proud, depressed, or indifferent. Their minds were already dead. Many of the mutilated bodies were beaten beyond recognition. Eyes and ears were missing from a great number. Old scars were opened anew, bones protruded through the taut, blotched skin, closely clipped heads showed bruises and bashing like old rotten apples.

What methods were used to end the lives of these "enemies of the Reich" besides starving? I soon found out. An Englishman led me into the inner sanctums of the crematorium. Here was mass murder at its best. Humans, dead or very near dead, were reduced from 80 to 90 pounds of skin and bones to a pound of ashes in a matter of seconds. Six ovens, with a capacity of 4 persons each, operated twenty-four hours per day to keep up with the Buchenwald death rate. Not 2,000 a month, but 4,000 a month here departed from our civilized world. The blazing ovens, for many weeks, had been unable to dispose of the ever increasing flow of starvation cases. For the surplus, a more crude, and less original disposition was used. The "SS" merely piled them up, sprinkled gasoline, and struck a match to them. The blaze failed to impress the prisoners; they had long ago forgotten everything except that their death was eminent. Many expressed an anxious desire to have been one of the human torches.

We milled around the stoves, still warm with charred remains, inspecting the organization which fed in humans as a baker feeds in loaves of bread, asking nationalities, length of time in the camp, age, relations, reasons for their persecution, etc. Not one of the answers gave even a hint of civil treatment with justice, kindness, or Christian emotions by the Germans.

Still I did not see what besides starvation killed so many before they were burned. I bent over to ask a miserable old man sitting in a gutter of excrement and vomit, but my German was not clear enough, and before I could explain further what I desired he collapsed in death. His eyes were big, brown, kindly, but very dead. His skin sagged further between his ribs, sores still festered on his back, his legs and broken feet were blue or gray from lack of blood and freezing nights. His hands, like blunt claws, clutched where his stomach had long since grown together. He was first of many who died talking to me in the few hours I spent there. From a five year old French boy destined to death within a few weeks I found out where the gory beatings were administered. Going down clean, whitewashed steps, I was led into a low, damp, white stone room, where frantic attempts were made by the Germans to erase the atrocious stories from the walls and ceiling. Much had been recently and hastily plastered, but plenty remained to burn a vivid picture into the already stunned minds of all who saw it. Hooks had been sunk into the walls, at a height of about seven feet, and spaced an arm's length apart. From here would dangle the emaciated, still living bodies of those doomed for the crematorium, while vampirish, mad, 'SS' guards improved their technique of torture. A club was left behind by the fleeing guards. It was a club well worn from the administration of years of savage use. As heavy as a big league baseball bat, and a foot shorter, it was stained dark brown, and dented. With these clubs groups of 24 humans at a time were being systematically broken and crushed while we went to college, or built tractors, or saw shows, or voted for a new president, or played football. It is odd that the shrieks and cries of agony and pain could not have reached our ears sooner. Could we have been too well deafened by security and contentment to hear Europe lose its freedom? If only the breaking limbs of the Jews, the Christians, the Poles, and all could have vibrated then around the world, if only the claw marks scraped in solid rock in depths of torture could have dug in our front doors, if only the blood splattered on the walls and ceilings could have been falling on our floors to stir us into the righteous deeds we were too hesitant to perform. Can there be a next time when 100s a day are made the targets of an inhuman lust of a warped mob? The elevator which hauled the bodies to the ovens could have been filled with our families, our friends, our leaders, and ourselves.

*Left: Captain Gordon Fisher, 321st CO at the end of the war. Right: Captain Gordan Fisher, CO, and Captain Jim Rinehardt, operations officer of the 321st on board ship heading for the States.*

The stench of the place drove us to seek fresh air. We stumbled into day-light, over dried bones and below the gallows where the Nazis illustrated to their students how dull and common hanging could be. They compared it against the barrel they drove spikes through, then tying a prisoner inside rolled it around the area till death through loss of blood finished the sport. Blood was still damp in the cracks of the barrel, and flesh clung to many of the spikes. Stumbling over more dead and dying, bumping into blind, not through loss of sight but through loss of eyes, we shoved our way into one of the more famous barracks, famous as the last home before the crematorium. A word picture could not be drawn to fully illustrate the atrocious conditions. The dark dirty wood building covered a chapter in our history. A chapter which should be read over and over, not before going to bed, but before voting for the leaders who can most successfully prevent a repetition of history. The vivid pictures of the suffering of thousands of our fellow men should be refreshed. If only I could describe each of the hundreds of naked men and boys, too weak and too packed to shiver on their wooden tiers. Too far gone to move, beyond hope of many days of life. All the medical care possible was being given, but it could not resurrect those already dead of mind and spirit. Food was useless without a stomach to put it in. Intravenous injections were being administered wherever hope flickered. The narrow aisle was slippery with milk and broth spit out because there was no place to swallow it. Death was occurring fast, too fast even to watch.

A French boy asked me if the Eiffel Tower still stood in Paris. Before I could answer that the Parisians in their jaunty spring outfits still strolled beneath the towering mass of steel which helped make Paris beautiful, he had died. Old men, asking names and places, passed quietly away, alone and without the consternation of their neighbors now inching closer to the live companion to keep warm. Living slept on dead. It was difficult to segregate many on the living from the dead. Only a moving eye, a mumble or grown would indicate life in these barracks of bones. A young Russian, illustrating his starvation, grabbed a handful of skin from his stomach, stretched it up and let is fall back into his body cavity, like dropping an inner tube into an empty bucket. That was his last move.

As I write this those barracks have been cleared. They have all died, and those that can be saved are being saved. Yet there is more to Commandant Kock's school of torture. There are phases which surpass the mass torture and eradication of so-called undesirables to the Reich. There are personal dealings which reflect further on the character and mentality of the would-be world conquerors. There are the thousands of human guinea pigs at Buchenwald who died as a result of countless failures of German doctors and scientists to perfect cures and toxins against prevalent army diseases. Many died from being drained of their blood. Then there is the woman angle. You have doubtless wondered why I have not mentioned women in my observations? I did see a few dead ones. The rest were evacuated days before. What else would you expect the "SS" troops to do with women other than to establish brothels for themselves and the more talkative prisoners. When the girls and elderly women were starved beyond usefulness or became pregnant, it is only natural sequence that they had to be beaten and burned. Then more were those put to death for other special reasons. On examination after arrival at camp many prisoners were found to have beautiful and unique tattoos upon their body, or possibly gold fillings and inlays in their teeth. These were killed instantly, with care not to mar the tattoos, for Madam Kock needed them after the skin had been tanned, to make handbags for her friends, or lamp shades, with gold inlay for her husband, the Commandant. Block 51 contained such a lamp shade, and many matched human skins.

We left amid the praise and thanks of the still-living prisoners. I felt we should be cursed for not arriving sooner.

As we drove along the highway leading from the camp, the citizens of Weimar were walking to their homes. General Patton had ordered 1,500 to go and view the products of their great government. Many were visibly impressed, weeping, stumbling, dazed by the horrors they had witnessed. Others already acquainted with the camp, through their association with the imprisoned slave laborers forced to work with them at the adjoining robot factory, laughed and joked, casting such remarks as "'We didn't know," and "they didn't tell us these things." Why didn't they tell them? Weren't they proud of their great achievements? They knew, but they did not care. Already they were alibiing by their unprepared air force, planning for the next time. Can we prevent there being a next time?

*310th Pilots, J.P. Predmore, Shields Krutzsch, "Jake" Jacobs, and Ralph Jenks.*

**Ralph Jenks was a pilot in the 310th Ferrying Squadron. After the end of hostilities he volunteered for a mission which turned into a grand adventure:**

I don't know who said it first, but it made the rounds in Europe. I always thought that the Irish were world class storytellers, but I think that they must take a back seat when it comes to a bunch of pilots telling about their heroic exploits. When you listen in, it sounds like "Dere' I wuz, on my back with two engines feathered, takin' code in Chinese."

Well, the tale that I will tell you now doesn't embrace quite the immediate hazard that the above situation might result in, but anyway, "Dere' I wuz," sitting out in front of the ready room, at my home base, "Burtonwood." Burtonwood was a huge air depot located between Liverpool and Manchester in northern England. Sitting next to me on the wooden bench was a good friend and fellow pilot named Ralph Jacobs. Ralph Jacobs had a nickname which he rather enjoyed. It was "Jake the Snake." Don't ask me where it came from or why he liked it, but he did.

It was a sunny and warm day for England, and we were waiting around for our flight assignments. Soaking up the sun was thoroughly enjoyable since we didn't get all that much in the UK. As I looked up, out strolled our Operations Officer, Captain Hartzell. "I need two C-47 crews to volunteer for a mission for the State Department, out of Paris. Any takers?" he said. I yelled, "To where? Where are we going?" "Don't know," he responded. "It's a take it or leave it kind of deal." One of the first things that I learned after joining the service was, don't volunteer for anything. I looked at Jake and he looked at me, shaking his head back and forth. "We don't volunteer for nothin," was his response. We sat there in the sun and pondered the situation for awhile. Wonder where someone wants to go? How long will it be? Why do they need two ships? These where just a few of the many questions that went through our minds.

The more that we talked about it, the more we were subconsciously talking ourselves into finding out more about it. I said to Jake, "Come on, it might be fun." So, off we went to Operations, to see who was going to take the other ship. Captain Hartzell said that Lt. Powell had inquired about it and that he would probably get a crew together and go. Hartzell said that if we decided to go, we had to depart for Villacoublay the next morning and go to the American Embassy in downtown Paris. Jake and I were still in the dark as to where! I guess that the intrigue of it all got the best of us, and we told Captain Hartzell that we would take the assignment if we could pick our crew.

Sgt. Charles Scafidi was a top notch radio operator and Bill Commins was the crew chief of the C-47, so we were all set.

We called Sgt. Scafidi "Skeeter" because he was such a little guy. He may have been small, but he was the best in the ETO. We went over and checked out the airplane. It was one of the later models. I was especially pleased to see it had been assembled in my hometown of Oklahoma City, at the Douglas plant where I had worked one summer. Everything looked OK, and the tanks were full of fuel.

As we walked back towards operations, the mystery and intrigue of it was about to get the best of us. We guessed about every place under the sun, except where we finally ended up. We asked Hartzell what kind of clothes we should take. Will it be a hot or a cold climate? He simply shrugged his shoulders and said, "Your guess is as good as mine. I haven't the slightest idea." We went back to our barracks and began to put our stuff together. It turned out to be our "pinks and greens" with the "Eisenhower style" battle jacket. That evening, we met with Lt. Powell and made plans to go to Paris the next morning. He was as much on pins and needles as we were. We knew that we had volunteered for something, but we didn't know what.

The next morning Jake and I went to the airplane and checked it over once more. It looked good. We decided to take turns flying pilot and co-pilot, on the various legs of the trip. Jake flew the first leg into Villacoublay at Paris. Villacoublay was like a second home for both of us, since we had both lived there for about three months earlier in the war.

When we landed, we were greeted by a Lt. Colonel. He told us he was the Assistant Director of Intelligence at the Seine base sector of the American Embassy. We were told to go to a certain address near the Arc de Triumphe, and to get our pictures taken. He then said, "Talk to no one about the anticipated trip, and be at the airport tomorrow morning, in your plane, at 0600." We asked, "Where are we going?" He responded with a smile, "I'll tell you in the morning."

Both crews boarded a GI bus and went to the address that the Colonel had given us. When we arrived, the building looked like an ordinary gray stone, like all the rest in that area of Paris. We went upstairs and entered a photographer's studio. We were instructed to takeoff all insignia of rank from our uniforms. All of us were then photographed wearing the same plaid sport coat. When I put it on, the sleeves came just below the elbows. It didn't make much difference, since all of the photos were bust shots for a passport. We then took the photos and went to the American Embassy to secure our passports. We still did not have a clue as to where we were going.

We got up pretty early the next morning. At 0600, our whole crew was on board and ready to go someplace. An Army command car pulled up near the plane, and the Lt. Colonel jumped out and boarded our C-47. It was my turn to fly the next leg of the flight to somewhere, and I was seated in the pilot's left seat. The colonel handed me a large brown manila envelope and said, "Well, here it is." Jake and I opened it up, and there was a map and a set of official orders. We examined the contents carefully, and Jake said, "Wow! We are going to Lisbon, Portugal, with stops at Bordeaux and Madrid." "Jenks," Jake said, "our first leg is from Paris to Bordeaux," and he gave me the heading and distance. I inquired as to what in the world was at Bordeaux. Jake responded, "Gas. We are going to need it, if we go up over the Pyrenees Mountains and drop down into Madrid, Spain."

The Lt. Colonel stayed on our ship, and a full "Bird Colonel" was on Lt. Powell's plane. I asked our Colonel as to what kind of cargo we might be hauling back. He said, "We are going to pick up the entire German Embassy and take them back to Germany. "Wow! What a deal!" we exclaimed. We had not had time, at that point, to look at our final leg of the flight to see where we were going. Stuttgart, Germany, was the last stop for us before returning home. But, a lot of water had to flow under the bridge before we got there.

The war had just ended a week before with the unconditional surrender of Germany to the Allies. General Franco, the Dictator of Spain, was dead, but the sympathy of the Spanish Government was still leaning toward the wrong side at that time. We didn't know what to expect from them. Dr. Salazar was the dictator of Portugal, and he seemed to be a good friend of President Roosevelt's, so we thought that we could expect a fairly friendly greeting from there.

"Let's get going," Jake yelled to the crew. We closed the door, contacted the tower, and I began to taxi out to the end of the runway. Our takeoff was smooth and to the east, toward Orly Airfield, which we could see off in the distance. I turned to the compass heading toward Bordeaux, France, and we settled down toward the first leg of the adventure. After a while we could see Bordeaux in the distance, and sure enough, there was the airfield just outside of town. As we circled the field, I exclaimed, "Man, there ain't much there, is there?" We landed and taxied over to an area where there were a couple of trucks and a bunch of fifty-five gallon drums. There were a half dozen people standing around the area waiting for us, so we pulled up near them and stopped. Jake said, "Don't tell me that our gas is in those drums! Man, we'll never get out of here." Jake's guess was correct, and furthermore, there was no electricity or other power source to pump the gas. You guessed it. It all had to be done by hand pump. Lt. Powell's ship had pulled up in the meantime, and both Colonels jumped out and were talking to the Frenchmen near the drums. Our Colonel came back and confirmed the worst. "It is going to be slow, but we'll make it," he said. Each ship holds about three hundred gallons, and we fortunately had quite a bit left. It was slow pumping, and we settled down for the wait.

We got out, stretched our legs, and enjoyed the sunny warm day. In the meantime, Jake and I were looking at the map trying to figure out the best route to go over the Pyrenees Mountains, which separate France from Spain. It looked like the mountains were ten to eleven thousand feet high, so we had to plan a route to safely clear the peaks. After several hours the refueling was complete for both ships, and we prepared to depart. This leg of the flight was to be piloted by Jake. He taxied out to the end of the runway and gave it the needle. The takeoff was smooth, as the ship lifted off and headed in a southerly direction. We were not too far from the French/Spanish border, so we began to gain altitude rather early. The French countryside was beautiful, and we could see the Bay of Biscay off to the West. The Pyrenees Mountains began to loom up in the far distance, and before we knew it, we were over the peaks as we entered Spain. The Pyrenees were beautiful with deep valleys. As we made our way further south, some of the countryside looked rather barren, and then we would see areas of intense green vegetation. Madrid is in the middle of the nation, and it did not take very long for us to be approaching that large sprawling city.

We landed at the municipal airport, and a jeep with a large sign on it which said, "Follow me," led us to a parking area, where we shut everything down. Our crew chief opened the back door of the airplane, and a man from the American Embassy came up to the cockpit and greeted us. He asked us to remove all signs of rank or insignia before we left the airplane. We all complied with the request, and two large black cars pulled up near the ships, and off we went. The two colonels left with the man from the embassy, and we then started on a sight seeing trip of Madrid.

The city was very ornate and beautiful. Lots of fountains and statues. We then drove to the outskirts of the city, and the embassy driver showed us the General Franco Memorial. It was a very large structure with a tall center piece and painted entirely in white. After a few hours we made our way back to the airport where the two colonels were waiting, and we prepared to depart.

This leg of the flight from Madrid to Lisbon was mine. We cleared with the tower and soon lifted our beautiful bird into the sky and headed west. At that time the western part of Spain looked rather dry and barren. We really didn't need a map to tell us when we entered Portugal, because everything suddenly turned green, with lush vegetation. The Portuguese countryside looked good and well cared for. Lisbon was our next stop. The city lies on the western part of the country and is on the Atlantic Ocean. Lisbon looked beautiful from the air as we circled and prepared to land at the airport. The weather was bright and sunny, and our landing was smooth. Once again the jeep went ahead of us with the familiar sign "Follow Me." Lt. Powell's ship was down by now, and we both parked the C-47s near one of the hangars. The back door popped open, and a guy with a leather jacket, two-tone shoes, and argyle socks came up front and said, "Strip off all rank and insignia, and welcome to Lisbon." I said, "Who in the heck are you?" He flushed and apologized, "Sorry, I'm Major Smith. I'm attached to the American Embassy here in Lisbon. Be sure and take your bags with you. I'll take you to your hotel." We prepared the airplane for the night stay and began to thumb through the brown manila envelope to see when we were supposed to depart. The orders read for us to leave within twenty-four hours.

We went with the Major to the big black automobiles and then to the Excelsior Hotel. It was a beautiful building, and the accommodations were excellent. The hotel was located in the center of Lisbon. For the two crews, this was more like a vacation holiday. Lisbon was a very pretty city with fountains, statues, and ornate buildings. During the afternoon we were free to roam around town and do some sight seeing. We also did some shopping, because everything seemed to be rather inexpensive compared to prices elsewhere. I recall that I bought six Omega wrist watches at a very low cost.

That night at dinner, in the hotel dining room, the colonel came over to our table with a very stern look on his face. He said, "Guys, I have some bad news. It seems that the Chief of Police of Lisbon has released our passengers, and it may take a while to round them up again." I asked, "Colonel, who are the passengers that you referred to?" "Our assignment was to pick up the entire German Embassy in Lisbon and take them to Stuttgart, Germany," he responded. I asked, "How many?" and the Colonel said, "About forty-five." "Well, what do we do now?" Jake inquired. The Colonel turned and asked, "Can you reach Paris by radio from here?" We all looked at "Skeeter" for an answer. "We can if you get me high enough," he said. The Colonel exclaimed, "Let's try it in the morning."

The next morning our crew, plus the two colonels, boarded the C-47, and we climbed to about twelve thousand feet over the Atlantic. Skeeter was given the instructions as to how to contact the embassy in Paris. Sure enough, they came in loud and clear. The Colonel talked to them for a few minutes, and then came up to the cockpit with, "We stay until we get them – no matter how long it takes." We went back to the airport and landed, and the search was on. Actually, the search had started the night before. I can only imagine what was said to the Lisbon Police Chief by their government authorities.

The crew had settled in the beautiful hotel for an extended stay, and that wasn't all bad for us. The next morning, Jake and I caught the train and went out to the coast to see a casino named Monte Estoril. When we exited from the train, an elderly gentleman approached us and said, "May I be your guide and show you the sights at Monte Estoril?" We said, "No thanks, we shall only be here a short time. We just want to see the beautiful flowers." The old gentleman said, "May I give you some good advice?" We said, "Sure!" He cocked his head and smiled and said, "Much money is taken into Monte Estoril – very little money is take out." We thanked him, took some pictures, and soon boarded the train back to Lisbon.

The next few days were rather uneventful for us. Our job was to simply sit tight and wait for the German Embassy to be rounded up again. The Major from the Embassy did come by one evening and took us out to dinner and to some unusual places, to see some night life. Frankly, I was glad to get back to our hotel. About five days after our arrival, the colonel came in at dinner and said, "OK, we are all set. We leave in the morning for Stuttgart."

The next morning started rather early for us. We were at the planes by 06:00, waiting for the buses to arrive, and here they came. Listen, if a Hollywood casting director had been there to pick them out, he could not have done a better job. We had every size and shape that you could imagine, but overall they looked like a pretty sharp bunch of guys. Then came the German Military Attaché. He was a tall, thin character, dressed to the hilt in his best uniform. He was wearing tall riding boots, with the britches to match, and carried a swagger stick. He had a monocle in his right eye and a chest full of service ribbons. Following along behind him was a young Lieutenant that was having a hard time keeping up with him.

Finally, we got them all on board the two planes and prepared to take-off. It was a long flight to Stuttgart, Germany, and Jake and I traded off piloting from time to time. When we were about half way back, one of the Germans came up to the cockpit. He was obviously a Jew. He was dressed like he was a model at a fashion show. We chatted with him for a few minutes, and he pulled out a roll of currency, made up of money from several countries. I'll bet that roll was four or five inches in diameter. I said to him, "You are a Jew, why did you work for those guys?" He responded by saying that the Nazi's threatened to kill his family if he did not work for them. I said, "How do you know that they are not already dead?" He said that he had seen his father in Berlin about a year prior, but he knew nothing about the rest of his family. As we approached Stuttgart, he came up to the cockpit again. When he saw the beat up airport, with the bomb pock marks all over the place, he said, "Look what you naughty boys did." I said, "Look, bud, we didn't start this war, but we sure as the devil ended it." He said nothing and returned to his seat.

After we landed, we were supposed to be met by the CIC (Counter Intelligence Corps) and turn our passengers over to them. But there was no one there yet. Jake and I had on top coats because it was rather cool in Germany at that time. We both had loaded .45 caliber automatics in our pockets, and both crews were armed. While we were waiting for the buses, I ask our Colonel, "What was the big rush to get this bunch out of Lisbon?" He said, "Ralph, almost every one of these men are experts in metallurgy, and from a jet engine standpoint, that is a very important subject. We had to get them out of there to beat Russians from getting them. And we did it! You bet we did!"

Here came the buses with several MPs, and they quickly loaded our passengers and away they went. We took the two colonels from Paris back to Villacoublay airport, and our mission was complete. Jake and I flew back to Burtonwood late that evening, and first thing the next morning, you know what – "Dere We Wuz" – sitting on a wooden bench just outside of our ready room, waiting for another assignment. What a grand adventure we had volunteered for ... maybe it helped us to get the metallurgists out first. Maybe a few of them, ultimately, ended up in the USA, like Dr. Werner Von Braun. Maybe they contributed to solving the jet engine metal tail pipe problem. Just maybe they even helped us get to the moon first. Just maybe their work contributed to making our everyday airline travel safer. Just maybe! I don't know for sure, but let's hope so!

**Les Veit, Aerial Engineer of the 86th TS, recalls the following incidents as the war ended. (At the time, Les was stationed at Grove, with the 808th Air Engineering Squadron):**

THE WAR ENDS !

The news of Japan's surrender set off the wildest celebration I have ever seen.

After things got back to some semblance of normal, we started the process of evacuating the base at Grove. That meant we made daily trips to other bases to get rid of supplies. One of the trips took us through the town of High Wycombe. We had to make a sharp left turn at the bottom of a steep hill. Some of the loads on our tractor-trailers were so heavy that we had a Jimmy 6x6 follow as a pusher to get them over the hump. The driver of the 6x6 would then return to Grove to resume regular duty there.

On one trip I made the fog rolled in while I was still on the base unloading. Thinking I knew where I was, I headed for the main gate. Imagine my surprise when the beautiful highway I was on turned out to be the main runway. I was lost! Using my head for a change, I climbed in a C-47 in a revetment and called the tower. They asked for the revetment number, then sent a "follow me" jeep out to guide me to the main gate. I made the trip back to Grove more by good luck than anything else, for I never saw the trailer wheels or the back end until I got back to Grove. The fog was that dense.

Finally, our orders came in and we were transported to Southampton where we boarded the *Queen Mary*, for what was to be the last load of American troops she would haul home. She was used from then on to return British troops from India and Egypt. Later on I was to have the pleasure of seeing her at her berth in Los Angeles, but that is another story.

As we stood by the rail waiting to leave England, we all had mixed emotions, thinking of the good times and the bad that we had been through. We occupied our time tossing scraps of food to the seagulls, and candy and gum (got any gum chum) to the kids on the dock. Amid much whistle blowing and excitement we were finally pulling away from the dock. Goodbye, Blighty, you were home to many of us for so long. How did you put up with us?

The trip home was made in 5 days, even though we came through a storm that sent a U.S. cruiser and a "baby flattop" back to Southampton for repairs. You no doubt have seen movies of the naval warfare in which the destroyers bury their bows under waves. This storm was so bad that the *Queen Mary* was doing the same. They had MPs stationed to keep us from going forward of the bridge. The waves were actually breaking over her bows. It was a crowded, but good time, for us – those that were not seasick, that is. We were only given two meals a day because of the crowding. As soon as they finished serving breakfast they started getting ready to serve supper. In between times we stuffed on cookies from the PX. Jane can't understand why for so many years I could not look a Fig Newton in the eye.

Our arrival in New York harbor was tumultuous to say the least. The Statue of Liberty was the most beautiful girl in the world. Even though so many had arrived home before us, they pulled out all the stops for us. The fire boats were shooting water high in the air, and every boat in the harbor was blowing its whistle. Talk about noise pollution! We were taken to New Jersey on ferry boats and arrived at Camp Kilmer to a steak dinner, in the middle of the night yet! That was SOP. Every one got their steak dinner as soon as they arrived. I never heard a complaint from anyone, even though we had to prop our eyes open to see the plates before us.

We were split up by home region, and I was among those sent to Indian Town Gap, near Harrisburg, PA, for separation. I arrived home December 19th during a snow storm. I had taken the elevated train from Pennsylvania Station. I went to the end of the line at Bridge Street. Dragging my duffel bag and carrying my Mauser rifle, I descended to street level. I was immediately approached by a cop. When he heard my story and that I wanted to take a cab to Bustleton, he shook his head. "I don't think a cabby will try to go there tonight," he said.

When a cab did finally show up, he flatly refused to take a trip to Bustleton. Unslinging my Mauser (he did not know it was empty), I stuck it in his ribs and said, well then get out, for this cab is going. The cop smiled, turned his back, and walked away.

The ride home to Bustleton had some anxious moments for me, as I had to get out and push the cab several times. My street was solid snow, so the cabby wisely refused to try and negotiate it. I walked the block home with my Mauser slung on my back and dragging my barracks bag.

As I got to the house the whole family was there to greet me. After our first long kiss, Jane came up for air and announced, "That mustache can stay tonight, but it goes in the morning." Welcome back to civilian life! My son may have wondered who the guy was embracing his mother, after all, he was all of six months old when I left, and he did not know me. He was starting his terrible twos.

As we settled down to getting reacquainted and getting into the routine of civilian life, I was starting to question my taking a discharge. Boy, things are rough in the real world. I got my old job back. The laws said they had to take me back, but the pay was not enough to support a family.

Somehow we managed to survive those first few years, and as I learned of the rationing and shortage of all consumer goods, I wondered how they survived at home. At least they did not have Nazi bombers and buzz bombs to contend with. The British people earned my admiration for their bull dog determination to see it through to victory.

**TOP SECRET – FINALLY OUT IN THE OPEN** by Ben Ramsey:

I was originally with the Eighth Air Force Service Command and stationed in Prestwick, Scotland, in 1942 and 1943, and then went to 27th ATG Headquarters as Adjutant at Cranford, about a mile from Heathrow Airport, in 1944. Then, after the invasion and the fall of Paris in August 1944, I was incorporated into the 302nd Transport Wing Headquarters as Assistant Adjutant General. A short time afterwards the Adjutant General was transferred back to the states, and I became the Adjutant for the 302nd Transport Wing Headquarters there in Paris. After the Battle of the Bulge, in probably April, we had an instruction from the Supreme Headquarters that the 302d Transport Wing was being transferred back to the States and those eligible could apply to return to the States. I did not apply, even though I had been in Europe three years, because I had a wife in England and I didn't want to return home until I could arrange to get her home. Therefore, around the 1st of May I was transferred out to Villacoublay, France, and became the Adjutant of the 27th Group again. Lt.Col. Reecher, who was in the 302d Wing Headquarters Air Control, was also transferred there as Commander of the 27th Group. Probably the first weekend I was there, which was probably about the 5th of May, a young lieutenant in security came to the headquarters and was very excited and asked to see the colonel. I told him the colonel was not in. He wanted to know when he would be back, and I told him sometime in the afternoon. He stood there for a few seconds, apparently thinking what to do, and then reached in his pocket and brought out a sheet of paper that appeared to be a telegram and handed it to me. The top of the instrument said "TOP SECRET." Below that, it said, "To Marshall," and below that it said, "The German Army will surrender May 8th" and gave a time. Below that it said "Eisenhower."

As you know, it was very unusual to see a TOP SECRET document, and I said, "where did you get this?" He said, "A WAC officer wanted to fly to London, and, of course, she had to sign an affidavit that she did not have any CONFIDENTIAL, SECRET, or TOP SECRET documents on her." She said she couldn't sign. I told her she couldn't fly. She said she had to because her family was meeting her in London. I told her that didn't make any difference. She reached in her purse and pulled out this instrument that he had just handed me. He said, "I was surprised," and asked, "Where did you get this?" She replied, "I work at SHAEF Headquarters, and this is the sort of instrument my group handles. Some of us girls decided to make a photostat copy as a souvenir."

The Lieutenant wanted to know what I was going to do with the document, and I said I would put it in the safe until the colonel arrived.

That afternoon when the colonel came in, I told him that I had a present for him. He looked surprised and asked what kind of present. I told him it was in the safe and that I would get it for him.

I procured the document and handed it to him. His eyes lit up and he said, "Where did you get this?"

I told him the story, and that is how I knew three or four days in advance that the German Army was going to surrender.

**Dick Seebers was a pilot in the 311th and 321st Squadrons. (Excerpts from Dick's diaries appear in chapter 4.) Dick has lasting memories of the first girl he ever saw in a bikini!:**

Several times, in recent years, I have been amused by answers to TV quiz show questions as to when the first bikini swim suit was shown. The answers, 1947 and 1948, were both wrong.

Shortly after the fighting in Europe ended, the 321st Squadron stood down and had a party. We were taken by truck to a swimming club on the Marne River, near Paris. Mostly, we sat around, talking, drinking, "horsing-around," relaxing, and looking. I remember a group of girls playing volleyball in the water.

The main event, silently, came upon us. Suddenly, the talking and drinking stopped, and all heads turned to the left. Descending a spiral staircase was a beautiful French girl with almost no swimsuit on. The silence continued for almost endless minutes. What she was wearing is what we now call a bikini. The year was 1945, and history was made that day!

**87th TS pilot, Charles H. Harbaugh, Jr., remembers a few incidents after the war was over:**

When the armistice was signed we heard it on our radio, and were heading back to Grove, empty from Germany. Brussels was in our line of flight, and when we got there the Belgians had found their hidden fireworks and the sky was lit up all over. We fired off our flares and got into the left bound circle with a bunch of others. I thought it was a little crowded, so we went on over to London. The fireworks were nothing, compared to Brussels.

Next day, Chaves came around with the proposal: "Since we know you are the best scrounger we have, if I can get a plane, would you get over to Germany and get some guns for the guys that don't get there so often?" Ike and I took him on and off we went, probably the only plane flying. Everybody on the field could hear us takeoff, and questions were asked. We went direct to Ike's old bomb base, refueled, and direct to Grove, Denmark, 700 miles over the North Sea.

*The first girl Dick Seebers (and several other guys) ever saw in a bikini!*

At Grove, Denmark, the Germans had overnight complied with the Armistice, and all props and tails were off of the large number of German fighters. We landed, taxied in, and parked on the perimeter.

We were met by a huge German officer, undoubtedly the base commander. He would not give us any side arms, so we started to leave. One of their Sgts., speaking English, knowing what was coming, wanted to trade a German aerial camera, 175mm I believe, maybe larger, for food. We didn't have much food, if any, so like a fool, I didn't make any kind of deal with him.

So off to Breman, and landing there, we were met by an American major in a German pre-war Opel Admiral convertible sedan with the top down. Driving up to the plane, that car looked similar to a '38 Buick.

We were being very careful this time, as the British were already there. Bear in mind, this is the day after the Armistice was signed. Major Spivak deduced quickly what we were after. "Get in, let's go." He took us to one of those huge concrete bunkers the Germans had built and started in. We were challenged by the British soldier guard, armed with a British rifle, and he demanded a pass. Spivak, who was with the Strategic Bomb Survey, leafed all through his wallet, couldn't find one – really didn't have one – so he said, "Come on boys, let's go," and we went, with the guard trailing behind, but not shooting. We had gone equipped with a couple of barrack bags, and the room he took us to was half full of German side arms of all kinds – Lugers, P-38s, P-35s – everything thrown in a large pile. Ike started picking up and inspecting each one, and the guard was getting more nervous. I told Ike to throw in the guns and let's get out of here, which we did, back to the plane, no sight-seeing, as Spivak said, "Get the hell out of here quick." What he knew I didn't know, but off we went. This was a beautiful, clear day, and we met a huge vulture, or at least he looked that way, and I ducked so hard I had a sore neck. I really thought he was coming through the windshield. He didn't hit the tail, either.

I don't remember where we refueled, but when we landed at Grove, England, Chaves was there to meet us. "I hope you guys got guns. Headquarters is asking questions." His eyes flew open when we showed him the barrack bags that were so heavy they were really a load to carry. We got what we wanted, and the rest were distributed strategically. We never heard anything more about that flight.

Next day we were back in business, as if nothing had happened. There were wounded to bring back. We had to watch for B-17s and B-24s at about 1,000 feet or lower, as they were flying their ground troops on sightseeing missions.

Right after the ground forces passed Kassel, we went there to pick up French POWs. We went over the field to make sure we had the right place. While we were doing that, a Troop Carrier Group came along with 15 or 20 planes and we had to follow them ten miles or more out of town to land. The field had something grey that appeared, at 1,000 feet, to have oozed out on the all grass field. When we taxied in, these were inmates that had been freed from the Buchenwald concentration camp. I don't know why we didn't find someone there lying on the ground that spoke English, and talk to them. We did talk to an American captain, dressed in an A-2 jacket and pinks. He said he, and his crew with him, had been shot down, and asked if we would we take him back to his bomb base. Our orders were explicit on taking people out of Germany, and I turned him down. I'm not sure who he was. He spoke perfect American English. Anyway, we went to see the camp, and it was a sight never to be forgotten. We picked up French POWs and took them to Le Bourget. Their families were there to greet them. With the way things were torn up, I wonder how the word got back to Paris to the exact families of these survivors.

Sometime later, my friend Ike had announced that he was going home to marry Ann, and he was gone. I was assigned to the U.S. Navy in London. I wasn't happy about that, but only stayed in London one week, and off to Frankfort for a soft job with the Navy. The Army didn't know where we were, and the Navy didn't care, as long as we met the flight schedule, which was about one trip a week, usually to London. We had five planes and five crews with Navy call signs. That lasted about a year, then to EATS to fly the Army's airlines until I came home.

*87th TS Pilot, Charles H. Harbaugh, Jr.*

I came home to the same house I left and I still live in today. To my mother and sisters, my father was gone, but we lost no one in the family, all having been in combat. Two first cousins, one a Navy pilot and the other in maintenance on B-29s. My little dog came up and took two sniffs, and he just ran around in circles in the yard. He knew me and was happy to see me. He lived on, another ten years.

Then, after 50 years plus, we start writing about what we did.

**A pilot of the 27th ATG, who asked to remain anonymous, had these recollections of the end of the war:**

The war in Europe was over, but we were still delivering supplies and evacuating POWs near the forward areas. One of my deliveries in a C-47 ended not too far from Berlin, so after unloading I thought I would fly over the big bombed out city and look at the damage. I neglected to consider Berlin was now Russian and neutral territory. My co-pilot and I, sightseeing Unter-den-Linden and other devastated areas, ended up over Tempelhof airdrome. It was pock-marked with bomb craters and surrounded by ruined hangars and apartment buildings. We were surprised to see on the ramp area a L-5 and a P-51. Close by the planes were two guys waving wildly – the American pilots interned by the Russians. I looked at the field, looked at my co-pilot, and he looked at me. I think at that time he wished he were someplace else. I cut the power, lowered the wheels and flaps, and landed the C-47 across the field towards the two planes, swerving to avoid bomb craters. I yelled at my co-pilot to hurry aft, open the fuselage door, and we would pick our boys up on the run. He swung both pilots into the cabin, slammed the door, and I was on my way, weaving across the field gaining speed. By then, the Russians were alerted with trucks chasing behind and motorcycles coming ahead. I yanked back on the control wheel and we were up and out. The two pilots had been forced down with mechanical problems (while sightseeing) and were immediately interned by the Russians. I thought it best not to get involved any deeper, so we dropped them off at a field near Paris with promises not to identify us. They were just glad to be free again. However, we did hear that Marshal Zukov complained to Ike. No big investigation – I think Ike may have been tickled by the episode.

He was not tickled by one of my other flights. The end of the war was a day of great celebration, in – and over – Paris. Planes were flying thick above the crowded town. I had a P-51 flying up and down the streets, under the big Eiffel Tower, rat racing around in the Place de Concord. All this at or below roof tops. Returning to base, I found a gang of M.P.s wanting to celebrate. So, I invited about a dozen into a C-47, pulled out the little five inch ventilating plugs from the windows, stacked the center aisle with very pistols (flare guns) and cases of multiple colored flares. I found a co-pilot and took off for the Champs Ellysis, a wide tree lined boulevard, the main street of Paris.

From curb to curb was solid with Frenchmen and women and soldiers. Telling my MP's to fire away, down the long boulevard I flew, just skimming the tree tops, below the tops of the apartment buildings, and stores. The M.P.s were yelling and flares were shooting out, bouncing off the sides of the buildings. My co-pilot could not bear to look sideways. He stared straight ahead, gripping his seat. Even that was not safe, because at the end of the Champs Ellysis was the Arc-de-Triumph, and we were well below its top. We came roaring towards it, flares arcing out of the plane. I noticed people on top of the Arc, cameramen and newsreel people looking down on us coming in. I peeled up and over their heads as they ducked for safety. We flew back to base, landing after knocking over a couple of haystacks with our prop wash. I knew none of the M.P.s would say a word, because that would be trouble for all of us, and the M.P.s were familiar with trouble. An order to all squadrons followed from Ike. No more flying over Paris. But, I bet the M.P.s have told their kids about that day. I am telling mine.

My last flying in Europe was another fun trip. We were in a staging area near Reims, France. It was a tent city, and as commanding officer of the squadron, I was getting it packed to take to China. The tents were arranged on a gentle slope in two long rows with a canvas, four sided, open top latrine at the end of each row. An old friend called from Group Headquarters saying he could get his hands on a couple of P-51s if I would be interested. Would I?! He and I took off from Paris, and naturally, headed for Reims and our tent city. Some of our guys had strung radio antennas across the rows from tent top to tent top. It was a large base camp, but we located my squadron and came down at them, Mustangs roaring. He took one row and I took the other, knocking down the antenna lines and pulling up sharply at the end of the rows, over the canvas latrine, collapsing all four sides with our prop wash. If there had been anyone inside suffering from constipation, we sure helped them out. We ended up leaving camp doing slow rolls. I lost count after 19, and was almost seasick by the time I stopped. The guys at camp really got a kick out of our last "buzz" job. And, so did we.

Well, it was not really my last. I had one more with a C-47 over my home town, Waukesha, Wisconsin. We were back in the States signing off the squadron and turning over equipment at La Fayette, Indiana. I needed my monthly flying time, so managed a trip to Indianapolis to pick up an aircraft part. I took a fresh young base pilot with me as co-pilot. At Indianapolis, I fueled up because I had a slight course change in mind returning to La Fayette. I would go via Waukesha ... only 200 miles out of my way. My brother was visiting Mom and Dad, and I wanted to say "hello" my favorite way.

We lived on a hill on the edge of town, so I could get a pretty good shot at them. I brought the C-47 low up the valley and up the side of our roof. This brought my brother out of the house, so I made another low pass, then went over to visit my in-laws on the other side of Waukesha. I came down their street, chasing my wife's mother up their back porch steps. We turned around, feathered my right engine, and made another pass at each of our homes. Then I left for La Fayette, feeling good. My new co-pilot was not feeling quite as good. It was a new experience for him, but a great way to end the war for me.

I was lucky. Even now, I often think of those who were not so lucky. The Rays, Esposites, Creechs, Daniels, Canevas, Francis's, Hollingsworths, Smittys, Smileys, Rebaczeks, and many more of my buddies who still lie in France and England. They never had the chance to have children and grandchildren. They all sacrificed everything so we could continue to live in a wonderful, free country. I will never forget them.

I hope you won't forget them.

# Chapter 9

# Aircraft Markings

Much like the fluid nature of the development of the 302nd Transport Wing, and the 27th and 31st Groups, the markings on the aircraft were in a state of evolution throughout the war. There does not appear to be a great deal of consistency of application of markings at any one particular time. Part of this may be due to the fact that aircraft were acquired from different sources at different times. Some aircraft were new, while others were transferred from Troop Carrier Command, ATC, etc. This allows for some of the variances, and explains why many photos show evidence of previous unit markings being painted over. Members of the same squadron have very different recollections of aircraft markings, and they are both probably right, in their own set of circumstances and memories. There is a lot of discussion among veterans over whether or not 27th ATG aircraft used code letters. The correct answer is yes, and no! The material presented here is based on the limited photographic evidence available, and numerous interviews with veterans of the 27th and 31st Transport Groups.

**Wing and Group Markings**

The one marking that was fairly consistently applied to all aircraft of the 302nd Wing was the yellow-black-yellow, bands or stripes, at the top of the vertical stabilizer. Some veterans referred to these stripes as "hornet" or "bee" stripes. The other marking that was applied with some consistency, although not 100% of the time, was the group geometric symbol. The 27th ATG used a solid white circle, and the 31st TG used a solid white triangle. This insignia was applied in two places on the C-47s. One, centered over the serial number, on the vertical stabilizer, and the other, on the center of the front of the nose. Other aircraft types may only have the tail markings. It also was somewhat common to see the last three numbers of the aircraft serial number painted on the lower portion of the front of the nose of C-47s, especially in the later part of the war.

At some point, in the later part of the war, the 312th, 321st, and possibly the 86th, 311th, and Headquarters Squadrons began to apply letter codes behind the cockpit area of their C-47s. The first letter was the squadron, and the second letter was the individual aircraft. The lettering was yellow with black shadowing, although the shadowing was not always applied. When this practice began the aircraft code was applied under the nose of the aircraft, as well. The 321st squadron letter was "C," and the 312th, "P." Photographic evidence suggests that the 86th used "T," the 311th used "S," and Headquarters Squadron, "W." It has been suggested by some that these codes were just a carry over on aircraft acquired from Troop Carrier units. This is simply not the case. Troop Carrier aircraft of the same squadron all carried the same two letters. The second letter did not change with each aircraft. Troop Carrier Command code letters were applied in white or gray, not yellow and black. The letter combinations which appear in the known photographs, at this time, are not attributable to Troop Carrier units.

*The yellow-black-yellow band of the 302nd Wing, and the white circle of the 27th ATG, can be seen on the tail of this C-47.*

*Left: The white circle of the 27th ATG can be seen on the nose of this C-47 in Paris, 1945. The man in front is Bill Reid. Right: The tail of a 31st TG Gooney Bird can be seen in the background of this photograph. Note the yellow-black-yellow stripe. It appears that the tip of the stabilizer is also painted black on this airplane. The black tip is sometimes found on other aircraft, as well. Also visible is the white triangle of the 31st TG.*

*The 27th ATG white circle is visible on the nose of this well worn Gooney Bird. Notice the areas behind the cockpit and on the nose have been painted over. This airplane likely came from Troop Carrier, and the markings were obliterated.*

*Left: The 302nd Wing stripe and the 31st TG triangle, are clearly visible on this C-46 "Commando." This is one of three C-46s assigned to Grove. All three were lost within two months. Right: The 31st TG triangle is visible on the nose of this "nosed-over" Gooney.*

*One "brave" pilot did a Split-S in this Norseman and tried to loop it. He was lucky to get back on the ground in one piece. The 302nd tail stripes are visible on what's left of the tail.*

**Squadron Markings**

The 86th, 87th, 311th, 312th, 320th, and 321st Squadrons each had individual aircraft markings. Again, they were not consistently applied, but we can draw some generalities.

**The 86th Transport Squadron.**

Aircraft of the 86th TS carried the 302nd Wing tail stripes, and the 27th ATG, circles. Additionally, the 86th had a squadron insignia, which depicted "Sad Sack" carrying a very large, red crate on his back, superimposed on a yellow circle, with a red border. This insignia was carried on both sides of the nose of the C-47s. Aircraft of the 86th did not use number or letter identification codes on their aircraft as a rule. However, at least one photograph exists, taken at the end of the war, showing what appears to be "TM" or "TA" (the second letter is not clearly visible) on an 86th bird, in yellow, with black shadowing. This suggests that these codes may have been applied to some aircraft near the end of the war. (This photo appears in the last section of the 302nd Wing History, reprinted at the first part of this book. A cropped version of the photo appears in this section, also.)

*This hazy photograph of the 86th TS, at the end of the war, shows the "Sad Sack" insignia on the nose, and code letters behind the cockpit. This is the only photo the author has seen of an aircraft of the 86th with code letters. The letters appear to be "TM" or "TA," but the second letter is difficult to see.*

*The squadron insignia of the 86th TS on the nose of a C-47.*

*Lt. Hayes, of the 321st, poses in front of an 86th C-47. Note the squadron insignia, white circle, and the last three numbers of the S/N painted on the nose.*

*A C-47 of the 86th TS, on operations in Sweden. Note the placement of the squadron insignia on the nose.*

### The 87th Transport Squadron

Aircraft of the 87th carried the yellow-black-yellow band of the 302nd Wing, as well as the circle of the 27th ATG. The 87th was reassigned to the 31st TG, and can therefore be found with the triangle of that unit later in the war. The squadron identification markings were natural metal (aluminum) engine cowlings with two blue bands around them. Aircraft of the 87th apparently did not use number or letter aircraft identification codes.

*Below: Gooney Birds of the 87th on the flight line. This is after the 87th was assigned to the 31st TG, as the tail markings are triangles. Note the two blue bands on the natural metal cowlings. The aircraft in the background was likely reassigned from Troop Carrier, as there is evidence of code letters having been painted over behind the cockpit area.*

*Detail of the cowlings of an 87th TS, C-47.*

*C-46 "Commando" of the 87th TS. The natural metal cowlings, with blue bands, and the yellow and black tail stripes are visible. Note the number 14 applied to the nose. There were three C-46s assigned to Grove, one per squadron. All three were lost within a short, two month time period.*

*Charles Harbaugh in the cockpit of an 87th TS C-47 in France. The squadron cowling markings are very clear. There is also a code letter behind the cockpit and a quickly applied number on the nose. Harbaugh is fairly certain that these markings were carried over from a previous unit, to which the aircraft was assigned, and not applied by the 87th. The first letter, carried also under the nose, is "B." The second letter, visible behind the cockpit, is "D" or "O."*

### The 311th Ferrying Squadron

C-47s of the 311th FS carried the 302nd Wing tail stripes and the 27th ATG circle, although it seems that these markings were less consistently applied than in the other squadrons. The squadron marking of the 311th was a yellow and black "tiger tooth" pattern, sometimes called a "tulip" pattern, painted around the cowlings. It is not common to see 311th aircraft with code letters, although one photograph exists of a 311th C-47 with "SX" behind the cockpit.

*Right: Lt. Dick Seebers in front of a 311th C-47. The yellow and black "tiger tooth" cowlings can be clearly seen.*

*Left: This 311th Gooney Bird on its belly sports the "tiger tooth" cowlings and the yellow-black-yellow tail stripe, but does not have the 27th ATG circle on the tail or nose. The circumstances of this accident are not known, but since only one prop is bent, it would indicate that only that engine was running at the time. Right: This ship of the 311th FS wears the "tiger tooth" cowlings, but lacks the wing and group markings.*

*Sgt. John Dargin, who served with 27th ATG HQ, Headquarters Squadron, and the 520th Service Squadron, and Sgt. Frank Wardlaw, pose in front of a 311th C-47. This airplane has the letters "SX" behind the cockpit and under the nose. The 27th ATG white circle is also visible on the nose.*

### The 312th Ferrying Squadron

The 312th FS Squadron aircraft were marked with the 302nd Wing tail stripes and the 27th ATG white circle. Additionally, the 312th had its own squadron insignia, which featured a caricature of a pilot, dressed in black, riding a yellow "Gooney Bird," superimposed on a white disc with a red border. This insignia was carried on the nose of their C-47s. The 312th also used an aircraft code, with "P" as the first letter, and the individual aircraft having its own letter as the second letter. Photographs have surfaced of "PX," "PW," and "PZ." This code appears behind the cockpit and under the nose, and is in yellow with black shadowing. These aircraft also had the last three numbers of the serial number, painted in white, between the circle and the aircraft code under the nose. To top it off, the front half of the cowlings were painted black, with the back half painted yellow.

*The rear portion of aircraft "PW" of the 312th FS. Note the last three numbers of the serial number have been over painted in white. Also visible are the yellow-black-yellow stripes and the 27th ATG white circle.*

*C-47 "PZ," #250, of the 312th FS, can be seen over the heads of the men of the 312th. Note the name "BABS," appears on the rear portion of the Gooney Bird in the squadron insignia.*

*C-47 "PW," #474, of the 312th FS. The squadron insignia, yellow with black shadowed lettering, aircraft number in white, and black and yellow cowling bands can all be seen in this photograph. Note on the squadron insignia, on the rear portion of the Gooney Bird, the name "STELLA" is written.*

*312th, C-47 "PX." The squadron insignia, code letters, white circle, and cowling bands are all visible in this photograph. The aircraft number is not painted on the nose of this bird, as it was on "PZ" (#250) and "PW" (#474). Dillard Hyden, of the 311th Squadron, was assigned to this plane when he became a flight engineer. Radio call letters were "Precious X-Ray."*

## The 320th Transport Squadron

The aircraft of the 320th were easily spotted by their yellow and black "checkerboard" cowlings. The C-47s and UC-64s were both marked in this fashion. The aircraft also were marked with the 302nd Wing yellow-black-yellow tail stripes. The UC-64s apparently did not carry the white circle over the serial number, but many of the C-47s did. No photographs have surfaced, to date, showing any squadron codes used in the 320th. It does appear that, at some point, some of the UC-64s were marked with a yellow cowling, with a single black band, with solid black cowlings, and with black and white cowlings. These markings may have been carried over from previous units to which the aircraft were assigned.

*Above: In this photo, "Nancy Gee" has a sold black cowling.*

*Left: This UC-64 #335377, "Nancy Gee," at Goxhill, England, was flown by Howard Gilberg. The cowling appears to be yellow, with "Nancy Gee" in white. The top of the tail also appears yellow.*

*A second view of "Nancy Gee" with black cowling.*

*This was the art work on the right side of "Nancy Gee."*

*Above: Crew chief, Nelson, and radio operator, Bill White, in front of UC-64 "Claire." Note cowling appears to be white and black. Also note yellow-black-yellow tail stripes. A color photo of this aircraft appears in the color section of this work, showing the aircraft with the yellow and black checkerboard cowling. The name "Claire" and the star on the wheel are in red.*

*Right: Lt. Marshall, in front of the distinctive yellow and black checkerboard cowling of a 320th TS, UC-64.*

*Below: Crew chief Marvin Diehl, working on 320th TS C-47, aircraft #046, at Le Bourget, November, 1944. Marvin remembers this aircraft as having come from service in North Africa, and described it as being "dirt colored," as opposed to the more familiar shade of olive drab commonly seen in the ETO.*

**The 321st Transport Squadron.**

The 321st Transport Squadron holds a very special place in the heart of the author, because my dad flew with them. As with most of the squadrons, there is a lot of inconsistency with the application of markings. Generally, the 321st C-47s were marked with the 302nd Wing tail stripes, and the 27th ATG white circle. The squadron marking of the 321st was a yellow "tear drop," or "lemon drop," on the cowlings. The 321st began to apply squadron codes in yellow, sometimes with black shadowing, behind the fuselage at some point also. Photos have surfaced of "CB," "CC," "CF," and "CS."

*Lt. Joe Maguire, in the cockpit of a 321st C-47. His original caption to wife, Jeanan, said, "Notice I am in the first pilot's seat," indicating he was now a first pilot. The 321st "lemon drop" is clearly visible on the cowling. There are no codes on this airplane.*

*Left: A second view of a 321st C-47, with the lemon drop on the cowling and no codes.*

*This photo is of a group of pilots of the 310th Ferrying Squadron on a trip to Italy in February of 1945. The taxi ship is a 321st bird. Note the lemon drop on the cowling and the 27th ATG circle on the tail. The yellow-black-yellow stripe is not on this aircraft.*

*Right: This is the aircraft Lts. Maguire and Barker were flying on April 12, 1945, when they were hit by flak and bounced by a Me 109. The code letters "CC," in yellow, with no black shadowing, can be seen behind the cockpit.*

*This photo of the 321st, cropped from a larger example in the 302nd Wing History, was taken at the end of the war. Interestingly, this bird also carries the letters "CC," this time with black shadowing. It is believed that the aircraft Maguire and Barker were shot up in, (also "CC," but with no shadowing) was used for spare parts. This photo suggests that that airplane may have been repaired and repainted, or there was a second aircraft, coded "CC," when that plane was taken out of service.*

*Above and left: These photos were taken 18 May 1945, in Germany. The Gooney Bird, of the 321st, was flown that day by Lt. Ray Zych and crew. The photos were taken by Zych's brother, a S/Sgt. The aircraft does not carry the squadron marking "lemon drop," but does have squadron codes "CF" or "CE." (It is not possible to see all of the second letter) Of particular interest is the fact that the "C," has black shadowing, while the second letter does not.*

*Below: This 321st Gooney Bird displays all markings, as it should. The lemon drop on the cowlings, the 302nd tail stripe, the 27th ATG circle on the nose and tail, and the "CS" codes, with shadowing, are all visible in this shot.*

**Headquarters**

I only have one photograph, with information, that I know to be a headquarters aircraft. That is of a C-47, #038. Radio operator Bill White was assigned this airplane. The aircraft carried the code "WA" in yellow, with black shadowing, behind the cockpit and under the nose. It also had the 27th ATG white circle on the nose. We do not have photographs of the tail, but must assume it had the white circle and yellow-black-yellow stripe. The last three numbers of the serial number are 038. The airplane also had the name "Puppeschön," painted below the cockpit on the left side.

*Left: Headquarters C-47 "Puppeschön." Note the lettering "WA," behind the cockpit and under the nose. The 27th ATG white circle is also visible. Right: Radio Operator Bill White in the cockpit of "Puppeschön." "Puppeschön" translates as "Beautiful Doll."*

*This photo is of the right side of "Puppeschön," according to Bill White. It must be assumed that this shot was taken prior to having 27th ATG markings applied. It appears that the letters TC, and a squadron insignia, have been removed, or painted over, and 038 has been newly applied. This would indicate the airplane came from another unit, but the code TC is, so far, unidentifiable to the author.*

*Left: This view of Bill White, in front of the aircraft, shows that the cowlings were plain.*

**Invasion Stripes.**

Aircraft of the 27th ATG continued to use black and white "invasion stripes" on the underside of the fuselage only after the Invasion period was over. It is unknown exactly how long this went on, but it appears it was well into 1945, and probably through the end of the war.

*F/O Jim Leverick, of the 311th FS, at A-54, in October of 1944. Note the invasion stripes on the lower half of the fuselage only.*

*This photo of a 321st C-47 was taken by Joe Maguire, in March of 1945. Note the invasion stripes on the underside of the fuselage only.*

*This C-45, on its back, has invasion stripes on the underside of the fuselage. The yellow and black tail stripes are barely visible in the grass.*

### Other Aircraft

The 310th Ferrying Squadron was assigned a B-26B, SN 41-31742. It was flown primarily by Captain Fay Brandis, and Crew Chief, S/Sgt. Ray Dlouhy. The aircraft was olive drab with gray undersurfaces. The entire engine nacelles and cowlings were natural metal. The vertical stabilizer was marked with the yellow and black stripes, and it had invasion stripes on the lower portion of the fuselage. The airplane wore the name and nose art "Demon Deacon."

*Right: Aircraft nick-name "DOTTIE" on one of the B-17s. Notice there are no guns in the nose, and the round patch where the chin turret was removed.*

*Below: The 27th ATG had some B-17s assigned, which were stripped of all guns to conserve weight and increase speed. These aircraft were used as taxi ships and as gas tankers. This example is in natural metal finish. The only real indication it is with the group is the yellow and black tail stripe. Also note the invasion stripes on the lower portion of the fuselage.*

*B-26B of the 310th Ferrying Squadron, "Demon Deacon."*

*The tail of the "Demon Deacon" can be seen in this photo, with a British B-25 in the background.*

*Cockpit of "Demon Deacon," with pilot's name, "Captain Fay Brandis," and "Crew Chief, S/Sgt. Ray Dlouhy" painted under the window.*

*Detail of the "Demon Deacon" nose art.*

*This photograph of Howard Gilberg could cause some confusion. The insignia of the Air Transport Command (ATC) is on the fuselage, just over Gilberg's head, of this C-47. Also visible is the 27th ATG white circle on the tail. The 27th ATG was not part of the ATC. It must be assumed that the 27th acquired this bird from ATC, and for some reason, the marking was not removed.*

**Miscellaneous 302nd Wing markings**

There is a marking visible in photographs from three different veterans of the 27th ATG, on three different airplanes, which as of now is unattributed. It is a white, oblong marking on the center of the nose of at least two C-47s and one C-87. There are numbers or letters in the center of the white area, but they are not clear enough to read in the photographs.

*Right: C-47 at Tempelhof, Berlin in 1945. Note the white marking on the nose of the airplane.*

*The old C-87 in the hangar at Burtonwood. Note the large white marking on the nose.*

*This photo was captioned by 310th pilot Vincent Alexander as "Taxi ship landing." The unidentified white marking on the nose is very apparent in this photo. Also notice there is a dark stripe under the serial number on the tail, which is not found in other known photographs.*

*Right: A group of enlisted men of the 27th ATG. Note on the far left the tail of a C-47 is visible, with a checkerboard pattern in yellow and black or white and black. This marking is unidentified at this point, but the other C-47 in the background displays the yellow and black tail stripes of the 302nd Wing.*

*Above: A C-47 on the ramp at Grove. I believe this is one of the squadrons of the 31st TG. Notice the large diamond shapes around the cowlings, which appear to be yellow and black.*

*Right: C-53 "Hairless Joe," 1944. 87th pilot Charles Harbaugh recalls that this aircraft was a requisitioned American airliner that had an engine fire over eastern France. The crew bailed out. All made it except the co-pilot, who forgot to buckle his leg straps and slipped out of his chute.*

# Epilogue

The 302nd Transport Wing lives on as the 302nd Airlift Wing (Air Force Reserve Command) flying C-130Hs out of Peterson AFB, Colorado. (As of 1997)

The 27th ATG was inactivated 15 October, 1945, and disbanded on 8 October, 1948.

The 86th TS (Cargo and Mail) was disbanded on 15 November 1945. Reconstituted, and redesignated 86th TS (Medium) on 20 June 1952. Activated on 20 July, 1952. Inactivated on 1 July, 1955. Activated 21 December 1962. Organized on 8 January 1963. Redesignated 86th Military Airlift Squadron on 8 January 1966.

The 87th TS was disbanded at Marfa AAF, Texas, on 15 November 1945.

The 320th TS was disbanded on 8 October 1948. Reconstituted and consolidated with the 320th Air Refueling Squadron on 19 September 1985, but remains inactive.

The 321st TS was disbanded on 15 November 1945. Reconstituted and consolidated with the 321st Air Refueling Squadron 15 September 1985, but remains inactive.

The 310th FS was disbanded on 8 October 1945.

The 311th FS was redesignated as the 321st Troop Carrier Squadron, European Air Transport Service (EATS). Inactivated at Bolling Field, Washington, D.C., 27 May, 1946. Redesignated 321st TCS (Medium) 24 May, 1955. Activated at Stewart AFB, Smyrna, Tennessee, 8 June, 1955. Inactivated 6 August, 1957.

The 312th FS became the 323rd Troop Carrier Squadron and was inactivated on 27 June 1949.

The 325th FS became the 324th Troop Carrier Squadron and was inactivated on 27 June 1949.

# Photo Gallery

*While collecting material for this project, I copied every photograph I could get my hands on relating to the 27th ATG. Many have appeared throughout the text, where they relate to given stories and anecdotes, but many more, which are still important parts of the history of the group, did not fit into the specific text of this work. That is where this section comes in. You will find here miscellaneous photographs from the albums of men of the 27th ATG. I have grouped them, to some extent, by subject and by the albums they came from. In many cases, there is little or no information available. In those cases, the picture must be "worth a thousand words."*

*Left: Lt. Sico at Nice in front of a C-47 "STELLA" (on the tail of the bird of the squadron insignia). Code letters were "PW" in yellow, with black shadowing. This was aircraft number 348474. The cowlings were yellow and black, and the 27th ATG circle was on the nose and tail. See also color profile illustration. Center: Lt. Marvin Bugg of the 310th Squadron in front of an A-20, in England. Right: 310th Pilot, Lt. Byron Carrell.*

*Above: C-47 "Arctic Queen." This is one of the C-47s from the 321st Squadron on the mission in Sweden.*

*Right: An original example of a 310th Ferrying Squadron patch.*

*Left: 310th pilot, Lt. Herman Estrada. Right: 2nd Lts. Larry Sims (P-38 pilot) and Richard Seebers, pilot in the 311th FS and the 321st TS.*

*A view of new B-17s at Burtonwood waiting to be delivered to frontline bomber units. These airplanes were delivered by ferrying squadrons. (U.S. Army via Lawrence.)*

*UC-64 Norseman aircraft of the 320th TS being loaded with blood for transportation to frontline hospitals. (Ethell)*

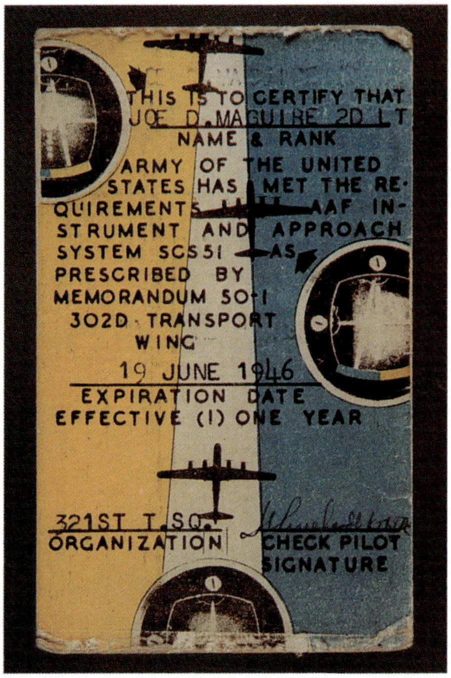


*Above left and center: Heavily painted A-2 jacket worn by 310th radio operator Larry "Mickey" McGuire. Right: This was the "Rainbow Card" referred to by Joe Maguire in Chapter 2. Many pilots of the 27th ATG and 302nd Wing held this card. The SCS-51 was an early ILS system used late in the war in the ETO.*

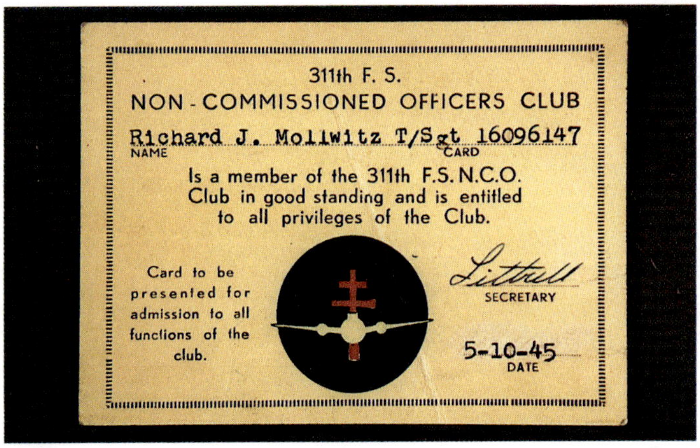


*Above: 311th FS NCO Club Card. Below and right: A Christmas card from the 27th ATG.*

*Left: General George J. "Jim" Eade pinning the Air Medal on Richard Seebers at the medal ceremony which was held at the reunion in Cocoa Beach, Florida, in 1995. Right: Some of the men who were presented with the Air Medal at Cocoa Beach. First row: Fay Brandis, Richard Seebers, Dean Sheets, Art Kane, Joe Maguire, Joe Stevens. Second row: Don Kogge, Ingwer Ketelsen, General Eade, Richard Cook, Ted Lucas, John Schneider. Eade, Maguire, and Stevens, also received the Distinguished Flying Cross. Other members awarded Air Medals at the ceremony were: Bert Astrove, James Beaird, Jacques Gordon, Elliote Holland, Dillard Hyden, Larry McGuire, Donald Kendrick, Robert Millar, Michael Palermo, and Christ Zivalich. A complete list of members who received decorations can be found in Appendix II.*

*Above left: The Memorial Plaque which was dedicated to the 27th ATG at the United States Air Force Academy Cemetery Memorial Wall, in 1994.*

*Above right: Marvin Diehl and Dick Seebers with the 302nd Wing, reunion flag, which is a reproduction of the War time flag.*

*Right: The 27th ATG Reunion Flag.*

***Some of what they wore.***

*Left: Uniform of Robert P. Walker which was tailor made in London at Hawkes & Co. Ltd. Walker had this uniform made when he transferred from the RCAF, 1 June 1943. His RCAF wings are on the right breast. "Paddy" Walker served as a ferry pilot in the early days of the 27th ATG out of Warton. He transferred to the 25th Bomb Group at Watton where he flew a number of OSS missions. Some of his recollections are in Chapter 3. Center: Uniform of 321st TS pilot Joe D. Maguire. Maguire's stories appear in Chapters 2, 5, and 8. Right: Summer Tan uniform of 321st TS pilot Joe D. Maguire with bullion insignia.*

*Left: French tailor made battle jacket worn by 311th FS and 321st TS pilot Richard H. Seebers. The buttons are marked "PARIS" on the reverse. The 9th AF patch is English made. Seebers wrote in his diary about having this jacket made (see Chapter 4). More of Dick's memories are recorded in Chapter 8. Center: Uniform coat of Richard H. Seebers. Dick wore the 9th AF patch on the right shoulder and the AAF patch on the left. Right: English tailor made battle jacket worn by 310th FS pilot Bert Astrove. Bert had the jacket made at Hawkes & Co., Ltd., in June of 1944. The insignia is also English made. Bert has several contributions found in Chapter 3.*

*Left: Uniform of 321st TS pilot Joseph W. Stevens. Joe continued to wear this coat after the war, when he served with the 116th Fighter Squadron, Washington ANG, flying P-51s. The distinctive insignia on the epaulets are for the 116th FS. Joe contributed stories located in Chapters 2, 5, and 8. Center: Officer's short overcoat, worn by 321st TS pilot Joe Stevens. Right: The A-2 jacket is one of the most recognized and beloved, pieces of American flying gear. It was a prized possession of USAAF flyers. This well worn example made many missions with Lt.Col. Robert P. Walker, USAF (Ret.), who served with the 27th ATG at Warton, in late 1943. Walker transferred from the RCAF as Flight Officer, in June of 1943.*

*Above left: English made EM "crusher" cap worn by crew chief Harold Susen.*

*Above right: "Summer Tan" officer's "crusher" cap worn by 321st Pilot Joseph W. Stevens.*

*Right: English made officer's cap by Thomas & Stone, London for Robert P. Walker.*

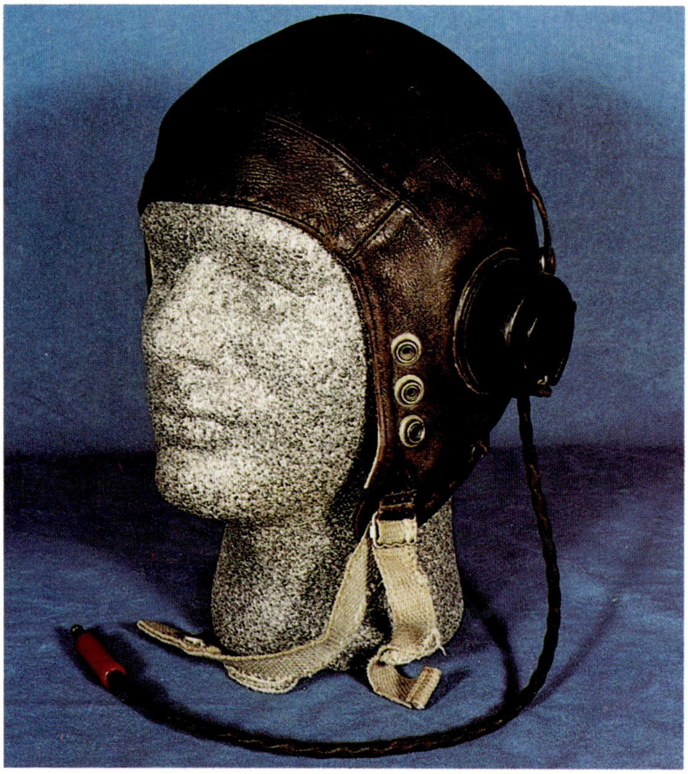

*Above: RAF late C-Type flight helmet with American receivers worn by Bert Astrove. Bert picked up this helmet on one of his stops at an RAF airfield.*

*Right: Uniform worn by Crew Chief Harold Susen. Harold was the crew chief on General Carl Spaatz's personal C-45, with Joe Clemow as pilot. Susen is mentioned in Chapter 3 in Joe Clemow's writings.*

***Other memorabilia***

*Aircraft identification flag of Lt. General Carl Spaatz. This flag was made in the parachute shop at USSTAF HQ and used on his C-45 "Expediter" flown by pilot Joe Clemow and crew chief Harold Susen. When the aircraft was on the ground Susen would raise this flag on a staff mounted in the flare port of the C-45. As Harold put it, "When we raised that flag, things would start to happen!"*

*Aircraft identification flag of Brigadier General E.P. Curtis, Spaatz's Chief of Staff. This flag was also made at the USSTAF HQ parachute shop and used on board the C-45 flown by Clemow and Susen.*

*Above: A grouping of material from 321st pilot Joe D. Maguire. The St. Christopher's medal was placed around his neck by an elderly French woman on the streets of Paris.*

*Right: Wings and photographs of 310th FS pilot G. Ralph Jenks. Ralph contributed a story in Chapter 8.*

*Two below: Groupings of memorabilia from pilot Robert P. "Paddy" Walker.*

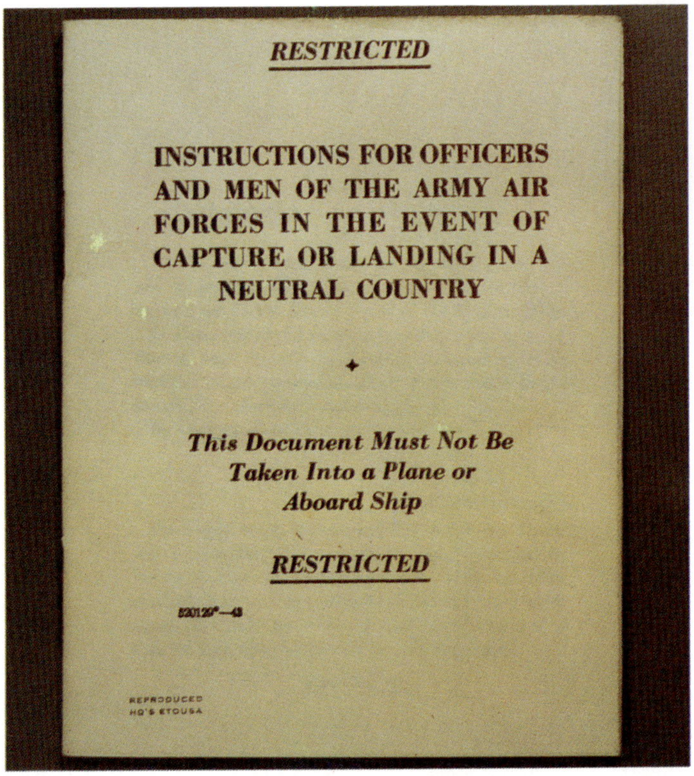


*Left: A group of items spanning a long flying career from pilot Richard H. Seebers. Seebers flew "Gooney Birds" in the 311th FS and the 321st TS. Right: An instruction booklet on conduct in the event of capture, or landing in a neutral country.*

*Above: Souvenirs of London. Right: A pamphlet to help soldiers familiarize themselves with operations and conduct on a troopship.*

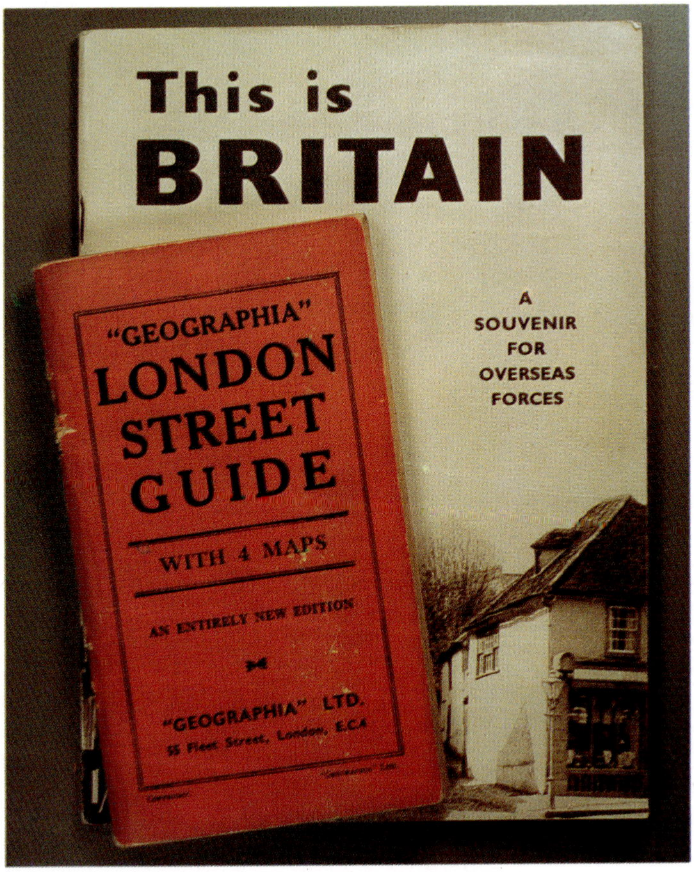

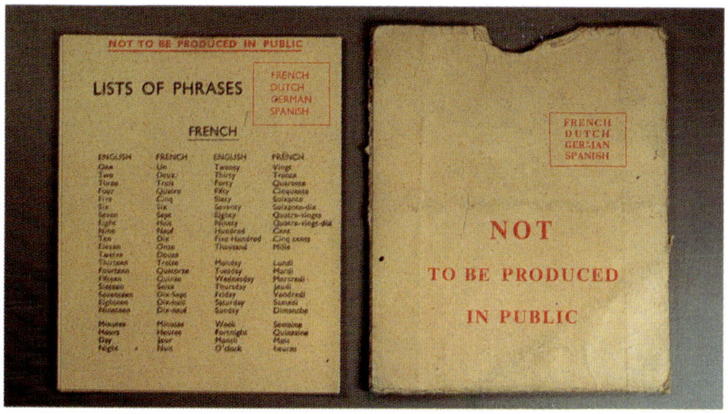


*A list of phrases to be used by downed American flyers.*

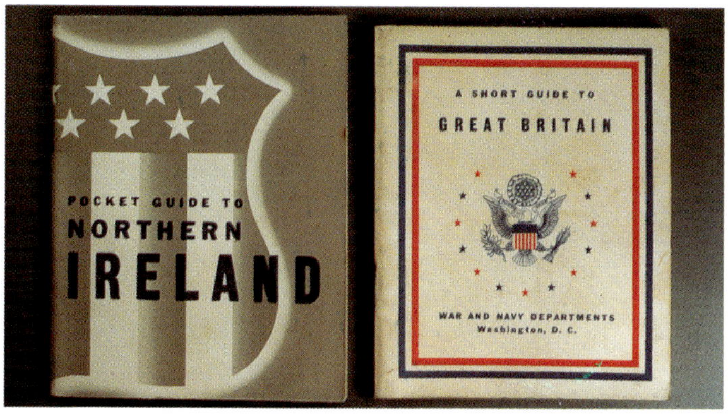


*These type booklets were produced in all theaters to help American soldiers get acquainted with their new surroundings.*

*The original diaries of Richard Mollwitz. Large portions of these are printed in Chapter 4.*

## *Aircraft profile descriptions*

*Page 284 top to bottom:*

**Douglas C-47-A-30-DK Skytrain**, s.n. 348247, "Vandra Min Vag" of the 86th TS, Lulea, Sweden, early 1945. "Vandra Min Vag" translates to "Going My Way."

**Douglas C-47-A-5-DL Skytrain**, s.n. 223637, of the 87th TS, Grove, England, 1945. This aircraft is depicted after the 87th was reassigned to the 31st ATG with the white triangle of that unit over the serial number. The triangles varied from one aircraft to another with some being equilateral and some isosceles. Note that there is evidence of Troop Carrier Command letter codes having been painted over behind the cockpit indicating previous service. This is apparent in several photographs of aircraft from the 87th TS.

**Curtiss C-46-D-10-CU Commando**, s.n. 477607, of the 87th TS, Grove, England.

**Martin B-26-B-20-MA Marauder**, s.n. 131742, "Demon Deacon" of the 310th Ferrying Squadron, Warton, 1944. This aircraft was used to check out new pilots on the B-26 and served as a squadron taxi ship. It was most frequently flown by pilot Capt. Fay Brandis and crew chief S/Sgt Ray Dlouhy.

*Page 285 top to bottom:*

**Boeing B-17-G-40 Flying Fortress**, s.n. 297103. This is one of several B-17s assigned to the 27th ATG. B-17s are known to have been operated by the 310th FS, the 87th TS, and possibly by other squadrons as well. Many of the B-17s assigned to the group were stripped of armament and refitted as gas haulers and taxi ships, as was the case with the aircraft depicted here.

**Douglas C-47-B-1-DK Skytrain**, s.n. 348487, of the 311th FS, Istres, France, late 1944.

**Douglas C-47-B-1-DK Skytrain**, s.n. 348474, "Stella" of the 312th FS, Villacoublay, France, 1945. The name "Stella" appears in a rectangle on the rear end of the "Gooney Bird" depicted in the 312th Squadron insignia on the nose of the aircraft.

**Douglas C-47-A-40-DL Skytrain**, s.n. 224046, of the 320th TS, Villacoublay, 1945. This illustration depicts an aircraft which served in North Africa prior to being transferred to the 27th ATG. It was extremely weather worn.

*Page 286 top to bottom:*

**Noorduyn C-64 Norseman**, s.n. 43-5392, of the 320th TS. Pilot Howard Gilberg made a successful forced landing in this aircraft on D-Day, 6 June 1944. (See Chapter 2 for full story)

**Noorduyn C-64 Norseman**, s.n. 335372, "Geraldine" of the 320th TS, Le Bourget, France, late 1944.

**Douglas C-47-B-5-DK Skytrain**, s.n. 348796, of the 321st TS, Villacoublay, 1945.

**Douglas C-47-B-10-DK Skytrain**, s.n. 349038, "Püppeschon" ("Beautiful Doll") of HQ Squadron 27th ATG.

348247

223637

477607
07

131742

297103

348487

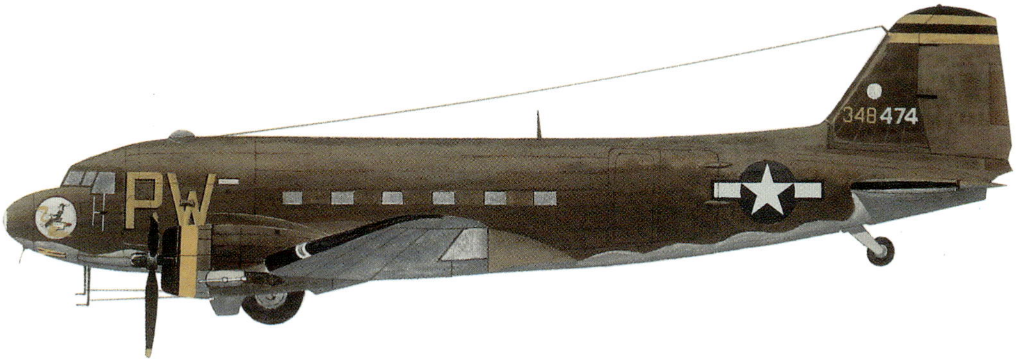
PW
348474

224046

35392

335372
Geraldine

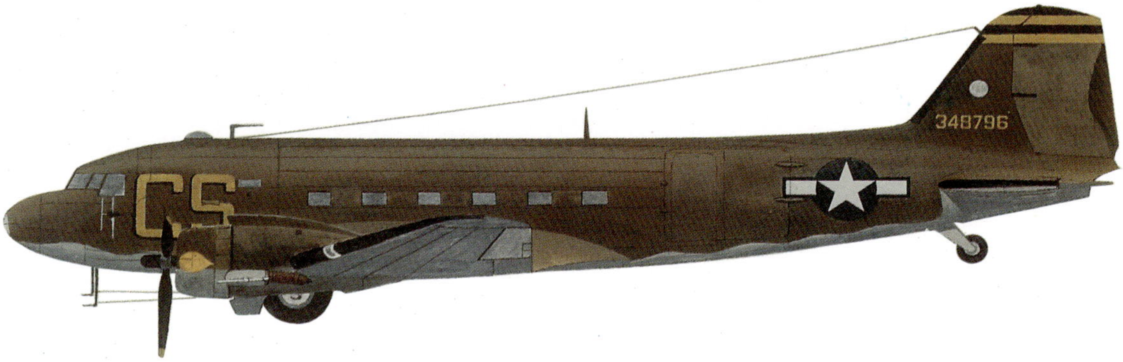
348796
CS

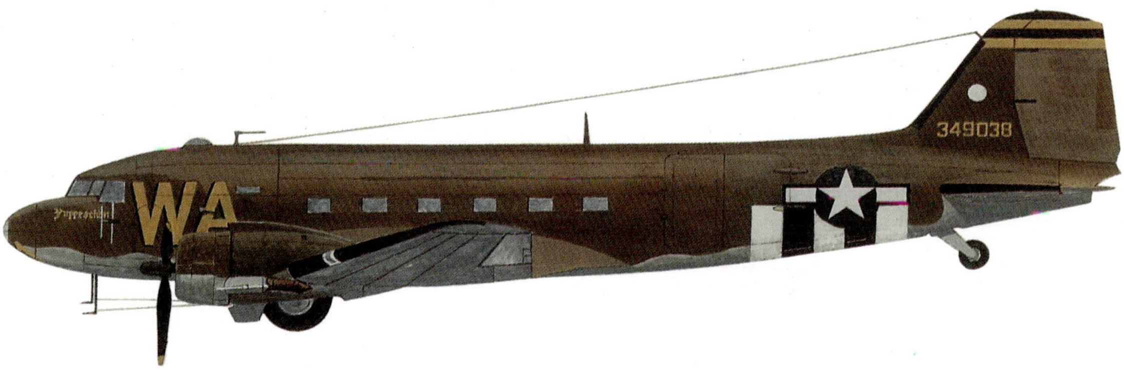
349038
WA

*A new B-24 after a taxiing mishap.*

*B-24 with collapsed nose gear.*

*P-38 on its nose.*

*P-47 Thunderbolt after a hard landing.*

*Early B-24D "Hoopoe" on its belly.*

*P-47 "Razorback" of the 368th FS, 359th FG.*

*This RAF "Dakota" nosed over in the mud under high power at Le Bourget.*

*P-38 crack up at Le Bourget.*

*P-51D on a ferrying trip.*

*Ralph Jenks at speed in a P-47D.*

*Ralph Jenks of the 310th by a P-51D "Little Chick" flown by a 78th FG "Ace."*

*Ralph "Jake the Snake" Jacobs by a new P-47D.*

*R/O Bill White in front of a P-38 "Little Buckaroo" flown by 367th FG "Ace" Major R.C. "Buck" Rogers.*

*310th pilot Vincent Alexander with a P-51D.*

R/O Bill White by B-24, S/N 42-52744, "Capricorn," of the 834th BS, 486th BG with art work by Phil Brinkman.

Vincent Alexander of the 310th with an F-5 (photo recon P-38).

Vincent Alexander with a P-61 "Black Widow" night fighter.

A 27th ATG E/M sitting on the wing of P-51 "Spare Parts."

P-38 on its nose of the 77th FS, 20th FG.

P-47 on its belly.

*Interesting modification to a B-17. In Howard Gilberg's album it was titled, "The Abortion." It appears to be an experimental attempt to fit a B-24 turret onto a B-17.*

*P-61 in flight.*

*A glass nosed P-38 "pathfinder" aircraft can be seen on the left, and to the right is a Douglas A-20 of the 410th BG, with collapsed nose gear.*

*B-26 Marauder.*

*An RAF Gloster Meteor on the field with an AT-6 "Texan."*

*"Ket" Ketelsen by B-24 "Black Widow"*

*P-51D.*

Billy L. Hyden (brother of 311th flight engineer, "Red" Hyden) in front of a Beech C-45. Bill was being processed to come home at Camp Twenty Grand about 90 miles from Paris, after having served with the 49th Armored Division under Patton. He got a pass and came to visit Red for a week. When it was time to go back, Red called operations to see if Bill could be flown back to his unit. Operations sent a pilot and co-pilot, and they took off. There was quite a line of ground forces along the line of the fence by the cow pasture where they landed to watch the event. Red was able to spend a week with his brother before he had to return.

A somewhat unusual, all natural metal, C-47.

***Luftwaffe Aircraft Encountered***

German "Mistel" guided bomb, made from an Fw 190, mounted on a "war weary" Ju 88. The pilot of the 190 would fly the aircraft to the target, then release the Ju 88, which was mounted with a hollow-charge warhead.

Other examples of Mistels in Germany, 18 May 1945.

*Radio operator Bill White with a late model Fw 190.*

*Scrapped Ju 88s. Note the light colored aircraft in the background is a night fighter version.*

*Italian Re 2002 fighter, in German markings.*

*Ju 88 in France.*

*Ju 88*

*John McDowell, with an He 111H at the airfield at Metz. This was on a trip delivering blood to Patton's bogged down army.*

*Left: Flight engineer Marvin Diehl by the fuselage cross of an He 111.*

*321st pilot Joe Maguire on the tail of an He 111.*

*A captured Bf 109G-6 in British markings.*

*McCarthy and Bonser, Le Bourget, October, 1944.*

*Chelchowsky, October, 1944.*

*Marvin Diehl in the cockpit of a Bf 109.*

*Bf 109 October, 1944.*

*Captured B-24 in German markings. Salzburg R-80.*

*Captured Fw 190F-8 in American markings.*

*Bf 109K.*

*Ju 88 in France.*

*Sgt. Frank Wardlaw and Sgt. John Dargin, in front of a Ju 88.*

*Bf 110G-2 nightfighter.*

***The following photographs, in the Luftwaffe section, were all acquired by Bob Lawrence, of the 310th FS. They were found in a billet, which had been recently vacated by the Luftwaffe.***

*A recent German grave.*

*A group of Luftwaffe officers many of whom are flyers. Probably a squadron photo.*

*An early Bf 109.*

*Above and below: An early version of the Bf 109 on its belly.*

*Landing gear was always a problem with the 109. Here is an early 109 with one wheel collapsed.*

*Germany's equivalent to the "Gooney Bird," the Ju 52, in flight.*

*Crewmen working on the gun position of a Ju 52.*

*Ju 52 in flight.*

*Ground crew servicing a Bf 109E.*

*Ju 87B "Stuka."*

*Bf 109E-4 of Stab/JG 1.*

*Arado Ar 68E the last biplane fighter of the Luftwaffe.*

*Czech Avia B-534 in German markings.*

***The next section of the photo gallery is made up of miscellaneous shots from the photo albums of individuals in the 27th ATG.***

*Navigating through the mud at Warton.*

*F/O Robert P. "Pat" Walker.*

*F/O John "Pee Wee" Morgan. Morgan was the pilot lost with Glenn Miller.*

*Johnny Davey, 1943. Davey served with the RAF prior to transferring to the 27th ATG.*

*Johnny Davey and John Morgan.*

*Pete Dustman.*

*Pete Dustman.*

*Ken "KA" Johnson.*

*Ken "KA" Johnson.*

*Captain Daniels.*

*Unknown, said to be an Eagle Squadron veteran.*

*Unknown.*

Unknown.

Johnson, Dustman and Harper.

Lts. Markle and Estrada, Dijon, France.

Lt. Stuart.

A group of 310th pilots – Standing: Alexander, Peres, Wade, Service, Estrada, Curtis. Front row: McConnell, Purdue, Canning.

*310th Pilots at Warton – Krutzsch, Manning, unknown, Jacobs, Jenks.*

*Lt. Langhorn Gee, in an A-26, at Warton.*

*Above: 310th Pilots, Markel, Trees, Burdick, Hoehne, and Blake, Italy, January, 1945.*

*Right: J.J. Canning enjoying the day.*

Estrada and Biales.

Jimmie Andrews.

John McDowell on control tower duty at Burtonwood, 1943.

Curtis, Gaw, Oswalt, Krutzsch, Estrada, and Jenks, at Manneken-Pis, September 1945.

McDowell and Bush.

*Left: McAlister at Burtonwood. Right: Kelly R. "Moose" Moutray and John McDowell. Moutray went MIA on January 8, 1945. He was shot down over one of the islands in the Channel and turned up a POW.*

*Left: Greenham Commons, before Arnhem. Right: From the cockpit of the old C-87 taxi ship waiting to pick up pilots delivering P-47s, in France.*

*Left: Crawford, in an A-20 over Beachy Head, England on the way to France. Right: John McDowell, on the side of a burned out German Panther tank, Place de Concord, Paris, 8 September, 1944. The tank was still warm!*

Flight engineer Johnson and a friend Tuileries Gate, Place de Concord, Paris.

*Villacoublay. "We had this car on detached service at Paris. It was a 1939 Ford previously owned by the Germans and had a wood burner on the back." – Lawrence*

*Strubar, Lawrence, and Lamb getting on the bus to return to the field after a night in Paris.*

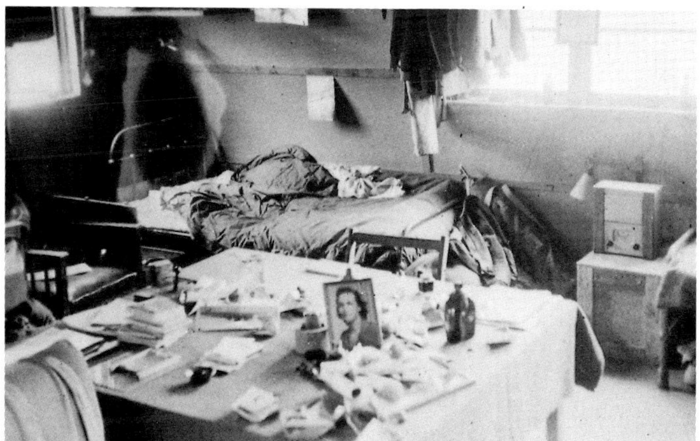

*Lawrence's bunk at Grove, 1945.*

*Left: Dick Washburn, 326th Sqdn.*

*Left: 310th Pilots waiting for the taxi somewhere in the ETO. Right: Ket Ketelsen by a new B-26.*

*Left: Ketelsen in the cockpit of a British Westland Lysander. Center: Lt. Earnest G. Garritt and Ket Ketelsen. Right: Ketelsen by the Eiffel Tower.*

*Left: Left to right – Lt. Marcus Barrett, Lt. George Logan, Lt. Ketelsen, unknown, Bert Astrove. The center of attention is a "whirligig" toy sent from the States by Ket's wife. There is plenty of expert advice available on how to fly it! Right: Ket with a friend in southern Germany, west of Munich.*

*Left: Lt. "Slim" Collins and Ket Ketelsen in front of some B-24 nose art. Center: Slim Collins and Ket Ketelsen in front of an RAF "Walrus" rescue aircraft. Right: Lt. I.W. Abernathy at Warton.*

*Lt. Martin Chaves on the wing of a P-51B.*

*Major Stenglein, Lt. Fisher, Lt. Creech.*

*Captains Brandis and Rawls, Warton, 1944.*

*Bob Taylor and Joe Clemow, facing camera, playing cards.*

*Left: Captain George Eade. Center: McDevitt, Clemow, and Rulow at Pompei. Right: Capt. Clemow and Sgt. Susen by General Spaatz's C-45.*

*Left: An E/M in front of a C-45. Right: Three E/Ms by the tail of a C-45. The third man is Sgt. Harold Susen, flight engineer/crew chief.*

*Left: This photo is simply titled, "Hot Rocks, 310th FS" from Larry "Micky" McGuire. Right: From Marvin Diehl – Front Row: Capt. Chandler, F/O Couch, 2nd Lt. Reed, F/O Morgan, 1st Lt. Malone, unknown. Second row: unknown, unknown, Lt. Rogge, W/O Wheat, Lt. Scheich, 1st Lt. Harper. Third row: unknown, 1st Lt. Hille, 1st Lt. Vague, Lt. Shuely, 2nd Lt. Stenerson, Lt. Batdorf, Lt. Ramer, unknown.*

*Art Kane wearing his A-2 jacket. Notice the 86th TS patch on his jacket.*

*Above and below: War correspondents flown by the 86th.*

*Left: "Andy and friend." Center: Dry. Right: Babcock.*

*A shower constructed from drop tanks.*

*86th Operations, Villacoublay.*

*Right: December 1944 trip to Marseilles – first American beer, in a long time.*

*Left: Sgt. Joe Louis, the "Brown Bomber," at Heston, 1944. Center: "Sarki" Sarkis Samarian. Right: "Flashlight" Clapper.*

*General Arnold at an Air Medal ceremony, at Villacoublay.*

*Fris and Clarey.*

*Louis Ruffio.*

*Jerry Denman.*

*Left: Doughty. Center: "Doc" Doherty. Right: Joan Turner, ARC.*

*Bill White with the 27th ATG HQ sign.*

*Left: R/O Bill White, in flight clothing, at Le Bourget. Right: White at his B-17 post.*

*Enlisted quarters, at Villacoublay.*

*White by an ARC AERO CLUB sign.*

A load of troops.

Left: A radio operator at Warton. Right: Bill White preparing to mount up.

Oops! A new B-17 meets a Bristol Beaufighter.

Prewar Le Bourget.

Left: Lts. Lee Powers and Joe Maguire at Grove. Center: F/O Robert Bailey and Lt. Lee Powers at Grove. Right: Lt. Maguire at Grove.

*Joe Maguire and Lt. Roy J. "Porky" Shilling on a cold morning at Le Bourget. Shilling was killed in a C-47 crash on January 18, 1945.*

*321st pilots, Joe Maguire, Dick Taylor, and Bob Bailey, at Le Bourget.*

*321st Pilots, Taylor, Maguire, Stevens, Messelt, and Mayer, late November, 1944, Le Bourget.*

*Cutting wood in the courtyard of the 321st billet at Le Bourget, 1945. Maguire, Bob Mayer, Roy Shilling, Ray Zych.*

*Right: Joe Maguire in flight helmet, $O_2$ mask and B-8 goggles – a rig seldom worn by Gooney Bird drivers. Joe jokingly referred to it as his "fighter pilot" helmet*

*Left: 321st pilot Lt. Charles Longshore, at Le Bourget. Center: F/O Robert Bailey at Le Bourget. Right: Maguire, Taylor, and Powers.*

*Left: Maguire, Bailey, and Powers. Right: A group of 321st pilots in front of 321st Operations, at Le Bourget, Winter, 1944.*

*Lt. Roy Shilling at Le Bourget a short time before his death in a C-47 crash.*

*The 321st officer's billet at Villacoublay.*

*Maguire in front of a B-26 at Le Bourget. A 27th ATG C-47 can be seen in the background.*

*Pilots relaxing on the balcony of the billet at Villacoublay. Seated far left, is Joe Stevens, while standing is Joe Maguire.*

*321st pilots, left to right: Rinehardt, Zych, Ambrose, and Simpson.*

*321st pilots at Villacoublay: Lee Powers, Art Meeks, Joe Maguire, and Carl Moxan.*

*Ray Zych, Dick Ambrose, Charles Longshore, and Joe Maguire, 321st pilots, at Villacoublay.*

*Lt. Harry Protzeller and Lt. Hayes enjoy lunch in the sun at Villacoublay.*

*321st pilots in the 321st jeep. Driving, is Jim Rinehardt. Kuntz is in the front seat. Legard and Meeks are in the back.*

*321st pilots. Protzeller is on the left.*

*A group of 321st pilots – left to right: Art Meeks, Harry Protzeller, Ray Zych (on bike), Charles Longshore, Dick Ambrose and the man kneeling, is unknown.*

*A group of pilots of the 321st ATS.*

*Above and below: 321st pilot Carl Moxan at Le Bourget.*

*Left: Dick Seebers sent this photo of Jim Rinehardt, when he made Captain. Rinehardt was well liked and respected, and was the operations officer of the 321st TS, at the end of the war. Center: Lt. Wendell L. "Tony" Hoppers. Tony did a tour in B-26s before joining the 321st. Right: Howard Gilberg at LLAD, March 1944.*

*Left: Gilberg and Psalidas. Center: Former RAF Pilot Capt. Nading at Maghaberry, April, 1944. Right: Lt. Smith, Maghaberry.*

LLAD, 4/44. Pointer, unknown, unknown, Hill (Killed in a P-38 7/44), Hall, unknown.

320th officers, Malone (KIA, 7/44 in a C-64), Hille, Batdorf, Vague, and Couch, Honington, 7/44.

Left: Lt. Patterson, Belfast, May, 1944. Center: F/O McCarthy. Right: Lt. Couch.

*Left: F/O Bonser. Center: Lt. Thaddeus Chelchowski. Right: Dr. W.P. Bradley.*

*Left: Lt. Roy T Marshall. Center: Capt. John Humke. Right: Lt. Reid.*

*Lts. Jim Rinehardt and John Schneider.*

*320th pilot Howard Gilberg piloting a motorcycle.*

*Left: Lt. Marshall. Center: Major Rosenblatt. Right: Baby, Rusty, and Batdorf, at Eccles, 9/44.*

*Evans and Ramer.*

*Hille, unknown, Stenerson, Vague, at Honington 6/44.*

*Left: H.T. Bonser, Wattisham, 8/44. Center: Howard Gilberg on the wing of a P-38. Right: Walt Lenox, KIA, in a B-24 on the Isle of Man, 7/44.*

*Ramer, Gilberg, Batdorf, at Eccles, 10/44.*

*Hunt, Harris, and Nulle, Wattisham, July 1944.*

*Left: Howard Gilberg in the cockpit of a P-47 "T" Bolt. Center: Sgt. Dawson, surgical tech., October, 1944. Right: "Doc" Bradley, Paris, 3/45.*

*Left: Captain Jarvis. Right: Marvin Diehl and Armond Palestini, in Paris.*

*320th Squadron navigator Tom Lynch sent this photo of a group of enlisted men outside of a 320th building at Le Bourget. The man in the center is "Moose" Hasselman, a very big guy, for that time period and he pumped iron wherever he was. He told Lynch that he played football for Columbia University and that he would return after the war. Lynch was not sure he believed him, at the time. In 1946, Lynch was reading the "New York Times," and found his name. He was playing tackle for the team. Tom Lynch went to see him play against Dartmouth and they had a small reunion at the game. That was the last time they saw each other.*

*Parris and Boyd.*

*LLAD*

*This picture comes from Gordon Fisher. "Gordy" served as a pilot, in the 310th, 312th, and at the end of the war was CO of the 321st. "I took this picture in early 1943, of a fighter flight on the wing of a P-47. I was flying with these guys out of Warton, England." Left to right : Hollingsworth (KIA), Gildersleeve, Glover, Rybaczek (KIA), Cameron, Daniels (KIA), Bruner, Smith (KIA), Jones (KIA). Daniels and Hollingsworth had left the 310th, and were killed in combat.*

*Kendricks, Hebb, Bradley and Walker.*

*Left: Harry Delick. Center: Bud Swank. Right: "Those GI helmets were handy. We even bathed in them."*

*Rinehardt and Oien.*

*Chow line – Le Bourget.*

*Wash-Rinse-Wash-Rinse.*

*A game of horseshoes at the 321st staging area, near Reims. "We were packing for the Orient."*

*"After a day off in Paris, we were waiting for transportation back to A-42."*

*Left: "This news rerouted us from heading for the Orient to heading for home – a welcomed surprise. We were on board the "General Morton" at the time." Right: George Eade in the doorway of our Nissen hut in northern Ireland.*

*George Eade standing on the wing of a P-51D.*

*Berry and crew Le Bourget.*

*Williams, Graham, Nickie, Artie Howard, Frank Terry.*

*Front row: Berry, Terry, Metz, Howard, Iacono, Graham. Second row: Diehm, Stitt, Stokes, Muller, Stanley.*

Iacono and Diehm.

Enlisted men of the 312th.

312th communications personnel.

312th EMs. Front row: Stokes, Diehm, Terry. Back row: unknown, Nash, Jessup, unknown, unknown, unknown.

Left: Diehm and Manty, front row. Note the 312th Squadron patch on Don Diehm's jacket. Right: Diehm with a Russian officer at Budapest.

Donald Diehm at Budapest.

*Left: Diehm and Manty with a Russian soldier at Budapest. Center: Don Diehm climbing into a staff car at Budapest. Right: 312th R/O Donald Diehm before he added the squadron patch to his A-2.*

*Jessup, Gordy, Hicks.*

*Unknown, Jessup, Howard, Hicks.*

*Right: Sgt. Larry Kelly.*

*Radio Shack.*

*Left: Manty stepping out of a C-53. Right: Mehalich.*

*Frenchy and Diehm at the tail of a C-47.*

*Gooney Birds in action.*

*Composite photo of the 312th area at Villacoublay.*

*Left: Berry. Right: Diehm and Knoblock both with 312th Squadron patches on their A-2s.*

*Front of 312th FS HQ.*

*Right and below: The 312th going home.*

*Donald Diehm on board ship going home.*

*Diehm's family had this sign waiting for him, when he got home.*

*311th pilot Lt. Eggers.*

*Public toilet facilities at Istres, France.*

*Elliott Holland in the 311th enlisted men's quarters at Versailles, France.*

*Left: Travis Taylor and Shorty Hartman. Right: August 2, 1944, Northern Ireland. Roger Knoblock and Howard Kopf.*

*Left: 312th R/O Manty, at Salzberg. Right: Trading on the "black market."*

*A C-53 of the 31st TG nosed over.*

An RAF Beech "staggerwing."

311th pilots Decker, Frazer, and Ryan.

Cpl. Taylor and F/O Leverick cooking at A-54, October 1944.

Decker and Thomas.

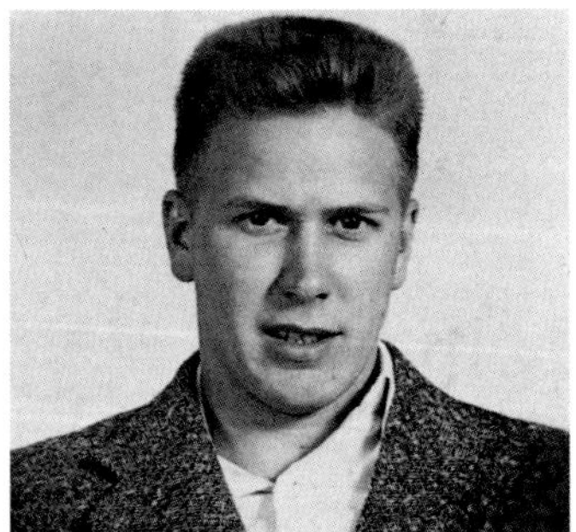

*Four photos above: Lt. Dick Seebers. Right: This type of photo, in civilian clothing, was taken of many flyers as part of the escape kit. They could be used to forge documents, etc. This photo is of Dick Seebers.*

*Bill Soloman, March 1945, the Martinez Hotel in Cannes.*

*Bill Soloman, Chuck Watley, and Dick Seebers, at the Martinez Hotel, Cannes, March, 1945.*

*Charles Watley, Cannes, March, 1945.*

*Bill Soloman, Cannes, March, 1945.*

*311th pilots, at Villacoublay.*

*Sgt. John Dargin with a P-38.*

*Sgt. John Dargin standing in the cockpit of a P-38.*

*Sgt. Dargin with his then new wife, Shirley Blackwood Dargin, on honeymoon on the island of Rothsay, off the western coast of Scotland.*

*Ed Madigan, Harry Amzen, a neighborhood French boy "adopted" by HQ Squadron, Red Manning and John Dargin.*

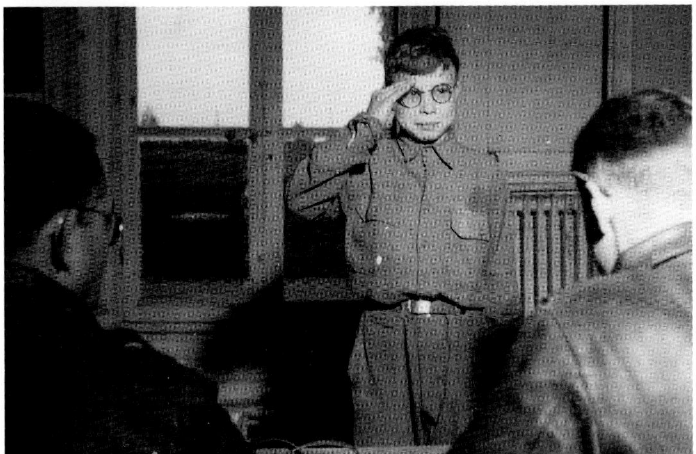

*A local orphaned French boy the men took under their wing.*

*Barracks life. Note the Merry Christmas sign.*

*A Headquarters Squadron party at Villacoublay to celebrate VE Day.*

*Sgt. Dargin and Sgt. Wardlaw examine a Ju 88 engine. Dargin was chief clerk, Group Materiel, and Wardlaw was chief clerk, Group Engineering.*

*Sgt. Dargin shaving in the field at Normandy.*

*Glenn Miller at Wattisham, July, 1944.*

*Above and right: The Glenn Miller Band at Warton.*

*Left: Grove looking straight out from the tower. In the foreground, is a late version of the Spitfire with Griffon engine and five bladed prop. This was the personal plane of an RAF Wing Commander who often visited the CO. He always put on a real show when he tookoff. He would retract the gear and lower the plane until the prop almost hit the ground. Near the end of the war he would fly in, in an early RAF jet. Right: A 31st TG C-47 on the hardstand at Grove.*

*Left: Fire truck and "meat wagon" looking to the left out of the tower across the field. In the distance, over the C-47 to the right of center, steam is visible from a train engine. This is about where Wantage Station would be. Right: Looking to the left out of the tower at Grove. This is the refueling area and one of the hangars. Behind it is a protected hardstand. We were never bombed here, but were strafed once.*

*Left: Looking toward the depot side of the field. A B-26 is parked on the unused runway. Right: The field at Grove, looking toward Wantage.*

*Looking to the right, out of the tower at Grove. Wantage would be just to the left, out of the picture. The large building is the freight terminal.*

*Group HQ building, Grove, as it appeared in 1958.*

*What was Site 13, at Grove Airfield, now a housing development (1958).*

*Hangar by the control tower, station side, Grove.*

*"The Shannon" – The little locomotive that used to pull the trains by our barracks to Wantage Road Station. The service was discontinued right after we left and the tracks were torn up about 1953. The engine (in 1958) was displayed at the Wantage Road Station.*

*Enlisted Mess on the depot side of the field viewed from the hospital, as it appeared in 1958.*

*Grove Officer's Club depot side of the field, 1958.*

*The town square of Wantage, 1958.*

*Statue of King Alfred at Wantage.*

*Another view of Wantage, England, familiar to those stationed at Grove.*

*Briefing photograph of the 321st TS. There is some discussion as to the location of this shot. Most feel it was at Grove, but one member remembers it to be at Marseilles.*

# *Appendix I*

# History of KIA and MIA Personnel of the 302nd Air Transport Wing

The information in this section is mainly due to the efforts of former group historian Marvin Diehl. Marvin compiled the information in a booklet he put together called "302 TRANSPORT WING, History of Killed and Missing Members, 43-44-45"

2nd Lt. Charles Agbashian, pilot, 310 FS
Killed on takeoff in a P-38 when he shut off the fuel switch instead of the booster pump.

Sgt. Mario J. Agnese, 39007788, 311 FS
Died at AAF-239, March 4, 1944, of multiple injuries.

2nd Lt. Vernon F. Albrecht, pilot, 314 TS
Albrecht was returning from a mercy mission in France in a C-47. As he buzzed the field, he didn't clear the trees at the end of the field and crashed. With him was R/O Cpl. Howard Hutchinson and flight engineer S/Sgt. Raywood Copell. Other crew unknown.

T/Sgt. Cecil A. Allen (No Information)

1st Lt. John M. Allen, pilot, 0-509015, 310 FS
Aircraft was lost in the Irish Sea on course between Warton and Langford Lodge. Lt. Pierce, piloting a C-47, witnessed the accident. He reported seeing the aircraft in trouble at about 1,800 feet. The plane hit the water, disintegrated, and sank rapidly, leaving small debris and one gas tank. A C-47 circled the area for about 90 minutes waiting for the arrival of air sea rescue. Nothing was seen to indicate survival of Lt. Allen. Died May 17, 1945.

Sgt. Anthony F. Bellini, flight engineer, 33368488, 312 FS
Killed in a B-24 due to bad weather, Isle of Man, June 8, 1944. With him was: Lt. Walter Lenox, pilot; 1st Lt. Sampson Sharff, co-pilot; and T/Sgt. Sam F. Joseph, R/O. Burial for all four took place June 14, 1944, at a Military Funeral in Belfast, Northern Ireland. Sgt. Joseph is buried on Sgt. Bellini's right at Lisnabreeny Cemetery, Belfast, Northern Ireland.

2nd Lt. John H. Boss, pilot, 311 FS or 310 FS
Flying a P-51 Boss did a slow roll over the field and went into the ground at Renfrew. Died 2/5/44.

Cpl. Chester D. Bright, R/O, 310 FS
Bright was a crew member on C-47 leaving Paris on a voluntary flight to pick up wounded close to the front. The C-47 was shot down by enemy ground fire. Crew members were as follows: 1st Lt. Ralph T. Parker, Sr., pilot; 2nd Lt. David L. Forbes, co-pilot; 2nd Lt. Reba Whittle, flight nurse T/3; Jonathan Hill, medic; and Cpl. Chester D. Bright, R/O. Full story under Sgt. Harold Bonser. Cpl. Bright was killed when the aircraft was forced down by enemy ground fire.

Pvt. Leslie A. Butler, 10th Airdrome Sqdn.
Killed by a "Buzz Bomb" at Heston Airfield on June 28, 1944. There were 6 other casualties (wounded). Sgt. Joseph Walsh, Pvt. Gibbs, and M/Sgt. Albert B. English, only once mentioned as wounded. Headquarters and Dispensary were completely destroyed. Damage to one C-47, hangars, 2 ambulances, passenger terminal, plus many buildings had glass blown out. Buzz Bomb landed at 2230 hours.

1st Lt. Donald K. Cameron, pilot, 310 FS
Last flight recorded was in a P-51A, Oct. 8, 1943. Killed in P-51 accident near Liverpool, England. Died October 9, 1943

2nd Lt. Herman G. Carey, pilot, 310 FS
Killed while flying a P-47 out of Renfrew, Scotland. Carey was flying on the deck when he took the wrong valley out of Renfrew. (There were three.) Weather was a factor that caused him to fly into a mountain. Died on December 28, 1943 according to archival records.

2nd Lt. Warren M. Chapman, 0-792803, 311th FS
Killed when his P-38 crashed on February 12, 1944.

M/Sgt. Loyd F. Cheek, flight engineer, 320 TS
Killed in a UC-64 on a flight to deliver tire and wheel for their Lockheed Hudson, which was damaged earlier at Preston, Scotland. On the flight their Norseman crashed into King Alfred's Tower near Zeal, Wiltshire, Yeovil, England. Cpl. Henry Mazzie is buried on his right, and on his left is Lt. Winfield Malone. All three died July 10, 1944 and were buried at Brookwood Cemetery near Cambridge, England. Lt. Jack H. Couch made identification and was an escort at funeral, July 18, 1944.

1st Lt. James P. Christy, pilot, 0-918971, 311 FS
Killed attempting to land his P-38 February 12, 1944. Bob Sweitzer reported that Christy was trying to land at Howarden as he had a date with a W.A.A.F. Fog was heavy, and he was making a tight circling approach. He lost his bottom engine in a tight turn at 100 ft. and crashed into two RAF Wellingtons.

Alphonse V. Cogozza, R/O, 310 FS, 321 TS
Cogozza was the Radio Operator on a C-47 with pilot, 2nd Lt. Roy Shilling, co-pilot, 2nd Lt. George Wood, and flight engineer, Cpl. Harold Grubb. They took off from A-54 (Le Bourget) to arrive at AAF-343 (Biggin Hill). Pilot of C-47 took off with 11 passengers at 9:23 AM. Eight minutes later at 9:30 AM., crashed at Plessis-Gossot, France. Reason for crash unknown. Only four passengers survived. January 18, 1945.

1st Lt. Charles P. Congden, pilot, 0-794470, 310th and 311th FS
An A-20 was converted to a weather plane so the 310 FS could get their own weather reports. Everyone wanted to fly the A-20 as it was light and fast. Wilton Hodges reports it was his turn to fly the airplane. Hodges sent his crew chief Joe Nagy and R/O Julius Sopo to preflight the A-20, as Hodges was busy in operations picking crews for the day's deliveries. He then took the jeep to the flight line and found the A-20 gone. He learned the A-20 had just departed with Chuck Congden and R/O Sopo on the weather flight. Hodges returned to operations and learned of the bad news that the aircraft had gone down four miles north of Chester, England. 310th pilot John McDowell gave the most plausible reason. The A-20 was seriously out of balance. The center of gravity was changed through modification, which could make it uncontrollable on a single engine. Indications were that they had a problem with

the right engine. The A-20 spun in, and from under 1,500 feet, the crew had no chance to bail out. Crash occurred in February of 1945. Congden and Sopo were killed.

S/Sgt. Raymond Copell, flight engineer, 314th TS
Copell was with Lt. Albrecht when they crashed. Returning from a mercy mission in France in a C-47, Albrecht buzzed the field. He didn't clear the trees at the end of the field and crashed. With him was R/O Cpl. Howard Hutchinson and flight engineer, S/Sgt. Raywood Copell. Other crew unknown.

T/Sgt. Cecil A. Allen (No Information)

S/Sgt. Victor C. Corsen, flight engineer, 311 FS
He was flying with Sgt. Robert Norris. Both were flight engineers on C-47s and were stationed at Istres, France. They were sent back to Grove, England, for a few weeks to help deliver material to the ETO. Upon leaving Istres with a load of mail for England and the USA, along with supplies for their C-47, they flew into bad weather and hit a mountain near the top. No reports on the rest of the crew.

1st Lt. Burl J. Creech, pilot, 0-664143, 87th TS, 310th FS and 311 F.S
Killed as reported officially on March 4, 1944, in a B-26G at Maghaberry. Beal was thought to be with him, but was not recorded on the 302 TW list. A defective generator was the cause of the crash, which happened on take-off.

PFC, Harry U. Daniels, 314th TS
Killed July 14, 1945, in a motor vehicle accident at Berkshire, England. Buried at Cambridge Cemetery July 17, 1945.

S/Sgt. John L. Demmer, flight engineer, 313th TS
Flight engineer on a C-47B, based at A-25 in Normandy, France. Two C-47s reported shot down over Dunkirk, France, that same day, one with S/Sgt Demmer, other believed to be Leroy Holiday. A.E. Loop was the original engineer on #118627. He was relieved of duty to be Sgt. of the Guard, and S/Sgt Demmer was assigned in his place for that day.

1st Lt. Clyde A. Depuy, pilot, 0-887751, RCAF, 313 TS, 326 FS, 87 TS
Dupuy was on final approach when his left engine cut out and the plane spun into the ground in France. He was a tent mate of John M. Lyons. He was in the RCAF until transferring into USAAF 6-14-44. Flying records closed January of 1945.

1st. Lt. William J. Dion, pilot, 0887821, RCAF, 326th FS
Dion was flying a P-38J on the deck and was hit by ground fire, October, 1944. He was reinterred in California by his mother and father after the war.

1st Lt. Ronald B. Dorrington, pilot, 0-745647, 312th FS
Dorrington was killed in a B-24 crash, 7-17-44. Prior to joining the 312th, 5-25-44, he had completed 36 missions in B-17s with the 381st BG.

Cpl. Henry H. Eagan, 310, 311, 312, 325 FS
Killed by a Buzz Bomb at Heston Aerodrome, London, 6-28-44.

Sgt. Cecil A. Edmonds, 34608953, 321 TS
Killed 10-14-44, with crew, when C-47 crashed near Halten, Buckinghamshire, England. PFC Merl E. Stutesman, 321 TS, is buried on his right, and T/Sgt. William Lulf, 321 TS, is on his left at Brookwood Cemetary near Cambridge, England.

Lt. Estosite, 310th FS
Died 2-2-43. He was the third to lose his life.

S/Sgt. Addison W. Fain, Jr., 326th FS.
S/Sgt. Fain was killed with Lt. Kilgore, September, 1944.

1st. Lt. Robert C. Fife, pilot, 0-693024, 31st TG
Fife was a B-17 pilot with the 305th and 306th Bomb Groups prior to his transfer to the 31st TG. No information on his death at this time.

2nd Lt. Max I. Fogg, pilot, 0-887762, RCAF, 314 TS, 326th FS, 87th TS
2nd Lt. Fogg was in a C-47 that spun in on final approach. Other crew members unknown on this flight. Last flying records are 1-5-45.

Captain Charles Francis, pilot, 0-660131, 87th TS, 310th FS
Killed 2-6-44 in a P-47 while flying formation on instruments, in bad weather, with F/O John R. Runnells. Francis and Runnells locked wings, and Francis was killed when his Thunderbolt spun in. Prior to joining the 310th, Francis flew with the 355th Fighter Group.

1st Lt. Frank S. Frazer, pilot, 0796043, 311th FS
Lt. Frazer was the pilot on a C-47 with F/O Weshofsha as co-pilot which had landed at a field northeast of Paris. The field was constructed of PSP (Pierced Steel Planking). While the plane was being unloaded, the crew went to eat dinner, with the exception of Lt. Frazer. After being loaded he took the C-47 onto the metal strip. Accounts vary as to the exact cause (some say a blown tire resulting from a buckled spot in the steel mat, others say the gear was accidentally raised and an enlisted crewman was in the co-pilot's seat at the time of the accident), but the left prop hit the ground, causing it to come off and spin into the cockpit, hitting Lt. Frazer. He died in hospital that evening. The crew was also injured, but survived. March 1945.

Sgt. Ottie L. French, 314 TS
Sgt. French and 2nd Lt. David R. Hughes, Jr., were killed in the line of duty when their plane crashed at Gunnislake, Davenshire, England, while flying a scheduled courier run.

F/O Ronald L. Garkie, pilot, 310th FS
Killed in B-17 crash due to weather, from Prestwick, Scotland, 11/23/43.

1st Lt. Theadore E. Garland, pilot, 0-664390, 87th TS
Killed on 12/23/43 with his crew when they hit a hill in Wales in a C-47. Other crew were: 2nd Lt. Daniel C. Lardin, 0-521760, S/Sgt. Paul W. Welter, 18025422, Sgt. Charles Miller, 35334261

Lt. Richard A. Gasperoni, pilot, 0-680203, 320 TS
Lt. Gasperoni was killed on 12/3/44 with flight engineer, Sgt. Robert Hadley. They crashed at Montge, France, in a UC-64. Bad weather was the cause of crash. Burial was at Solers Cementary No.1 Montge, France.

2nd St. Hillyer C. Godfrey, pilot, 0-667692, 310th FS
Killed in P-47D crash 3/1/44. Prior to joining the 310th Godfrey was with the 62nd Fighter Sqdn., 56th FG.

Cpl. Henry A. Gorechie, radio operator, 311 FS (No Information)

2nd Lt. William G. Gough, pilot, 0-804152, 86th TS
No information on cause of death.

Cpl. Harold A. Grubb, flight engineer, 9950421
Killed in the crash of a C-47, 1/18/45, at Plessis-Gassot, France, with a load of GIs on board. Crash occurred seven minutes after takeoff at 9:23 a.m. Destination was AAF-343, England. Other crew member were: 2nd Lt. Roy J. Shilling, Pilot; 2nd Lt. George A. Wood, co-pilot; and Cpl. Alphonse Cogozza, R/O. There were 18 passengers, 4 survived.

Sgt. Robert L. Hadley, flight engineer, 320 TS
Hadley was killed on 12/3/44 with Pilot, Lt. Gasperoni. They crashed at Montge, France, in a UC-64 on a return trip from Liege, Belgium. Bad weather was the cause of crash. Burial was at Solers Cementary No.1, Montge, France.

Capt. Hagaman, pilot, 310 FS
Left A-84 to 590, failed to arrive 6/10/45

2nd Lt. Algie M. Hill, pilot, 0-515002, 311 FS and 310 FS
Killed when his P-38 blew up on takeoff, 8/14/44.

1st Lt. Eugene A. Howard, service pilot, 0-511201, 312th and 310th FS
Killed when his B-17 stalled on base leg for landing, 1/3/45. Lt. Roy Parker is believed to have been with him. (Also reported, a pilot Parker was killed in an A-20 of the 310 FS in 1944 by hut 3.)

2nd Lt. David R. Hughes, Jr., service pilot, 0-822722, 314 TS
2nd Lt. Hughes and Sgt. Ottie L. French were killed in the line of duty when their plane crashed at Gunnislake, Davenshire, England, while flying a scheduled courier run. Lt. Hughes was flying in Lee Smith's place for the day in a UC-64 Norseman. With him was his pet dog. No survivors. Last flying time on record was in a C-47A. Records closed in June 1944.

1st Lt. Donald L. Hunter, pilot, 0-737426, 310th FS
Completed missions in B-26s before transferring into 310 FS in March of 1945. Last flight on record was March 22, 1945, in B-17G. Total flying time 841.50 hrs. Records closed. Deceased.

Cpl. Howard Hutchinson, R/O, 314 TS
11/16/44, Hutchinson was returning from a mercy mission in France in a C-47 with pilot Lt. Vernon Albrecht. As he buzzed the field, he didn't clear the trees at the end

of the field and crashed. Flight engineer, S/Sgt. Raywood Copell, was with them. Other crew unknown. Cpl. Hutchinson is buried beside Lt. Vernon Albrecht at St. Mere Eglise, France.

2nd Lt. Kenneth W. Johnson, pilot, 00826986, 313th TS, 312th FS
Last flight recorded Dec. 29, 1944. Records closed in Jan. 1945. Records show he only flew C-47, C-53, UC-64s. Can find no P-51 flying time on record in the ETO. It was reported that he and Lt. Clyde R. McDow were flying P-51s in formation and hit a snow covered hill in Belgium or France. (This may have actually been F/O Ed Johnston with McDow)

F/O Edward Johnston, pilot, 310 FS
Killed 1/3/45 when his airplane crashed near Little Walton, England. Reported killed in a P-51 by Hut 3, Burtonwood

Sgt. Sam F. Joseph, R/O, 13011890, 312 FS
Killed 6/8/44 in a B-24 which crashed into a hill on the Isle of Man, due to bad weather. Pilot was Lt. Walter Lenox, co-pilot, Lt. Sampson Sharff, and flight engineer, Anthony F. Bellini. Sgt. Joseph received the Air Medal for a tour of duty on anti-submarine patrol.

2nd Lt. Summen A. Kiligore, pilot, 0-886278, 326th FS
Transferred from RCAF to USAF January of 1944. Last recorded time Sept. 14, 1944, in a B-26B. Crew member with him was S/Sgt. Fain. Records closed. Deceased.

Cpl. Claude King, Jr., 311 FS
Lost in C-46 (Dragon Lady) from Grove,

2nd Lt. Robert E. Knowles, Jr., pilot, 0-778841, 326th FS, 314th TS, 325th FS
Knowles went down in the bay 1/2 mile southwest of Cragmore Point, near Gatehouse Fleet, Scotland. He was in a flight of three P-47s flying from Renfrew, Scotland, to Burtonwood. Ceiling was very low, and they were on the deck. As they approached landfall after flying over the Irish Sea, the leader said he was going up through the overcast. Bobby Knowles didn't make it. A fisherman reported that Knowles attempted to make a turn to avoid cliffs, drug a wing in the water, and the airplane cart wheeled. Last flight recorded was 2/4/45.

2nd Lt Daniel C. Lardin, service pilot, 0-521760, 310th FS
Killed 12/23/43 when their C-47 crashed into a hill in Wales due to weather. Also killed were 1st Lt. Theodore Garland, S/Sgt. Paul Welter, and Sgt. Charles Miller.

2nd Lt. Alva W. Leeper, Jr., pilot, 326th FS
Died 2/9/44 in the ETO.

2nd Lt. Douglas C. Legear, 0-887764, 313 TS, 326th FS, 325th FS
Killed in an accident at Cormeille, France, 2/8/45 in a fighter aircraft.

1st Lt. Walter L. Lenox, service pilot, 0-497983, 87th TS, 311th FS, 312 FS
Killed 7/8/44 approximately 5:00 PM flying a B-24 on instruments. The aircraft with full crew on board hit a mountain on the Isle of Man. The crew with him was: co-pilot, 1st Lt. Sampson Sharff; flight engineer, Sgt. Anthony F. Bellini; and R/O Sam F. Joseph.

F/O Willard Leutenegger, pilot, 325 FS
Killed in December, 1944, delivering an airplane with T/Sgt. John J. Veicik. Cpl. Kelak and PFC. Riley were injured in the crash, but recovered.

Cpl. Hyman Levitsky (No Information)

T/Sgt. William P. Lulf, 321 TS
Killed in a C-47, 10/21/44, at Halten, Buckinghamshire, England. Also with him were Sgt. Cecil A. Edmonds and PFC Merl E. Stutesman. All three are buried together at Brookwood Cemetery.

1st Lt. William B. Lustig, pilot, 0-7474445, 310th FS, 325 FS
Killed in a C-47 after the war. Aircraft crashed into a hill due to weather.

Capt. Howard B. Lynch, pilot, 312 FS
Killed in a B-24, 7/6/44.

2nd Lt. Jimmie Mah, service pilot, 0-530881, 310 FS
Killed 11/44 when the B-17G, #445, he was ferrying struck a mountain in bad weather near Oakly, Kettering, Northamptonshire; 132 degrees out of Grafton Underwood Airfield (3 miles by air). Jimmie Mah was a U.S. citizen of Chinese ancestry. Sgt. Geo. F. Sherman and Cpl. Henry A. Garechi, R/O, were with him.

1st Lt. Winfield H. Malone, pilot, 0-797861, 325 FS, 320 TS
Killed 7/10/44, in a UC-64 on a flight to deliver a tire and wheel for a Lockheed Hudson which was damaged earlier at Preston, Scotland. On the flight, their Norseman crashed into King Alfred's Tower near Zeal, Wilts, Yeovil, England. Cpl. Henry Mazzie and M/Sgt. Loyd Cheek are buried with him at Brookwood Cemetery near Cambridge, England. Lt. Jack H. Couch made identification and was escort at the funeral, July 18, 1944.

F/O Kenneth A. Maloney, T-223066, 310 FS
Killed 2/12/44 in the ETO. Served with the RAF before transferring to the USAAF

1st Lt. James C. Martin, pilot, 325 FS
Last flight reported Sept. 6, 1944. Reported from Hut 3 in England that Lt. Martin was killed in a UC-64.

Cpl. Henry A. Mazzie, 320 TS
Killed 7/10/44, in a UC-64, on a flight to deliver a tire and wheel for a Lockheed Hudson which was damaged earlier at Preston, Scotland. On the flight, their Norseman crashed into King Alfred's Tower near Zeal, Wilts, Yeovil, England. 1st Lt. Winfield Malone and M/Sgt. Loyd Cheek are buried with him at Brookwood Cemetery near Cambridge, England. Lt. Jack H. Couch made identification and was escort at the funeral, July 18, 1944.

2nd Lt. Clyde K. McDow, pilot, 313 TS
Last flight recorded 1/2/45. Killed flying possibly with F/O Edward Johnston. They were fighting bad weather with a low ceiling and hit a snow covered hill in France or Belgium. Both were flying P-51s.

1st Lt. Ernest G. McGehee, pilot
McGehee was the first pilot killed on 7/12/42, in a P-47. He hit a balloon cable near Burtonwood. He was one of the pilots of the first three C-47s which started the 27 TG

1st. Lt. Bernard S. McGuire, pilot, 311 FS
Killed 3/15/44

S/Sgt. Kirk McLoren (No Information)

Pvt. Rex J. Measom, 312 FS
Arrived in England September 1943, sent to a casual pool, and assigned to 312 FS He was killed on 6/6/44 in Northern Ireland in a converted Lockheed Hudson V.

Capt. Loren L. Miles, 86 TS
Died 9/4/43 in the ETO. Age 44

Sgt. Charles Miller, crew chief, 35334261, 310 FS
Killed 12/23/43 on a flight in a C-47. Accident caused by bad weather, which caused them to fly into a mountain in Wales. Other crew members were: Pilot, 1st Lt. Theodore E. Gailand; co-pilot, 2nd Lt. Daniel C. Larden; and R/O, S/Sgt. Paul W. Weltner. There were no survivors

Capt. Everett L. Miller, pilot, 0-725765, 310 FS
Pilot of a B-26 lost in flight from Warton, England, to Toome, North Ireland, on 11/6/43. Crew members were as follows: co-pilot Ray G. McDonnell; S/Sgt. Wilfred G. Belk; and Major George F. King, Jr. McDonnell and King are not listed on the death list of 302 Transport Wing. The flight was supposed to take 1 hour. Cause was listed as routine flight forced down at sea. British and Americans gave up the search on December 1, 1943.

F/O John V. Monasmith, pilot, 325 FS
Monosmith was a close friend of Capt. Charles J. Purcell. The friendship started in the RCAF in Toronto, Canada, in June 1941. Both arrived at Oshawa, Ontario, Canada, the morning of December 7, 1941. Both received their wings on June 19, 1942.

In December 1943 they were sent overseas to England in the RCAF They were both transferred into the U.S. Air Corp in June or July 1944. Later both served in the 325 FS Capt. Purcell had a detachment of the 325 FS at Warton.

In late 1944 they converted to C-47s. On March 13, 1945, they were flying some ammo and parts to a fighter base near the front, east of Paris, and they were jumped by a Me 109. Monasmith's aircraft caught fire, and he and the crew bailed out.

F/O Monasmith failed to fasten his leg straps, and when the chute opened he fell through and was killed. Other crew members were: Cpl. Muth; Sgt. Link; Sgt. Worley; and Sgt. Holden. Location of accident was near Vitry Le Francois, France.

2nd Lt. Craig C. Moore, pilot, 325 FS
Crashed at Tangnese, England, 2/11/45, in a C-47. He was a Sgt. Pilot with the RAF and transferred into the U.S. Air Corps as a F/O. Also reported he was ferrying a P-47 by W. Jones .

Sgt. Walter A. Morin, 31 TG (No Information)

Pvt. Wilbur L. Murray, 312 FS. Died 7/6/44.

2nd Lt. Ralph M. Nathan, Pilot- 311 FS- 325 FS
Pilot of a C-47 in early spring of 1945. He crashed with a full crew, plus a flight nurse, in bad weather in Eastern France or Western Germany. The cause of the crash was low ceiling, fog, and poor visibility. Lt. Nathan was in the 325 FS being transferred into the 311 FS Other crew unknown as of now. Reported by Charles A. Watry, Pilot 311-325 FS

Sgt. Robert S. Norris, flight engineer, 311 FS
Sgt. Norris was the engineer on a flight from Istres, France, with engineer S/Sgt. Corsen to Grove, England. Their job was to help for a few weeks to relieve work overload at Grove. After leaving Istres with a load of mail and other materials en route to England, they encountered bad weather and hit near the top of a mountain. No report as of yet who the other crew members were.

1st Lt. Roy H. Parker Jr., pilot, 325 FS
It is believed Parker was with Lt. Eugene H. Howard in a B-17 that stalled on base leg and spun in. Hut 3 claims he was killed in a L-5. Last flight recorded March 25, 1945, in a L-4A. Records closed. Deceased.

1st Lt. Howard R. Pederson, 321 TS
Killed in a jeep, it is believed, by an American MP.

Capt. John Perrin, pilot, 312 FS
Died 7/4/44. Last flight recorded 6/16/44.

1st Lt. Richard L. Pogue, pilot, 311 FS
Pogue was flying a C-47 with 2nd Lt. Robert H. Robinson when they hit a hill in southern England. Both were killed. Other crew members are unknown.

1st Lt. Rex L. Pond, pilot, 314 TS
Killed 5/23/45 flying a C-46 with Lt. Claude Weid to eastern France with a load of cargo. Having delivered their cargo, they loaded up patients for return to a hospital in Paris or England. The engine caught on fire from a bad oil leak. They tried to make the nearest airfield at Creil, but could not make it as the wing burned off and all were lost. Crew chief is believed to have been Sgt. Vermillion. Buried at Marne, France. (See entry for Weid for more information.)

1st Lt. William H. Powers, pilot, 325 FS
Last flight recorded 10/10/44 in a C-47.

2nd Lt. Joe F. Quintana, 326 FS
Killed 3/21/44 in the ETO flying a P-47 aircraft, which exploded. Reported by Col. Richards, USAF (Retired)

Lt. Ray, pilot, 310 FS
Killed 2/2/43. He was the second pilot to lose his life.

2nd Lt. Dennis E. Robinson, 310 FS
He was flying a P-38 and hit a mountain on 1/19/44

2nd Lt. Robert H. Robinson, pilot, 311 FS
Robinson was flying a C-47 with 1st Lt. Richard L. Pogue when they hit a hill on the southern coast of England. Both were killed. Other crew members are unknown to date.

2nd Lt. Ralph G. Robinson, pilot, 311 FS
This report is from Louis Gale: "The food was lousy at our mess hall, and Ralph and his roommate asked me to scare up some more firewood as they were going hunting for some rabbits. Rabbits were plentiful at Istres. Ralph and his friend, Lt. Bill Keenan, took off to shoot some rabbits, and Ralph was killed when he stepped on a land mine. Lt. Keenan received shrapnel wounds in the thigh and shoulder and was hospitalized for some time. They never saw the signs reading 'Land Mines.'"

2nd Lt. Richard R. Rolfe, pilot, 86 TS
Last flight recorded 10/29/44 in a C-47.

2nd Lt. Richard C. Rowe, pilot, 325 FS
Died 2/3/45

F/O Samuel P. Rubinowitz, pilot, 321 TS
Killed in crash of C-47 in May of 1944 due to bad weather. Other crew unknown.

F/O John R. Runnells, pilot, 310 FS
Died 2/6/44 while flying a P-47 in formation, with Capt. Francis, on instruments. The aircraft locked wings and crashed. Bad weather was again the cause. (It was also reported that F/O Runnells ran out of gas, hit a hill, and he died 4 days later from injuries and exposure.)

F/O Eugene S. Rybaczak, pilot, 310 FS
Rybaczak was flying a P-51 on 2/16/44, in bad weather, low over Liverpool, England, and hit a high smoke stack while trying to buzz his wife's house. Report from Hut 3.

Sgt. Harry Segal, 31 TG (No Information)

2nd Lt. William J. Shaffer, pilot, 326 FS
Last flight recorded June 6, 1944, in P-47. Records closed Deceased.

1st Lt. Sampson Sharff, pilot, 312 FS
Killed in a B-24, 7/8/44, with Lt. Walter Lenox on the Isle of Man. They were flying on instruments due to bad weather. Lt. Sharff was co-pilot on the B-24. Other crew was as follows: flight engineer, Anthony F. Bellini; and radio operator, Sgt. Sam F. Joseph. Lt. Sharff had completed a tour of combat missions (30), and held the DFC and Air Medals.

Lt. J. Shaughnessy, pilot, 311 FS
Crashed/died March 4, 1944

Sgt. George F. Sherman, 310 FS
He was with Lt. Jimmie Mah when they crashed.

2nd Lt. Roy J. Shilling, pilot, 0-696907, 321 TS
1/18/45, left A-54C to go to AAF-343 with 18 Govt. troops. C-47 took off at 9:23 from A-54C, and 7 minutes later crashed at Pleasis-Gassot, France. All aboard were killed except 4 passengers. Reason for crash unknown. Other crew members who lost their lives were as follows: co-pilot, 2nd Lt. George A. Wood, radio operator, Cpl. Alphonse V. Cogozza, and Cpl. Harold W. Grubb, crew chief.

2nd Lt. Redene W. Simenson, pilot, 310 FS
Killed in P-47. Moutray was his wingman navigating.

2nd Lt. Robert Smillie, pilot, 310 FS (Former RAF Pilot)
Killed in bad weather flying a C-61 aircraft.

Lt. Floyd Smith, pilot, 321 TS
Lt. Smith was killed 3/22/44 in a Lockheed Hudson V. Lt. Smith was first pilot with R.A. Schremp as co-pilot. The Hudson crashed on take-off and caught on fire. R.A. Schremp was severely burned and suffered a broken arm. Schremp does not recall from the crash at midday, until 5 PM when he woke up in the 79th General Hospital near base. The other crew member was Sgt. Jerman, flight engineer. Remaining people on board unknown to date. R.A. Schremp spent 1 year in the hospital.

Cpl. Jerome J. Smith, radio operator, 311 FS
Smith was on the same aircraft with Bob Norris and S/Sgt Victor Corsen of the 311 FS.

Cpl. Julius J. Sopo, radio operator, 310 FS
An A-20 was converted to a weather plane, so the 310 FS could get their own weather reports. Everyone wanted to fly the A-20 as it was light and fast. Wilton Hodges reports it was his turn to fly the airplane. Hodges sent his crew chief Joe Nagy and R/O Julius Sopo to preflight the A-20 as Hodges was busy in operations picking crews for the day's deliveries. He then took the jeep to the flight line and found the A-20 gone. He learned the A-20 had just departed with Chuck Congden and R/O Sopo on the weather flight. Hodges returned to operations and learned of the bad news that the aircraft had gone down four miles north of Chestes, England. 310th pilot John McDowell gave the most plausible reason. The A-20 was seriously out of balance. The center of gravity was changed through modification which could make it uncontrollable on a single engine. Indications were that they had a problem with the right engine. The A-20 spun in and from under 1,500 feet, the crew had no chance to bail out. Crash occurred in February of 1945. Congden and Sopo were killed.

2nd Lt. William L. Stutesman, 31 TG (No Information)

PFC Merl E. Stuteman, 321 TS
Died on 10/21/44 in a C-47 with Sgt. Edmonds and T/Sgt. Lulf. They are buried side by side with PFC Merl Stutesman at Brookwood Cementary, Cambridge, England. Burial time 1500 hours. 10/24/44. Pilots of C-47 unknown of this date.

Cpl. James F. Syron Jr., radio operator, 312 FS
Died 7/6/44 in the crash of a B-17 on the Isle of Man, while on a ferrying trip between LLAD and a base in England. The aircraft burned, leaving only the tail section. Syron had asked Henry Twitty to take his place on the flight as he had a date that night. Twitty declined. Twitty served as a pall bearer at Syron's funeral.

Lt. O. Sullivan, pilot, 310 FS
Died 11/23/43 in a B-17 crash with F/O Ronald L. Garkie on a return flight from Prestwick, Scotland, due to bad weather.

1st. Lt. Benjamin A. Taylor, pilot, 310 FS
Could be same person as reported from Hut 3 killed in P-47, 8/45

1st Lt. Ron Taylor, pilot, 325 FS
Former RAF pilot who crash landed at Rambury. Died 12/22/44.

Cpl. James D. Todd, flight engineer, 310 FS
Killed in a C-47 crash on a flight from Grove, England, to a destination in France, early Fall, 1944.

F/O Oliver E. Tudor, pilot, T-223886, 31 TG
C-47, #434890, crashed at A-54, resulting in death of F/O Tudor in January 1945.

F/O William A. Vallee, pilot, T-190584, 310 FS
Killed in a P-38 crash on March 18, 1944.

Sgt. Edward V. Vermillion, flight engineer, 314 TS
Killed 5/23/45 flying a C-46 with Lt. Claude Weid and Lt. Rex Pond, to eastern France with a load of cargo. Having delivered cargo, they loaded up patients for return to a hospital in Paris or England. The engine caught on fire from a bad oil leak. They tried to make the nearest airfield at Creil, but could not make it as the wing burned off and all were lost.

T/Sgt. John J. Vejcik
Not listed as killed overseas during WWII, but 302 Wing history states he was with F/O Willard Leutenegger.

1st Lt. Edwin E. Walker, pilot, 311 FS
Reports from Hut 3 state that Walker was killed in a C-47 in June of 1945. Lt. Walker was a co-pilot to Howard Stillwell for a period of time until March 7, 1945. He appears in squadron pictures taken at Viroflay, France, on April 8, 1945

1st Lt. Claude W. Weid, pilot, 314 TS
Killed 5/23/45 flying a C-46 with Lt. Rex Pond to eastern France with a load of cargo. Having delivered cargo, they loaded up patients for return to a hospital in Paris or England. The engine caught on fire from a bad oil leak. They tried to make the nearest airfield at Creil, but could not make it as the wing burned off and all were lost.

The following statement was sent to Marvin Diehl from Cloyd A. Taylor on 20 January 1992:

"On page 42 in your book, you list the death of Lt Weid and others in a C-46 explosion along with the statement that the rest of the crew is unknown, accident 5-25-45.

I can't help with who the medics were on the mission, but I know who the radio operator was ... me – Cloyd Taylor.

"Seems the regular operator normally assigned that day had the day off, and the rule was, as the chief operator, I would fill in the absentee's place. By the time the word came down from operations that he hadn't shown and I had gathered up my flight equipment, scheduled take-off time had passed and the flight was late. From the radio shack to the dispersal area was only a short distance, but by the time I got there, the C-46 had started its taxi to the runway without an operator. I couldn't get Lt. Pond's attention, so I just watched the rear of that monster airplane as it taxied away.

"When word came in that afternoon about the loss of the plane and all aboard, I was both very sad for the crew and passengers, and relieved that both myself and the regular operator missed the flight. Although I can't remember the operator's name, I remember the look on his face when he got the word, but the most vivid recollection is the sight of that plane taxiing away ... I still see the picture as if it were yesterday!"

S/Sgt. Paul W. Weltner, radio operator, 18025422, 310 FS
Killed on 12/23/43 when they hit a hill in Wales in a C-47. Other crew members were: pilot, 1st Lt. Theodore E. Garland; co-pilot, 2nd Lt. Daniel C. Lardin; and crew chief, Sgt. Charles Miller.

PFC Edward M. White, radio operator, 313 TS
Lost with a full crew, due to fog in February or March of 1945, in the crash of a C-47.

T/Sgt. Stanley L. Wisneskie (No Information)

Lt. George A. Wood, pilot, 0748306, 321st TS
1/18/45, left A-54C to go to AAF-343 with 18 Govt. troops. C-47 took off at 9:23 from A-54C and 7 minutes later crashed at Pleasis-Gassot, France. All aboard were killed except 4 passengers. Reason for crash unknown. Other crew members who lost their lives were as follows: pilot, 2nd Lt. Roy Shilling; radio operator, Cpl. Alphonse V. Cogozza; and Cpl. Harold W. Grubb, crew chief.

Pvt. Nick Yaksich – 325 FS
Died 9/1/44. Cause of Death, intestinal obstruction and peritonitis. Buried Sept. 5 '44 at Cambridge, England.

**Missing in Action**

Lt. Herman Adolfae, pilot, 313 TS
Adolfae and Lt. Glenn Goodwin were presumed to be shot down while flying from England to the far shore. Intelligence said Dunkirk was secured, but was incorrect. That same day aircraft from the group flew over or near Dunkirk, and some were shot down. Report shows that two were shot down in February 1945. R/O Edward White was with Lt. Herman Adolfae, and S/Sgt. Demmer was with Lt. Goodwin as R/O.

1st Lt. William G. Bavin (No Information)

S/Sgt. Wilfred S. Belk, 20742211, 87 TS
Sgt Belk, with Pilot, Everett L. Miller, co-pilot, Ray G. McDonnall, and Major George F. King, Jr., took off in a B-26 from Warton, England, destined for Toome, Northern Ireland, November 6, 1943. Aircraft is believed to have been forced down at Sea. Flight from Warton to Toome only took 1 hour. Aircraft never arrived at Toome, Ireland. American and British searched the area until December 1, 1943, when the sea search was given up. Reason of crash listed as forced down at sea. S/Sgt. Wilfred Belk was married to an English girl. He lived off base with S/Sgt. Herman Avery and his wife, who was also English. S/Sgt. Avery had the unpleasant job of telling S/Sgt. Belk's wife of his death. S/Sgt. Belk took James Besird's place on the flight, as James was grounded with the flu.

S/Sgt. Clarence R. Benge, radio operator, 312 FS
Missing 12/15/44 on a flight from Hendon Aerodrome, England to France. Never arrived. Other crew members were: pilot, 1st Lt. Malcolm S. Brown; co-pilot, 2nd Lt. Gordon J. Kinsella; and crew chief, T/Sgt. Eugene L. Conroy. Reported by James H. Hammett that the destination was to a landing strip near the German border with a load of gas. Not knowing that the Germans had retaken the air strip, they were captured upon landing.

1st Lt. Robert B. Blackler, pilot, 313 TS
Blackler was shot down over the Island of Jersey or Guernsey off the coast of the continent. He became a POW and was the sole survivor of his C-47 crew. Crew consisted of: 1st Lt. Ermene G.J. Pallatine, drowned; S/Sgt. James R. Carroll, Jr., body never recovered; Sgt. Joseph E. Fiset, drowned; Private William A. Westeimier, drowned; Plus 7 passengers, drowned. Crew was reburied at U.S. Military Cemetery, Blosville, France.

Lt. Blackler, flying C-47, #43-48592, took off from Villacoublay, France, Oct. 30, 1944, for a flight to Querqueville, France. Last radio contact 15 miles from destination. Pilot reported electrical failure. The C-47 was shot down by German ack-ack, and they crash landed at Sea, in Bowley Bay. Lt. Blackler was picked up by the Germans. He was the only survivor. Seas were very high. All drowned and were washed up on shore later, except Sgt. Carroll. His body was not recovered. Lt. Blackler last saw him trying to hang on to a large straight wall of rocks at shore. There was no way to get to safe ground, because of high cliffs. They were only 200 yards off shore. The crash happened at 8:00 P.M. near Bonneuit, France. Lt.Blackler reported that because of high seas the crew were knocked unconscious and drowned. Lt. Blackler became a POW. All were declared combat casualties.

Sgt. Harold Bonser, 310 FS
Not listed on 302 TW missing list, but other crew members were as follows:
Pilot 1st Lt. Ralph T. Parker Jr., POW
Co-pilot 2nd Lt. David L. Forbes, POW

Flight Nurse 2nd Lt. Reba A. Whittle, POW
Flight Engineer Sgt. Harold Bonser, POW
R/O Cpl. Chester D. Bright was killed at crash sight.
See Chapter 7 for complete details.

1st Lt. Malcolm S. Brown, pilot, 312 FS
Missing 12/15/44 on a flight from Hendon Aerodrome, England to France. Never arrived. Other crew members were: pilot 1st Lt. Malcolm S. Brown; co- pilot, 2nd Lt. Gordon J. Kinsella; and crew chief, T/Sgt. Eugene L. Conroy.

Reported by James H. Hammett that the destination was to a landing strip near the German border with a load of gas. Not knowing that the Germans had retaken the air strip, they were captured upon landing.

Brown radioed his take off time from England to Paris, but never arrived. Nothing was heard from him or his crew.

S/Sgt. Robert P. Campbell, radio operator
He was a crew member on the flight that was lost when the 311 FS flew from Grove to Istres, France, in 1944. (See Lt. Halverson below)

S/Sgt. James R. Carroll
Story under Lt. Blackler

T/Sgt. Eugene J. Conroy, crew chief, 312 FS
Missing 12/15/44 on a flight from Hendon Aerodrome, England to France. Never arrived. Other crew members were: pilot 1st Lt. Malcolm S. Brown; co-pilot, 2nd Lt. Gordon J. Kinsella. Reported by James H. Hammett that the destination was to a landing strip near the German border with a load of gas. Not knowing that the Germans had retaken the air strip, they were captured upon landing.

Lt. Raymond E. Davis (No Information)

T/Sgt. Joseph A. Filkins, radio operator, 86 TS
Lost in a C-47 over Europe with a load of of gas. Other crewmembers were:
1st. Lt. Paul E. Mellers, pilot
1st Lt. John D. Lampman, Jr., co-pilot
T/Sgt. John T. Ruddy, crew chief

S/Sgt. Joseph C. Fiset, 313 TS
Story under Lt. Blackler.

2nd Lt. David L. Forbes, pilot, 310 FS
Listed as POW. Story under Sgt. Harold Bonser on missing list.

Lt. Ted M. Freeman, pilot , 0-686737, 310 FS
Nicknamed "Tex." Dick Richards and "Tex" were ferrying two P-38s from Langford Lodge to Grove (England). Skies were overcast above 200 feet. Over Ireland, at takeoff, the overcast was a few thousand feet thick, and it ended over England at their destination. They climbed up through the cloud layer and headed out over the Irish Sea toward England. Tex radioed Dick that his right tank was siphoning fuel. Dick decided he would return to Langford Lodge and have it checked. Tex said he would follow him down through the clouds. They decided to let down over the Irish Sea to eliminate any chances of hitting a mountain or hill. Dick told Tex he would make a long and easy let down through the clouds. Dick leveled out at 100 ft. above the water, and in the clear he proceeded to Langford Lodge. Dick circled the base several times calling on the radio, but Tex did not answer. In the meantime, Dick's fuel tank had stopped siphoning from the wing tank and he proceeded to Grove to deliver his P-38. Dick never heard from Tex again. Upon arrival at Grove he discovered that Tex had not shown up yet. This is not unusual since Tex might have decided to stop at Burtonwood, England, and spend the night there. A couple of weeks later Dick delivered to Grove again and once more checked on Tex. Tex had not arrived with his P-38. A month or so after the original take off from Langford Lodge, Tex's leather coat was found floating near the coast of Scotland, near Prestwick. No one really knows what happened to Tex. He was known to have ulcer cramps once in a while, but it didn't cause him any undue alarm and he never turned himself in for a medical check-up. He was reported missing August 4, 1944, and presumed dead August 5, 1944.

1st Lt. Reeves K. Gauthier, pilot, 311th FS
Lt. Gauthier was with 2nd Lt. Halverson on the flight to Istres, France. See below.

1st Lt. Glenn E. Goodwin, 313 TS
Lt. Goodwin and Lt. Herman Adolfae were presumed shot down over Dunkirk, France. Reports were that Dunkirk was secured, but that information was incorrect.

Lt. Kenneth V. Halverson, pilot, 311 FS
Halverson was lost on a flight from Grove, England, to Istres, France. They were given two routes to fly either over Cherbourg and ESE to the Rhone Valley, through to Istres, or from Cherbourg SE to the Pyrennes Mountains and then east to Istres, France. Lt. Halverson took the latter route and was lost in the Pyrennes Mountains. His C-47 was found later after the war with all aboard dead. Crew chief was Sgt. Paylak. co-pilot was Lt. Gauthier, and radio operator was Sgt. Robert Campbell.

Sgt. LeRoy W. Holliday Jr., 313 FS
Lost over Dunkirk, France, due to enemy flak. They were en route to Brussels, Belgium, with a load of beef quarters in a C-47. Also lost that day was S/Sgt. Demmer.

2nd Lt. Raymond E. Jones (No Information)

2nd Lt. Gordon J. Kinsella, pilot, 312 FS
Missing 12/15/44 on a flight from Hendon Aerodrome, England to France. Other crew members were: pilot 1st Lt. Malcolm S. Brown; crew chief, T/Sgt. Eugene L. Conroy. Reported by James H. Hammett that the destination was to a landing strip near the German border with a load of gas. Not knowing that the Germans had retaken the air strip, they were captured upon landing.

T/Sgt. William E. Kirwan (No Information)

1st Lt. John D. Lampman, Jr., pilot, 86 TS
Lost in a C-47 over Europe with a load of gas. Other crew members were as follows: 1st Lt. Paul E. Mellers, pilot; T/Sgt. John T. Ruddy, crew chief; and T/Sgt. Joseph A. Filkins, R/O. Missing early 1945, no survivors

Lt. Paul E. Mellers, pilot, 86 TS
Lost on flight with Lampman, above.

1st Lt. Ray G. McDonnall, pilot, 0-470106, 87 TS
McDonnall was flying with Capt. Everett Miller in a B-26 from Warton, England, to Toome, North Ireland, on 11/6/43. Flight should have taken one hour, but they never arrived at Toome. British and Americans searched till 12/1/43. Cause listed as "forced down at sea." Other crew members were: Capt. Everett Miller; S/Sgt. Wilfred Belk; and Major George F. King. Records from archives.

2nd Lt. Kelly R. Moutray, 310 FS
Shot down over one of the Islands in the English Channel. He was flying a P-47 with J.J. Canning as reported. They were separated, and "Moose" Moutray went down. He became a POW and spent time in a German hospital. He recovered and returned to service later on. (Also reported he was wing man for 2nd Lt. Redene W. Simenson in P-47s.)

Sgt. Floyd R. Myers (No Information)

T/Sgt. John A. Neilson (No Information)

Lt. Ermene Pallatine
Story under Lt. Blackler

Lt. Ralph T. Parker Jr., pilot, 310 FS
Listed under Sgt. Harold Bonser story.

S/Sgt. Charles D. Pavlak, 311 FS
Possibly a member of C-47 crew with Lt. Halverson on flight from Grove England to Istres, France, when they moved. More under Lt. Halverson.

Lt. Donald S. Phillips, pilot, 314th TS, 325 or 326 FS
Phillips and Lt. Elmer Born, were each flying an A-26. They flew into a front over the English Channel and were never heard from again.

Lt. Robert T. Reed, pilot, 310 FS
Killed in P-51 in May of 1945.

Sgt. John T. Ruddy, crew chief, 86 TS
See Lt. John D. Lampman.

T/Sgt. Joseph P. Filkins, R/O
Missing in early 1945.

2nd Lt. Wallace M. Smyth, pilot, 325 FS, 310 FS
Smith was ferrying a P-47 on 3/27/45. He flew into a weather front over the English Channel and was never heard from again.

Pvt. William H. Westeimier
Story under Lt. Blackler

**Following Names are not on KIA or MIA List of the 302nd TW.**

Lt. Apple, 313 TS, 325, 326 FS?
Apple was flying in and out of Switzerland and was killed at the end of August 1945. He flew into a mountain in southern Germany. Other crew unknown at this time. His name is not on the 302 TW list because it happened after VE Day.

PFC Wilbur Baumgardner, 310 FS (No Information)

Beal (rank unknown), 311 FS
Killed March 4, 1944, in a B-26G that crashed because of a defective generator. He was flying with Lt. Burl J. Creech. Other crew member (unknown).

2nd Lt. Henry M. Bishop, 313 TS
Co-pilot with Capt. Stiles as pilot, crashed at Grove, England, on take-off in a B-26. Lt. Bishop died in the hospital as a result.

Blanchard, Pilot, 310 FS
Killed in a P-51 in June 1944 as reported by Hut 3.

1st Lt. John Bloemendal, pilot, BAD 2
Bloemendal, with T/Sgt. Jimmie Parr, and flight engineer, Gordon Kinney, were taking a B-24 for a test flight. The B-24 was to be assigned to the 2nd Air Division after completion of the flight. Sometime after takeoff they encountered a violent thunderstorm with sheer winds. The control tower had ordered them to return to base on account of the storm. After they received orders to return to base they were in the storm and broke out into an open spot. Lightning struck the plane and it broke apart. Within seconds, the aircraft slammed into the village of Freckleton. Parts of the plane hit a classroom, and parts landed in a school yard and on sidewalks. A snack bar was also hit. Several buildings were set afire and destroyed. Total life lost was 38 children, 9 civilian adults, 4 RAF personnel, and 10 USAAF personnel. Total of 61 people killed. Some of you might remember this dreadful day. Date August 23, 1944, in Warton, England. (See Chapter 3 for more information)

Tony Canena, pilot, 312 FS
Reports are that he was killed in a C-47 in 1945. One report says he went in near Casablanca.

Bretta, pilot, 310 FS
Killed in June 1945 as reported by Hut 3. Werner Kolthe thought he was killed in B-26.

Cpl. Busch, 311 FS
Villacoublay. Busch came from a squadron in England, to the 311th, in October or November, 1945, as a replacement for flight engineers who were getting ready to go home. Reports were that he had a load of mail and other material on his C-47. They were trying to reduce weight by throwing out anything to make the C-47 lighter. Reports are that they went down near WWI trenches in France. He was a roommate of Marvin Diehl.

Clearwater, pilot (unknown rank)
Killed in a P-51, October 1944.

Cosgrove, radio operator, 311 FS
R/O Cosgrove radioed back to base from Germany that they were going down and had no parachutes. This crash happened after the war was over.

1st Lt. Clint Cowden, pilot, 31 TG or 313 TS
Cowden served as a Sgt. Pilot in the RAF He was shot down by enemy ground fire. Latest reports say he was in a C-78.

Cpl. Henry A. Hartman, 39531872
Died January 1944.

T/3 Herbert H. Hill, 31 TG
Hill went down in a C-47 in southern England due to engine trouble.

Hogamon, pilot, 310 FS
Killed in an A-20 aircraft in June 1945.

Hollingsworth, pilot, 310 FS
Killed in a P-38 in June 1944. Reported by Hut 3.

Hurst, pilot
Killed in a P-51. Burtonwood. Reported by Hut F-3

Major George F. King, Jr., 0-418300, 31 TG
Major King and 1st Lt. McDonnall are not listed in the 302 TW. Death list of 43-44-45 history book. (See McDonnall)

Lawson, pilot, 310 FS
Killed in a P-51 in June 1944.

McCraig, pilot, 310 FS
Killed in a P-51 in June 1944.

F/O John R.S. Morgan, 87 TS 325 FS detachment E of the 320 TS
(Pilot of Glenn Miller's last flight 12/15/44)
At one time F/O Morgan was a member of the 302 TW. He transferred into the 87 TS June 25, 1943, from the RCAF. In May 1944 he was transferred into 325 FS detachment E at AAF-547. He flew mostly C-64 Norsemans in the 87th and 325th. August 3, 1944, was transferred into 35 ADG 35 Repair Sqdn. AAF-547. Many have said he was from our outfit. They are correct that he was at one time, but when his flight went missing he was in the 35 ADG.

McElroy Nangle, 313 TS
He was flying a C-47 with crew chief Buford Compton, while stationed at A-25 France. He asked and was transferred into a P-47 squadron near Rheims. He was reported killed on his first combat mission by Buford Compton.

Neisser, pilot
Killed in a B-24 which was overloaded with parts for Switzerland drop outs in May 1944. Reported by Hut 3. Pilot with him was Smith.

Flight Nurse Sollie Shay, 313 TS
She may have been the nurse on the C-46 flight, lost with Lt. Pond and Lt. Weid with a load of patients in France.

Smith, pilot, 310 FS
Killed in light plane, possibly a L-5, in June of 1944, reported by Hut 3.

Sullivan (rank unknown), 310 FS
Killed in B-17 with Lt. Gaskie in November or December of 1943 on a flight returning to Prestwick, Scotland, when they hit a hill.

2nd Lt. Jim Weatherford
Killed in a crash on the way to pick up a colonel at a base south of London. He was on TDY assigned to Loges.

2nd Lt. or F/O Glenn Youtsey, 325 FS
One member thinks he lost his life in a jeep accident after he arrived in France from England.

# *Appendix II*

# Decorations

The men of the 27th ATG flew long and tough hours under adverse conditions. Some would say they were in a non-combatant role, but as the photographs and stories in this volume demonstrate, they were shot at, shot down, captured, flew front line support missions, and flew when the rest of the USAAF was grounded.

Regardless, not many decorations were awarded to these men during WWII. This was partly due to the fact that because of the spread out "Anywhere, Anything, Anytime" nature of the group, good records simply were not kept. The men were often moved frequently from base to base, and their assignments changed daily in many cases.

It was through the efforts of past Group Historian Marvin Diehl and General George J. "Jim" Eade, USAF (Retired), that this situation was partially remedied. In General Eade's letter of recommendation for decorations to the USAF, he states, "The 27th ATG had a number of detachments that moved around the theater, often with little contact with higher headquarters, which itself was pretty fluid. While not surprising, it is nonetheless regrettable that the administrative process failed to cover all the air crew members who deserved timely consideration for the missions they flew."

Flight records were assembled for many members of the 27th ATG veterans organization and submitted to the USAF for review. Here follows a list of those men who were awarded The Distinguished Flying Cross, The Air Medal, and The Purple Heart, fifty years later! (At the time of this writing this list is complete. However, other names may have been submitted later and would therefore not be included on this list. I regret any omissions)

|  |  |
|---|---|
| Vincent E. Alexander | Air Medal |
| Bert Astrove | Air Medal |
| George E. Batchelor | Air Medal |
| James O. Beaird | Air Medal |
| Harold L. Boatright | Air Medal |
| Harold R. Bonser | Air Medal and Purple Heart |
| Harvey T. Bonser | Air Medal |
| Anton Bogdan | Air Medal |
| Fay W. Brandis | Air Medal |
| Joseph E. Brannock | Air Medal |
| Carlos B. Brown | Air Medal |
| John J. Canning | Air Medal |
| Martin J. Chaves | Air Medal |
| Joseph V. Cioffi | Air Medal |
| Donald M. Clark | Air Medal |
| Warren L. Clark | Air Medal |
| Richard M. Cook | Air Medal |
| Jack H. Couch | Air Medal |
| John H. Crawford | Air Medal |
| Elmer H. Davis | Air Medal |
| Raymond F. Dlouhy | Air Medal |
| William E. Doherty, Jr. | Air Medal |
| Loris L. Dorris | Air Medal |
| George J. Eade | DFC - Air Medal five Oak Leaf Clusters |
| Jacob C. Eckert | Air Medal |
| Herman J. Estrada | Air Medal |
| Edwin C. Eubanks | Air Medal |
| Goerge H. Flibbert | Air Medal |
| Fred T. Garcia | Air Medal |
| Durward K. Gaw | Air Medal |
| Jacques A. Gordon | Air Medal |
| Samuel A. Graves | Air Medal |
| Robert E. Hafley | Air Medal |
| James F. Harded | Air Medal |
| Edwin F. Henke | Air Medal |
| Elliotte Holland | Air Medal |
| John B. Howard | Air Medal |
| Dillard T. Hyden | Air Medal |
| Ralph C. Jacobs | Air Medal |
| Grover R. Jenks | Air Medal |
| Walter E. Jones | Air Medal |
| Arthur C. Kane | Air Medal |
| Donald C. Kendrick | Air Medal |
| Ingwer C. Ketelsen | Air Medal |
| Harry G. King | Air Medal |
| Richard M. Kirkes | Air Medal |
| Roger Knoblock | Air Medal |
| Donald K. Kogge | Air Medal |
| Edward W. Kollar | Air Medal |
| Shields H. Krutzsch | Air Medal |
| Louis J. Lamosek | Air Medal |
| Preston H. Lawrance | Air Medal |
| Robert R. Lawrence | Air Medal |
| James E. Leverick | Air Medal |
| Stanley L. Loftsgard | Air Medal four Oak Leaf Clusters |
| Theodore M. Lukas | Air Medal |
| Lawrence W. McCartney | Air Medal |
| John McDonald | Air Medal |
| John I. McDowell | Air Medal |
| Larry W. McGuire | Air Medal |
| Joe D. Maguire | DFC - Air Medal six Oak Leaf Clusters |
| Robert E. Millar | Air Medal |
| Edward Miller | Air Medal |
| Ambrose P. Moore | Air Medal |
| Harry P. Morrow | Air Medal |
| Solomon Padia | Air Medal |
| Michael Palermo | Air Medal |
| Lionel L. Palmer | Air Medal |
| Joseph Pastular | Air Medal |
| Thomas Laughlin Perdue | Air Medal |
| Robert A. Pfluger | Air Medal |
| Thomas V. Powers | Air Medal |
| Wayne Preston | Air Medal |
| Virgil P. Reimer | Air Medal |
| James S. Rinehardt | Air Medal |
| Fred W. Rue | Air Medal |
| Sarkis Samarian | Air Medal |
| John J. Schneider, Jr. | Air Medal three Oak Leaf Clusters |
| Richard A. Seebars | Air Medal two Oak Leaf Clusters |
| Dean F. Sheets | Air Medal |
| Frank Simpson, Jr. | DFC - Air Medal seven Oak Leaf Clusters |
| Dallas O. Southwick | Air Medal |
| Hubert A. Stabler | Air Medal |
| Morris Stauffer | Air Medal |
| Jenkin N. Stenerson | Air Medal |
| Joseph W. Stevens | DFC - Air Medal six Oak Leaf Clusters |
| Robert J. Sweitzer | Air Medal |
| Burl Taylor | Air Medal |
| Cloyd A. Taylor, Jr. | Air Medal |
| Harold H. Taylor | Air Medal |
| Henry E. Twitty | Air Medal |
| Lawrence J. Uter | DFC - Air Medal six Oak Leaf Clusters |
| Fredrick Wahl | Air Medal |
| Harry Weinshank | Air Medal |
| Gordon F. Wiley | Air Medal |
| Llewelyn Williams | Air Medal |
| Thomas G. Work, Jr. | Air Medal |
| Joseph G. Worthington | Air Medal |
| William A. Wright, Jr. | Air Medal |
| Christ P. Zivalich, Jr. | Air Medal |

Due to the efforts of Marvin Diehl and General Eade, Harold Bonser received the Purple Heart for his wound which occurred in the shoot down of his C-47, 9/27/44. (see chapter 7 for complete story.)

Many of the men who participated in the Swedish missions were recommended for multiple Air Medals, and some may have received them during the war, but certainly, many did not. There were also a few other men in the group who were awarded the Air Medal during the war. This is a list of those who were recommended from the Swedish missions and other known war time awards. This list is, most likely, not complete.

**War Time Air Medal List**

| | |
|---|---|
| John W. Abercrombie | (four OLC) |
| Samuel B. Alexander, Jr. | (four OLC) |
| Roy F. Allemeier | (four OLC) |
| Benjamin W. Benson | (four OLC) |
| Norman C. Bishop | (three OLC) |
| Victor J. Boynton, Jr. | (four OLC) |
| Leonard C. Calloway | (three OLC) |
| Joe Clemow | |
| Phillips M. Clinton | (four OLC) |
| Posie M. Clinton | (two OLC) |
| Jacob M. Cohen | (eight OLC) |
| Wilbur L. Cowley, Jr. | (four OLC) |
| John A. Ellis | (four OLC) |
| Jackson H. Evans | (four OLC) |
| Gordon Fisher | |
| Joseph H. Gasslein | (two OLC) |
| Frank R. Griffith | (seven OLC) |
| Paul A. Hagerup | (two OLC) |
| Nicholas J. Haglietto | |
| Revis H. Hicks | |
| Charles G. Holliman | (five OLC) |
| Stanley D. Jensen | (six OLC) |
| Howard L. Karsak | (four OLC) |
| Robert L. King | (nine OLC) |
| Arthur H. Krafft | (four OLC) |
| Albert Lai | (two OLC) |
| Robert R. Lawrence | |
| Irvin J. Levy | (two OLC) |
| Burnie C. Lindle | (seven OLC) |
| Charles Longshore | DFC, Air Medal (multiple OLC) |
| Joseph J. Luke | (five OLC) |
| John A. McAlpine | (four OLC) |
| William J. Mahon | (seven OLC) |
| Harlow A. Marsh | (four OLC) |
| Robert C. Merritt | (four OLC) |
| M.T. Messelt | (three OLC) |
| Thomas E. Mostyn | |
| Wesley Muller | |
| Troy W. Newsome | (four OLC) |
| William J. Otts | (four OLC) |
| John A. Rieggle | (four OLC) |
| Bennett Robertson | (one OLC) |
| William J. Rosenthal | (four OLC) |
| George H. Rottner | (four OLC) |
| Chandler R. Royal | (nine OLC) |
| John G. Rudzonis | (four OLC) |
| Albert J. Rydzynski | (four OLC) |
| Maurice P. Saliman | (six OLC) |
| John J. Schneider | (four OLC) |
| Floyd J. Schultz | (four OLC) |
| Stanton H. Small | (seven OLC) |
| Everett Stevens | (eight OLC) |
| Howard A. Stillwell | |
| Richard C. Stone | (three OLC) |
| John H. Sversull | |
| Richard Taylor | (four OLC) |
| Franklyn J. Terry | |
| Melvin L. Torrey | (four OLC) |
| Conrad Utecht | |
| Thomas C. Wahrmund | (four OLC) |
| Willie D. Whipple | (four OLC) |
| William T. White | |
| William H. Winnett | |
| Sydney M. Wood | (three OLC) |

**Other known Decorations awarded to 27th ATG members.**

Pfc. Harold Koontz was authorized the Soldier's Medal per paragraph 1, General Orders No. 11, headquarters, Air Technical Service Command in Europe, dated 10 March, 1945, for his heroic actions in saving the life of a pilot of a crashed B-26, and the saving of the bodies of the rest of the crew from cremation.

| Name | Decoration |
|---|---|
| PFC Clarence Owinge | Soldier's Medal |
| Captain Curtis | Soldier's Medal |
| Sgt. Harold Susen | Bronze Star |
| Robert P. Walker | Silver Star, DFC (one OLC), Purple Heart, Air Medal (five OLCs), Air Force Commendation Medal |

# Glossary

| | |
|---|---|
| Ablutions | English term for baths, showers, bathrooms, etc. |
| ADF | Automatic Direction Finder – Radio Compass |
| A-20 | "Havoc" Douglas attack bomber |
| A-26 | "Invader" Douglas attack bomber, later redesignated B-26, during Korea. |
| BAD | Burtonwood Air Depot (HQ BADA) |
| BAD2 | Warton Air Field |
| B3M | new Morse ground station call letters for Maghaberry. |
| Basic/521 | Army classification for no specific training or job assignment |
| "Biscuits" | British mattresses – three cushions to a bunk. |
| "Belshaft" | GI slang for Belfast. |
| "Browned off" | upset, disturbed, slightly angry |
| B-17 | "Flying Fortress" Boeing heavy bomber |
| B-24 | "Liberator" Consolidated heavy bomber |
| B-26 | "Marauder" Martin medium bomber |
| CAVU | Ceiling and Visibility Unlimited. |
| CO | Commanding Officer |
| CQ | Charge of Quarters - usually a rotating night time clerical type position |
| C-47 | "Skytrain" – Military cargo transport version of the Douglas DC-3 |
| C-53 | "Skytrooper" Military passenger transport version of the Douglas DC-3 |
| C-45 | "Expediter" twin engine Beech transport aircraft |
| C-46 | "Commando" – twin engine Curtis transport aircraft |
| C-87 | "Liberator Express" – transport version of the B-24 Liberator |
| Darkey | Emergency call to anyone listening for navigational help |
| DF | Direction Finding |
| DS | Detached Service |
| EM | Enlisted Man |
| ETO | European Theater of Operations |
| FIDO | Fog Intensive Dispersal Of |
| Flight Engineer | Synonymous with Aerial Engineer and, in the 27th ATG, "Crew Chief." |
| FOIBLE | Call sign for Grove Air Field, England |
| FC | Flight Command |
| "Flack Home" | Rest area for combat crews |
| Flimsy | Daily sheet of radio codes, flare signals, challenges for radio ID, etc. – named because it was usually typed on tissue-like paper |
| GCA | Ground Control Approach |
| GI | Government Issue |
| "Gooney Bird" | Common nick-name for the Douglas C-47 |
| "Hand Job" | Dirty slang for poor pilot |
| HQ | Headquarters |
| IG | Inspector General |
| ILS | Instrument Landing System |
| "Kite" | British slang for airplane |
| KP | Kitchen Police/mess hall duty |
| L3Q | Morse code for Langford Lodge Airfield |
| LLAD | Langford Lodge Air Depot |
| "Latrine-o-gram" | GI slang for "Big Rumor" |
| LOC | Lockheed Overseas Corporation |
| "Mosquito" | British attack aircraft made of wood |
| MP | Military Police |
| NYZA | Morse Code for ground radio station at Maghaberry |
| Nissen Hut | Half round metal roofed barracks hut – British style |
| OP | Operational Priority – Radio term for emergency clearance |
| OPS | Operations |
| PX | Post Exchange |
| "Piccadilly Commandos" | London's "ladies of the night" |
| POE | Port of Embarkation |
| PWK | Prestwick, Scotland |
| Putt-putt | Auxiliary gasoline engine |
| P-38 | "Lightning" Lockheed twin engine fighter |
| P-51 | "Mustang" North American fighter |
| P-47 | "Thunderbolt" affectionately called "the Jug", Republic fighter |
| P-61 | "Black Widow" North American twin engine night fighter |
| P-39 | "Aeracobra" Bell fighter |
| QDMs | "What is the magnetic course to steer, with no wind, to make for – a navigational heading |
| Q-sigs | International Morse code abbreviations |
| Quonset Hut | Larger version of a Nissen hut |
| R/O | Radio Operator |
| RON | Remain Over Night |
| "Ship" | Slang for airplane |
| Site | lodging area, including barracks huts, mess hall, etc. |
| SNAFU | Situation Normal All "Fouled" Up |
| "Sweating Out" | Waiting impatiently |
| SPIKE | Special radio frequency for emergency |
| TANOY | British loud speaker system on air fields |
| TO | Table of Organization (also "tech order") |
| UC-64 | Noordyn "Norseman" single engine utility aircraft |
| VHF | Very High Frequency |
| World Guard | Emergency radio frequency |
| WPM | Words Per Minute – Morse code speed – sending or receiving |
| WT | Wireless Transmitter |
| WX | Weather |
| XMTR | short for transmitter |

**Airfield Codes**

The USAAF used a series of codes to refer to airfields in the ETO. Many of the stories in this book use those codes. While a complete list is beyond the scope of this work, I do want to provide the reader with the ones most commonly referred to.

| | |
|---|---|
| Y-11 | Cannes/Mandelieu |
| Y-35 | Compiegne/Margny |
| Y-17 | Istres/Le Tube |
| A-54 | Le Bourget |
| A-93 | Liege/Bierset |
| Y-14 | Marseilles/Marignane |
| Y-34 | Metz |
| A-95 | Nancy/Azelot |
| Y-42 | Nancy/Essey |
| Y-52 | Nice |
| A-47 | Orly |
| A-62 | Reims/Champagne |
| A-46 | Toussus le Noble |
| A-82 | Verdun |
| Y-28 | Verdun/Charny |
| A-42 | Villacoublay |